Microsoft® Windows® 2000 Professional Edition

Illustrated Complete

Patrick Carey
Steven M. Johnson
Neil J. Salkind

ONE MAIN STREET, CAMBRIDGE, MA 02142

Australia • Canada • Denmark • Japan • Mexico • New Zealand • Philippines
Puerto Rico • Singapore • South Africa • Spain • United Kingdom • United States

Microsoft Windows 2000—Illustrated Complete is published by Course Technology

Managing Editor: Nicole Pinard
Senior Product Manager: Kathryn Schooling
Product Manager: M.T. Cozzola
Developmental Editor: M.T. Cozzola
Associate Product Manager: Emily Heberlein
Production Editor: Elena Montillo
Marketing Manager: Andrea Loeb
Editorial Assistant: Stacie Parillo
Composition House: GEX, Inc.
QA Manuscript Reviewer: Ashlee Welz, Jeff Schwartz, John Freitas
Text Designer: Joseph Lee, Joseph Lee Designs
Cover Designer: Doug Goodman, Doug Goodman Designs

For more information contact:

Course Technology
One Main Street
Cambridge, MA 02142

or find us on the World Wide Web at: www.course.com

ISBN 0-7600-5476-2

Printed in the United States of America

1 2 3 4 5 6 7 8 9 BM 04 03 02 01 00

Exciting New Products

Master Microsoft Office 2000

Master Microsoft Office 2000 applications with the Illustrated series. With *Microsoft Office 2000—Illustrated Introductory* students will learn the basics of Microsoft Office 2000 Professional. For deeper coverage, *Microsoft Office 2000—Illustrated Second Course* focuses on the more advanced skills of Office 2000 applications.

Illustrated also offers individual application books on Access, Excel, Word, and PowerPoint 2000. Each book covers basic to advanced skills for the application and meets Microsoft Office User Specialist (MOUS) Expert certification.

Other titles include:

- Microsoft Access 2000—Illustrated Introductory and Complete
- Microsoft Excel 2000—Illustrated Introductory and Complete
- Microsoft Publisher 2000—Illustrated Essentials
- Microsoft Publisher 2000—Illustrated Introductory
- Microsoft Outlook 2000—Illustrated Essentials
- Microsoft FrontPage 2000—Illustrated Introductory
- Microsoft FrontPage 2000—Illustrated Essentials
- Microsoft Office 2000—Illustrated Introductory and Second Course
- Microsoft Office 2000—Illustrated Brief
- Microsoft PowerPoint 2000—Illustrated Brief and Introductory
- Microsoft Word 2000—Illustrated Introductory and Complete
- Microsoft PhotoDraw (Version 2) —Illustrated Essentials

Check Out Computer Concepts

Computer Concepts—Illustrated Brief and Introductory, Third Edition is the quick and visual way to learn cutting-edge computer concepts. The third edition has been updated to include advances to the Internet and multimedia, changes to the industry, and an introduction to e-commerce and security.

Create Your Ideal Course Package with CourseKits™

If one book doesn't offer all the coverage you need, create a course package that does. With Course Technology's CourseKits—our mix-and-match approach to selecting texts—you have the freedom to combine products from more than one series. When you choose any two or more Course Technology products for one course, we'll discount the price and package them together so your students can pick up one convenient bundle at the bookstore.

Try out Illustrated's New Product Line: Multimedia Tools

What are Multimedia Tools?

Multimedia tools teach students how to create text, graphics, video, animations, and sound; all of which can be incorporated for use in printed materials, Web pages, CD-ROMs, and multimedia presentations.

New Titles

- Adobe Photoshop 5.5—Illustrated Introductory (0-7600-6337-0)
- Adobe Illustrator 8.0—Illustrated Introductory (0-619-01750-3)
- Adobe InDesign 1.0—Illustrated Introductory (0-619-01751-1)
- Macromedia Director 7—Illustrated Introductory (0-619-01772-4)
- Macromedia Director 7—Illustrated Complete (0-619-01779-1)

Preface

Welcome to *Microsoft Windows 2000—Illustrated Complete*. This highly visual book offers users a full introduction to Microsoft Windows 2000, Professional Edition, and also serves as an excellent reference for future use.

▶ Organization and Coverage

This text contains fifteen units that cover basic through advanced Microsoft Windows 2000 skills. In these units, students learn how to manage files and hardware, share information between programs, and administer their computer.

▶ About this Approach

What makes the Illustrated approach so effective at teaching software skills? It's quite simple. Each skill is presented on two facing pages, with the step-by-step instructions on the left page, and large screen illustrations on the right. Students can focus on a single skill without having to turn the page. This unique design makes information extremely accessible and easy to absorb, and provides a great reference for after the course is over. This hands-on approach also makes it ideal for both self-paced or instructor-led classes.

Each lesson, or "information display," contains the following elements:

Each 2-page spread focuses on a single skill.

Clear step-by-step directions explain how to complete the specific task, with what students are to type in green. When students follow the numbered steps, they quickly learn how each procedure is performed and what the results will be.

Concise text that introduces the basic principles discussed in the lesson. Procedures are easier to learn when concepts fit into a framework.

Windows 2000

Viewing Hardware Settings

One reason you might want to view hardware settings is if you plan to install any legacy hardware. **Legacy hardware** is any device that is not designed for Windows 98 or 2000 plug-and-play support. If you have a hardware device that is not designed for Plug and Play, then it is important to find out current hardware resource settings to avoid **conflicts**, two devices with the same resource settings, during installation. Before you actually place a legacy hardware device into your computer, you should browse through the devices currently attached to your computer system and ensure that your computer has the available resources to install the hardware device. With the Device Manager, you can view the device resources that are being used with your system hardware and determine whether your computer has the available resources to install a legacy or Plug and Play hardware device. Generally, you cannot install non-Plug and Play hardware without performing some manual setup with the Device Manager. John has an old scanner and wants to examine current hardware resource settings to determine whether he can install the legacy hardware.

Steps

QuickTip
To scan for any hardware changes in the Device Manager, click the Scan for hardware changes button on the toolbar.

QuickTip
To get additional information about Device Manager, click the Help button on the toolbar.

1. In the Device Manager window, click **View** on the menu bar, then click **Resources by connection**
2. Click the **plus sign** ⊞ next to the Interrupt request (IRQ) icon
   The Device Manager displays the resource settings currently in use and the hardware that is using each resource, as shown in Figure L-14. Each installed device requires a communication line called an **interrupt request line (IRQ)**, which allows the hardware device to communicate with your computer's software. Each device must have its own IRQ. If two devices attempt to share an IRQ, you will have an IRQ conflict, and neither device will work properly.
3. Drag the **scroll bar** to the bottom of the window, if necessary
   Take note of the available IRQs on your computer. Any IRQ number between 0 and 15 that is not listed is available. When you install a legacy hardware device, the device's instructions might ask you to provide an IRQ setting. When prompted by the device instructions, provide an IRQ that is not already in use. Instead of writing down your computer resource information on paper, you can print a system summary report.
4. Click **View** on the menu bar, then click **Print**
   The Print dialog box opens, as shown in Figure L-15. Table L-3 describes the report options available in the Print dialog box. Before you print, make sure that an available printer is selected.
5. Click **Print**
   Figure L-16 shows the first part of the summary report. If you are having trouble installing a hardware device, a technical support person might ask you questions that this summary report will help you answer.
6. Click the **Close button** ☒ in the Device Manager window, then click **OK** to close the System Properties dialog box

Using the hardware troubleshooter

Hardware conflict can occur when two or more devices try to use the same IRQ. In many cases, one of the devices will not work. If you have a conflict, you can use the hardware troubleshooter. To use the troubleshooter, click Help on the Start menu, click the Contents tab, click the Troubleshooting and Maintenance book, click the Windows 2000 Troubleshooters book, click the Hardware link in the right pane of the Help window, click Next at the bottom of the right pane, then follow the instructions and suggestions listed.

WINDOWS L-14 MANAGING HARDWARE

Hints as well as trouble-shooting advice, right where you need it – next to the step itself.

Clues to Use boxes provide concise information that either expands on one component of the major lesson skill or describes an independent task that is in some way related to the major lesson skill.

Other Features

The two-page lesson format featured in this book provides the new user with a powerful learning experience. Additionally, this book contains the following features:

► Real-World Case

The case study used throughout the textbook, a fictitious coffee company called Wired Coffee Company, is designed to be "real-world" in nature and introduces the kinds of activities that students will encounter when working with Microsoft Windows 2000. With a real-world case, the process of solving problems will be more meaningful to students.

► End of Unit Material

Each unit concludes with a Concepts Review that tests students' understanding of what they learned in the unit. The Concepts Review is followed by a Skills Review, which provides students with additional hands-on practice of the skills. The Skills Review is followed by Independent Challenges, which pose case problems for students to solve. The Visual Workshops that follow the Independent Challenges help students develop critical thinking skills. Students are shown completed screens and are asked to re-create them.

Every lesson features large-size, full-color representations of what the students' screen should look like after completing the numbered steps.

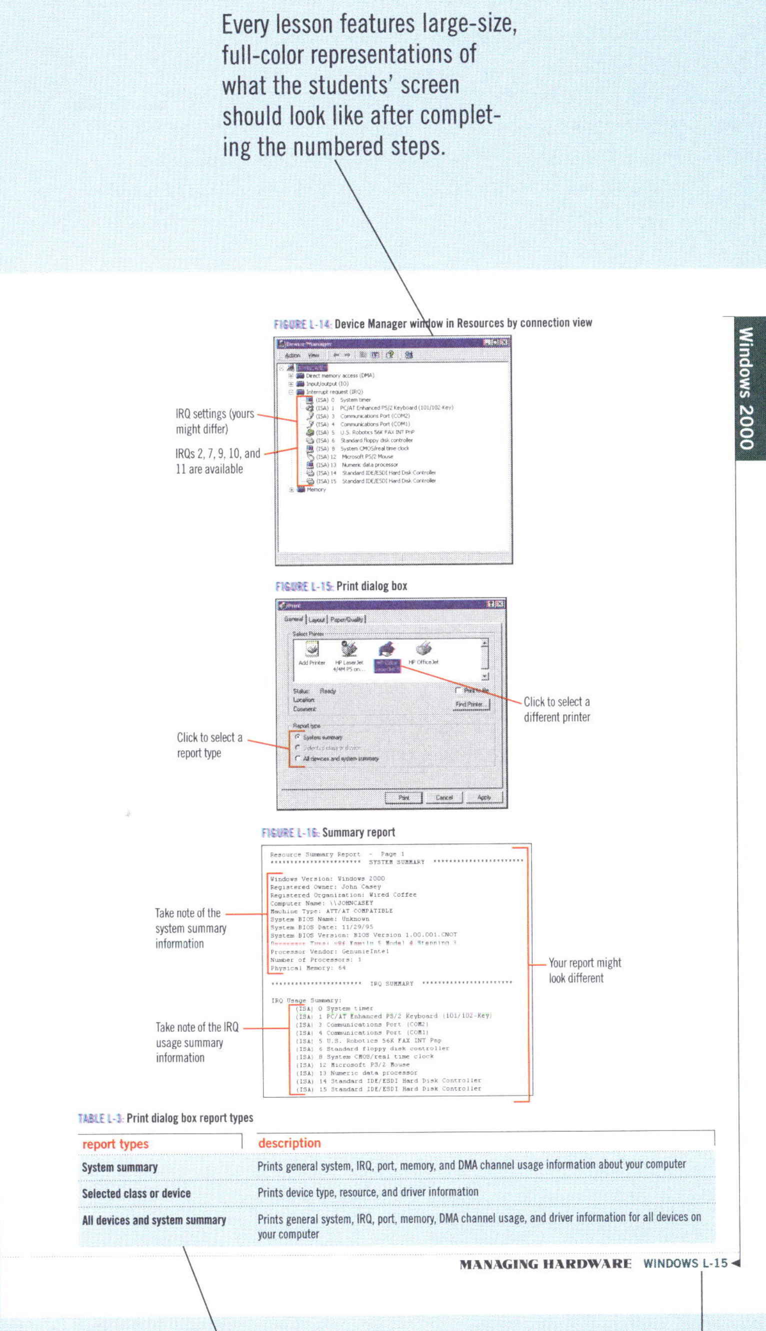

Windows 2000

FIGURE L-14: Device Manager window in Resources by connection view

IRQ settings (yours might differ)

IRQs 2, 7, 9, 10, and 11 are available

FIGURE L-15: Print dialog box

Click to select a different printer

Click to select a report type

FIGURE L-16: Summary report

Take note of the system summary information

Take note of the IRQ usage summary information

Your report might look different

TABLE L-3: Print dialog box report types

report types	description
System summary	Prints general system, IRQ, port, memory, and DMA channel usage information about your computer
Selected class or device	Prints device type, resource, and driver information
All devices and system summary	Prints general system, IRQ, port, memory, DMA channel usage, and driver information for all devices on your computer

MANAGING HARDWARE WINDOWS L-15

Quickly accessible summaries of key terms, toolbar buttons, or keyboard alternatives connected with the lesson material. Students can refer easily to this information when working on their own projects at a later time.

The page numbers are designed like a road map. Windows indicates the text subject, L indicates the twelfth unit, and 15 indicates the page within the unit.

Instructor's Resource Kit

The Instructor's Resource Kit is Course Technology's way of putting the resources and information needed to teach and learn effectively into your hands. With an integrated array of teaching and learning tools that offers you and your students a broad range of technology-based instructional options, we believe this kit represents the highest quality and most cutting edge resources available to instructors today. Many of these resources are available at www.course.com. The resources available with this book are:

Instructor's Manual Available as an electronic file, the Instructor's Manual is quality-assurance tested and includes unit overviews, detailed lecture topics for each unit with teaching tips, an Upgrader's Guide, solutions to all lessons and end-of-unit material, and extra Independent Challenges. The Instructor's Manual is available on the Instructor's Resource Kit CD-ROM, or you can download it from **www.course.com**.

Course Test Manager Designed by Course Technology, this Windows-based testing software helps instructors design, administer, and print tests and pre-tests. A full-featured program, Course Test Manager also has an online testing component that allows students to take tests at the computer and have their exams automatically graded.

Course Faculty Online Companion You can browse this textbook's password-protected site to obtain the Instructor's Manual, Solution Files, Project Files, and any updates to the text. Contact your Customer Service Representative for the site address and password.

Project Files Project Files contain all of the data that students will use to complete the lessons and end-of-unit material. A Readme file includes instructions for using the files. Adopters of this text are granted the right to install the Project Files on any standalone computer or network. The Project Files are available on the Instructor's Resource Kit CD-ROM, the Review Pack, and can also be downloaded from www.course.com.

Solution Files Solution Files contain every file students are asked to create or modify in the lessons and end-of-unit material. A Help file on the Instructor's Resource Kit includes information for using the Solution Files.

Figure Files Figure files contain all the figures from the book in bitmap format. Use the figure files to create transparency masters or in a PowerPoint presentation.

WebCT WebCT is a tool used to create Web-based educational environments and also uses WWW browsers as the interface for the course-building environment. The site is hosted on your school campus, allowing complete control over the information. WebCT has its own internal communication system, offering internal e-mail, a Bulletin Board, and a Chat room.

Course Technology offers pre-existing supplemental information to help in your WebCT class creation, such as a suggested Syllabus, Lecture Notes, Figures in the Book / Course Presenter, Student Downloads, and Test Banks in which you can schedule an exam, create reports, and more.

Brief Contents

Contents

Windows 2000

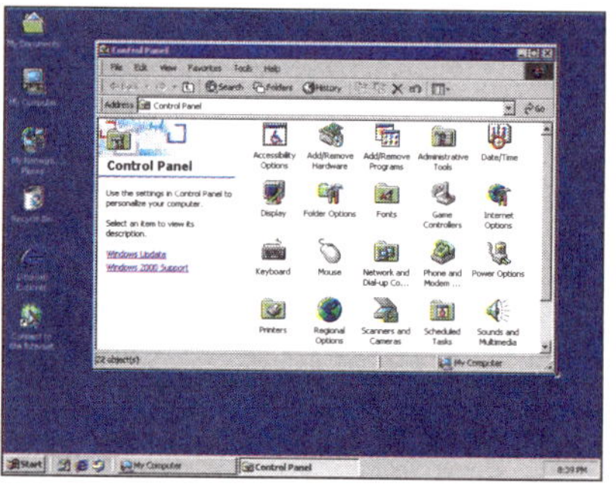

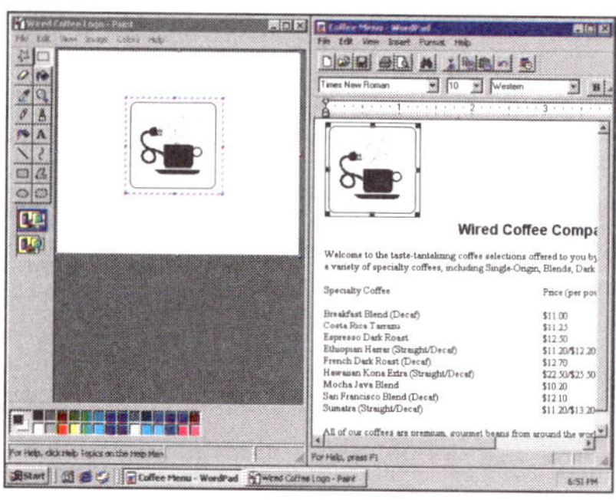

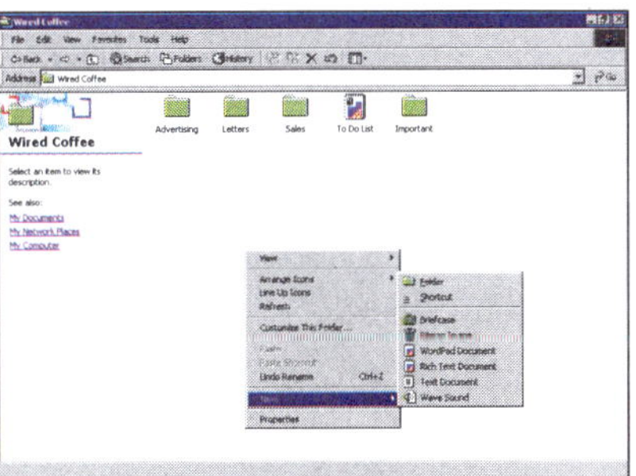
Wired Coffee

Contents

Managing Folders and Files Using Windows Explorer

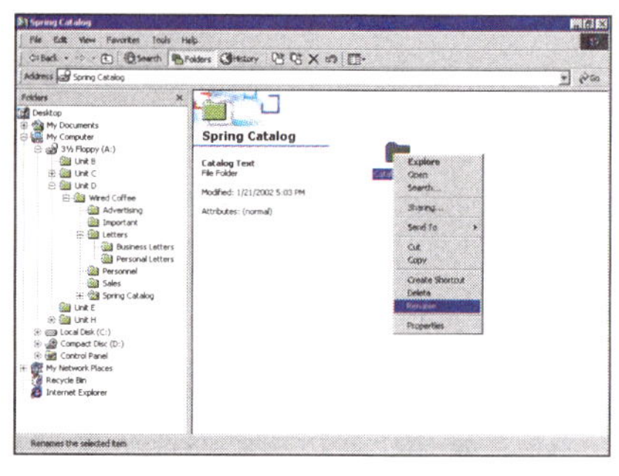

Customizing Windows Using the Control Panel

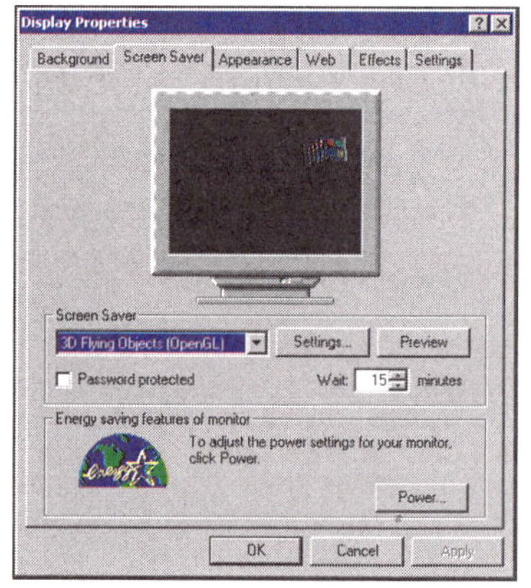

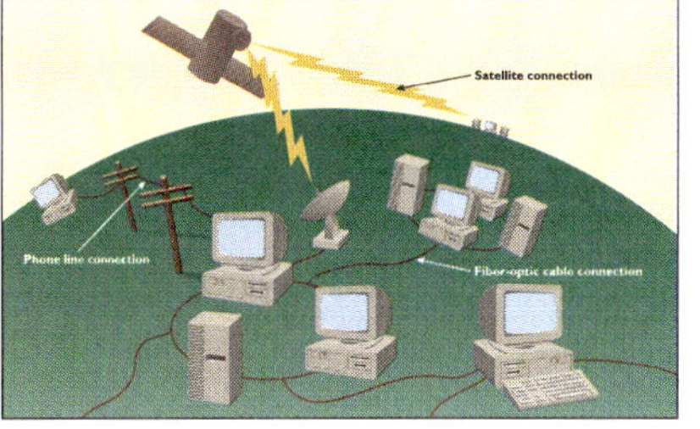

Satellite connection
Phone line connection
Fiber-optic cable connection

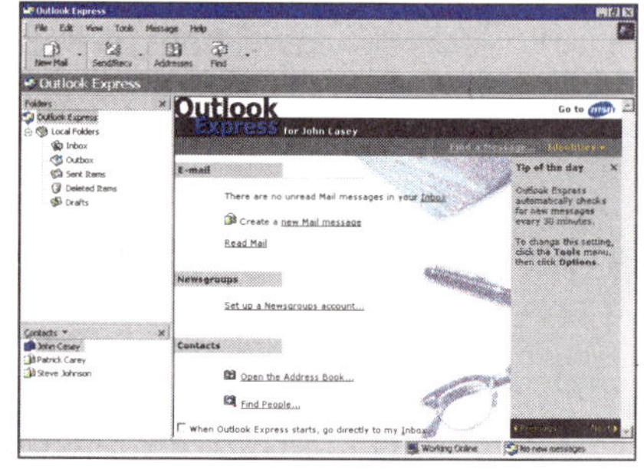

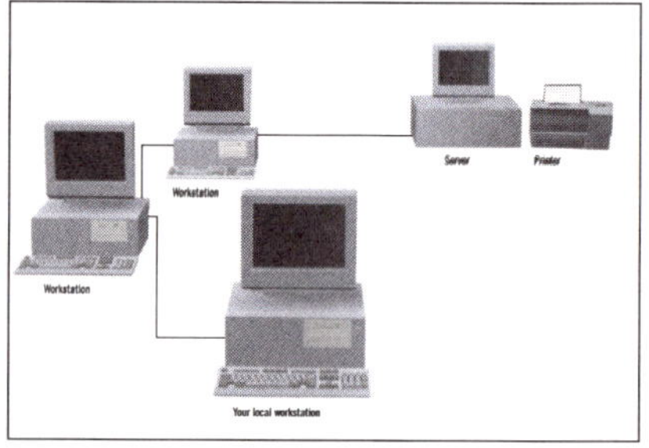
Workstation
Workstation
Server
Printer
Your local workstation

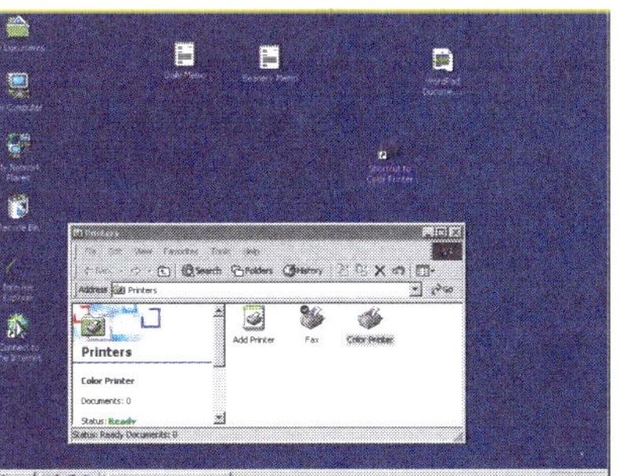

Contents

Insert Object
Object Type:
Create New
Create from File
Bitmap Image
Image Document
Media Clip
MIDI Sequence
Package
Paintbrush Picture
Video Clip
Wave Sound
OK
Cancel
Display As Icon
Result
Inserts a new Bitmap Image object into your document.

Unit L
Printers

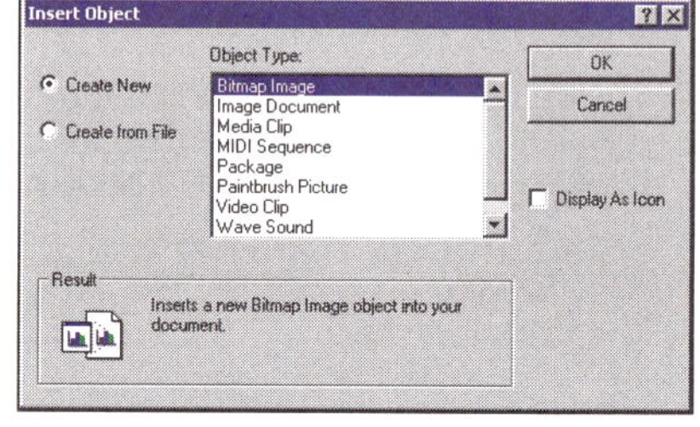

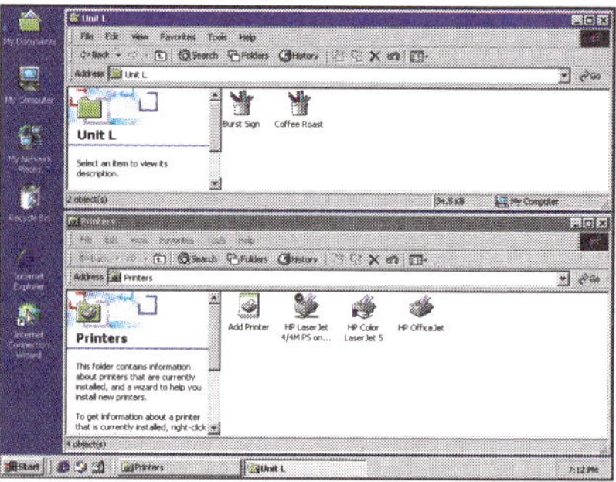

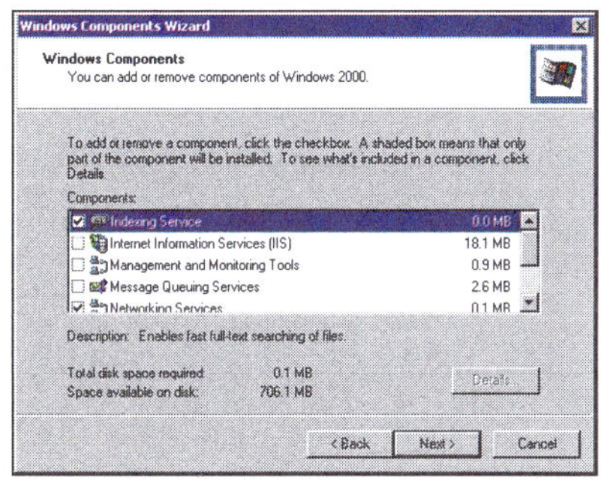

Windows Components Wizard
Windows Components
You can add or remove components of Windows 2000.
Components:
Indexing Service
Internet Information Services (IIS)
Management and Monitoring Tools
Message Queuing Services
Description: Enables fast full-text searching of files.
< Back
Next >
Cancel

Contents

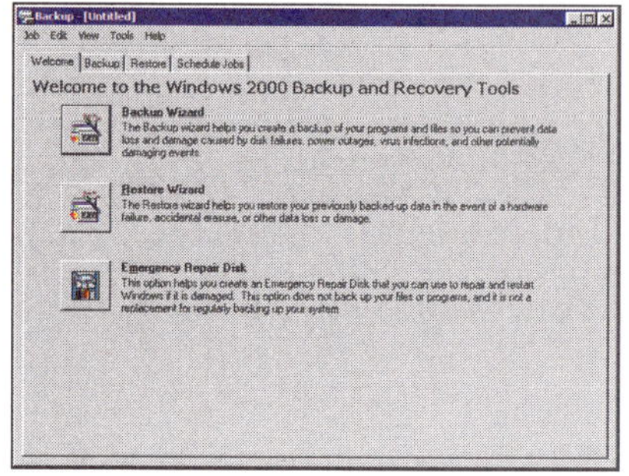

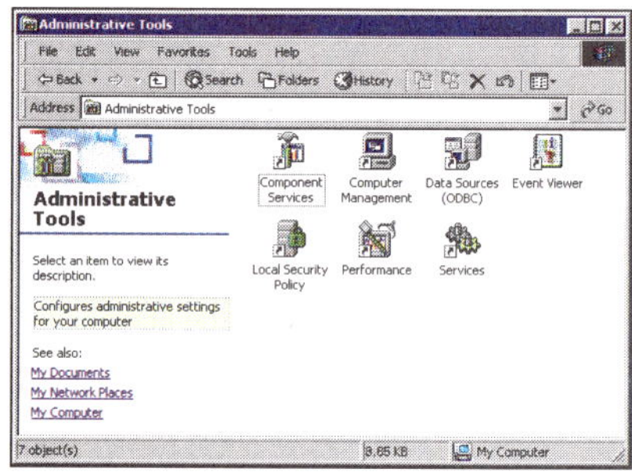

Getting Started with Windows 2000

Objectives

- Start Windows and view the Windows desktop
- Use the mouse
- Get started with the Windows desktop
- Move and resize windows
- Use menus and toolbars
- Use scroll bars
- Use dialog boxes
- Use Windows Help
- Shut down Windows

Microsoft Windows 2000 is an **operating system**, a computer program that controls the basic operation of your computer and the programs you run on it. **Programs**, also known as **applications**, are task-oriented software you use to accomplish specific tasks, such as word processing, managing files on your computer, and performing calculations. When you work with Windows 2000, you will notice many **icons**: small pictures on your screen intended to be meaningful symbols of the items they represent. You will also notice **windows**: rectangular frames that can contain icons, the contents of a file, or other usable data. This use of icons and windows is called a **graphical user interface** (**GUI**), meaning that you interact ("interface") with the computer through the use of graphics. This unit introduces you to basic Windows skills.

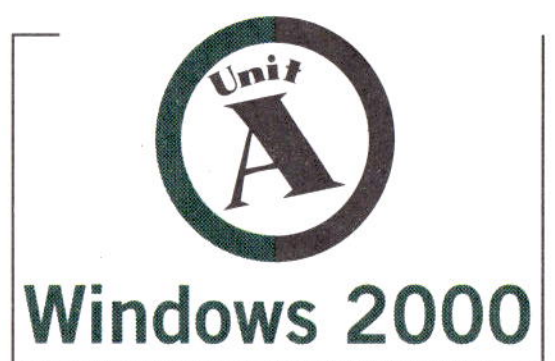

Windows 2000

Starting Windows and Viewing the Windows Desktop

Microsoft Windows 2000 is an operating system that provides a secure file management system in which you can work on your computer and share information with others on a network. When you first start Windows, you will see the logon screen. In the logon procedure, you identify yourself to Windows using a user name and password. After completing the logon procedure, you see the Windows Active Desktop. The **Active Desktop** is an on-screen version of a regular desk, containing all the information and tools you need to accomplish your tasks. From the desktop, you can access, store, share, and explore information in a seamless manner, whether it resides on your computer, a network, or the Internet. (The **Internet** is a worldwide collection of over 40 million computers linked together to share information.) The desktop is called "active" because (unlike other Windows desktops) it allows you to access the Internet and view content from the desktop. Figure A-1 shows what the desktop looks like when you start Windows 2000 for the first time. The bar at the bottom of your screen is called the **taskbar**, which allows you to start programs and switch among currently running programs. (At the moment, none are running.) At the left end of the taskbar is the **Start button**, which you use to start programs, find and open files, access Windows Help and so on. Next to the Start button on the taskbar is the **Quick Launch toolbar**, which contains buttons you use to quickly start Internet-related programs and show the desktop. Use Table A-1 to identify the icons and other elements you see on your desktop. Windows 2000 automatically starts when you turn on your computer. If Windows is not currently running, follow the steps below to start it now.

Steps 1 2 3 4

1. **Turn on your computer**

   Windows automatically starts, and the desktop appears, as shown in Figure A-1. If you are working on a network at school or at an office, you might see a Welcome to Windows dialog box or a Network Password dialog box. If so, continue to Step 2 for the Windows dialog box or continue to Step 3 for the Network Password dialog box; if not, continue to Step 5. When you start Windows 2000, the Getting Started with Windows 2000 dialog box might appear. You can click Register Now to register your Windows 2000 software, Discover Windows to learn about Windows 2000, or Connect to the Internet to set up your computer to access the Internet.

2. **Press [Ctrl][Alt][Del] to begin the logon process**

   After you press the three keys, the Log On to Windows dialog box opens, with spaces for you to enter your user name and password. Your instructor or technical support person (the person in charge of your network) assigns your user name. If you are using your own computer, you selected your user name when you installed Windows 2000. A user name might automatically appear. If your user name appears on the screen, proceed to Step 4.

3. **In the User name box, type your user name, then press [Tab]**

4. **Type your password, then click OK**

   When you type the password, only asterisks will appear as you type. This helps to prevent other people from learning your password. When you enter a valid password, you are given privileges to use the network.

5. **In the Getting Started with Windows 2000 dialog box, click to clear the Show this screen at startup check box, then click Exit**

   The Windows desktop appears on your screen, as shown in Figure A-1.

Trouble?

To perform this step, you press all three keys at the same time. Hold down [Ctrl] and [Alt] with one hand, then press [Del] with the other.

Trouble?

If you don't know your password, see your instructor or technical support person.

QuickTip

To open this dialog box, click the Start button, point to Programs, point to Accessories, point to System Tools, then click Getting Started.

FIGURE A-1: Windows Active desktop

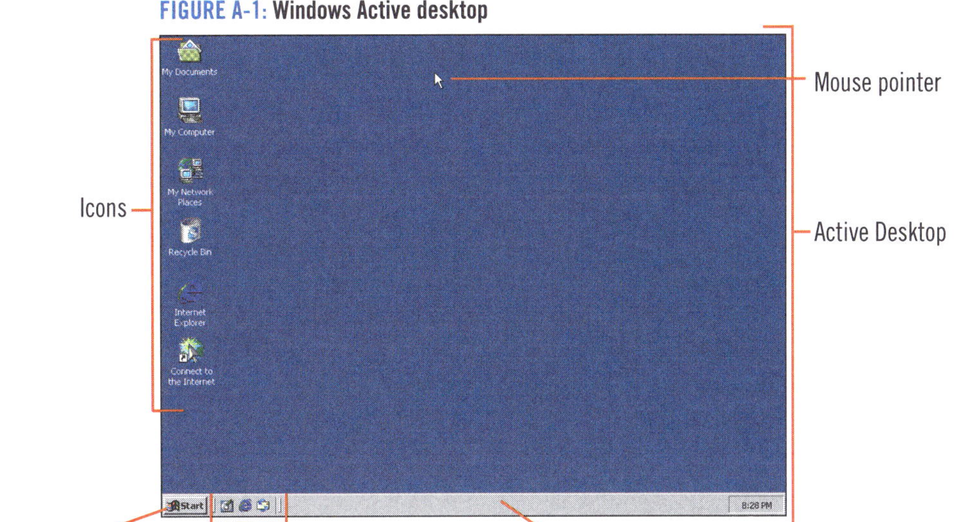

TABLE A-1: Elements of the Windows desktop

desktop element	allows you to
My Documents folder	Store programs, documents, graphics, or other files
My Computer	Work with different disk drives and printers on your computer system
My Network Places	Work with different disk drives and printers on a network
Recycle Bin	Delete and restore files
Internet Explorer	Start Internet Explorer, a program you use to access the Internet
Internet Connection Wizard	Set up your computer to access the Internet; changes to Connect to the Internet icon after you create a connection
Taskbar	Start programs and switch among open programs
Start button	Start programs, open documents, find a file, and more
Quick Launch Toolbar	Show the desktop, start Internet Explorer, and start Outlook Express

Using and changing a password

Passwords are used to maintain security on a local or network computer. When choosing a password, remember that the Windows 2000 password program is case-sensitive. Your password should be at least six to eight characters long. It should include, if possible, combinations of capital letters, lowercase letters, and non-alphabetic characters. Using a word from the dictionary as a password is not a good idea, as someone trying to gain unauthorized access to your account could guess it more easily than a non-dictionary password that you can remember easily. Never write down your password on paper or let someone look over your shoulder as you log on to the system. Always be sure to log out when you walk away from your desk. To change your password, press [Ctrl][Alt][Del], click Change Password in the Windows Security dialog box, type the old password in the Old Password text box, type the new password in the New Password and Confirm New Password text boxes, then click OK.

Windows 2000

Using the Mouse

A **mouse** is a handheld input device you roll across a flat surface (such as a desk or a mousepad) to position the **mouse pointer**, the small symbol that indicates the pointer's relative position on the desktop. When you move the mouse, the mouse pointer on the screen moves in the same direction. The shape of the mouse pointer changes to indicate different activities. Table A-2 shows some common mouse pointer shapes. Once you move the mouse pointer to a desired point on the screen, you use the **mouse buttons**, shown in Figure A-2, to "tell" your computer what you want it to do. Table A-3 describes the basic mouse techniques you'll use frequently when working in Windows. Try using the mouse now to become familiar with these navigational skills.

Steps 1 2 3 4

1. Place your hand on the mouse, locate the mouse pointer on the Windows desktop, then move the mouse back and forth across your desk
   As you move the mouse, the mouse pointer moves correspondingly.
2. Move the mouse to position the mouse pointer over the **My Computer icon** in the upper-left corner of the desktop
   Positioning the mouse pointer over an icon or over any specific item on the screen is called **pointing**. When you position the mouse pointer over an icon or button, a **ScreenTip** appears, which describes the icon or gives the name of the button.
3. Press and release the **left mouse button**
   The act of pressing a mouse button once and releasing it is called **clicking**. The icon is now highlighted, or shaded differently than the other icons on the desktop. The act of clicking and highlighting an item, such as an icon, indicates that you have **selected** it to perform some future operation on it. To perform any type of operation on an icon (such as moving it), you must first select it.
4. Point to the **My Computer icon**, press and hold down the **left mouse button**, move the mouse down and to the right, then release the mouse button
   The icon becomes dimmed and moves with the mouse pointer. When you release the mouse button, the icon relocates on the desktop. This skill is called dragging and allows you to move icons and other Windows elements. Next you will use the mouse to display a pop-up menu.
5. Point to the **My Computer icon**, then press and release the **right mouse button**
   Clicking the right mouse button is known as **right-clicking**. Right-clicking an item on the desktop displays a **pop-up menu**, shown in Figure A-3. This menu lists the commands most commonly used for the item you have clicked; the available commands are not therefore the same for every item.
6. Click anywhere outside the menu to close the pop-up menu
7. Move the **My Computer icon** back to its original position in the upper-left corner of the desktop using the pointing and dragging skills you have just learned
8. Point to the **My Computer icon**, then click the **left mouse button** twice quickly
   The My Computer window opens, containing several icons. Clicking the mouse button twice is known as **double-clicking**, and it allows you to open a window, program, or file that an icon represents. Leave the desktop as it is and move on to the next lesson.

Trouble?

If pointing to the icon highlights it, you are not using default Windows 2000 settings. Consult your instructor or technical support person. This book assumes you are using the Windows 2000 default double-click mouse setting.

QuickTip

When a step tells you to "click," it means, by default, to left-click. The directions will say "right-click" if you are to click with the right mouse button.

FIGURE A-2: Typical mouse

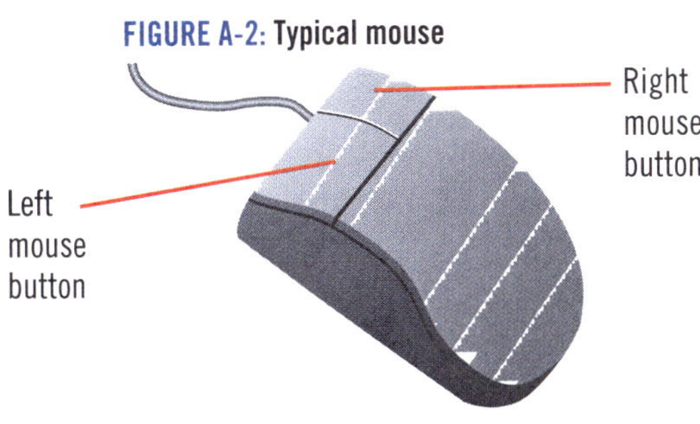

FIGURE A-3: A pop-up menu

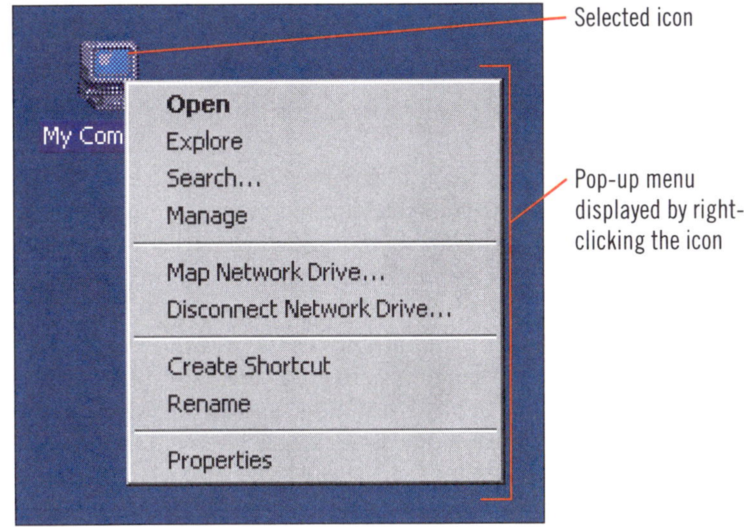

TABLE A-2: Common mouse pointer shapes

shape	used to
	Select items, choose commands, start programs, and work in programs
	Position mouse pointer for editing or inserting text; called the insertion point or cursor
	Indicate Windows is busy processing a command
	Position mouse pointer on the border of a window for changing the size of a window
	Position mouse pointer for selecting and opening Web-based content

TABLE A-3: Basic mouse techniques

task	what to do
Pointing	Move the mouse to position it over an item on the desktop
Clicking	Press and release the left mouse button once
Double-clicking	Press and release the left mouse button twice quickly
Dragging	Point to an item, press and hold the left mouse button, move the mouse to a new location, then release the mouse button
Right-clicking	Point to an item, then press and release the right mouse button

Using the mouse with the Internet

When you use the Internet, you point to an item to select it and single-click an item to open it, which is different from the standard Windows operating system. Because Windows 2000 integrates use of the Internet with its other functions, it allows you to choose whether you want to extend the way you click on the Internet to the rest of your computer work. Windows 2000 gives you two choices for selecting and opening icons using the mouse buttons: single-click mode (known as the Internet or Web style) or double-click mode (known as the Classic style). To change the way Windows 2000 uses the mouse button to select and open icons, click the Start button on the taskbar, point to Settings, click Control Panel, double-click Folder Options, and click the Single-click to open an item or Double-click to open an item option. Windows 2000 is set by default in double-click mode.

Getting Started with the Windows Desktop

The key to getting started with the Windows desktop is learning how to use the Start button on the taskbar. Clicking the Start button on the taskbar displays the **Start menu**, which is a list of commands that allows you to start a program, open a document, change a Windows setting, find a file, or display help information. Table A-4 describes the available categories on this menu that are installed with Windows 2000. As you become more familiar with Windows, you might want to customize the Start menu to include additional items that you use most often and change Windows settings in the Control Panel to customize your Windows desktop. **Personalized Menus** is a Windows setting that reduces the size of the Programs menu to reflect how you use your computer. When Personalized Menus is turned on, Windows keeps track of which programs you use and hides the programs you have not used recently, while still keeping all of your programs easily accessible. To view hidden programs, click the down arrow at the bottom of the Programs submenu. Begin by viewing the Start menu and opening the **Control Panel**, a window containing various programs that allow you to specify how your computer looks and performs. The My Computer window should still be open on your screen.

1. Click the **Start button** on the taskbar

   The Start menu opens.

2. Point to **Settings** on the Start menu

   An arrow next to a menu indicates a **cascading menu**, or a **submenu**—a list of commands for the menu item with the arrow next to it. Pointing at the arrow displays a submenu from which you can choose additional commands. The Settings submenu opens, as shown in Figure A-4, listing commands to open the Control Panel, Network and Dial-up Connections, and Printers; and to change settings for the Taskbar & Start Menu.

3. Click **Control Panel** on the submenu

   The Control Panel window opens, as shown in Figure A-5, containing icons for various programs that allow you to specify how your computer looks and performs. Leave the Control Panel window open for now, and continue to the next lesson.

QuickTip

To turn on Personalized Menus, click Taskbar & Start Menu on the Settings submenu, then click the Use Personalized Menus check box on the General tab.

Accessing the Internet from the desktop

One of the important differences between Windows 2000 and other versions of Windows is that Windows 2000 allows you to access the Internet right from the desktop. This is possible because a program called Internet Explorer is integrated into the Windows 2000 operating system. **Internet Explorer** is an example of a **browser**, a computer program designed to access the Internet. Windows 2000 adds Web enhancements to the Start menu and the taskbar. The Favorites command on the Start menu makes it easy to access places on the Internet you visit frequently. New commands on the Search submenu (On the Internet and For People) make it easy to find and access places on the Internet you want to visit. To provide additional Internet access, the Quick Launch toolbar is available on the taskbar to help you launch Internet-related programs and show the desktop. Windows 2000 makes it easier than ever to access the Internet.

FIGURE A-4: Cascading menus

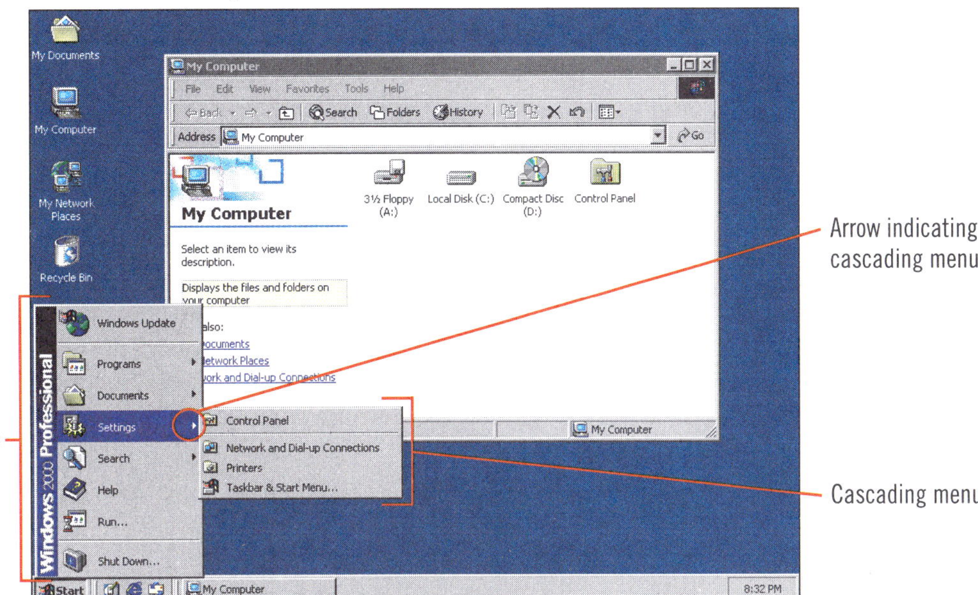

FIGURE A-5: Control Panel

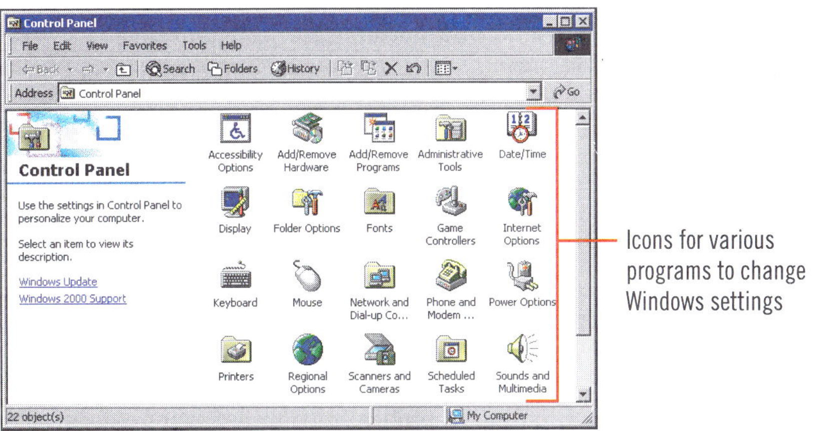

TABLE A-4: Start menu categories

category	description
Windows Update	Connects to a Microsoft Web site and updates your Windows 2000 files as necessary
Programs	Opens programs included on the Start menu
Favorites	Connects to favorite Web sites, or opens folders or documents that you previously selected; available when the Display Favorites feature is turned on in the Taskbar & Start Menu dialog box
Documents	Opens documents most recently opened and saved
Settings	Allows you to set user preferences for system settings, including the Control Panel, Network and Dial-Up Connections, Printers, and Taskbar & Start Menu
Search	Locates programs, files, folders, or computers on your computer network, or finds information or people on the Internet
Help	Lists Windows help information by topic, alphabetical index, or search criteria
Run	Opens a program or file based on a location and filename that you type or select
Log Off	Allows you to log off the system and log on as a different user; available when the Display Logoff feature is turned on in the Taskbar & Start Menu dialog box
Shut Down	Provides options to shut down the computer, restart the computer, or log off a user and restart the computer

Windows 2000

Moving and Resizing Windows

One of the powerful things about working in Windows is that you can open more than one window or program at once. This means, however, that the desktop can get cluttered with many open windows for the various windows and programs you are using. To organize your desktop, sometimes it is necessary to change the size of a window or move it to a different location. Each window, no matter what it contains, is surrounded by a standard border that you can drag to change the size of the window. Each window also has three standard buttons in the upper-right corner that allow you to change the size of windows. Table A-5 shows the different mouse pointer shapes that appear when resizing windows. Try moving and resizing the Control Panel window now.

Steps

1. Click anywhere in the My Computer window or click the **My Computer button** on the taskbar
   The My Computer window moves in front of the Control Panel window. The My Computer window is now **active** (title bar color changes from gray to blue); this means that any actions you perform will take place in this window.

QuickTip

You can click the Show the Desktop button on the Quick Launch toolbar to minimize all open windows and programs in order to show the desktop.

2. Click the **Minimize button** in the My Computer window
   The window no longer appears on the desktop, but you can still see a button named My Computer on the taskbar. When you **minimize** a window, you do not close it but merely reduce it to a button on the taskbar so that you can work more easily in other windows. The button on the taskbar reminds you that the program is still running.
3. Point to the **title bar** on the Control Panel window
   The **title bar** is the area along the top of the window that contains the name of the file and the program used to create it. When a window is active, the title bar color changes from gray to blue. You can move any window to a new location on the desktop by dragging the window's title bar.
4. With the mouse pointer over any spot on the title bar, click and drag the **title bar** to center the window on the desktop
   This action is similar to dragging an icon to a new location. The window is relocated.

QuickTip

You can double-click the title bar of a window to switch between maximizing and restoring the size of a window.

5. Click the **Maximize button** in the Control Panel
   When you **maximize** a window, it takes up the entire screen.
6. Click the **Restore button** in the Control Panel
   The **Restore button** returns a window to its previous size, as shown in Figure A-6. The Restore button only appears when a window is maximized. Now try making the window smaller.

QuickTip

You can resize windows by dragging any corner, not just the lower-left. You can also drag any border to make the window taller, shorter, wider, or narrower.

7. Position the mouse pointer on the lower-right corner of the Control Panel window until the pointer changes to ↘, as indicated in Figure A-6, then drag the corner up and to the left
   The window is now resized. In the next lesson you will work with the menus and toolbars in the Control Panel, so you can leave this window open.
8. Click the **My Computer button** on the taskbar
   The My Computer window returns to the size it was before it was minimized and is now active.
9. Click the **Close button**, located in the upper-right corner of the My Computer window
   The My Computer window closes. You will learn more about My Computer in later lessons.

FIGURE A-6: Restored Control Panel window

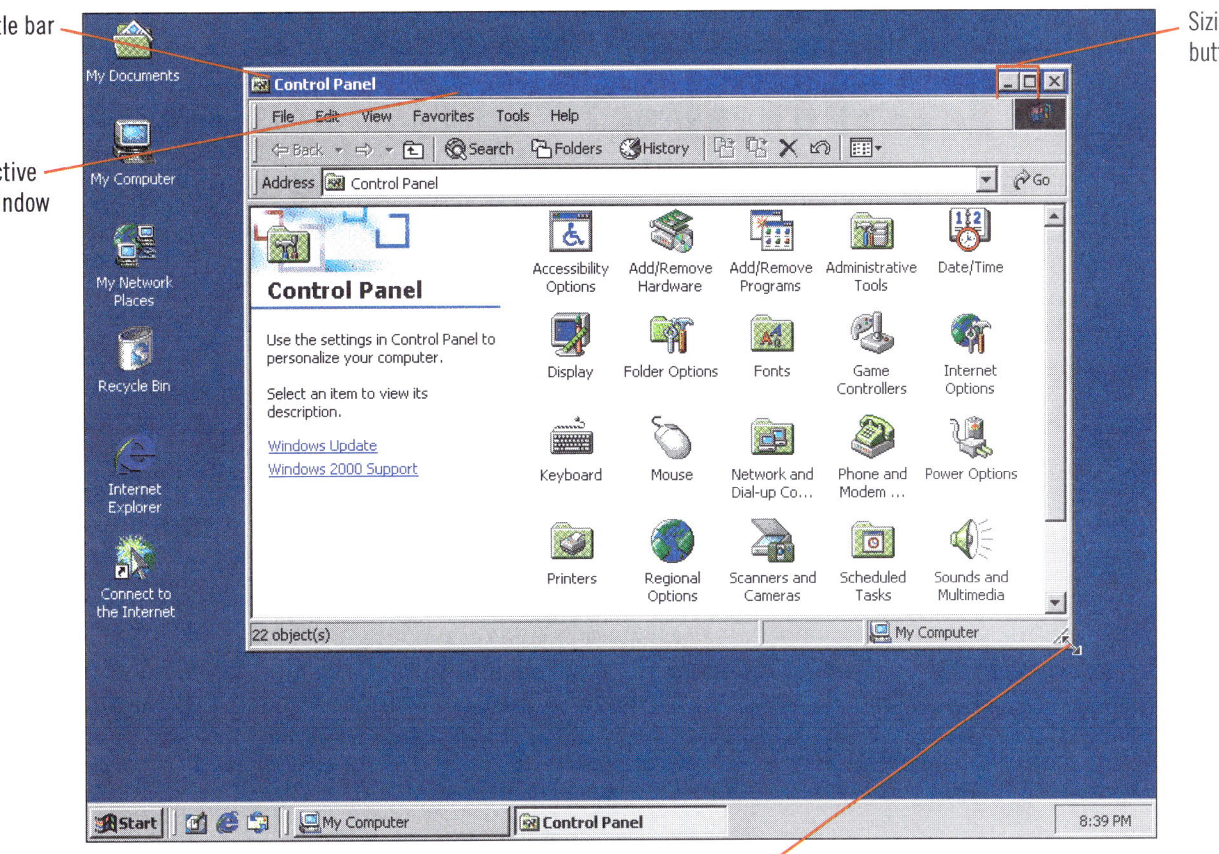

TABLE A-5: Mouse pointer shapes that appear when resizing windows

mouse pointer shape	use to
↔	Drag the right or left edge of a window to change its width
↕	Drag the top or bottom edge of a window to change its height
⤡ or ⤢	Drag any corner of a window to change its size proportionally

Moving and resizing the taskbar

In addition to windows, you can also resize and move other elements on the desktop, such as the taskbar, using the methods in this lesson. You can move the taskbar by dragging it to any edge (right, left, top, or bottom) of the desktop. You can also change the size of the taskbar by dragging its edge.

Using Menus and Toolbars

A **menu** is a list of commands that you use to accomplish certain tasks. You've already used the Start menu to open the Control Panel. A **command** is a directive that provides access to a program's features. Each Windows program also has its own set of menus, which are located on the menu bar along the top of the program window. The **menu bar** organizes commands into groups of related operations. Each group is listed under the name of the menu, such as "File" or "Help." To access the commands in a menu, you click the name of the menu. See Table A-6 for examples of items on a typical menu. Some of the most frequently used commands on a menu can also be carried out by clicking a button on a toolbar. A **toolbar** contains buttons that are convenient shortcuts for menu commands. Use a menu and toolbar button to change how the contents of the Control Panel window appear.

QuickTip

You can add or remove buttons to or from a toolbar to customize it. To customize the toolbar, click View on the menu bar, click Toolbars, then click Customize.

1. Click **View** on the menu bar

   The View menu for the Control Panel appears, listing the View commands available in the Control Panel, as shown in Figure A-7. When you click a menu name, a general description of the commands available on that menu appears in the status bar. On a menu, a **check mark** identifies a feature that is currently selected (that is, the feature is enabled or "on"). To disable ("turn off") the feature, you click the command again to remove the check mark. A menu can contain more than one enabled check mark. A **bullet mark** also indicates that an option is enabled, but a menu can contain only one enabled bullet mark. To disable a command with a bullet mark next to it, you must select a different bullet option on the menu. On the View menu, the Large Icons bullet option is enabled, so the Control Panel window displays large icons.

Trouble?

If you do not see the views button, click the More Buttons button » to display it.

2. On the View menu, click **Small Icons**

   The window now displays smaller icons, so they take up less room. The Control Panel toolbar includes buttons for the commands that you use most frequently while you are in the Control Panel window. When you position the mouse pointer over a button, a ScreenTip appears. Use the ScreenTip feature to view the name of a button on the toolbar.

3. On the Control Panel toolbar, position the pointer over the **Views button** to view the ScreenTip

   Some toolbar buttons appear with an arrow, which indicates that the button contains several choices. You can click the button arrow to display a menu of choices.

4. On the Control Panel toolbar, click the **Views button**, as shown in Figure A-8, then click **Details**

   The Details view includes a description of each Control Panel program. The ellipsis (. . .) at the end of a column line of text indicates more text to the right. You can adjust the column width to see the additional text. To adjust the column width, position the pointer (which changes to ↔), then drag to the right.

FIGURE A-7: View menu in the Control Panel

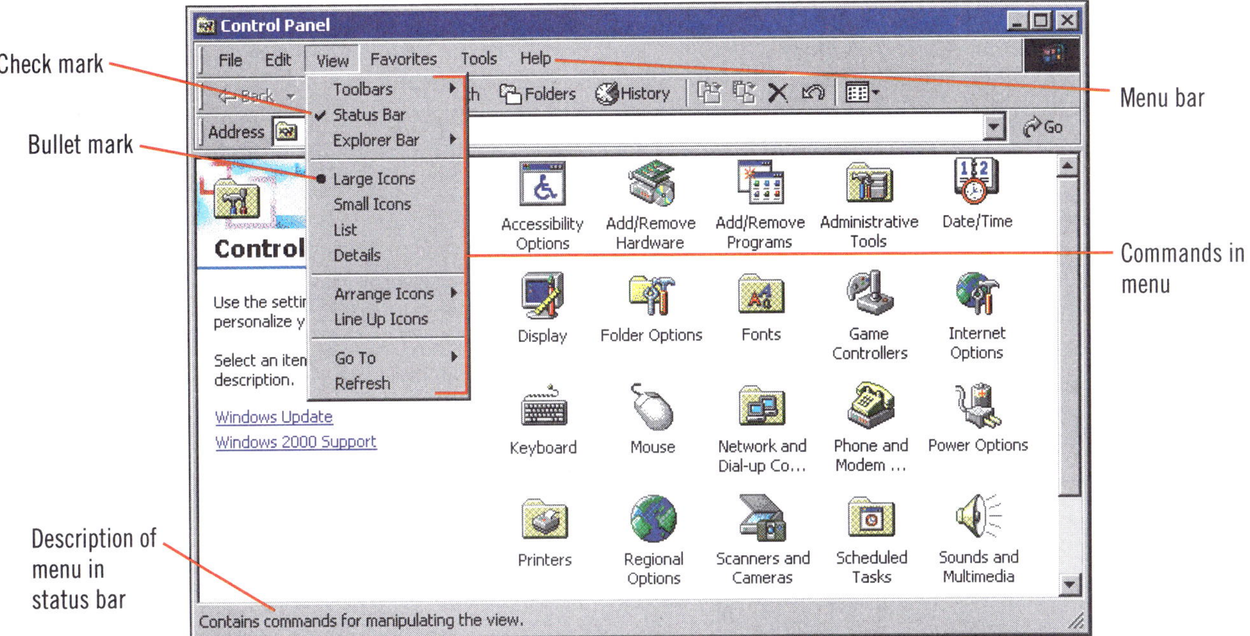

FIGURE A-8: Control Panel toolbars

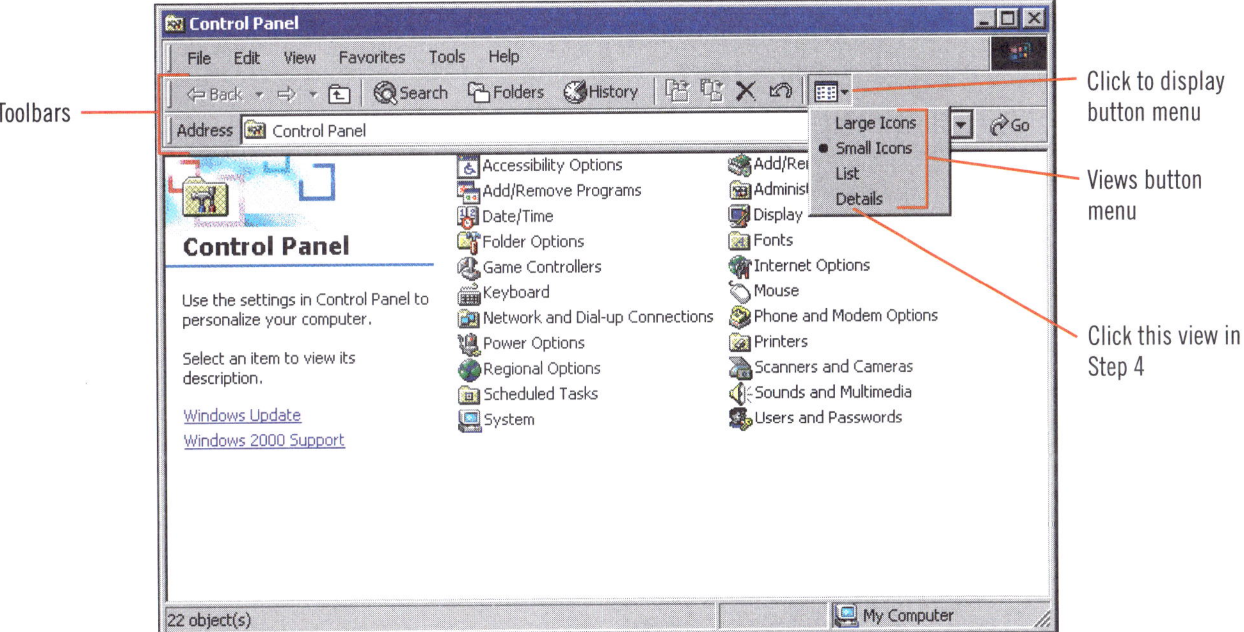

TABLE A-6: Typical items on a menu

item	description	example
Dimmed command	A menu command that is not currently available	Undo Ctrl+Z
Ellipsis	Choosing this menu command opens a dialog box that allows you to select from several options	Save As...
Triangle	Choosing this menu command opens a cascading menu containing an additional list of menu commands	Zoom ▸
Keyboard shortcut	An alternative to using the mouse for executing a menu command	Paste Ctrl+V
Underlined letter	Pressing the underlined letter while the [Alt] key is also pressed executes the menu command	Print Preview

Windows 2000

Using Scroll Bars

When you cannot see all of the items available in a window, scroll bars appear on the right and/or bottom edges of the window. **Scroll bars** allow you to move around in a window to display the additional contents of the window. See Figure A-9 for the components of scroll bars. The vertical scroll bar moves your view up and down through a window; the horizontal scroll bar moves your view from left to right. There are several ways you can use scroll bars. When you need to scroll only a short distance, you can use the scroll arrows. When you need to scroll more quickly, you can click in the scroll bar above or below the scroll box, which moves the view up or down one window's height (the line that was at the bottom of the screen is moved to the top, and vice versa). Dragging the scroll box moves you even more quickly to a new part of the window. See Table A-7 for a summary of the different ways to use scroll bars. Use the scroll bars to view and read the description of each Control Panel program.

Steps

QuickTip

When scroll bars don't appear in a window, it means that all the information fits completely in the window.

1. **In the Control Panel window, click the down scroll arrow once in the vertical scroll bar, as shown in Figure A-9**
   Clicking this arrow once moves the view down one line. Clicking the up arrow once moves the view up one line at a time.
2. **Click the up scroll arrow in the vertical scroll bar**
   The view moves up one line.
3. **Click anywhere in the area below the scroll box in the vertical scroll bar**
   The contents in the window scroll down in a larger increment.
4. **Click the area above the scroll box in the vertical scroll bar**
   The contents in the window scroll back up. To move in even greater increments, you can drag the scroll box to a new position.

QuickTip

If you have a mouse with a wheel button in between the left and right buttons, you can roll the wheel button to quickly scroll up and down or click the wheel button and move the mouse in any direction.

5. **Drag the scroll box to the middle of the scroll bar**
   The scroll box indicates your relative position within the file, in this case, the halfway point.
6. **On the Control Panel toolbar, click the Views button, then click Large Icons**
   This restores the Control Panel to its original display.

FIGURE A-9: Scroll bars in Control Panel

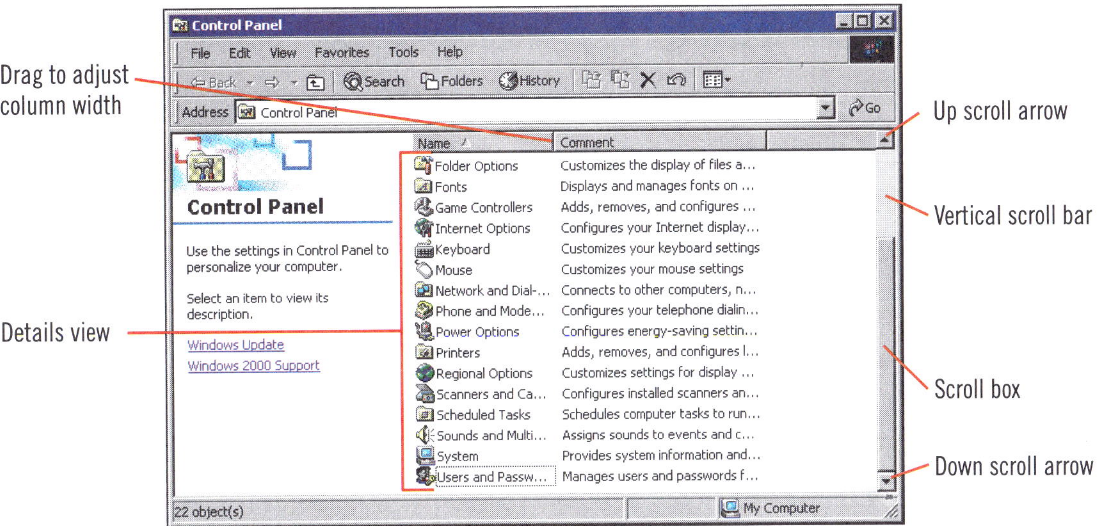

TABLE A-7: Using scroll bars in a window

to	do this
Move down one line	Click the down arrow at the bottom of the vertical scroll bar
Move up one line	Click the up arrow at the top of the vertical scroll bar
Move down one window's height	Click in the area below the scroll box in the vertical scroll bar
Move up one window's height	Click in the area above the scroll box in the vertical scroll bar
Move up or down a greater distance in the window	Drag the scroll box in the vertical scroll bar
Move a short distance side to side in a window	Click the left or right arrows in the horizontal scroll bar
Move to the right one window's width	Click in the area to the right of the scroll box in the horizontal scroll bar
Move to the left one window's width	Click in the area to the left of the scroll box in the horizontal scroll bar
Move left or right a greater distance in the window	Drag the scroll box in the horizontal scroll bar

Accessibility for special needs

If you have difficulty typing or using a mouse, have slightly impaired vision, or are deaf or hard of hearing, you can adjust the appearance and behavior of Windows 2000, making your computer easier to use. The **Accessibility Wizard** helps you configure Windows for your vision, hearing, and mobility needs. The Accessibility Wizard also enables you to save your settings to a file that can be used on another computer. To open the Accessibility Wizard, click Start, point to Programs, point to Accessories, point to Accessibility, then click Accessibility Wizard. You can also use the Control Panel to adjust the way your keyboard, display, and mouse function to suit varying vision and motor abilities. Some of the accessibility tools available include StickyKeys, which enables simultaneous keystrokes while pressing one key at a time; FilterKeys, which adjusts the response of your keyboard; ToggleKeys, which emits sounds when certain locking keys are pressed; SoundSentry, which provides visual warnings for system sounds; ShowSounds, which instructs programs to provide captions; High Contrast, which improves screen contrast; MouseKeys, which enables the keyboard to perform mouse functions; and SerialKeys, which allows the use of alternative input devices.

Using Dialog Boxes

A **dialog box** is a window that opens when you choose a command from a menu that is followed by an ellipsis (. . .). The ellipsis indicates that more information is required before the program can carry out the command you selected. Dialog boxes open in other situations as well, such as when you open a program in the Control Panel. In a dialog box, you specify the options you want using a variety of elements. See Figure A-10 and Table A-8 for some of the typical elements of a dialog box. Practice using a dialog box to control your mouse settings.

Steps

1. In the Control Panel window, double-click the **Mouse icon** (you might need to scroll down the Control Panel window to find this icon)
   The Mouse Properties dialog box opens, shown in Figure A-11. The options in this dialog box allow you to control the way the mouse buttons are configured, select the types of pointers that appear, choose the speed of the mouse movement on the screen, and specify what type of mouse you are using. **Tabs** at the top of the dialog box separate these options into related categories.
2. Click the **Motion tab**
   This tab has three boxes. The first, labeled Speed, has a slider for you to set how fast the mouse pointer moves on the screen in relation to how you move the mouse in your hand. The slider lets you specify the degree to which the option is in effect—the speed of the mouse pointer.
3. In the Speed box, drag the **slider** to the left
   As you move the mouse, notice the slower speed.
4. Click the other tabs in the Mouse Properties dialog box and examine the options that are available in each category
   Now, you need to select a command button to carry out the options you've selected. The two most common command buttons are OK and Cancel. Clicking OK accepts your changes and closes the dialog box; clicking Cancel leaves the settings intact and closes the dialog box. The third command button in this dialog box is Apply. Clicking the Apply button accepts the changes you've made and keeps the dialog box open so that you can select additional options. Because you might share this computer with others, it's important to return the dialog box options back to the original settings.
5. Click **Cancel**
   The original settings stay intact and the dialog box closes.
6. Click the **Close button** in the upper-right corner of the Control Panel window

FIGURE A-10: Dialog box elements

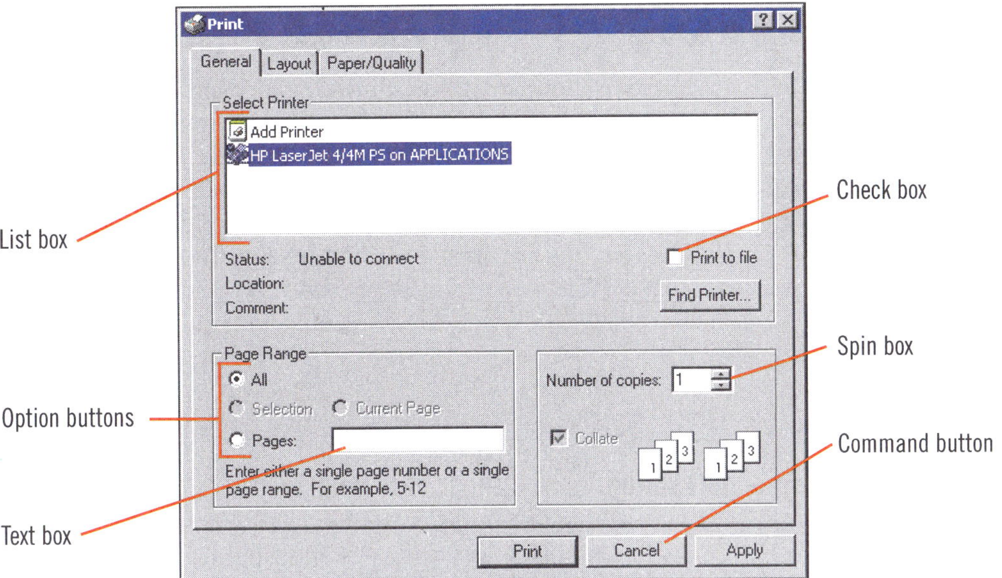

FIGURE A-11: Mouse Properties dialog box

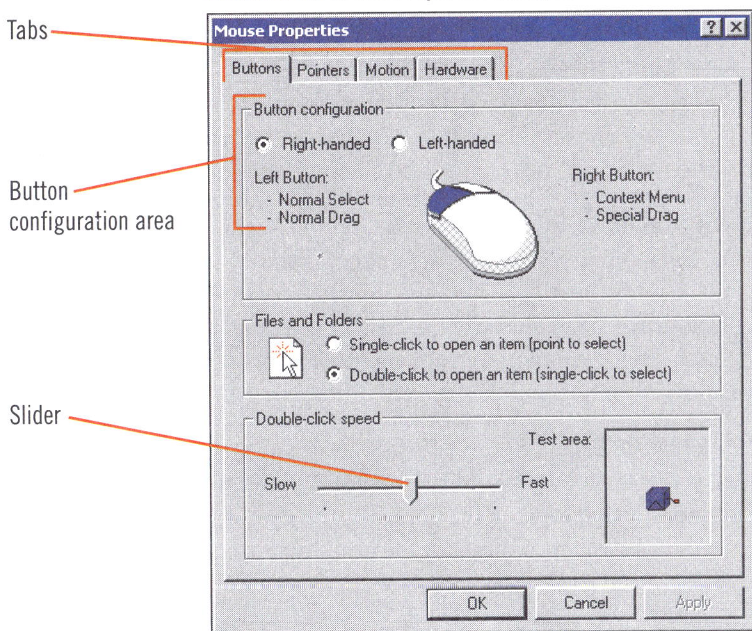

TABLE A-8: Typical items in a dialog box

item	description
Check box	A square box that turns an option on (when the box is checked) and off (when the box is blank)
Command button	A rectangular button with the name of the command on it; it carries out a command in a dialog box
List box	A box containing a list of items; to choose an item, click the list arrow, then click the desired item
Option button	A small circle that selects a single dialog box option (you cannot check more than one option button in a list)
Spin box	A box with two arrows and a text box; allows you to scroll numerical increments or type a number
Slider	An icon you slide to set the degree to which an option is in effect
Tab	A place to organize related options
Text box	A box in which you type text

Using Windows Help

When you have a question about how to do something in Windows 2000, you can usually find the answer with a few clicks of your mouse. There are a variety of different ways to access **Windows Help**, which is like a book stored on your computer, complete with an index and a table of contents to make finding information easier. You can click Help on the Start menu to open the main Windows Help dialog box. To get help on a specific program, you can click Help on the program's menu bar. You can also access **context-sensitive help**, help specifically related to what you are doing, using a variety of methods that you will practice (such as pointing to or right-clicking an object). Use Help to find out about the Windows desktop.

Steps

1. **Click the Start button on the taskbar, click Help, then click the Contents tab if necessary**
   The Windows Help dialog box opens, as shown in Figure A-12, with the Contents tab in front. The Contents tab provides you with a list of help categories. Each book icon has several "chapters" (subcategories) that you can see by clicking the book icon or the name of the help category next to the book.

2. **Point to the Introducing Windows 2000 Professional category, then click to view the subcategories underneath**
   When you point to a help category, the mouse changes to the hand pointer and the help category text is selected. The text changes to blue and underlined. This is similar to the way selecting on the Internet works. You continue to click categories to find the help topic you want.

QuickTip

You can hide the left pane of the Help window to make reading the help information easier. Click the Hide button on the Help toolbar to hide the left pane; click the Show button to re-open it.

3. **Click the What's new? topic**
   The What's New topic appears in the right pane, as shown in Figure A-13. **Panes** divide a window into two or more sections. Read the information on the new features in Windows 2000 Professional. Within a help topic, you can click [+] to expand a topic heading or click [−] to collapse a topic heading. You can move back and forth between help topics you have already visited by clicking the Back button and the Forward button on the Help toolbar.

4. **Click the Favorites tab**
   The Favorites tab allows you to add a frequently used help topic to the Topics list. If you want to add the selected topic to the Topics list, known as a **bookmark**, click Add. Later, you can return to this list and double-click the bookmark to quickly display the topic.

5. **Click the Index tab**
   The Index tab provides you with an alphabetical list of all the help topics that are available, much like an index at the end of a book. You can find out about any Windows feature by either entering the topic in the text box, or by scrolling down to the topic for which you want help, selecting a topic, and then clicking Display.

QuickTip

To print all or part of the help information, click the Options button on the Help toolbar, then click Print.

6. **Click the Search tab**
   The Search tab helps you locate the topic you need using keywords. You can find a topic by entering a keyword in the text box, clicking List Topics, selecting a topic, and then clicking Display.

7. **Click the Web Help button on the Help toolbar**
   Windows online support and information appears in the right pane. You can access the Windows Web site by clicking any one of the topics. The Web site topics provide technical support, answers to frequently asked questions, upgrade information, and late-breaking tips about working with Windows 2000.

8. **Click the Close button in the Windows Help window**
   The Help window closes.

FIGURE A-12: Windows 2000 dialog box

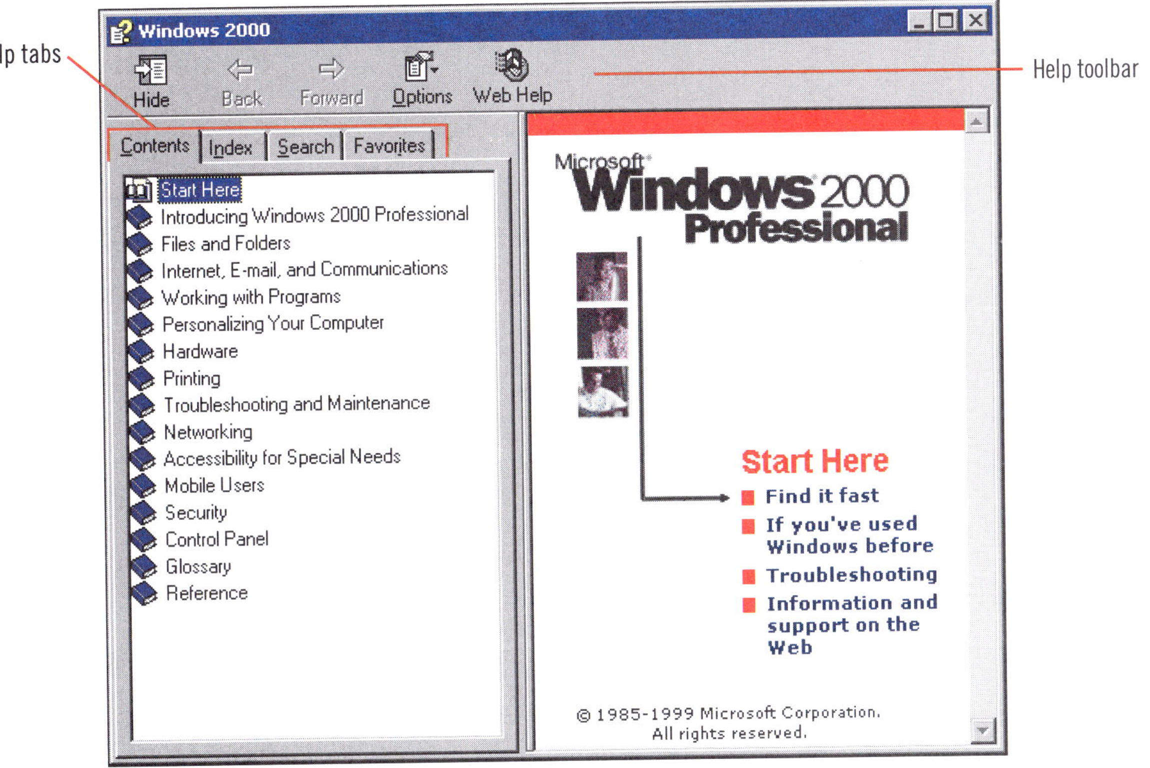

FIGURE A-13: Getting help on a particular topic

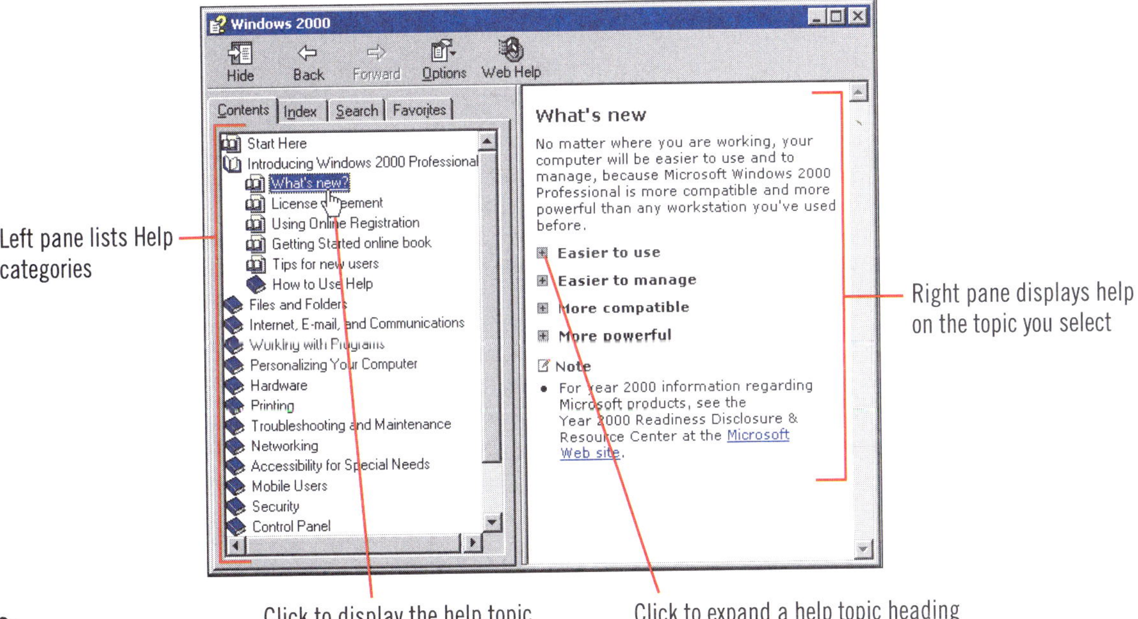

Clues to Use

Context-sensitive Help

To receive help in a dialog box, click the Help button [?] in the upper-right corner of the dialog box; the mouse pointer changes to ?. Click on the item in the dialog box for which you need additional information. A pop-up window opens, providing a brief explanation of the selected feature. You can also click the right mouse button on an item in a dialog box, then click the What's This? button to view the explanation. In addition, when you click the right mouse button in a help topic window, you can choose commands to annotate, copy, and print the contents of the topic. Help windows always appear on top of the currently active window, so you can see help topics while you work.

Windows 2000

Shutting Down Windows

When you are finished working at your computer, you need to make sure to **shut down**, or turn off, your computer properly. This involves several steps: saving and closing all open files, closing all open windows, exiting all running programs, shutting down Windows itself, and, finally, turning off the computer. If you turn off the computer while Windows or other programs are running, you could lose important data. Once all files, windows, and programs are closed, you choose the Shut Down command from the Start menu. The Shut Down Windows dialog box opens with several options, as shown in Figure A-14. See Table A-9 for a description of each option. Depending on your Windows settings, your shut down options might be different. Close all your open files, windows, and programs, and then exit Windows.

1. If you have any open windows or programs, click the **Close button** in the upper-right corner of the window
   Complete the remaining steps to shut down Windows and your computer only if you have been told to do so by your instructor or technical support person.
2. Click the **Start button** on the taskbar, then click **Shut Down**
   The Shut Down Windows dialog box opens, as shown in Figure A-14. In this dialog box, you have the option to shut down the computer, restart the computer, log off a user, stand by for a while, or hibernate.
3. Click the **What do you want the computer to do? list arrow**, then click **Shut down**, if it isn't already selected, or click outside the list to close it.
4. If you are working in a lab, click **Cancel** to return to the Windows desktop; if you are working on your own machine or if your instructor or technical support person told you to shut down Windows, click **OK** to exit Windows
5. If you see the message "It's now safe to turn off your computer", turn off your computer and monitor
   Some computers power off automatically, so you may not see this message.

FIGURE A-14: Shut Down Windows dialog box

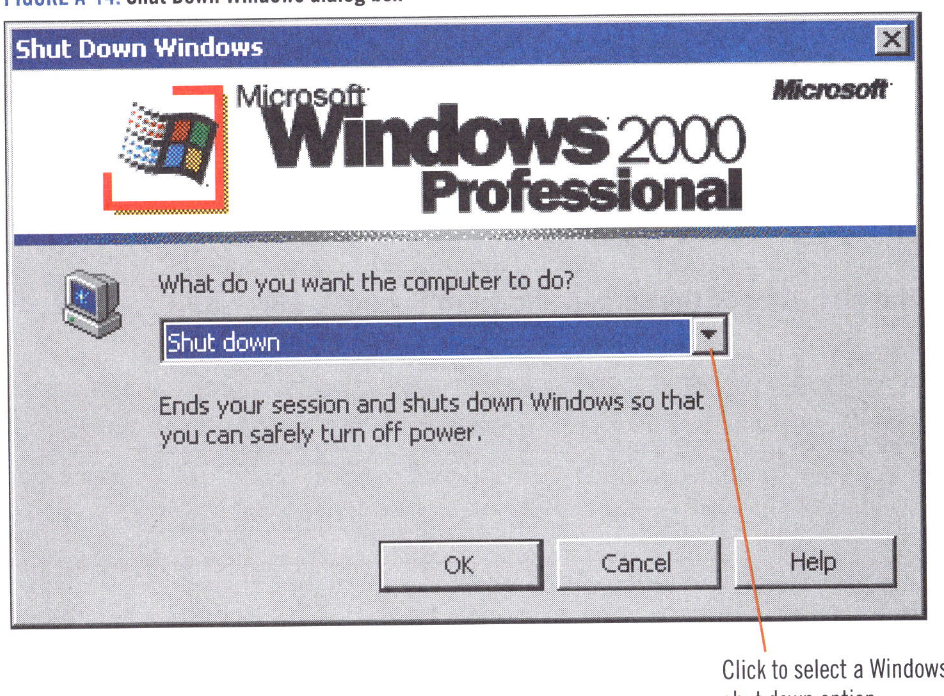

TABLE A-9: Shut down options

option	function	when to use it
Shut down	Prepares the computer to be powered off	When you are finished working with Windows and you want to shut off your computer
Restart	Restarts the computer and reloads Windows	When you want to restart the computer and begin working with Windows again (your programs might have frozen or stopped working)
Log off	Ends your session and restarts the computer for a new user	When you want to change to another user on the same computer
Stand by	Maintains your session, keeping the computer running on low power	When you want to stop working with Windows for a few moments and conserve power (for a laptop or portable computer)
Hibernate	Saves your session to disk so that you can safely turn off power; your session is restored the next time you start Windows	When you want to stop working with Windows for a while and start working again later; available when the Power Management setting (in the Control Panel) is turned on

Logging off Windows

Many users may use the same computer, so each user has his or her own identity in Windows. This allows many users to use the same machine with complete privacy over their files, and with the ability to customize the operating system for their own preferences. Windows manages these separate identities by giving each user a unique user name and password. For a quick change between users of the same computer, you can choose the Log Off command on the Start menu or in the Shut Down Windows dialog box. This command identifies the name of the user who is currently logged on. When you choose this command, Windows 2000 shuts down and automatically restarts to the Enter Network Password dialog box. When the new user enters a user name and password, Windows starts with their configuration settings and network permissions.

Practice

Concepts Review

Label each of the elements of the screen shown in Figure A-15.

FIGURE A-15

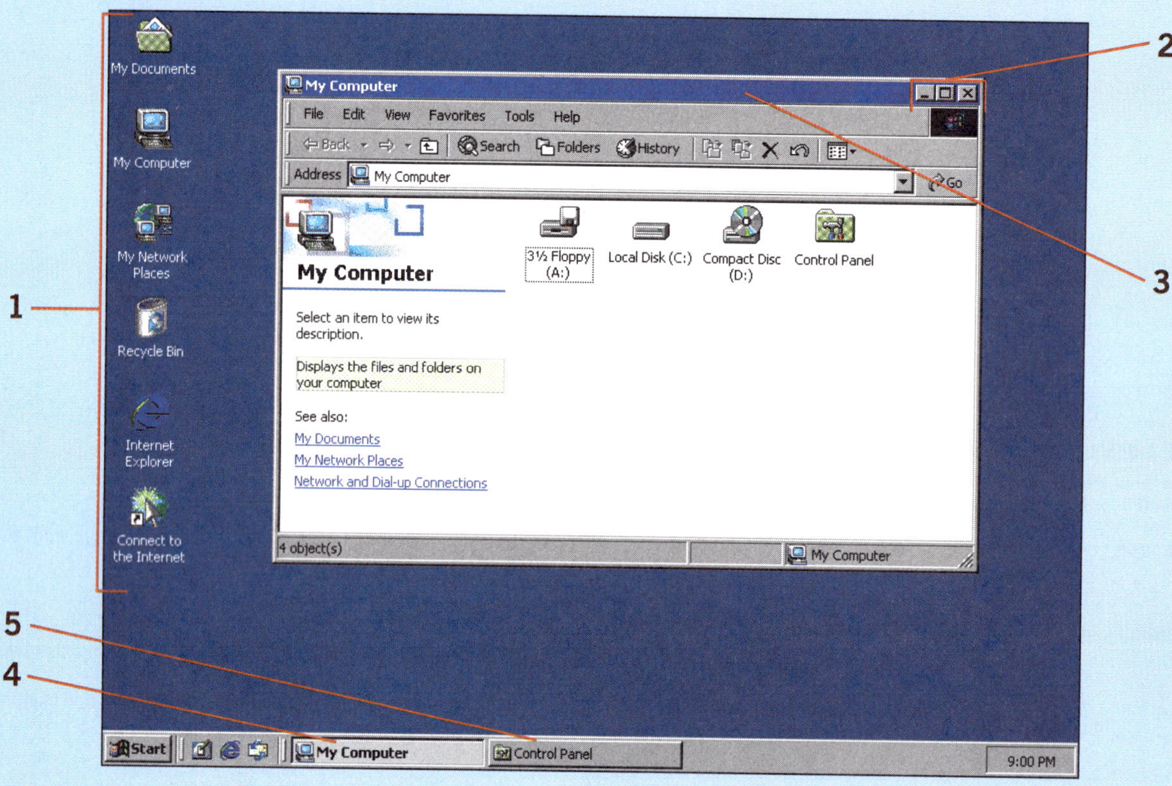

Match each of the terms with the statement that describes its function.

6. **Recycle Bin**
7. **Sizing buttons**
8. **Start buttons**
9. **Taskbar**
10. **Title bar**
11. **Mouse**

a. Allows you to minimize, maximize, and restore windows
b. The item you first click to start a program using the Start menu
c. Used to point to screen elements and make selections
d. Area where the name of an open program and file appear
d. Area where deleted files are placed
e. Displays the Start button and buttons for currently open programs and windows

Select the best answer from the list of choices.

12. The term for moving an item to a new location on the desktop is
- a. pointing.
- b. clicking.
- c. dragging.
- d. restoring.

13. The Maximize button is used to
- a. return a window to its original size.
- b. expand a window to fill the entire screen.
- c. scroll slowly through a window.
- d. reduce a window to a button on the taskbar.

14. The Minimize button is used to
- a. return a window to its original size.
- b. expand a window to fill the entire screen.
- c. scroll slowly through a window.
- d. reduce a window to a button on the taskbar.

15. The Menu bar provides access to a program's functions through
- a. toolbar buttons.
- b. scroll buttons.
- c. commands.
- d. dialog box elements.

16. To move the contents of the window up one screen,
- a. click the up scroll arrow.
- b. click the down scroll arrow.
- c. click in the scroll bar above the scroll box.
- d. click in the scroll bar below the scroll box.

▶ Skills Review

1. Start Windows and view the Windows desktop.
- a. Identify and write down as many items on the desktop as you can, without referring to the lesson material. Write them down as a list.
- b. Compare your results to Figure A-1.

2. Use the mouse.
- a. Move the mouse on your desk and watch how the mouse pointer moves across the screen.
- b. Point to the My Documents icon on the desktop.
- c. Click the My Documents icon once. Notice that the icon's title is highlighted.
- d. Press and hold down the mouse button, then drag the My Documents icon to the opposite side of the desktop. Release the mouse button when you are finished.
- e. Drag the My Documents icon back to the original location.
- f. Practice clicking and dragging other icons on the desktop.
- g. Double-click the My Documents icon.

3. Get started with Windows desktop.
- a. Click the Start button on the taskbar.
- b. Point to Settings.
- c. Click Control Panel.

4. **Move and resize windows.**
   a. Click the My Documents button on the taskbar.
   b. Click the Minimize button.
   c. Point to the title bar on the Control Panel window, then drag the window to the center of the desktop.
   d. Click the Maximize button.
   e. Click the Restore button.
   f. Position the mouse pointer on any corner of the Control Panel window and drag to resize the Control Panel window smaller, so that the vertical and horizontal scroll bars appear.
   g. Click the My Documents window button on the taskbar.
   h. Click the Close button on the My Documents window.
5. **Use menus and toolbars.**
   a. Click View on the menu bar, then click Small Icons.
   b. Click View on the menu bar, then click List.
   c. Click the Views button on the toolbar, then click Details.
6. **Use scroll bars.**
   a. Click below the vertical scroll box.
   b. Click the vertical up scroll arrow.
   c. Drag the horizontal scroll box to the middle of the scroll bar.
   d. Click the View button arrow on the toolbar, then click Large Icons.
7. **Use dialog boxes.**
   a. Double-click the Display icon.
   b. Click the Appearance tab.
   c. Click the Scheme list arrow.
   d. Select a color scheme.
   e. Click Apply (do not click OK).
   f. Click the Scheme list arrow, then click Windows Standard to return the color scheme back to the way it was.
   g. Click OK, then close the Control Panel window.
8. **Use Windows Help.**
   a. Click the Start button, then click Help.
   b. Click the Index tab.
   c. In the Type in the keyword to find text box, type **accessibility**.
   d. Click Accessibility Wizard in the list of topics, then click Display twice.
   e. Read the help topic in the right pane. Use the buttons on the vertical scroll bar if necessary to read all of the information.
   f. Click the Close button.
9. **Shut down Windows.**
   a. Click the Start button, then click Shut Down.
   b. Click the What do you want the computer to do? list arrow, then click Restart.
   c. Click OK if you are not working in a lab or if your lab manager approves of shutting down the computer. Otherwise, click Cancel.

Independent Challenges

1. Windows 2000 provides extensive online Help. At anytime, you can select Help from the Start menu and get the assistance you need. Use the Help options to learn about the topics listed below.

To complete this independent challenge:

a. Locate and read the help information on the following topics: My Computer, adjusting the double-click speed of the mouse, changing the color of the desktop, changing the appearance of scroll bars, and exiting programs.
b. If you have a printer connected to your computer, print one or more of the help topics you located.
c. Close the Windows Help window.

2. You can customize many Windows features to suit your needs and preferences. One way you do this is to change the appearance of the taskbar on the desktop.

To complete this independent challenge:

a. Position the mouse pointer over a blank area of the taskbar, then drag to the top of the screen to move the taskbar.
b. Position the mouse pointer over the bottom border of the taskbar. When the pointer changes shape, drag upwards to increase the size of the taskbar.
c. Click the Start button, point to Settings, and click Taskbar & Start Menu. On the General tab, click the Show Clock check box to deselect the option and observe the effect on the taskbar in the Preview window.
d. Print the Screen using the Windows Paint accessory (Press the Print Screen key to make a copy of the screen. Start the Paint program by clicking the Start button, pointing to Programs, pointing to Accessories, then clicking Paint. Click Edit on the menu bar, click Paste to paste the screen into Paint, then click Yes to paste the large image if necessary. Click File on the menu bar, click Print, then click Print in the dialog box.)
e. Restore the taskbar to its original setting, size, and location on the screen.

3. You have accepted a new job in New York City. After moving into your new home and unpacking your stuff, you decide to set up your computer. Once you set up and turn on the computer, you decide to change the date and time settings to reflect the time zone in New York.

To complete this independent challenge:

a. Open the Control Panel window, then double-click the Date/Time icon.
b. Click the Time Zone tab.
c. Select Eastern Time (US & Canada) from the list.
d. Click the Date & Time tab, change the month and year to September 2001, then click Apply.
e. Print the screen. (See Independent Challenge 2, Step d for screen printing instructions.)
f. Return the date and time zone back to their original settings, then click OK.
g. Close the Control Panel window.

4. You are a student in a Windows 2000 course. After learning basic Windows 2000 desktop skills, you want to learn how to customize the desktop. Use the online version of the Getting Started Book in Windows Help to find information on customizing your desktop and then print the related help topics.

To complete this independent challenge:

a. Open the Windows Help window.
b. In the Contents tab, go to the Introducing Windows 2000 Professional category.
c. Go to the Getting Started online book topic.
d. In the right pane, click Windows 2000 Professional Getting Started, then open Ch 1 – Welcome.
e. View the Windows 2000 Professional at a Glance topic, then print the topic.
f. Close the Windows Help windows.

FIGURE B-5: Positioning the insertion point

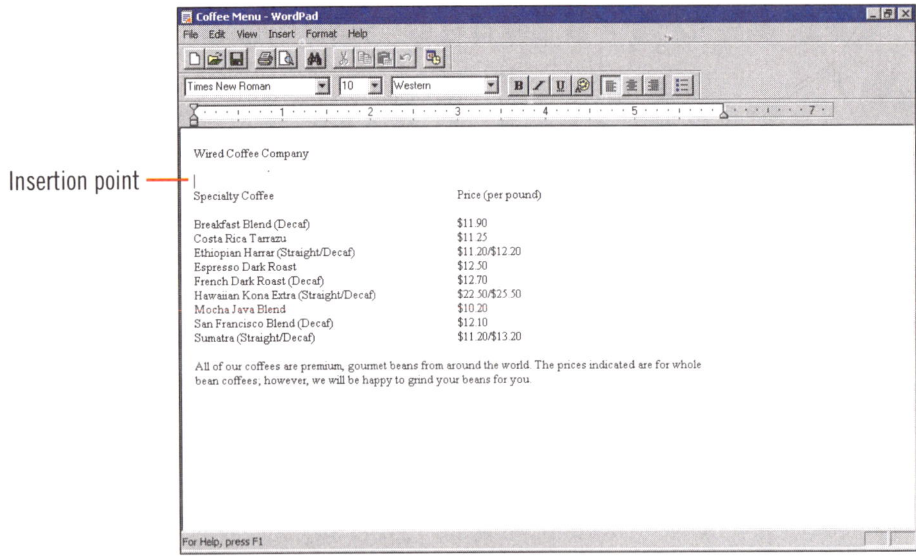

FIGURE B-6: Editing a WordPad file by cutting and pasting

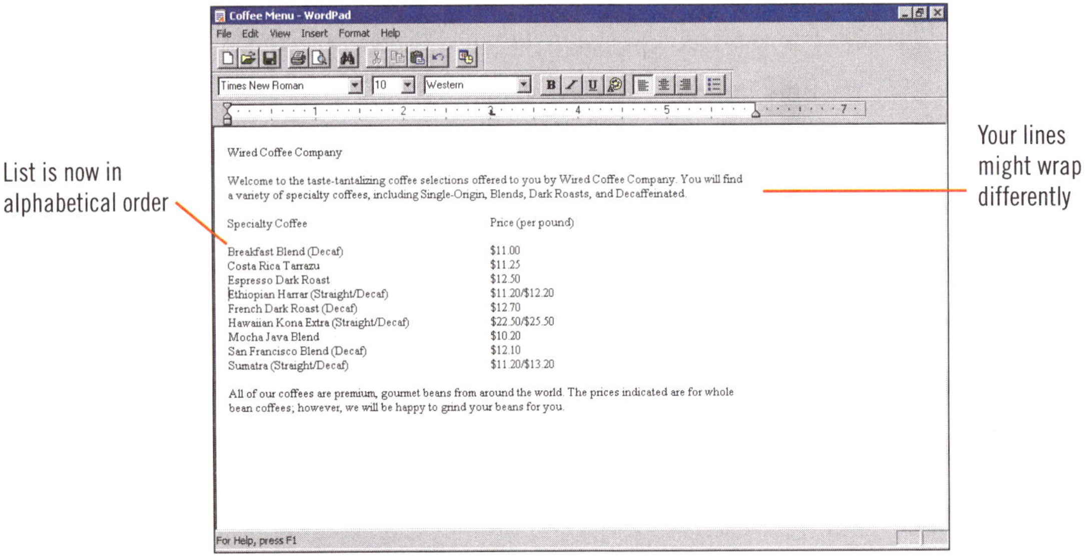

TABLE B-1: Moving around a WordPad document

key(s)	navigation
↑	Move up one line
↓	Move down one line
←	Move left one character
→	Move right one character
[PgUp]	Move to the previous page
[PdDn]	Move to the next page
[Ctrl][End]	Move to the end of the document
[Ctrl][Home]	Move to the beginning of the document
[Ctrl]→	Move to the beginning of the next word to the right
[Ctrl]←	Move to the beginning of the previous word to the left

Windows 2000

Formatting Text in a WordPad Document

You can change the **format**, or the appearance of the text and graphics in a document, so that the document is easier to read or more attractive. Almost all formatting changes in WordPad can be achieved using the Format Bar, which appears below the Toolbar in the WordPad window. Table B-2 describes the function of each button on the Format Bar. John wants to make the Coffee Menu document more attractive. He does this by centering the title, bolding it, and increasing its size.

Steps

QuickTip

To insert a special character, such as a trademark or symbol, click the Start button on the taskbar, point to Accessories, point to System Tools, and then click Character Map. Click a character, click Select, click Copy, place the insertion point in your document at the desired location, and then click the Paste button on the Toolbar.

1. Select the text **Wired Coffee Company**

   Remember that the first step in making any editing or formatting change is to select the text you want to change. Then, you can carry out the desired command.

2. Click the **Center button** on the Format Bar

   Notice that the title is centered and the button appears indented.

3. Click the **Bold button** on the Format Bar

   The selected material appears in bold. If you wanted to turn bold off, you would click the button again. Buttons act as **toggle** switches—click once to turn the format feature on, click again to turn it off.

4. Click the **Italic button** on the Format Bar

   Italicizing does not provide the effect that John wanted.

5. Click the **Undo button** on the Toolbar

   This command reverses the last change that was made, such as typing new text, deleting text, and formatting existing text. Undo cannot reverse all commands (such as scrolling or saving a document), but it is a quick way to reverse most editing and formatting changes.

6. Click the **Font list arrow** on the Format Bar, then click **Arial**

   The **font**, or typeface, of the text changes from Times New Roman to Arial.

7. Click the **Font Size list arrow** on the Format Bar, then click **14**

   The selected text increases in size from 10-point to 14-point. One **point** is 1/72 of an inch in height. Whenever you want to know the type and size of a font on your screen, place the insertion point anywhere in the text and look at the size that appears in the Font list box and Font Size list box.

8. Click anywhere in the document to deselect the text

   As Figure B-7 shows, the title is centered and changed in typeface to Arial and size to 14-point.

9. Click the **Save button** on the toolbar

   The changes made to the Coffee Menu are saved.

FIGURE B-7: Formatted text

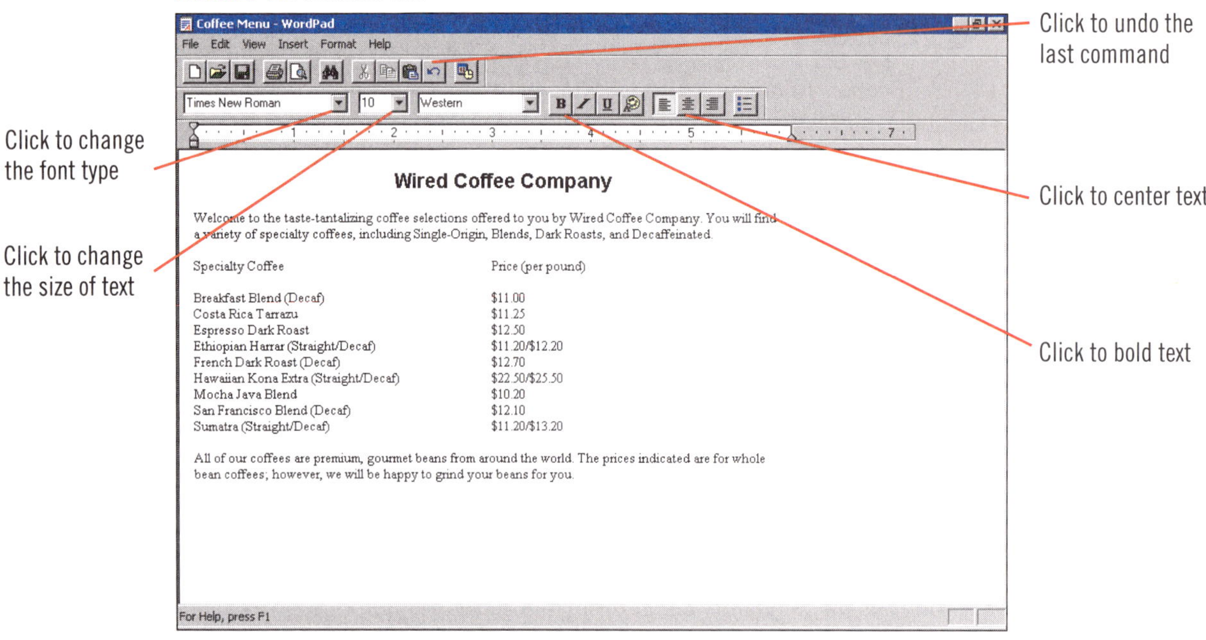

TABLE B-2: Format Bar buttons and list arrows

button	function	button	function
Times New Roman	Select a font		Add or change color
10	Select a font size		Left align
B	Bold		Center align
I	Italic		Right align
U	Underline		Create bulleted list

CLUES TO USE

Formatting text as you type

As you've learned, one way to format text is to select it, then apply a formatting change. Another way is to first apply the formatting you want, then enter text. This approach is helpful when you are starting a new document and are familiar with the effect that different formatting options create. For example, if you were creating a new list of items and knew that you wanted the title to be 24-point underlined text, you could click the Underline button U on the Format Bar, then click 24 in the Font Size list box. Anything that you type from that point will have those format characteristics. When you finish typing the title, you can change the font back to a smaller point size and click the Underline button to toggle the option off, then continue typing.

Windows 2000

Using Paint

When it comes to creating and working with images, Paint is a useful Windows accessory. You can draw images and manipulate them with commands such as rotate, stretch, and invert colors. You can open more than one Windows program at a time, so while WordPad is still running, you can open Paint and work on drawings and images. This is called **multitasking**. John already created a logo for his coffee company. Now he wants to review the logo and revise it as necessary before using it on his promotional materials.

Steps

1. Click the **Start button** on the taskbar, point to **Programs**, point to **Accessories**, click **Paint**, then click the **Maximize button** on the Paint title bar
   The Paint window opens and is maximized in front of the WordPad window. You can find buttons for frequently used commands in the Paint Tool Box, located along the left edge of the window. Table B-3 describes these tools.

QuickTip

To provide a consistent place to store all your images, Windows 2000 saves and opens all your image files to and from the My Pictures folder located in the My Documents folder.

2. Click **File** on the menu bar, click **Open**
   The Open dialog box opens.
3. Click the **Look in list arrow**, click **the drive that contains your Project Disk**, then double-click the **Unit B folder**
   A list of the files stored in this folder on the Project Disk appears.
4. In the file list, click **Win B-2**, then click **Open**
   The file named Win B-2 opens, shown in Figure B-8. If you cannot see the logo on your screen, use the scroll buttons to adjust your view. John decides the logo could use some final modifications.
5. Click **File** on the menu bar, click **Save As**, then save the document as **Wired Coffee Logo** to your Project Disk
   A copy of the file is saved under the new name, and the original file remains intact. John wants to add a rounded border around the logo. To use any tool in Paint, you first click it in the Tool Box, and then "paint" or "draw" with it using the mouse.

QuickTip

You can press and hold down [Shift] while you drag a drawing tool to create a proportional drawing, such as a square or circle.

Trouble?

If your rounded rectangle doesn't match Figure B-9, click Edit on the menu bar, then click Undo to reverse the last command. If Undo is not available, click the Erase tool, drag to erase the rounded rectangle, then repeat Step 6.

6. Click the **Rounded Rectangle tool** in the Tool Box, then move the cursor into the Paint work area
   When you move the mouse pointer back into the work space, it changes to +, indicating that the Rounded Rectangle tool is active.
7. Beginning above and to the left of the logo, drag + so that a rounded rectangle surrounds the image, then release the mouse button below and to the right of the image, as shown in Figure B-9
   John likes this new look.
8. Click **File** on the menu bar, then click **Save**
   Now John can use the logo in his other documents.

FIGURE B-8: Company logo in Paint

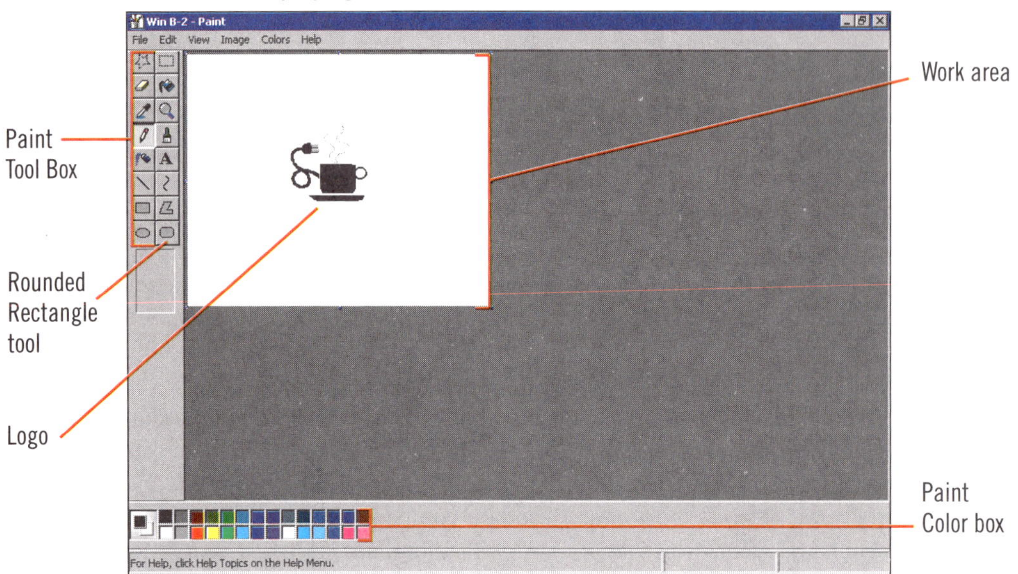

FIGURE B-9: Company logo with rounded rectangle

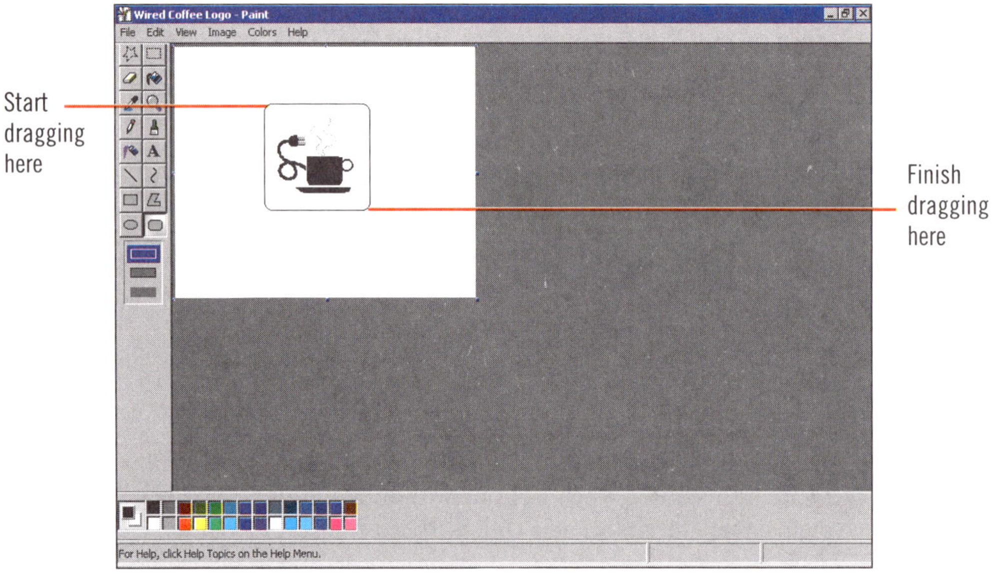

TABLE B-3: Buttons in the Paint Tool Box

tool	description	tool	description
	Selects a shape that is not regular		Creates dispersed lines and patterns
	Selects a shape that is regular		Enters text in drawings
	Erases part of a drawing		Draws a straight line
	Fills a shape with a color or texture		Draws a free-form line
	Picks up a color from the picture for drawing		Draws a regular shape
	Magnifies part of an image		Draws an irregular shape
	Draws freehand		Draws an oval or circle
	Designates the size and shape brush to draw with		Draws a rectangle or square with rounded corners

Windows 2000

Copying Data Between Programs

One of the most useful features that Windows offers is the ability to use data created in one document in another document, even if the two documents were created in different Windows programs. To work with more than one program or document at a time, you simply open each of them on your desktop. Any window that is open on the desktop is represented by a **program button** on the taskbar. When you want to switch from one open window to another, click the correct program button on the taskbar. If you **tile** or arrange open windows on the desktop so that all are visible, you can switch among them simply by clicking in the window you want to work in. Just as you used the Clipboard to rearrange text in WordPad, you can use it to move and copy data between two different documents. Table B-4 reviews the Cut, Copy, and Paste commands and their associated keyboard shortcuts, which can be used in Paint, WordPad, and many other Windows programs. John wants to add the company logo, which he created with Paint, to the Coffee Menu document, which he created with WordPad. He'll first switch to WordPad, which is still running, to decide exactly where he wants to place the logo. Then he'll switch to Paint, copy the logo, and finally switch back to WordPad and paste it in the menu.

Trouble?

If your windows don't appear tiled, click the program button on the taskbar for each program (Paint and WordPad) to ensure that both windows are maximized, then repeat Step 1.

1. Make sure both WordPad and Paint are open, place the mouse pointer on an empty area of the taskbar, **right-click**, then click **Tile Windows Vertically** from the shortcut menu
   The windows (Paint and WordPad) are arranged next to one another vertically, as shown in Figure B-10, so that John can maneuver quickly between them while working.
2. Click the **Paint program button** on the taskbar or click anywhere in the Paint window
   The Paint program becomes the **active program** (the title bar changes from gray to blue).
3. Click the **Select tool** in the toolbox, then drag a rectangle around the coffee logo to select it
   Dragging with the Select Tool selects an object in Paint for cutting, copying, or performing other modifications.

QuickTip

When Windows are tiled, you can drag a selected item from one program to another to copy the item between programs.

4. Click **Edit** on the Paint menu bar, then click **Copy**
   The logo is copied to the Windows Clipboard. The Copy command is similar to the Cut command you used when working with the coffee list, but when you copy a selection, the original remains intact and a copy is placed on the Clipboard.
5. Click the first **blank line** of the WordPad document, above the title
   The WordPad program becomes active and the insertion point is placed on the WordPad page, where John wants the logo to appear. If you cannot see enough of the page, use the scroll buttons to adjust your view.
6. Click the **Paste button** on the WordPad Toolbar
   The logo is pasted into the document, as shown in Figure B-11.
7. Click the **Maximize button** in the WordPad window, click the **Center button** on the Format Bar, then click below the logo to deselect it
   The logo is centered in the document.
8. Click the **Save button** on the WordPad Toolbar
   The document is complete and ready for John to print.
9. Click the **Paint program button** on the taskbar, then click **Close button** in the Paint window

FIGURE B-10: Tiled windows

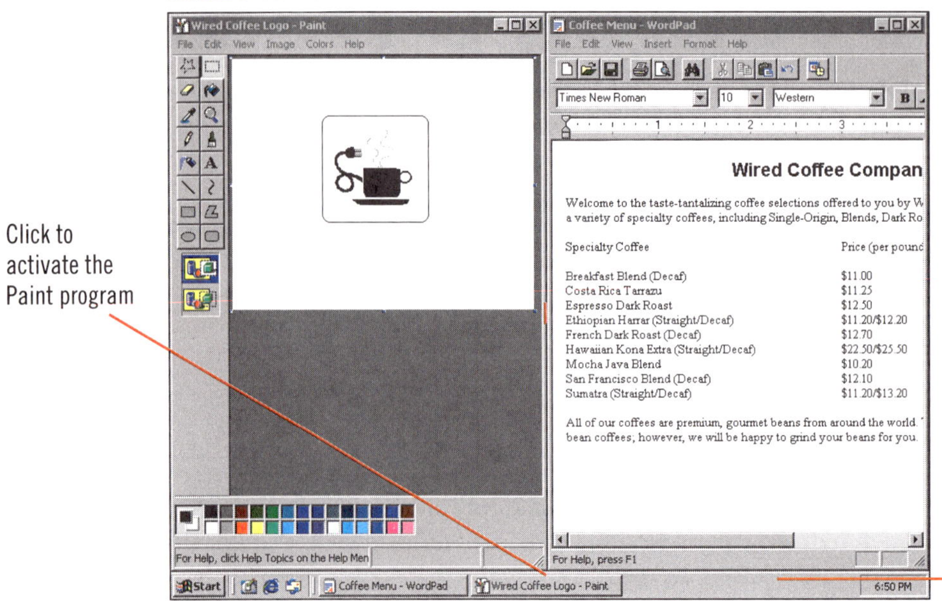

FIGURE B-11: Copying a selection between programs

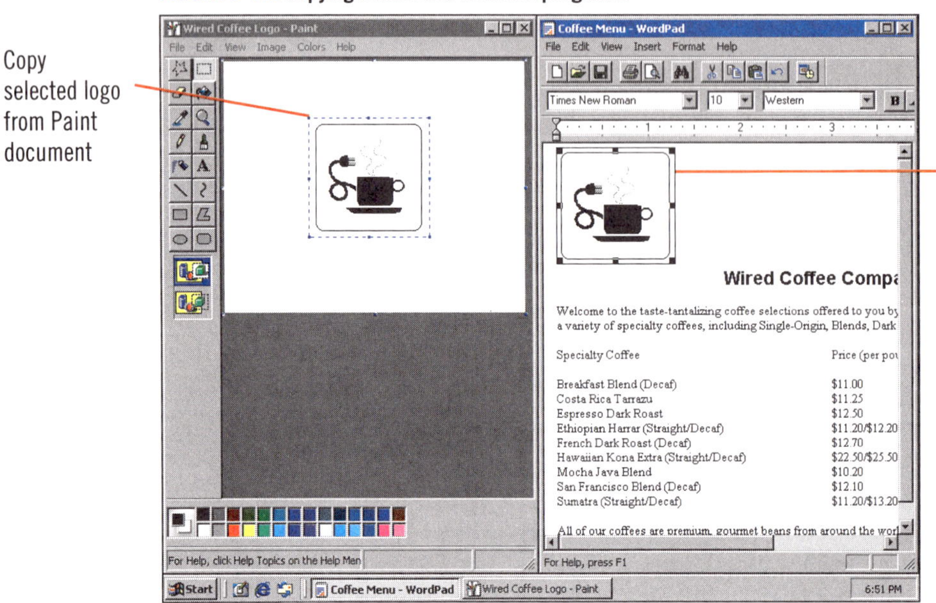

TABLE B-4: Overview of cutting, copying, and pasting

function	toolbar button	keyboard shortcut
Cut: Removes selected information from a file and places it on the Clipboard		[Ctrl][X]
Copy: Places a copy of selected information on the Clipboard, leaving the file intact		[Ctrl][C]
Paste: Inserts whatever is currently on the Clipboard into another location (within the same file or in a different file)		[Ctrl][V]

Windows 2000

Printing a Document

Printing a document creates a **printout** or **hard copy**, a document on paper that you can share with others or review as a work in progress. Most Windows programs have a print option that you access through the Print Dialog box and a Print button on the Toolbar. Although your printing options vary from program to program, the process works similarly in all of them. It is a good idea to use the **Print Preview** feature to look at the layout and formatting of a document before you print it. You may catch a mistake, find that the document fits on more pages than you wanted, or notice formatting that you want to do differently. Making changes before you print saves paper. John decides to preview the coffee menu before printing the document.

Steps 1 2 3 4

1. **In the WordPad window, click the Print Preview button on the Toolbar**
   A reduced but proportionate image of the page appears in the Preview window, as shown in Figure B-12.

> **QuickTip**
> To zoom out from the zoom in position, click the print preview area or click the Zoom Out in Print Preview.

2. **Move the mouse pointer (which changes to) over the logo and click, or click Zoom In in Print Preview**
   The preview image of the page appears larger, easier to see. John notices extra space around the dotted rectangle, the area determined by the **margin** setting, so he is not yet ready to print.
3. **Click Close in Print Preview**
   The Preview window closes and you return to the Coffee Menu document.
4. **Click File on the menu bar, then click Page Setup**
   The Page Setup dialog box opens. In this dialog box, you can change the margin setting to decrease or increase the area outside the dotted rectangle. You can change other printing options here, such as paper size, page orientation, and printer source. Table B-5 describes the Page Setup dialog box options.
5. **Select the number in the Top text box, then type 1.25, select the number in the Bottom text box, type 1.25, then click OK**
   You return to the WordPad document. You should verify that you like the new margins before printing.
6. **Click**
   The menu contains smaller margins.

> **QuickTip**
> To quickly print a document, click the Print button on the Toolbar. To open the Print dialog box, click File on the menu bar, then click Print.

7. **Click Print in the Print Preview window**
   The Print dialog box opens, as shown in Figure B-13, showing various options available for printing. Check to make sure you are printing to the correct printer. If you need to change printers, select a printer. If you want to add a printer, double-click the Add Printer icon, then follow the Add Printer Wizard instructions. When you are done, accept all of the settings.

> **QuickTip**
> To see the number of documents waiting to print, right-click the printer in the Print dialog box, then click Open.

8. **Click Print**
   The WordPad document prints. While a document prints, a printer icon appears in the status area on the taskbar. You can point to the printer icon to get status information. To **close**, or quit, a program and any of its currently open files, you select the Exit command from the File menu. You can also click the Close button in the upper right-corner of the program window.
9. **Click the Close button in the WordPad window**

FIGURE B-12: Coffee Menu in Print Preview

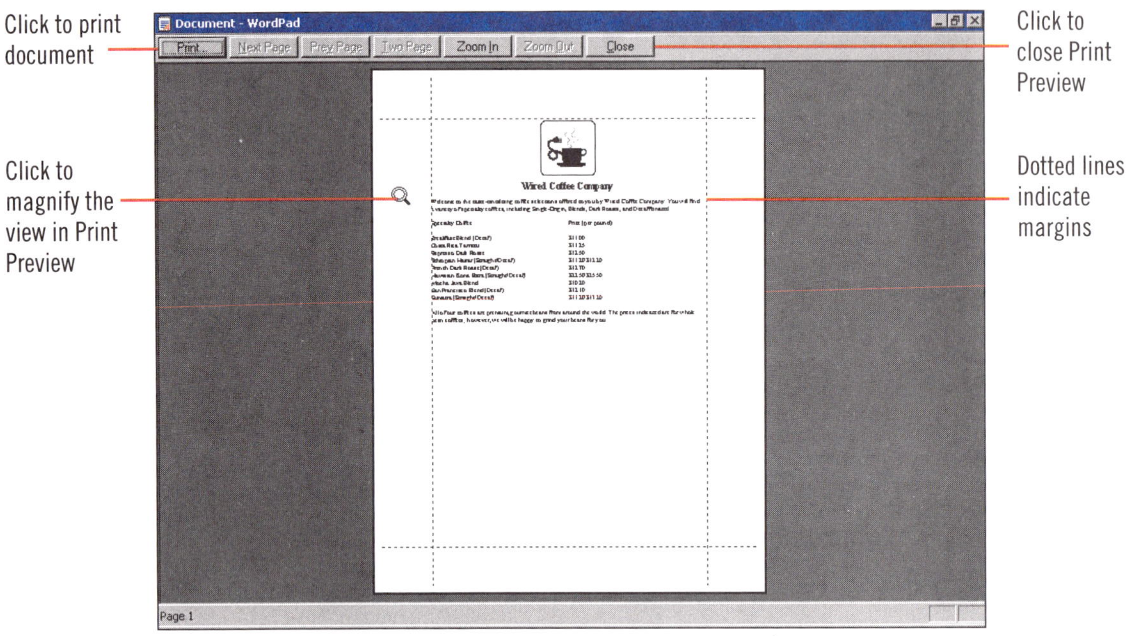

FIGURE B-13: Print dialog box

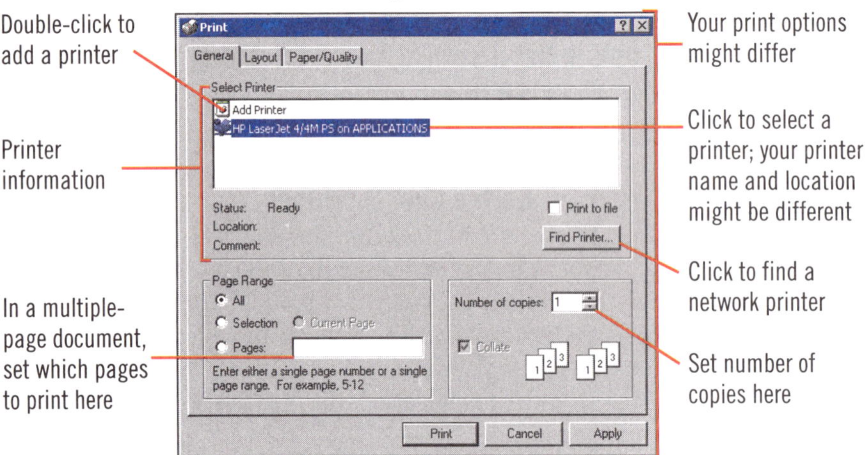

TABLE B-5: Page Setup dialog box options

page setup option	function
Size	Defines the size of the paper on which you want to print
Source	Defines the location of the paper, such as another paper bin or an envelope feeder
Orientation	Allows you to select between Portrait (the page being taller than it is wide) and Landscape (the page being wider than it is tall)
Margins	Allows you to define top, bottom, left, and right page margins

Printer properties

You can select Layout or Paper/Quality tabs from the Print dialog box and adjust several facets of the printing operation. For example, to control the intensity with which graphics images are printed, you would click the Paper/Quality tab, then adjust the intensity slider. You can also adjust fonts, paper sizes, and other printing dimensions in the Print dialog box.

Windows 2000

Playing a Video Clip

Windows 2000 comes with a built-in accessory, called **Windows Media Player**, that you can use to play video, sound, and mixed-media files. You can use it to play movies, sounds, and other multimedia files from your computer, a local network, or the Internet. The Windows Media Player delivers high-quality continuous video and sound playback, known as **streaming media**. With the Windows Media Player, you can modify the media and control settings. John wants to play a video, so he needs to use the Windows Media Player.

Steps

QuickTip

To make sure you are using the most recent version of Windows Media Player, click Help on the menu bar, then click Check for Player Upgrade. (You must have an open connection to the Internet to perform this check.)

QuickTip

You can change the size of the Windows Media Player window by clicking View on the menu bar, then clicking Standard, Compact, or Minimal.

QuickTip

To customize playback settings, click View on the menu bar, click Options, click the Playback tab, select the settings you want, then click OK.

1. Click the **Start button** on the taskbar, point to **Programs**, point to **Accessories**, point to **Entertainment**, then click **Windows Media Player**
   Windows Media Player opens, as shown in Figure B-14.
2. Click **File** on the menu bar, click **Open**, then click **Browse**
   The Open dialog box opens.
3. Click the **Look in list arrow**, click the **drive that contains your Project Disk**, then double-click the **Unit B folder**
   A list of the files in this folder on the Project Disk appears in the file list.
4. In the file list, click **Coffee Cup**, click **Open**, then click **OK** in the Open dialog box
   The video opens in the Media Player window and starts to play. A **Seek bar** in the Windows Media Player window moves indicating the progress of the video, as shown in Figure B-15. You can drag the Seek bar backward or forward to play different parts of the video. Below the Seek bar is the Control bar. The **Control bar** allows you to play all or part of a video. Table B-6 describes the function of each button on the Control bar. Above the Seek bar is the Navigation bar. With the **Navigation bar** buttons, you can move backward and forward between open files and start your Web browser and open media Web sites on the Internet. (You must have an open connection to the Internet to perform this check.)
5. Click the **Play button** on the toolbar
6. Click **File** on the menu bar, then click **Close**
   The video closes. Leave the Windows Media Player window open for the next lesson.

FIGURE B-14: Windows Media Player window

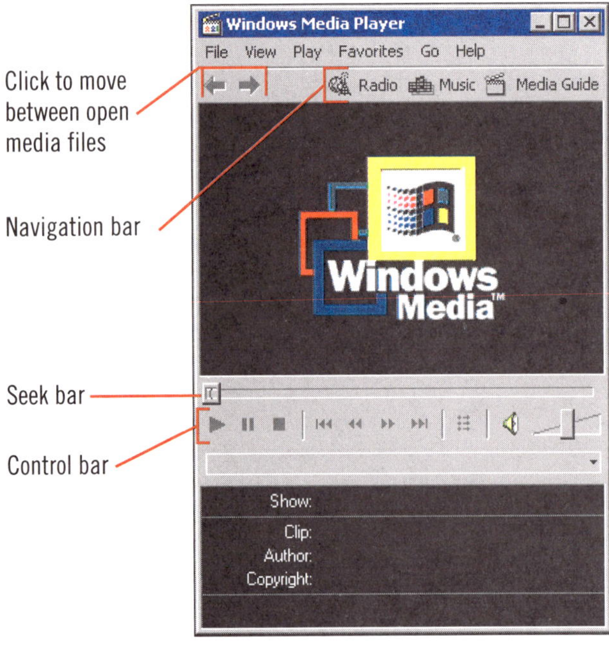

FIGURE B-15: Windows Media Player window playing a video

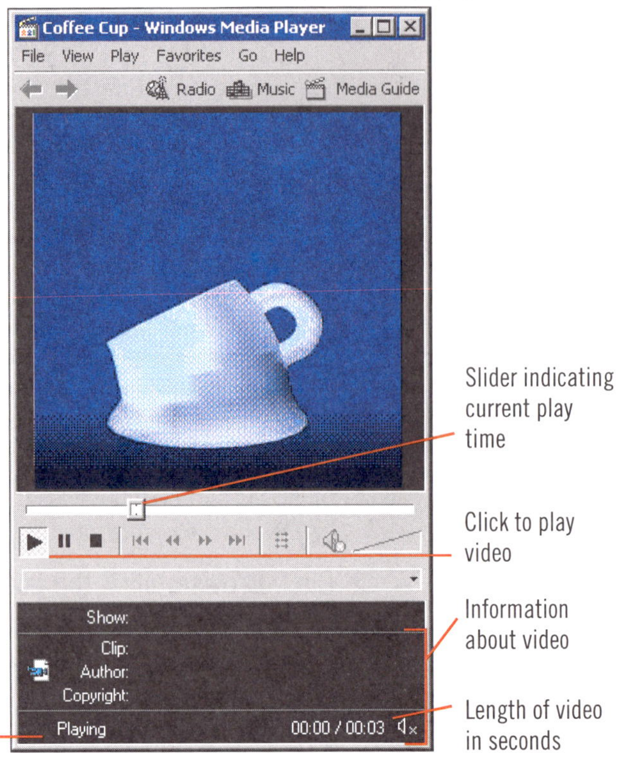

TABLE B-6: Control bar buttons on the Windows Media Player

button	description
	Play a video or sound
	Pause a video or sound
	Stop a video or sound
	Return to the beginning of the current video or sound
	Rewind the video or sound
	Advance forward through the video or sound
	Begin to play the beginning of the next video or sound
	Play a short section of each video or sound in a show
	Silence the audio content of the file
	Control the volume level of the content you are viewing

Changing Windows Media Player Options

You can change the way Windows Media Player plays video and audio, the way the player opens, the size of the player window, and the types of files you can play. To change Windows Media Player options, click View on the menu bar, then click Options. In the Options dialog box, click the Playback tab to change audio volume, balance, playback options such as whether files should repeat and rewind; click the Player tab to specify how Windows Media Player opens and the window appears; click the Custom Views tab to specify what controls appear in Compact and Minimal view; click the Advanced tab to change streaming settings; and click the Formats tab to specify the file formats you want to use with Windows Media Player.

Windows 2000

Playing a Sound

You can play sounds using the Windows Media Player. In order to listen to sounds, your computer must have a sound card and self-powered speakers. Windows Media Player can play a variety of sounds. To play a sound, you click the Play button. If you want to pause while playing the sound, you click the Pause button. If you want to change the starting position of the sound, you drag the slider. John enjoyed playing a video, so he decides to play a sound.

Steps

1. Make sure the Windows Media Player is open, click **File** on the menu bar, then click **Open**
   The Open dialog box opens. John decides to play a sound located on your Project Disk.
2. Click **Browse**, click the **Look in list arrow**, then click the drive that contains your Project Disk
   A list of the files and folders stored on the Project Disk appears in the file list.
3. In the file list, click **Better Coffee**, click **Open**, then click **OK**
   The sound plays, as shown in Figure B-16. The Seek bar in the Windows Media Player window moves, indicating the current play time of the sound. John decides to pause the sound, change the starting position of the sound, and then resume playing.
4. Click the **Play button** on the toolbar, then before the sound finishes, click the **Pause button** on the toolbar
   You can drag the Seek bar backward or forward to play different parts of the sound.
5. Drag the **Seek bar** back to the beginning, then click the **Play button** to restart the sound
6. When you are finished playing the sound, click the **Close button** on the Windows Media Player window

QuickTip

To adjust the volume, use [↑] and [↓] on the keyboard to raise and lower the volume.

QuickTip

To display the volume control icon on the taskbar, double-click the Sound and Multimedia icon in the Control Panel, click the Sound tab, click the Show volume control on the taskbar check box, then click OK.

FIGURE B-16: Windows Media Player window playing a sound

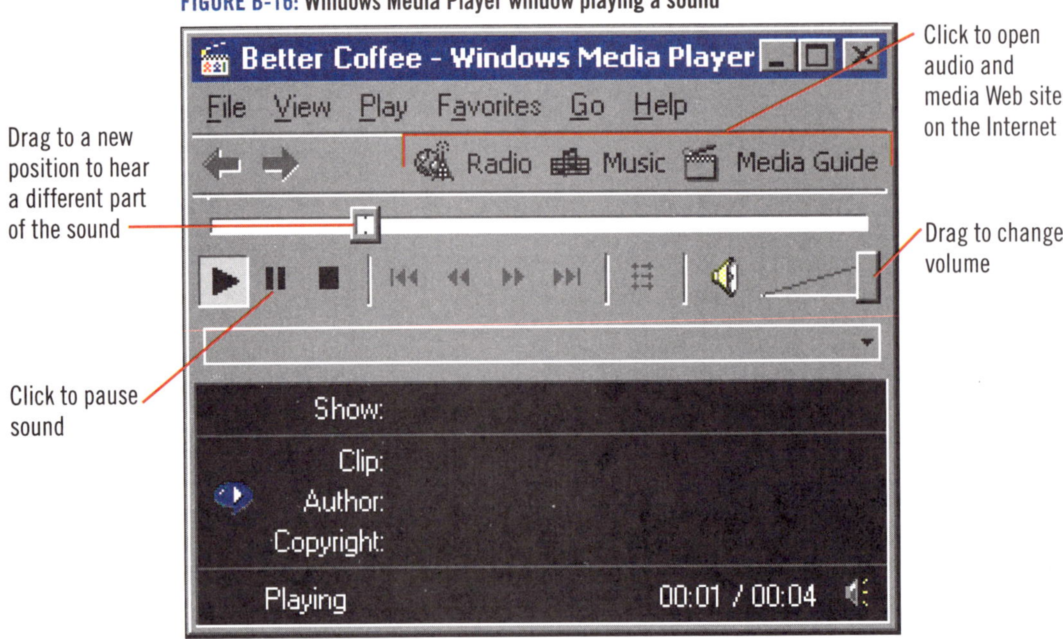

Playing a music CD

To accommodate the many people who like to play audio CDs in their CD-ROM drives while working, Windows 2000 includes the CD Player program in its accessories. The controls on the player, shown in Figure B-17, look just like those on a regular CD player. The Windows 2000 CD Player supports many of the same features found in CD players, such as random play, programmable playback order, and the ability to save programs so that users don't have to re-create their playlists each time they play a CD. To play an audio CD, insert the CD in your CD-ROM drive; the CD Player will automatically start playing the audio CD. You can click the CD Player button on the taskbar to open the CD Player window

FIGURE B-17: CD Player window

Practice

▶ Concepts Review

Label each of the elements of the screen shown in Figure B-18.

FIGURE B-18

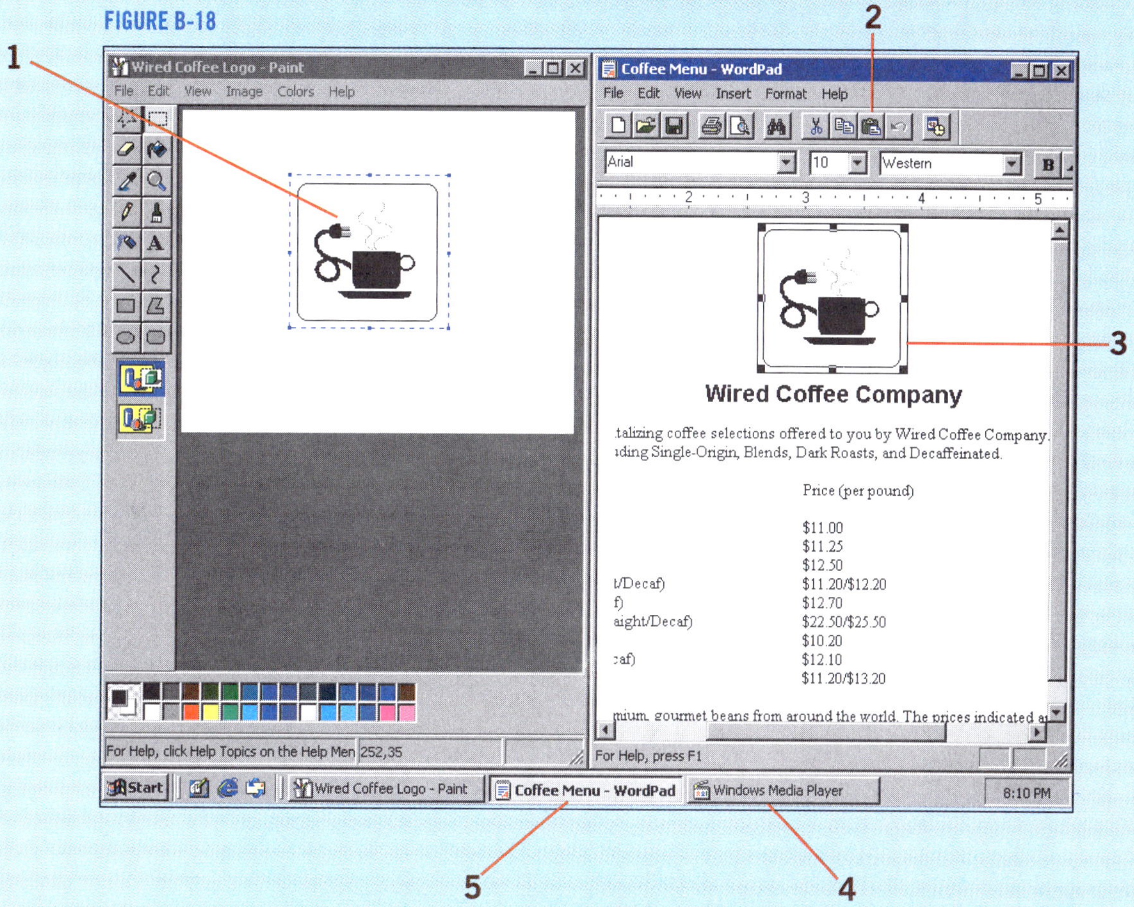

Match each of the terms with the statement that describes its function.

6. Copy	**a.**	Removes selected text or an image from its current location
7. Accessories	**b.**	Copies selected text or an image from its current location
8. Cut	**c.**	A set of characters you assign to a collection of information
9. Select	**d.**	A collection of programs that come built-in with Windows and enable you to perform certain tasks
10. filename	**e.**	What you must first do to existing text before you can format, move, or copy it

Select the best answer from the list of choices.

11. The first step in starting any Windows accessory is to click
- **a.** the Start button.
- **b.** the taskbar.
- **c.** the Open icon.
- **d.** anywhere on the desktop.

12. **What program command makes a copy of a file?**
    - **a.** Save
    - **b.** Save As
    - **c.** Copy
    - **d.** Duplicate
13. **The WordPad feature that automatically moves words to the next line when there is not room for them on the previous line is called**
    - **a.** Wordwrap.
    - **b.** Format insert.
    - **c.** Margin.
    - **d.** Tab.
14. **Which of the following is NOT a way to select text?**
    - **a.** Double-click a word
    - **b.** Drag over the text
    - **c.** Click File on the menu bar, then click Select
    - **d.** Click to the left of the first character in a line of text
15. **What is the name of the Windows location where information is placed after it is cut or copied?**
    - **a.** Clipboard
    - **b.** Paint
    - **c.** Start Up menu
    - **d.** Hard drive
16. **Which of the following is an option to change the outside edge size of a document?**
    - **a.** Paper Size
    - **b.** Paper Source
    - **c.** Orientation
    - **d.** Margins

Skills Review

1. **Start a program.**
    - **a.** Start WordPad.
    - **b.** Review the elements of the WordPad program window.
2. **Open and save a WordPad document.**
    - **a.** Open the WordPad file named Win B-3 on your Project Disk.
    - **b.** Save the file as *Choose Coffee* to your Project Disk.
3. **Edit text in a WordPad document.**
    - **a.** Change the spelling of the word *neuances* to *nuances* in the first paragraph.
    - **b.** Insert a space between the characters *r* and *a* in *ora* in the second paragraph.
    - **c.** Delete the word *heavy* in the last line of text and replace it with *medium.*
4. **Format text in a WordPad document.**
    - **a.** Select all the text in the file named Choose Coffee.
    - **b.** Change it from the present font to Garamond, and change the size to 12-point.
    - **c.** Center the title (*Wired Coffee*) and change it to bold, 16-point.
    - **d.** Underline each title (*How to Choose a Coffee* and *How to Taste the Difference*) and change them to 14-point.
    - **e.** Click anywhere in the WordPad window outside of the selected text.
    - **f.** Save the document.

5. **Use Paint.**
   a. Start Paint.
   b. Open the Paint file named Win B-2 on your Project Disk, then save it as *Wired Coffee Logo 2* to your Project Disk.
   c. Draw a circle around the logo.
   d. Use the Undo command or Eraser tool as necessary if the circle doesn't fit around the logo.
   e. Save the file.
6. **Copy data between programs.**
   a. Tile the WordPad and Paint windows vertically. (*Hint:* Maximize both windows first.)
   b. Select the logo in the Paint window, then copy it to the Clipboard.
   c. In WordPad, insert the cursor at the beginning of the document.
   d. Maximize WordPad, then paste the logo in the blank line.
   e. Center the logo.
   f. Save the Choose Coffee file.
   g. Close the Wired Coffee Logo 2 file and Paint.
7. **Print a document.**
   a. Print two copies of the file named Choose Coffee.
   b. Close all open documents.
   c. Close WordPad.
8. **Play a video clip.**
   a. Start Windows Media Player.
   b. Open the video file named Coffee Cup on your Project Disk.
   c. Play the video, then close it.
9. **Play a sound.**
   a. Open the sound file named AM Coffee on your Project Disk.
   b. Play the sound, and then pause it.
   c. Drag the Seek bar to the beginning of the sound, then replay it.
   d. Close the Windows Media Player window.

Independent Challenges

1. You just opened a small, independent bookstore and are working on your inventory. You need to create a list of books that can be consulted when customers come in and want to know what kind of books you carry. Start WordPad and create a new document that lists the first 10 books in your stock. Above the list, include your name, the name of your book store; a street address, city, zip code, and phone number for the store. For each book in the list, include the author's name (last name first), the title, and the date of publication.

To complete this independent challenge:

a. Start WordPad.
b. Type the heading (the name of the bookstore, address, city, state, zip code, and phone number).
c. Center the heading information.
d. Enter the information for at least 10 books, using [Tab] to create columns for the author's name, the title, and the date of publication. Be sure that the columns line up with one another.
e. Proofread your list and correct any errors you may have made.
f. Italicize the last and first name of each author, and bold the name of each book.
g. Save the list as *Book Inventory* to your Project Disk.
h. Print two copies of the list.
i. Exit WordPad.

2. You parents are celebrating their 25th wedding anniversary. You want to create an invitation to a party for them. Using WordPad, create an invitation, including the invitation title, your parents' names, date and time of the party, location of the party (use *35 Crow Canyon Road* for the address), written directions to the party, your name, and the date to respond by and phone number to reach you. Using Paint, then paste a map of the party location into the invitation. Remember that you can open more than program at a time, and you can easily switch between programs using the taskbar.

To complete this independent challenge:

a. Start WordPad and type the information needed for the invitation.
b. Select the title text and click the Center button on the toolbar.
c. Change the title text to 18-point, bold.
d. Change the rest of the text to 14-point Arial.
e. Save the WordPad document as *Invitation* to your Project Disk.
f. Start Paint, then open the *Invitation Map* file on your Project Disk.
g. Copy the map to the Clipboard.
h. Place the insertion point above the written instructions in the Invitation document.
i. Click the Paste button on the toolbar.
j. Save the document, preview the document, make any necessary changes, then print the document.
k. Close WordPad and Paint.

3. As the vice-president of Things-That-Fly, a kite and juggling store, you need to design a new type of logo, consisting of three simple circles, each colored differently. You'll use Paint to design the logo, and then paste it into a WordPad document.

To complete this independent challenge:

a. Start Paint and create a small circle using [Shift] and the Ellipse tool.
b. Use the Select tool to select the circle, click the Edit menu, then click Copy. Now you can paste the circle so you don't have to try to re-draw the exact same shape.
c. Click Edit on the menu bar, click Paste, then use the mouse to move the second circle below the first and slightly to the right of the first.
d. Click Edit on the menu bar, then click Paste to paste another copy of the circle. Use the mouse to move the third circle below the first and slightly to the left of the first.
e. For each circle, click the Fill tool, click the color you want the circle to be, then click inside the circle you want filled with that color.
f. Using the Select tool, select the completed logo, click Edit on the menu bar, then click Copy.
g. Open WordPad and click the Center button on the toolbar.
h. Click the Paste button on the toolbar, click to the right of the logo to deselect it, press [Enter] twice, then type *Things-That-Fly*.
i. Using the Format Bar, change the text to 18-point, bold.
j. Save the document as *Stationery* to your Project Disk.
k. Preview the document, make any necessary changes, then print the document.
l. Close WordPad and Paint.

4. As the creative director at Digital Arts, a computer music company, you need to find sample sounds to include on a demo CD. You'll use Windows Media Player to open sound files located on your computer and play each one. You'll also use WordPad to keep track of the sounds you listened to and which ones you liked the best.

To complete this independent challenge:

a. Open Windows Media Player.
b. Open all the sound files in the Media folder (in the Windows folder) on your computer.
c. Play each sound file.
d. In WordPad, create a list of the sound files that you played, and indicate the sounds you liked the best.
e. Save the list as *Sound List* to your Project Disk.
f. Print the list, then close Windows Media Player.

▶ Visual Workshop

Re-create the screen shown in Figure B-19, which shows the Windows desktop with more than one program window open. You can use the file Win B-2 for the coffee cup logo (save it as *A Cup of Coffee* to your Project Disk). Create a new WordPad document, save it as *Good Time Coffee Club* to your Project Disk, and enter the text as shown in the figure. Print the Screen (Press the Print Screen key to make a copy of the screen, open Paint, click Edit on the menu bar, click Paste to paste the screen into Paint, then click Yes to paste the large image if necessary. Click File on the menu bar, click Print, then click Print.)

FIGURE B-19

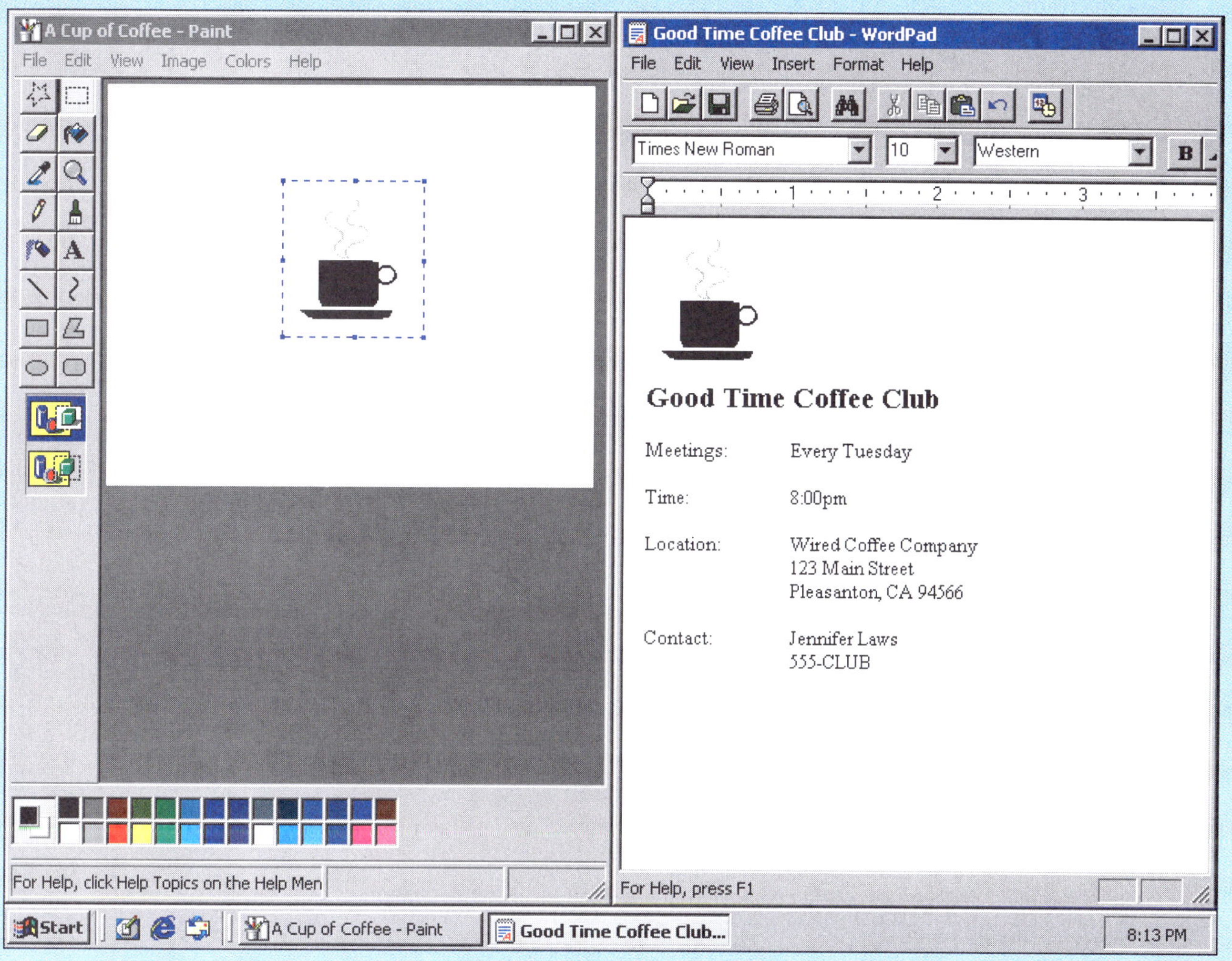

Windows 2000

Managing

Files Using My Computer

Objectives

- Understand file management
- Open and view My Computer
- View folders and files
- Create a folder
- Move files and folders
- Delete and restore files and folders
- Create a shortcut to a file
- Display drive information

An important Windows 2000 skill is **file management**, organizing and keeping track of files and folders. Windows 2000 provides you with two file management programs: My Computer and Windows Explorer. You can use both of these tools to view the files on your computer or computer network, and how they are arranged. You can also use either tool to rearrange the files by creating new folders, and by moving, renaming, and deleting files and folders. A **folder** is an electronic collection of files and other folders. This unit concentrates on My Computer, the simplest file management tool in Windows 2000; the next unit focuses on Windows Explorer, which contains more powerful features for accomplishing the same tasks. In this unit, John Casey will use My Computer to organize the files on his computer.

Windows 2000

Understanding File Management

Managing folders and files enables you to quickly locate any file that you have already created and need to use again. Working with poorly managed files is like looking for a needle in a haystack—it's frustrating and time-consuming to search through several irrelevant, misnamed, and out-of-date files to find the one you want. Figure C-1 shows the files and folders that John uses in the course of running his business.

As you examine the figure, note that file management can help you do the following:

Organize folders and files in a file hierarchy, so that information is easy to locate and use

A **file hierarchy** is a logical structure of files and folders, so that files are located in appropriate folders, and folders are located in other folders as necessary, to make everything easy to find. For instance, John stores all of his correspondence files in a folder called Letters. Within that folder are two more folders. One is named Business Letters and holds all business correspondence. The other is named Personal Letters and holds all of John's personal correspondence.

Save files to the folder in which you want to store them for future use

John has a folder named Sales in which he stores all information about sales for the current year. He also places files related to accounting information in this folder.

Create a new folder so you can reorganize information

Now that John is doing more advertising for Wired Coffee Company, he wants to create a new folder to store files related to these marketing efforts.

Delete files and folders that you no longer need

John deletes files once he's sure he will no longer use them again, to free up disk space and keep his disk organized.

Create shortcuts

If a file or folder you use often is located several levels down in a file hierarchy (for example, if it is in a file within a folder, within a folder), it might take you several steps to access it. To save you time in accessing the files and programs you use most frequently, you can create shortcuts to them. A **shortcut** is a link that you can place in any location that gives you instant access to a particular file, folder, or program on your hard disk or on a network. John created a shortcut on the desktop to the Wired Coffee folder. To view or access the contents of his folder all he has to do is double-click the shortcut icon on the desktop.

Find a file when you cannot remember where it is stored

John knows he created a letter to a supplier earlier this week, but now that he is ready to revise the letter, he cannot find it. Using the Search command on the Start menu, he can quickly find that letter and revise it in no time.

Open a file when you don't know the type of program in which it was created

If John wants to open a file but doesn't know which program to use to open it, he can use the Open With command. To open a file of unknown type, John can right-click the file icon, point to Open With, and then click one of the programs that are known to open that type of file, or he can click Any Program to open the Open With dialog box, where he can select a program to open the file.

FIGURE C-1: How John uses Windows to reorganize his files

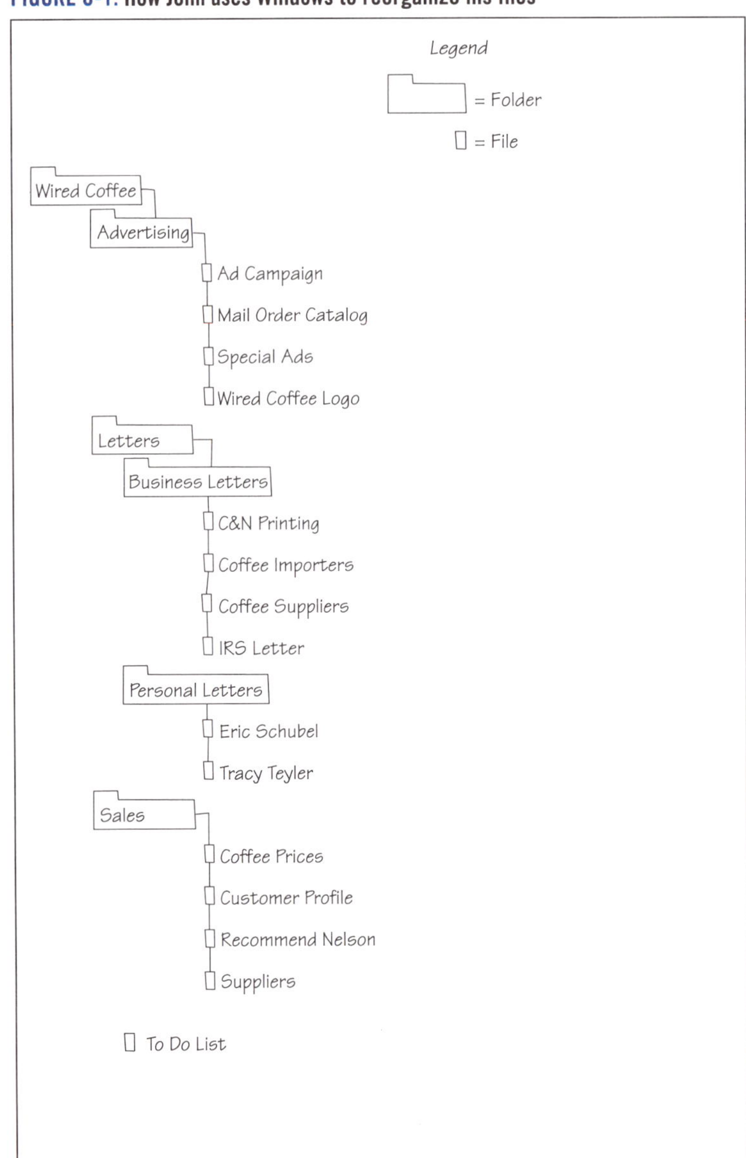

Planning a file hierarchy

Windows 2000 allows you to organize folders and files into a file hierarchy that imitates the way you would actually store paper document files in real folders. Just as a filing cabinet contains several folders each containing a set of related documents, and several dividers grouping related folders together, a file hierarchy allows you to place files into folders, then folders into other folders, so that your files are neat and organized. When creating a file hierarchy, create folders for top-level categories, such as a business or major project, and create folders within them to hold subcategories, such as departments in the business or major tasks within the project. For example, Figure C-1 shows the file hierarchy of the Wired Coffee folder on your Project Disk. At the topmost level of the hierarchy is the name of the folder, Wired Coffee. This folder contains a file and several folders that are related to the Wired Coffee Business: Advertising, Letters, Business Letters, Personal Letters, and Sales. Within each of these folders are files and any additional folders related to each subcategory.

Windows 2000

Opening and Viewing My Computer

The key to organizing folders and files effectively within a hierarchy is storing related things together and naming folders informatively. That way, you can get a good idea of what's on your system just by looking at the higher levels of your file hierarchy, and not having to examine every individual file or memorize a coding system. As the previous lesson showed, the file hierarchy on John's disk contains several folders and files organized by topic. Now he is ready to use My Computer to review this organization and see if it needs to be changed.

Steps

Trouble?

To prevent unwanted changes to your Project Disk, make sure you have made a copy of it. If you need assistance, see your instructor or technical support person.

Trouble?

If the toolbar is not visible, click View on the Menu bar, point to Toolbar, then click Standard Buttons.

QuickTip

To open Windows Explorer from My Computer, right-click any disk or folder icon, then click Explore.

1. Make sure a copy of your Project Disk is in the appropriate drive, then double-click the **My Computer icon**

   This icon is usually located in the upper-left corner of the desktop. My Computer opens, displaying the contents of your computer, including all the disk drives and printers, as shown in Figure C-2. Because computers differ, your My Computer window will probably look different. There are icons that represent drives and icons that represent folders. As with most other windows, there is a toolbar, a status bar providing information about the contents of the window, a menu bar, and a list of contents in the My Computer window.

2. If necessary, click the **Maximize button** in the My Computer window

   This enables you to see the entire toolbar as you work. The toolbar contains a set of buttons that makes using My Computer easier. Table C-1 lists what each of these buttons does and how they are used.

3. Double-click the **drive that contains your Project Disk**

   You can see the files and folders that are contained on the disk drive. When you open a disk drive or folder, the Address bar changes to indicate the new location. Notice that the Address bar and the title bar have changed from My Computer to 3½ Floppy (A:).

4. Double-click the **Unit C folder**, then double-click the **Wired Coffee folder**

   Now you can see the folders that are contained in the Wired Coffee folder.

5. Double-click the **Sales folder**

   You can now see the files contained in the Sales folder. These are files that John created using WordPad and saved in the Sales folder.

FIGURE C-2: My Computer window

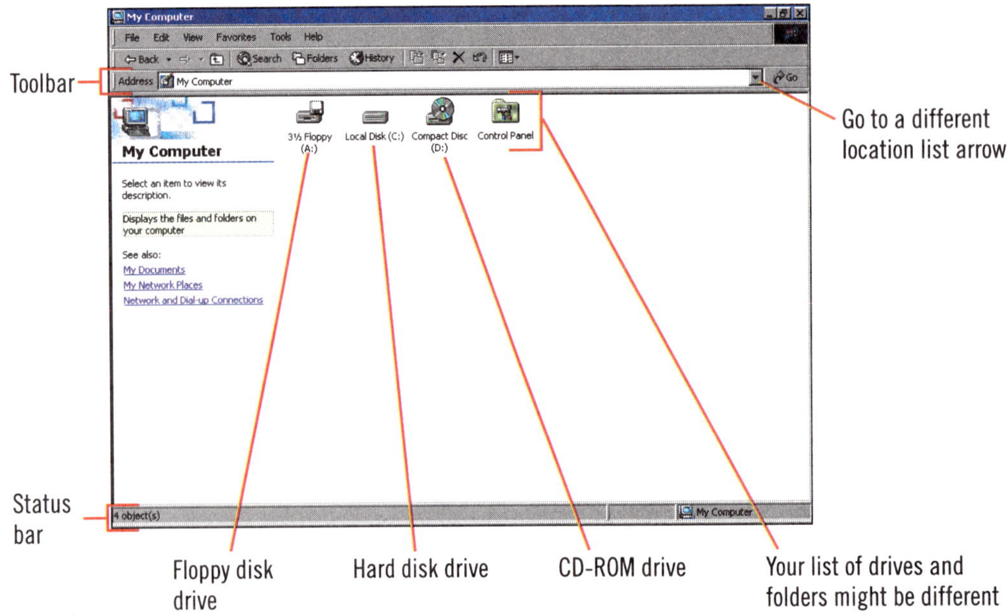

TABLE C-1: My Computer toolbar buttons

button	name	function
Back	**Back**	Moves to the last previous location you visited
	Forward	Once you have moved back, moves to the location you visited before moving back
	Up	Moves up one level in the file hierarchy
	Search	Lets you search for folders or files
	Folders	Displays a list of folders on your computer
	History	Displays a list of recently used folders and files
	Move To	Moves a folder or file to another folder
	Copy To	Copies a folder or file to another folder
	Delete	Deletes a folder or file
	Undo	Undoes the most recent My Computer operation
	Views	Displays the contents of My Computer in different views

Formatting a disk

All disks have to be formatted before they can be used. Often, new disks come preformatted, but if not, you can easily perform this function yourself. You can also format a disk that already contains data to quickly erase its files and folders. To format a floppy disk, select the disk drive in My Computer that contains the disk, click File on the menu bar, then click Format, or right-click the disk drive, then click Format. Specify the size of the disk and format type, then click Start. If you are formatting a disk that has never been formatted, select the Full format type. If the disk has already been formatted and you simply want to clear its contents, select the Quick format type to reduce the time it takes. Be absolutely certain you want to format a disk before doing so, because formatting removes all the data from a disk.

Windows 2000

Viewing Folders and Files

Once you have opened one or more folders, you can use buttons on the toolbar to help you move among folders quickly in My Computer. If you want to move up one step in the hierarchy, you can click the Up One Level button. Each time you open a folder, Windows 2000 keeps track of where you have been. If you want to go back or forward to a folder you have already visited, you can click the Back button or the Forward button. Each time you click the Back or Forward button, you go back or forward to the folder you previously visited. If you want to go to a folder you visited two or more locations ago, you can click the list arrow next to the button to display a menu of places you have been, and then click the place you want to go. When you view a folder in the My Computer window, you can use the Views button on the toolbar to change the way folder and file icons appear. As he works with My Computer, John moves between folders and changes the view depending upon the type of information that he needs.

Steps

1. Click the **Up button** on the toolbar
   The Wired Coffee folder and its contents appear in the Wired Coffee window. Each time you click the Up button, you move up one step in the hierarchy to the folder that contains the folders and files you currently see on the screen.

QuickTip

You can also click the Address bar list arrow to move to another location up or down the file hierarchy.

2. Click again
   You should now be at the topmost level of your disk drive file hierarchy showing several folders and files. See Figure C-3. Instead of double-clicking the Wired Coffee folder icon again to reopen the folder, you can click the Back button on the toolbar to go back to the previous folder (Wired Coffee) you visited.
3. Click the **Back button** Back on the toolbar
   Clicking the Back button displays the last folder you visited. The Wired Coffee folder and its contents appear in the My Computer window.

Trouble?

If Microsoft Word is installed on your computer, the Word icon will appear in Figure C-4. If not, the WordPad icon will appear.

4. Double-click the **Advertising folder**
   The Advertising folder and its contents appear in the My Computer window. Instead of using the Up button to go back to the Wired Coffee folder and then clicking the Sales folder, you can click the list arrow next to the Back button to display a menu of places you have been, and then select the Sales folder.
5. Click the **Back button list arrow** Back on the toolbar, then click **Sales**
   The Back button list arrow, as shown in Figure C-4, displays the last several locations you opened. You can click any place in the list to return to that location.
6. Click the **Forward button** on the toolbar
   Once you have returned to a previously opened folder or drive, clicking the Forward button on the toolbar opens the location you visited just prior to the return. The Wired Coffee folder opens in the My Computer window because this is the location that was open before you clicked the Back button list arrow and then clicked Sales.

QuickTip

The target location of the Back and Forward buttons change frequently as you navigate files and folders. To see the target location of either button, point to it and read the ScreenTip.

7. Click the **Views button** on the toolbar, then click **Details**
   In the Details view, the name, size of the object, type of file, and date on which each folder or file was last modified appear, as shown in Figure C-5. This might be the most useful view because it includes a great deal of information about the folder or file, in addition to the icon of the application that was used to create the file.
8. Click the **Views button** on the toolbar, then click **Large Icons**
   The files appear as large icons, without additional file information.

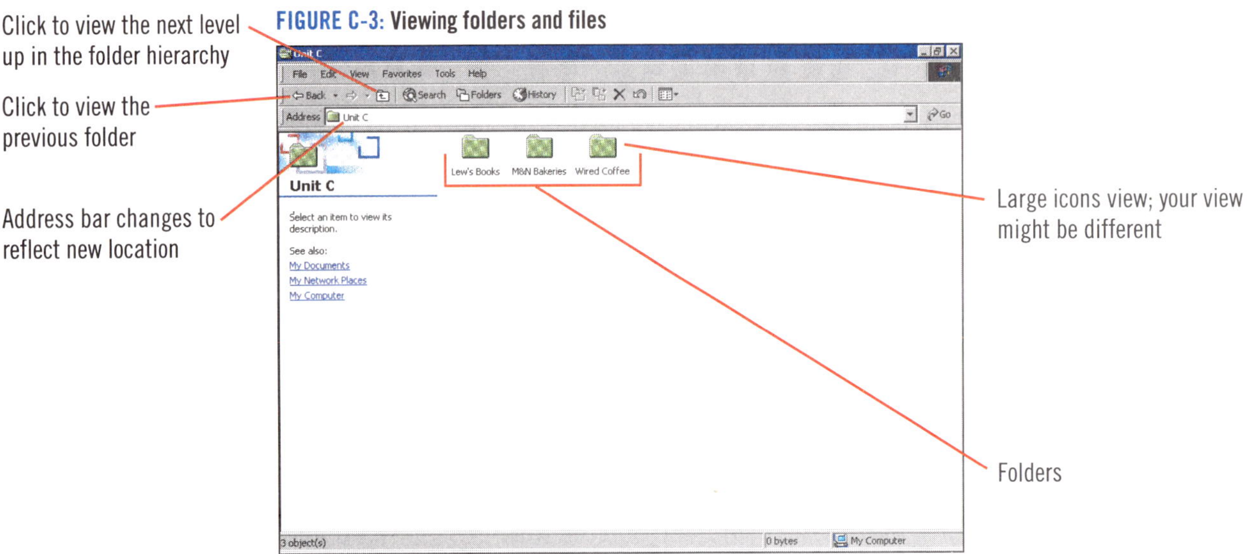

FIGURE C-3: Viewing folders and files

FIGURE C-4: My Computer window

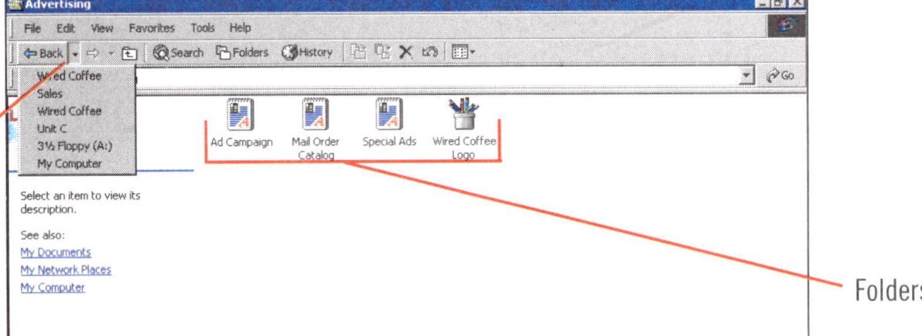

Click to view list of recently opened locations

Folders

FIGURE C-5: Viewing folders and files in Details view

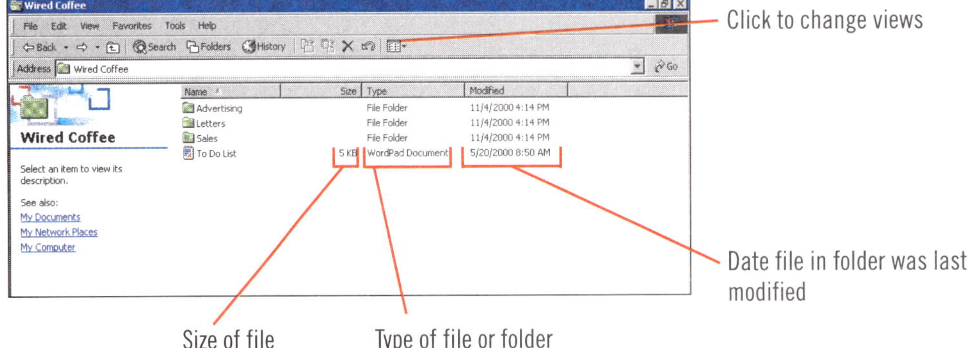

Size of file

Type of file or folder

CLUES TO USE

Viewing image and picture files

The My Pictures folder does the same thing for images and pictures as the My Documents folder does for documents—it provides a consistent storage location. The My Pictures folder is the default location for storing images from digital cameras, scanners, and other digital imaging devices. If you store your images and pictures in the My Pictures folder, you can see a preview of a file in the My Computer or Windows Explorer window without having to open the file in an editing program. In the My Computer or Windows Explorer window, the right pane contains a file list, which you can view in a number of different formats, including large icons or **thumbnails** (miniature views), and a preview area. Above the preview area is the selected image or picture. Along the top of the preview area is a row of buttons that allows you to zoom in and out, view the image or picture in actual size, best fit size, or full screen, and print the image or picture. If you want to open the image or picture, you can double-click the file.

Creating a Folder

You can create one or more new folders to store files and even other folders. Creating and informatively naming new folders makes it easy to organize files and other folders in a logical hierarchy. To create a folder in Windows 2000, you can click the New command on the File menu or you can right-click anywhere in any My Computer window and point to New, then click Folder. John needs to create two new folders. One will contain his To Do List. The other will contain information about his employees.

Steps

1. Click **File** on the menu bar, point to **New**, then click **Folder**
   A new folder appears in the Wired Coffee window, as shown in Figure C-6. All new folders are initially named New Folder. A border appears around the newly created folder, meaning that it is selected and ready to be renamed.
2. Type **Important**, then press **[Enter]**
   The folder is now named Important, a name that reflects the type of documents it will contain—important files relating to John's work week.
3. Place the mouse pointer anywhere in the Wired Coffee window (except on a file or folder), **right-click**, then point to **New**
   The pop-up menu opens, as shown in Figure C-7.
4. Click **Folder**
   A new folder appears, named New Folder, where you right-clicked the mouse in the Wired Coffee window.
5. Type **Personnel**, then press **[Enter]**
   The Wired Coffee window now has two new folders, Important and Personnel, as shown in Figure C-8. Once you create new folders, you can quickly rearrange them into orderly rows and columns.
6. Click **View** on the menu bar, point to **Arrange Icons**, then click **By Name**
   The folder and file icons in the Wired Coffee folder are sorted by name in alphabetical order and automatically moved in line with the other icons. You can change the way individual files and folders are sorted by using other Arrange Icons options on the View menu. Table C-2 describes these options.

QuickTip

To rename a folder, right-click the folder you want to rename, click Rename, then type a new name.

FIGURE C-6: Creating a new folder

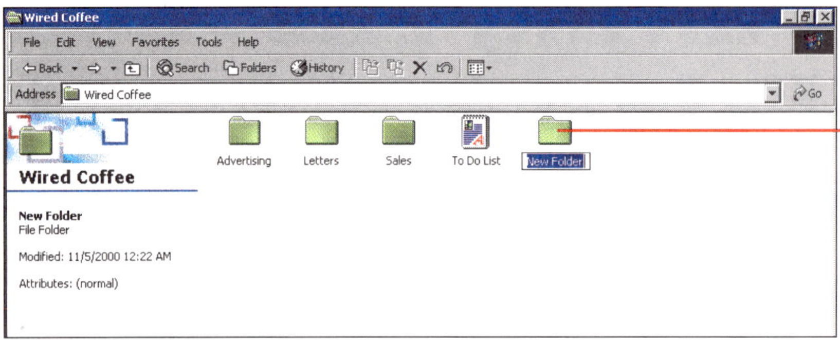

New folder, ready to be named, in the Wired Coffee folder

FIGURE C-7: Right-clicking to create a new folder

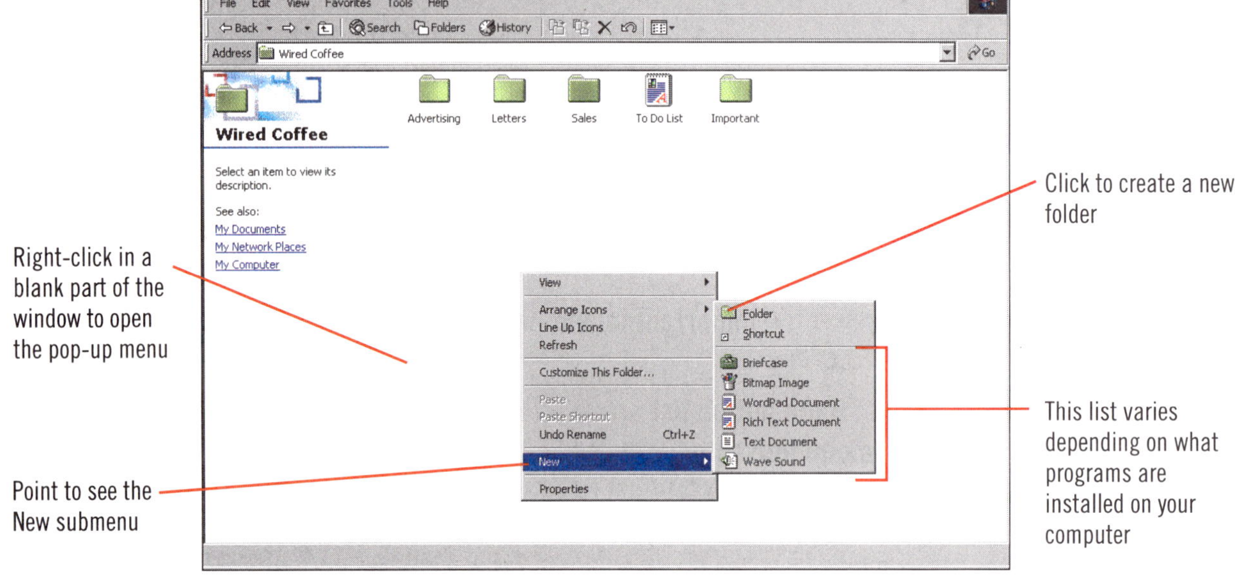

Right-click in a blank part of the window to open the pop-up menu

Point to see the New submenu

Click to create a new folder

This list varies depending on what programs are installed on your computer

FIGURE C-8: Two new folders

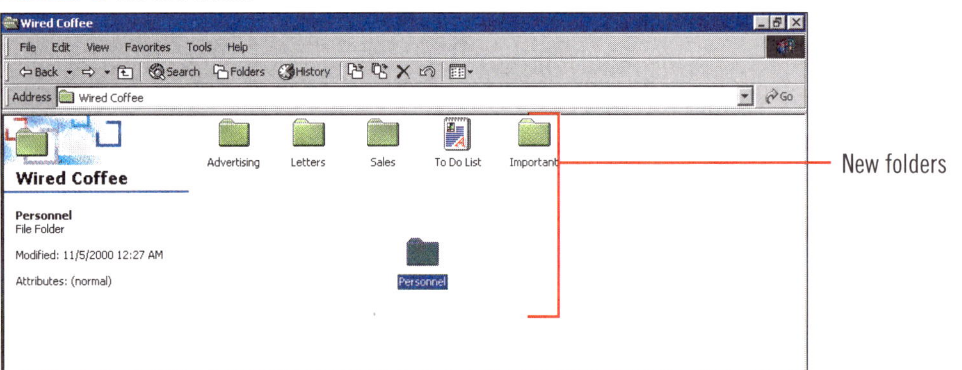

New folders

TABLE C-2: Options on the View menu for arranging files and folders

option	arranges files and folders
By Name	Alphabetically
By Type	By type, such as all documents created using the WordPad program
By Size	By size, with the largest folder or file listed first
By Date	By the date they were last modified with the latest modification being listed last
Auto Arrange	Automatically in orderly rows and columns

Moving Files and Folders

You can move a file or folder from one location to another using a variety of methods in My Computer. See Table C-3 for a description of moving and copying methods. If the file or folder and the location to which you want to move it are visible in a window or on the desktop, you can simply drag the item from one location to the other. When the location is not visible, you can use the Cut, Copy, and Paste commands on the Edit menu or the buttons on the toolbar. Now that John has created the Important folder to store files relating to his weekly tasks, he is ready to move the To Do List file into it. He also needs to move a letter (a recommendation for a new marketing person) currently contained in the Sales folder to the new Personnel folder.

Steps

1. Drag the **To Do List file** from the Wired Coffee window to the Important folder
   The icon representing the To Do List file is removed from the Wired Coffee folder and is placed in the folder named Important. Folders are moved in the same manner. Dragging a file or folder from one place to another on the same disk moves it; whereas dragging it from one disk drive location to another copies it. If you want to copy an item on the same disk by dragging, press and hold [Ctrl] while dragging.
2. Double-click the **Important folder** and confirm that the file has been moved
   The folder named Important now contains John's To Do List.
3. Click the **Back button list arrow** Back on the toolbar, click **Sales**, then click the **Recommend Nelson** file to select it
   When the folder you want to move a file into is not visible, you can use the Cut and Paste commands to move a file from one folder to another.
4. Click **Edit** on the menu bar, then click **Cut**
   The file is removed from its original location and stored on the Windows Clipboard. When you cut or copy a file, the file icon turns gray, as shown in Figure C-9.
5. Click the **Back button** Back on the toolbar, then double-click the **Personnel folder**
6. Click **Edit** on the menu bar, then click **Paste**
   The file is now pasted into the Personnel folder, as shown in Figure C-10.
7. Click Back
   You return to the Wired Coffee folder.

QuickTip

If you want to perform a file management operation such as moving or copying on more than one file or folder at a time, first select all the files or folders by holding [Ctrl] and clicking each one you want to select. Then perform the operation.

QuickTip

To move or copy a folder or file, you can click the Move To button or Copy To button on the toolbar, select the folder in which you want to place the folder or file, then click OK.

FIGURE C-9: Preparing to move a file

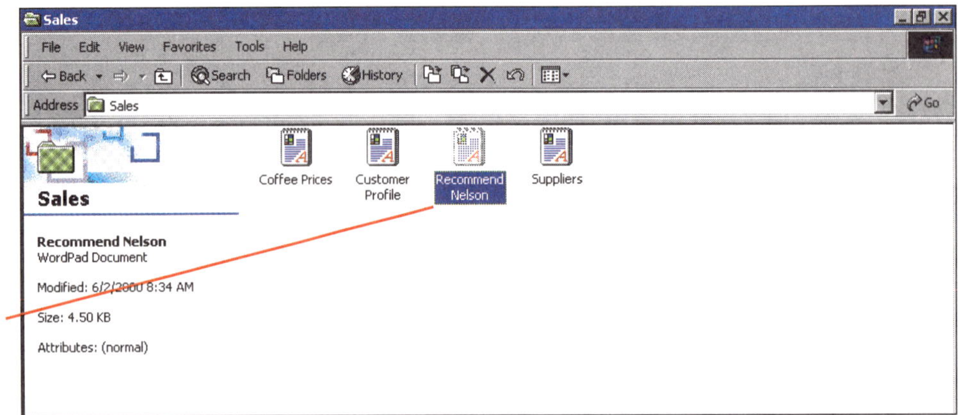

FIGURE C-10: Relocated file

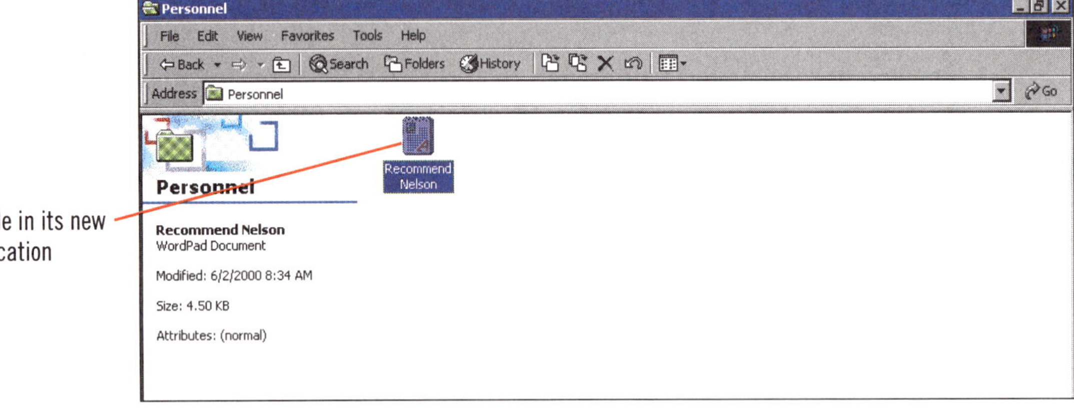

TABLE C-3: Methods for moving and copying files

action	methods
Move	Drag the file or folder to new location on the same disk Right-click the file or folder, drag to folder or drive, then click Move Here Select the file or folder, click the Move To button on the toolbar, click a folder or drive, then click OK Select the file or folder, click File on the menu bar, click Cut, display a folder or drive, click File on the menu bar, then Paste
Copy	Press and hold [Ctrl], then drag the file or folder to new location Right-click the file or folder, drag to folder or drive, then click Copy Here Select the file or folder, click the Copy To button on the toolbar, click a folder or drive, then click OK Select the file or folder, click File on the menu bar, click Copy, display a folder or drive, click File on the menu bar, then Paste

Sending files and folders

The Send To command, located on the pop-up menu of any desktop object, lets you "send" (or move) a file or folder to a new location on your computer. For example, you can send a file or folder to a floppy disk for a quick backup copy of the file or folder, a mail recipient for receiving electronic messages, or the desktop for creating a shortcut. You can also use the Send To command to move a file or folder from one folder to another. To send a file or folder, right-click the file or folder you want to send, point to Send To on the pop-up menu, and then click the destination you want. You can determine the options that appear in the Send To command by creating a shortcut to the program or folder you want included and moving it to the SendTo folder, located within the Windows folder.

Windows 2000

Deleting and Restoring Files and Folders

When you organize the contents of a folder, disk, or the desktop, you might find files and folders that you no longer need. You can **delete** these items, or remove them from the disk. If you delete a file or folder from the desktop or from the hard disk, it goes into the Recycle Bin. The **Recycle Bin**, located on your desktop, is a temporary storage area for deleted files. If you delete a file that you still need, you can restore it by moving it from the Recycle Bin to another location. Be aware that if you delete a file from your floppy disk it will not be stored in the Recycle Bin—it will be permanently deleted. See Table C-4 for a summary of the deleting and restoring options. To demonstrate how the Recycle Bin works, John first moves a file to the desktop, deletes that file, and then restores it.

Steps 1 2 3 4

Trouble?

If you cannot find the Recycle Bin, click the title bar in the My Computer window, then drag the window to the right to see the Recycle Bin.

QuickTip

To quickly move files or folders from one disk to another, select the files or folder, press and hold [Shift], then drag the selected items to the new location.

Trouble?

If you are unable to find the deleted file in the Recycle Bin, it may be because your Recycle Bin is full or too small (so that files are deleted right away rather than being stored in the Recycle Bin). See your instructor or technical support person for assistance.

QuickTip

Your deleted files remain in the Recycle Bin until you empty it. To empty the Recycle Bin, right-click the Recycle Bin icon, then click Empty Recycle Bin. This permanently removes the contents of the Recycle Bin from your hard disk.

1. Double-click the **Advertising folder**, then click the **Restore Down button** in the Advertising window
   The Advertising folder and its contents appear in the Advertising window. Before you can delete a file from a floppy disk to the Recycle Bin, you need to move it to the desktop or hard drive. If you want to delete a file directly from a floppy disk without the possibility of restoring it, you can drag the file directly to the Recycle Bin or press [Delete].
2. Right-click and hold the **Ad Campaign file**, drag it to the desktop from the Advertising folder on your Project Disk, then click **Move Here**
   The file now appears on the desktop and can be moved to the Recycle Bin, as shown in Figure C-11.
3. Drag the **Ad Campaign file** from the desktop to the Recycle Bin (you might have to move the Advertising folder window), then click **Yes** if necessary
   The Recycle Bin icon should now look like it contains paper.
4. Double-click the **Recycle Bin icon**
   The Recycle Bin window opens. It contains the file that was deleted. The Recycle Bin window is like most other windows in that it contains a menu bar, a toolbar, and a status bar. Because John still needs this file he decides to restore it. The windows overlap, making it difficult for John to see the contents of both folders.
5. Right-click an empty area of the **taskbar**, then click **Tile Windows Vertically**
   This option allows you to see all open windows on the desktop at one time. The Recycle Bin window and the Advertising window appear side-by-side, as shown in Figure C-12.
6. Select the **Ad Campaign file** in the Recycle Bin window, then drag it back to the Advertising folder window
   The file is restored—it is intact and identical to the form it was in before you deleted it.
7. Click the **Close button** in the Recycle Bin window

FIGURE C-11: Selecting files to drag to the Recycle Bin

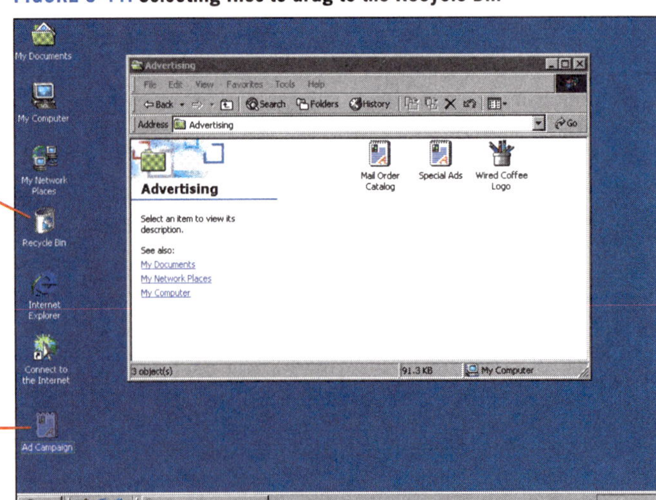

FIGURE C-12: Deleted file from the Advertising folder in the Recycle Bin

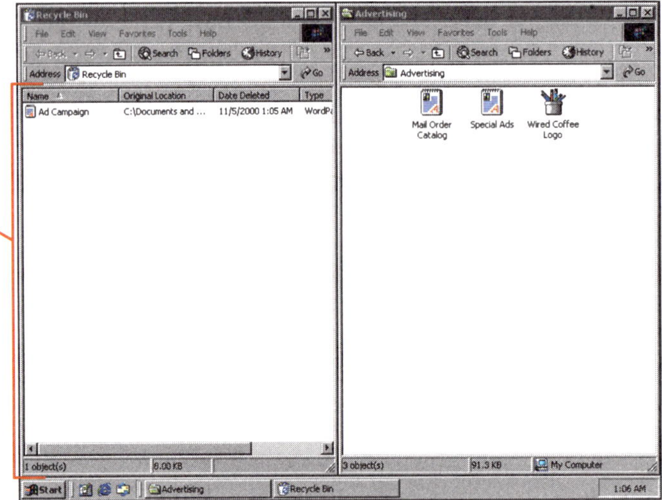

TABLE C-4: Deleting and restoring files

ways to delete a file	ways to restore a file from the recycle bin
Select the file, then click the Delete button on the toolbar	Click the Undo button on the Recycle Bin toolbar
Select the file, then press [Delete]	Select the file, click File on the menu bar, then click Restore
Right-click the file, then click Delete	Right-click the file, then click Restore
Drag the file to the Recycle Bin	Drag the file from the Recycle Bin to any location

Recycle Bin properties

You can adjust several Recycle Bin settings by using the Properties option on the Recycle Bin pop-up menu. For example, if you do not want files to go to the Recycle Bin when you delete them, but, rather, want them to be immediately deleted, right-click the Recycle Bin, click Properties, then click the Do Not Move Files to the Recycle Bin check box to select the option. Also, if you find that the Recycle Bin is full and cannot accept any more files, you can increase the amount of disk space devoted to the Recycle Bin by moving the Maximum Size of Recycle Bin slider to the right. The percentage shown represents how much space the contents of the Recycle Bin takes up on the drive.

Creating a Shortcut to a File

If a file or folder is buried several levels down in a file hierarchy, it could take you a while to access it. To save you time in getting to the items you use frequently, you can create shortcuts. A shortcut is a link between two points: a "home" folder where a file, folder, or program is actually stored and any other location where you want to access that file or program. The actual file, folder, or program remains stored in its original location, but you place the icon representing the shortcut in a convenient location, whether that is a folder or the desktop. John always uses his Wired Coffee logo on stationery, in flyers and in general advertising materials. Rather than having to go through the steps to start Paint and then open the file, he simply places a shortcut for this Paint file on the desktop.

1. In the Advertising folder, right-click **Wired Coffee Logo**, then click **Create shortcut**
   An icon for a shortcut to the Wired Coffee Logo now appears in the Advertising window. Compare your screen to Figure C-13. All shortcuts are named the same as the file on which they are based, with the words "Shortcut to" in front of the original name.

Trouble?

If you can't see an empty area of your desktop, your My Computer window is maximized. Click the Restore Down button to resize it.

2. Click the **Shortcut to Wired Coffee Logo** file, click the **Move To button** on the toolbar, click **Desktop**, then click **OK**
   The shortcut appears on the desktop, as shown in Figure C-14. A shortcut can be placed anywhere on the desktop.
3. Double-click the **Shortcut to Wired Coffee Logo icon**
   The Paint program opens with the file named Wired Coffee Logo.
4. Click the **Close button** in the Paint window
   The logo file and the Paint program close. The shortcut to Wired Coffee Logo remains on the desktop until you delete it, so you can use it again and again. If you are working in a lab environment, you should delete this shortcut.
5. Right-click the **Shortcut to Wired Coffee Logo icon**
   When you right-click folders and files (as opposed to the blank area in a window), a pop-up menu opens that offers several file management commands, as described in Table C-5. The commands on your pop-up menu might be different depending on the Windows 2000 features installed on your computer.
6. Click **Delete** on the pop-up menu, then click **Yes** in the Confirm File Delete dialog box
   The shortcut is deleted from the desktop and placed in the Recycle Bin, where it will remain until John empties the Recycle Bin or restores the shortcut. When you delete a shortcut, only the shortcut is removed. The original file remains intact in its original location.
7. Click the **Maximize button** in the Advertising window

CLUES TO USE

Placing shortcuts on the Start menu or taskbar

You can place shortcuts to your favorite files and programs on the Start menu or on a toolbar on the taskbar. To do this, simply drag the folder, file, or program to the Start button or a toolbar on the taskbar, and the item will appear on the first level of the Start menu or on the toolbar.

FIGURE C-13: Creating a shortcut

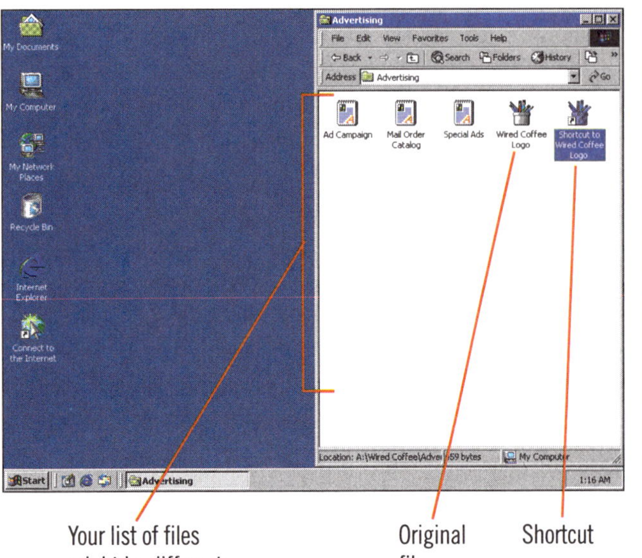

FIGURE C-14: Dragging shortcut to a new location

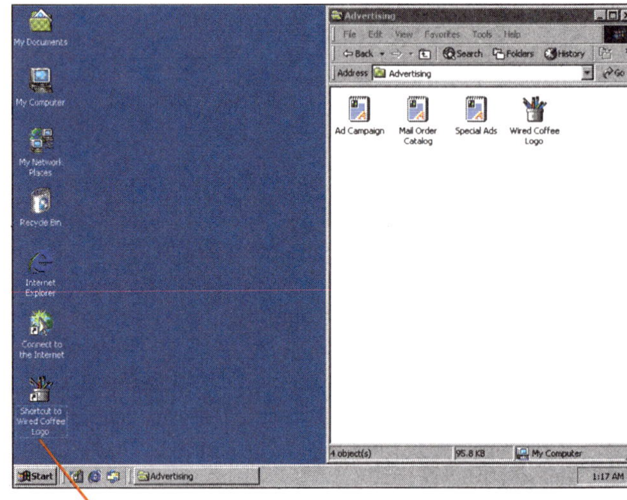

TABLE C-5: Shortcut menu options for files and folders

option	description
Copy	Copies the file or folder to the Windows Clipboard
Create Shortcut	Creates a shortcut to the file or folder
Cut	Cuts the file or folder from its original location to the Windows Clipboard
Delete	Deletes the file or folder
Explore	Opens a folder or drive in Windows Explorer
Open	Opens the selected file or folder
Open with	Opens the file with a designated program
Paste	Pastes the file or folder from the Windows Clipboard to a new location
Preview	Previews the selected file
Print	Prints the selected file
Properties	Displays the properties of the file or folder
Rename	Renames the file or folder
Search	Searches for files in a folder or drive
Send To	Sends the selected file or folder to new location
Sharing	Displays the sharing properties of the folder

Windows 2000

Displaying Drive Information

You should know as much about your system as possible. You might have to tell your instructor or system administrator certain information if you encounter a problem with your computer, or you might want to know how much space is left on a disk or change a **disk label** (a name you can assign to a hard or floppy disk). When you label a hard disk, the label will appear in the My Computer and Windows Explorer windows. Besides checking hard drive or floppy disk information, you can also use Windows 2000 tools to check your disks for damage, optimize your disk for better performance, make copies of your disks for safe keeping, and share your disk contents with others. You can perform these activities by using the Properties command. John wants to find out how much free space is available on his floppy disk.

QuickTip

To display drive information in the My Computer window, display the My Computer window, then click an icon.

1. Click the **Back button list arrow** on the toolbar, then click **My Computer**
2. Right-click the **icon in the My Computer window for the drive that contains your Project Disk**
   The icon representing the 3½ disk drive is highlighted. Now John can examine the property information for this disk. In the left pane, you can see a graphical representation of the amount of space being used relative to the amount available in the pie chart for the floppy disk. John reviews the chart and determines that the floppy disk contains plenty of free space.
3. Click **Properties** on the pop-up menu
   The 3½ Floppy (A:) Properties dialog box opens with the General tab in front, as shown in Figure C-15. Click the General tab if it is not the frontmost tab.
4. Click the **Label text box** if necessary, then type **ProjectDisk**
   A disk label can contain up to 11 characters but no spaces.
5. Click the **Tools tab**
   The Tools tab becomes the frontmost tab, as shown in Figure C-16, showing you three utilities that can make Windows work more efficiently: error-checking, backup, and defragmentation. You can use the Defragmentation feature to speed up the performance of a disk. **Defragmenting** means that files will be rewritten to the disk in contiguous blocks rather than in random blocks. When you click any one of these options, Windows will update you as to when that tool was last used on the currently selected disk. Although these tools are mostly used for keeping a hard disk healthy, they can be used on a floppy disk as well. Table C-6 describes what each tool does.
6. Click **OK**
   The Properties dialog box closes.
7. Click the **Close button** in the My Computer window

FIGURE C-15: General tab options in the 3½ Floppy (A:) Properties dialog box

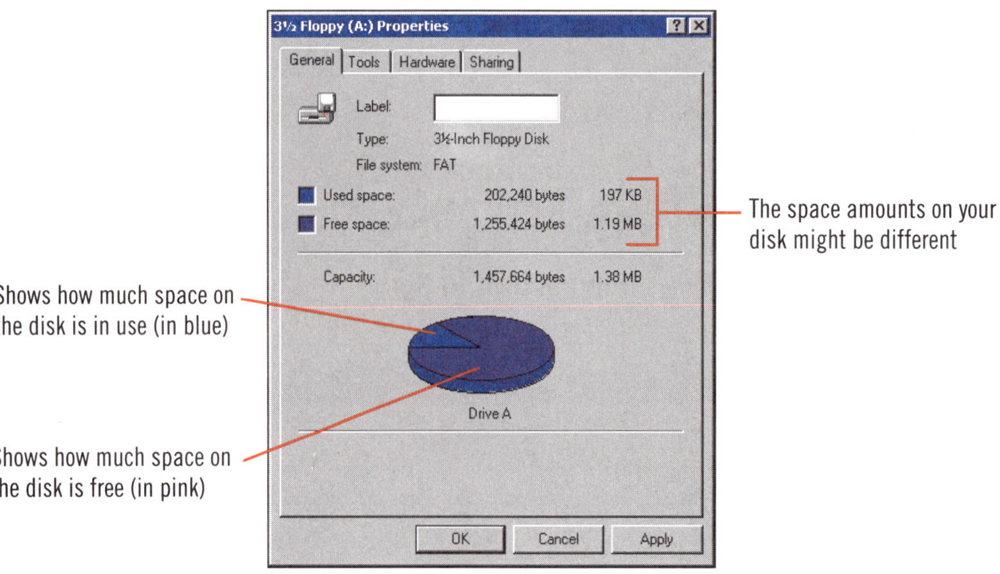

FIGURE C-16: Tool tab options in the 3½ Floppy (A:) Properties window dialog box

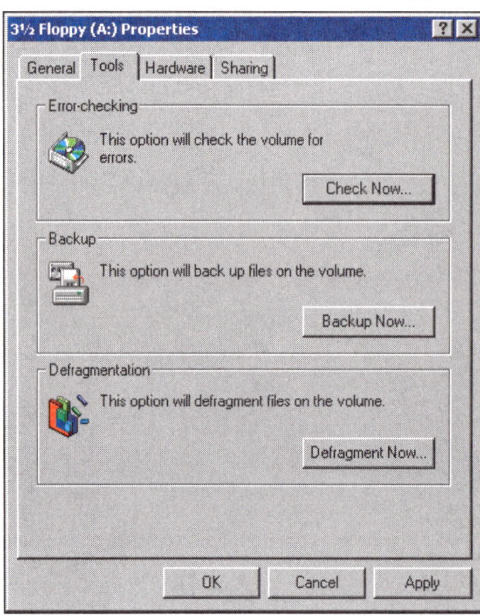

TABLE C-6: Tools in the Properties dialog box

tool	action
Error-checking	Checks for the last time you checked the disk for damage and, if you want, attempts to correct files that are damaged
Backup	Displays the last time you have backed up the contents of the disk, and if you want, starts the Windows 2000 backup program
Defragmentation	Checks for the last time you optimized the disk, and if you want, starts the Windows 2000 Defragmentation procedure

Backing up files

The more you work with a computer, the more files you'll create. To protect yourself from losing critical information, it's important to **back up** your files (make copies on a separate disk) frequently. The Backup option in the disk drive Properties dialog box walks you through a series of dialog boxes to help you back up the files on your hard disk to a floppy or tape drive. You can back up the contents of an entire disk, or only certain files.

Practice

▶ Concepts Review

Label each of the elements of the screen shown in Figure C-17.

FIGURE C-17

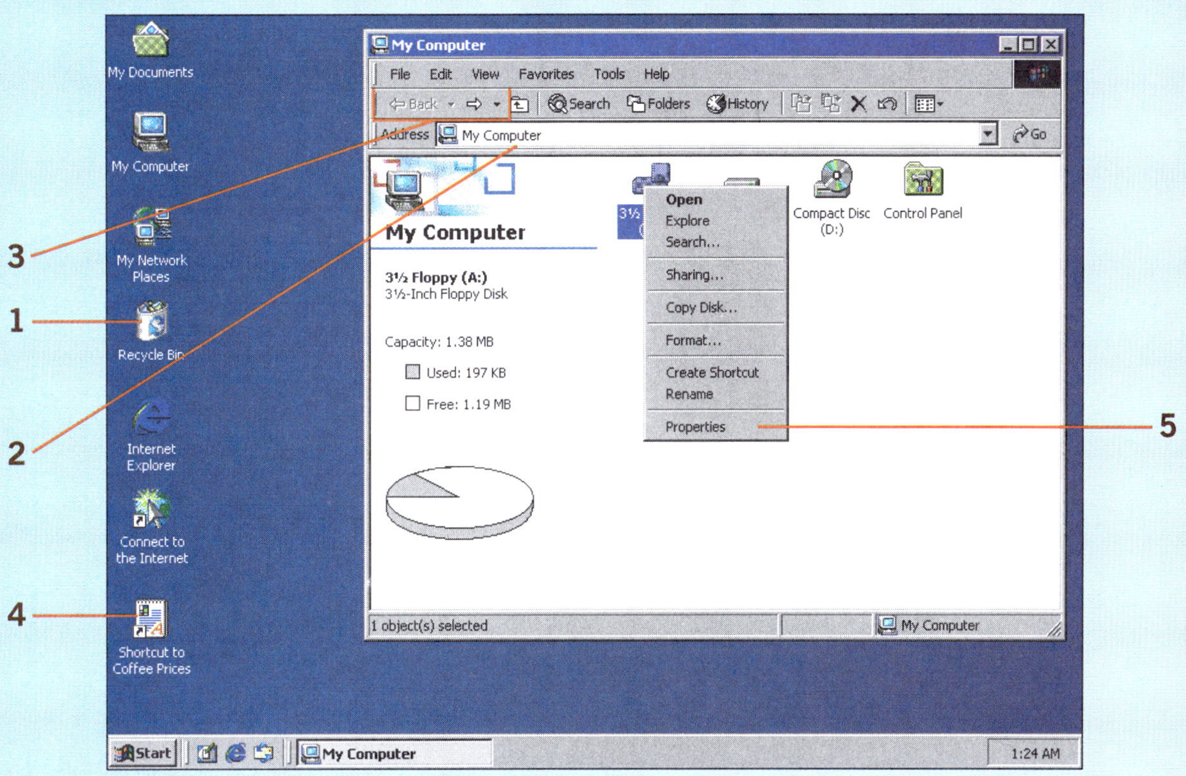

Match each of the terms with the statement that describes its function.

6. **My Computer**
7. **Shortcut**
8. **File**
9. **Recycle Bin**
10. **Folder**

a. A collection of files and folders
b. Location of deleted files
c. A file and folder management tool
d. A collection of information
e. A link to a file or folder

Select the best answer from the list of choices.

11. When a file is deleted, it is placed in
- **a.** My Computer.
- **b.** My Documents.
- **c.** the Recycle Bin.
- **d.** the Desktop Container.

12. My Computer is used to
- **a.** manage files and folders.
- **b.** delete files.
- **c.** add folders.
- **d.** all of the above.

13. Which of the following is not an option for viewing files and folders?
- **a.** Large icons
- **b.** Small icons
- **c.** File names
- **d.** Details

14. When files and folders are arranged by date, they are arranged by
- **a.** the current date.
- **b.** the date they were last modified.
- **c.** the date they were created.
- **d.** the date they were last opened.

15. When right-clicking on a folder, which of the following cannot be done?
- **a.** Explore the folder
- **b.** Find a file
- **c.** Print the contents of the folder
- **d.** Create a shortcut

16. Which of the following is NOT an option for arranging files and folders?
- **a.** By Name
- **b.** By Size
- **c.** By Location
- **d.** By Date

17. Which of the following is NOT disk property information?
- **a.** Used space
- **b.** File type
- **c.** Capacity
- **d.** Free space

Skills Review

1. **Open and view My Computer.**
   a. Insert your Project Disk in the appropriate disk drive.
   b. Double-click My Computer.
   c. Click the Maximize button in the My Computer window.
   d. Double-click the 3½ Floppy drive (A: or B:) icon.
   e. Double-click the Unit C folder, then double-click the Wired Coffee folder.
   f. Double-click the Sales folder.

2. **View folders and files.**
   a. Click the Views button, then click List.
   b. Click the Up button on the toolbar twice.
   c. Click the Back button on the toolbar.
   d. Open the Personnel folder.
   e. Click the Back button list arrow on the toolbar, then click Sales.
   f. Click the Forward button on the toolbar.
   g. Click View on the menu bar, then click Details.
   h. Click View on the menu bar, then click Large Icons.

3. **Create a folder.**
   a. Right-click a blank area of the window, point to New, then click Folder.
   b. Type **Marketing** and press [Enter].
   c. Click View on the menu bar, point to Arrange Icons, then click By Name.

4. **Move files and folders.**
   a. Double-click the Advertising folder.
   b. Click the Mail Order Catalog file.
   c. Click Edit on the menu bar, then click Copy.
   d. Click the Back button on the toolbar.
   e. Double-click the Marketing folder.
   f. Click Edit on the menu bar, then click Paste.
   g. Click the Back button on the toolbar.

5. Delete and restore files and folders.

a. Click the Marketing folder.
b. Click the Restore Down button on the toolbar.
c. Right-click the Marketing folder, drag it to the desktop, then click Move Here.
d. Drag the Marketing folder from the desktop to the Recycle Bin, then click Yes, if necessary.
e. Double-click the Recycle Bin.
f. Right-click an empty area of the taskbar, then click Title Windows Vertically.
g. Click File on the Recycle Bin menu bar, click Empty Recycle Bin, then click Yes. (To restore the Marketing folder, you would drag it back to the Wired Coffee folder.)
h. Click the Close button in the Recycle Bin window.

6. Create a shortcut to a file.

a. Double-click the Advertising folder.
b. Right-click the Special Ads file, then click Create Shortcut.
c. Right-click and drag the Shortcut to Special Ads file to the desktop, then click Move Here.
d. Right-click the Shortcut to Special Ads file, then click Delete.
e. Click Yes.
f. Right-click the Recycle Bin icon, then click Empty Recycle Bin.
g. Click Yes.

7. Display drive information.

a. Click the Back button list arrow on the toolbar, then click My Computer.
b. Right-click the icon representing your Project Disk in the My Computer window, then click Properties.
c. Write down the capacity of the disk, how much capacity is being used, and how much is available for further use.
d. Click OK.
e. Click the Close button in the My Computer window.

Independent Challenges

1. As a manager at Lew's Books and Cappuccino bookstore, you need to organize the folders and files on the store's computer. These are located on your Project Disk in the folder named Lew's Books.

To complete this independent challenge:

a. Open My Computer, and open and view the contents of the folder named Lew's Books in the Unit C folder on your Project Disk.
b. In the Lew's Books folder, create four new folders named *Q1*, *Q2*, *Q3*, and *Q4*.
c. Move the quarterly folders in the 2001 and 2002 folders (2001Q1, 2001Q2, etc.) and place them in the respective Q1, Q2, Q3, and Q4 folders, so that there are two quarterly folders in each of these folders.
d. Create a shortcut for the Collectors' Newsletter file (located in the Letters folder) and place it in the Lew's Books folder.
e. In the Store Locations folder, create a new folder and name it *New Stores*.
f. Move the New Store Location file in the Letters folder to the New Stores folder.
g. Using paper and pencil, draw out the new organization of all the folders and files in the Lew's Books folder.
h. Close My Computer.

2. You are the vice president of a small carton manufacturing company, Apex Cartons, and need to organize your Windows 2000 folders and files. As with any typical business, you have correspondence (business and personal), contracts, inventory, personnel documents, and payroll information. You may have other folders as well. Your job is to organize these separate folders.

To complete this independent challenge:

- **a.** Open My Computer and create a new folder named *Apex Cartons* in the Unit C folder on your Project Disk, within which the rest of the organization of files and folders will be created.
- **b.** Create a folder in the Apex Cartons folder named *Manufacturing*.
- **c.** Create another folder in the Apex Cartons folder named *Material Suppliers*.
- **d.** Create two more folders in the Apex Cartons folder; one named *East Coast* and one named *West Coast*.
- **e.** Move (do not copy) the East Coast and West Coast folders into the Material Suppliers folder.
- **f.** Create a file using WordPad (it doesn't need to contain any text) and save it as *Suppliers Bid* to the Manufacturing folder.
- **g.** Move the Suppliers Bid file into the Materials Suppliers folder.
- **h.** Using paper and pencil, draw out the new organization of all the folders and files in your Apex Cartons folder.
- **i.** Close My Computer.

3. You and your college roommate have decided to start a mail order PC business called MO PC, and you decide to use Windows 2000 to organize the business. Your job is to organize the following folders and files, as well as create shortcuts.

To complete this independent challenge:

- **a.** Open My Computer and create a new folder named *MO PC* in the Unit C folder on your Project Disk, within which the rest of the organization of files and folders for this Independent Challenge will appear.
- **b.** Create a new folder in the MO PC folder named *Advertising*.
- **c.** Create another new folder in the MO PC named *Customers*.
- **d.** Use WordPad to create a form letter welcoming new customers (one paragraph long), then save it in the Customers folder as *Customer Letter*.

e. Use WordPad to create a list of tasks that need to get done before the business opens (at least five items), and save it as *Business Plan* in the MO PC folder.
f. Use Paint to create a simple logo, then save it as *MO Logo* to the Advertising folder.
g. Create a shortcut to the MO Logo file.
h. Delete the Business Plan file and then restore it.
i. Using paper and pencil, draw out the new organization of all the folders and files in your MO PC folder.
j. Close My Computer.

4. M & N Bakeries just opened. You have been hired to help the owners sort their recipes into different categories and work on the design of their company logo. For this independent challenge, use the files Icing 1, Icing 2, Brownies, Passover & Easter Torte, located in the M&N Bakeries folder on your Project Disk.

To complete this independent challenge:

a. Open My Computer and open the folder called M&N Bakeries in the Unit C folder on your Project Disk, within which the rest of the organization of files and folders for this Independent Challenge will appear.
b. Create a folder in the M&N Bakeries folder named *Cakes*.
c. Create a folder in the M&N Bakeries named *Flourless Cakes*, and move it into the Cakes folder.
d. Create a folder in the M&N Bakeries named *Flour Cakes*, and move it into the Cakes folder.
e. In the M&N Bakeries folder, create a folder named *Cookies & Bars*.
f. Move the Brownies file to the Cookies & Bars folder.
g. Move the file named Passover & Easter Torte into the Flourless Cakes folder.
h. Move the Icing 1 recipe file to your desktop, then drag the file to the Recycle Bin.
i. Double-click to open the Recycle Bin and restore the Icing 1 recipe to the M&N Bakeries folder on your Project Disk.
j. Using paper and pencil, draw out the new organization of all the folders and files in your M&N Bakeries folder.
k. Close My Computer.

▶ Visual Workshop

Re-create the screen shown in Figure C-18, which displays the My Computer window for the floppy disk drive with the Project Disk. Use Figure C-1 to help you located the Coffee Price file on your Project Disk. Print the screen (Press the Print Screen key to make a copy of the screen, open Paint, click Edit on the menu bar, click Paste to paste the screen into Paint, then click Yes to paste the large image if necessary. Click File on the menu bar, click Print, then click Print in the Print dialog box.)

FIGURE C-18

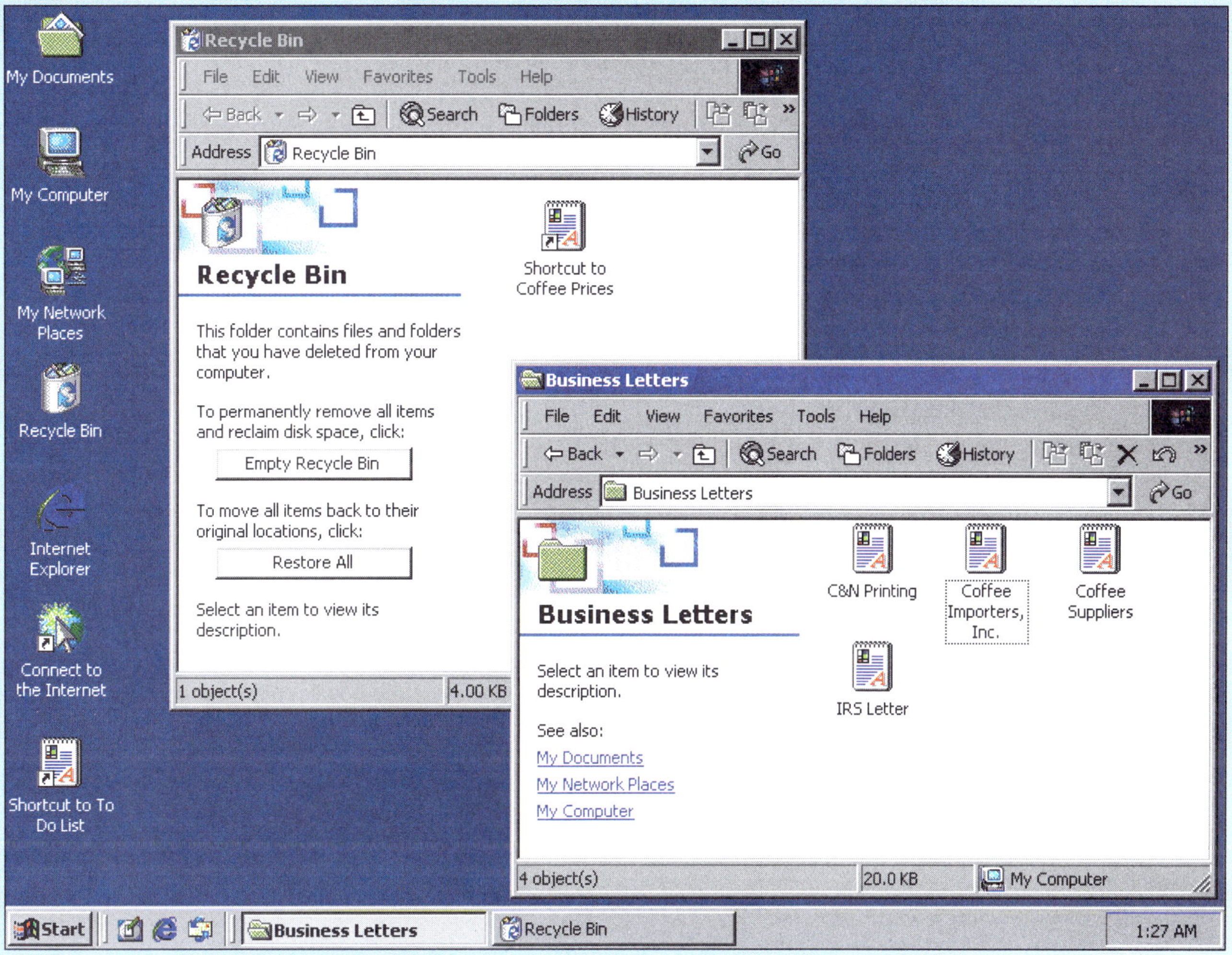

Windows 2000

Managing

Folders and Files Using Windows Explorer

Objectives

- View the Windows Explorer window
- Open and view folders in Windows Explorer
- Customize the Windows Explorer window
- Create and rename folders in Windows Explorer
- Search for a file
- Move and copy a file to a folder
- Restore a deleted file using Undo
- Customize a folder

Windows 2000 offers another useful feature for managing files and folders, named Windows Explorer. Windows Explorer is more powerful than My Computer, offers more features, and most importantly, allows you to work with more than one computer, folder, or file at once. This is because the Windows Explorer window is split into two panes, or frames, so that you can view and compare information from two different locations. You can also use Windows Explorer to copy, move, delete, and rename files and folders, just as you can with My Computer. In this unit, John will use Windows Explorer to perform some general file management tasks and also to prepare for the upcoming Wired Coffee Spring Catalog.

Viewing the Windows Explorer Window

The most important aspect of the Windows Explorer window is the two panes shown in Figure D-1. The pane on the left side of the screen, known as the **Explorer Bar** (or simply "the left pane"), displays all drives and folders on the computer, and the right pane displays the contents of whatever drive or folder is selected in the Explorer Bar. This arrangement enables you to simultaneously view the file hierarchy (the overall structure of the contents of your computer) and the contents of specific folders within that structure. In order to manage his files, John needs to start Windows Explorer and view the contents of his computer.

Steps

Trouble?

If you do not see the toolbar, click View on the menu bar, point to Toolbars, then click Standard Buttons to place a checkmark next to it and display the toolbar; follow the same procedure if you don't see the Address Bar.

Trouble?

To prevent any changes to the original disk, be sure you have made a copy of your Project Disk before using it. For assistance, see your instructor or technical support person.

1. Click the **Start button** on the taskbar, point to **Programs**, point to **Accessories**, click **Windows Explorer**, then click the **Maximize button** if necessary
   Windows Explorer opens, displaying the contents of your My Documents folder, as shown in Figure D-1. Note that the contents of your screen will vary depending on the programs and files installed and also depending on where Windows is installed on your hard disk or network. Windows Explorer has its own toolbar. Below the toolbar is the Address Bar, which you can use to change what is selected in the left pane, and therefore what appears in the right pane. Notice that the toolbar and the Address Bar are the same ones used in the My Computer window. Windows 2000 provides a consistent look and feel to make it easier to accomplish your tasks.
2. In the Explorer Bar, click the **Desktop icon**
   The icons on the desktop are listed in the right pane. You can change what appears in the right pane by clicking the drive or folder in the Explorer Bar, which is the left pane.
3. In the Explorer Bar, click the **My Computer icon**
   The drives and system folders on your computer appear in the right pane.
4. Make sure a copy of your Project Disk is inserted in the appropriate disk drive, click the **Address list arrow** on the Address Bar, then click **3½ Floppy (A:)** or **(B:)**
   The 3½ floppy drive opens, as shown in Figure D-2. The Address Bar makes it easy to open items on the desktop and the drives and in the folders and system folders in your computer. The contents of the floppy drive appear in the right pane of Windows Explorer. You can open a folder or open a document in the right pane of Windows Explorer. When you double-click a drive or folder icon in the right pane, the contents of that item appear in the right pane of the Windows Explorer. When you double-click a document icon, the program associated with the file starts and opens the document.
5. Click the **Back button** Back on the toolbar
   The contents of My Computer (the last location you displayed, in Step 3) appear in the right pane of Windows Explorer. You can move back and forth to the last drive or folder you displayed by using the Back and Forward buttons on the toolbar in Windows Explorer just as you do in the My Computer window.
6. Click the **Forward button** on the toolbar
   The contents of the 3½ floppy drive reappear in the right pane of Windows Explorer. Leave Windows Explorer open and move on to the next lesson.

FIGURE D-1: Viewing the contents of a computer's drives and folders

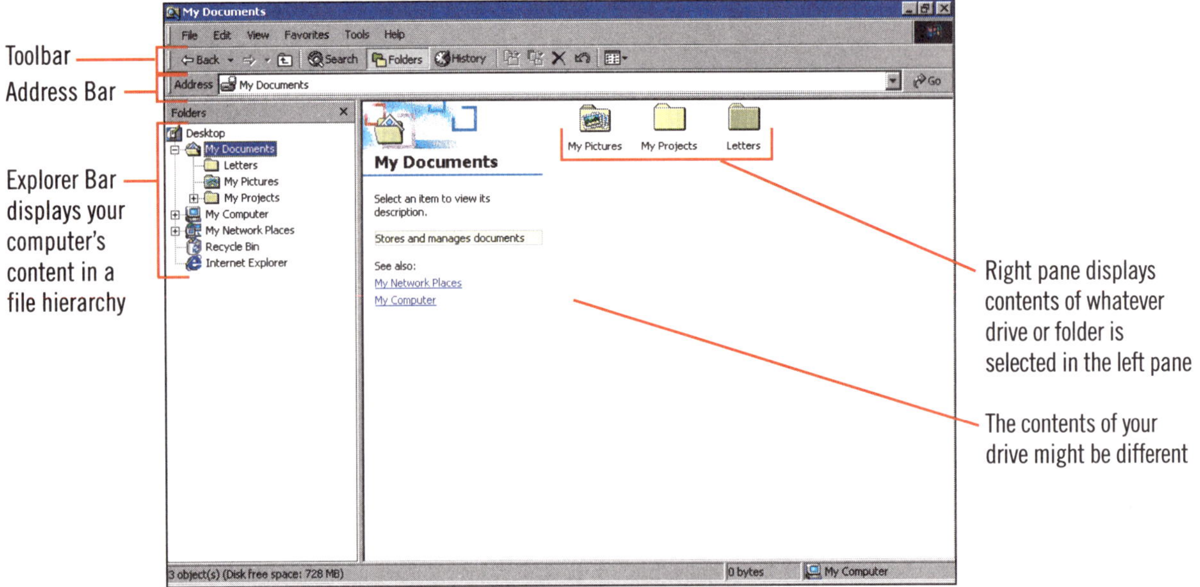

FIGURE D-2: Contents of 3½ Floppy disk

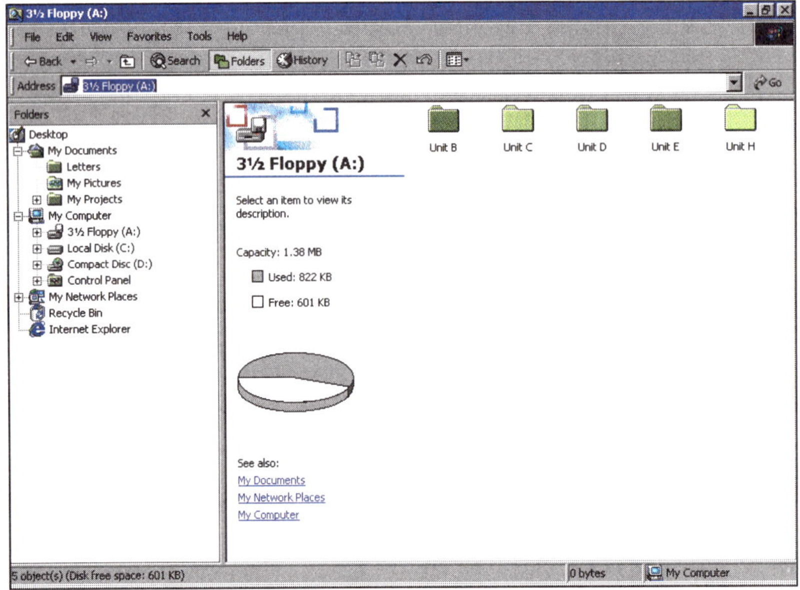

Changing folder options

You can change your view of the current folder in Windows Explorer by changing the folder view settings. You can choose to display the full path of the folder in the Address Bar or title bar, show or hide hidden files and folders in the folder, show the My Documents folder on the desktop, and show pop-up descriptions of folders and desktop items. To change view settings, click Tools on the menu bar, click Folder Options, click the View tab, then click check boxes and option buttons in the Advanced settings window for the settings you want. If you don't like the options you have set in the Folder Options dialog box, you can restore the dialog box settings back to Windows default settings by clicking Restore Defaults. If you want the new settings to apply to all folders on your computer, click Like Current Folder under Folder views. To restore all folders back to original Windows settings, click Reset All Folders.

Windows 2000

Opening and Viewing Folders in Windows Explorer

The Explorer Bar (the left pane of Windows Explorer) displays your computer's contents in a file hierarchy. The top of the file hierarchy is the desktop, followed by the drives, and then the folders. The dotted gray lines indicate the different levels. You can display or hide the different levels by clicking the plus sign (+) or minus sign (−) to the left of an icon in the Explorer Bar so that you don't always have to look at the complicated structure of your entire computer or network. Clicking the + to the left of an icon displays (or expands) the contents of the drive or folder under the icon, and clicking the – hides (or collapses) them. Clicking the icon itself displays the contents of the item in the right pane. When neither a + nor a – appears next to an icon, it means that the item does not have any folders in it (although it may have files, which you could display in the right pane by clicking the icon). Using the + and – in the Explorer Bar allows you to quickly display the file hierarchy on your computer without having to open and display the contents of each folder. John wants to open the Personnel and Letters folders without having to open and display the contents of each folder in the file hierarchy.

QuickTip

To get tips about Windows 2000, click View on the menu bar, point to Explorer Bar, then click Tip of the Day.

1. Click the **– (minus sign) next to the My Documents folder** in the Explorer Bar
   The folders in the My Documents folder collapse to display only the My Documents folder icon. The – changes to a + indicating the hard drive contains folders and files. Because you did not click the My Documents folder icon, the right pane still displays the contents of the A: drive as it did before.

2. Click the **+ (plus sign) next to the 3½ Floppy drive icon** in the Explorer Bar
   The folders on the floppy disk drive, which is where your Project Disk is located, appear in the Explorer Bar.

3. Click the ⊞ **next to the Unit D folder** in the Explorer Bar, then click the **+ next to the Wired Coffee folder icon** in the Explorer Bar
   The folders in the Wired Coffee folder appear in the Explorer Bar, as shown in Figure D-3.

4. Click the **Personnel folder** in the Explorer Bar
   The contents of Personnel folder appear in the right pane, as shown in Figure D-4. When you click a folder in the Explorer Bar, the contents of that folder appear in the right pane of Windows Explorer.

5. Click the **Letters folder** in the Explorer Bar, then double-click the **Business Letters folder** in the right pane of Windows Explorer
   The Business Letters folder opens, as shown in Figure D-5. The folders in the Letters folder are expanded in the Explorer Bar and the contents of the Business Letters folder appear in the right pane.

Opening each folder in its own window

Instead of using the same window to display each folder, you can open each folder in its own window. This can be helpful when you want to use drag and drop to copy or move files. To choose this folder view option, click Tools on the menu bar, click Folder Options, click the General tab, click the Open each folder in its own window option button, then click OK.

FIGURE D-3: Folders on the 3½ Floppy drive

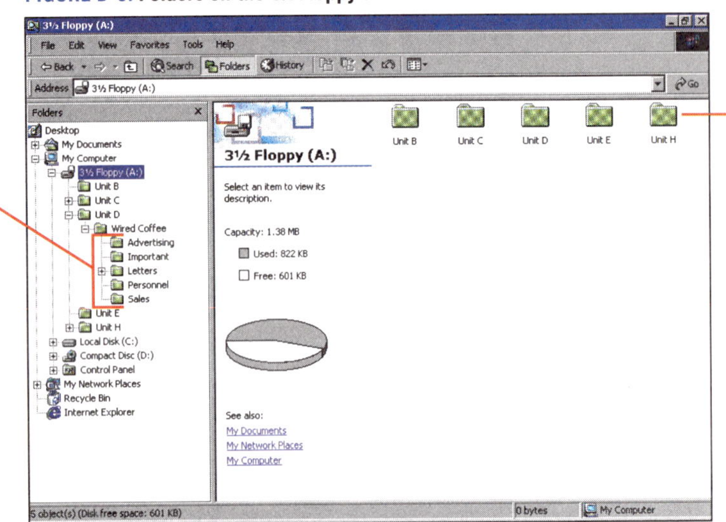

Folders in the Wired Coffee folder expanded in the Explorer Bar

Contents of the 3½ Floppy drive

FIGURE D-4: Personnel folder

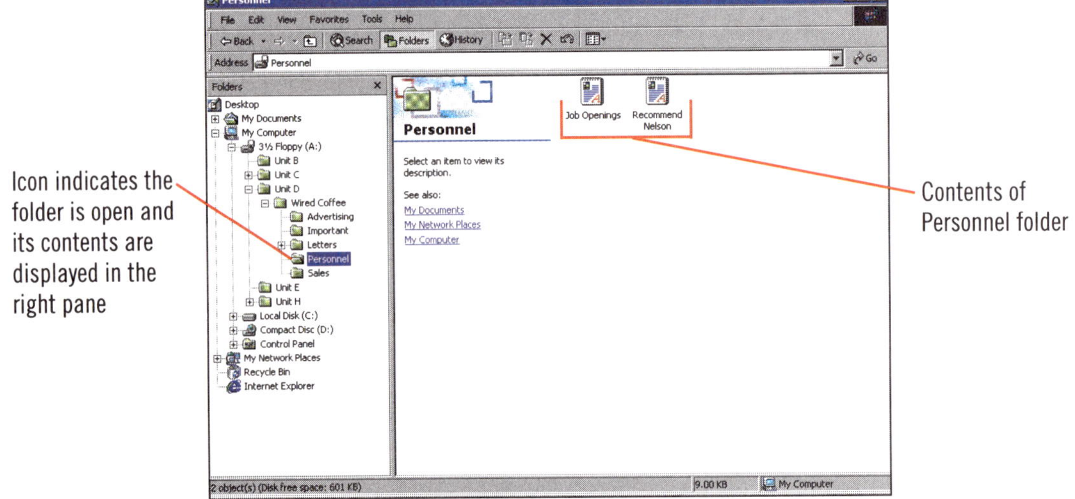

Icon indicates the folder is open and its contents are displayed in the right pane

Contents of Personnel folder

FIGURE D-5: Business Letters folder

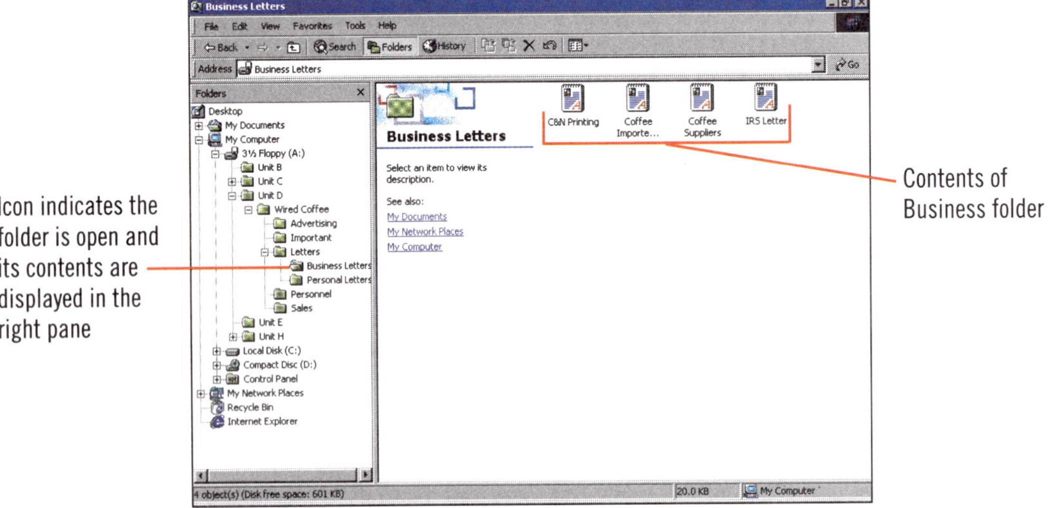

Icon indicates the folder is open and its contents are displayed in the right pane

Contents of Business folder

Windows 2000

Customizing the Windows Explorer Window

You can display Windows Explorer and your file hierarchy in a variety of different ways depending on what you want to see and do. For example, if you have a lot of files and folders to display, you can hide the Explorer Bar or status bar to free up more viewing room. If you need to change the way Windows Explorer sorts your files and folders, you can use the column indicator buttons in the right pane in Details view. When you click one of the column indicator buttons, such as Name, Size, Time, or Modified (date) in Details view, the folders and files are sorted by the type of information listed in the column. John wants to find out the date he last modified the Coffee Suppliers file, so he decides to sort the files in the Business Letters folder.

Steps

1. Point to **Business Letters** in the Explorer Bar
   A ScreenTip appears, displaying the full name of the folder. When you are unable to view the entire folder name in the Explorer Bar, you can point to any part of the folder name to display a ScreenTip.
2. Position the pointer on the vertical bar that separates the two panes of the Explorer window; when the mouse changes to ↔, drag the **vertical bar** to the right until the full name of each folder appears
3. Click the **Views button** on the toolbar, then click **Details**
   The files and folders on your Project Disk (in the 3½ floppy disk drive) appear in Details view, shown in Figure D-6.
4. Click the **Close button** in the Explorer Bar
   The Explorer Bar closes.
5. Position the pointer between the Name column indicator button and the Size column indicator button; when the pointer changes to ✛, drag to the right until the full name of each file appears
   You know that all file names are completely visible when no ellipses appear after a file name. You can sort by any category listed by clicking the column indicator button located at the top of the folders and files list in the right pane. The files in the Business Letters folder are currently sorted in alphabetical order.
6. Click the **Modified column indicator button**
   The files and folders are sorted by the date they were last modified, from earliest to latest, as shown in Figure D-7.
7. Click the **Name column indicator button**
   The files and folders are sorted by name in alphabetical order. John finds the Coffee Suppliers file and sees the date he last modified the file.
8. Click the **Folders button** on the toolbar
   The Explorer Bar opens and displays folders. In the Explorer Bar, you can change the view from the file hierarchy to a search feature, list of favorite Web pages, or list of Web pages you've recently visited, known as History.
9. Click the **Views button** on the toolbar, then click **Large Icons**

QuickTip

In Details view, you can select the columns that you want to be visible. Click View on the menu bar, click Choose Columns, click the columns you want show or hide, then click OK.

QuickTip

Each of the column indicator buttons works as a toggle; clicking once sorts the files in one order, and clicking again reverses the order.

QuickTip

To change the view in the Explorer Bar, click View on the menu bar, point to Explorer Bar, then click Search, Favorites, History, or Folders.

FIGURE D-6: Windows Explorer in Details view

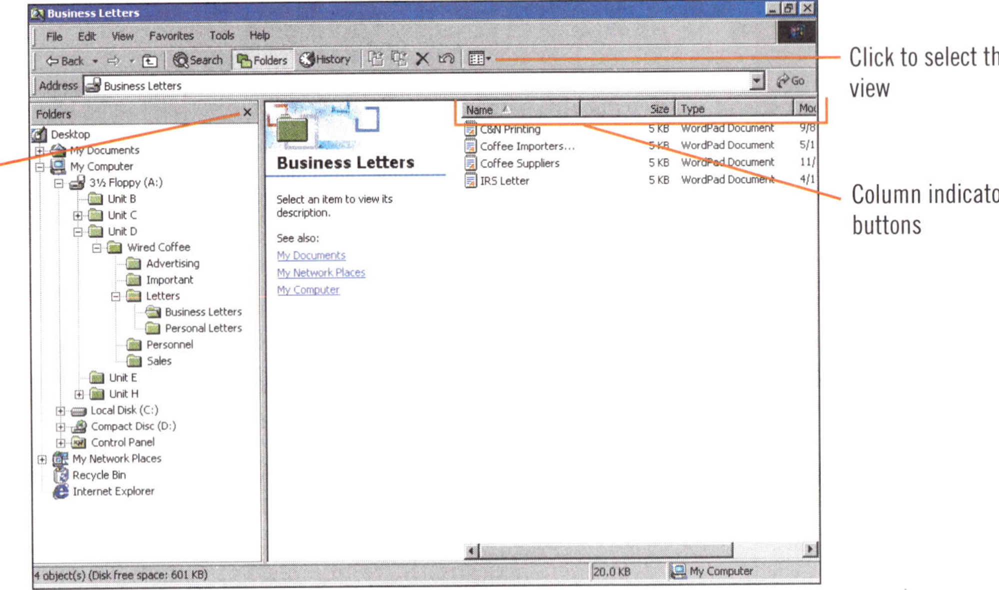

FIGURE D-7: Sorting files and folders by date

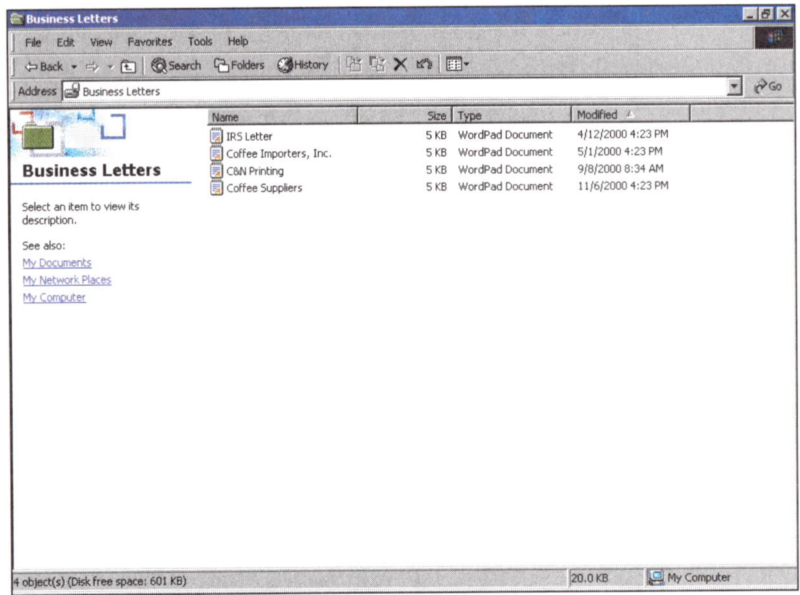

Using the status bar

The status bar at the bottom of the Windows Explorer window gives you information about drives, folders, and files on your computer. You can quickly find out how many items a drive or folder contains, the total size of its contents, where it is located on your computer and (for drives) the amount of free disk space. If you don't want to use the status bar, you can turn the status bar off by clicking View on the menu bar and then clicking Status Bar.

Windows 2000

Creating and Renaming Folders in Windows Explorer

To effectively manage all the files on your computer, you need folders in convenient locations to store related files. You should give each folder a meaningful name so that merely glancing at the folder reminds you what is stored there. Creating a new folder in Windows Explorer is much like doing so in My Computer. First, select the location where you want to store the new folder, then create the folder, and finally, name the folder. You can create a folder in Windows Explorer by using the New command on the File menu, or by right-clicking in the right pane, clicking New, then clicking Folder. You can rename a folder or file in Windows Explorer using the Rename command. John wants to create a set of new folders that will hold the files related to the creation of the Wired Coffee Spring Catalog.

1. Click the **Wired Coffee folder** in the Explorer Bar
   To create a new folder, you must first select the drive or folder where you want the folder, which in this case is the Wired Coffee folder.
2. Click **File** on the menu bar, point to **New**, then click **Folder**
   A new folder, temporarily named New Folder, appears highlighted with a rectangle around the title in the right pane of Windows Explorer, as shown in Figure D-8.
3. Type **Spring Catalog**, then press **[Enter]** or click an empty area in the right pane
   The name of the folder changes to Spring Catalog, as shown in Figure D-9.
4. In the right pane, double-click the **Spring Catalog folder**
   Nothing appears in the right pane because the folder is empty; there have been no new files or folders created or moved here. Because Spring Catalog is the currently selected folder, any folders you create will be located here.
5. Right-click anywhere in the right pane, point to **New** on the pop-up menu, then click **Folder**
   A new folder, named New Folder, appears in the right pane of Windows Explorer.
6. Type **Catalog Text**, then click an empty area in the right pane
   The new folder is named Catalog Text. Notice also that there is a + (or a – if the folder is expanded) next to the Spring Catalog folder in the left pane, indicating that this folder contains other folders or files.
7. Right-click the **Catalog Text folder** in the right pane, then click **Rename** on the pop-up menu
   The folder appears highlighted with a rectangle around the title in the right pane of Windows Explorer.
8. Type **Catalog Pages**, then press **[Enter]**
   The folder is renamed from Catalog Text to Catalog Pages.

Trouble?

If nothing happens when you type the name, you pressed [Enter] or clicked outside the new folder. Select the folder, click the name "New Folder" so a rectangle surrounds it (with the insertion point inside), then repeat Step 3.

QuickTip

To rename a file, you can also select the item, click the name so a rectangle surrounds it, type the new name, and then press [Enter].

FIGURE D-8: Newly created folder

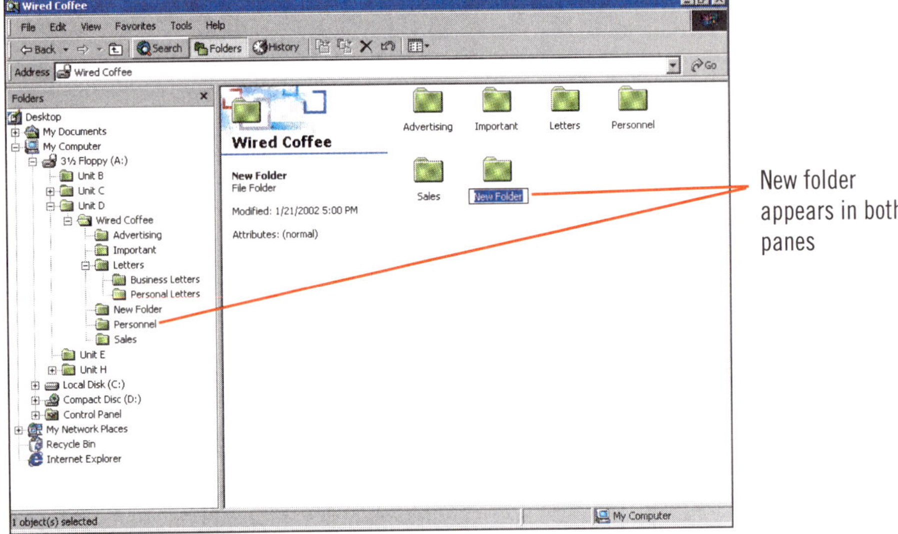

New folder appears in both panes

FIGURE D-9: Creating a new folder using the right-click method

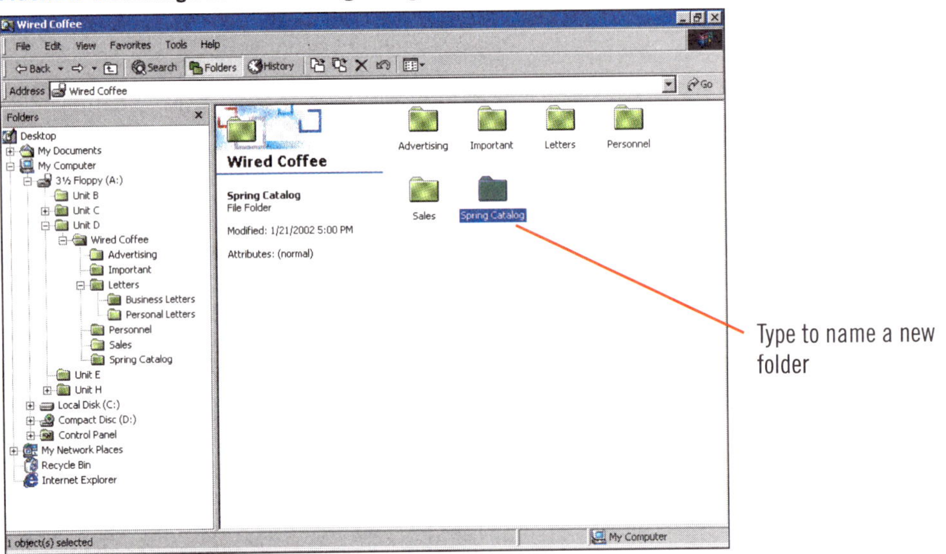

Type to name a new folder

FIGURE D-10: Renaming a folder using the right-click method

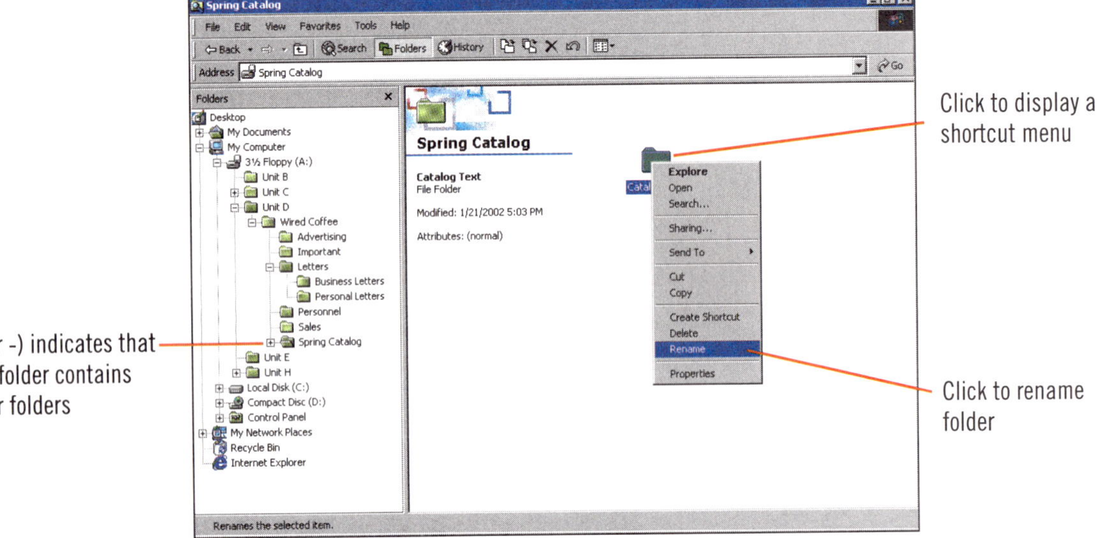

Click to display a shortcut menu

+ (or -) indicates that this folder contains other folders

Click to rename folder

Searching for a File

Sometimes it is difficult to remember precisely where you stored a file. Windows Explorer provides a Search feature located in the Explorer Bar to help you find files or folders on your computer or network, computers on your network, and people and information on the Internet. The Search feature also gives you advanced options to find a file or folder by name, location, size, type, and the date on which it was created or last modified. The Search feature is also available on the Start menu to help you locate the information you are looking for when you are not using Windows Explorer. John wants to find a file he created several months ago with a preliminary outline for the Spring Catalog. He cannot remember the exact name of the file or where he stored it, so he needs to do a quick search.

Steps

1. Click the **Search button** on the toolbar
   The Spring Catalog window opens, as shown in Figure D-11.

QuickTip

Insert the * (asterisk) wildcard symbol in a file name when you're unsure of the entire name. For example, type "S*rs" to find not only the file named Suppliers, but also all other files beginning with S and ending with rs (such as Stars and Sportscars).

2. Type **Catalog** in the Search for files or folders named text box
   You can supply the full name of the folder or file you want to find, or only the part you're sure of. If, for example, John were unsure as to whether he had saved the file as Spring Catalog or Catalog Outline, he could type "Catalog," because he's sure of that much of the name. If John didn't know the name of the file but did know some text contained in the file, he could enter the text in the Containing text box. Before you can start the search, you need to indicate where you want the Search feature to search. The Search feature initially enters the currently displayed folder in Windows Explorer, but you can choose the location you want.
3. Click the **Look in list arrow**, then click the **drive that contains your Project Disk**
   Before you start the search, you can set additional search criteria. Table D-1 describes the additional search options available using the Search feature.

QuickTip

To perform a new search, click the New button in the Explorer Bar.

4. Click **Search Now**
   The Search feature searches all the folders and files on your Project Disk and lists those folders and files whose names contain the word "Catalog" in the box at the bottom of the Search Results window. The full names, locations, sizes, types, and the dates on which the folders or files were created or last modified are listed.
5. Position the pointer between the In Folder column indicator button and the Relevance column indicator button; when the pointer changes to ↔, drag to the right to display the location of the files, as shown in Figure D-12
   At this point, John can either double-click the file to start the associated program and open the file, or he can note the file's location and close the Search Results window.
6. Click the **Folders button** on the toolbar, then click the **Spring Catalog folder** in the Explorer Bar

TABLE D-1: Search options in Explorer Bar

option	use to search for
Files or Folders	File or folders on your computer or network
Computers	Other computers on your network
People	People and groups on the Internet or in your organization
Internet	Information on the Internet

FIGURE D-11: The search for Files and Folders in the Explorer Bar

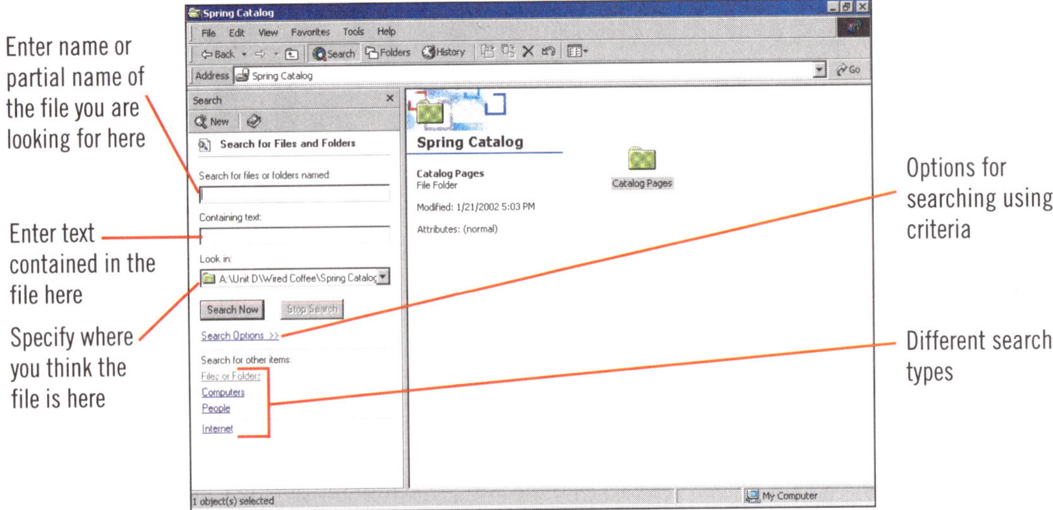

FIGURE D-12: Results of search for Suppliers file

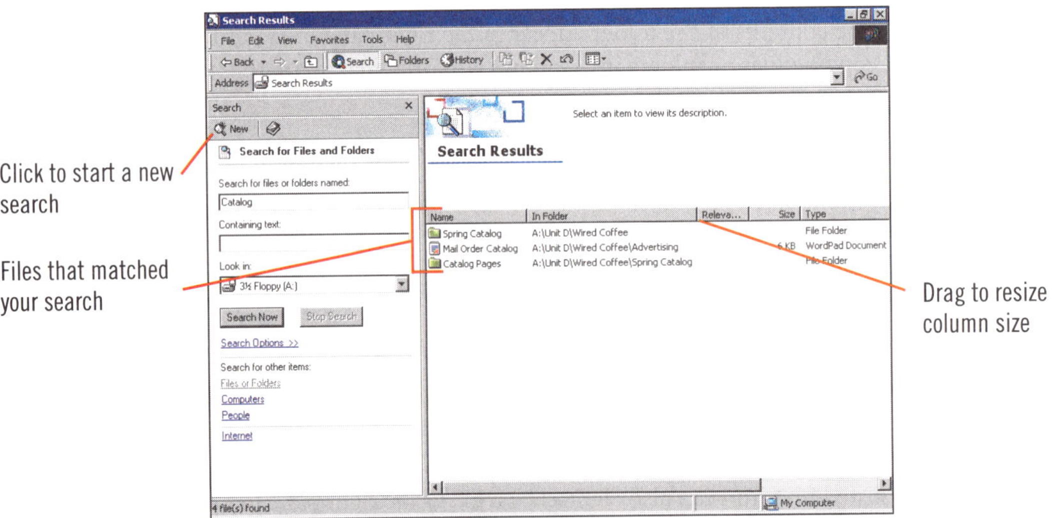

Performing an advanced search

You can also complete an advanced search in Windows Explorer that uses **criteria**, or information, beyond just the name or partial name of a file. If you have no idea what the name or content of the file is, but can recall the type of file (such as a WordPad document), then click the Search button on the toolbar, click Search Options, and then click the Type check box, as shown in Figure D-13. When you click Search Now, Windows will search for and display all the files for the type you specified. This can take a long time, although probably less time than it would take to re-create the missing file. You can also search for files and folders by date and size.

FIGURE D-13: Using Advanced Search features

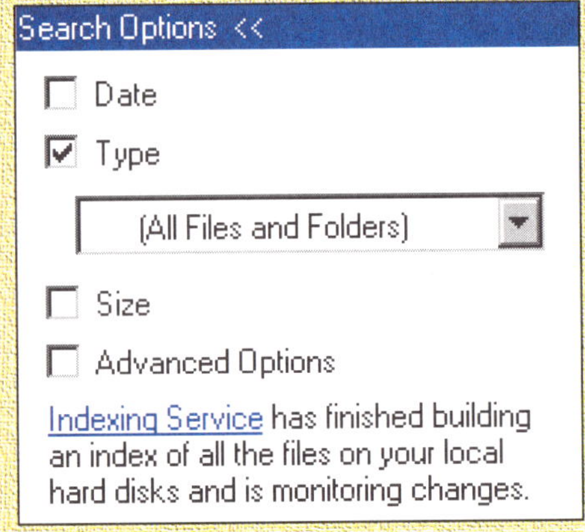

Windows 2000

Moving and Copying a File to a Folder

You should always store your files in the appropriate folders. Sometimes this involves moving a file from one folder to another (removing it from the first and placing it in the second) and sometimes it involves copying a file from one folder to another (leaving it in the first but placing a copy of it in the second). You can move and copy files and folders in several different ways in Windows Explorer. You can use the Cut, Copy, and Paste buttons on the Windows Explorer toolbar, use the drag and drop method, or right-click the file or folder and click the appropriate command in the pop-up menu. John plans to use text from the Mail Order Catalog file (currently located in the Advertising folder) in the Spring Catalog, so he wants to move the Mail Order Catalog file from the Advertising folder to the Catalog Pages folder. He also wants to make a copy of the Wired Coffee Logo file and place it in the Spring Catalog folder.

1. Click the + (plus sign) **next to the Spring Catalog folder** in the Explorer Bar
   The Spring Catalog folder expands, displaying the folder it contains.

QuickTip

To select files or folders that are not consecutive, press and hold [Ctrl], then click each item.

2. Click the **Advertising folder** in the Explorer Bar
   The contents of the folder appear in the right pane of Windows Explorer. When moving or copying files or folders in Windows Explorer, make sure the file or folder you want to move or copy appears in the right pane.
3. Drag the **Mail Order Catalog file** across the vertical line separating the two panes to the Catalog Pages folder, as shown in Figure D-14, then release the mouse button
   Once you release the mouse button, the Mail Order Catalog file is relocated in the Catalog Pages folder. If you decide that you didn't want the file moved, you can move it back easily using the Undo button on the toolbar.
4. Point to the **Wired Coffee Logo file**, press and hold down the **right mouse button**, drag the file across the vertical line separating the two panes to the Spring Catalog folder, then release the mouse button
   As Figure D-15 shows, the pop-up menu offers a choice of options. The Copy Here option is listed first. You can also right-click a file in the right pane to open a pop-up menu—another way to copy or move the file to a new location.

QuickTip

To quickly copy a file from one folder to another on the same disk, select the file, press and hold down [Ctrl], then drag the file to the folder. You can also copy a file from a hard disk to a floppy disk by right-clicking the file, pointing to Send To, and clicking the appropriate disk drive icon.

5. Click **Copy Here**
   The original file named Wired Coffee Logo remains in the Advertising folder and a copy of the file has been placed in the Spring Catalog folder.
6. Click the **Spring Catalog folder** in the Explorer Bar
   The Wired Coffee Logo file was copied from the Advertising folder (where the original is still located) to the Spring Catalog folder (where the copy is located).
7. Click the **Catalog Pages folder** in the Explorer Bar
   The folder opens, and the Mail Order Catalog file appears in the right pane.

FIGURE D-14: Copying a file

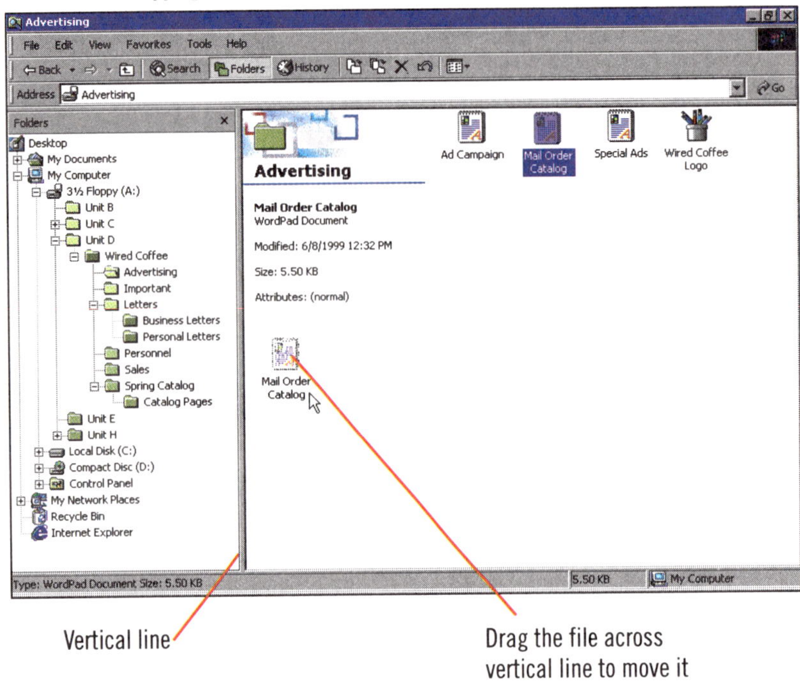

FIGURE D-15: Copying or moving a file

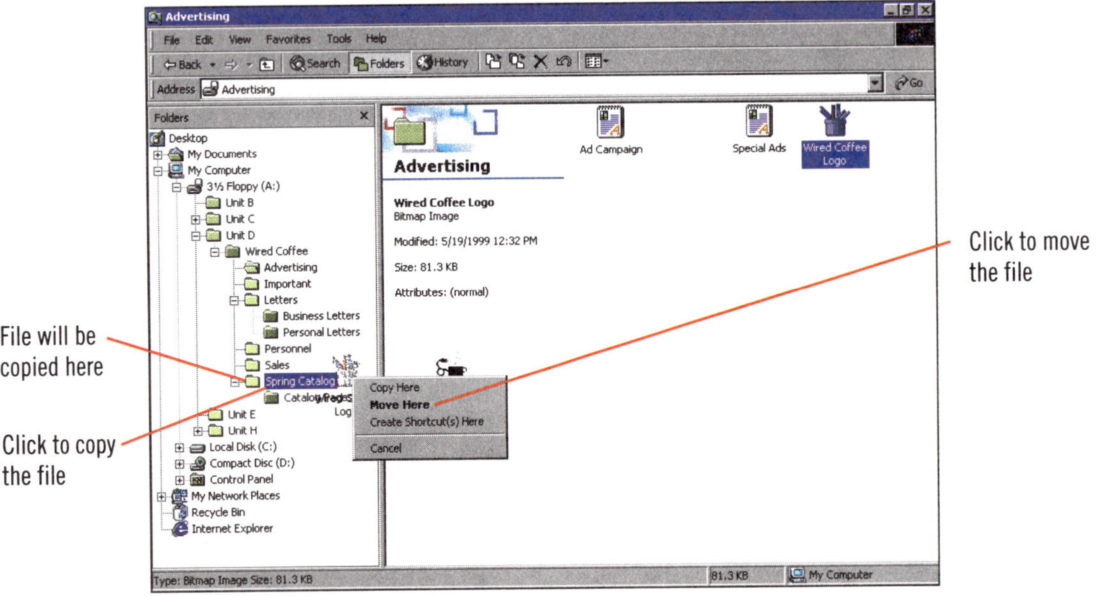

CLUES TO USE

Finding files or folders using the History folder

Windows 2000 keeps a list of your most recently used files, folders, and network computers in the History folder. To display the History folder, click the History button on the toolbar. You can view the History folder is several ways: by date, by size, by most visited, and by order visited today. In the Explorer Bar, click the View button, then click the view you want.

Restoring a Deleted File Using Undo

To keep your files and folders manageable, you should delete files and folders you no longer need. All the items you delete from your hard disk are stored in the Recycle Bin, so that if you accidentally delete an item, you can move it out of the Recycle Bin window to restore it, or you can use the Undo command. You cannot restore files and folders that you delete from a floppy disk or that you drag from a floppy disk to the Recycle Bin. Windows does not store items deleted from a floppy disk in the Recycle Bin; they are permanently deleted (after a confirmation). See Table D-2 for the various methods of deleting and restoring items. John wants to delete a file and then restore it using the Undo command. Because you cannot restore files deleted from a floppy disk, you will start by moving a file from your Project Disk to the desktop.

QuickTip

Some computers are set up so that the Recycle Bin isn't used—deleted files are removed from the hard drive immediately. To check whether your Recycle Bin is enabled, right-click the Recycle Bin on the desktop, then click Properties; if the Do not move files to the Recycle Bin check box has a check in it, click the check box to turn this option off.

1. Click the **Spring Catalog folder** in the Explorer Bar
   The contents of the Spring Catalog folder appear in the right pane.

2. Right-click the **Wired Coffee Logo file** in the right pane, hold down the right mouse button, drag the file to the My Documents folder in the Explorer Bar, then click **Move Here**
   The Wired Coffee file is now moved to the My Documents folder.

3. Click the **My Documents folder** in the Explorer Bar
   The My Documents folder is a general folder where you can store files and folders.

4. Drag the **Wired Coffee Logo file** in the right pane to the Recycle Bin in the Explorer Bar
   You can also right-click the file and then click Delete, or select the file and then press [Delete]. The Wired Coffee Logo file is now removed from My Documents and stored in the Recycle Bin.

5. Click the **Recycle Bin icon** in the Explorer Bar
   The Recycle Bin window opens, as shown in Figure D-16.

QuickTip

To restore an individual file in the Recycle Bin, click the file, then Restore in the Recycle Bin window.

6. Click the **Undo button** on the toolbar
   The Wired Coffee Logo file is now restored to the My Documents folder. The Undo command also lets you reverse multiple actions, so you can use the Undo command again to return the Wired Coffee Logo file back into the Spring Catalog folder on your Project Disk.

QuickTip

Files and folders that you delete from your hard drive remain in the Recycle Bin until you either restore them or empty the Recycle Bin. To empty the Recycle Bin, right-click it (on the desktop or in Windows Explorer), then click Empty Recycle Bin.

7. Click again
   The Wired Coffee Logo file is now moved back to the Spring Catalog folder on your Project Disk.

8. Click the **Spring Catalog folder** in the Explorer Bar
   The contents of the Spring Catalog folder, including the Wired Coffee Logo file, appear in the right pane.

9. Click **View** on the menu bar, point to **Arrange Icons**, then click **by Name**
   The items are arranged by name in the right pane, as shown in Figure D-17.

FIGURE D-16: Recycle Bin window

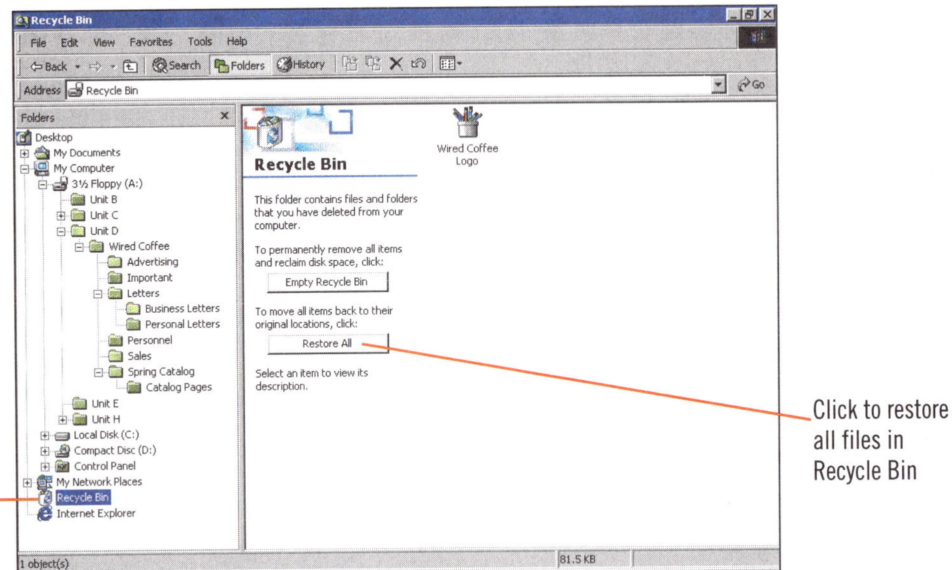

FIGURE D-17: Results of using Undo to restore a file to its original location

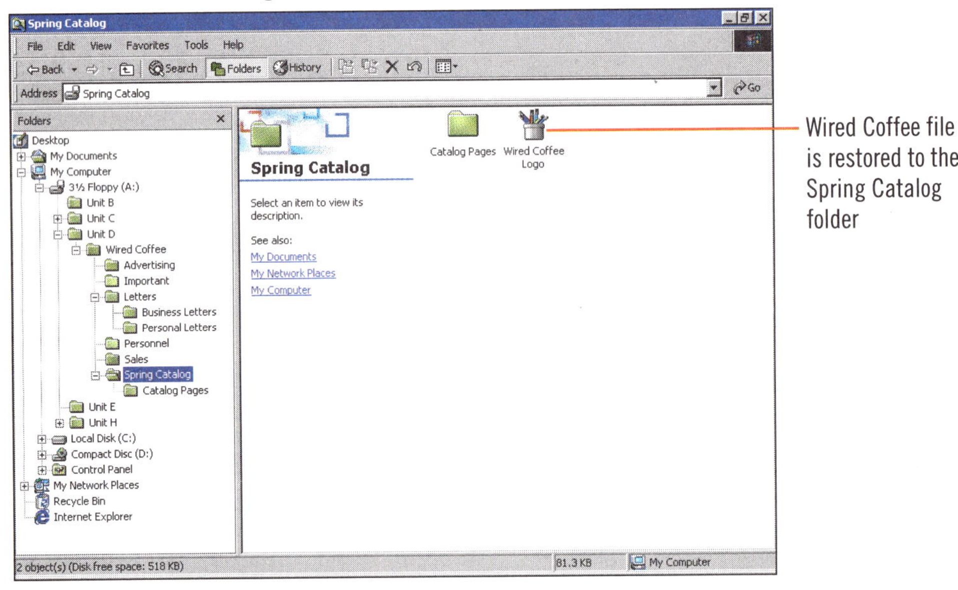

TABLE D-2: Methods for deleting and restoring files in Windows Explorer

action	methods
Delete	• Right-click the file or folder you want to delete, then click Delete • Drag the file or folder to the Recycle Bin • Select the file or folder, click File on the menu bar, then click Delete • Select the file or folder you want to delete, then press [Delete]
Restore	Open the Recycle Bin, then • Select the file or folder you want to restore, click File, then click Restore • Right-click the file or folder you want to restore, then click Restore • Drag the file or folder to a new location on the desktop

Windows 2000

Customizing a Folder

To make working in Windows Explorer more interesting and appealing, you can customize the way a folder looks when it is open (when its contents are displayed in the right pane). As you have seen, by default, folders appear against a white background. However, you can change the background color, select a picture to use as a background, or even create your own Web page view of the folder. Windows Explorer comes with a **wizard** (a series of dialog boxes) that walks you through the steps of customizing a folder. John wants to customize the background of the Wired Coffee folder to display the Wired Coffee logo.

Steps

1. Click the **Wired Coffee folder** in the Explorer Bar
   The contents of Wired Coffee folder appear in the right pane of Windows Explorer.
2. Click **View** on the menu bar, click **Customize This Folder**, then click **Next**
   The Customize This Folder Wizard opens, as shown in Figure D-18. This wizard helps you change the background appearance of the currently displayed folder. See Table D-3 for a description of the wizard options.
3. Click the **Choose or edit on HTML template for this folder check box** to clear it if necessary
4. Click the **Modify background picture and filename appearance check box** to select it if necessary, then click **Next**
   Now you need to select a background picture for the Wired Coffee folder. You can select a picture from the list provided, or you can click the Browse button to select a picture stored elsewhere on your computer.
5. Click **Browse**
   The Open dialog box opens, displaying the My Documents folder.
6. Click the **Look in list arrow**, click the **drive that contains your Project Disk**, double-click the **Unit D folder**, double-click the **Wired Coffee folder**, double-click the **Advertising folder**, then double-click **Wired Coffee Logo**
   The Wired Coffee Logo file appears in the left pane of the Customize this Folder dialog box and is selected in the list of available background pictures.
7. Click **Next**
   The wizard displays the file name and location of the background picture you have selected. You can click the Back button to change the picture you have selected or click the Finish button to complete the wizard with the selected picture.
8. Click **Finish**
   The right pane of Windows Explorer displays the Wired Coffee logo in the background, as shown in Figure D-19.
9. Click the **Close button** in Windows Explorer
   Windows Explorer closes.

QuickTip

To remove a background picture, follow Steps 1 through 4, click None, click Next, then click Finish.

FIGURE D-18: Customize This Folder Wizard

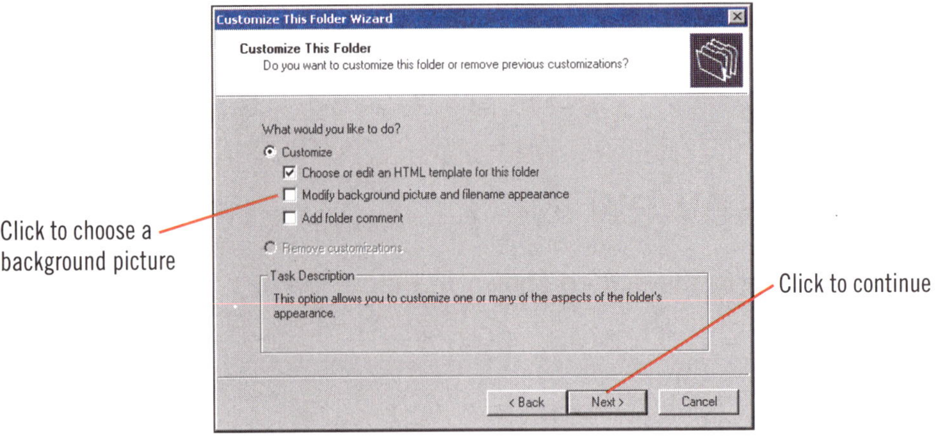

FIGURE D-19: Customized Wired Coffee folder

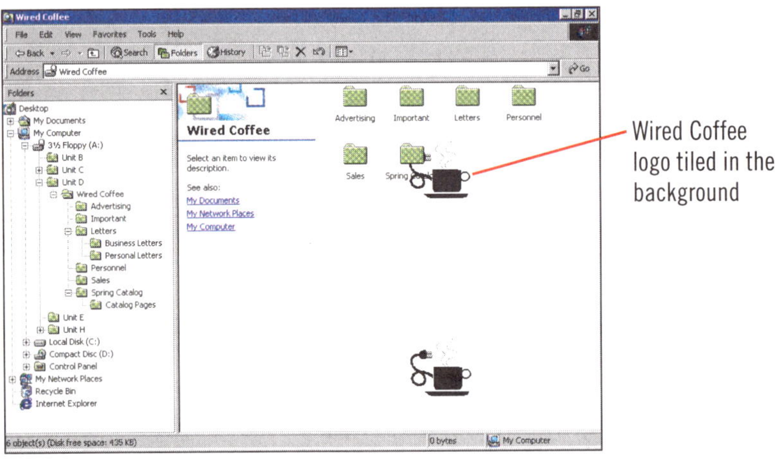

TABLE D-3: Customize This Folder Wizard options

option	allows you to
Choose or edit on HTML template for this folder	Choose or edit an Internet document to view the folder as a Web page (you must know how to use HTML, a computer programming language, to use this option)
Modify background picture and filename appearance	Change the background and file name color or select a picture as a background for the folder
Add folder comment	Add a ScreenTip comment for a folder

Displaying a thumbnail of a graphic

In Windows Explorer you can view a thumbnail version of files in selected folders, as shown in Figure D-20. A thumbnail is a miniature version of an image that is often used for quick browsing through multiple images. Thumbnail versions are available for graphical format only. Click the folder that contains the files you want to view in a thumbnail version. Click View on the menu bar, then click Thumbnails.

FIGURE D-20: Thumbnail of graphic file

Practice

▶ Concepts Review

Label each of the elements of the screen shown in Figure D-21.

FIGURE D-21

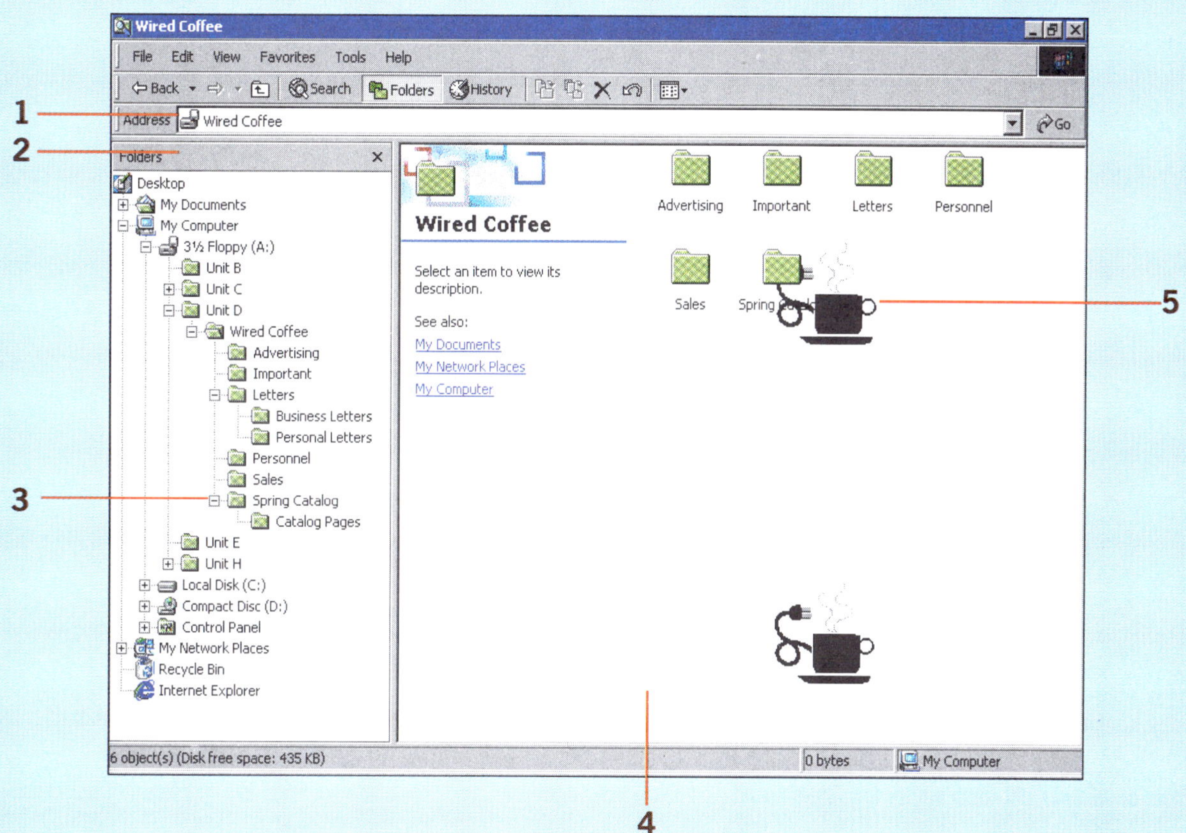

Match each of the terms with the statement that describes its function.

6. Move a file or folder to the Recycle Bin
7. Column indicator
8. Pane
9. + icon
10. Right-click an icon

a. Icon that is clicked to expand folder contents
b. Frames that display information from two different locations
c. Delete selected file or folder
d. Opens pop-up menu
e. Sorts files and folders

Select the best answer from the list of choices.

11. Windows Explorer is different from My Computer in that it allows you to

a. view the structure of your computer's content.
b. view the contents of a folder or drive.
c. change the view.
d. move between folders.

12. Where is the Explorer Bar located in Windows Explorer?

a. Right pane
b. Left pane
c. Folder
d. Hard drive

13. In Windows Explorer, which of the following do you click to list the contents of a folder or drive in the Explorer Bar?

a. +
b. -
c. [Up button]
d.  [← Back button]

14. To sort files and folders in Windows Explorer, click

a. View on the menu bar, then click Sort.
b. a column indicator button.
c. the Views button on the toolbar, then click List.
d. View on the menu bar, then click Arrange.

15. Which of the following is NOT a valid *search criterion* for a file using the Find program?

a. Name
b. Location
c. Type
d. Date opened

16. To copy a folder or file in Windows Explorer,

a. double-click the folder or file.
b. left-click the folder or file and click Copy.
c. press [Ctrl] and drag the folder or file.
d. drag the folder or file.

17. When a folder or file is moved to another disk,

a. the original is moved.
b. a copy of the original is created.
c. a copy of the original is created and moved.
d. a shortcut is created and moved.

18. Which of the following locations is NOT a valid place from which to delete a file and sent it to the Recycle Bin?

a. Hard drive
b. My Computer
c. Floppy disk
d. My Documents folder

19. **Which of the following is NOT a Customize This Folder Wizard option?**
    a. Choose a background picture
    b. Create and edit an HTML document
    c. Remove customization
    d. Choose a color scheme

► Skills Review

1. **View the Windows Explorer window.**
    a. Insert your Project Disk in the appropriate disk drive.
    b. Click the Start button on the taskbar, point to Programs, point to Accessories, then click Windows Explorer.
    c. In the Explorer Bar, click My Computer
    d. Click the Address list arrow, then click the 3½ Floppy Drive (A:) or (B:).
    e. Click the Back button on the toolbar.
    f. Click the Forward button on the toolbar.

2. **Open and view folders in Windows Explorer.**
    a. Click the – next to the My Documents folder icon in the Explorer Bar.
    b. Click the + next to the 3½ Floppy drive icon in the Explorer Bar.
    c. Click the ⊞ next to the Unit D folder icon in the Explorer Bar.
    d. Click the + next to the Wired Coffee folder icon in the Explorer Bar.
    e. Click the Personnel folder in the Explorer Bar.
    f. Click the Letters folder in the Explorer Bar.
    g. Double-click the Business Letters folder in the right pane.

3. **Customize the Windows Explorer window.**
    a. Click the Views button on the toolbar, then click Details.
    b. Click the Close button in the Explorer Bar.
    c. Click the Modified column indicator button.
    d. Click the Name column indicator button.
    e. Click View on the menu bar, point to the Explorer Bar, then click Folders.
    f. Click the Views button on the toolbar, then click Large Icons.

4. **Create and rename folders in Windows Explorer.**
    a. Click the Wired Coffee folder in the Explorer Bar.
    b. Right-click in a blank area of the right pane of Windows Explorer.
    c. Point to New on the pop-up menu, then click Folder.
    d. Name the folder *Money*, press [Enter], then click in a blank area of the right pane.
    e. Click File on the menu bar, point to New, then click Folder.
    f. Name this folder *Legal*, then press [Enter].
    g. Right-click the Money folder, then click Rename.
    h. Rename this folder *Financial*, then press [Enter].

5. **Search for a file.**
    a. Click the Search button on the toolbar.
    b. Type **IRS** in the Search for files or folders named text box.
    c. Click the Look in list arrow, then click 3½ Floppy (A:) or (B:).

d. Click Search Now.
e. Write down the location of the IRS Letter file.
f. Click the Folders button on the toolbar.

6. Move and copy a file to a folder.

a. Drag the IRS Letter file in the right pane to the Financial folder in the Explorer Bar.
b. Click the Business Letters folder in the Explorer Bar.
c. Right-click and then drag the Coffee Importers, Inc. file from the Business Letters folder in the right pane to the Legal folder in the Explorer Bar.
d. Click Copy Here on the pop-up menu.
e. Click the Legal folder in the Explorer Bar.

7. Restore a deleted file using Undo.

a. Right-drag the Coffee Importers, Inc. file (right-click and hold down the right mouse button while dragging) from the Legal folder in the right pane to the My Documents folder in the Explorer Bar, then click Move Here.
b. Click the My Documents folder in the Explorer Bar.
c. Drag the Coffee Importers, Inc. file from the My Documents folder in the right pane to the Recycle Bin in the Explorer Bar.
d. Click the Recycle Bin in the Explorer Bar.
e. Click the Undo button on the toolbar.
f. Click the Undo button on the toolbar again.
g. Click the Legal folder in the Explorer Bar.

8. Customize a folder.

a. Click the Wired Coffee folder in the Explorer Bar.
b. Click View on the menu bar, click Customize This Folder, then click Next.
c. Click the Modify background picture and filename appearance check box to select it.
d. Click Next, then click None.
e. Click Next, then click Finish.
f. Click the Close button in Windows Explorer.

► Independent Challenges

1. You have just started Sewing Works, a sewing machine repair business, and want to use Windows 2000 to organize your documents. For this challenge, you will create on your Project Disk a set of files that are relevant to the business and organize them in a set of folders that will make it easy for you to locate what you need when you need it.

To complete this independent challenge:

a. Create a WordPad file named *Wilson Letter* on your Project Disk thanking Mr. Wilson for his business.
b. On your Project Disk, create another WordPad file named *Suppliers*. List the following suppliers in the file:

Apex Sewing Machine Parts
POB 3645
Tempe, AZ 12345
Jones Sewing Repair
18th and 3rd
Brooklyn, NY 12345

c. On your Project Disk, create a third WordPad file and name it *Bills*. List the following information in the file:

Apex	16453	$34.56
Jones	47354	$88.45
Ott	44412	$98.56

d. On your Project Disk, create a folder named *Sewing Works*.

e. In the Sewing Works folder, create three folders. Name the folders *Letters*, *Contacts*, and *Accounts*.

f. Expand the Sewing Works folder in the Explorer Bar.

g. Move the Wilson Letter file to the Letters folder, the Suppliers file to the Contacts folder, and the Bills file to the Accounts folder.

h. Open the Letters folder.

i. Print the screen. (Press the Print Screen key to make a copy of the screen, open Paint, click Edit on the menu bar, click Paste to paste the screen into Paint, then click Yes to paste the large image if necessary. Click File on the menu bar, click Print, then click Print in the Print dialog box.)

j. Close Windows Explorer.

2. As manager of the summer program at a day camp, you need to keep your folders and files organized so information can be easily and quickly found. Your files fall into two main categories: children and activities. You need to create a folder for each category and place them in a separate folder named Day Camp, to distinguish it from other years you've managed the camp.

To complete this independent challenge:

a. On your Project Disk, create three folders. Name the folders *Camp 2001*, *Campers*, and *Activities*.

b. Create a WordPad file named *Camper Data*. Save the file to your Project Disk. In this file, create information on five campers, including their name, age, bunk, and favorite sports. Here's a sample of two:

Name	Age	Bunk #	Sports
Bill Moore	11	3	Swimming, Horseshoes
Michael Morley	12	4	Basketball

c. Move the Camper Data file into the Campers folder.

d. Create a WordPad file named *Activities Overview*. Save the file to your Project Disk. In this folder, create information on five camp activities, including the name, equipment or supplies the children need to supply, number of children, and name of the activity leader. Here's a sample of two:

Activity	Children provide	Number allowed	Leader
Swimming	Swimsuit, water wings if needed	18	John Lee
Soccer	Shoes, shin guards	24	Madeline Harman

e. Move the Activities Overview file into the Activities folder.

f. Move the Activities folder and the Campers folder into the Camp 2001 folder.

g. Expand the Camp 2001 folder in the Explorer Bar.

h. Open the Campers folder.

i. Copy the Camper Data file to the Activities folder.

j. Open the Activities folder.

k. Print the screen. (See Independent Challenge 1, Step K for screen printing instructions.)

l. Close Windows Explorer.

3. The summer fine arts program that you manage has different categories of participation for young adults, including two-week and four-week programs. In order for you to keep track of who is participating in each program, you have to organize the files with program information into folders. For this challenge, you'll have to create new folders, create a list of participants, and then move the document lists into folders.

To complete this independent challenge:

a. On your Project Disk, create a folder named *Summer Program.*
b. Within the Summer Program folder, create a folder named *Arts.*
c. Within the folders you created named Arts, create two other folders named *2 Weeks* and *4 Weeks.*
d. Create a WordPad file named *2 Weeks Art* on your Project Disk with the following:

Leni Welitoff	2 weeks painting
Tom Stacey	2 weeks ceramics and jewelry

e. Create a WordPad file named *4 Weeks Art* on your Project Disk with the following:

Kim Dayton	4 weeks painting and landscape design
Sara Jackson	4 weeks set construction

f. Move the files you created into their respective folders named 2 Weeks and 4 Weeks.
g. Rename the Arts folder to *Fine Arts.*
h. Collapse and expand the Summer Program 2001 folder.
i. Expand the Fine Arts folder.
j. Open the 4 Weeks folder located in the Fine Arts folder.
k. Print the screen. (See Independent Challenge 1, Step K for screen printing instructions.)
l. Find the files on your Project Disk that contain "painting" in the text (not the title).
m. Print the screen. (See Independent Challenge 1, Step K for screen printing instructions.)
n. Close Windows Explorer.

4. As the head of the graphics department in a small design firm, one of your jobs is to organize the clip art images used by the company. The two categories in which you can place an image are Lines and Shapes. You can place clip art images in more than one category as well. For this challenge, you'll have to create several folders and Paint images and move and copy them to different folders.

To complete this independent challenge:

a. On your Project Disk, create two different small Paint images and save them using the following names: *Ellipses* and *Lines.*
b. On your Project Disk, create two folders named *Lines* and *Shapes.*
c. Move the Lines file to the Lines folder.
d. Move the Ellipses file to the Shapes folder.
e. Copy the Curves file into the Shapes folder.
f. Rename the Ellipses file to *Ovals.*
g. Customize the Lines folder with the Curves file as a background.
h. Open the Lines folder.
i. Print the screen. (See Independent Challenge 1, Step K for screen printing instructions.)
j. Close Windows Explorer.

► Visual Workshop

Re-create the screen shown in Figure D-22, which displays the Windows Explorer window. Print the screen. (See Independent Challenge 1, Step K for screen printing instructions.)

FIGURE D-22

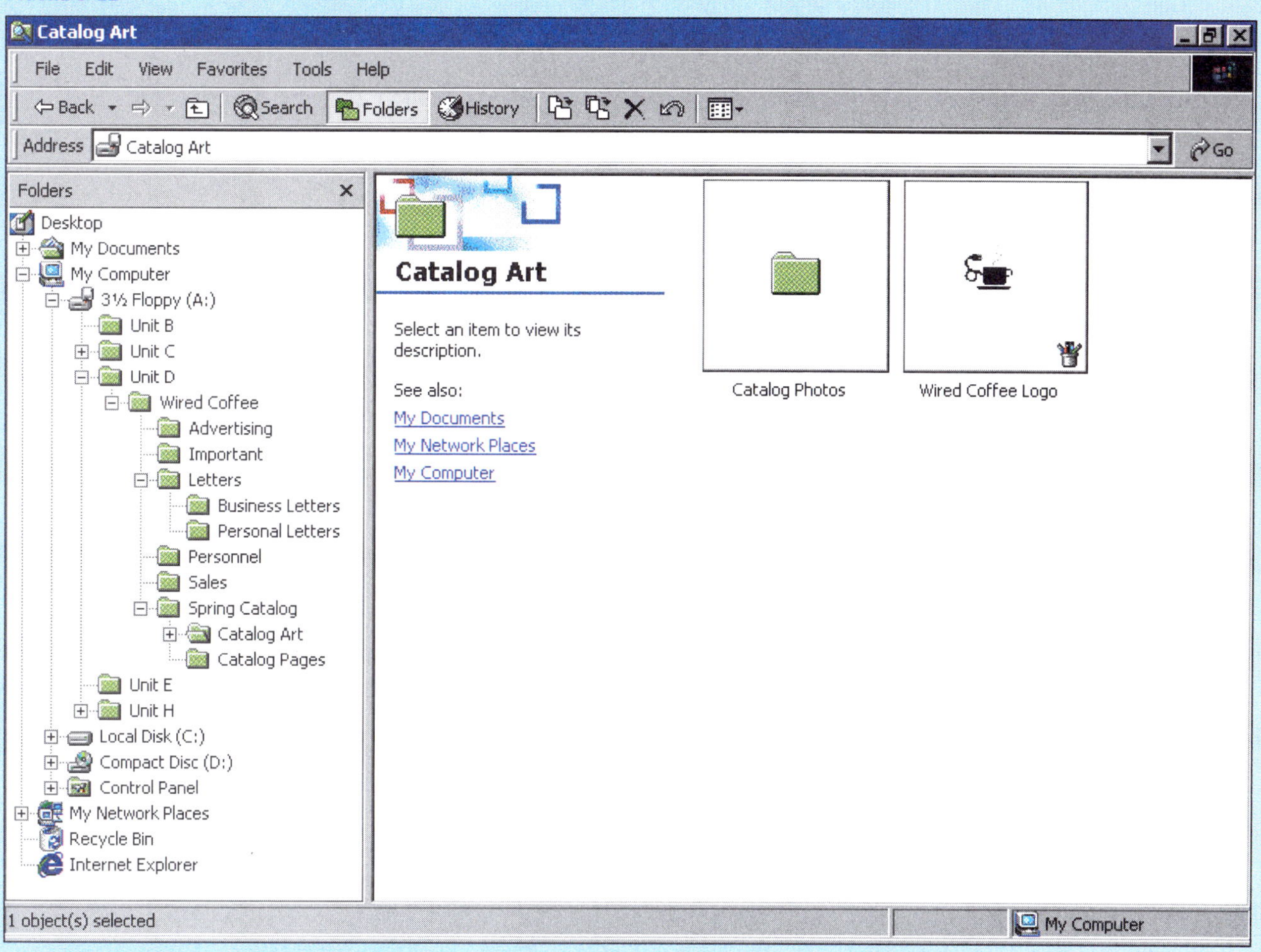

Windows 2000

Customizing
Windows Using the Control Panel

Objectives

- Customize the Active Desktop
- Change the desktop background and screen saver settings
- Change the desktop scheme
- Set the date and time
- Work with fonts
- Manage power options
- Add a scheduled task
- Customize the taskbar
- Customize the Start menu

In this unit, you will learn how to customize Windows 2000 to suit your personal needs and preferences. Most Windows features can be adjusted through the **Control Panel**, a central location where you can change Windows settings. The Control Panel contains several icons, each of which opens a dialog box for changing the **properties**, or characteristics, of a specific element of your computer, such as the desktop, the taskbar, or the Start menu. John wants to customize some Windows 2000 settings. *If you are concerned about changing the aspects of Windows 2000 at your location, or your instructor or technical support person does not wish you to customize, simply read through this unit without completing the steps, or click the Cancel button in any dialog box where a change could be made.*

Windows 2000

Customizing the Active Desktop

Because more and more people are using the Internet, Windows 2000 includes Active Desktop, a feature that allows you to view Web content, or Active Desktop items, on your desktop as you would a document on the Internet, known as a **Web page**. **Active Desktop items** are elements you can place on the desktop to access or display information from the Internet. For example, you can add an Active Desktop item to continuously display Web information such as a home page, stock prices, or weather information. Using the Control Panel Display Properties dialog box, you can customize the desktop to display the Active Desktop items you want to use. John wants to learn how to customize the Active Desktop.

Trouble?

In order for Web content to appear when you click Show Web Content, you need to be connected to the Internet.

QuickTip

You can change the way you click on desktop icons from double-clicking to open an item to single-clicking (like a document on the Internet). Double-click the Mouse icon in the Control Panel, click the Single-click to open an item option button on the Buttons tab, then click OK.

QuickTip

You can quickly turn off all Active Desktop items from the desktop by right-clicking the desktop, pointing to Active Desktop, and then clicking Show Web Content to remove the checkmark.

1. Right-click in an empty area on the **desktop**, point to **Active Desktop**, then click **Show Web Content**
   All Active Desktop items, such as a home page, that are turned on are retrieved from the Internet and displayed on the desktop, as shown in Figure E-1. A **home page** is the Web page that opens when you start your Web browser.
2. Right-click in an empty area on the **desktop** (to the left of the Web page), point to **Active Desktop**, then click **Customize My Desktop**
   The Display Properties dialog box opens with the Web tab in front, as shown in Figure E-2. The Web tab displays a list of Active Desktop items and a preview of the items. To turn on or turn off items on the Active Desktop, you select or deselect the Active Desktop item check boxes.
3. Click the **My Current Home Page check box** to deselect it
   The My Current Home Page is removed from the preview display. You can turn off all Active Desktop items by clicking the Show Web content on my Active Desktop check box to deselect the option.
4. Click **Apply**
   The My Current Home Page is removed from the Active Desktop.
5. Click the **My Current Home Page check box** to select it
   The My Current Home Page appears in the preview display.
6. Click the **Show Web content on my Active Desktop check box** to deselect it
   The Show Web Content feature is turned off.
7. Click **Apply**
   The Display Properties dialog box remains open.

FIGURE E-1: Active Desktop with Web content

FIGURE E-2: Display Properties dialog box

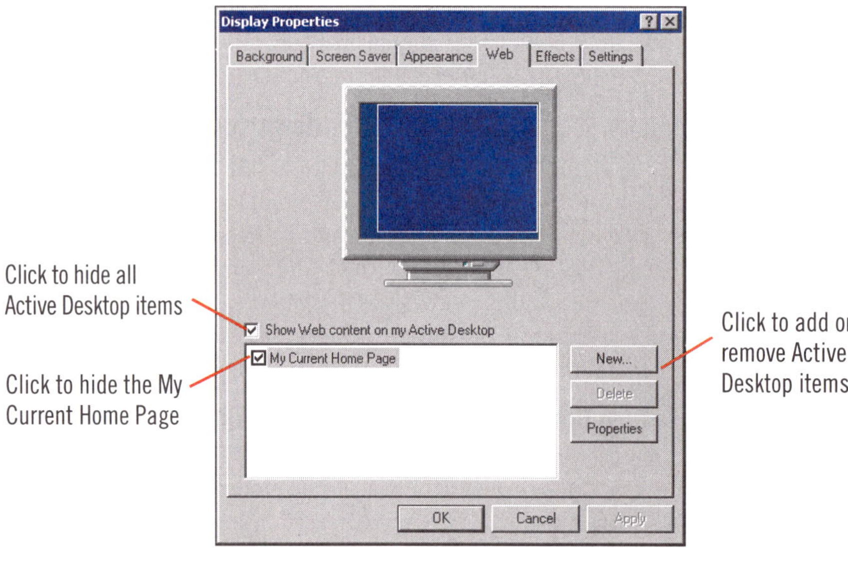

CLUES TO USE

Adding a new Web item to the Active Desktop

You can add new desktop items, live Web content, or pictures to your Active Desktop. Right-click in an empty area on the desktop, point to Active Desktop, then click Customize My Desktop. Click the Show Web content on my Active Desktop check box to select it, then click New. The New Active Desktop Item dialog box opens, as shown in E-3. To add a Web page or picture from the Internet, type its Web address in the Location box. To add a new desktop item, click Visit Gallery to access and display Microsoft's Active Desktop Gallery on the Internet, then select the item in which you want to add. To access and display a Web page, you need to be connected to the Internet.

FIGURE E-3: Creating a new Active Desktop item

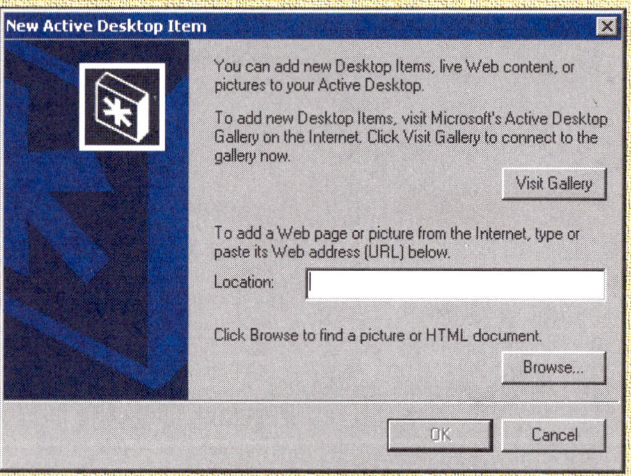

Changing the Desktop Background and Screen Saver Settings

You can change the look of your Windows desktop using the Display Properties dialog box. You can adjust your screen's **background**, the basic surface on which icons and windows appear. You can use a **screen saver**, a moving display that protects your monitor from burn-in, which can occur when there is no movement on your screen for a long time. You can also assign a password to your screen saver to prevent others from using your computer. John wants to choose a new background for his desktop and set one of the standard screen savers to start when his computer is idle for more than five minutes.

Steps

QuickTip

You can also open the Display Properties dialog box by right-clicking an empty area of the desktop, then clicking Properties.

1. In the Display Properties dialog box, click the **Background tab**
   The Background tab appears, as shown in Figure E-4. Table E-1 describes the tabs in this dialog box.
2. In the Wallpaper section, click the **up** or **down scroll arrow**, then click **Coffee Bean** (or a wallpaper of your choosing if this one is not available on your system)
   The preview window shows how the wallpaper will look on your screen. **Wallpaper** is a picture that serves as your desktop's background. Acceptable formats for wallpaper files are Bitmap (the format of a Paint file) or JPEG (the format of an Internet document). You can use Paint to create new wallpaper designs or change existing ones. Besides the wallpaper, you can also choose a desktop **pattern**, a design that can be modified by clicking the None Wallpaper icon and then clicking the Pattern button.
3. Click the **Picture Display list arrow**, then click **Tile**
   You can determine how a wallpaper or pattern appears on the screen using the Picture Display list arrow. **Tile** displays the wallpaper picture or pattern consecutively across the screen; **Center** displays the picture or pattern in the center of the screen; and **Stretch** displays the picture or pattern enlarged in the center of the screen.
4. Click **Apply**
   The new wallpaper appears on the desktop.
5. Click **(None)** in the Wallpaper section, then click **Apply**
6. Click the **Screen Saver tab**
   The default setting is for no screen saver, meaning that your screen will not be replaced by a constantly changing image no matter how long your computer remains idle. If someone else used this machine before you, a screen saver might already be set.

QuickTip

To assign a password to your screen saver, click the Password protected check box to select it, then click Apply.

7. Click the **Screen Saver list arrow**, then click **3D Flying Objects**
   The 3D Flying Objects screen saver appears in the preview window, as shown in Figure E-5.
8. In the Wait box, click the **up arrow** (or **down arrow**) until it reads 5 minutes
   This is the amount of time between when your computer detects no mouse or keyboard activity and when the screen saver begins.
9. Click **Preview**, move the mouse or press any key to stop the preview, then click **Apply**
   The entire desktop previews the screen saver pattern.

FIGURE E-4: Background tab of Display Properties dialog box

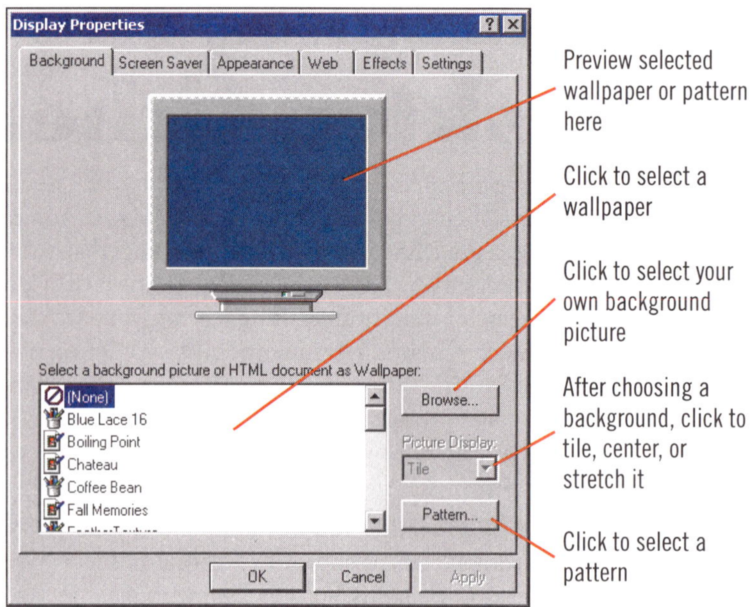

FIGURE E-5: Screen Saver tab of Display Properties dialog box

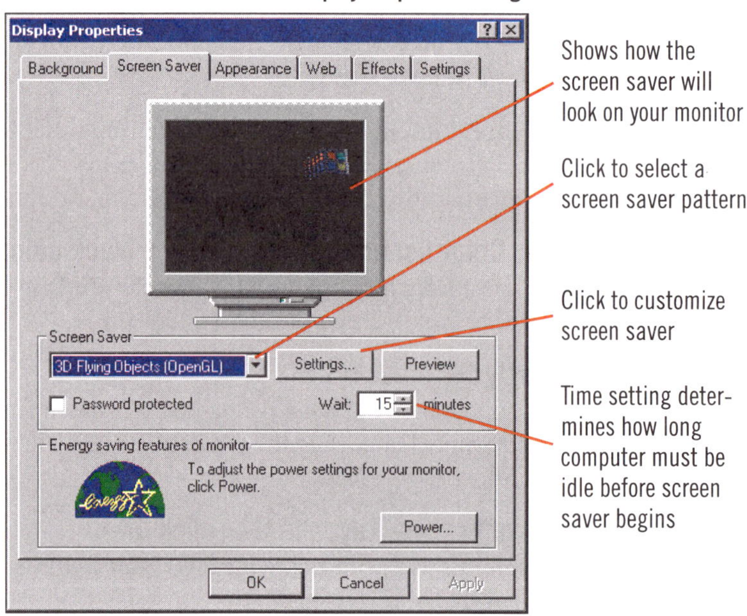

TABLE E-1: Display Properties tab description

display tab	allows you to
Background	Choose a picture or pattern to display on the desktop
Screen Saver	Choose and preview a screen saver pattern, set pattern characteristics, and adjust some power settings depending on your monitor
Appearance	Choose colors, sizes, and fonts for Windows screen items such as title bars, icons, etc., or choose a coordinated Windows Scheme for these items
Web	Choose whether to view the desktop as a Web page, and add or delete Active Desktop items
Effects	Change appearance of desktop icons and set visual effects such as large icons
Settings	Set the maximum number of colors viewable at one time, change the screen resolution, and change advanced settings such as monitor settings

Changing the Desktop Scheme

You can change the appearance of colors, fonts, and sizes used for major window elements such as title bars, icons, menus, borders, and the desktop itself. You can change each item individually, or use a **scheme**, a predefined combination of settings that assures all items are visually coordinated. Windows includes many predefined schemes, and you can also create your own. When you create a custom scheme or modify an existing scheme, you save the changes you've made with a unique name. Ray Adams, an employee of Wired Coffee, is visually impaired and needs a display configuration in which the window elements are larger than the standard size and in which the background color provides greater contrast with window elements. John decides to create a scheme for Ray, who can switch to the scheme whenever he uses the computer.

1. Click the **Appearance tab** in the Display Properties dialog box
   The Appearance tab, as shown in Figure E-6, allows you to change the appearance of individual desktop elements, such as the menu bar, message box, and selected text, or to select one of several predefined schemes that Windows provides, and modify it as necessary.
2. Click the **Scheme list arrow**, then click **Windows Standard (large)**
   In Figure E-7, you can see that the size of everything in the Preview box is increased from standard size to extra large.
3. Click the **Item list arrow**, then click **Desktop** if necessary
   The desktop color can now be changed. Notice that the Item size option and Font option are grayed out, indicating that these options do not apply to the desktop.
4. Click the **Color list arrow**, then click the **black color box** in the first row
   You can select from a matrix of different colors. Before you save the scheme, you can apply the scheme to the desktop to see how it looks.
5. Click **Apply**
   The desktop changes, but the dialog box remains open. Use the Apply button when you want to test your changes and the OK button when you want to keep your changes and close the dialog box.
6. Click **Save As**, type **Ray**, and then click **OK**
   The scheme is saved with the name Ray. Now, anytime Ray wants to use the computer, he can easily switch to this scheme.
7. Click **Delete** to remove the Ray scheme, click the **Scheme list arrow**, click **Windows Standard**, then click **Apply**
8. Click the **Screen Saver tab**, click the **Screen Saver list arrow**, then click **None**
   The screen saver is turned off.
9. Click **OK**

FIGURE E-6: Appearance tab of the Display Properties dialog box

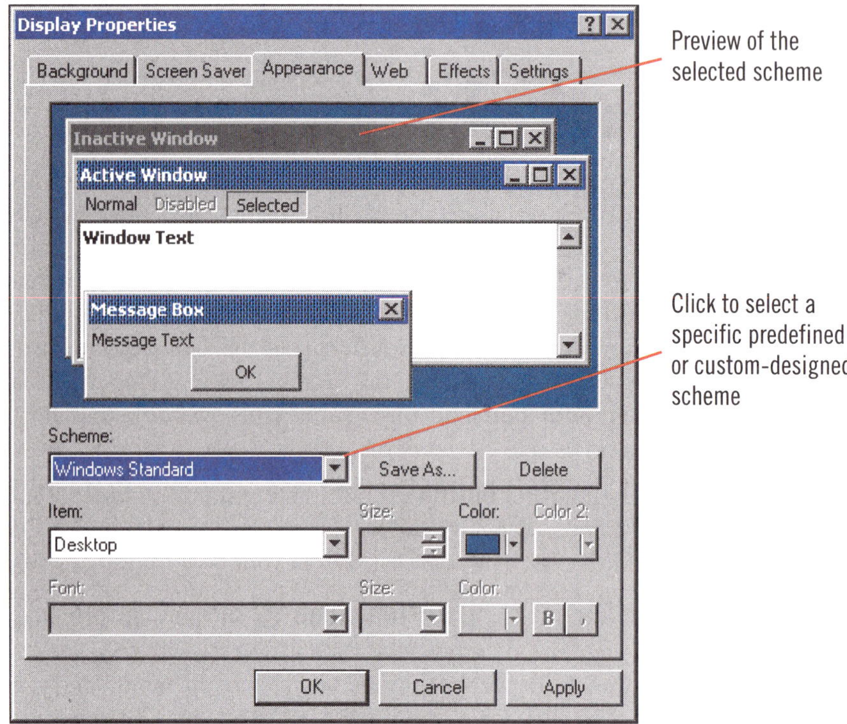

FIGURE E-7: Changing the desktop color scheme

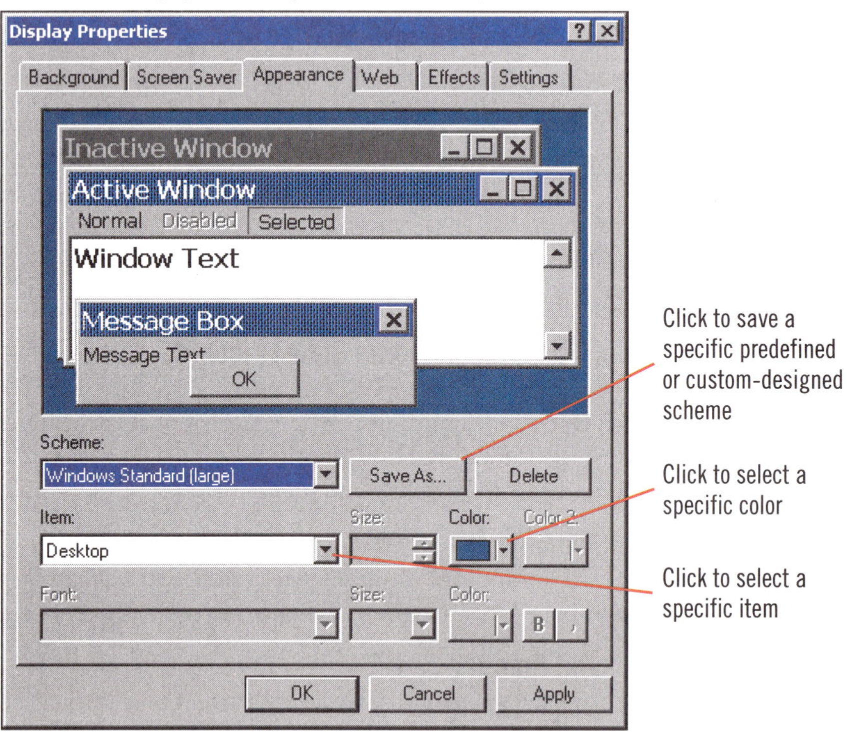

CLUES TO USE

Changing the size of the desktop

You can change the size of the desktop that appears on your monitor. In the Display Properties dialog box, click the Settings tab, then drag the Screen Area slider. The settings available depend upon the hardware that Windows detects when it is installed. In some cases, you might even have higher settings than 640 × 480 or 800 × 600 (such as 1024 × 768) available. A higher setting means higher resolution, so more information can fit on the screen.

Windows 2000

Setting the Date and Time

The date and time you set in the Control Panel appears in the lower-right corner of the taskbar and is used by programs to establish the date and time that files and folders are created and modified. To change the date and time, you modify the date and time settings in the Date/Time Properties dialog box. In addition to changing the date and time, you can also change how the date and time appear. This can be handy if you are working on documents from a different country or region of the world. To change the date and time display, you modify the date or settings on the Date/Time tab in the Regional Settings Properties dialog box. John is working on an international document and wants to change his date and time settings.

1. Click the **Start button** on the taskbar, point to **Settings**, then click **Control Panel**
   The Control Panel window opens, as shown in Figure E-8. Each icon represents an aspect of Windows that can be adjusted to fit your own working habits and personal needs.

QuickTip

To quickly open the Date/Time Properties dialog box, double-click the time on the taskbar.

2. Double-click the **Date/Time icon** in the Control Panel window
   The Date/Time Properties dialog box opens with the Date & Time tab in front, as shown in Figure E-9. To change the date, you choose the month and year you want in the Date section, and then click the day you want in the calendar. To change the time, you choose the hours, minutes, or seconds you want in the text box in the Time section, and then type a new number or click the up or down arrow to select the new time.
3. Double-click the **current hour** in the text box in the Time section, then click the **up arrow** three times
   The new time appears in the running clock.

QuickTip

To change the time zone setting, click the Time Zone tab in the Date/Time Properties dialog box, click the list arrow, and then select the time zone you want.

4. Click **Apply**
   The new time appears in the right corner of the taskbar.
5. Double-click the **current hour**, click the **down arrow** three times to restore the correct time, then click **OK**
6. Double-click the **Regional Options icon** in the Control Panel window
   The Regional Settings dialog box opens, displaying tabs for General, Number, Currency, Time, Date, and Input Locales (for international keyboard support). Using these tabs, you change the format, symbols, and international languages used for text, numbers, currency, time, and date in your files and programs.

QuickTip

To specify how your computer interprets two-digit years, click the Date tab in the Regional Settings dialog box, then click the up or down arrows to set the ending year.

7. Click the **Date tab**
   The Date tab appears, displaying the current date formats being used. You can click the short date or long date list arrows to change the two date formats, as shown in Figure E-10.
8. Click the **Time tab**
   The Time tab appears, displaying the current time formats being used.
9. Click **OK**

FIGURE E-8: Control Panel window

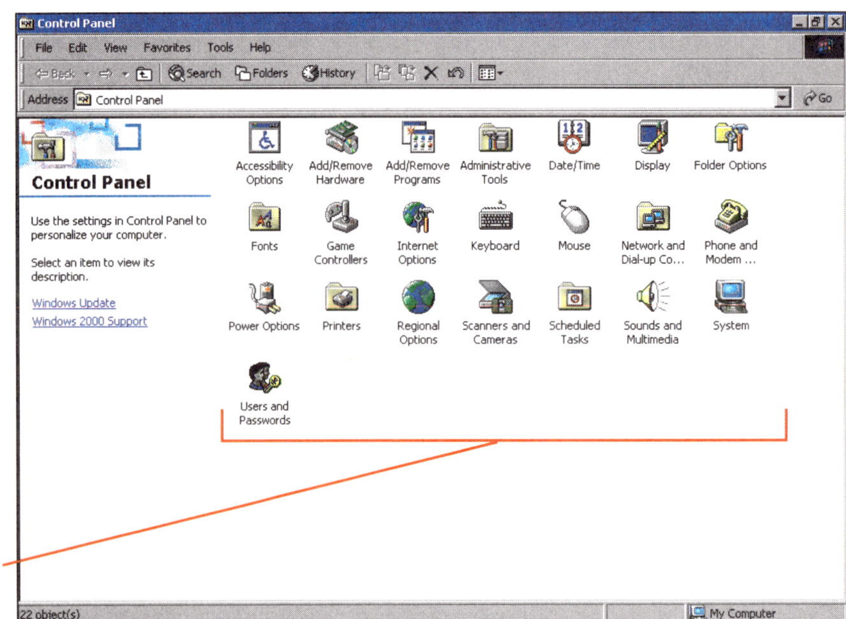

Depending on your computer, your icons might be different

FIGURE E-9: Date/Time Properties dialog box

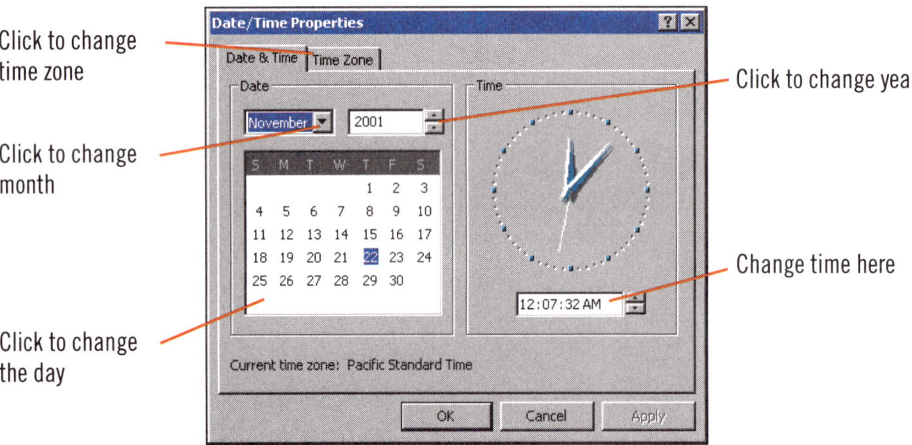

Click to change time zone

Click to change month

Click to change the day

Click to change year

Change time here

FIGURE E-10: Regional Options dialog box

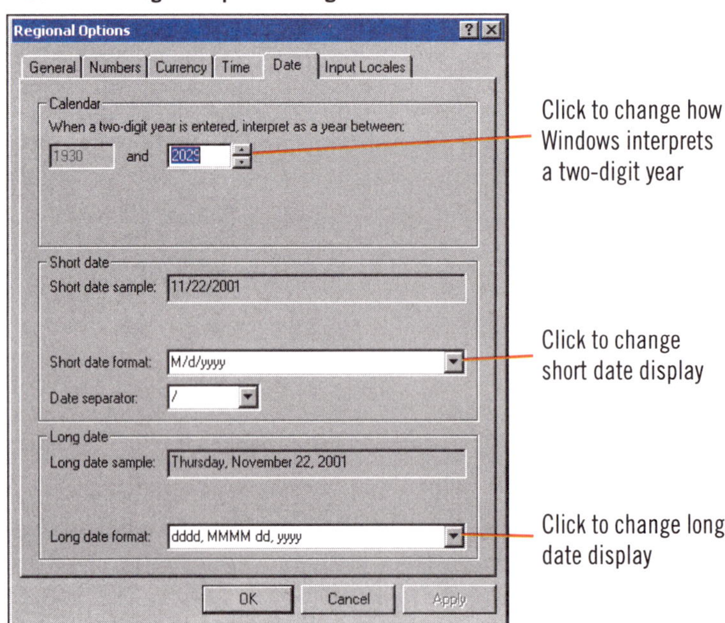

Click to change how Windows interprets a two-digit year

Click to change short date display

Click to change long date display

Working with Fonts

Everything you type appears in a font, such as Times New Roman, Arial, Courier, or Symbol. A font describes the design of a set of characters, known as a typeface, along with other qualities, such as size and spacing. Windows comes with a variety of fonts that appear and print in programs that are part of Windows, such as WordPad and Paint. Using the Fonts window, you can view these fonts, compare them to each other, see a sample of how a font would appear if printed, and even install new fonts. John wants to examine different fonts in preparation for an upcoming flyer he wants to make.

Steps

1. Double-click the **Fonts icon** in the Control Panel window, then click the **Maximize button** in the Fonts window if necessary
   The Fonts window opens, as shown in Figure E-11. The window displays the fonts available on your system and indicates whether each is an OpenType or a screen font. An **OpenType** font is based on a mathematical equation so the curves are smooth and the corners are sharp. A **screen font** consists of **bitmapped characters**, small dots organized to form a letter. Table E-2 lists the various options on the Font toolbar and describes what they do.
2. Click **View** on the menu bar, then click **Hide Variations (Bold, Italic, etc.)**
   The main font styles appear in the Font window.
3. Double-click the **Arial font icon**
   As shown in Figure E-12, the window displays information about this font and shows a sample of the font in different sizes.
4. Click **Print** in the Arial (OpenType) window, then click **Print** again
   A copy of the font information prints.
5. Click **Done**
   The Arial (OpenType) window closes.
6. Click the **Similarity button** on the Fonts toolbar
   The Similarity tool helps you find fonts that are similar to the selected font. All the fonts are listed by how similar they are to Arial, the font listed in the List fonts by similarity to box. You can choose a different font to check which ones are similar to it by clicking the List fonts by similarity to list arrow, and then selecting the font you want to check.
7. Click the **Large Icons button** on the Fonts toolbar, then click the **Back button** Back on the toolbar
   You return to the Control Panel.

Installing a font

Windows 2000 might not come with all the fonts you need or want, but you can purchase additional fonts and easily install them. To install a new font, click Install New font on the File menu in the Fonts window, indicate the location of the font you want to install (on the hard drive or a floppy disk), and then click OK. The new font will be installed and will be available in the Fonts window of the Control Panel and in all your Windows programs.

FIGURE E-11: Fonts window

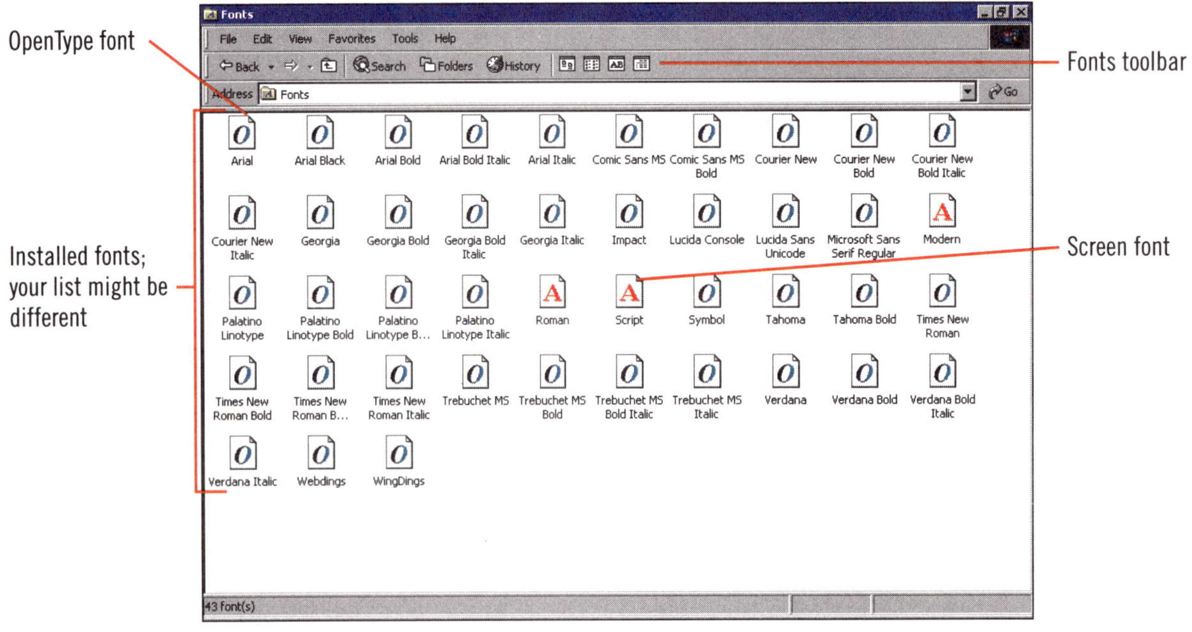

FIGURE E-12: Information on the selected font

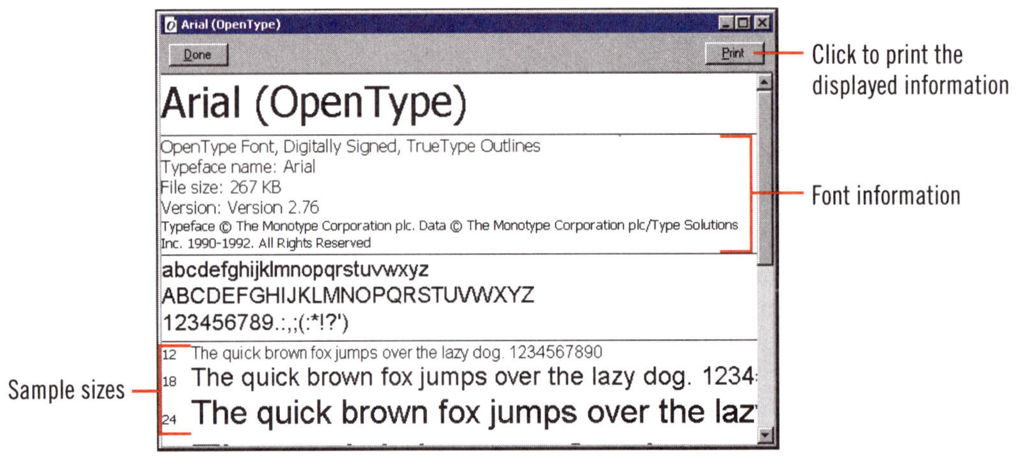

TABLE E-2: Font toolbar options

toolbar icon	name	description
Back	**Back**	Moves you back to a previous folder
	Forward	Moves you forward to a previously opened folder
	Up	Moves to the next level up in the hierarchy of folders
	Search	Searches folder or file
	Folders	Displays a list of folders on your computer
	History	Displays a list of recently used folders and files
	Large Icons	Lists fonts by large icon
	List	Lists fonts alphabetically
	Similarity	Lists fonts by similarity to the selected font
	Details	Lists details of fonts, including file name, font name, size, and date last modified

Managing Power Options

You can change power options properties on your computer to reduce the power consumption of your entire system or a specific device. For example, if you are often away from your computer for a short time while working, you can set your computer to go into **standby**, a state in which your monitor and hard disks turn off, after standing idle for a set time. When you bring the computer out of standby, your desktop appears exactly as you left it. Because standby does not save your desktop settings to disk, a power failure while on standby can cause you to lose unsaved information. If you are often away from your computer for an extended time or overnight but like to leave the computer on, you can set it to go into **hibernation**, a state in which your computer shuts down but first saves everything in memory on your hard disk. When you restart the computer, your desktop is restored exactly as you left it. Table E-3 lists common tabs in the Power Options Properties dialog box and describes the power options each offers. During the day, John takes short breaks from his computer to attend meetings, so he wants to change power options for his computer to save power.

Steps

1. Double-click the **Power Options icon** in the Control Panel window
   The Power Options Properties dialog box opens with the Power Schemes tab in front, as shown in Figure E-13. A **power scheme** is a predefined collection of power usage settings. You can choose one of the power schemes included with Windows or modify one to suit your needs. The Power Options you see will vary depending on your computer's hardware configuration. The Power Options feature automatically detects what is available on your computer and shows you only the options that you can control.

> **QuickTip**
> To create your own power scheme, click the Power Schemes tab in the Power Options Properties dialog box, select the Turn off monitor and Turn off hard disks power options you want, click Save As, type a name, then click OK.

2. Click the **Power schemes list arrow**, then click **Portable/Laptop**
   Settings for the Portable/Laptop power scheme appear in the bottom section of the Power Schemes tab.
3. Click the **Turn off monitor list arrow**, then click **After 1 min**
4. Click **Apply**, then wait one minute without moving the mouse or pressing a key
   After a minute, the screen goes on standby (a blank screen). While on standby, your entire computer switches to a low power state where devices, such as the monitor and hard disks, turn off and your computer uses less power.

> **QuickTip**
> To show a power option icon in the taskbar, click the Advanced tab, click the Always show icon on the taskbar check box to select it, then click Apply or OK.

5. Move the mouse to restore the desktop
   The computer comes out of standby, and your desktop is restored exactly as you left it.
6. Click the **Power schemes list arrow**, then click **Always On**
   The Turn off monitor and Turn off hard disks options change to reflect power settings for this scheme. For the computer shown in Figure E-13, the power settings change to Never, the preset option.

> **Trouble?**
> If you do not see the Hibernate tab, skip to Step 8. For most laptop computers, other tabs appear instead of the Hibernate tab.

7. Click the **Hibernate tab**
   The Hibernate tab appears, displaying settings for hibernation support, as shown in Figure E-14. In this case, the hibernation support is turned on. When you shut down your computer, the Hibernation option is available for you to select.
8. Click **OK**

FIGURE E-13: Power Options Properties dialog box

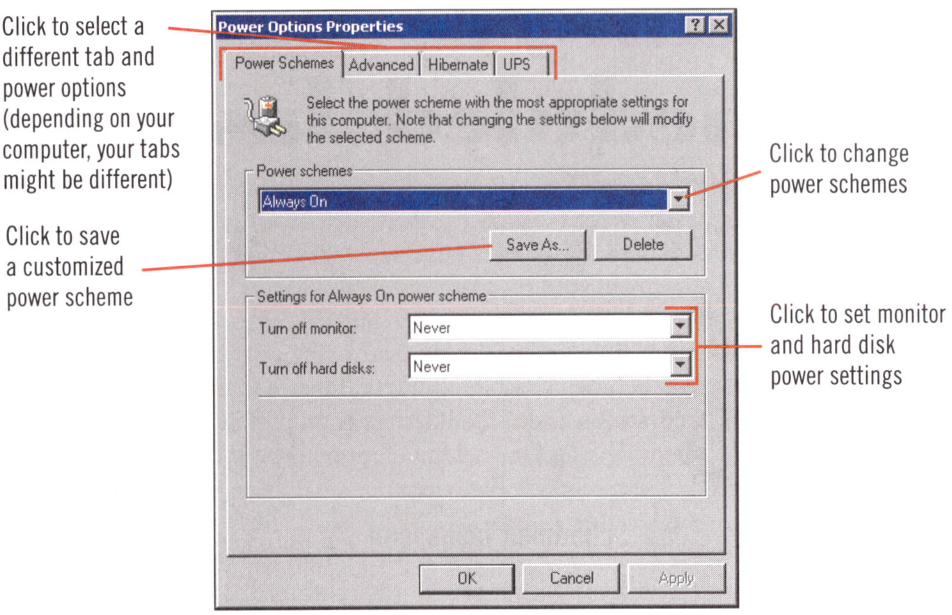

FIGURE E-14: Hibernate tab of Power Options Properties dialog box

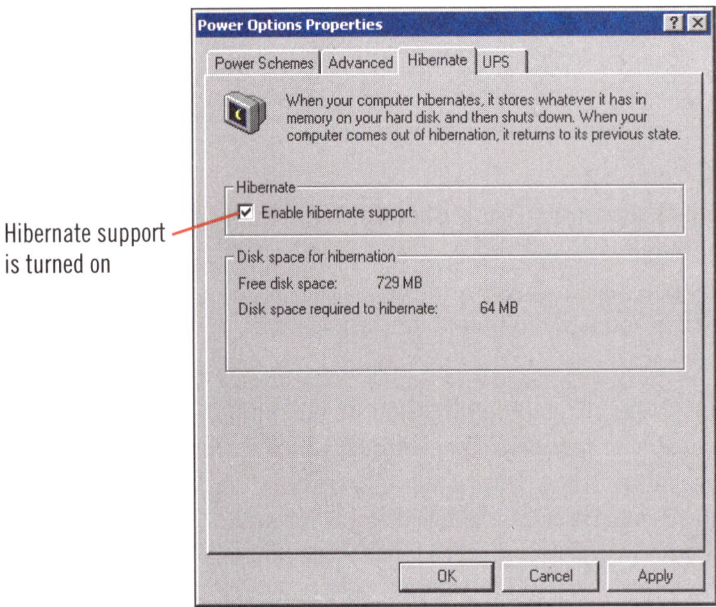

TABLE E-3: Common Power Options Properties tabs

tab	allows you to
Power Schemes	Change power settings for your monitor and hard disks
Advanced	Change user power options
Hibernate	Turn on and off hibernate support
UPS	Select and configure an Uninterruptible Power Supply (UPS) device (availability depends on the specific UPS hardware installed on your computer)
Alarms	Change settings for low battery notification alarms (available on most laptop computers)
Power Meter	Display power usage details for each battery in your computer (available on most laptop computers)
APM	Turn on or turn off Advanced Power Management (APM) support in order to reduce overall power consumption (available on most laptop computers)

Windows 2000

Adding a Scheduled Task

Task Scheduler is a tool that enables you to schedule tasks (such as Disk Cleanup, a program that removes unnecessary files) to run regularly, at a time that is convenient for you. Task Scheduler starts each time you start Windows. When Task Scheduler is running on your computer, its icon appears next to the clock on the taskbar. With Task Scheduler, you can schedule a task to run daily, weekly, monthly, or at certain times (such as when the computer starts or is idle), change the schedule for or turn off an existing task, or customize how a task will run at its scheduled time. Before you schedule a task, be sure that the system date and time on your computer are accurate, as Task Scheduler relies on this information to run scheduled tasks. John schedules a task to back up files on his computer.

QuickTip

To modify a scheduled task, right-click the task you want to modify, and then click Properties.

1. Double-click the **Scheduled Tasks icon** in the Control Panel window
   The Scheduled Tasks window opens, as shown in Figure E-15.

2. Double-click the **Add Scheduled Task icon**, then in the Scheduled Task Wizard dialog box, click **Next**
   The Scheduled Task Wizard displays a list of programs you can schedule to run. If the program or document you want to use is not in the list, you can click Browse to locate the program on your computer disk drive or network.

3. In the list of programs, click **Backup**, click **Next**, click the **Weekly option button**, then click **Next**
   The next Scheduled Task Wizard dialog box opens, as shown in Figure E-16, asking you to select the time and day you want to the task to start.

4. In the Start time box, change the time to one minute ahead of the current time, click the current day of the week check box to select it, then click **Next**
   The next Scheduled Task Wizard dialog box opens, asking you to enter the name and password of the current user. The task will run as if it were started by that user.

5. In the Enter the password box, type your **password**, press **[Tab]**, then type your password again

QuickTip

To stop a scheduled task that is running, right-click the task that you want to stop, then click End Task.

6. Click **Next**, then click **Finish**
   The scheduled task appears in the Scheduled Task window, as shown in Figure E-17.

7. Wait for the backup to take place, then click the **Close button** in the Backup Window

QuickTip

To notify you when a scheduled task is missed, click Advanced on the menu bar, then click Notify Me of Missed Tasks to select the option.

8. Right-click the **Backup icon**, click **Delete**, then click **Yes**
   The scheduled task is deleted.

9. Click the **Close button** on the Scheduled Tasks window

FIGURE E-15: Scheduled Tasks window

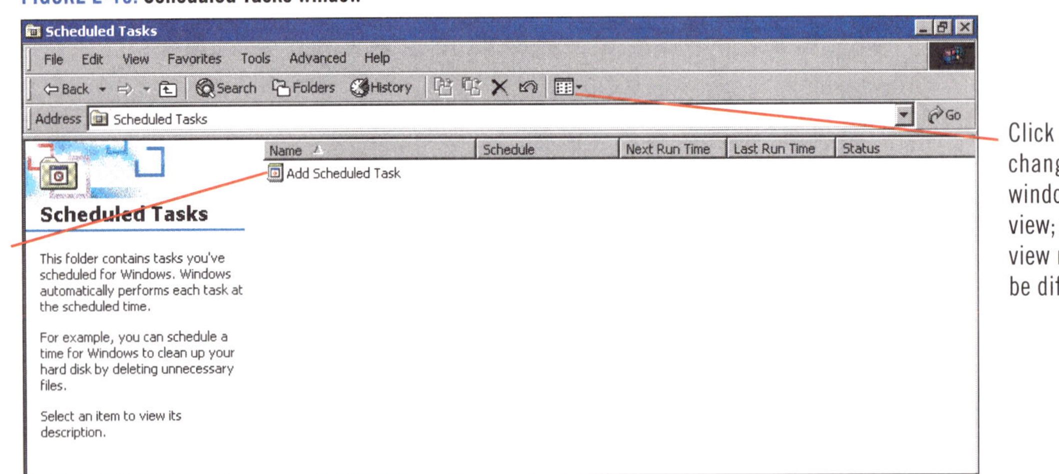

FIGURE E-16: Scheduled Task Wizard

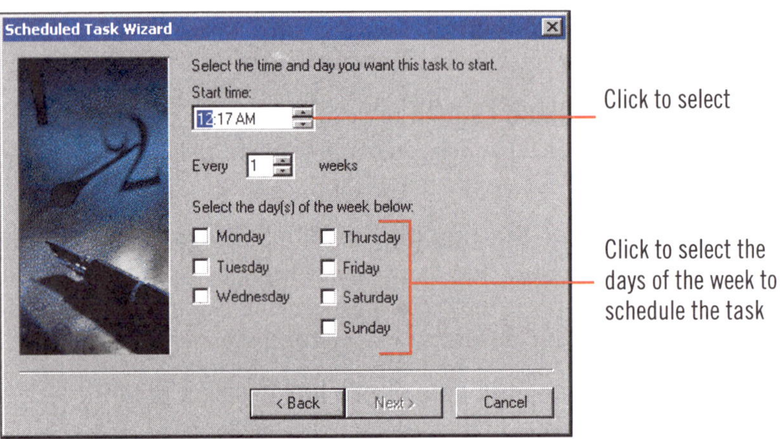

FIGURE E-17: Task added to Scheduled Tasks window

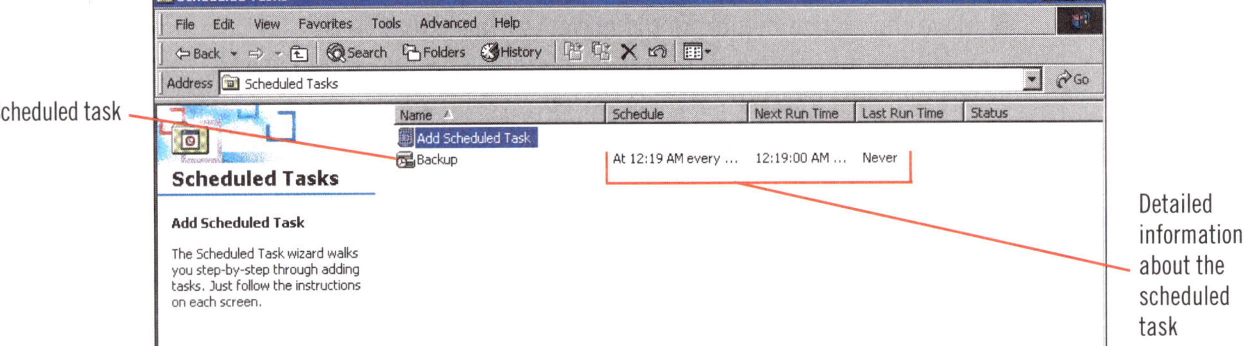

CLUES TO USE

Adding new hardware and software to Windows

You can add new hardware, such as a printer, and add or remove programs by using tools on the Control Panel. The Add New Hardware and Add/Remove Programs dialog boxes walk you through the necessary steps. To start the add new hardware procedure, click the Add New Hardware icon in the Control Panel, then click the Next button and follow the prompts. To add or remove a program, click the Add/Remove Program icon, click Install, then follow the prompts. In both cases, Windows 2000 should recognize that there are new hardware needs to be added or that there is an installation file that needs to be executed.

Customizing the Taskbar

The taskbar is most often used for switching from one program or document to another. The taskbar is initially located at the bottom of the Windows desktop. As with other Windows elements, you can customize the taskbar; for example you can change its size and location, or add or remove toolbars to it that help you perform the tasks you need to do. Sometimes you need more room on the screen to display a window, and it would help to hide the taskbar. You can use the **Auto hide** feature to help you automatically hide the taskbar when you don't need it. John wants to remove and add a toolbar to the taskbar. He also wants to learn how the Auto hide feature works.

Steps

QuickTip

You can show the toolbar title or toolbar button names for a toolbar on the taskbar. Right-click an empty area of the toolbar, then click Show Title or Show Text.

1. Place the mouse pointer in a blank section of the taskbar (not on a button), right-click the **taskbar**, then point to **Toolbars**

   The Toolbars submenu appears, as shown in Figure E-18. You can add or remove a variety of existing toolbars to the taskbar or create a new one.

2. Click **Quick Launch** to deselect it

   The Quick Launch toolbar is removed from the taskbar. Now you have more room on the taskbar for program buttons.

3. Click the **Start button**, point to **Settings**, then click **Taskbar & Start Menu**

   The Taskbar and Start Menu dialog box opens, displaying the General tab, as shown in Figure E-19. You can show how items (such as the clock and small icons on the Start menu) appear on the taskbar or how the taskbar appears on the screen.

4. Click the **Auto hide check box** to select it

   The taskbar in the preview box is hidden.

5. Click **OK**

   The taskbar is hidden at the bottom of the screen.

6. Move the mouse pointer to the bottom of the screen

   While the mouse pointer is located at the bottom of the screen, the taskbar appears. When you move the mouse pointer up, the taskbar is hidden.

Trouble?

If the Quick Launch toolbar reappears on the right side of the taskbar, position the mouse pointer over the small bar (which changes to ↔) to the left of the Internet Explorer icon, then drag to the left until you reach the Start button.

7. Right-click in an empty section of the taskbar, point to **Toolbars**, then click **Quick Launch** to select it

   The Quick Launch toolbar is added to the taskbar.

8. Click the **Start button**, point to **Settings**, then click **Taskbar & Start Menu**

   The Taskbar and Start Menu dialog box opens.

9. Click the **Auto hide check box** to deselect it, then click **Apply**

FIGURE E-18: Removing a toolbar from the taskbar

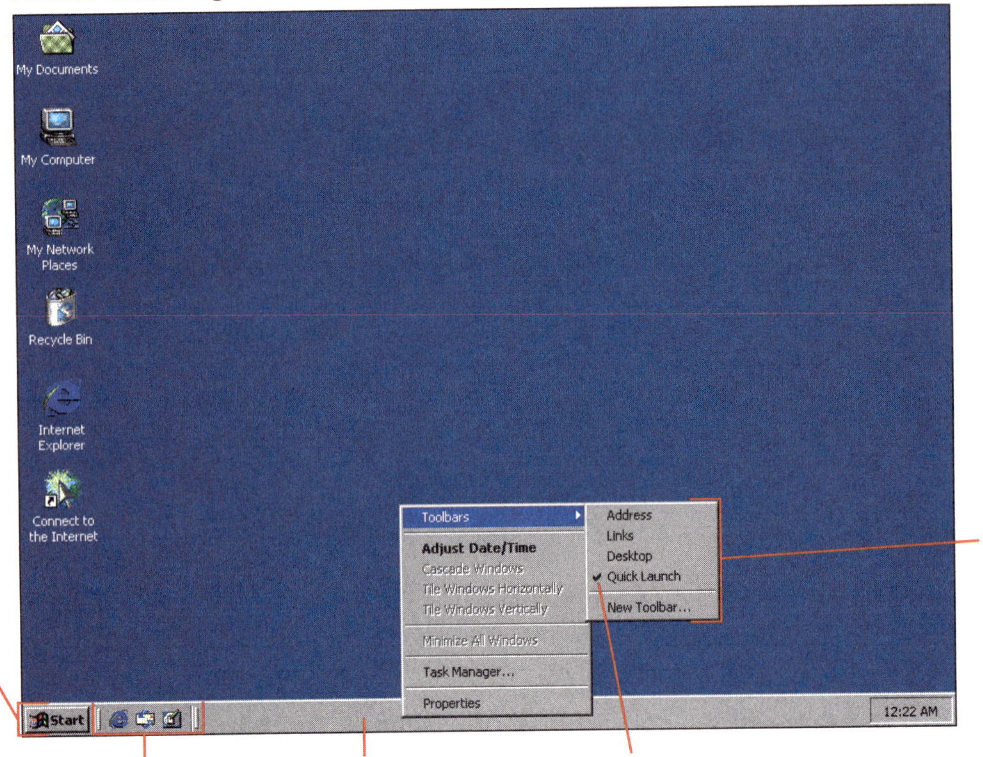

FIGURE E-19: Taskbar and Start Menu Properties dialog box

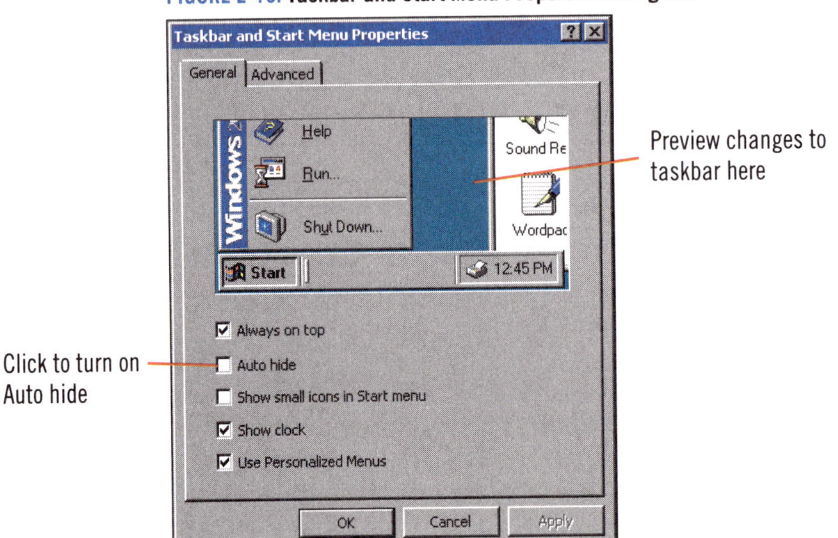

Starting a program as a taskbar button

You can change how Windows 2000 displays a program each time you start it using its Start menu shortcut. The program can open in a standard window, in a maximized window, or minimized as a button on the taskbar. Starting a program as a taskbar button is useful for a program you don't need maximized but want quick access to. To set a program to start in minimized form, click the Start button on the taskbar, point to Settings, click Taskbar & Start Menu, click the Advanced tab, then click Advanced. In the Start Menu folder, locate the shortcut to the program you want to start, and then click it. Click File on the menu bar, click Properties, then click the Shortcut tab. Click the Run list arrow, click Minimized, click OK, click File, click Close, then click OK again.

Windows 2000

Customizing the Start Menu

You can add shortcuts to programs, files, or folders to the Start menu, so that instead of having to navigate several levels of the Start menu to start a program or access a file, you can simply click the Start button and then click the item you want on the Start menu. Of course, if you add too many items to the Start menu, you defeat the purpose. To further customize the Start menu, you can display additional menu items on the Start menu, including Favorites, Log Off, and Administrative Tools, or extend a submenu from the Control Panel, Printers, or Dialup and Network Connections menu items on the Settings submenu. When you extend a menu item, a submenu appears with additional menu items. For example, when you extend the Control Panel, a submenu appears with a menu item for each icon in the Control Panel to provide easy access to each one. Because John uses the Wired Coffee logo so often in his work, he decides to add the file as a menu item to the Start menu.

QuickTip

To remove all recently used documents on the Documents submenu, click the Advanced tab in the Taskbar and Start Menu Properties dialog box, then click Clear.

1. Click the **Advanced tab** on the Taskbar and Start Menu Properties dialog box
   The Advanced tab appears, as shown in Figure E-20. You can use this tab to add and delete items from the Start menu.
2. Make sure your Project Disk is in the floppy disk drive, click **Add**, then click **Browse**
   The Browse For Folder dialog box opens, where you search for and select a file, folder, or program you want to add to the Start menu.
3. Click the **+ (plus sign) next to the drive containing your Project Disk,** then click the **+ next to the folder containing the Project files for this unit**
4. Click the **Wired Coffee Logo**, click **OK**, then click **Next**
5. Click the **Start Menu folder** in the Select Program Folder dialog box, click **Next** to accept the default name, then click **Finish**
   The shortcut will be placed in the Start Menu with the name Wired Coffee Logo. The Taskbar and Start Menu Properties dialog box appears with the Advanced tab in front.
6. In the Start Menu Settings section of the Advanced tab, click the **Display Favorites check box** to select it, then click **OK**
   This adds the Favorites menu to the Start menu.

QuickTip

You can also add an item to the Start menu by creating a shortcut to it (on the desktop or in Explorer, for example) and dragging the icon to the Start button.

7. Click the **Start button** on the taskbar
   Notice that the Favorites menu item appears below Programs, and the Wired Coffee logo appears at the top of the Start menu, as shown in Figure E-21. To open the Wired Coffee logo file, all you need to do is click the icon on the Start menu.
8. Press **[Esc]** to close the Start menu, right-click an empty area on the **taskbar**, click **Properties**, click the **Advanced tab**, then click **Remove**
   The Remove Shortcuts/Folders dialog box opens.

QuickTip

To start a program each time you start Windows 2000, click the Advanced tab, click Advanced, find the shortcut to the program you want to start each time you start Windows, then drag it to the Startup folder.

9. Click **Wired Coffee Logo** in the list of shortcuts and folders, click **Remove**, click **Yes** to confirm the deletion, click **Close**, click the **Display Favorites check box** to deselect it, then click **OK**
   The Taskbar and Start Menu Properties dialog box closes, and the menu items are removed from the Start menu.

FIGURE E-20: Advanced tab of the Taskbar and Start Menu Properties dialog box

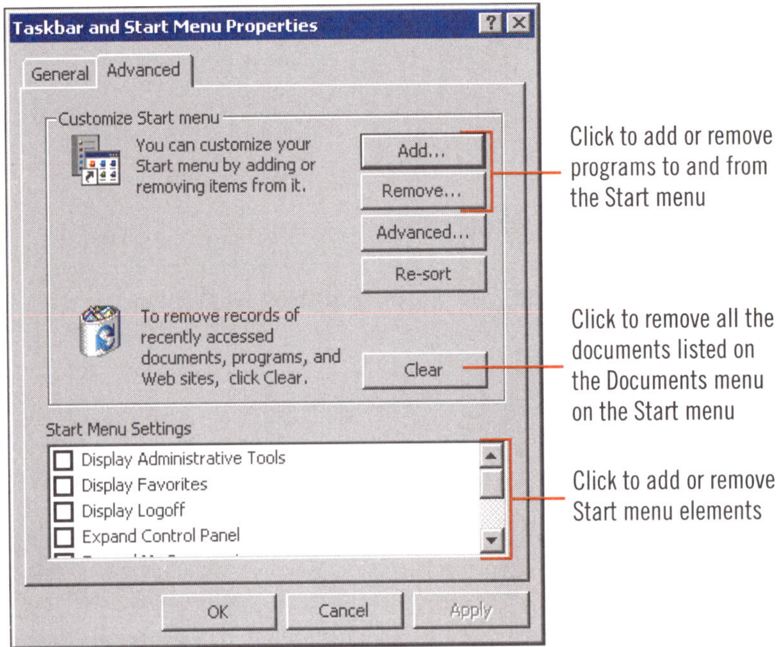

FIGURE E-21: Items added to the Start menu

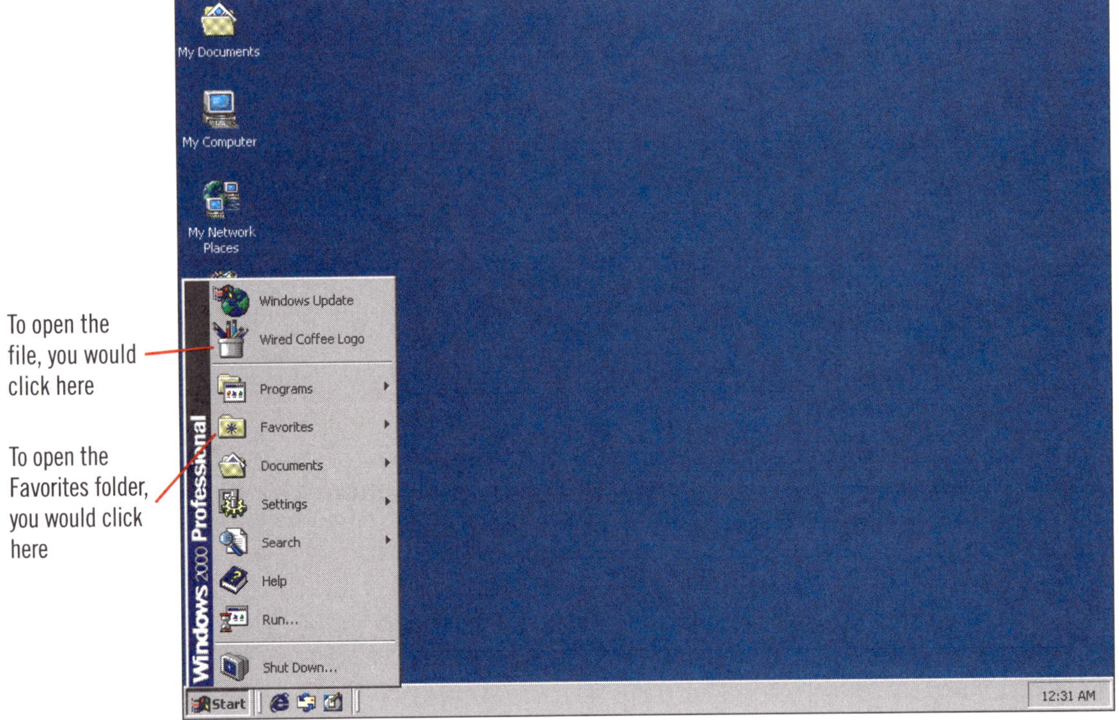

CLUES TO USE

Rearranging Start menu items

If you don't like the location of an item on the Start menu, you can move the item to a different location by dragging it to the desired location. A black line appears as you move the mouse pointer indicating the new location of the item. For example, to move the Windows Explorer menu item from the Program submenu to the Start menu, open the Start menu, then drag the Windows Explorer item to the Start menu.

Practice

▶ Concepts Review

Label each of the elements of the screen shown in Figure E-22.

FIGURE E-22

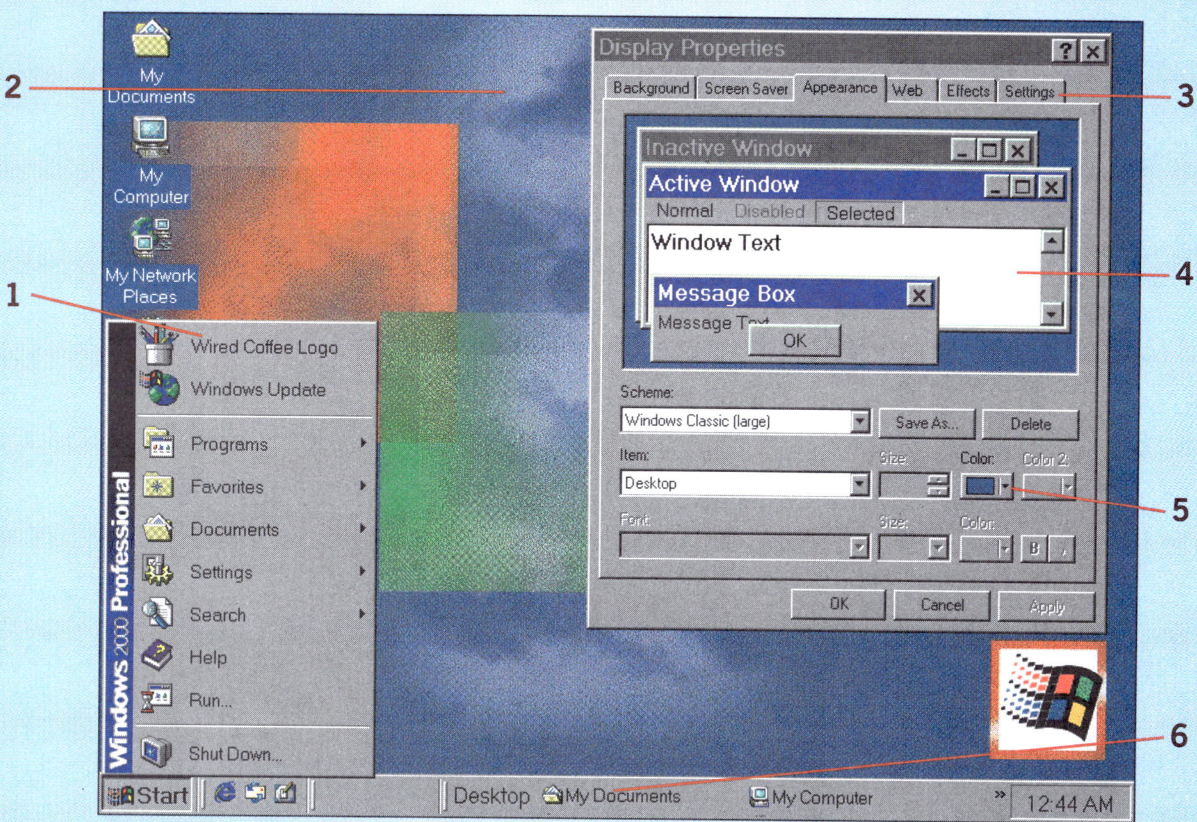

Match each of the terms with the statement that describes its function.

7. **Patterns**
8. **Screen saver**
9. **Desktop schemes**
10. **Control Panel**
11. **Start menu**

a. Used to change properties of various computer elements
b. Preset combinations of desktop colors
c. Used to prevent damage to the monitor
d. Preset designs for the desktop
e. Used to start programs and open documents

Select the best answer from the list of choices.

12. To customize the Active Desktop, you need to open the
- **a.** Folder Options dialog box.
- **b.** Display Properties dialog box.
- **c.** Desktop Settings dialog box.
- **d.** Custom Desktop dialog box.

13. To change the pattern on the desktop from the Display window in the Control Panel, click the
- **a.** Background tab.
- **b.** Screen Saver tab.

c. Appearance tab.
d. Settings tab.

14. An Internet document or Paint file used as a background is called a
a. pattern.
b. wallpaper.
c. display.
d. shortcut.

15. To set the date and time using the Control Panel, you double-click the
a. Regional Settings icon.
b. Date/Time icon.
c. Scheduled Tasks icon.
d. System icon.

16. A power failure when your computer is in this state can cause you to lose unsaved information.
a. Sleep
b. Standby
c. Hibernation
d. Locked

Skills Review

1. Customize the Active Desktop.
a. Right-click in an empty area on the desktop.
b. Point to Active Desktop, then click Customize My Desktop.
c. Click the Show Web content on my Active Desktop check box to select it.
d. Click Apply.
e. Click the Show Web content on my Active Desktop check box to deselect it.
f. Click Apply.

2. Change the desktop background and screen saver settings.
a. Click the Background tab in the Display Properties dialog box.
b. Click Greenstone in the Wallpaper section, then click Apply
c. Click the Screen Saver tab, click the Screen Saver list arrow, click 3D Pipes, then click Preview.
d. Move the mouse to end the Screen Saver preview.
e. Click the Screen Saver tab, click the Screen Saver list arrow, then click (None).
f. Click the Background tab, click (None) in the Wallpaper section, then click Apply.

3. Change the desktop scheme.
a. Click the Appearance tab.
b. Click the Item list arrow, then click Desktop.
c. Click any color you want for the desktop, then click Apply.
d. Click Save As, type **Fred**, then click OK.
e. Click Delete.
f. Click the Scheme list arrow, then click Windows Standard, then click OK.

4. Set the date and time.
a. Click the Start button, point to Settings, then click Control Panel.
b. Double-click the Date/Time icon.
c. Double-click the number of minutes.
d. Click the up arrow three times, then click Apply.

e. Double-click the number of minutes.
f. Click the Down Arrow button three times, then click OK.

5. **Work with fonts.**
   a. Double-click the Fonts icon in the Control Panel.
   b. Double-click a Times New Roman icon.
   c. Click Print, click Print again, click Done, then click the Back button on the toolbar.
6. **Manage power options.**
   a. Double-click the Power Options icon in the Control Panel.
   b. Click the Turn off monitor list arrow, then click After 1 min.
   c. Click Apply, then wait one minute without moving the mouse or pressing a key.
   d. Move the mouse to restore the desktop.
   e. Click the Turn off monitor list arrow, click Never, then click OK.
7. **Add a scheduled task.**
   a. Double-click the Scheduled Tasks icon in the Control Panel.
   b. Double-click the Add Scheduled Task icon, then click Next.
   c. Click Character Map, click Next, click the One time only option button, then click Next.
   d. Change the time to one minute ahead, select the current day, then click Next.
   e. Type your password, press [Tab], type your password again, then click Next.
   f. Click Finish, wait for the task to take place, then click the Close button on the program window.
   g. Right-click the Character Map icon, click Delete, then click Yes.
   h. Close the Scheduled Tasks window.
8. **Customize the taskbar.**
   a. Right-click the taskbar, point to Toolbars, then click Quick Launch to remove that toolbar from the taskbar.
   b. Click the Start button, point to Settings, then click Taskbar & Start Menu.
   c. Click the Auto hide check box to select it, then click OK.
   d. Move the mouse pointer to the bottom of the screen.
   e. Right-click the taskbar, point to Toolbars, then click Quick Launch to add the toolbar back to the taskbar.
   f. Click the Start button, point to Settings, then click Taskbar & Start Menu.
   g. Click the Auto hide check box, then click Apply.
9. **Customize the Start menu.**
   a. Click the Advanced tab.
   b. Click the Expand Control Panel check box to select it.
   c. Click Apply.
   d. Click the Start button, point to Settings, point to Control Panel, then press [Esc].
   e. Click the Expand Control Panel check box to deselect it, then click OK.

Independent Challenges

1. You have been retained as a consultant by a large law firm that has just installed Windows 2000. The firm's employees need to be taught how to customize Windows 2000 to fit their needs. As you prepare your presentation, you decide to customize the display so it is easier for them to see. Make the following changes and be sure to change them back to the default setting or setup when you are finished.

To complete this independent challenge:

a. Open the Display Properties dialog box from the Control Panel.
b. Change the background to a background of your choice.
c. Set the screen saver for one minute so you can show them how it works without waiting too long.
d. On the Appearance tab, set the scheme to High Contrast Black (extra large).

e. Save the scheme as *Demo*, then apply the changes.
f. Print the screen. (Press the Print Screen key to make a copy of the screen, open Paint, click Edit on the menu bar, click Paste to paste the screen into Paint, click Yes to paste the large image if necessary, click File on the menu bar, click Print, then click Print in the Print dialog box.)
g. Delete the Demo scheme, then select the Windows Standard scheme.
h. Set the screen saver for five minutes.

2. As the owner of a small optical laboratory, you want to abide by the Americans with Disabilities Act, which states that employers should make every reasonable effort to accommodate workers with disabilities. You have one worker who is visually impaired. Customize the Windows desktop for this employee so that it is easier to work in, desktop items are easier to see and read, and desktop colors are strongly contrasted with each other, but still easy on the eyes. Save this custom configuration so that this employee can use it when necessary.

To complete this independent challenge:

a. Open the Display Properties dialog box from the Control Panel.
b. Change the Desktop color to red.
c. Change the font size of menu text to 12.
d. Change the size and color of the text in the title bar for the Active Window to 24 and light blue (the second color in the fifth row).
e. Change the font style for the message box to bold.
f. Save the custom configuration as *Visible*.
g. Apply the scheme.
h. Print the screen. (See Independent Challenge 1, Step f for screen printing instructions.)
i. Delete the Visible scheme.
j. Select the Windows Standard.

3. As the system administrator of a small computer network for a chain of specialty book stores, you want to make sure all the computers run efficiently. To accomplish this goal, you want to set up a scheduled task to clean up the hard disk drives of all the computers on a weekly basis.

To complete this independent challenge:

a. Open the Scheduled Tasks window from the Control Panel.
b. Schedule the Disk Cleanup program as a task.
c. Schedule the task for a weekly time period.
d. Set the time one minute ahead of the current time.
e. When the Disk Cleanup program appears, print the screen. (See Independent Challenge 1, Step f for screen printing instructions.)
f. Delete the Disk Cleanup scheduled task.

4. As the owner of Lew's Office Supply, you need to make your business computers easier for your employees to use. One way to do this is to add programs to the Start menu. Your employees use WordPad and Paint almost exclusively, and they also use the same documents quite often.

To complete this independent challenge:

a. Add a WordPad shortcut to the Start menu. (*Hint*: Select WordPad.exe located in the Accessories folder within the Program Files folder.)
b. Add a Paint shortcut to the Start menu. (*Hint*: Select MSpaint.exe located in the same place as WordPad.)
c. Create a memo to employees about the upcoming company picnic using WordPad, then save the memo on your Project Disk as *Company Picnic Memo*.
d. Close the memo and WordPad.
e. Add the Company Picnic Memo to the Start menu.
f. Open the Company Picnic Memo from the Start menu.
g. Print the screen. (See Independent Challenge 1, Step f for screen printing instructions.)
h. Remove all the shortcuts you created.

Visual Workshop

Re-create the screen shown in Figure E-23, which displays the Windows desktop, then print the screen. (See Independent Challenge 1, Step f for screen printing instructions.)

FIGURE E-23

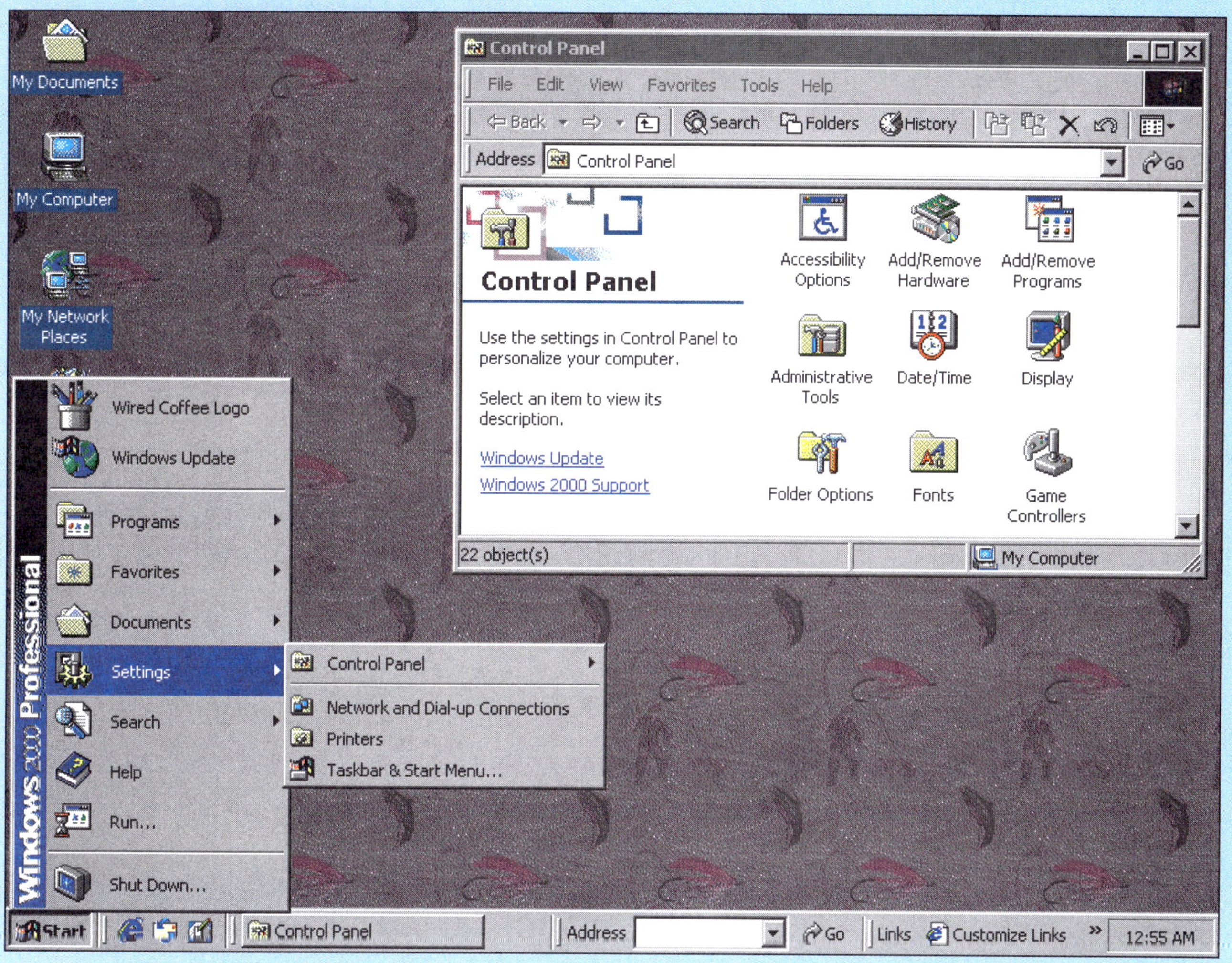

Windows 2000

Exploring the Internet with Microsoft Internet Explorer

Objectives

- Understand Web browsers
- Start Internet Explorer
- Explore the browser window
- Open a Web page and follow links
- Add a Web page to the Favorites list
- Make a Web page available offline
- Change your home page and add a link button
- Search the Web
- Print a Web page

A valuable component included with Windows 2000 is Microsoft Internet Explorer 5, a software program that helps you access the World Wide Web. In this unit, you will learn about the benefits of the World Wide Web, examine the basic features of Internet Explorer 5, and access Web pages. This unit requires a connection to the Internet. If your computer is not connected to the Internet, check with your instructor or technical support person to see if it's possible for you to connect. If not, simply read the lessons to learn about using Internet Explorer. Wired Coffee Company is a growing business that wants to take advantage of Internet technology. John uses Internet Explorer to open the company Web page and find information related to the coffee business.

Understanding Web Browsers

The Internet is a worldwide collection of more than 40 million computers from all over the world linked together to share information. The Internet's physical structure includes telephone lines, cables, satellites, and other telecommunications media, as depicted in Figure F-1. Using the Internet, computer users can share many types of information, including text, graphics, sounds, videos, and computer programs. The **World Wide Web** (also known as the Web or WWW) is a part of the Internet that consists of Web sites located on different computers around the world. A **Web site** contains Web pages that are linked together to make looking for information on the Internet easier. **Web pages** are documents that contain highlighted words, phrases, and graphics, called **hyperlinks** (or simply **links**) that open other Web pages when you click them. Some Web pages contain frames. A **frame** is a separate window within a Web page. Frames give you the ability to show more than one Web page at a time. Figure F-2 shows a sample Web page. **Web browsers** are software programs that you use to "browse the Web," or access and display Web pages. Browsers make the Web easy to navigate by providing a graphical, point-and-click environment. This unit features Internet Explorer 5, a popular browser from Microsoft that comes with Windows 2000. Netscape Communicator is another popular browser. John realizes that there are many uses for Internet Explorer in his company.

Display Web pages from all over the world

John can look at Web pages for business purposes, such as checking the pages of other coffee companies to see how they are marketing their products.

Display Web content on your desktop

John can make his desktop look and work like a Web page. John can display Web content, such as the Microsoft Investor Ticker, ESPN SportsZone, Expedia Maps Address Finder, or MSNBC Weather Map, directly on his desktop and have the content updated automatically.

Use links to move from one Web page to another

John can click text or graphical links (which appear as either underlined text or as graphics) to move from one Web page to another, investigating different sources for information. Because a Web page can contain links to any location on the Internet, you can jump to Web pages all over the World.

Play audio and video clips

John can click links that play audio and video clips, such as the sound of coffee grinding or a video of workers picking coffee beans. He can also play continuous audio and video broadcasts through radio and televisions stations over the Internet.

Search the Web for information

John can use search programs that allow him to look for information about any topic throughout the world.

Make favorite Web pages available offline

John can create a list of his favorite Web pages to make it easy for him to return to them at a later time. He can also make a Web page available offline. When he makes a Web page available offline, he can read its content when his computer is not connected to the Internet.

Print the text and graphics on Web pages

If John finds some information or images that he would like to print, he can easily print all or part of the Web page, including the graphics.

FIGURE F-1: Structure of the Internet

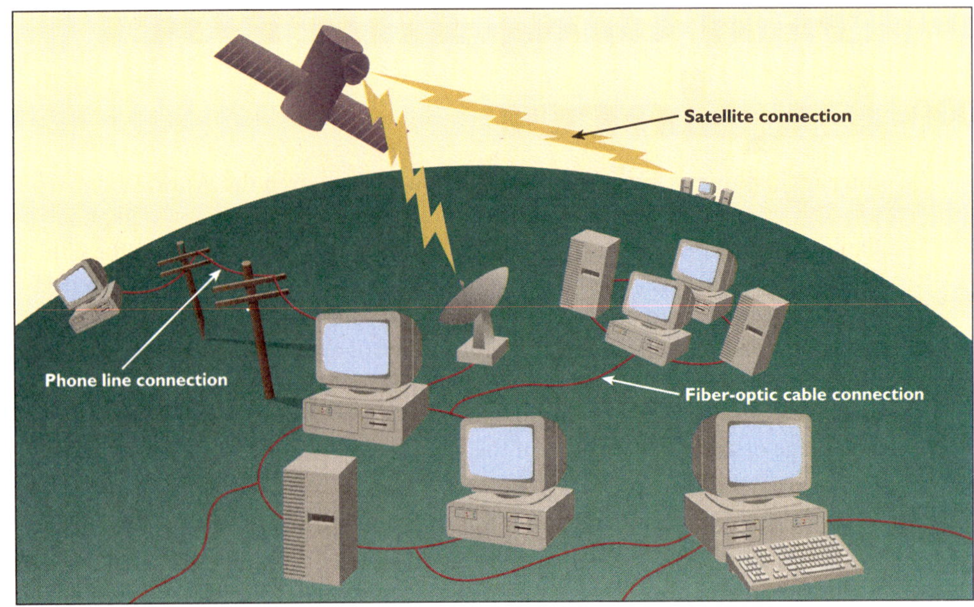

FIGURE F-2: Sample World Wide Web page

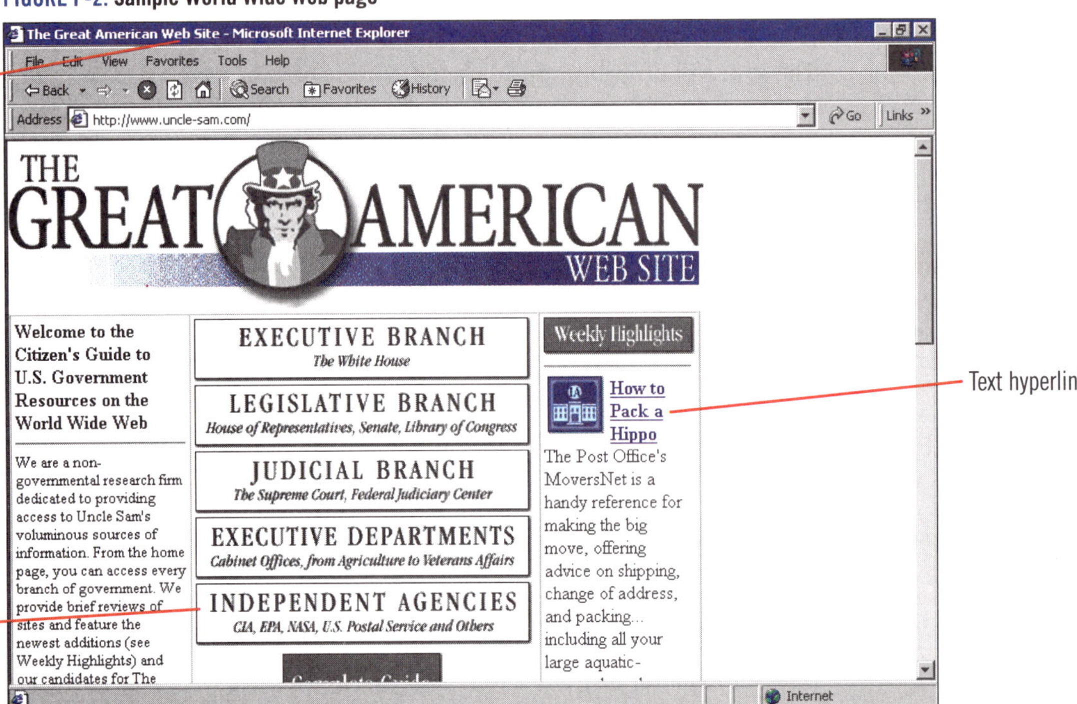

The history of the Internet and World Wide Web

The Internet has its roots in the Advanced Research Projects Agency Network (ARPANET), which the United States Department of Defense started in 1969. In 1986, the National Science Foundation formed NSFNET, which replaced ARPANET. NSFNET expanded the foundation of the U.S. portion of the Internet with high-speed, long distance data lines. In 1991, the U.S. Congress expanded the capacity and speed of the Internet further and opened it up to commercial use. The Internet is now accessible in over 300 countries. The World Wide Web was developed in Switzerland in 1991 to make finding documents on the Internet easier. Software programs designed to access the Web (Web browsers) use "point-and-click" interfaces. The first such Web browser, Mosaic, was introduced at the University of Illinois in 1993. Recently, Microsoft Internet Explorer and Netscape Communicator have become the two most popular Web browsers.

Windows 2000

Starting Internet Explorer

Internet Explorer is a Web browser that you use to search the World Wide Web (you also need a physical connection to the Internet). When you install Windows 2000, an icon for Internet Explorer will appear on the desktop and a button for it will appear on the Quick Launch toolbar on the taskbar. You can also make your desktop look and work like a Web page. You can display a Web page or custom Web content directly on your desktop and have the content updated automatically. The specialized Web content, known as a **channel**, is designed to deliver content from the Internet to your computer. To display Web content on your desktop, simply right-click the desktop, point to Active Desktop, then click Show Web Content. Before John can take advantage of the many features of the World Wide Web, he must start Internet Explorer.

Steps

Trouble?

If your computer is not connected to the Internet, check with your instructor or technical person to see if it's possible for you to connect.

Trouble?

If the Internet Explorer icon isn't on your desktop, click the Start button, point to programs, then click Internet Explorer.

1. **Establish a connection to the Internet via the network or telephone**
   If you connect to the Internet through a network, follow your instructor's or technical support person's directions to establish your connection. If you connect by telephone, create a new connection using the Connection Wizard to establish your connection or use an existing Dial-Up Networking connection.
2. **Locate the Internet Explorer icon on your desktop**
   The icon will probably appear on the left side of your screen, as shown in Figure F-3, but it doesn't matter where it is or even if it is not on your desktop. There are several different ways to start Internet Explorer, depending on your circumstances. If you have upgraded from Internet Explorer 4 or Windows 98, the desktop Channel Bar and the View Channels button on the Quick Launch toolbar are also available on the desktop.
3. **Double-click or click the Launch Internet Explorer Browser button on the Quick Launch toolbar**
   Internet Explorer opens. If you connect to the Internet through a network, follow your instructor's or technical support person's directions to log on. If you connect to the Internet by telephone using a Dial-Up Networking connection, you need to enter your user name and password to connect to the Internet. See your instructor or technical support person for this information.
4. **If necessary, enter your user name, press [Tab], enter your password, then click Connect**
   Upon completion of the dial-up connection, you are connected to the Internet (unless an error message appears).
5. **If necessary, click the Maximize button to maximize the Internet Explorer window**
   Internet Explorer displays a Web page, as shown in Figure F-4. It's okay if the Web page on your screen is not the same as the one shown in Figure F-4. Later in this unit, you will learn how to change the Web page that appears when you first start Internet Explorer. Continue with the next lesson to view the various elements of the browser window.

FIGURE F-3: Windows desktop

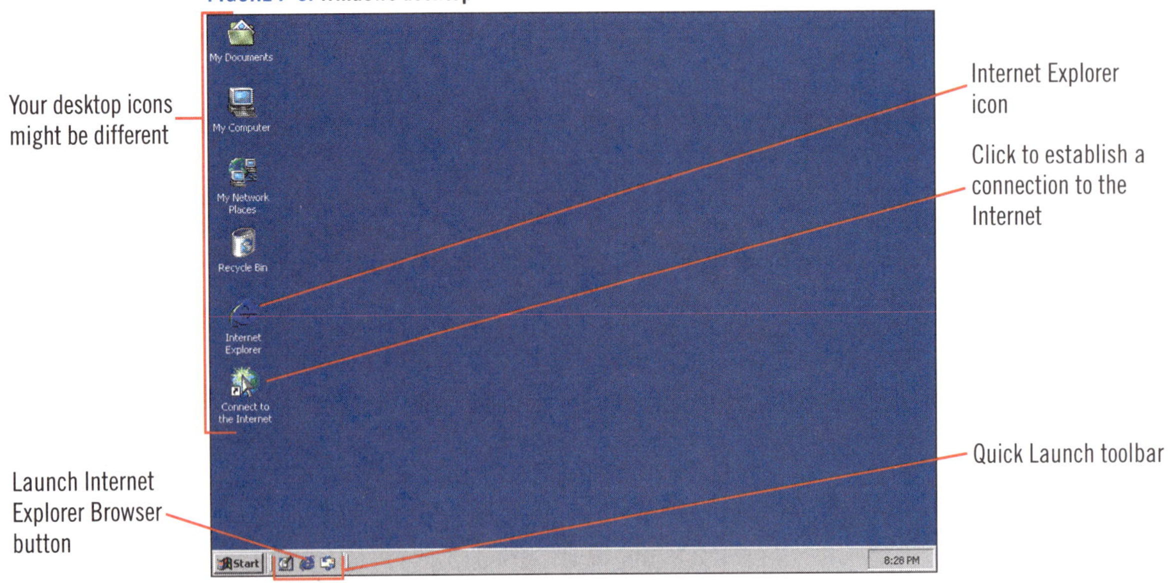

FIGURE F-4: Web page featuring the Microsoft Corporation

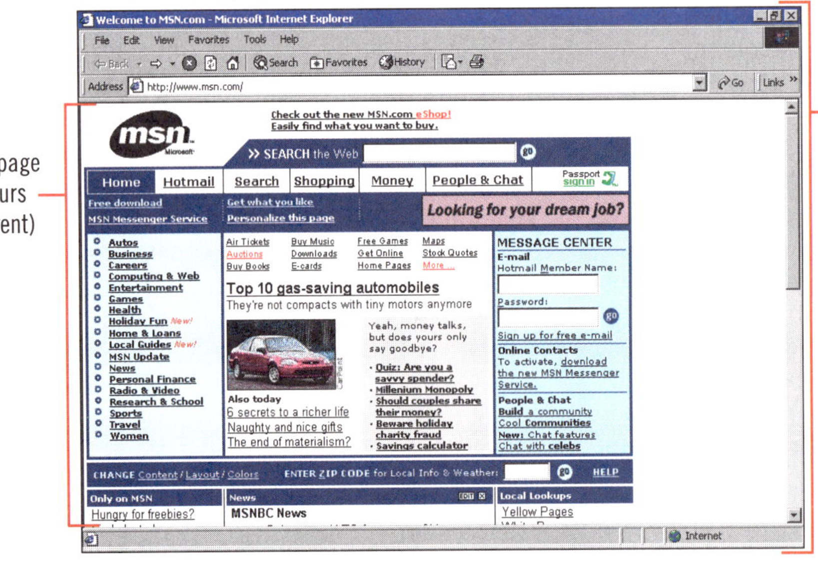

CLUES TO USE

Connecting to the Internet

Sometimes connecting your computer to the Internet can be the most difficult part of getting started. The Connection Wizard simplifies the process, whether you want to set up a new connection using an existing account or you want to select an **Internet Service provider (ISP)**—a company that provides access to the Internet for a fee—and set up a new account. You might need to obtain connection information from your ISP or your system administrator. To get connected to the Internet using the Connection Wizard, double-click the Internet Connection Wizard icon on the desktop or click the Start button, point to Programs, point to Accessories, point to Communications, click Internet Connection Wizard, and then follow the step-by-step instructions. If you are on a network, you might need to use a **proxy server**, which provides a secure barrier between your network and the Internet and prevents other people from seeing confidential information on your network. To configure your computer to use a proxy server, click View on the menu bar, click Internet Options, click the Connections tab, and click LAN Settings. See your instructor or technical support person for setting details to connect to your network.

Windows 2000

Exploring the Browser Window

The elements of the Internet Explorer program window, shown in Figure F-5, allow you to view, print, and search for information on the Internet. Before exploring the Web, John decides to familiarize himself with the components of the browser window.

He notes the following features:

 The **title bar** at the top of the page displays the name of the Web page and the name of the browser you are using.

 The **menu bar** provides access to a variety of commands, much like other Windows programs.

 The **toolbar** provides buttons for easy access to the most commonly used commands in Internet Explorer. See Table F-1 for a description of each toolbar button. These button commands are also available on the menus.

 The **Address bar** displays the address of the current Web page or the contents of a local or network computer drive. The **Web address,** like a postal address, is a unique place on the Internet where you can locate a Web page. The Web address is also referred to as the **URL**, which stands for **Uniform Resource Locator**.

 The **Links bar** displays link buttons to Web pages on the Internet or documents on a local or network drive.

 The **status indicator** (the Internet Explorer logo) spins to indicate a new Web page is loading.

 The **document window** displays the current Web page or the contents of a local or network computer drive. You may need to scroll down the page to view the entire contents.

 The **vertical scroll bar** allows you to move up or down the current Web page. The **scroll box** indicates your relative position within the Web page.

 The **status bar** displays information about your connection progress with new Web pages that you open, including notification that you have connected to another site and the percentage of information that has been transferred. This bar also displays the locations of the links in the document window as you move your mouse pointer over them.

FIGURE F-5: Elements of the Internet Explorer program window

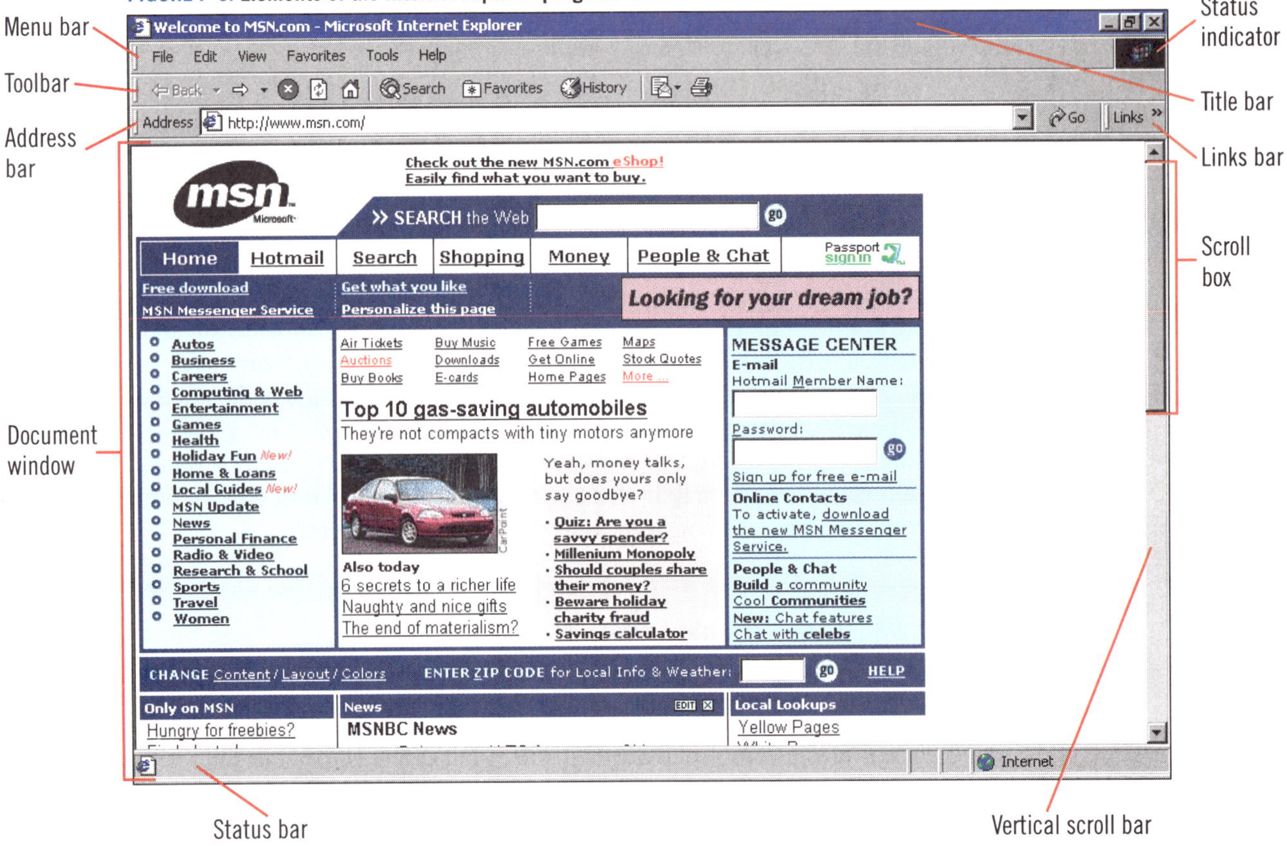

Menu bar · Toolbar · Address bar · Document window · Status bar · Vertical scroll bar · Scroll box · Links bar · Title bar · Status indicator

TABLE F-1: Internet Explorer toolbar buttons

button	name	description	button	name	description
Back	**Back**	Opens the previous page		**Favorites**	Opens the Favorites list
	Forward	Open the next page		**History**	Opens the History list
	Stop	Stops loading a page		**Mail**	Displays options for working with Mail and News
	Refresh	Refreshes the contents of the current page		**Print**	Prints the current Web page
	Home	Opens the Home page		**Go**	Displays the current Web address
	Search	Opens the Search Bar			

Getting Help with Internet Explorer

If you are new to the Internet or to Internet Explorer, you can take a tour to learn how Internet Explorer can help you efficiently browse the Web. To take the tour, click Help on the menu bar, click Tour, then follow the step-by-step instructions. If you want to get information on a general topic or a specific task, you can find the information you are looking for in Microsoft Internet Explorer Help. To access Help, click Help on the menu bar, then click Contents and Index. The Microsoft Internet Explorer Help window appears and works in the same way the Windows 2000 Help does. If you need more help, you can probably find what you need about Internet Explorer on the Web by clicking Help on the menu bar, then clicking Online Support. You can also get tips on how to use Internet Explorer more effectively. To display a tip, click Help on the menu bar, then click Tip of the Day. A Tip pane appears at the bottom of the Internet Explorer window. Read the tip, then click the *Next tip* link to display another tip. Click the Close button in the Tip pane to close the pane.

Windows 2000

Opening a Web Page and Following Links

You can open a Web page quickly and easily using the Address bar. If you change your mind, or the Web page takes too long to **download**, or open on the screen, you can click the Stop button on the toolbar. If you stop a Web page while it is downloading and the page doesn't completely open, you can click the Refresh button on the toolbar to update the screen. Web pages can be connected to each other through links, which you can follow to obtain more information about a topic, as shown in Figure F-6. A link can move you to another location on the same Web page, or it can open a different Web page altogether. To follow a link, simply click the highlighted word, phrase, or graphic (the cursor changes to the hand pointer when it is over a link). John contracted a Web development company to create a Web site for Wired Coffee. He wants to access the Web site and follow some of the links in order to give feedback to the developer. John knows that the URL for the Web page is http://www.course.com/illustrated/wired/.

1. Click anywhere in the Address bar
   The current address is highlighted and any text you type will replace the current address. If the current address isn't highlighted, select the entire address.

Trouble?

If you receive an error message, type one of the URLs listed in Table F-2 instead to open a Web page, then follow a link.

2. Type **www.course.com/illustrated/wired/**, then press **[Enter]** or click the **Go button** on the toolbar
   Be sure to type the address exactly as it appears. When you enter a Web address, you don't have to type *http://* in the Address bar. Internet Explorer inserts it for you. The status bar displays the connection process. After downloading for a few seconds, the Web page appears in the document window.

QuickTip

You can browse folders on your hard disk drive and run programs from the Address bar. Click anywhere in the Address bar, then type the location of the folder or program. For example, typing **C:\My Documents** opens the My Documents folder.

3. Locate the **menu link** on the main page, and move the mouse pointer over the link, as shown in Figure F-7
   When you move the mouse pointer over a link, the mouse pointer changes to . This indicates that the text or graphic is a link. The address of the link appears in the Status bar.
4. Click the **menu link**
   The status indicator spins as the new Web page is accessed and opens. The menu Web page appears in the document window.
5. Move the mouse pointer over the **Wired Coffee logo** (the image in the upper-left corner), then click it
   The Wired Coffee Company page appears in the document window.
6. Click the **Back button** Back on the toolbar
   The previous Web page appears in the document window.
7. Click the **Forward button** on the toolbar
   The Company page appears in the document window again. You could have also clicked the Wired Coffee logo link to return to the Company page again.

QuickTip

To expand the document window to the full screen, click View on the menu bar, then click Full Screen. Press [F11] to return to the normal view.

8. Click the **Back button list arrow** Back on the toolbar, then click **Wired Coffee Home Page**
   The Wired Coffee Home Page appears in the document window. Notice that when you have already visited a link, the color of the link changes.

FIGURE F-6: Web pages connected through links

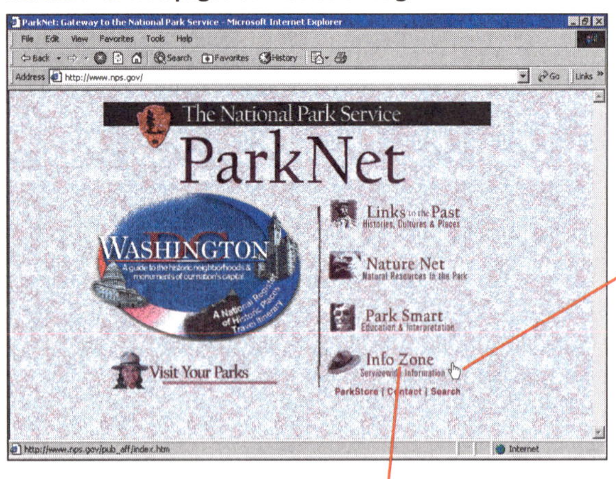

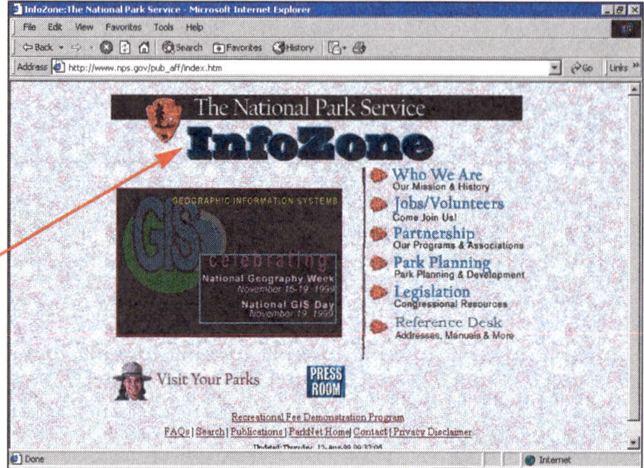

Graphic hyperlink; click to jump to the InfoZone Web page

FIGURE F-7: Wired Coffee Company Web page

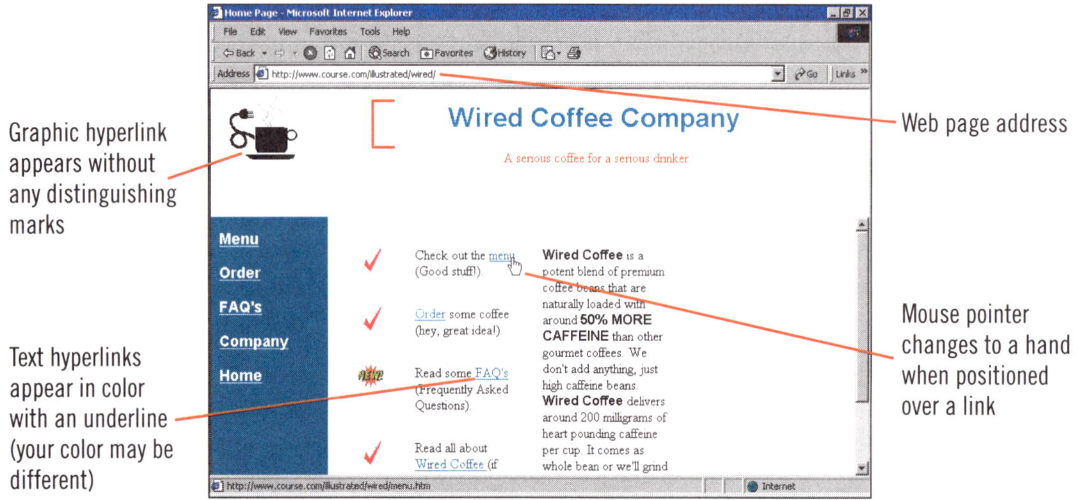

Graphic hyperlink appears without any distinguishing marks

Text hyperlinks appear in color with an underline (your color may be different)

Web page address

Mouse pointer changes to a hand when positioned over a link

TABLE F-2: URLs of Web sites dealing with coffee

name of company	url
Boyd Coffee Company	*http://www.boyds.com*
Peet's Coffee & Tea	*http://www.peets.com*
Seattle's Best Coffee	*http://www.seabest.com*
Starbucks Coffee	*http://www.starbucks.com*

CLUES TO USE

Understanding a Web address

The address for a Web page is referred to as a URL. Each Web page has a unique URL that begins with "http" (HyperText Transfer Protocol) followed by a colon, two slashes, and the name of the Web site. The Web site is the computer where the Web pages are located. At the end of the Web site name, another slash may appear, followed by one or more folders and a filename. For example, in the address, http://www.course.com/illustrated/wired/wired_main.htm, the name of the Web site is *www.course.com*; a folder at that site is called */illustrated/wired*; and within the wired folder is a file called *wired_main.htm*.

Windows 2000

Adding a Web Page to the Favorites List

Rather than memorizing the URLs or keeping a handwritten list of Web pages you want to return to, you can use a feature called **Favorites** to store and organize the addresses. When you display a Web page in your document window that you want to display again at a later time, you can add the Web page to your Favorites list. Once you add the Web page to the Favorites list, you can return to the page by opening your Favorites list and selecting the link to the page you want. John wants to add the Wired Coffee Web page to his Favorites list.

QuickTip

To view Web pages offline, click File on the menu bar, then click Work Offline. If you want to access other Web pages, you'll need to reconnect to the Internet.

1. Click **Favorites** on the menu bar, then click **Add to Favorites**

   The Add Favorites dialog box opens, as shown in Figure F-8. You have the option to make the Web page available for offline viewing. When you make a Web page available for **offline viewing**, the page is copied to your computer for later viewing when your Internet connection is disconnected. This is helpful when you want to read a Web page without having to worry about your connect time.

2. In the Name text box, select the current text, type **Wired Coffee Company**, then click **OK**

   The Web page is added to your Favorites list with the name "Wired Coffee Company."

Trouble?

URLs may be case-sensitive, meaning that you must type them exactly as they appear, using uppercase and lowercase letters.

3. Click anywhere in the Address bar, type **www.course.com**, then press **[Enter]**

   When you type a Web address in the Address bar, a feature called **AutoComplete** suggests possible matches from previous entries you have made for Web addresses. If a suggestion in the list matches what you want to enter, click the suggestion from the Address bar list.

4. Click the **Favorites button** on the toolbar

   The Explorer Bar opens on the left side of the document window and displays the Favorites list. The Favorites list contains several folders, including a Links folder, a Media folder, and individual favorite Web pages that come with Windows 2000.

QuickTip

You can import favorites, know as bookmarks, from Netscape Navigator by clicking File on the menu bar, then clicking Import and Export.

5. Click **Wired Coffee Company** in the Favorites list

   The Wired Coffee Company Web page appears in the document window, as shown in Figure F-9. The Favorites list also includes folders to help you organize your Favorites list. You can click a folder icon in the Favorites list to display its contents.

6. Click the **Links folder** in the Favorites list

   The Favorites list in the Links folder expands and appears in the Explorer Bar, as shown in Figure F-10. To open a favorite in the Links folder, position the mouse pointer over the favorite you want to open (the mouse pointer changes to a hand and the favorite appears underlined), then click the mouse button.

QuickTip

To start Internet Explorer and open a favorite, click the Start button, point to Favorites, then click a favorite Web page.

7. Click the **Links folder** in the Favorites list again

   The Favorites list in the Links folder collapse to display only the Links folder icon. If you no longer use a favorite, you can delete it from the Favorites list.

FIGURE F-8: Add Favorites dialog box

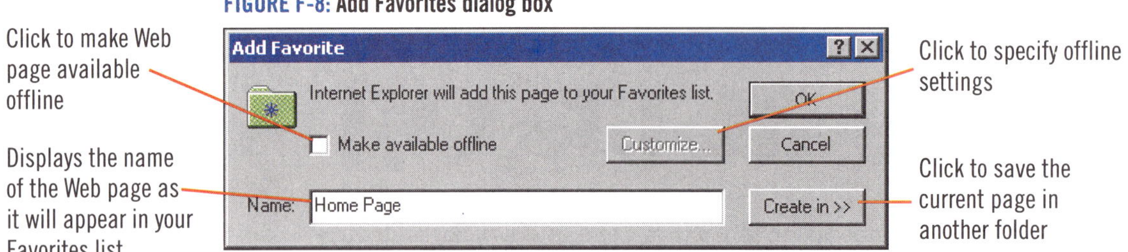

FIGURE F-9: Internet Explorer window with the Favorites list

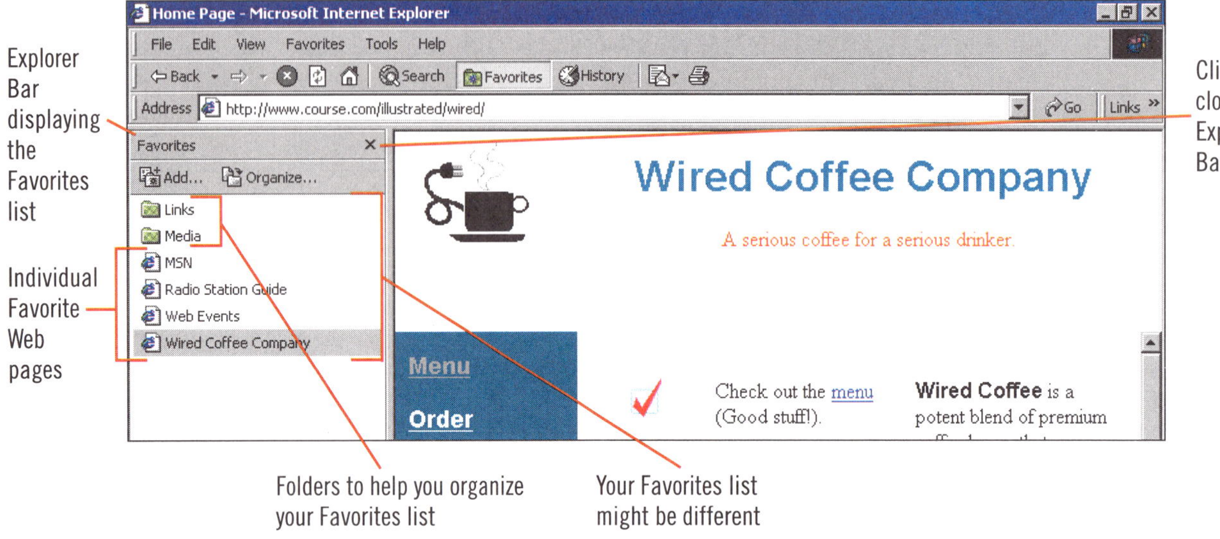

FIGURE F-10: Links folder with Favorites displayed

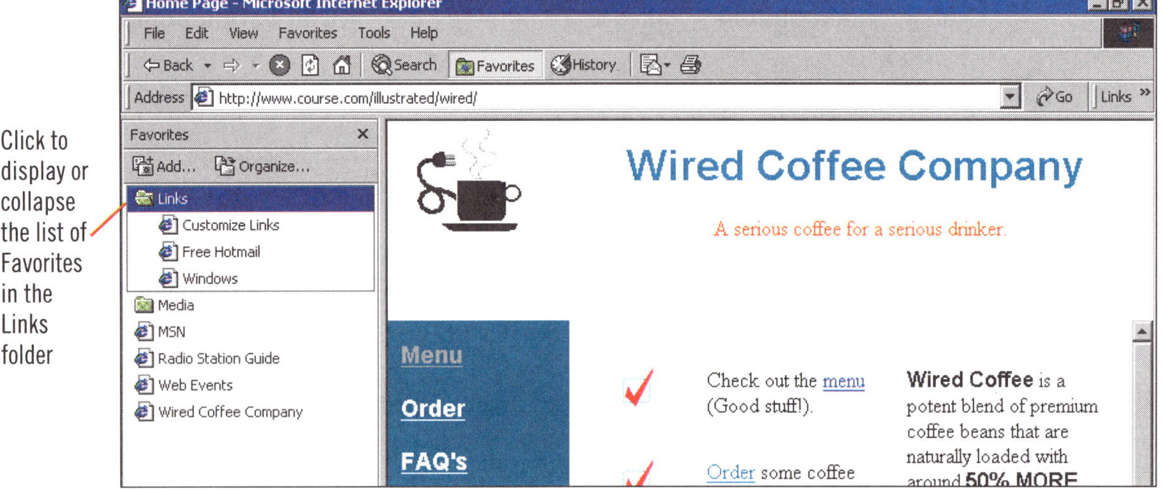

CLUES TO USE

Organizing favorites

If your list of favorites gets long, you can delete favorites you don't want anymore or move favorites into folders. To delete and move your favorites, click the Favorites menu, click Organize Favorites, select one or more files from the Favorites list, then click the Delete or Move to Folder buttons. If you want to add a new folder in your Favorites list, click the Create Folder button, type the new folder name, then press Enter. If you prefer to use another name for a favorite, you can select the favorite you want to rename, click the Rename button, type the new name, then press [Enter]. When you're finished making changes, you can click Close to exit.

Making a Web Page Available Offline

When you make a Web page available offline, you can read its content when your computer is not connected to the network and Internet. For example, you can view Web pages on your laptop computer when you don't have a network or Internet connection. Or you might want to read Web pages at home but do not want to tie up a phone line. When you make a Web page available offline, the latest online version of your Web page is saved, or **synchronized**, to your hard disk drive for offline viewing. You can specify how much content you want available, such as an individual Web page or a Web page and all its links, and choose how you want to update that content on your computer. John wants to make the Wired Coffee Company Web site on the Favorites list available for offline viewing. After viewing the offline version of the Web site, John updates the offline version to make sure he has the latest data.

QuickTip

To make the current Web page available offline, click Favorites on the menu bar, click Add to Favorites, click the Make available offline check box to select it, click Custom, follow the wizard instructions, click Finish, then click OK.

QuickTip

When you choose to work offline, Internet Explorer starts in offline mode until you click File on the menu bar, then click Work Offline again to clear the check mark.

QuickTip

To specify a schedule for updating that page and how much content to download, click Properties. You can also click Setup to schedule updating when you log on to your computer and when your computer goes on idle, no activity.

1. Click **Favorites** on the menu bar, then click **Organize Favorites**
   The Organize Favorites dialog box opens.
2. In the Favorites list, click **Wired Coffee Company**
   Status information about the Wired Coffee Company favorite appears in the Organize Favorites dialog box, as shown in Figure F-11.
3. Click the **Make available offline check box** to select it, then click **Close**
   The Synchronize dialog box opens and the Wired Coffee Company Web page is synchronized; the latest version of your Web page is saved to your hard disk drive for offline viewing.
4. Click **File** on the menu bar, then click **Work Offline**
   Internet Explorer is disconnected from the network and Internet.
5. Click the **Home button** on the toolbar, then click **Wired Coffee Company** in the Favorites list
   When you access the Wired Coffee Company Web site in offline mode, Internet Explorer displays the offline version of the Web page that is on your hard disk drive. You can view any of the offline Web pages, but if you click a link to Web page not available offline, Internet Explorer reconnects you to the network and Internet.
6. Click **File** on the menu bar, then click **Work Offline**
   When the connection to the network and Internet is re-established, you can synchronize to the latest online version of the Wired Coffee Web page to update the offline version on your hard disk drive.
7. Click **Tools** on the menu bar, then click **Synchronize**
   The Items to Synchronize dialog box opens, as shown in Figure F-12. You can select which Web pages or files you want to synchronize and specify when and how you want them to be updated.
8. Click the **Wired Coffee Company check box** to select it if necessary, deselect all other check boxes, then click **Synchronize**
   The Wired Coffee Company Web page is re-synchronized with the latest online version of the Web page to your hard disk drive and ready for offline viewing.
9. Right-click **Wired Coffee Company** in the Favorites list, click **Delete**, click **Yes**, then click the **Close button** in the Explorer Bar
   The Wired Coffee Company Web page is deleted from the Favorites list, and the Explorer Bar closes.

FIGURE F-11: Organize Favorites dialog box

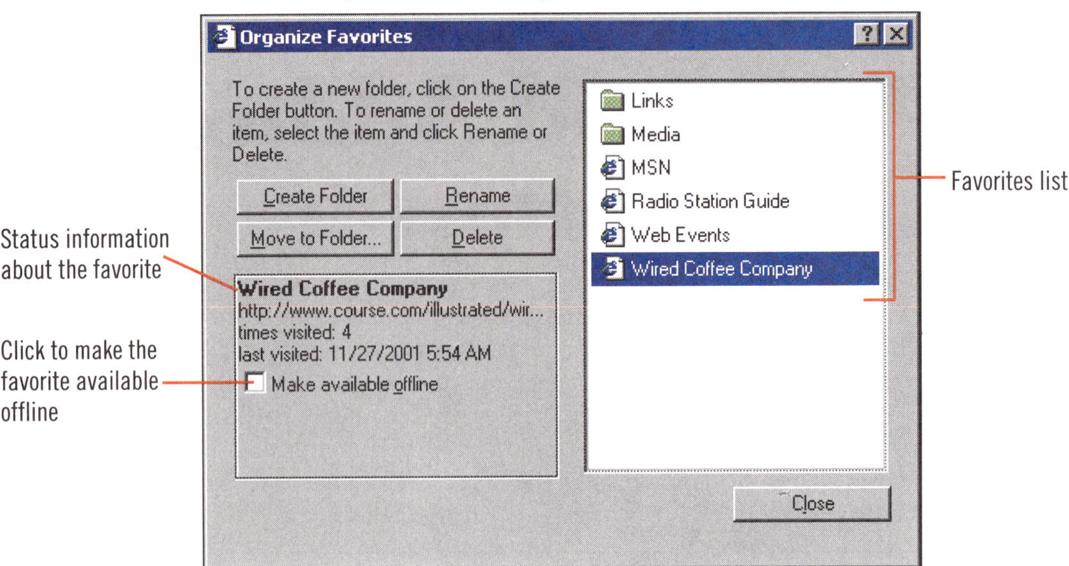

FIGURE F-12: Items to Synchronize dialog box

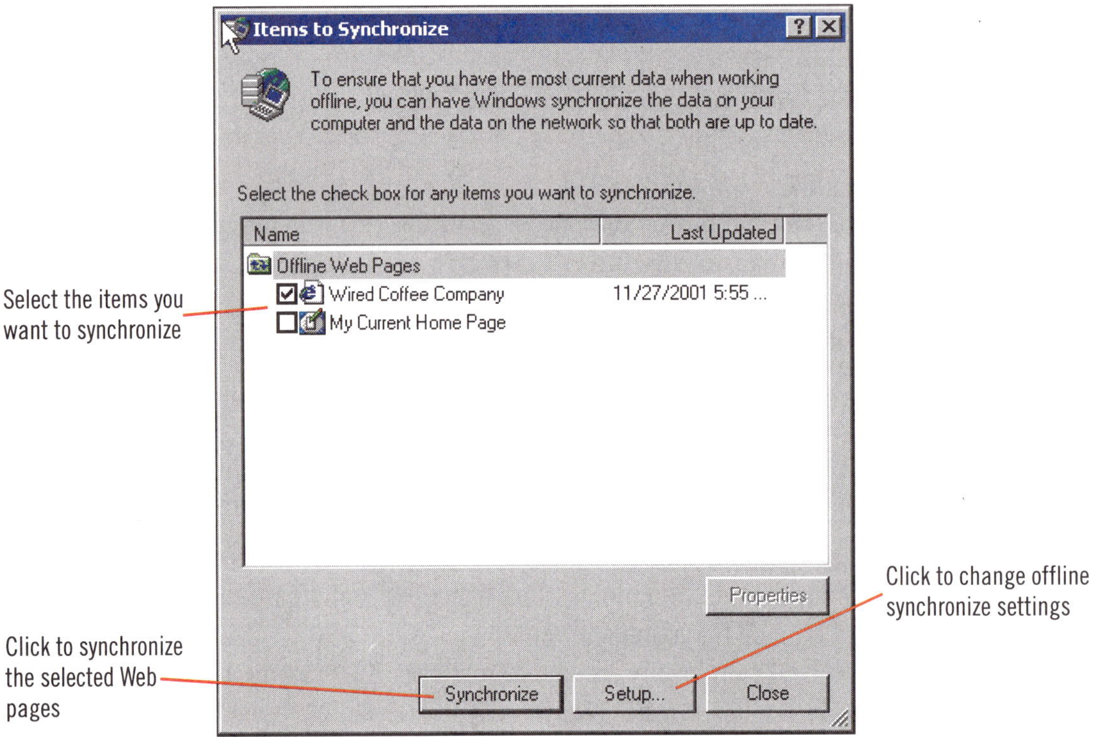

Saving a Web page

If you want to view a Web page offline, and you don't need to update the content, you can save the page on your computer. There are several ways you can save the Web page, from just saving the text to saving all of the graphics and text needed to display that page as it appears on the Web. To save a Web page, click File on the menu bar, then click Save As. Specify the drive and folder in which you want to save the file, type the name you want for the file, click the Save As Type list arrow, select the file format type you want, then click Save. When you save a complete Web page, Internet Explorer saves all the graphic and text elements in a folder.

Windows 2000

Changing Your Home Page and Adding a Link Button

Your **home page** in Internet Explorer is the page that opens when you start the program. When you first install Internet Explorer, the default home page is the Microsoft Network (MSN) Web site. If you want a different page to appear when you start Internet Explorer (and whenever you click the Home button), you can change your home page. You can choose one of the millions of Web pages available through the Internet or you can select a particular file on your hard drive. You can also change the Web pages associated with the buttons on the Links bar. John decides to change his home page to the Wired Coffee Web page and add a link button to the Links bar.

Steps

QuickTip

You will change your home page back to http://www.msn.com in the Skills Review exercise at the end of this unit. If you want to change it back at any other time, type *www.msn.com* in the Address bar, press [Enter], then complete Steps 1 through 3 from this lesson.

1. Click **Tools** on the menu bar, click **Internet Options**, then click the **General tab** if necessary

   The Internet Options dialog box opens, as shown in Figure F-13. The Internet Options dialog box allows you to change a variety of Internet Explorer settings and preferences. See Table F-3 for a description of each tab.

2. In the Home page section, click **Use Current**

   The address of the Wired Coffee Company Web page appears in the Address text box.

3. Click **OK**

   The Home button on the toolbar is now associated with the current Web page, Wired Coffee Company.

4. Click the **FAQ's link**, then click the **Home button** on the toolbar

   The home page appears in the document window.

QuickTip

You can move the Links bar by dragging it to a new location.

5. Double-click the word **Links** on the Links bar

   The Links bar opens and may hide the Address bar. The Links bar contains buttons with links to Web pages. You can drag a link on a page or a Web site address in the Address bar to a blank area on the Links bar to create a new Links button.

6. Drag the **Order link** on the main page to the left of the first button on the Links bar (the mouse pointer changes to a black bar to indicate the placement of the button), then release the mouse button

   A new link button appears on the Links bar with the name associated with the Web site, as shown in Figure F-14. You can delete or change the properties of a links button. Simply right-click the link button you want to change, then click the Delete or Properties command on the shortcut menu.

7. Click the **Order button** on the Links bar, then click the **Back button** Back on the toolbar

8. Right-click the **Order button** on the Links bar, click **Delete**, then click **Yes**

   The home page appears in the document window.

9. Position the mouse pointer over the word **Links**, then drag the **Links bar** to the right to hide it

FIGURE F-13: Internet Options dialog box

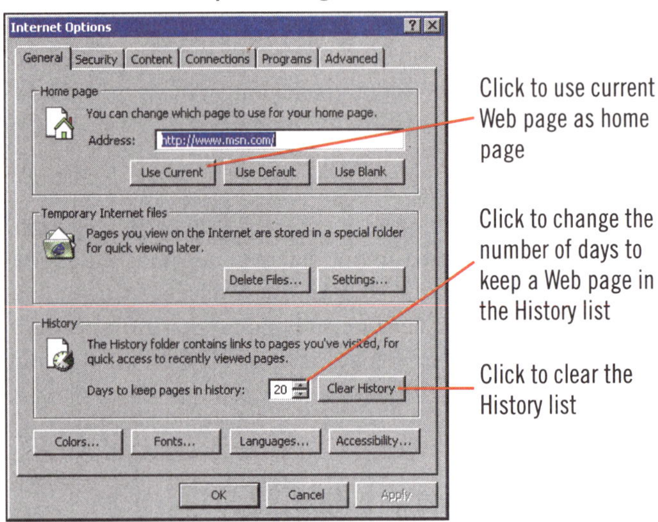

FIGURE F-14: New button on the Links bar

TABLE F-3: Internet Options dialog box tabs

tab	allows you to
General	Change your home page, temporary file settings, and history settings
Security	Select security levels for different parts of the Internet
Content	Set up a rating system for Internet content and personal information for typing Web addresses and buying items over the Internet
Connections	Change connection settings (phone and network)
Programs	Choose which programs (Mail, News, and Internet call) you want to use with Internet Explorer
Advanced	Change individual settings for browsing, multimedia, security, printing, and searching

Viewing and maintaining a History list

Sometimes you run across a great Web site and simply forget to add it to your Favorites list. With Internet Explorer there's no need to try to remember all the sites you've visited. The History feature keeps track of where you've been by date, site, most visited, or order visited today. To view the History list, click the History button on the toolbar and click a day or week in the Explorer Bar to expand the list of Web sites visited. Because the History list can grow to occupy a large amount of space on your hard drive, it's important that you control the length of time Web sites are retained in the list. Internet Explorer deletes the History list periodically based on the settings you specify in the General tab of the Internet Options dialog box, as shown in Figure F-13.

Searching the Web

You can find all kinds of information on the Web. The best way to find information is to use a search engine. A **search engine** is a program you access through a Web site and use to search through a collection of Internet information to find what you are looking for. There are many search engines available on the Web, such as Yahoo! and Excite. When performing a search, the search engine compares the words or phrases, known as **keywords**, you submit with words the search engine has found on various Web sites on the Internet. If it finds your keywords in the stored database, the matched sites are listed on a Web page (these matched sites are sometimes called **hits**). The company who manages the search engine determines what information is stored in their database, so search results for different search engines will vary. John wants to search for other coffee-related Web sites to check out the competition.

Steps

QuickTip

To customize the search options, click the Customize button in the Explorer Bar, click the option button to use the Search Assistant or one search engine, select the search options you want, then click OK or Update.

1. **Click the Search button on the toolbar**

   A search engine appears in the Explorer Bar, as shown in Figure F-15. In this case, the search engine is MSN Web Search; your search engine might be different. If you prefer another search engine, you can choose the search engine you want to use from the custom search options.

2. **Click the Find a web page option button in the Explorer Bar if necessary**

   You can select search options to find a person's or business address, display a list of links to previous searches, and find a map for a specific address. Each search option requires different search criteria, which is information related to what you want to find. To search for a Web page with the information you are looking for, you need to enter a keyword or words (a word or phrase that best describes what you want to retrieve) in the search text box. The more specific you are with your search criteria, the better list of matches you'll receive from the search engine.

3. **In the Find a Web page containing text box, type coffee imports**

   Now you're ready to start the search.

QuickTip

To search for other items using a search engine, such as a file, computer, or person, click the Files or Folders link, Computers link, or People link in the Explorer Bar.

4. **Click Search in the Explorer Bar**

   The search engine retrieves and displays a list of Web sites that match your criteria, as shown in Figure F-16. The total number of Web sites found is listed at the top. The search results appear in decreasing order of relevance. The percentage next to each Web site indicates the degree of relevance. If the search results return too many hits, you should narrow down the search by adding more keywords. As you add more keywords, the search engine will find fewer Web pages that contain all of those words. See Table F-4 for other techniques to narrow down a search.

QuickTip

To perform a new search, click the New button in the Explorer Bar.

5. **Click any link to a Web site in the list of matches**

   The Web site that you opened appears in the right pane of the document window. You can follow links to other pages on this Web site or jump to other Web sites. Once you are finished, close the Explorer Bar.

6. **Click Close button in the Explorer Bar**

   The Explorer Bar closes.

QuickTip

To find text on the current Web page, click Edit on the menu bar, click Find (on This Page), type the text you want to find, then click Find Next.

7. **Click the Home button on the toolbar**

   John returns to the Wired Coffee Company home page.

FIGURE F-15: Explorer Bar with a search engine

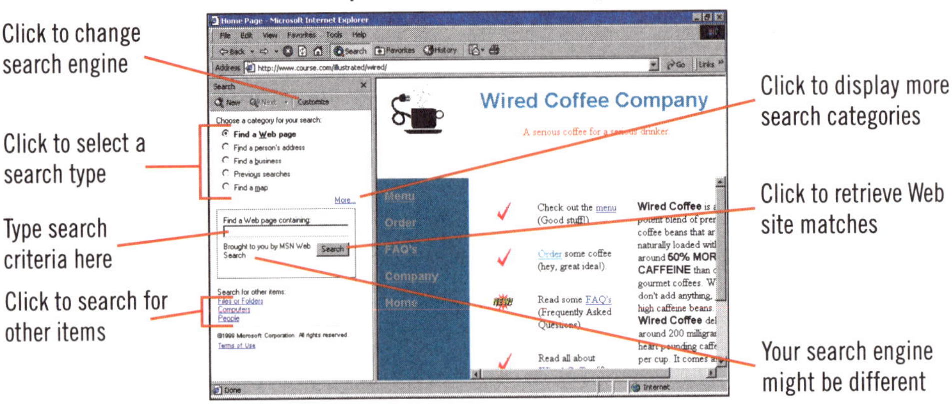

FIGURE F-16: Search engine results

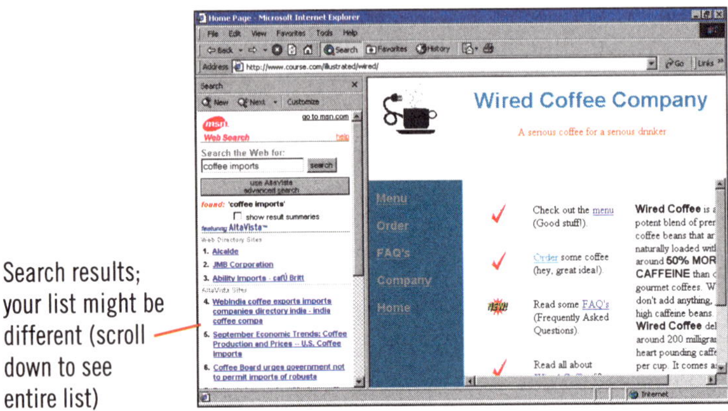

TABLE F-4: Techniques to narrow down a search

technique	example
Use descriptive, specific words	Beaches surfing pacific
Use plain English sentences	Surfing beaches on the pacific ocean
Place exact phrases and proper names in quotes	"Sunset beach"
Use "+" sign for words your results *must* contain	Surf + beach
Use "–" sign for words your results should *not* contain	Surf + beach - Atlantic
Use AND to find results with all words	Surf AND sea AND sand
Use OR to find results with at least one word	Surf OR beach

CLUES TO USE

Searching for people on the Web

Internet Explorer includes several directory services to help you find people you know who may have access to the Internet (one service, Bigfoot, is shown in Figure F-17). To find a person on the Internet, click the Start button, point to Search, click For People, select the directory service you want to use, type the person's name, and click Find Now. Each directory service accesses different databases on the Internet, so if you don't find the person you want using the first service you use, try looking with a different directory service.

FIGURE F-17: Find People dialog box

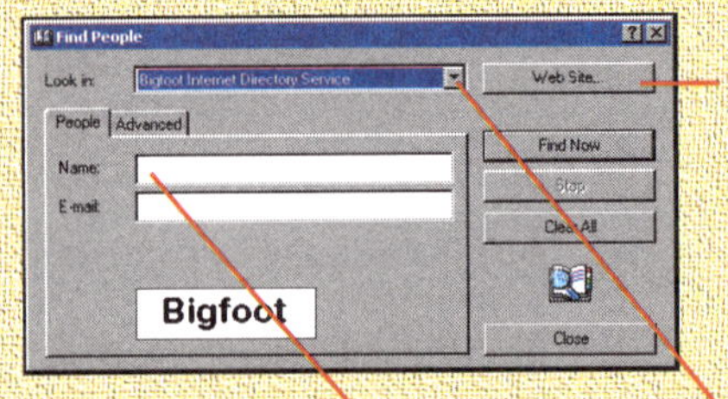

Printing a Web Page

Web pages are designed for viewing on a computer screen, but you can also print all or part of one. Internet Explorer provides many options for printing Web pages. For Web pages with frames, you can print the page just as you see it, or you can elect to print a particular frame or all frames. You can even use special Page Setup options to include the date, time, or window title on the printed page. You can also choose to print the Web addresses from the links contained in a Web page. John prints a Web page and then exits Internet Explorer.

Steps

1. Click **File** on the menu bar, then click **Print**
   The Print dialog box opens, as shown in Figure F-18. See Table F-5 for a description of each tab. Make sure the printer you want to use is connected to your computer.
2. In the Select Printer box, select the printer you want to use
3. Click the **Current Page option button**
   This option prints the currently displayed Web page.
4. Click the **Options tab**
   The Options tab appears, as shown in Figure F-19. When a Web page contains one or more frames, the Print dialog box gives you several options to print the frames. You can print the Web page as laid out on the screen, only the selected frame, or all frames individually.
5. Click the **All frames individually option button**
   Instead of writing down links on a Web page, you can automatically print the Web site addresses for each link.
6. Click the **Print table of links check box** to select it
7. Click **Print**
   The Web page prints on the selected printer.
8. Click the **Close button** in the Internet Explorer window
   The Internet Explore window closes. If you connected to the Internet by telephone, a disconnect dialog box opens. If you are connected to the Internet through a network, follow your instructor's or technical support person's directions to close your connection.
9. If the disconnect dialog box opens, click **Disconnect**

QuickTip

There is no need to save before you exit, because you only view documents with Internet Explorer; you do not create or change documents.

Trouble?

If you connected by telephone, you can right-click the Connect Icon on the right side of the taskbar, then click Disconnect.

TABLE F-5: Print dialog box tabs

tab	allows you to
General	Select a printer and specify the page range and number of copies
Options	Print all or parts of Web site frames, all linked documents, and table of links
Layout	Specify page orientation and number of pages per sheet
Paper/Quality	Specify the paper source and quality

FIGURE F-18: Printing a Web page

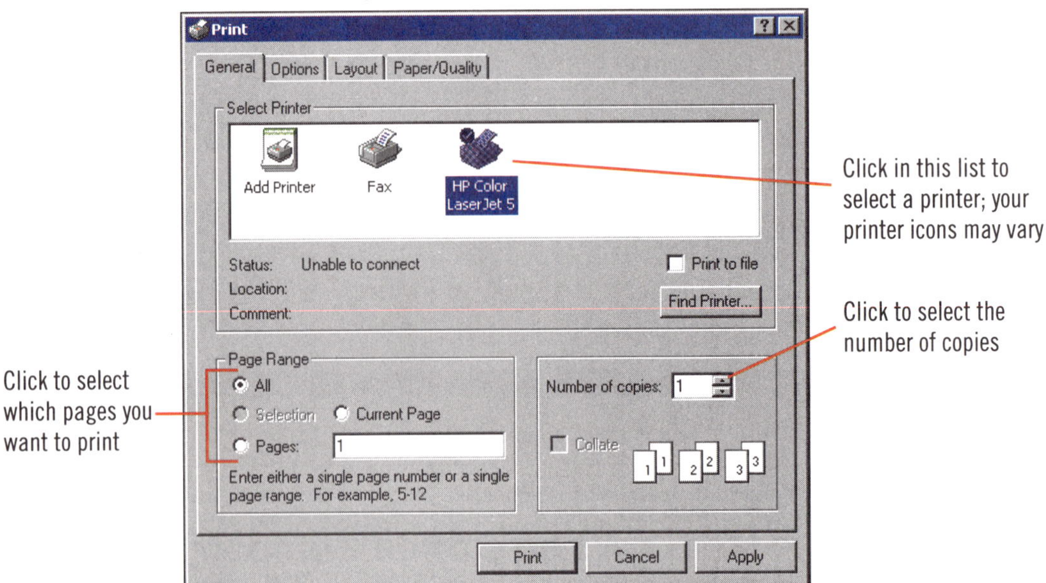

FIGURE F-19: Options tab in the Print dialog box

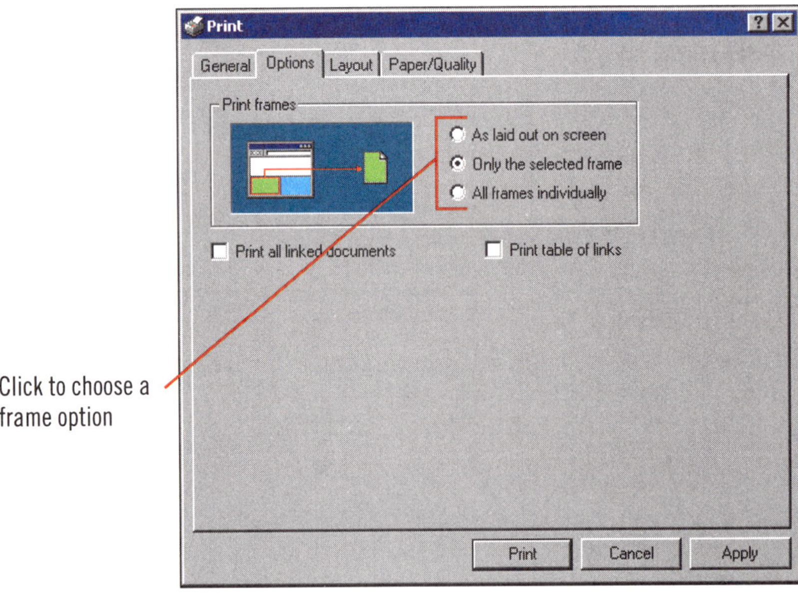

Setting up the page format

When you print a Web page, you can use the Page Setup dialog box to control the way text and graphics are printed on a page. The Page Setup dialog box, shown in Figure F-20, specifies the printer properties for page size, orientation, and paper source; in most cases, you won't want to change them. From the Page Setup dialog box, you can also change header and footer information. In the Headers and Footers text boxes, you can type in text that will appear as a header and footer of a Web page you print. In these text boxes, you can also use variables to substitute information about the current page, and you can combine text and codes. For example, if you type *Page &p of &P* in the Header text box, the current page number and the total number of pages will be printed at the top of each printed page. Check Internet Explorer Help for a complete list of header and footer codes.

FIGURE F-20: Page Setup dialog box

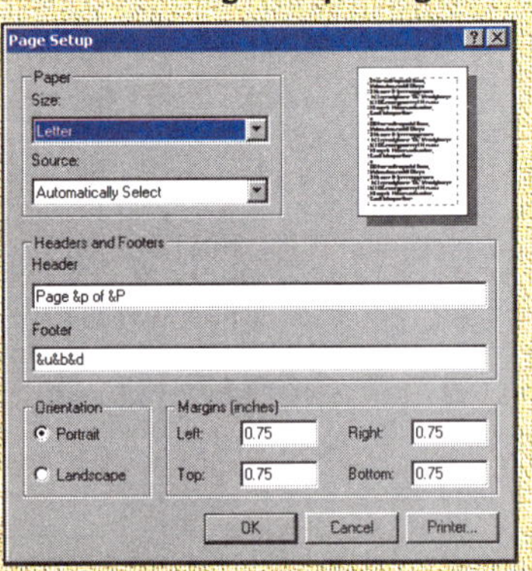

Practice

▶ Concepts Review

Label each of the elements of the screen shown in Figure F-21.

FIGURE F-21

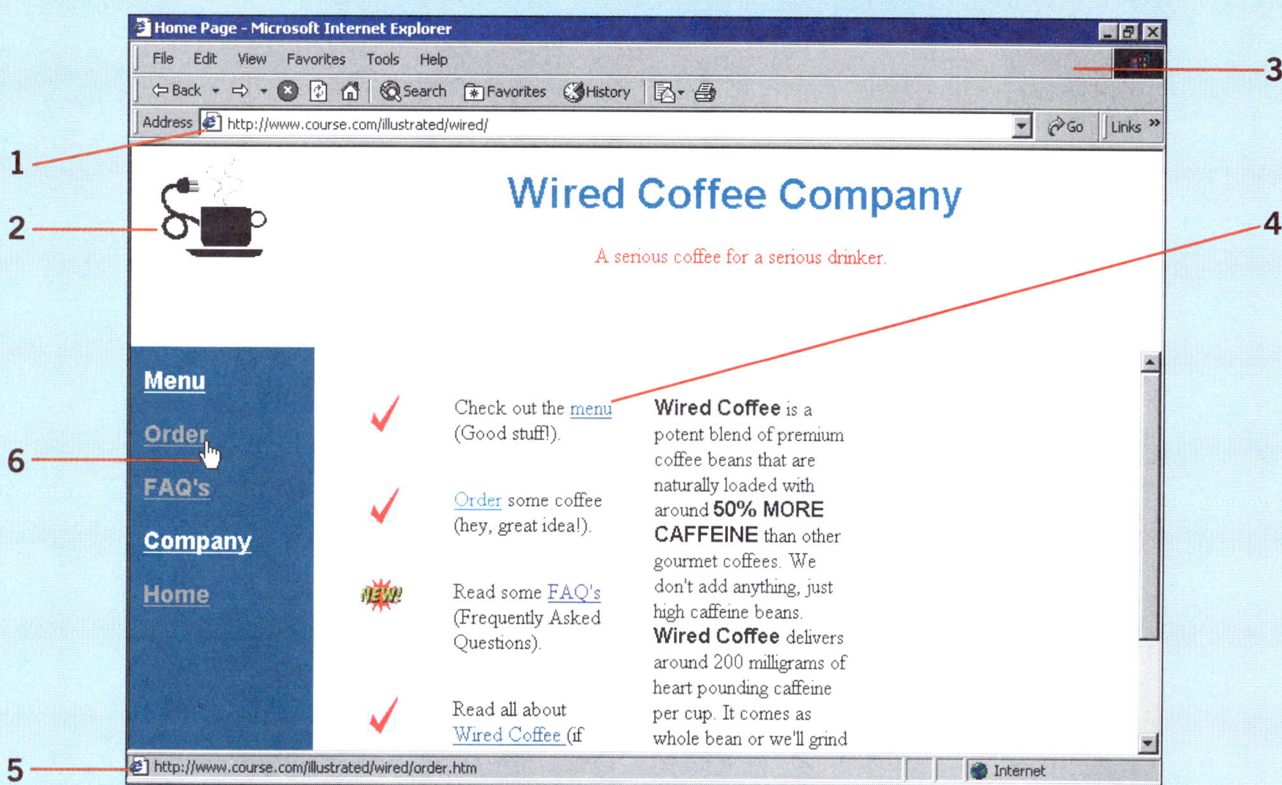

Match each of the terms with the statement that describes its function.

7. **Address bar**
8. **Toolbar**
9. **Favorites button**
10. **Status indicator**
11. **Back button**

a. Spins when Internet Explorer is loading a page
b. Displays the URL for the current page
c. Provides shortcuts for options on the menu bar
d. Displays a list of selected Web pages and folders to organize them
e. Displays the previously viewed page

Select the best answer from the list of choices.

12. Software programs that are used to access and display Web pages are called
  a. Web sites.
  b. search engines.
  c. Web utilities.
  d. Web browsers.

13. If you want to save the name and URL of a Web page in Internet Explorer and return to it later, you can add it to a list called
  a. Favorites.
  b. Bookmarks.
  c. Home pages.
  d. Preferences.

14. An international telecommunications network that consists of linked documents is called the
  a. NSFNET.
  b. Netscape Communicator.
  c. Internet Explorer.
  d. World Wide Web.

15. In Internet Explorer, where are the buttons located that perform common functions such as moving to a previous Web page?
  a. Address bar
  b. Toolbar
  c. Status bar
  d. Menu bar

16. Which of the following is a valid URL?
  a. http:/www.usf.edu/
  b. htp://www.usf.edu/
  c. htp:/ww.usf.edu/
  d. http//www.usf.edu/

17. Underlined words that you click to jump to another Web page are called
  a. explorers.
  b. favorites.
  c. Web browsers.
  d. hyperlinks.

18. The URL of the current Web page is displayed in the
  a. title bar.
  b. document window.
  c. Address bar.
  d. status bar.

Skills Review

1. **Start Internet Explorer.**
   a. Connect to the Internet.
   b. Start Internet Explorer.

2. **Explore the browser window.**
   a. Identify the toolbar, menu bar, Address bar, Links bar, status bar, status indicator, URL, document window, and scroll bars.
   b. In the toolbar, identify icons for searching, viewing favorites, viewing history, viewing Internet Explorer in full screen, and moving to the previous page.

3. **Open a Web page and follow links.**
   a. Click in the Address bar, type **www.cnet.com**, then press [Enter].
   b. Explore the Web site by using the scroll bars, toolbar, and hyperlinks.
   c. Click in the Address bar, type **www.sportsline.com**, then press [Enter].
   d. Follow the links to investigate the content.

4. **Add a Web page to the Favorites list.**
   a. Click in the Address bar, type **www.loc.gov**, then press [Enter].
   b. Click Favorites on the menu bar, then click Add to Favorites.
   c. Click OK.
   d. Click the Favorites button.
   e. Click the Home button.
   f. Click the link Library of Congress Home Page in the Favorites list.

5. **Make a Web page available offline.**
   a. Click Favorites on the menu bar, then click Organize Favorites.
   b. In the Favorites list, click Library of Congress.
   c. Click the Make available offline check box to select it, then click Close.
   d. Click File on the menu bar, then click Work Offline.
   e. Click Library of Congress Home Page in the Favorites list.
   f. Click File on the menu bar, then click Work Offline.
   g. Click Tools on the menu bar, then click Synchronize.
   h. Click the Library of Congress Home Page check to select it if necessary, then deselect all other check boxes.
   i. Click Synchronize.
   j. Right-click Library of Congress Home Page in the Favorites list, click Delete, then click Yes.
   k. Click the Close button in the Favorites list.

6. **Change your home page and add a link button.**
   a. Click in the Address bar, type ***www.msn.com***, then press [Enter].
   b. Click View on the menu bar, then click Internet Options.
   c. Click the General tab.
   d. Click Use Current.
   e. Click OK.
   f. Click the Back button.
   g. Click the Home button.

7. Search the Web.

a. Click the Search button.
b. Click the Find a Web page option button
c. Type **job computer training** in the search text box.
d. Click the Search button.
e. Click a link to a Web site from the match list.
f. Click the Close button in the Explorer Bar.
g. Click the Home button.

8. Print a Web page.

a. Click File on the menu bar, then click Print.
b. In the Select Printer box, click a printer.
c. Click the Pages option button (use the range 1 to 1).
d. Click Print.
e. Click the Close button to exit Internet Explorer.
f. Click Yes to disconnect, if necessary.

▶ Independent Challenges

1. You will soon graduate from college with a degree in business management. Before entering the workforce, you want to make sure that you are up-to-date on all of the advances in the field. You decide that checking on the Web would provide the most current information. In addition, you can look for companies with employment opportunities. Use Internet Explorer to investigate the All Business Network at http://www.all-biz.com/. When you find a promising site, print the page.

2. You are leaving tomorrow for a business trip to France. You want to make sure that you take the right clothes for the weather and decide that the best place to check France's weather might be the Web. Access one or two of the following weather sites and print at least two reports on the weather in Paris.

The Weather Channel	http://www.weather.com/
World Weather Guide	http://www.weatherlabs.com
CNN Weather	http://www.cnn.com/WEATHER/

3. Your boss wants to buy a new desktop computer (as opposed to a laptop). He assigns you the task of investigating the options. You decide that it would be more expedient to look on the Web than to visit the computer stores in the area. Visit the following Web sites and print a page from the two that you think offer the best deal.

IBM	http://www.ibm.com/
Apple	http://www.apple.com/
Dell	http://www.dell.com/

4. During the summer, you want to travel to national parks in the United States. Use one of the search engines available through your Web browser to find Web sites with maps of the national parks. Visit four or five Web sites from the match list and print a page from the three that you think offer the best maps and related information for park visitors.

Visual Workshop

Re-create the screen shown in Figure F-22, which displays the document window with a search engine and a Web site. Your search results might be different. (*Hint:* Use the Custom button to change search engines.) Print the Web page and then print the screen. (Press the Print Screen key to make a copy of the screen, open Paint, click Edit on the menu bar, click Paste to paste the screen into Paint, then click Yes to paste the large image if necessary. Click File on the menu bar, click Print, then click Print in the Print dialog box.)

FIGURE F-22

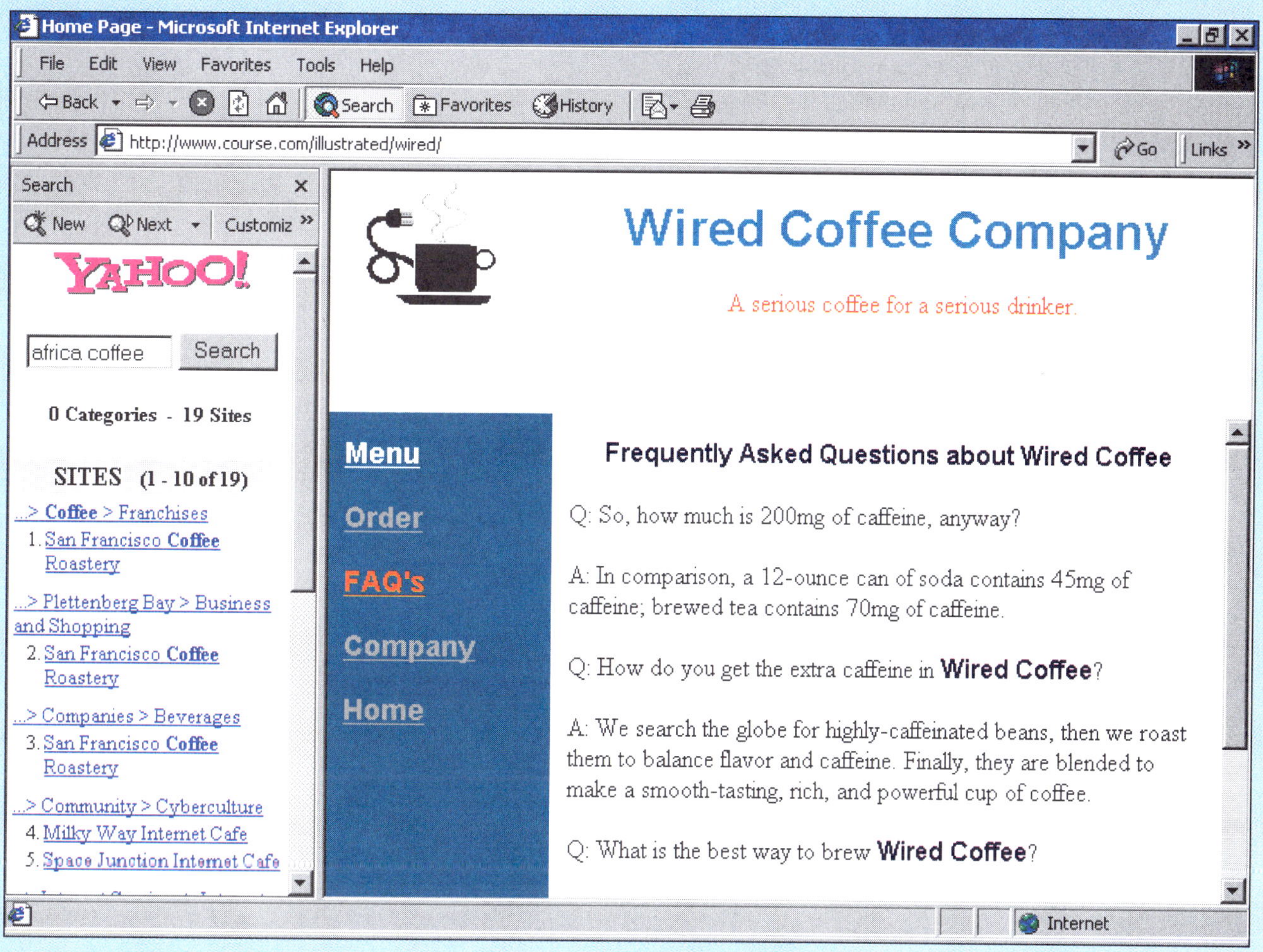

Windows 2000

Exchanging

Mail and News

Objectives

- Start Outlook Express
- Explore the Outlook Express window
- Add a contact to the Address Book
- Compose and send e-mail
- Retrieve, read, and respond to e-mail
- Manage e-mail messages
- Select a news server
- View and subscribe to a newsgroup
- Read and post a news message

Windows 2000 includes Microsoft Outlook Express, a powerful program for managing **electronic mail** (known as e-mail). With an Internet connection and Microsoft Outlook Express, you can exchange e-mail messages with anyone on the Internet and join any number of **newsgroups**, which are collections of e-mail messages on related topics posted by individuals to specified locations on the Internet. If you are not connected to the Internet, you will not be able to work the steps in this unit; however, you can read the lessons without completing the steps to learn what you can accomplish using Outlook Express. In this unit John Casey, owner of the Wired Coffee Company, will use Outlook Express to send and receive e-mail messages and join a newsgroup about the coffee industry.

Starting Outlook Express

Outlook Express puts the world of online communication on your desktop. Whether you want to exchange e-mail with colleagues and friends or join newsgroups to trade ideas and information, the tools you need are here. When you install Windows 2000, a button for Outlook Express appears on the Quick Launch toolbar, which is located on the taskbar. If your computer is not connected to the Internet or you don't have an e-mail account, check with your instructor or technical support person to see if it's possible for you to connect or set up an e-mail account. John wants to use Outlook Express to exchange e-mail with his employees.

1. If necessary, establish a connection to the Internet via the network or telephone
   If you connect to the Internet through a network, follow your instructor's or technical support person's directions to establish your connection. If you connect by telephone, create a new connection using the Connection Wizard to establish your connection, or use an existing Dial-Up Networking connection.

Trouble?

If a Browse For Folder dialog box opens, click OK to accept the default folder where Outlook Express should store your messages, then continue.

2. Click the **Launch Outlook Express button** on the Quick Launch toolbar, as shown in Figure G-1
   The Outlook Express window opens and displays the Outlook Express Start Page, as shown in Figure G-2. If you connect to the Internet through a network, follow your instructor's or technical support person's directions to log on. If you connect to the Internet by telephone using a dial-up networking connection, you might need to enter your user name and password to connect to the Internet. See your instructor or technical support person for this information.

3. If necessary, type your **user name**, press **[Tab]**, type your **password**, then click **Connect**
   Upon completion of the dial-up connection, you are connected to the Internet (unless an error message appears). When you start Outlook Express for the first time, the Internet Connection Wizard opens, asking you about your e-mail account setup information. See your instructor or technical support person for this information.

QuickTip

To modify or add an account, click Tools on the menu bar, click Accounts, click an account and click Properties, or click Add, click an account type, and follow the wizard instructions.

4. If necessary, enter the information required by the Internet Connection Wizard; type your **name**, click **Next**, type your **e-mail address**, click **Next**, type the **name of the incoming mail server**, type the **name of the outgoing server**, click **Next**, type your **e-mail account name**, type your **password**, click **Next**, then click **Finish**
   Your mail account is set up.

5. If necessary, click the **Maximize button** to maximize the Outlook Express window

FIGURE G-1: Windows desktop

FIGURE G-2: Outlook Express window

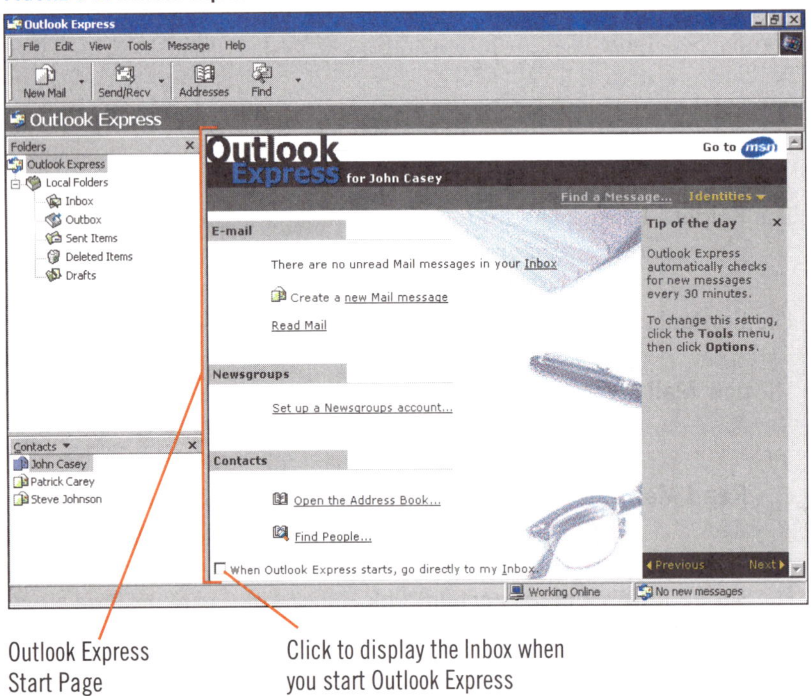

Starting Outlook Express from your Web browser

You can set Outlook Express to be your default e-mail program, so that whenever you click an e-mail link on a Web page or choose the mail command in your Web browser, Outlook Express opens. Likewise, you can set Outlook Express to be your default news reader, so that when you click a newsgroup link on a Web page or choose the news reader command in your Web browser, Outlook Express opens. To set Outlook Express to be your default e-mail or newsgroup program, start Internet Explorer, click Tools on the menu bar, click Internet Options, click the Programs tab, click either the E-mail or Newsgroups list arrow, click Outlook Express, then click OK.

Windows 2000

Exploring the Outlook Express Window

After you start Outlook Express, the Outlook Express window displays the Outlook Express Start Page, as shown in Figure G-3. The **Outlook Express Start Page** displays tools that you can use to read e-mail, set up a newsgroup account, read newsgroup messages, compose e-mail messages, enter and edit Address Book information, and find people on the Internet. Before reading his e-mail, John decides to familiarize himself with the components of the Outlook Express window.

He notes the following features:

 The **title bar** at the top of the window displays the name of the program.

 The **menu bar** provides access to a variety of commands, much like other Windows programs.

 The **toolbar** provides icons, or buttons, for easy access to the most commonly used commands. See Table G-1 for a description of each toolbar button. These commands are also available on menus.

 The **Go to MSN link** opens your default Web browser program and displays the MSN Web page.

 The **Folders list** displays folders where Outlook Express stores e-mail messages. You can also use folders to organize your e-mail messages.

 The **Contacts list** displays the contact names in the Address Book.

 The **new Mail message link** opens the New Message dialog box where you can compose and send e-mail messages.

 The **Read Mail link** jumps to the Inbox where you can read and reply to incoming e-mail messages.

 The **Set up a Newsgroups account link** (appears instead of the Read News link if you have not set up a news group account) creates a newsgroups account.

 The **Read News link** connects to newsgroups that you can view and subscribe to.

 The **Open the Address Book link** opens the Address Book where you can enter and edit your contacts list.

 The **Find People link** opens the Find People dialog box where you can search for people on the Internet or in your Address Book.

 The **Tip of the day** on the right side of the window displays an Outlook Express tip; click Next and Previous to move between the tips.

 The **status bar** displays information about your Internet connection with a mail or newsgroup server.

FIGURE G-3: Outlook Express window with the Start Page

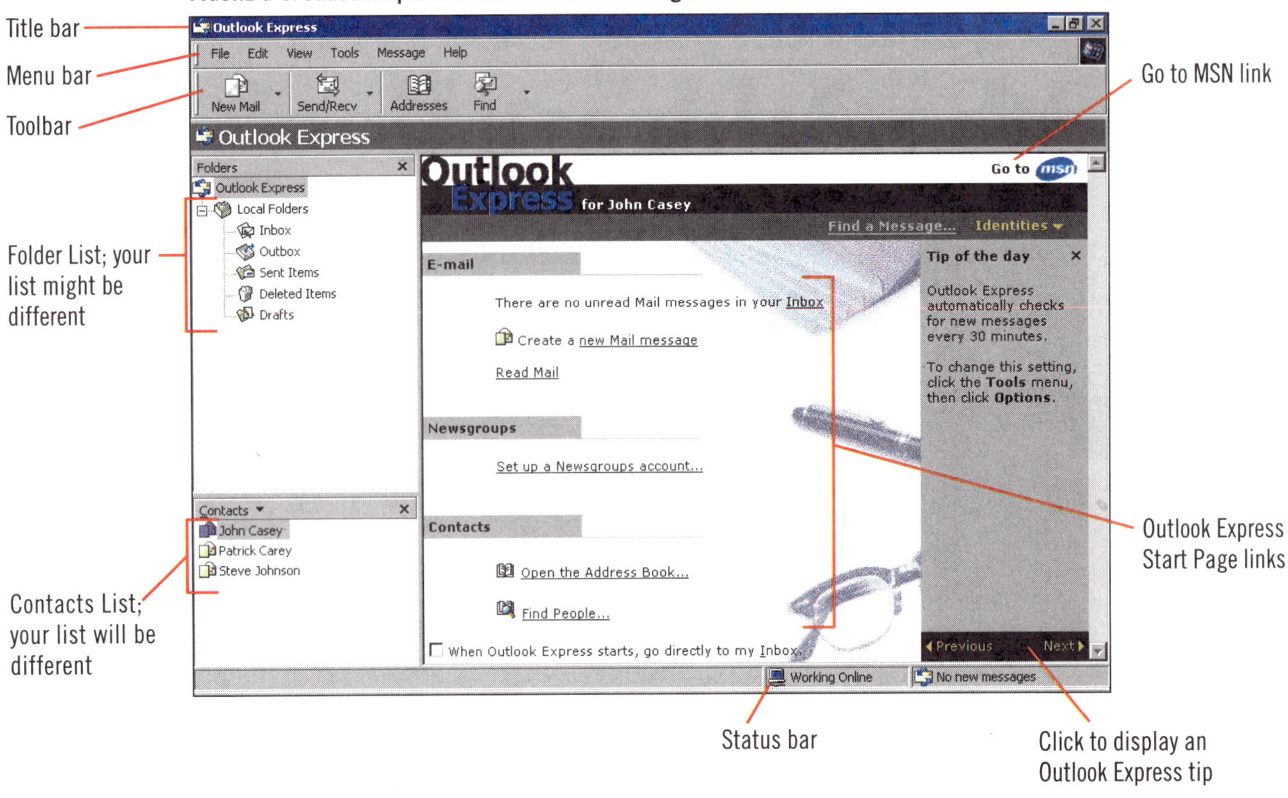

TABLE G-1: Outlook Express Start Page toolbar buttons

button	description
[New Mail icon]	Opens the e-mail message composition window
[Send/Recv icon]	Sends e-mail messages and checks for new messages
[Addresses icon]	Opens the Address Book
[Find icon]	Finds e-mail messages, text in an e-mail message, or people on the Internet

Getting help in Outlook Express

If you need help connecting to the Internet to get mail or learning how to use Outlook Express features, you can get help from several different sources. To get Outlook Express Help, you can use the online Help system that comes with the program or view Outlook Express Web sites on the Internet. To open Outlook Express online Help, click Help on the menu bar, then click Contents and Index. To learn more about Outlook Express from Web sites on the Internet, click Help on the menu bar, point to Microsoft on the Web, then click Product News. Internet Explorer starts and displays the Outlook Express Web site.

Adding a Contact to the Address Book

A **contact** is a person or company that you communicate with. One contact can have several mailing addresses, phone numbers, e-mail addresses, or Web sites. You can store this information in the **Address Book**, along with other detailed information—such as the contact's title, street address, phone number, and personal Web page addresses. When you want to create a new contact or edit an existing one, you use the Properties dialog box to enter or change contact information. You can organize your contacts into **contact groups**, which are groups of related people you communicate with on a regular basis, or into folders. One contact group might be your family members or people at work. John wants to add a new employee to his Address Book.

QuickTip

You can also click the Address Book button on the toolbar to open the Address Book.

1. Click the **Open the Address Book link** on the Outlook Express Start Page
   The Address Book window opens, as shown in Figure G-4, displaying the current contacts in the Address Book. Your list of contacts might be different or empty. The Address Book toolbar is above the list of contacts. See Table G-2 for a description of each toolbar button. These commands are also available on the menus.

QuickTip

To create a contact group, click the New button on the toolbar, click New Group, type a group name, click Select Members, double-click names from the Address Book, click OK, then click OK again.

2. Click the **New button** on the Address Book toolbar, then click **New Contact**
   The New button allows you to create new contacts, contact groups, and folders to organize contacts. The Properties dialog box opens, displaying the Name tab with empty text boxes. See Table G-3 for a description of each tab in the Properties dialog box.
3. Type **Shawn** in the First text box, press **[Tab]** twice to move to the Last name text box, then type **Brooks**
   The complete name of the new contact appears in the Display box; this is the name that will be displayed in the list of contacts unless you click the Display list arrow and choose a different name.

QuickTip

To modify an e-mail address, select it, then click Edit. To delete an e-mail address no longer in use, select it, then click Remove.

4. Click the **E-Mail Addresses text box**, type **shawnbrooks@course.com**, then click **Add**
   The e-mail address appears in the box below the E-Mail Addresses text box, as shown in Figure G-5. E-mail addresses are not case-sensitive (capitalization doesn't matter) and cannot contain spaces.
5. Click **OK**
   The Properties dialog box closes and you return to the Address Book. Instead of opening the Properties dialog box every time you want to see a more complete listing of a contact's information, you can position the mouse pointer over a contact in the Address Book to display a ScreenTip summary of the contact's information.

QuickTip

To print a phone list or business cards, click the Print button on the toolbar, click a print option, then click Print.

6. Position the mouse pointer over **Shawn Brooks** in the Address Book
   A ScreenTip summary appears on the screen. You can move the mouse pointer to remove the ScreenTip or wait. To edit a contact, simply double-click anywhere on the contact entry in the Address Book.
7. Double-click **Shawn Brooks**
   The Shawn Brooks Properties dialog box opens and displays the selected contact's information. You can use any of the tabs in this dialog box to add to or change the contact information.
8. Click the **Business tab**, click the **Phone text box**, type **925-555-3084**, then click **OK**
   Shawn's business phone number appears in the Address Book.
9. Click the **Close button** in the Address Book window

FIGURE G-4: Address Book window

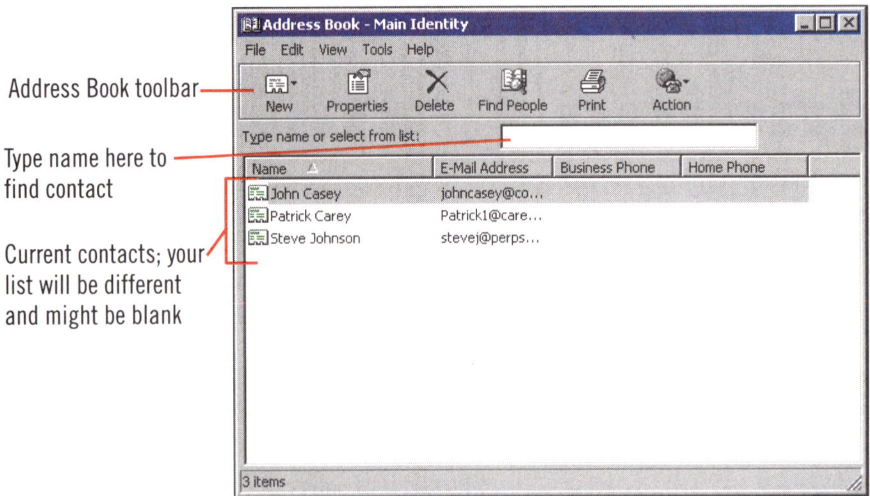

FIGURE G-5: Properties dialog box with a new contact

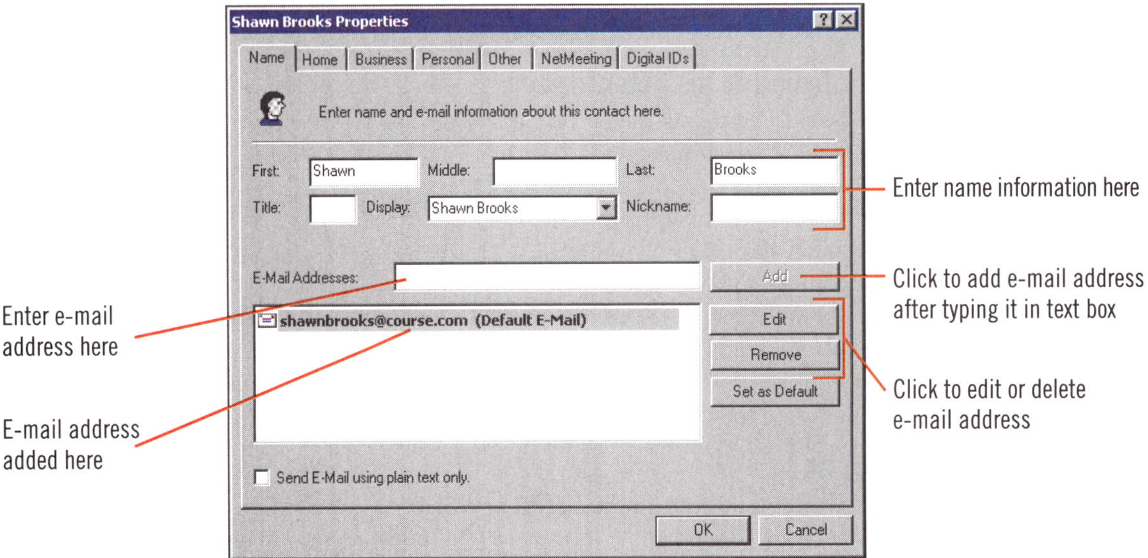

TABLE G-2: Address Book toolbar buttons

button	description	button	description
New	Creates a new contact, group, or folder	Find People	Finds people on the Internet
Properties	Opens the selected contact	Print	Opens the Print dialog box
Delete	Deletes the selected contact	Action	Sends mail, dials a connection, or places an Internet call

TABLE G-3: New contact Properties dialog box tabs

tab	description	tab	description
Name	Enter name and e-mail information	**Other**	Enter notes about contact
Home	Enter information related to the contact's home	**NetMeeting**	Add and modify e-mail conferencing addresses and servers
Business	Enter business-related information	**Digital Ids**	Add, remove, and view security identification numbers for the contact
Personal	Enter personal information		

Windows 2000

Composing and Sending E-mail

E-mail is quickly becoming the primary form of written communication for many people. E-mail messages follow a standard memo format with fields for the sender, recipient, date, and subject of the message. To send an e-mail message, you need to enter the recipient's e-mail address, type a subject, and then type the message itself. You can send the same message to more than one individual, to a contact group, or to a combination of individuals and groups. You can personalize your e-mail messages (and newsgroup messages) with built-in stationery, or you can design your own. John wants to send an e-mail message to the new employee whose contact information he added to the Address Book in the previous lesson.

Steps

QuickTip

To create a new message without stationery, you can click the New Mail button on the toolbar, click the new Mail message link in the Outlook Express window, or double-click a name in the Contacts list.

QuickTip

To remove a name from the Message recipients list, click the person's name in the Message recipients list box, then press [Delete].

QuickTip

To save an Incomplete message, click the Save button on the toolbar. The e-mail message is saved with the name of the subject and placed in the Drafts folder.

QuickTip

If you don't want to send the e-mail message right now, click File on the menu bar, then click Send Later. The e-mail message is placed in the Outbox but not sent.

1. Click the **New Mail button list arrow** on the toolbar, click **Clear Day**, then click the **Maximize button**
   The New Message window opens and is maximized, as shown in Figure G-6, displaying the Clear Day stationery in the message box.
2. Click **To** next to the To text box
   The Select Recipients dialog box opens, as shown in Figure G-7, displaying the contacts from the Address Book.
3. In the list of contacts, click the **down scroll arrow** if necessary, click **Shawn Brooks**, then click **To**
   The contact, Shawn Brooks, appears in the Message recipients list box. You can also add additional recipients to this list, select another recipient and click the Cc (carbon copy) button to send a copy of your e-mail message to that person, or click the Bcc (blind carbon copy) button to send a copy of your e-mail message to another person without displaying the names of the blind copy recipients in the e-mail message.
4. Click **OK**
   Shawn's name appears in the To text box. Shawn's e-mail address is associated with the name selected even though it is not displayed. John includes a subject title.
5. Click the **Subject text box**, then type **Welcome aboard!**
   The message title bar changes from New Message to the subject text, Welcome aboard!
6. Click the **text box** at the bottom of the message window
   The Formatting toolbar, just below the Subject text box, is activated. The Formatting toolbar works just like the Formatting toolbar in WordPad or other Windows programs. You can use it to change the format of your message text at any time.
7. Type **Dear Shawn:**, press **[Enter]** twice, type **I would like to welcome you to the Wired Coffee Company. We are excited that you have joined our team. Wired Coffee is a growing company, and I believe your contributions will make a big difference. Please come to a luncheon for new employees this Thursday at 12:30 in the company cafe.**, press **[Enter]** twice, then type **John**
8. Click the **Send button** on the toolbar, then click **OK** in the Information box, if necessary
   The New Message window closes, and the e-mail message is placed in the Outbox, a folder where outgoing messages are stored, and then automatically sent to the recipient. A copy of the outgoing message is saved in the Sent Items folder so you can reference the message later.

FIGURE G-6: New Message window with Clear Day stationery

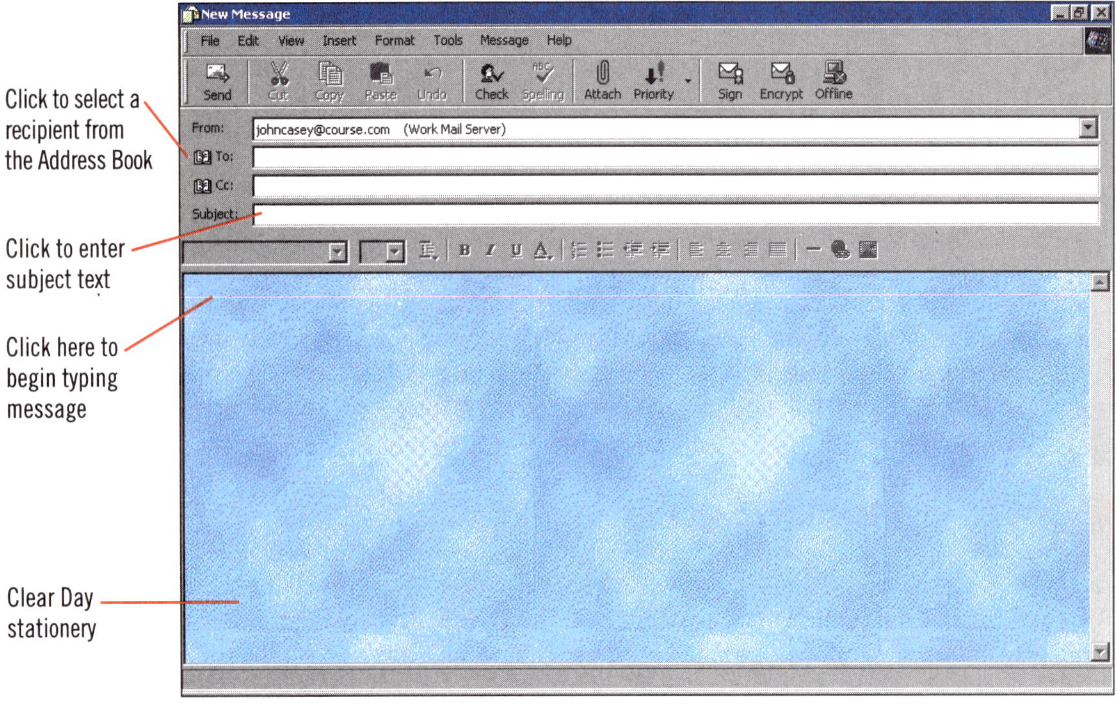

FIGURE G-7: Selecting recipients for an e-mail message

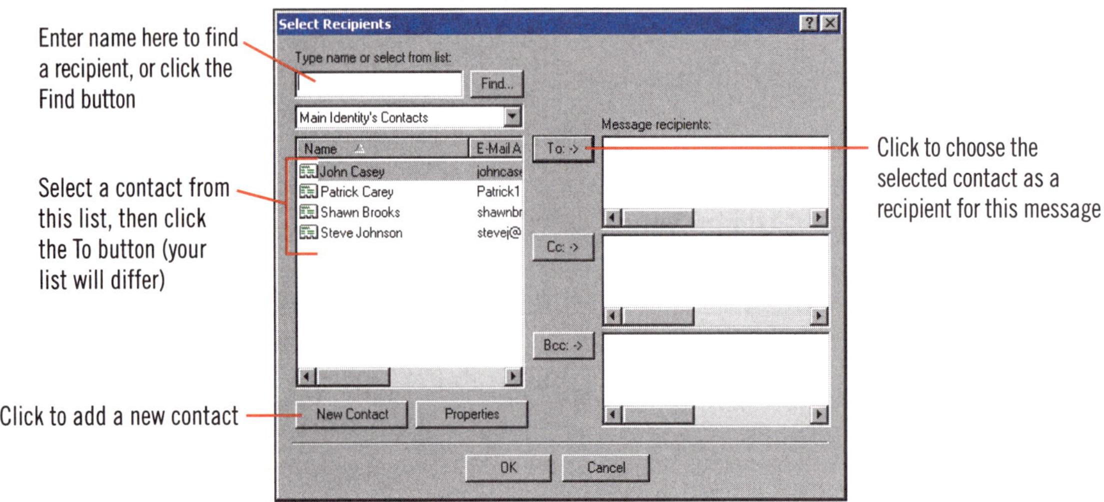

CLUES TO USE

Attaching a file to an e-mail message

You can easily share files using e-mail. You can send a file, such as a picture or a document by attaching it to an e-mail message. When the e-mail is received, the recipient can open the file in the program in which it was created or save it to disk. For example, suppose you are working on a report that you created using WordPad and that a colleague working in another part of the country needs to present it today. After you finish the report, you can attach the report file to an e-mail message and send the message to your colleague, who can then open, edit, and print the report. To attach a file to an e-mail message, create the message, click the Attach button on the toolbar, navigate to the drive and folder location of the file you want to attach, select the file, then click Attach.

Windows 2000

Retrieving, Reading, and Responding to E-mail

You can retrieve your e-mail manually or set Outlook Express to automatically retrieve your messages. New messages appear in the Inbox along with any messages you haven't yet stored elsewhere or deleted. One or more **message flags** may appear next to a message to indicate that the message has a certain priority, that it has a file attached to it, and whether or not it has been read. See Table G-4 for a description of the message flags. John forwards an e-mail message he received from Shawn Brooks to another person at the company.

Steps

QuickTip

To automatically check for messages every few minutes, click Tools on the menu bar, click Options, then click the check for messages option.

QuickTip

To display the Inbox when you start Outlook Express, click the When Outlook Express starts, go directly to my Inbox check box on the Outlook Express Start Page.

Trouble?

If you didn't receive a message from Shawn Brooks, click the Send/Recv button on the toolbar again. It may take a few minutes for the message to arrive.

Trouble?

If you don't know an e-mail address to send the forwarded message to, click the Close button in the message window, then continue with the next lesson.

1. Click the **Send/Recv button** on the toolbar
   An information box displays the progress of the e-mail messages you are sending and receiving. After your e-mail messages have been sent or received, the dialog box closes. When you receive new e-mail, the Inbox folder in the Folders list is bold, indicating that it contains unread messages, and a number in parentheses indicates the number of new e-mail messages you have received.
2. In the Folders list, click **Inbox**
   The Inbox folder opens, as shown in Figure G-8. The **preview pane** displays the messages in your Inbox. The **display pane** displays the e-mail message that is selected in the preview pane. E-mail messages in the preview pane with the subject or heading text in bold are messages that have not been opened.
3. Click the **message** you received from Shawn Brooks
4. Double-click the **message** you received from Shawn Brooks in the preview pane, then click the **Maximize button** in the message window
   When a message you receive is short, you can quickly read it by clicking the message and then reading the text in the display pane. Longer messages, like the one from Shawn Brooks, are easier to open and read in a full window. After reading a message, you can reply to the author, reply to all of the recipients, forward the message to another person, or simply close or delete the message. John forwards the message to his human resources administrator to ask her to add Shawn Brooks to the list of luncheon attendees. You will forward the message to your instructor or technical support person or to someone else whose e-mail address you know.
5. Click the **Forward button** on the message toolbar
   The Forward Message window opens, as shown in Figure G-9, displaying the original e-mail message you sent. At the top of the message box, you can add additional text to the message.
6. Click in the upper-left corner of the message box, then type **Please add Shawn Brooks to Thursday's luncheon guest list.**
7. Click the **To text box**, type the e-mail address of your instructor, technical support person, or someone else you know, then click the **Send button** on the toolbar
   The e-mail message is sent.
8. Click the **Address Book button** on the toolbar, click **Shawn Brooks**, click the **Delete button**, click **Yes**, then click the **Close button**
   Shawn is deleted from John's Address Book.

FIGURE G-8: Outlook Express window with the Inbox

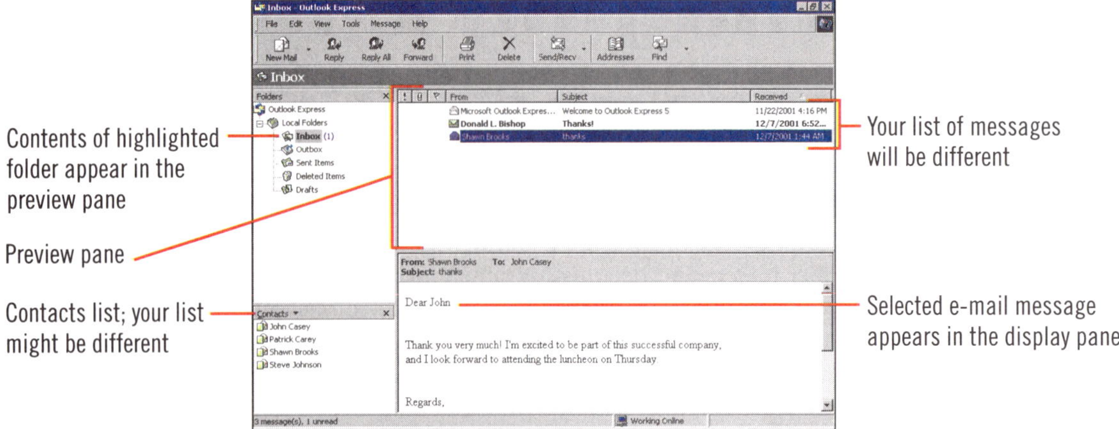

FIGURE G-9: Forward Message window

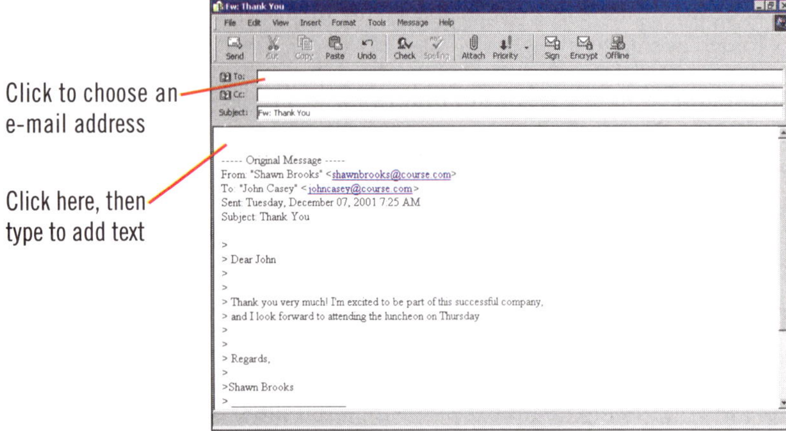

TABLE G-4: Mail message flag icons

icon	description
	Message has not been read; message heading text appears bold
	Message has been read
	Message has one or more files attached to it
	Message has been marked as high priority by the sender
	Message has been marked as low priority by the sender

Printing e-mail messages and contacts

You can print your e-mail messages from any folder at any time using Outlook Express. To print an e-mail message, open the message, then click the Print button on the toolbar. You can also open the Address Book and print contact information in a variety of formats, such as Memo, Business Card, and Phone List. The Memo style prints all the information you have for a contact with descriptive titles. The Business Card style prints the contact information without descriptive titles. The Phone List style prints all the phone numbers for a contact or for all your contacts. To print contact information, open the Address Book, select a specific contact (if desired), click the Print button on the toolbar, select a print range, print style, and the number of copies you want to print, then click Print.

Windows 2000

Managing E-mail Messages

A common problem with using e-mail is an overcrowded Inbox. To help you keep your Inbox organized, you should move messages you want to keep to other folders and subfolders, delete messages you no longer want, and create new folders as you need them. Storing incoming messages in other folders and deleting unwanted messages makes it easier to see the new messages you receive and to keep track of messages to which you have already responded. John wants to create a new folder for his important messages in the Local Folders location, move a message from the Inbox to the new folder, and then delete the messages he no longer needs.

1. **Click File on the menu bar, point to New, then click Folder**
   The Create Folder dialog box opens, displaying the list of folders contained in the Outlook Express folder, as shown in Figure G-10.
2. **Type Important, then click Local Folders in the Folders list**
   The new folder will be named Important and will appear in the Folders list under Local Folders. To create a subfolder (a folder in a folder), you would select one of the folders in the Folders list under Local folders. The Folders list works like the left pane of Windows Explorer. When a subfolder is created, a plus sign (+) appears next to the folder that contains the subfolder.
3. **Click OK**
   The new folder, Important, appears in the Folders list under Local Folders.

QuickTip

To block all messages from a sender, click a message from the sender, click Message on the menu bar, then click Block Sender.

4. **In the preview pane of the Inbox, right-click the message you received from Shawn Brooks**
   A pop-up menu appears, displaying commands, such as move, copy, delete, print, and add sender to Address Book, to help you manage your e-mail messages.
5. **Click Move To Folder on the pop-up menu**
   The Move To dialog box opens, allowing you to specify the folder where you want to move the selected message.

QuickTip

To move a message to a folder, drag the message from the preview pane to the folder in the Folder's list.

6. **Click the Important folder, then click OK**
7. **In the Folders list, click the Important folder**
   The e-mail message you just moved appears in the preview and display panes, as shown in Figure G-11.

QuickTip

To sort messages by sender, subject, date, priority or flag, click a header in the preview pane.

8. **In the Folders list, right-click the Important folder, click Delete, then click Yes**
   The Important folder is placed in the Deleted Items folder. The Delete Items folder works just like the Recycle Bin. Deleted messages are temporarily stored in the folder until they are automatically or manually deleted.
9. **In the Folders list, right-click the Deleted Items folder, click Empty 'Deleted Items' Folder**
   The Important folder and all of its contents are permanently deleted.

FIGURE G-10: Create Folder dialog box

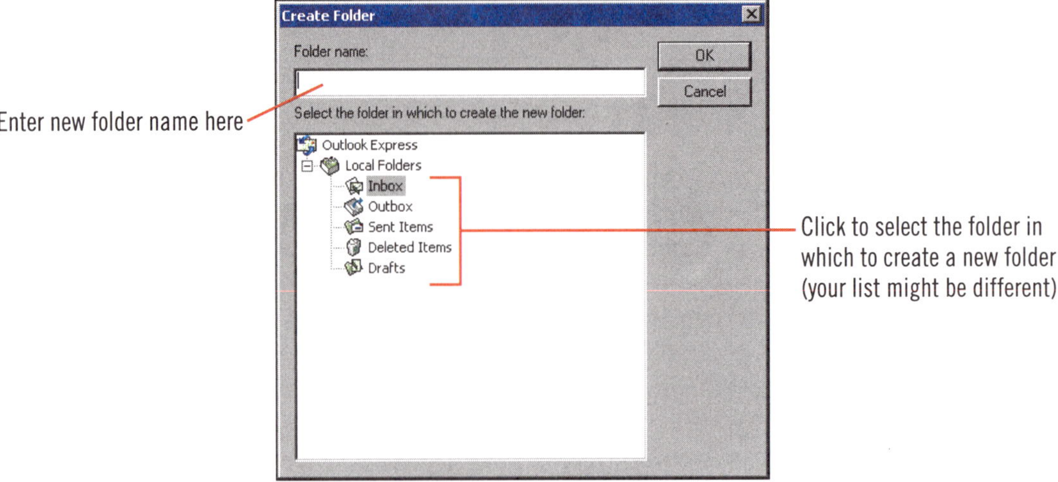

FIGURE G-11: Important folder

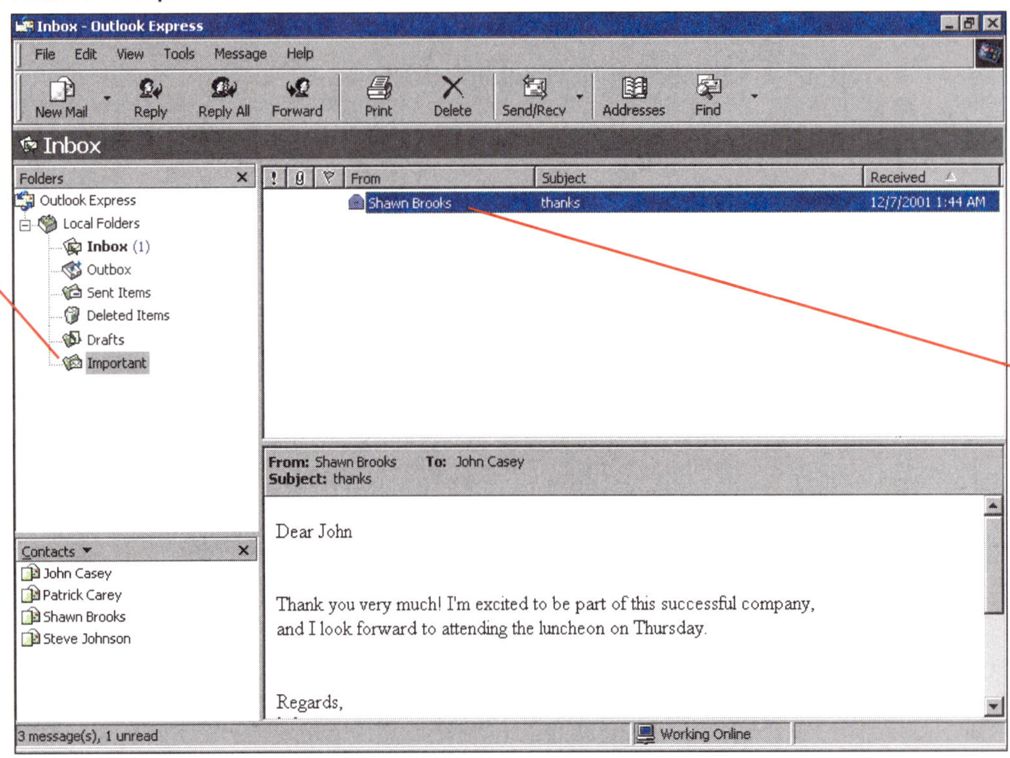

Diverting incoming e-mail to folders

Outlook Express can direct incoming messages that meet criteria to other folders in the Folders list rather than to your Inbox. Let's say that you have a friend who loves sending you funny e-mail, but you often don't have time to read it right away. You can set message rules to store any messages you receive from your friend in a different folder so they won't clutter your Inbox. When you are ready to read the messages, you simply open the folder and access the messages just as you would in the Inbox. To set criteria for incoming messages, click Tools on the menu bar, point to Message Rules, then click Mail. If the New Mail Rule dialog box opens, no previous message rules exist. Otherwise, the Message Rules dialog box opens; click New to create a new message rule. The New Mail Rule dialog box opens. Select the conditions for your rule, select the actions for your rule, click any undefined value (such as the e-mail address you want to divert and the folder where you want to store the diverted messages) and provide information, type a name to identify the rule, then click OK.

Selecting a News Server

A newsgroup is an electronic forum where people from around the world with a common interest can share ideas, ask and answer questions, and comment on and discuss any subject. You can find newsgroups on almost any topic, from the serious to the lighthearted, from educational to controversial, from business to social. Before you can participate in a newsgroup, you must select a news server. A **news server** is a computer located on the Internet where newsgroup messages, also called **articles**, on different topics are stored. Each news server contains several newsgroups from which to choose. The Internet Connection Wizard walks you through the process of selecting a news server. This wizard also appears the first time you use Outlook Express News. To complete the wizard and the steps in this lesson, you'll need to get the name of the news server you want to use from your instructor, technical support person, or Internet service provider (ISP), and possibly an account name and password. John wants to add a news server account so he can access coffee-related newsgroups.

Steps

Trouble?

If you do not already have a news server selected, the Internet Connection Wizard will open, and you should skip to Step 4 to complete the wizard. If you already have a news server, continue with the next step.

1. In the Folders list, click Outlook Express, then click the **Read News link** or click the **Set up a Newsgroups account link** in the Outlook Express Start Page

2. Click **Tools** on the menu bar, click **Accounts**, then click the **News tab**
   The Internet Accounts dialog box opens, as shown in Figure G-12, displaying the News tab with your list of available news servers. Using the Internet Accounts dialog box, you can add, remove, and view properties for news servers, mail servers, and directory services.

QuickTip

To add a new e-mail account, click Add, click Mail, then follow the Internet Connection Wizard instructions.

3. Click **Add**, then click **News**
   The Internet Connection Wizard dialog box opens.

4. Type your **name**, if necessary, then click **Next**
   The name you enter appears in messages you post to a newsgroup.

5. Type your **e-mail address**, if necessary, then click **Next**
   Individuals participating in the newsgroup need to know your e-mail address so they can reply to your news messages either by posting another news message or by sending you an e-mail message.

6. Type the **name of the news server** provided by your instructor, technical support person, or ISP, as shown in Figure G-13, then click **Next**

QuickTip

To change a news server name, right-click the news server in the Folders list, click Properties, type a name in the News Accounts text box, then click OK.

7. Click **Finish**, click **Close** if the Internet Accounts dialog box opens, then click **No** to download a list of available newsgroups
   The news server name appears in the Folders list, as shown in Figure G-14. You'll view a list of available newsgroups in the next lesson.

FIGURE G-12: Internet Accounts dialog box

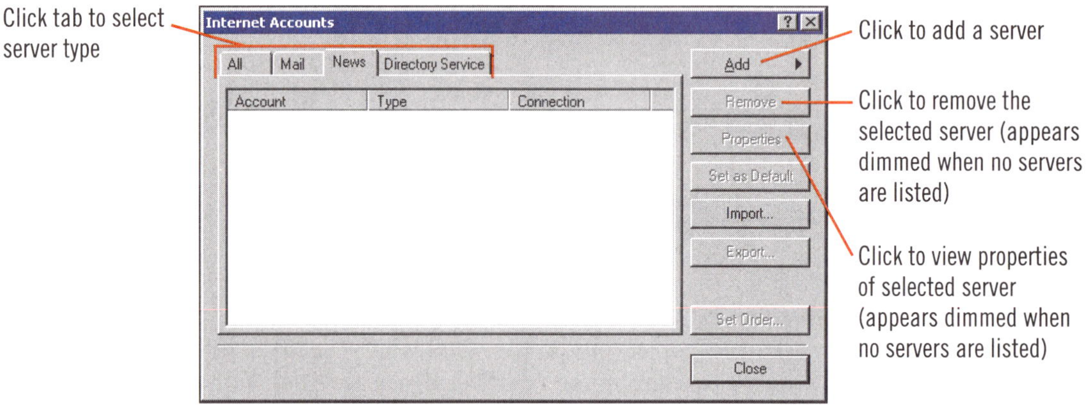

Click tab to select server type
Click to add a server
Click to remove the selected server (appears dimmed when no servers are listed)
Click to view properties of selected server (appears dimmed when no servers are listed)
Internet Accounts
All
Mail
News
Directory Service
Account
Type
Connection
Add
Remove
Properties
Set as Default
Import...
Export...
Set Order...
Close

FIGURE G-13: Internet Connection Wizard dialog box

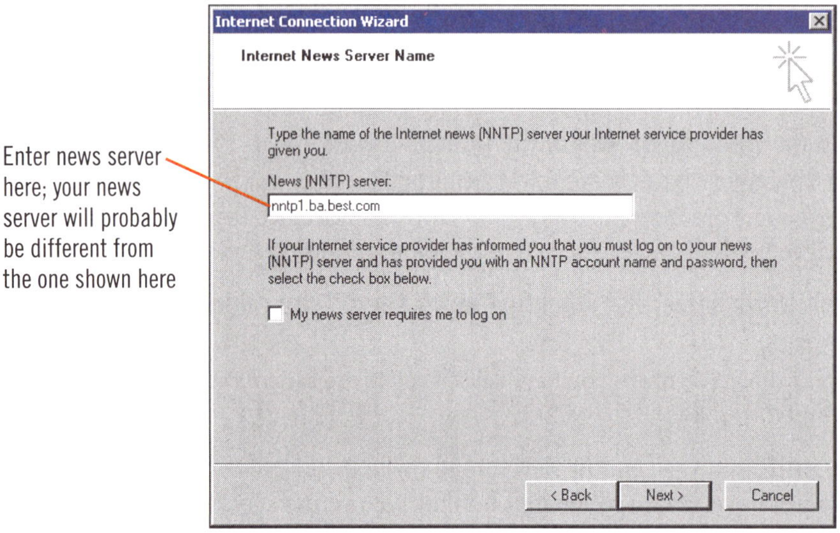

Enter news server here; your news server will probably be different from the one shown here
Internet Connection Wizard
Internet News Server Name
Type the name of the Internet news (NNTP) server your Internet service provider has given you.
News (NNTP) server:
nntp1.ba.best.com
If your Internet service provider has informed you that you must log on to your news (NNTP) server and has provided you with an NNTP account name and password, then select the check box below.
My news server requires me to log on
< Back
Next >
Cancel

FIGURE G-14: Outlook Express window with news server

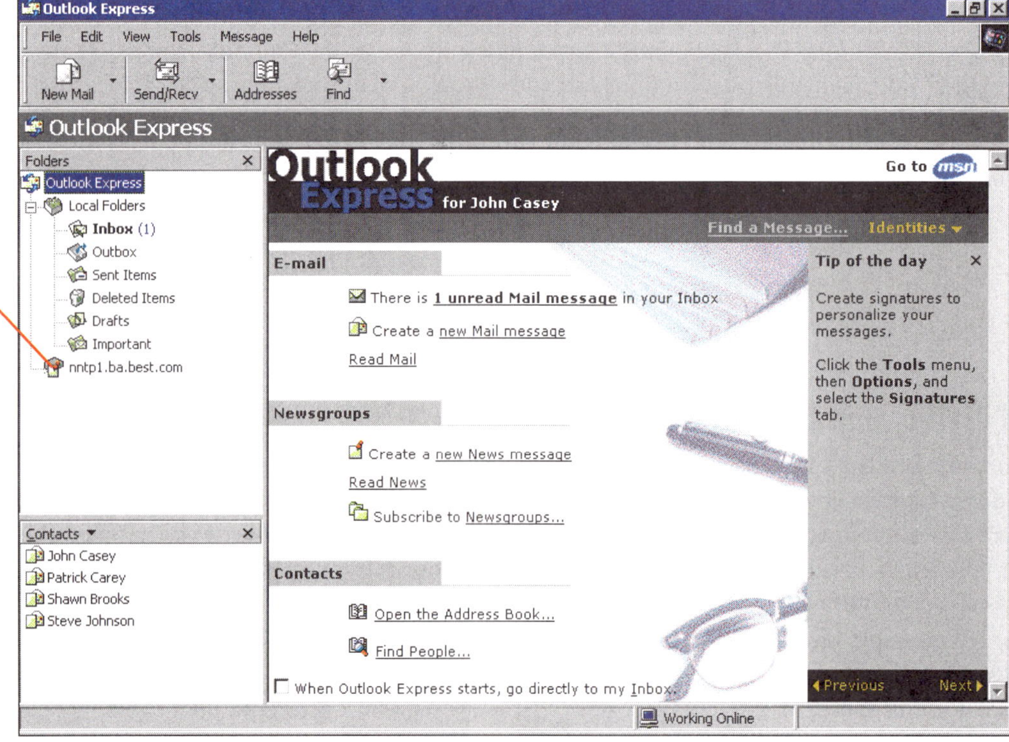

News server; your news server name might be different
Outlook Express
File Edit View Tools Message Help
New Mail
Send/Recv
Addresses
Find
Folders
Local Folders
Inbox (1)
Outbox
Sent Items
Deleted Items
Drafts
Important
nntp1.ba.best.com
Contacts
John Casey
Patrick Carey
Shawn Brooks
Steve Johnson
Outlook Express for John Casey
Go to msn
Find a Message...
Identities
E-mail
There is 1 unread Mail message in your Inbox
Create a new Mail message
Read Mail
Newsgroups
Create a new News message
Read News
Subscribe to Newsgroups...
Contacts
Open the Address Book...
Find People...
When Outlook Express starts, go directly to my Inbox.
Tip of the day
Create signatures to personalize your messages.
Click the Tools menu, then Options, and select the Signatures tab.
Previous
Next
Working Online

Windows 2000

Viewing and Subscribing to a Newsgroup

When you add a news server account to Outlook Express, it retrieves a list of newsgroups available on that server. Often this list is quite lengthy. Rather than scroll through the entire list looking for a particular topic, you can have Outlook Express search the list for that topic. Similarly, you can search a newsgroup for a particular message from all the messages you retrieve from a newsgroup. Once you select a newsgroup, you can merely view its contents, or, if you expect to come back to the newsgroup often, you can subscribe to it. Subscribing to a newsgroup places a link to the group in the news server folder in your Outlook Express Folders list, providing easy access to the newsgroup. John wants to find and subscribe to a newsgroup for coffee drinkers, so he can keep track of what people want from a coffee company.

1. **Click the Read News link in the Outlook Express Start Page, then click Yes if necessary, to view a list of available newsgroups**
   The Newsgroups dialog box opens, as shown in Figure G-15, displaying news servers on the left (if more than one exists) and related newsgroups on the right.
2. **In the News server list, click the news server you added in the previous lesson if necessary**
   A list of the newsgroups you have subscribed to appears in the preview pane. Your list might be empty.
3. **Type coffee in the Display Newsgroups which contain text box**
   Newsgroups related to coffee appear in the News groups list box, as shown in Figure G-16.
4. **Scroll if necessary, click the newsgroup rec.food.drink.coffee (if available), or click a different newsgroup from your list, then click Go To**
   The newsgroup name you have chosen appears selected in the Folders list and the newsgroup messages appear in the preview pane of the Outlook Express window, as shown in Figure G-17. John thinks this newsgroup looks promising, so he decides to subscribe to it.
5. **Right-click the newsgroup server in the Folders list, then click Subscribe**
   The number of newsgroup messages appears next to the newsgroup name in the Folders list. The icon next to the newsgroup changes from gray to color to indicate the subscription is complete.

QuickTip

To subscribe to a newsgroup, double-click it in the Newsgroup Subscriptions dialog box.

QuickTip

To download new newsgroup messages, click the newsgroup in the Folders list, then click Synchronize Account.

Filtering unwanted newsgroup messages

After you become familiar with a newsgroup, you might decide that you don't want to retrieve messages that are from a particular person, about a specific subject, of a certain length, or older than a certain number of days. This is called **filtering** newsgroup messages. To filter unwanted messages, click Tools on the menu bar, point to Message Rules, then click News. If the New News Rule dialog box opens, no previous message rules exist. Otherwise, the Message Rules dialog box opens; click New to create a new message rule. The New News Rule dialog box opens. Select the conditions for your rule, select the actions for your rule, click any undefined value (such as the e-mail address you want to divert and the folder where you want to store the unwanted messages) and provide the information, type a name for the rule, then click OK.

FIGURE G-15: Newsgroup dialog box

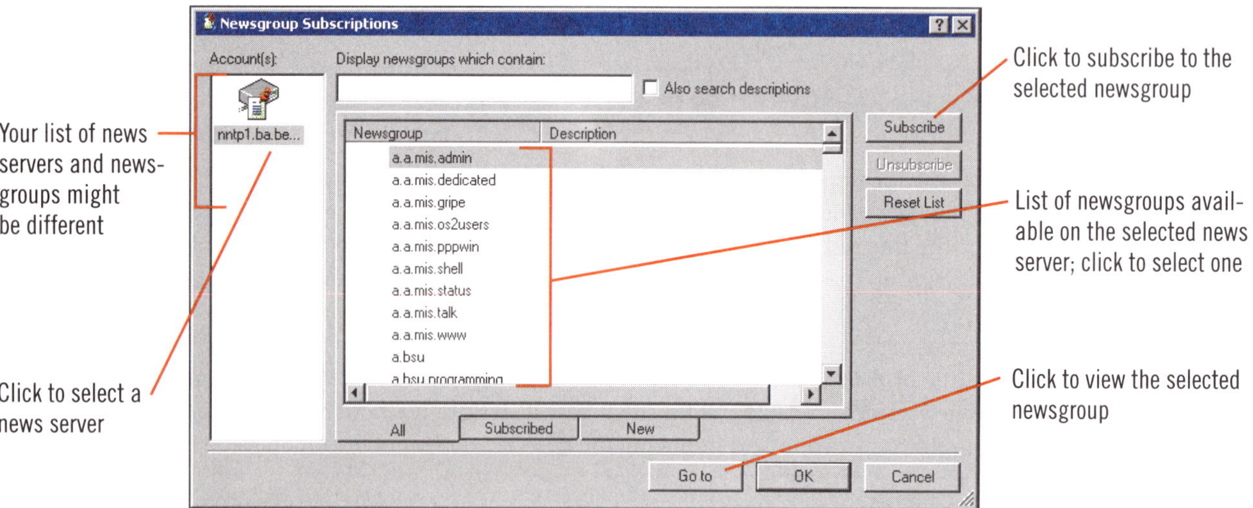

FIGURE G-16: List of newsgroups relating to coffee

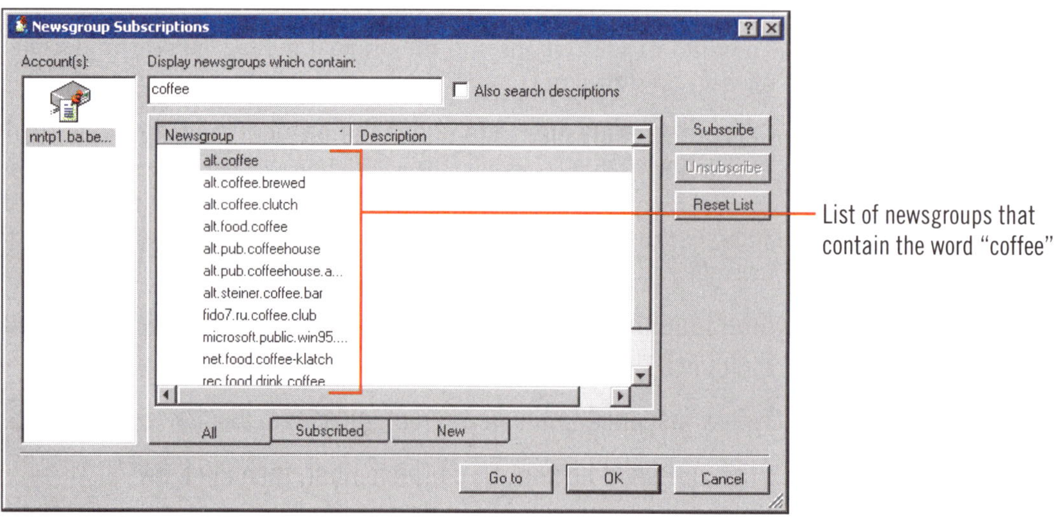

FIGURE G-17: Outlook Express window with a newsgroup

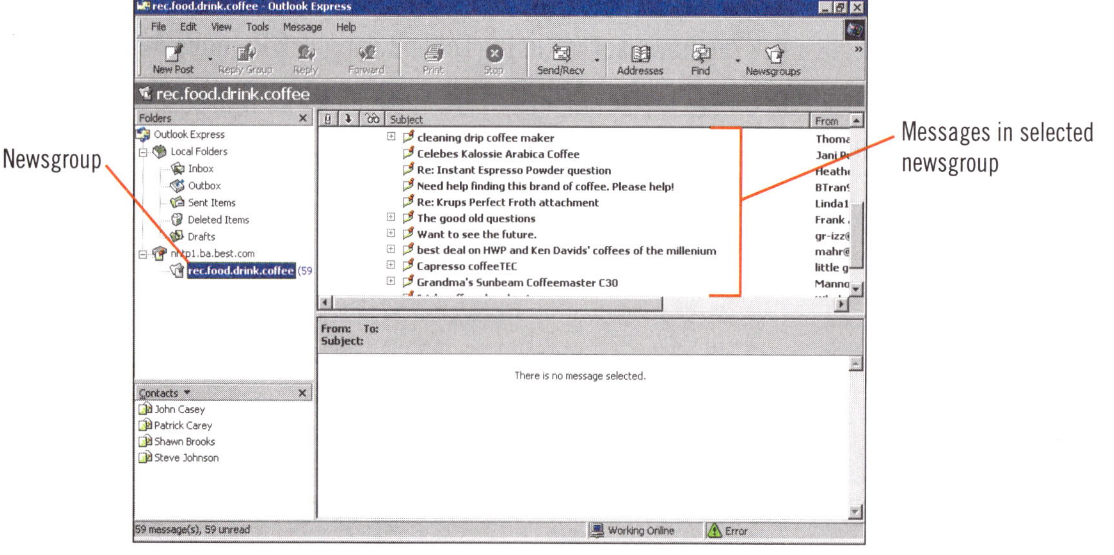

Windows 2000

Reading and Posting News Messages

After retrieving new newsgroup messages, you can read them. Newsgroup messages appear in the preview pane, just as e-mail messages do. To view a newsgroup message in the display pane, click the title of the message in the preview pane. If a plus sign (+) in a box appears to the left of a newsgroup message, then the message contains a conversation thread. A **conversation thread** consists of the original message on a particular topic along with any responses that include the original message. To read the responses, click the + to display the message titles, and then click the title of the message you want to read. John decides to read some of the messages in the newsgroup. When he is finished, he will restore his news server settings by unsubscribing from this newsgroup and removing the news server from the Folders list.

Steps

Trouble?

If a newsgroup message doesn't have a +, click a message without a +, then skip to Step 3.

QuickTip

To view only unread messages, click View on the menu bar, point to Current View, then click Hide Read Messages.

QuickTip

To watch a conversation of messages and replies, click a message in the thread, click Message on the menu bar, then click Watch Conversation.

1. Click a **newsgroup message** in the preview pane with a + to the left of the title, then read the message in the display pane
   The newsgroup message appears in the display pane.
2. Click the + next to the newsgroup message
   The titles of the responses to the original message appear under the original newsgroup message, as shown in Figure G-18.
3. Click **each reply message under the original message**, and read the reply
   As you read each message, you have the choice to compose a new message, send a reply message to everyone viewing the newsgroup (known as posting), send a reply message to the author's private e-mail address (rather than posting it on the newsgroup), or forward the message you are reading to another person.
4. After reading the last reply message, click the **Reply Group button** on the toolbar, then click the **Maximize button** if necessary
5. Type a response to the newsgroup message, as shown in Figure G-19
6. Click the **Send button** on the toolbar, then click **OK**
   Your reply message appears in the preview pane along with the other replies to the original message. Everyone viewing the newsgroup can download and read your response.
7. Right-click the **newsgroup** in the Folders list, click **Unsubcribe**, then click **OK** (if necessary, click No to subscribe to the Newsgroup and click No to view a list of the newsgroups)
8. Right-click the **news server** in the Folders list, click **Remove Account**, then click **Yes**
9. Click **File** on the menu bar, click **Exit**, then click **Yes** if necessary to disconnect from the Internet

FIGURE G-18: Reading a newsgroup message

Click + to display or – to hide replies to newsgroup messages
Click a message to display it in the display pane
Your list of messages might be different
Message selected in preview pane appears here

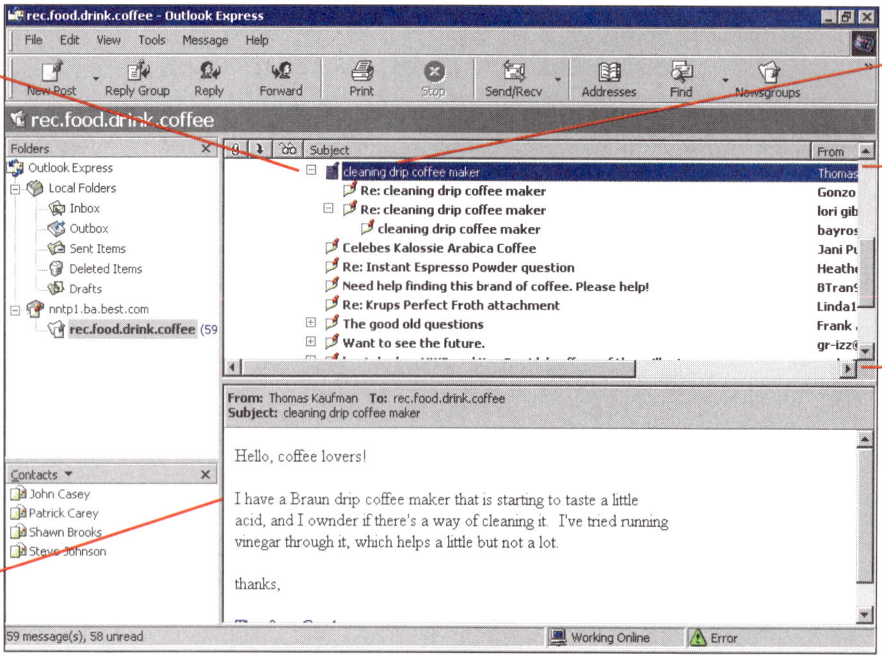

FIGURE G-19: Posting a newsgroup message

Click to post the message to the newsgroup
Type your reply to the message here
Your message will be different

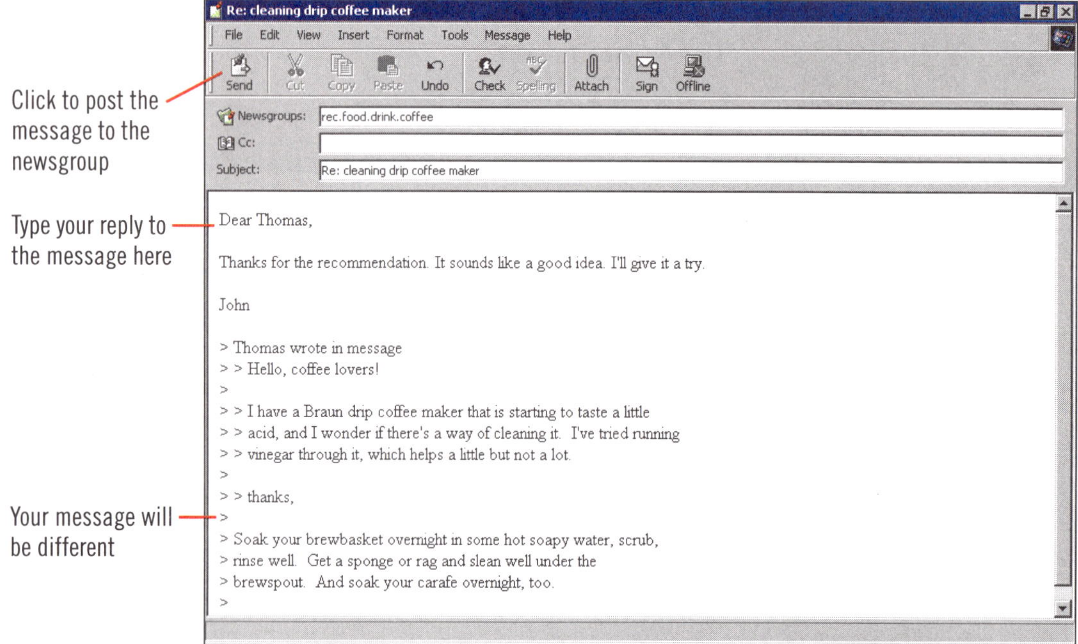

CLUES TO USE

Deleting old news messages

Newsgroup messages are stored on your hard drive, so you should delete messages you don't need to free up disk space. Outlook Express gives several cleanup options to help you optimize your hard drive space. You can delete entire messages (titles and bodies), compress messages, remove just the message bodies (leaving the title headers), or reset the information stored for selected messages, which allows you to refresh messages (download again). To clean up files on your local hard drive, select a news server in the Folders list, click Tools on the menu bar, click Options, then click the Maintenance tab. You can select any of the cleanup options to delete or compress news messages at a specified time or click Clean Up Now, then click the button for the cleanup option you want to perform now.

Practice

Concepts Review

Label each of the elements of the screen shown in Figure G-20.

FIGURE G-20

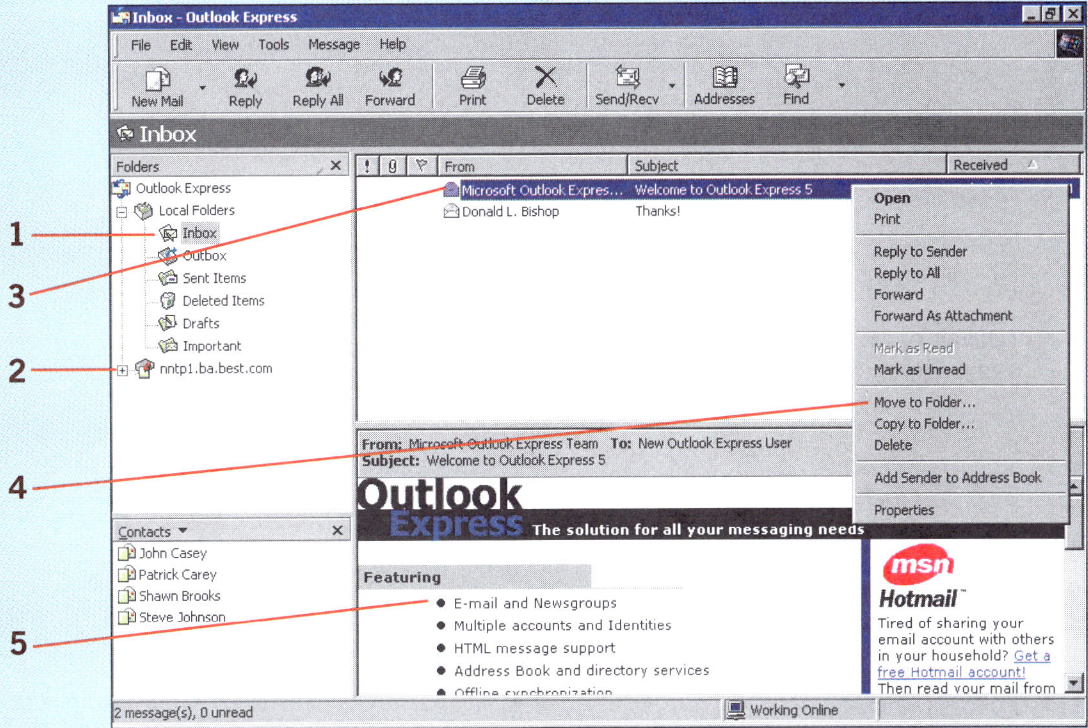

Match each of the terms with the statement that describes its function.

6. Message flag
7. Outlook Express Start Page
8. Message Rules
9. Outlook Express window
10. News server

a. A computer on the Internet where articles are stored
b. Displays e-mail and newsgroups
c. An icon that indicates e-mail to folders
d. Diverts selected incoming e-mail status
e. Jumps to folders and opens tools

Select the best answer from the list of choices.

11. The location that allows you to jump to folders and open tools is called the
    a. Outlook Express window.
    b. Outlook Express Start Page.
    c. Folders list.
    d. Outlook Express Link Page.
12. To compose a message, you can
    a. click the new Mail message link.
    b. click New Mail button on the toolbar.
    c. click Message on the menu bar, then click New Message.
    d. All of the above.

13. A contact is a
  - **a.** person you communicate with.
  - **b.** mailing address.
  - **c.** newsgroup.
  - **d.** program.

14. When you click the Send button on the toolbar in the New Message window, an e-mail message is sent first to the
  - **a.** e-mail address.
  - **b.** outbox.
  - **c.** Internet.
  - **d.** Cc and Bcc addresses.

15. [icon] indicates that the message has
  - **a.** not been read.
  - **b.** been read.
  - **c.** one or more files attached to it.
  - **d.** been marked as low priority by the sender.

Skills Review

1. Start Outlook Express and explore the Outlook Express window.
  - **a.** Connect to the Internet.
  - **b.** Click the Launch Outlook Express button on the Quick Launch toolbar.
  - **c.** Identify the title bar, menu bar, toolbar, Internet Explorer link, Folders list, Read Mail link, Read News link, new Mail message link, Open the Address Book link, Find People link, and status bar.
  - **d.** On the toolbar, identify icons for opening the Address Book, sending and receiving e-mail messages, composing a message, and finding a message.
  - **e.** If necessary, enter your user name and password, then click Connect.

2. Add a contact to the Address Book.
  - **a.** Click the Address Book button.
  - **b.** Click the New button, then click New Contact.
  - **c.** Type **John** in the First name text box, press [Tab] twice, then type **Asher**
  - **d.** Click in the E-Mail Addresses text box, then type **JohnA@course.com**
  - **e.** Click Add, then click OK.
  - **f.** Click the Close button.

3. Compose and send e-mail.
  - **a.** Click the New Mail button, then click the Maximize button if necessary.
  - **b.** Click the To button.
  - **c.** Click the name John Asher.
  - **d.** Click To, then click OK.
  - **e.** Click the Subject text box, then type **Financial Update Request**
  - **f.** Press [Tab] to move to the message window, then type **John: Please send 2001 year-end financial report ASAP. Thanks**.
  - **g.** Click the Send button.

4. Retrieve, read, and respond to e-mail.
  - **a.** Click the Send/Recv button. It may take a few minutes before you receive a message from John Asher.
  - **b.** In the Folders list, click Inbox.
  - **c.** Click the message you just received from John Asher.

d. Click the Forward Message button, then click the Maximize button if necessary.
e. Click the To text box, then enter your e-mail address.
f. Enter a response in the message window.
g. Click the Send button.

5. Manage e-mail messages.

a. Click File on the menu bar, point to New, then click Folder.
b. Type **Archive**.
c. Click Local Folders in the Folders list, then click OK.
d. Right-click the message received from John Asher, then click Move To Folder on the shortcut menu.
e. Click Archive, then click OK.
f. In the Folders list, click the Archive folder.
g. Right-click the message received from John Asher, then click Delete on the shortcut menu.
h. Right-click the Archive folder, click Delete, then click Yes.
i. Click the Address Book button.
j. Click John Asher, click the Delete button, then click Yes.
k. Click the Close button.

6. Select a news server.

a. In the Folders list, click Outlook Express.
b. Click the Read News link or the Set up a Newsgroup account link.
c. If the Internet Connection Wizard appears, skip to Step e. Otherwise, click Tools on the menu bar, click Accounts, then click News tab.
d. Click Add, then click News.
e. Type your name, then click Next.
f. Type your e-mail address, then click Next.
g. Type the name of a news server (see your instructor, technical support person, or ISP for a name), then click Next.
h. Click Finish, click Close (if necessary), then click No.

7. View and subscribe to a newsgroup.

a. Click the Read News link, then click Yes if necessary.
b. In the News server list, click the news server you just added (if available).
c. Type **caffeine** (If no items appear, type **tea** or **chocolate**.)
d. Click a newsgroup.
e. Click Go To.
f. Right click the newsgroup in the Folders list, then click Subscribe.

8. Read and post a news message.

a. Click a newsgroup message with a +.
b. Click the + next to the newsgroup message.
c. Click each reply and read it.
d. Click the Reply Group button, then type a response.
e. Click the Send button, then click OK.
f. Right-click the newsgroup in the Folders list, click Unsubscribe, then click OK.
g. Right-click the news server in the Folders list, click Remove Account, then click Yes.
h. Click File on the menu bar, click Exit, then click Yes if necessary to disconnect.

Independent Challenges

1. You are a new lawyer at Bellig & Associates. You have a computer with Windows 2000 and Outlook Express. Because email is an important method of communication at the law firm, you want to start Outlook Express, open the Address Book, and enter colleagues' e-mail addresses.

To complete this independent challenge:

- **a.** Start Outlook Express, then open the Address Book.
- **b.** Enter the following names and e-mail addresses:

  Greg Bellig **gregb@bellig_law.com**
  Jacob Bellig **jacobb@bellig_law.com**
  Jarod Higgins **jarodh@bellig_law.com**
- **c.** Print the Address Book in both the Business Card and Memo styles.
- **d.** Delete the names and e-mail addresses you just entered in the Address Book.

2. As president of Auto Metals, you have just negotiated a deal to export metal auto parts to an assembly plant in China. Your lawyer, Josh Higgins, has drawn up a preliminary contract. You want to send Josh an e-mail indicating the terms of the deal so he can finish the contract. When Josh responds, move the e-mail into the Legal folder. (*Note*: If you do not have a connection to the Internet, ask your instructor or technical support person for help completing this challenge.)

To complete this independent challenge:

- **a.** Open a New Message window using the stationery called Technical.
- **b.** Type **jhiggins@course.com** in the To text box in the message window and **China Deal Contract** in the Subject text box.
- **c.** Enter the following message:

  Dear Josh,
  I have completed the negotiations with the assembly plant. Please modify the following terms in the contract:
  1. All parts shall be inspected before shipping.
  2. Ship 10,000 units a month for 3 years with an option for 2 more years.
  Sincerely yours,
  [your name here]
- **d.** Send the e-mail.
- **e.** Print the e-mail you receive from Josh Higgins.
- **f.** Create a new folder called *Legal*, then move the e-mail message you received from Josh Higgins to the new folder.
- **g.** Delete the Legal folder.

3. You are a legal assistant at a law firm specializing in international law. Your boss has asked you to research international contracts with China. You decide to start your research with newsgroups on the Internet.

To complete this independent challenge:

- **a.** Select a news server (see your instructor, technical support person, or ISP to provide you with a news server).
- **b.** Subscribe to a newsgroup about China, then read several newsgroup messages and replies.
- **c.** Reply to a message, then post a new message.
- **d.** Print the newsgroup messages including the original message and replies.
- **e.** Unsubscribe to the newsgroup, then remove the newsgroup server.

4. You like to play sports, watch sports, read about sports, and talk about sports all the time, so you decide to join a sports newsgroup.

To complete this independent challenge:

- **a.** Select a news server (see your instructor, technical support person, or ISP to provide you with a news server).
- **b.** Subscribe to a newsgroup about sports, then read several newsgroup messages and replies.
- **c.** Reply to a message, then post a new message.
- **d.** Print the newsgroup messages including the original message and replies.
- **e.** Unsubscribe to the newsgroup, then remove the newsgroup server.

▶ Visual Workshop

Re-create the screen shown in Figure G-21, which displays the Outlook Express window with a message that has been sent. Print the Outlook Express window. (To print the screen, press the Print Screen key, open Paint, click File on the menu bar, click Paste to paste the screen into Paint, then click Yes to paste the large image if necessary. Click File on the menu bar, click Print, then click Print in the Print dialog box.)

FIGURE G-21

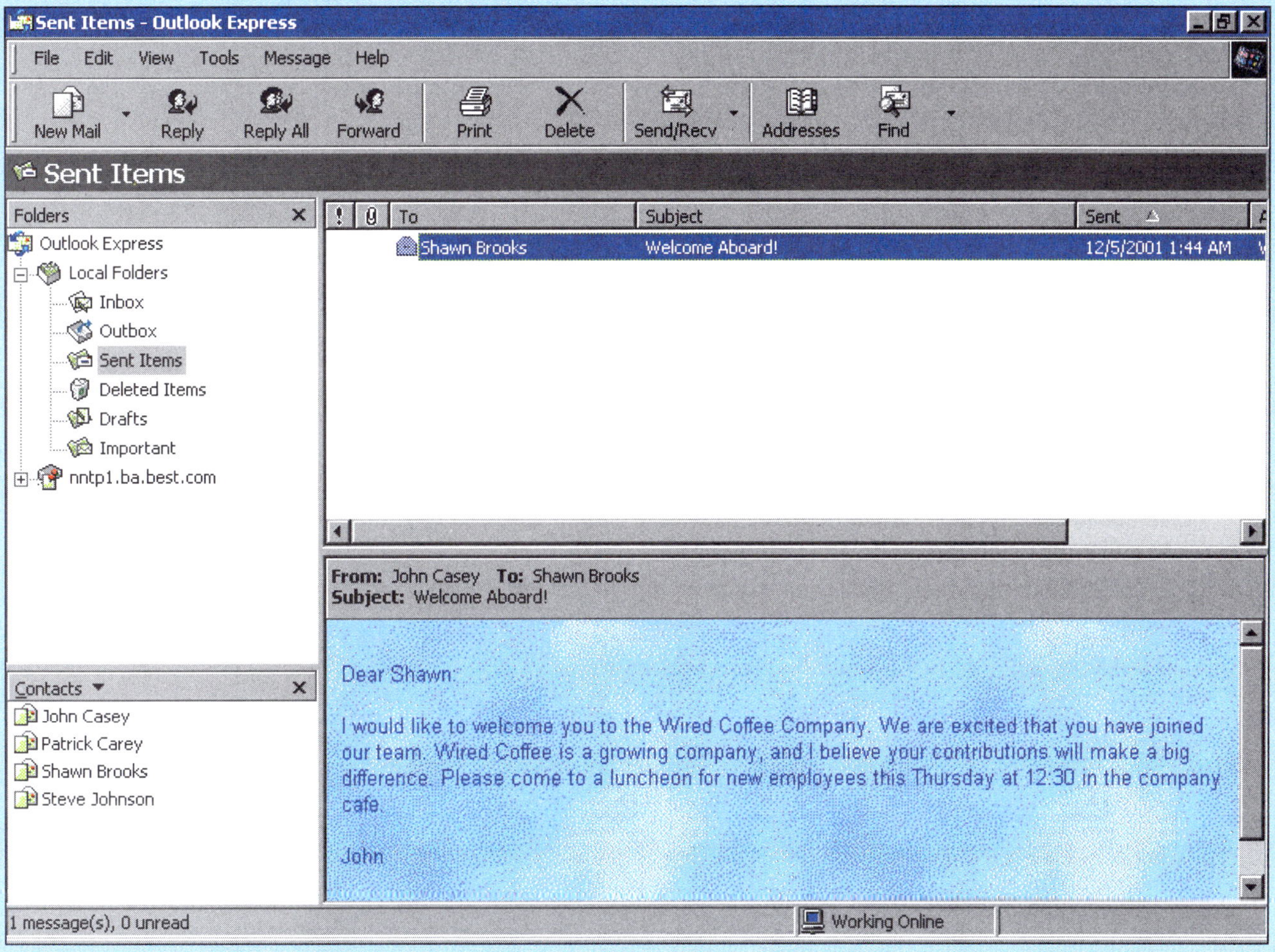

Windows 2000

Managing Shared Files Using My Network Places

Objectives

- Understand network services
- Examine network computer properties
- Open and view My Network Places
- Create a shared folder
- Map a network drive
- Copy and move shared files
- Open and edit a shared file
- Disconnect a network drive

Windows 2000 includes My Network Places, a powerful tool for managing files and folders across a network. A **network** is a system of two or more computers connected together to share resources. **My Network Places** is integrated with Windows Explorer, allowing you to view the entire network and share files and folders with people from other parts of the network. If you are not connected to a network, you will not be able to actually work the steps in this unit. However, you can read the lessons without completing the steps to learn what is possible in a network environment. In this unit, John will use My Network Places to manage files and folders that will be used by multiple users on the Wired Coffee network.

Understanding Network Services

Windows 2000 is a secure, reliable network operating system that allows people using many different computers to share programs, files, folders, and printers that are stored on computers other than their own. A single computer, called a **server**, can be designated to store these resources. Other computers on the network, called **clients** or **workstations**, can access the resources on the server instead of having to store them. You can share resources using two or more client computers, or you can designate one computer to serve specifically as the server. Windows 2000 provides software specifically designed for a server or a client computer. See Table H-1 for a description of the different Windows 2000 versions. If the network computers are close together, the network is called a **local area network**, or **LAN**. If the computers are spread out over a wider area, the network is called a **wide area network**, or **WAN**. **File sharing** allows many people to work on the same files without the need for creating or storing multiple copies. In this unit, you will integrate the essential Windows file management skills you have already acquired with the specific methods required to take full advantage of Windows networking capabilities. John realizes there are many benefits to using the Wired Coffee network to manage files and folders.

Share central resources through client/server networking

Windows 2000 provides the option of using a setup called **client/server networking**. Under this arrangement, a single computer is designated as a server, allowing access to resources for any qualified user. Client/server networking provides all users on a network a central location for accessing shared files. Figure H-1 shows an example of a typical network configuration.

Share resources through peer-to-peer networking

The Windows 2000 network operating system also offers a network configuration called peer-to-peer networking. **Peer-to-peer networking** enables two or more computers to link together without designating a central server. In this configuration, any computer user can access resources stored on any other computer, as long as those resources aren't restricted. Peer-to-peer networking allows individual computer users to share files and other resources, such as a printer, with other users on the network. Using peer-to-peer networking, you can transfer files from one computer directly to another without having to access a server.

Share resources through network and dial-up connections

Windows 2000 provides connectivity between your computer and a network, another computer, or the Internet using Network and Dial-up Connections. **Network and Dial-up Connections** enables you to access network resources, whether you are physically connected using a direct cable or remotely connected using a modem. You can connect securely to a network over the Internet using a **Virtual Private Network** connection. You can also connect your computer to another computer or network by having another computer call your computer. For example, you can enable your office computer to be accessed by your home computer.

Grant permission to share designated files and folders on your computer with other users

Windows 2000 provides support for security, so that even though your computer is connected to a network, you can designate which resources on your computer you want to share with others on the network. Before being able to take advantage of any resources on your computer, other users must be granted the required permission.

Map drives on your computer to automatically connect to resources of another client or server

If you have rights to share resources on another computer, Windows 2000 includes a method for connecting automatically to the other computer. You can add a drive letter to your computer that is automatically linked to the shared folder on the other computer every time you log on.

FIGURE H-1: A typical client/server network

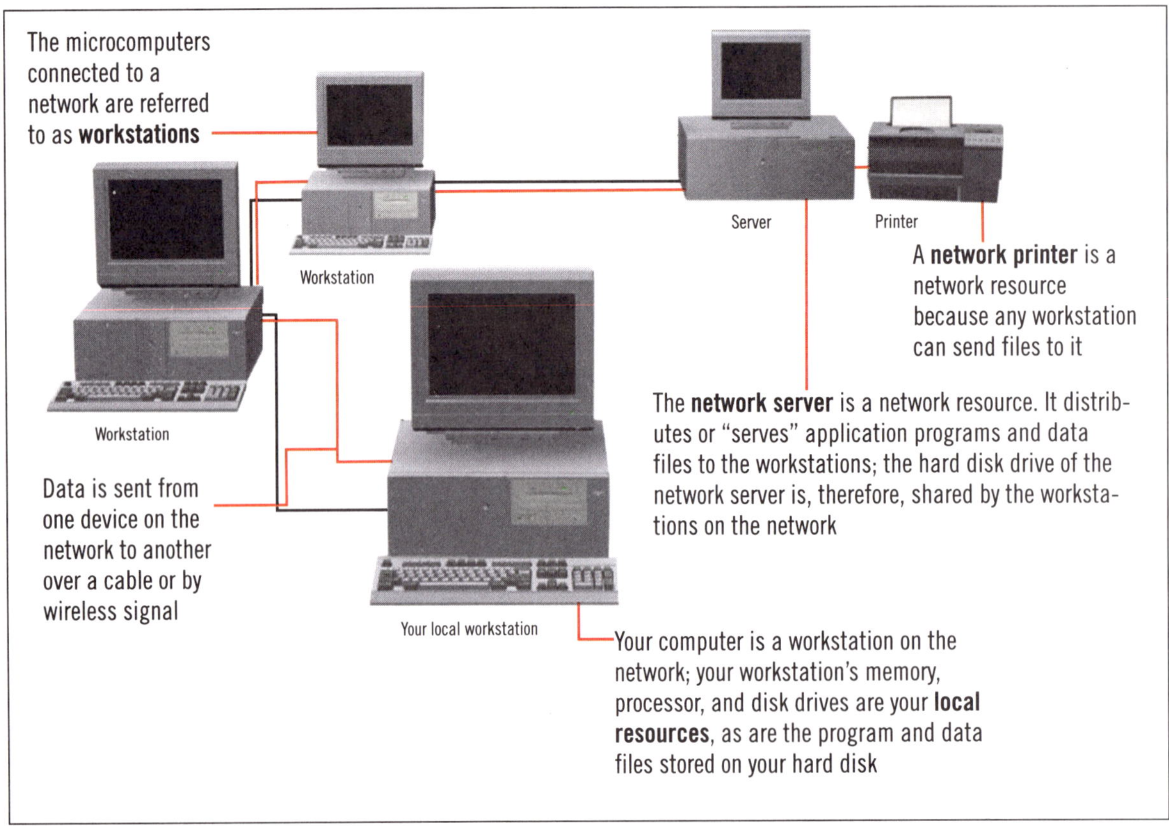

TABLE H-1: Windows 2000 versions

Windows 2000 version	description
Professional	A client computer for a client/server network or a peer-to-peer network; successor to Windows NT Workstation 4.0
Server	A standard server computer to perform file, print, application, Web, and communications services; successor to Windows NT Server 4.0
Advanced Server	A server computer for large networks to handle more database-intensive work as well as standard file, print, application, Web, and communication services; successor to Windows NT Server 4.0, Enterprise Edition
Datacenter Server	A server computer for large networks to handle large data storage, ISPs, online transaction processing, and large-scale science and engineering simulations

File permission properties

Every file in the Windows 2000 file system includes **permissions** for each user, or settings that designate what each user can and cannot do to each file. Two basic types of file permissions are available for users: read and full. **Read permission** allows the user to open and view the file, but not to make changes that can be saved to the file. When you open a read-only file, the words "Read Only" appear in the title bar. You can makes changes to the file, but an error message appears when you try to save it. You can save the file with a new name in a different location (one you have full access to). **Full permission** allows the user to edit and save changes to the file (or "write") and execute programs on server or client computers. Qualified users or system administrators use file permissions and passwords to control who has access to any specific area of the network. In this way, the network remains secure against unauthorized use.

Windows 2000

Examining Network Computer Properties

Computers are identified on networks by names and locations. The computer's name refers to the individual machine, whereas the computer's location refers to how the machine is grouped together with other computers. In a peer-to-peer network, individual computers are often organized into workgroups. A **workgroup** is a group of computers that performs common tasks or belongs to users who share common duties and interests. In a client/server network, individual computers are often grouped into domains. A **domain** is a collection of computers that the person managing the network creates to group computers that are used for the same tasks together and to simplify the set up and maintenance of the network. The difference between a domain and a workgroup is that the network administrator defines the domains that exist on the network and controls access to computers with those domains. In a workgroup, each user determines who has access to his or her computer. Computers anywhere on the network can be located easily through the naming hierarchy and can be addressed individually by name. You can find out the name and workgroup or domain of a computer on the network by examining the network computer properties. John decides to check the properties of his network computer.

Steps 1 2 3 4

QuickTip

To view the current status of the local area connection, double-click the Local Area Connection icon in the Network and Dial-up Connections window.

QuickTip

To examine network properties for your computer, you can also right-click the My Computer icon, click properties, then click the Network Identification tab.

1. Right-click the **My Network Places icon** on the desktop, click **Properties**, then click the **Maximize button** if necessary

   The Network and Dial-up Connections window opens, as shown in Figure H-2, and displays an icon to make a new network connection and an icon to connect to for the local area connection. When you start your computer and log on to the network, Windows 2000 automatically detects your local area network and creates a connection (unless you have previously disconnected your local area connection).

2. Click the **Network Identification link**

   The System Properties dialog box for your network computer opens with the Network Identification tab in front, as shown in Figure H-3. In Figure H-3, the network computer name appears at the top of the tab. The domain or workgroup name appears below the network computer name. In this case, the network computer name is JOHNCASEY and the domain name is NETONE.

3. Click **Properties**

   The Identification Changes dialog box opens. In the Properties dialog box, you can change the computer name and domain or workgroup name.

4. Click **Cancel**

   The Identification Changes dialog box closes.

5. Click **OK** to close the System Properties dialog box

6. Click the **Close button** in the Network and Dial-up Connections window

FIGURE H-2: Network and Dial-up Connections window

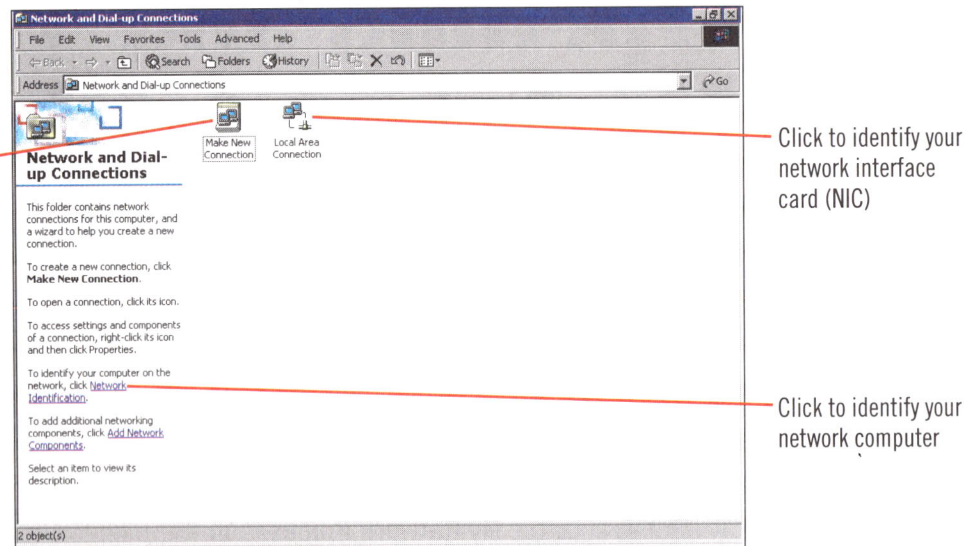

FIGURE H-3: Network Identification tab of System Properties dialog box

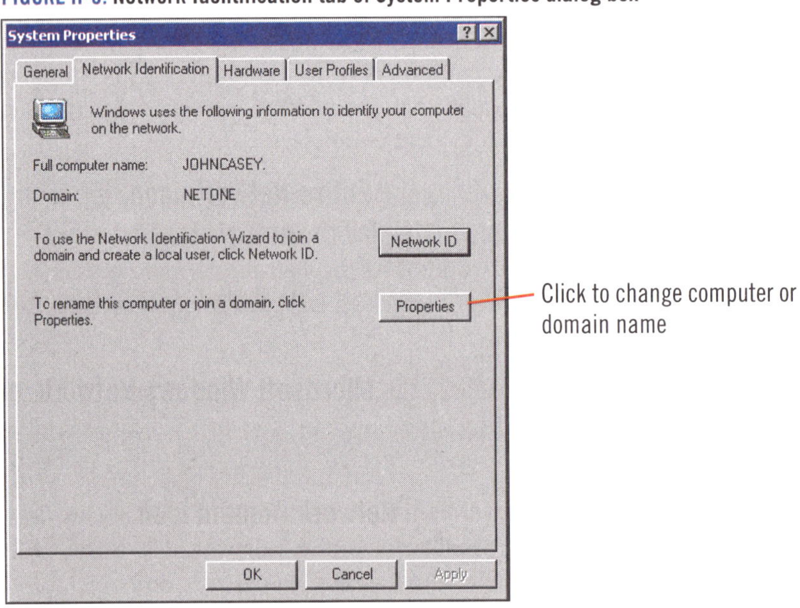

Viewing network properties

A computer that uses a Windows 2000 network must be configured so that other machines on the network recognize it. On a small network, you might be responsible for configuring your computer or that responsibility might fall to the network administrator. You can view and modify some of the network settings for your computer using the Network and Dial-up Connections dialog box. Right-click the My Network Places icon, click Properties, click Advanced on the menu bar, then click Advanced Settings. The network configuration consists of four components: adapter, protocol, service, and binding. The **adapter** is a device that connects your computer to the network. Adapters are usually cards, called **network interface cards**, or **NICs**, inserted into a slot in the back of your computer. To display the name of your NIC, click the Local Area Connection icon in the Network and Dial-up Connections window. The **protocol** is the language that the computer uses to communicate with other computers on the network. The **service** allows you to share your computer resources, such as files and printers, with other networked computers. A **binding** is a connection that enables communications among the adapters, protocols, and services installed in Windows 2000. Understanding which components have been installed on your computer helps you understand the capabilities and limitations of your computer on the network.

Windows 2000

Opening and Viewing My Network Places

The key to managing files and folders in a network environment is understanding the structure of your particular network. Most networks are comprised of multiple types of computers and operating systems. My Network Places lets you view the entire network or just your part of the network at a glance. The My Network Places window gives you access to the servers, domains, and workgroups on the network. From the My Network Places window, you can open the Entire Network window. The Entire Network window allows you to view a list of servers not in your workgroup and to view other network domains. If you want to add a server to your workgroup, you can use the Add Network Place wizard to help you through the process. John uses My Network Places to see where his computer fits in with all the others on his network.

QuickTip

To search for a computer on the network, double-click the My Network Places icon, click Search on the toolbar, type the name of the computer you want to find, then click Search Now.

1. Double-click the **My Network Places icon**, then click the **Maximize button** if necessary
   The icon is usually located right below the My Computer icon on the desktop. The My Network Places window opens, as shown in Figure H-4, and displays icons for all of the networked computers in John's immediate network, an icon for the Entire Network, and an icon to add a network to My Network Places. John's immediate network is currently running server and client computers.
2. Double-click the **Entire Network icon**, then click the **entire contents link** in the left pane to display the entire network
   My Network Places displays the various types of networks connected to John's computer. If you are on a large network, you might have other choices that will display more segments of the network.

QuickTip

To search for computers in the same workgroup, click Computers Near Me.

3. Double-click the **Microsoft Windows Network icon**
   The Microsoft Windows Network window displays the computer network domains and workgroups connected to John's computer, as shown in Figure H-5.
4. Double-click a **Network Domain icon** in your immediate network
   The My Network Places window displays the individual computers (including one for John) associated with the selected network domain.

QuickTip

My Network Places automatically keeps track of all your favorite folders on the local network. The first time you open a file on your network, a shortcut to its folder appears in My Network Places for easy access next time.

5. Double-click a **Network Computer icon** in your immediate network
   The computer connected to your network opens and displays the contents of the drive or folder.
6. Click the **Back button list arrow** Back on the toolbar, then click **My Network Places**
   The My Network Places window again displays the active computers in John's immediate network.

FIGURE H-4: My Network Places window

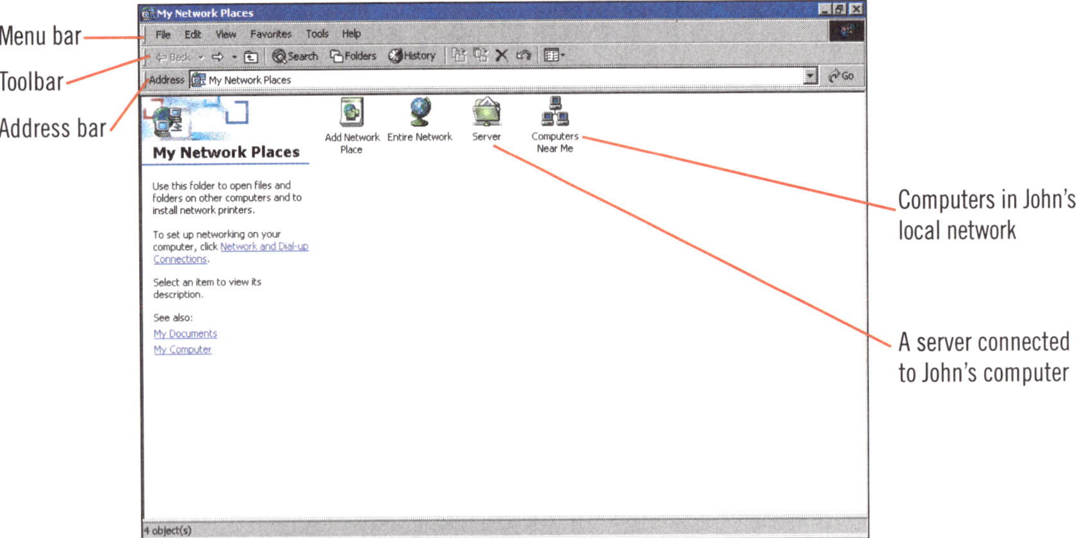

FIGURE H-5: Microsoft Windows Network window

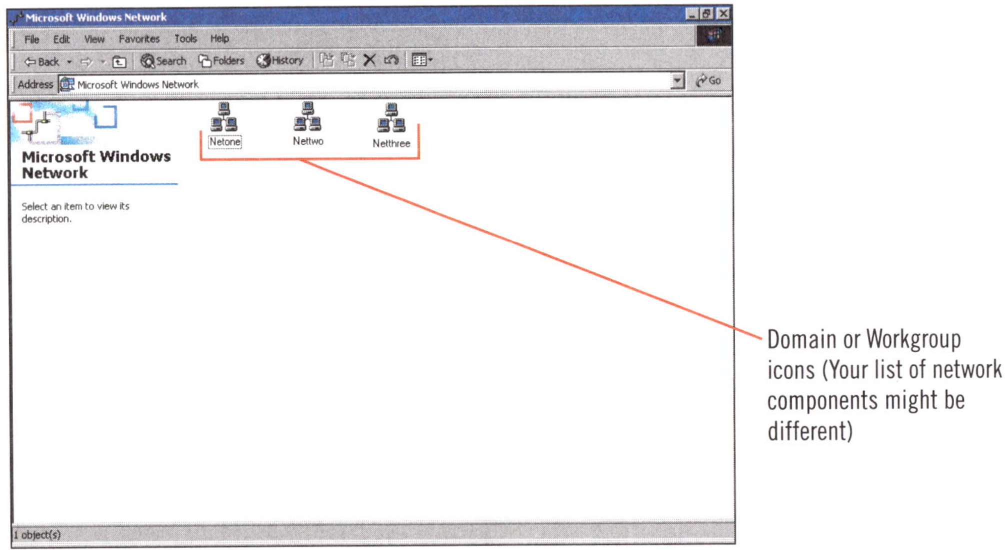

CLUES TO USE

Searching for network services

Search Assistant makes it easier to search for files or folders, printers, people, and other computers on your network. Search Assistant has an indexing service that maintains an index of all the files on your computer, making searches even faster. To search for computers on your network using the Search Assistant, double-click the My Network Places icon on the desktop, click Search on the toolbar, type the computer name you want to find, then click Search Now. If you want to find files or folders, people, or information on the Internet, you can click a search option link below the Search Now button. You can also use the Search Assistant to search Active Directory for network services, such as a printer that prints in color and is located near your computer, a group of users managed by a particular individual, or a shared folder to which a unique keyword has been assigned. **Active Directory** catalogs information about all the objects on a network, including people, computers, shared folders, and printers, and distributes that information to all the computers throughout your network. Before you can use Active Directory, the feature must be installed on your network server and tailored for your organization. To perform a search using Active Directory, double-click the My Network Places icon, double-click the Entire Network icon, click the entire contents link in the left pane, double-click Directory, right-click a directory object, and then click Find.

Creating a Shared Folder

A folder on your computer can be shared with others on the network. When you share a folder, you can decide the permissions that others will be allowed or denied when they access the files in that folder over the network. To create a shared folder in My Network Places, you use many of the file management skills you learned with Windows Explorer. You must first decide where you will put the new folder. John has decided to create a shared folder called Sales on his computer that will allow employees from anywhere on the network to add information to Sales files. If you are working at your own computer, you might create this shared folder in a subfolder within your My Documents folder. Otherwise, you may have to ask your instructor or technical support person for permission to create a folder in another location, or you can simply read through the steps without actually creating a folder.

1. Click the **Address list arrow** on the Address bar

   My Network Places displays the desktop and drives of your own computer. You can now work with the files and folders from your computer and still have the option of connecting to various other parts of the network.

2. Click the **My Documents folder**

   My Network Places displays the contents of the My Documents folder on your hard drive.

3. Right-click anywhere in the My Documents window (except on a file or folder), point to **New**, then click **Folder**

   A new folder, named New Folder, appears in the window.

4. Type **Sales**, then press **[Enter]**

   The folder is now named Sales.

5. Click **File** on the menu bar, then click **Sharing**

   The Sales Properties dialog box opens. The Sales Properties dialog box is where you adjust the settings to allow other users access to the files in your shared folder. The Sharing tab allows you to designate the kind of access you want other users to have for the folder you just created.

6. Click the **Share this folder option button**

   The sharing information about the Sales folder is shown in Figure H-6. This tab includes a text box for entering the shared name of the folder. Unless you have a very good reason for naming it differently, it's best to make the shared name the same as the folder name. Keeping the names consistent will help avoid confusion. By default, Windows automatically enters the name of the folder as the shared name.

7. Click **Permissions**

   The Permissions for Sales dialog box opens. By default, Windows automatically sets the file permission to Full Control, Change, and Read.

8. Click **OK**

9. Click **OK** to close the Properties window

   The Sales folder, shown in Figure H-7, is now accessible by anyone with the right permission from anywhere on the network. A Shared Folder icon appears with a hand underneath the folder.

FIGURE H-6: Sharing tab of Sales Properties dialog box

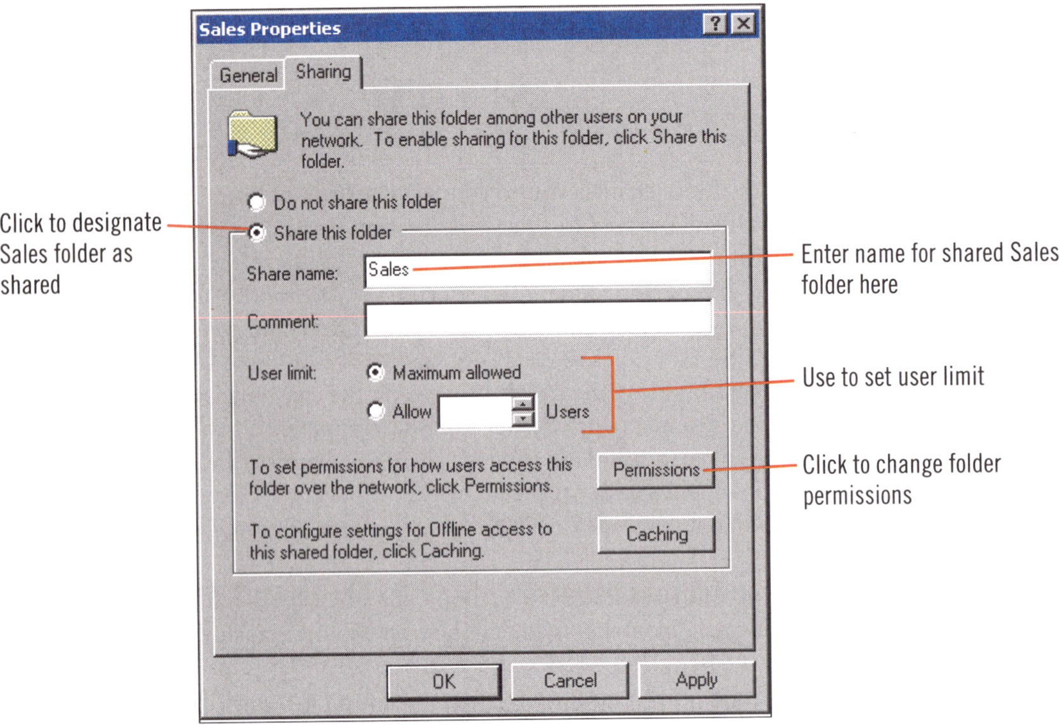

FIGURE H-7: Shared folder within My Documents folder

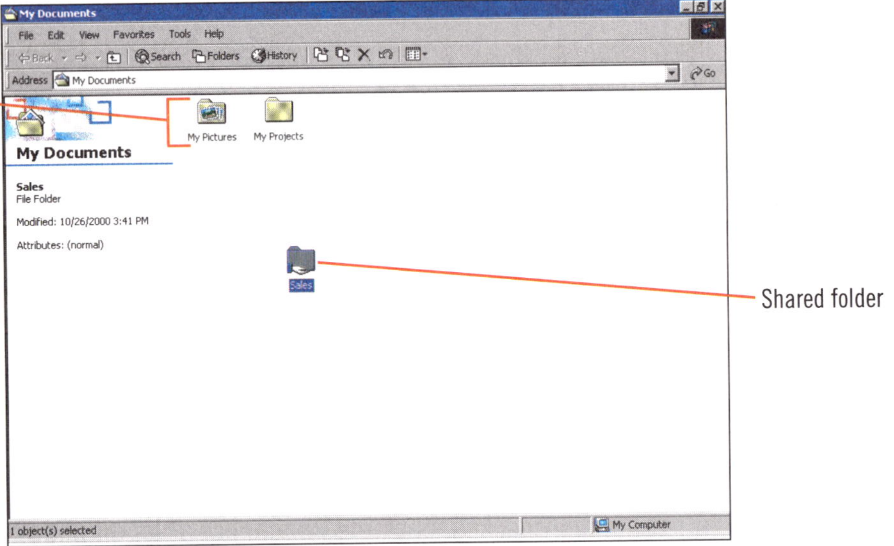

Password protection

With Windows 2000, you can use passwords to control access to your computer, the network, and specific files and folders. You can set different passwords and varying degrees of access for the different drives, folders, and files. You can also manage your files and printers from a remote computer and set password protection to limit access. To set or change password protection in Windows 2000 Professional, open the Control Panel and double-click the Users and Passwords icon, click the Users tab, click a user name, click Set Password, and then enter a new password. To change a user name and access privileges, click a user name, click Properties, click the General or Group Membership tab, then specify the changes you want. You can also use the Display utility to password protect files when in screen saver mode.

Windows 2000

Mapping a Network Drive

My Network Places enables you to connect your computer to other computers on the network quite easily. If you connect to a network location frequently, you might want to designate a drive letter on your computer as a direct connection to a shared drive or folder on another computer. Instead of spending unnecessary time opening My Network Places and the shared drive or folder each time you want to access it, you can create a direct connection, called **mapping** a drive, to the network location for quick and easy access. At John's request, the network administrator created a shared folder called Wired Coffee on the computer named Server. Next John uses My Network Places to map a drive letter from his computer to that folder so that he can easily move files to this central location for others to share. To complete these steps, you need to map to a network computer and a folder specified by your instructor or technical support person. If you don't have a networked computer available, read the steps without completing them.

1. Click the **Address list arrow**, then click **My Network Places**
   My Network Places shows you all the active computers in your immediate network.

2. Click **Tools** on the menu bar, then click **Map Network Drive**
   The Map Network Drive dialog box opens, as shown in Figure H-8. By default, the Map Network Drive dialog box highlights the next available drive letter.

3. If you want to use a different drive letter, click the **Drive list arrow**, then click the **drive letter** you want to use

4. Click **Browse**
   The Browse dialog box opens and displays a tree structure of My Network Places and My Computer.

5. Click the **+** next to the drive with the networked computer you can map onto your computer (specified by your instructor or technical support person), click the **Wired Coffee folder** (or the shared folder specified by your instructor or technical support person) to select it, then click **OK**
   The Browse dialog box closes and the Map Network Drive dialog box opens.

6. If not already checked, click the **Reconnect at logon check box**, then click **Finish**
   The Map Network Drive dialog box closes, and My Network Places maps a drive connecting your computer to the Wired Coffee shared folder (or to the shared folder specified by your instructor or technical support person). When the connection is complete, a window opens for the newly mapped drive, allowing you to view the files within the mapped drive, as shown in Figure H-9. John can now easily copy folders and files from his floppy disk into the shared folder.

7. Click the **Close button** on the mapped drive window

8. Click the **Back button list arrow** on the toolbar, then click **My Network Places**
   The My Network Places window displays the active computers in your immediate neighborhood.

QuickTip

If you already know the network path for the drive you want to map, right-click the My Network Places icon, click Map Network Drive, enter the network path in the Path box, then click OK.

Trouble?

If your mapped drives are not automatically reconnecting when you log on, make sure your user name and password are the same for all the networks to which you connect.

FIGURE H-8: Map Network Drive dialog box

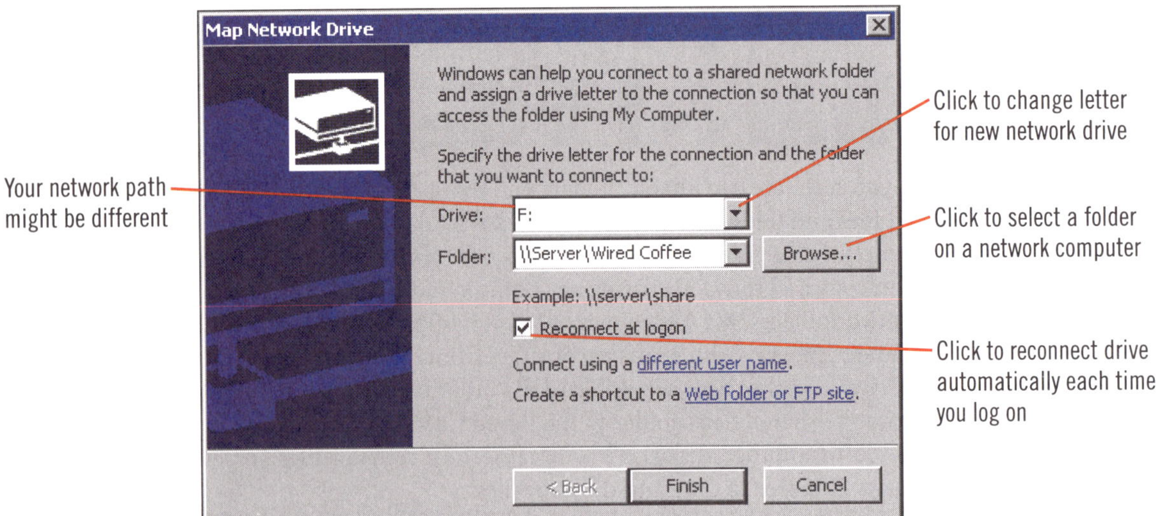

FIGURE H-9: Wired Coffee folder window

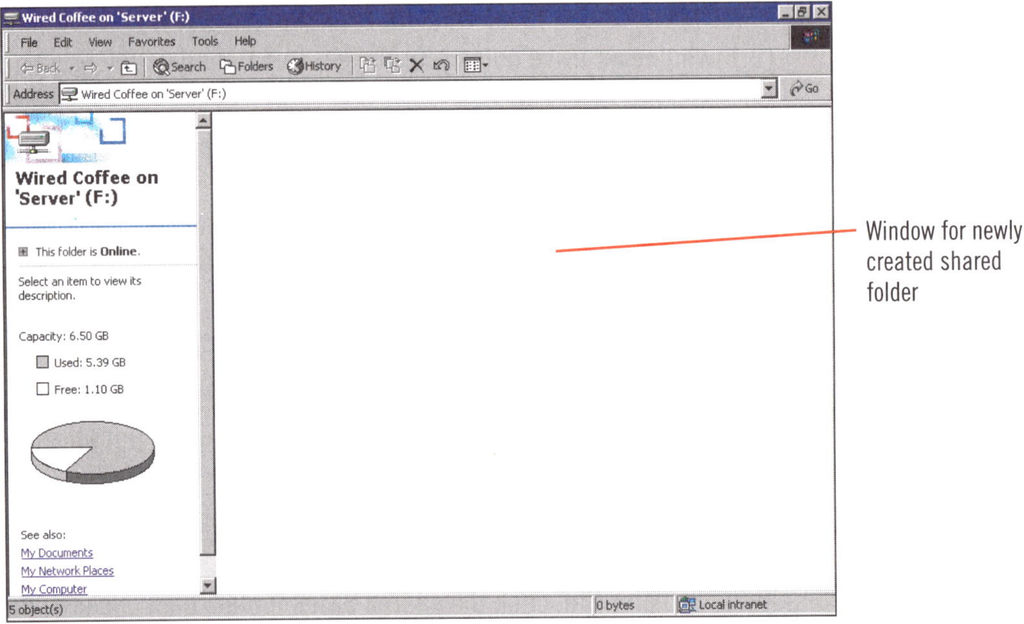

Creating a network or dial-up connection

Network and Dial-up Connections provide connectivity between your computer and a network, another computer, or the Internet. You can create outgoing or incoming connections. **Outgoing connections** contact a remote access server by using a cable or modem to establish a connection with your computer. **Incoming connections** enable your computer to be contacted by other computers. This means your computer running Windows 2000 can operate as a remote access server. With Network and Dial-up Connections, you can establish a Virtual Private Network connection through the Internet, a direct computer connection, or a dial-up connection. To establish any one of these connection types, click the Start button on the taskbar, point to Settings, click Network and Dial-up Connections, double-click Make New Connection, click Next, click the connection option you want, and then follow the instructions in the Network Connection wizard. To grant incoming connection access rights to your computer, open Network and Dial-up Connections, right-click Incoming Connections, click Properties, click the General tab, then select the devices through which incoming connections can connect.

Windows 2000

Copying and Moving Shared Files

Once you have created shared folders and mapped your network drives, copying and moving shared files and folders in Windows is as easy as managing files on your own computer. The only difference is data transfer can take longer over a network than it does on your local computer. You can copy and move files using any of the Windows 2000 Professional file management tools: My Network Places, My Computer, or Windows Explorer. My Network Places works just like My Computer. John wants to copy files from his floppy disk to the shared Sales folder on his hard drive to make them accessible to the other users on his network. He also needs to move a file from the shared Sales folder to the Wired Coffee folder on the network drive (F:) to make it accessible to another department. Because he's copying files to several locations, John uses Windows Explorer to drag and drop the files.

Steps 1 2 3 4

QuickTip

To prevent any changes to your Project Disk, make sure you have made a copy of it. If you need assistance, see your instructor or technical support person.

1. Make sure a copy of your Project Disk is inserted in the appropriate floppy drive
2. In the My Network Places window, click the **Address list arrow**, click **3½ Floppy (A:)** or **(B:)** (whichever drive holds your Project Disk), then double-click the **Unit H folder**
   My Network Places displays the contents of the 3½ floppy drive.
3. Right-click the **Wired Coffee folder**, click **Explore**, then click the **Sales folder** in the Explorer Bar
   Windows Explorer opens, displaying the available folders and drives in the left pane, as shown in Figure H-10. You can now copy or move files easily from your computer to anywhere on the network.

Trouble?

If you click the Sales folder by mistake, click the Sales folder on the floppy disk, then go to Step 5.

4. In the Explorer Bar, click the + next to the My Documents folder to display the shared Sales folder, as shown in Figure H-11, but *do not click the folder*
5. Click **Edit** on the menu bar, click **Select All**, then drag the files from the right pane to the shared **Sales folder** in the Explorer Bar
   The files are copied to the shared Sales folder on the hard drive. The employees who have access to John's computer can now share the files.
6. In the Explorer Bar, click the shared **Sales folder**, then click the **down scroll arrow** in the Explorer Bar if necessary until you can see the icon representing the mapped network folder
   Windows Explorer lists the contents of the Sales folder, as shown in Figure H-11.
7. Right-drag the **Suppliers file** to the mapped networked folder in the Explorer Bar, then click **Move Here**
   The Suppliers file is moved to the networked folder.
8. Click the **mapped networked folder** in the Explorer Bar to view the Suppliers file, then click the **Close button** in both the Exploring Sales and **Unit H** windows

FIGURE H-10: Exploring Sales folder

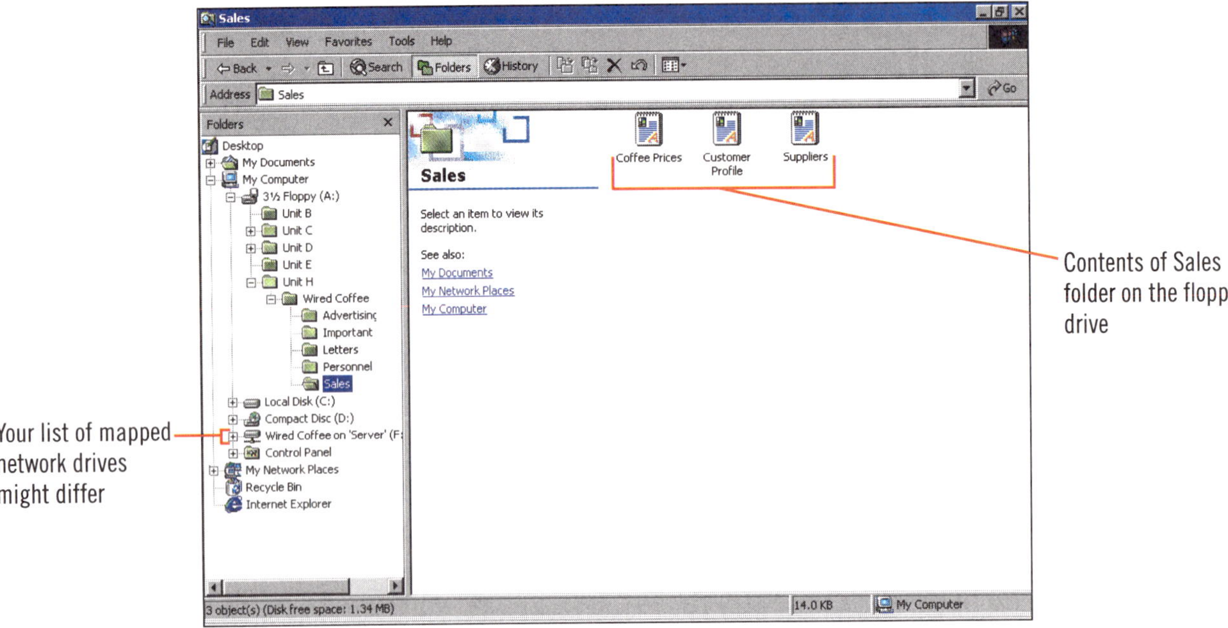

FIGURE H-11: Location of Wired Coffee folder on mapped network drive (F:)

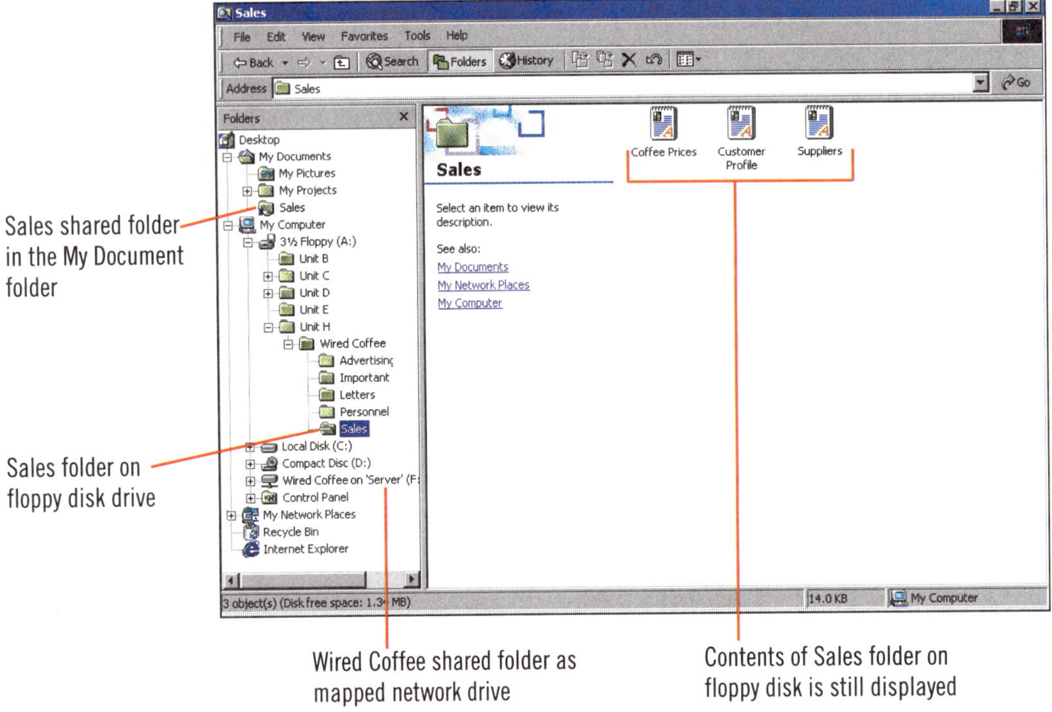

Network traffic

Large networks may serve hundreds of users simultaneously. Like water flowing through pipes, only a certain amount of data can pass through the wires connecting the individual computers at any given time. If the amount of network traffic is of sufficient volume, then the flow of data may slow considerably, causing file operations such as opening, saving, and copying to take longer to complete.

Windows 2000

Opening and Editing a Shared File

Working with shared files on a network is a simple task with Windows. Once you have mapped all the necessary drives to your network folders, you can use network files in any program from your computer. For example, you can use WordPad to edit text files, or Paint to create a graphic. You may also be able to use programs installed on the server specifically for the use of individual clients (ask your system administrator about available options). John uses WordPad to make corrections in the Suppliers file that he placed in the Wired Coffee folder on the server.

1. Click the **Start button** on the taskbar, point to **Programs**, point to **Accessories**, then click **WordPad**
   The WordPad window opens.
2. Click **File** on the menu bar, click **Open**, then click the **Look in list arrow**
   The Open file dialog box, shown in Figure H-12, displays the Look in list with local and networked drives. From here you can open files located on all drives and folders, including the drives mapped to the network.
3. Click the **icon for the mapped network drive to the Wired Coffee shared folder**
   The contents of the networked folder appear in the File list, as shown in Figure H-13.
4. Click **Suppliers**, then click **Open**
   The file named Suppliers opens.
5. Click the bottom of the list, then type **Homegrown USA Coffee**
6. Click the **Save button** on the toolbar
   WordPad saves the changes to the file Suppliers.
7. Click the **Close button** in the WordPad window

FIGURE H-12: Open dialog box

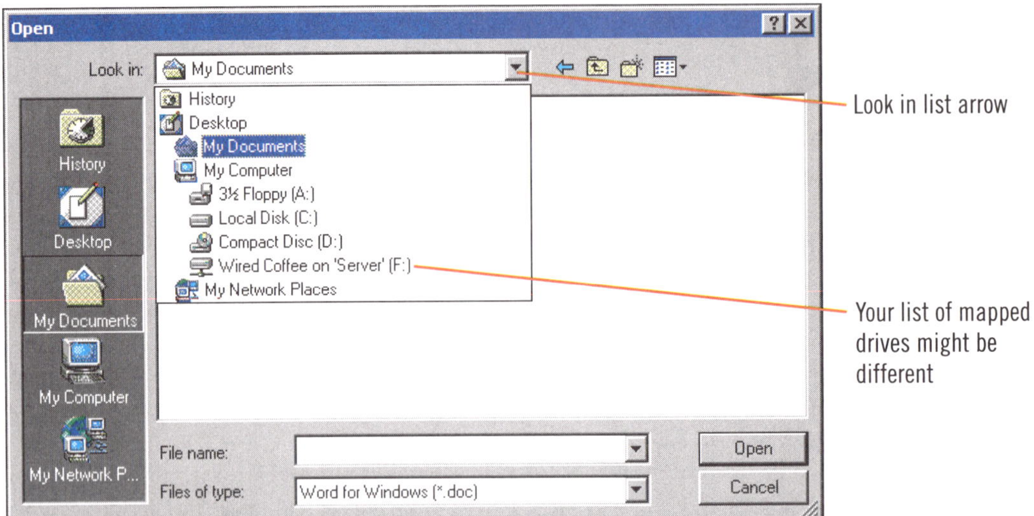

FIGURE H-13: Files in Wired Coffee shared folder

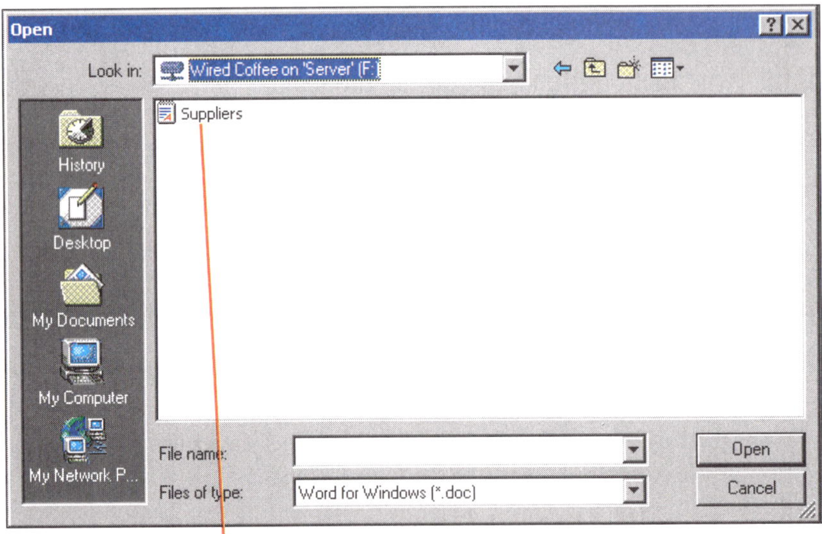

Working with shared network files offline

You can make shared files available offline. The Offline Files feature stores a version of them in a reserved portion of disk space on your computer called **cache**. The computer can access this cache regardless of whether it is connected to the network. You can use manual or automatic caching for documents. **Manual caching** for documents provides offline access to only those files that someone using your shared folder specifically identifies, while **automatic caching** for documents makes every file that someone opens from your shared folder available to them offline. Automatic caching does not make every file in your shared folder available offline, only those files that are opened. In Windows 2000, the Offline Files feature is enabled by default. If it's necessary to set up your computer to use Offline Files, double-click the My Computer icon, click Tools on the menu bar, click Folder Options, click the Offline Files tab, click to select the Enable Offline Files check box, then click OK.

Windows 2000

Disconnecting a Network Drive

Usually, you map a network drive to automatically reconnect every time you log on. However, sometimes you may find it necessary to manually disconnect a mapped drive. Your system administrator may have added new hard drives to the server, or he or she may have reorganized the directory structure, in which case the network path for the mapped drive may now be incorrect. Windows makes the process of disconnecting a mapped drive very easy in the case of such an event. John was informed by the system administrator of a network reorganization that will take place over the weekend. He disconnects the drive mapped to (F:) until he finds out what changes have been made. Before disconnecting the mapped drive, John cleans up his hard drive and the mapped drive.

Steps

1. Double-click the **My Computer icon**, then double-click the **mapped drive**
   The contents of the mapped drive appears.
2. Right-click the **Suppliers file**, click **Delete**, then click **Yes** to confirm the deletion
3. Click the **Back button** Back on the toolbar
4. Click the **Address list arrow**, then click **My Documents**
   John wants to delete the Sales folder.
5. Right-click the **Sales shared folder**, then click **Delete**
   The Confirm Folder Delete dialog box opens.
6. Click **Yes,** click **Yes** again, then click the **Close button** in the My Documents window
7. Right-click the **My Network Places icon** on the desktop
   A pop-up menu appears for My Network Places, as shown in Figure H-14. This menu provides several commands for working in a network environment. See Table H-2 for a description of the commands available through this menu.
8. Click **Disconnect Network Drive** on the pop-up menu
   The Disconnect Network Drive dialog box opens, as shown in Figure H-15. The dialog box displays a list of all the network drives that you have mapped from your computer. You should check with your system administrator or instructor before actually disconnecting a drive. To quit without actually disconnecting a drive, click Cancel.
9. Click the **mapped drive** with the Wired Coffee folder (or the one you previously mapped), click **OK**, then click **Yes** if necessary to the warning message
   Windows disconnects the drive you have selected and closes the Disconnect Network Drive dialog box.

QuickTip

To disconnect a network drive in Windows Explorer, right-click a mapped network drive in the left pane, then click Disconnect.

Network paths

The path to a shared network directory is like the path to a file on a hard or floppy disk. For example, the path to the Suppliers file on your Project Disk is A:\Wired Coffee\Sales\Suppliers. Network paths replace the drive designation with the host computer name, as in \\Server\Wired Coffee. In either example, the path tells the computer where to look for the files you need.

FIGURE H-14: Shortcut menu for My Network Places

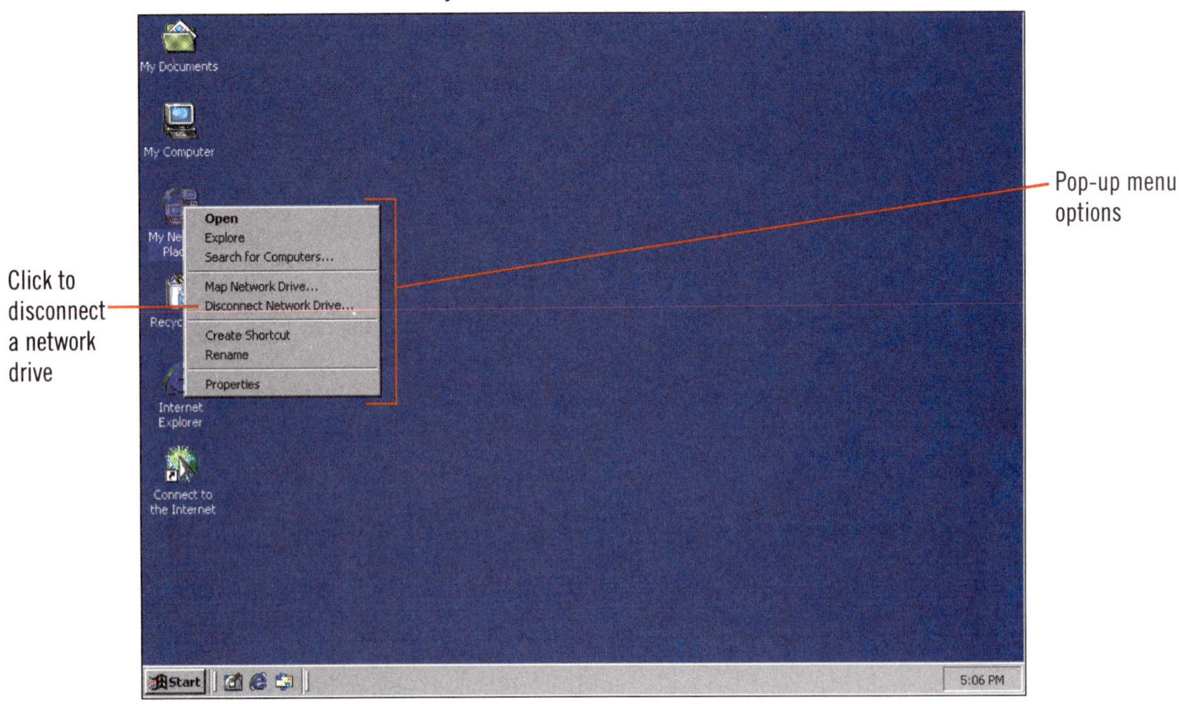

FIGURE H-15: Disconnect Network Drive dialog box

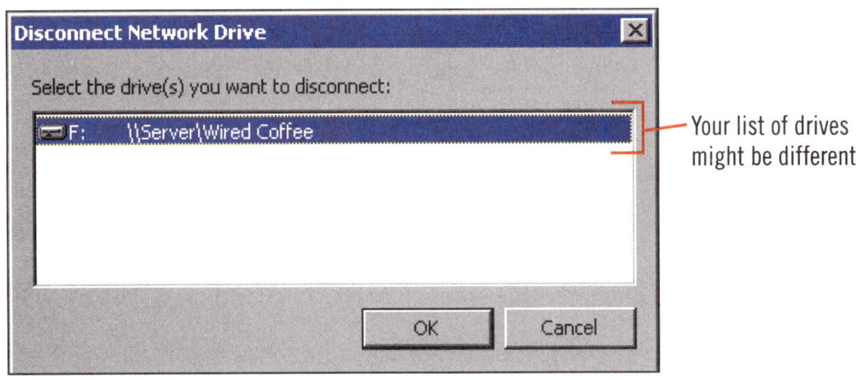

TABLE H-2: Pop-up menu commands for My Network Places

command	function
Open	Opens My Network Places
Explore	Opens Windows Explorer in order to copy and move files from one folder to another, whether on your local computer or the network
Search for Computers	Finds a computer whose name you know but not its location
Map Network Drive	Maps a drive from your computer to a shared directory on another computer
Disconnect Network Drive	Disconnects a drive on your computer from a shared directory on another computer
Create Shortcut	Creates a shortcut to My Network Places
Rename	Renames the My Network Places icon
Properties	Displays the properties of your network

Practice

► Concepts Review

Label each of the elements of the screen shown in Figure H-16.

FIGURE H-16

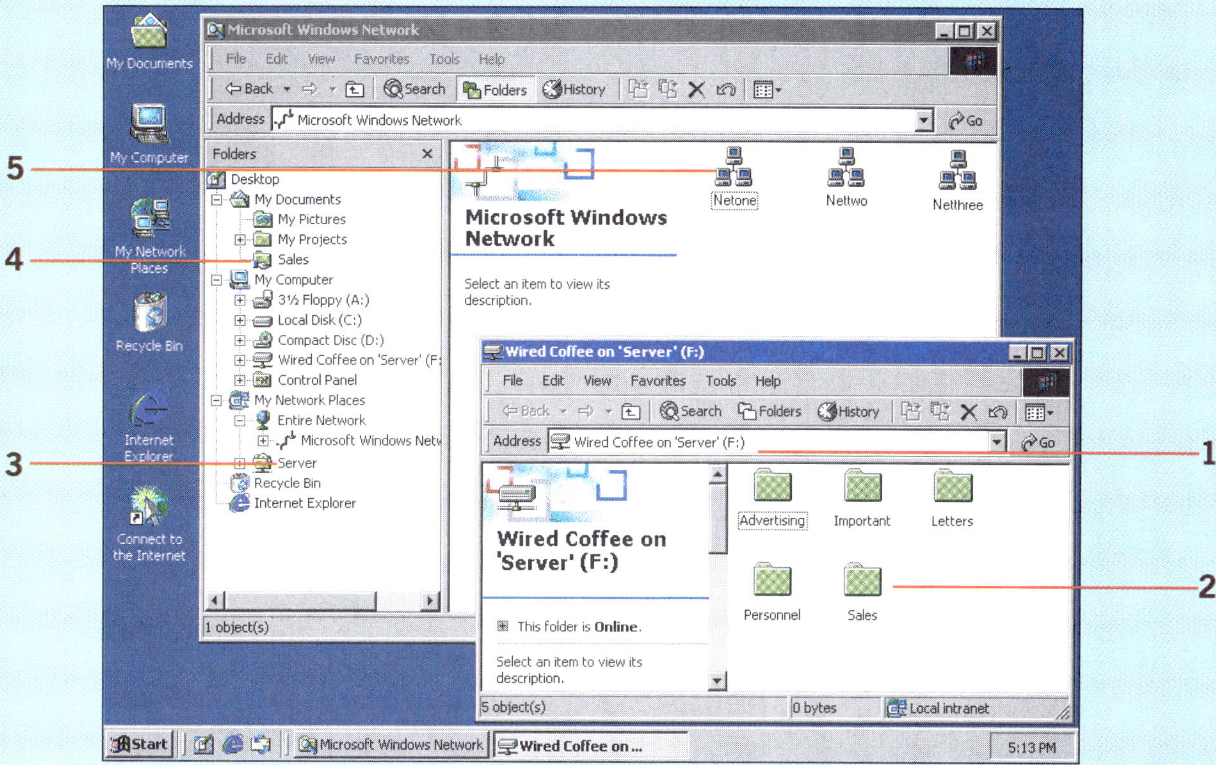

Match each of the terms with the statement that describes its function.

6. Shared folder
7. File permissions
8. Entire Network icon
9. Network path
10. Disconnect Network Drive command

a. Lists all workgroups and computers attached to a network
b. The address for an individual computer on a network
c. Determines who can read, write, or execute files
d. A location where multiple users can access the same files
e. Removes a mapped drive from the local computer

Select the best answer from the list of choices.

11. The windows network management tool that allows you to manage the files and folders of your network is called
- **a.** Windows Explorer.
- **b.** My Computer.
- **c.** My Network Places.
- **d.** File Manager.

12. To disconnect a network drive,
- **a.** Double-click the drive letter in My Network Places.
- **b.** Highlight the drive letter, click File, then click Delete.
- **c.** Click the drive letter, then drag it to the Recycle Bin.
- **d.** Right-click the My Network Places icon, then click Disconnect Network Drive.

13. When you highlight a drive letter in My Network Places, click File on the menu bar, then click Explore,
- **a.** My Computer starts, allowing you to manage files and folders.
- **b.** My Network Places lists the entire network.
- **c.** Windows Explorer starts, allowing you to manage files and folders.
- **d.** File Manager starts, allowing you to manage files and folders.

14. When you map a networked drive,
- **a.** My Network Places displays a graphic of the entire structure of the network.
- **b.** You can use the shared files and folders of another computer on the network.
- **c.** The computer you are using is attached to the network.
- **d.** My Network Places adds your computer to the network path.

15. If the file permissions for a shared folder are set to read-only,
- **a.** No one can read the files in the folder.
- **b.** You can edit the file and save your changes.
- **c.** Everyone can read the files but not write to the files.
- **d.** Everyone can write to the files but not read the files.

Skills Review

1. Examine network computer properties.
- **a.** Right-click the My Network Places icon.
- **b.** Click Properties on the pop-up menu.
- **c.** Click the Network Identification link.
- **d.** View the network properties.
- **e.** Click OK.
- **f.** Click the Close button.

2. **Open and view My Network Places.**
   - a. Double-click the My Network Places icon.
   - b. Double-click the Entire Network icon.
   - c. Click the entire contents link.
   - d. Double-click the Microsoft Windows Network icon.
   - e. Double-click a network domain icon.
   - f. Double-click a network computer icon.
   - g. Click the Back button list arrow, then click My Network Places.

3. **Create a shared folder.**
   - a. Click the Address list arrow, then click the My Document folder.
   - b. Right-click in the My Documents window, point to New, then click Folder.
   - c. Name the new folder *Memos*, then press Enter.
   - d. Click File on the menu bar, then click Sharing.
   - e. Click the Share this folder option button.
   - f. Click OK.

4. **Map a network drive.**
   - a. Click the Address list arrow, then click My Network Places.
   - b. Click Tools on the menu bar, then click Map Network Drive.
   - c. Click Browse, then find the shared folder to which you want to map.
   - d. Click the shared folder.
   - e. Click OK.
   - f. Click the Reconnect at logon check box to select it if necessary.
   - g. Click Finish.
   - h. Click the Close button on the mapped drive window.

5. **Copy and move shared files.**
   - a. Insert a copy of your Project Disk into the appropriate floppy drive.
   - b. Click the Address list arrow, click 3½ Floppy (A:) or (B:), then double-click the folder that contains your Project files.
   - c. Click the Wired Coffee folder.
   - d. Click File on the menu bar, then click Explore.
   - e. Click the Letters folder in the Explorer Bar.
   - f. Click the + next to the My Documents folder.
   - g. Click Edit on the menu bar, then click Select All.
   - h. Drag all the files to the shared Memos folder you created in the My Documents folder.
   - i. Click the shared Memos folder in the Explorer Bar.
   - j. Right-drag the IRS Letter file to the mapped networked folder in the Explorer Bar, then click Move Here.
   - k. Click the mapped networked folder in the Explorer Bar to view the file.
   - l. Click the Close buttons in the Explorer and Unit H windows.

6. **Open and edit a shared file.**
   - a. Start WordPad.
   - b. Open the IRS Letter file located on the mapped networked folder.
   - c. In the document, change *April 25* to *May 10.*
   - d. Save the file, print it, then close the file and WordPad.

7. Disconnect a network drive.
- **a.** Double-click the My Computer icon, then double-click the mapped drive.
- **b.** Click the IRS Letter File, press [Delete], then click Yes.
- **c.** Click the Address list arrow, then click My Documents.
- **d.** Right-click the shared Memos folder, then click Delete.
- **e.** Click Yes, then click Yes again to confirm the deletion.
- **f.** Click the Close button.
- **g.** Right-click the My Network Places icon.
- **h.** Click Disconnect Network Drive.
- **i.** Select the drive you mapped in Step 4.
- **j.** Click OK, then click Yes if necessary.

Independent Challenges

1. As the new clerk at Holly's (a craft store), you have been asked to create a list of suppliers' names. Your task is to enter the supplier information into a new file and place that file in two places for others to use. You must create a shared folder on your computer that will store the file, then map a drive to a network folder that will also contain the file. (*Note*: Ask your instructor or technical support person which networked computer you can map onto your computer. If you are working in a lab environment, you may not be able to create a shared folder. If so, do not create a shared folder, and instead use the folder supplied by your instructor.)

To complete this independent challenge:

- **a.** Open My Computer on the desktop.
- **b.** Open your local hard drive.
- **c.** Open the My Documents folder.
- **d.** Create a shared folder called *Suppliers* with read only permissions.
- **e.** Open WordPad and enter the following information in a new document:

Name	Address	City & State
Baskets & Things	101 Hopyard Road	Chicago, IL
Frames R Us	1934 Hummingbird Lane	Los Angeles, CA
Season's	125 34th Street	New York, NY

- **f.** Save the file as *Supplier List* in the newly created Suppliers folder.
- **g.** Print the Supplier List file.
- **h.** Map a drive to a shared folder on another computer to which you have permission.
- **i.** Create a *US Suppliers* folder on that drive.
- **j.** Copy the Supplier List file from the Suppliers folder on the local computer to the US Suppliers folder on the mapped drive.
- **k.** Print the Screen (Press the Print Screen key to make a copy of the screen, open Paint, click Edit on the menu bar, click Paste to paste the screen into Paint, then click Yes to paste the large image if necessary. Click File on the menu bar, click Print, then click Print in the Print dialog box.)
- **l.** Delete the Suppliers folder on your hard drive and the US Suppliers folder on the mapped drive.
- **m.** Disconnect the network drive you mapped and delete the shared folder you created.

2. As the president of your company, you have decided to increase the pay rates for two of your employees, Jessica Thielen and Debbie Cabral. You will use WordPad to write a memo that you can edit and use for both employees. After completing the memos, you will print the documents for the employees. You also want to copy the documents to the company server so they can be stored in their employee folders.

To complete this independent challenge:

a. Create a *Memos* folder on your Project Disk.
b. Open WordPad and enter the following memo in a new document:
Dear Jessica,
Your service to this company is greatly appreciated. To show my appreciation to such an outstanding employee as you, I have decided to give you a 10% raise in salary. The raise will go into effect with the next pay period.
Sincerely yours,
[your name here]
c. Use the Save As command to name the document *Thielen Raise* and save it in the Memos folder, then print the document.
d. Change *Dear Jessica* to *Dear Debbie* in the Thielen Raise memo.
e. Save the file as *Cabral Raise* in the Memos folder and print the document.
f. Close the file and WordPad.
g. Map a drive to a shared folder on another computer to which you have permission.
h. Create a shared folder on that mapped drive called *Thielen* and copy the Thielen Raise file from your Project Disk into the Thielen folder.
i. Create a shared folder on that mapped drive called *Cabral*, and copy the Cabral Raise file from your Project Disk to the Cabral folder.
j. Print the screen. (See Independent Challenge 1, Step k for screen printing instructions.)
k. Delete the Thielen and Cabral shared folders on the mapped drive.
l. Disconnect the network drive you mapped.

3. You are the system administrator for your company's computer network. During peak usage of the network, you want to monitor who is on the network. You will use the Properties command in the My Network Places to find out who is connected to the network. You also want to check the properties for a few servers to verify the connect information.

To complete this independent challenge:

a. Using My Network Places, open Computers Near Me.
b. Display the network identification for two connected computers to find out their name and domain.
c. Print the screen for the Computers Near Me window and the network identification for the connected computers (see Independent Challenge 1, Step k for screen printing instructions).
d. Map two drives to a shared folder on another computer to which you have permission.
e. Display the network identification for the mapped drives.
f. Print the screen for the network identification for the mapped drives (see Independent Challenge 1, Step k for screen printing instructions).
g. Disconnect the network drives you mapped.

4. The system administrator for your network calls and informs you that he needs to make some changes to the directory structure. He advises you to move any files you have put on the server recently and to disconnect any mapped drives.

To complete this independent challenge:

- **a.** Map a drive to a shared folder on another computer to which you have permission, and copy two files from your Project Disk to this mapped drive.
- **b.** Using My Network Places, create a folder on your local hard disk called *Network Files*.
- **c.** Move the files from the folder on the network drive to the Network Files folder on the local hard disk.
- **d.** Print the screen. (See Independent Challenge 1, Step k for screen printing instructions.)
- **e.** Disconnect the mapped drive from the network.
- **f.** Delete the Network Files folder on your local hard drive.

Visual Workshop

Re-create the screen shown in Figure H-17, which displays the My Network Places window. Print the screen. (See Independent Challenge 1, Step k for screen printing instructions.)

FIGURE H-17

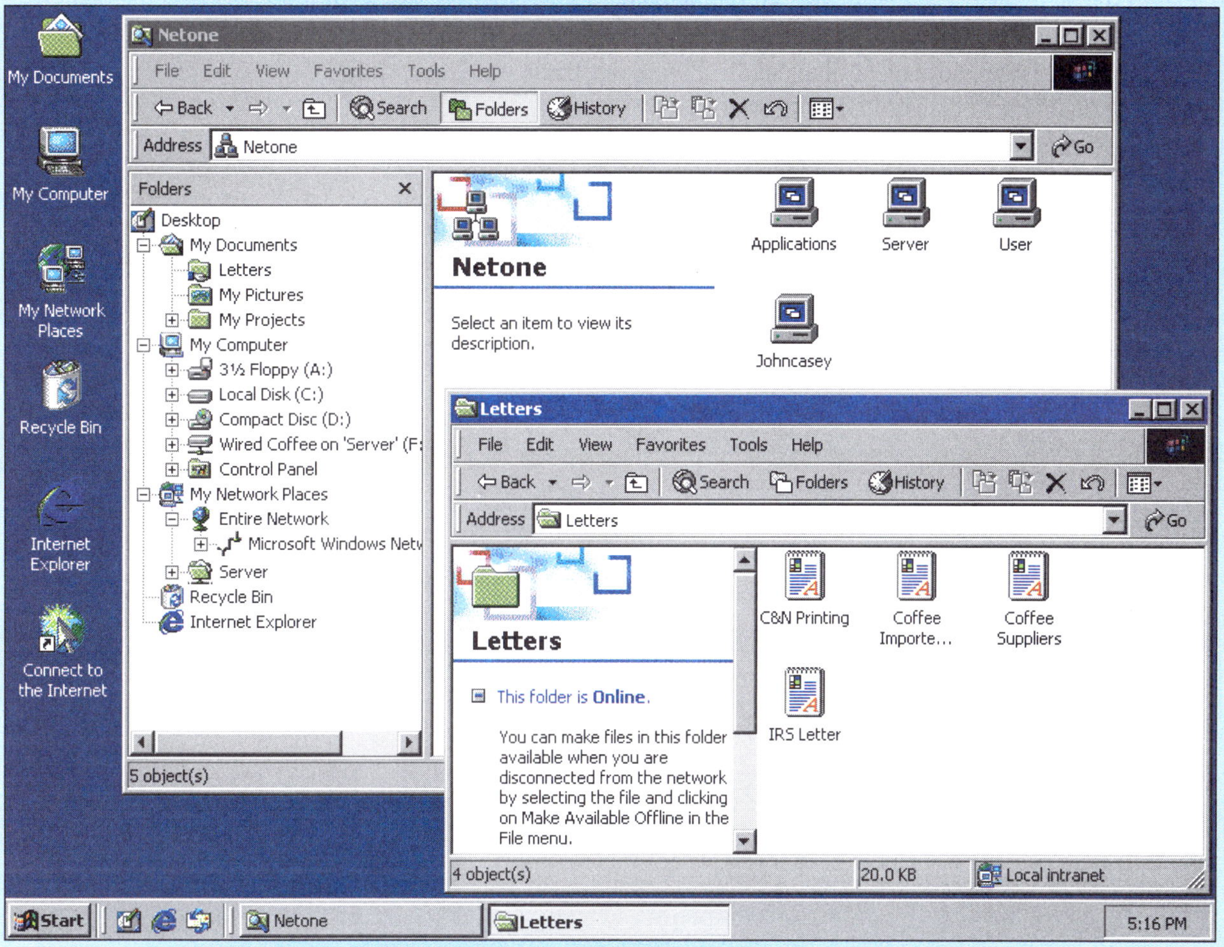

Exploring Windows 2000 Communication Features

Objectives

- Understand Windows connection tools
- Set up a Dial-Up Networking connection
- Use Connection Wizard advanced settings
- Connect to a dial-up service
- Make an Internet phone call with Phone Dialer
- Manage phone numbers
- Set Up NetMeeting
- Contact others with NetMeeting
- Share graphical content using NetMeeting

Windows 2000 makes communicating over computers easier than ever. It includes accessories that allow you to connect to other computers and to the Internet, to dial phone numbers automatically, to chat with users on other computers, and to collaborate with others during online conferences. This unit shows you how to set up a Dial-Up Networking connection to the Internet, and how to use Windows 2000 communication features such as Phone Dialer and NetMeeting, which are useful for home and business. John Casey recently purchased a computer so he can work from home. He wants to take advantage of Windows 2000 communication features for his business.

Understanding Windows Connection Tools

Computers at universities or large companies are mostly likely connected to the Internet via expensive, high-speed wiring that transmits data very quickly. Home computer owners, however, usually can't afford to run similar cables and wires to their homes, and instead must rely on phone lines that are already in place, as shown in Figure I-1. When a modem uses an ordinary voice phone line, which uses analog signals, it converts the modem's digital signals to analog, as shown in Figure I-2. The receiving computer converts the analog signal back to digital. Data usually travels much more slowly over phone wires than over the networking infrastructure that makes up the Internet, and if there are any problems with the phone connection, data can be lost. But regular phone lines are often the only practical choice for homes and small businesses. In some areas, **ISDN lines** or **DSL lines**, wires that provide a completely digital path from one computer to another, are becoming more widely available and affordable. Whether you use a regular phone line or a faster ISDN or DSL line, Windows 2000 can help you establish a connection between your home or office computer and the Internet. To do so, you will need to select an Internet Service Provider (ISP), which is a company that sets up an **Internet account** for you that provides Internet access. ISPs maintain servers that are directly connected to the Internet 24 hours a day. You dial into your ISP's server over your phone line to use its Internet connection. You pay a fee for this service, sometimes by the hour, but more often with a flat monthly rate.

Windows 2000 includes the following tools to help you connect to the Internet:

Dial-up Networking

Some computer users have one Internet account for home use and a different one for business use. The Dial-up Networking accessory helps you manage the accounts that you use to connect to the Internet. You might have just one or several accounts listed in the Dial-up Networking folder, which you can access through My Computer.

Internet Connection Wizard

The Internet Connection Wizard, available by clicking Tools on the Internet Explorer menu bar, clicking Internet Options, and then clicking the Connections tab, makes it easy for you to create an Internet account by prompting you for the needed information through a series of dialog boxes.

FIGURE I-1: Phone line connection to the Internet

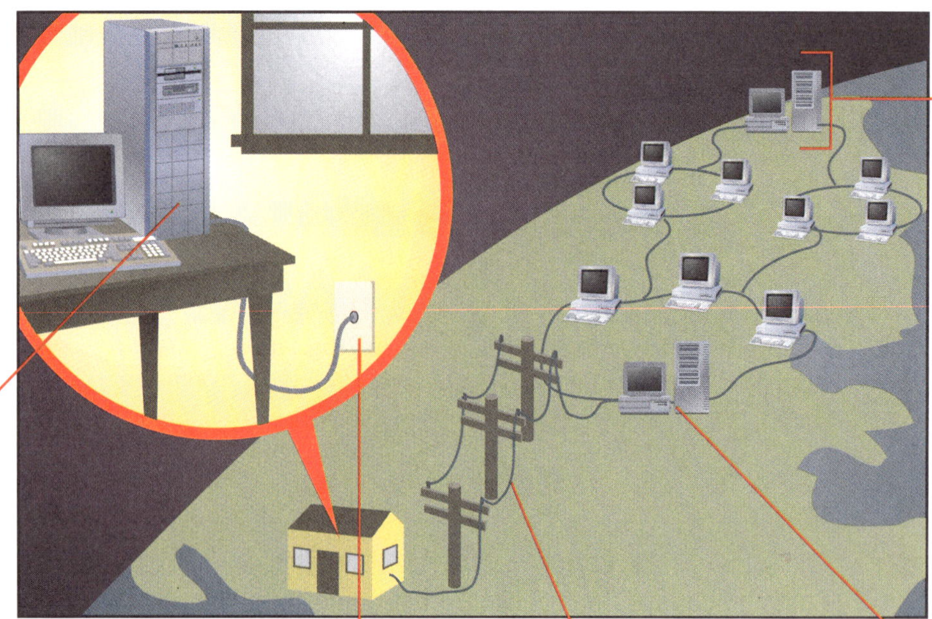

FIGURE I-2: Data traveling over a phone line

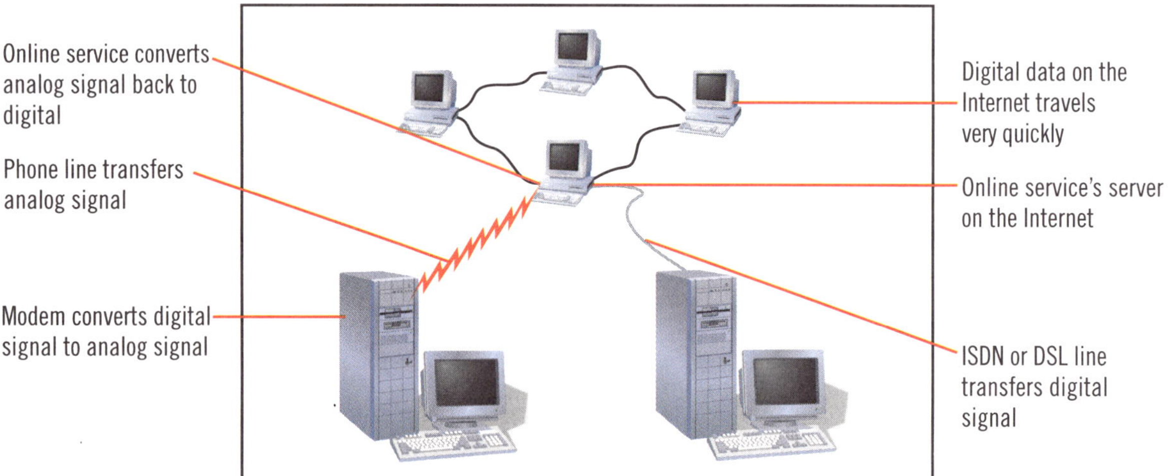

Online services

ISPs are sometimes referred to as **online services**, and vice versa. There used to be several differences between the two kinds of companies, but today they provide such similar services that the two terms are almost interchangeable. Online services include Internet access, e-mail, and much more. For example, **chat rooms and forums** allow users who share common interests to come together electronically and exchange messages on a specific topic in "real time." Many online services also offer newsgroup support. **Newsgroups** are similar to forums in that they bring people together who share common interests, but they exchange messages in an e-mail format rather than in real time. Some online services offer specialized Internet services, such as tools for searching the Internet, space for storing Web pages, and information services. When you are choosing your online service, make sure you consider your needs and compare the services you want for the price you want to pay.

Setting Up a Dial-Up Networking Connection

If you want to be able to connect to the Internet and other compatible networks using your home computer, you can set up a Dial-up Networking connection using the Internet Connection Wizard. *If your ISP has provided you with an installation program that sets up the connection for you, install and run that program rather than using the Windows 2000 Internet Connection Wizard, and skip this and the next lesson.* John has signed up with an ISP and has received the necessary information on his account. He will use the Internet Connection Wizard to set up the service.

QuickTip

If you are in a university or institutional setting, you are probably already connected to the Internet, so you can read through this lesson without completing the steps.

1. Click the **Start button**, point to **Programs**, point to **Accessories**, point to **Communications**, then click **Internet Connection Wizard**
2. Click the **I want to set up my Internet connection manually option button**, then click **Next**
   John chooses this option because he has an account with an ISP but isn't yet connected to it. The first option connects you to a referral service that helps you select an ISP, but you only use that option if you haven't already opened an account with an ISP. The second option is used only if you already have an Internet connection with an ISP supported by the Internet Connection Wizard. This list of supported ISPs might not include all the ISPs in your area.
3. Click the **I connect through a phone line and a modem option button**, then click **Next**
   John chooses this option, as shown in Figure I-3, because he is not on a local area network.

Trouble?

If you're not sure if you need to set up advanced options, check with your Internet Service Provider.

4. Type the area code and telephone number of your ISP in the appropriate boxes, then click **Next**; if you need to set up advanced options for your connection, stop here and skip to the next lesson, "Using Connection Wizard Advanced Settings"
   Your ISP documentation will provide you with the numbers you should use. John uses those shown in Figure I-4; yours will be different.

Trouble?

If you can't find your user name in your documentation, it might be called User ID, Member ID, Login Name, or something similar.

5. Type your user name in the User name text box, then press **[Tab]**
   Your ISP documentation will provide you with the user name and password you should use.
6. Type your password in the Password text box
   As you type the password, asterisks appear instead of the letters you type, as shown in Figure I-5. This protects your password from the eyes of people who might be walking by your computer.

QuickTip

You should keep your password secret so that unauthorized users cannot access your account.

7. Click **Next**, type a name for this dial-up connection in the Connection text box, then click **Next**
8. Because you're only setting up your network connection now and not your e-mail program, click the **No option button**, then click **Next**

QuickTip

If you want to connect to the Internet immediately, leave the check box selected.

9. To avoid connecting to your ISP immediately, deselect the **To connect to the Internet immediately check box**, then click **Finish**

FIGURE I-3: Connection options

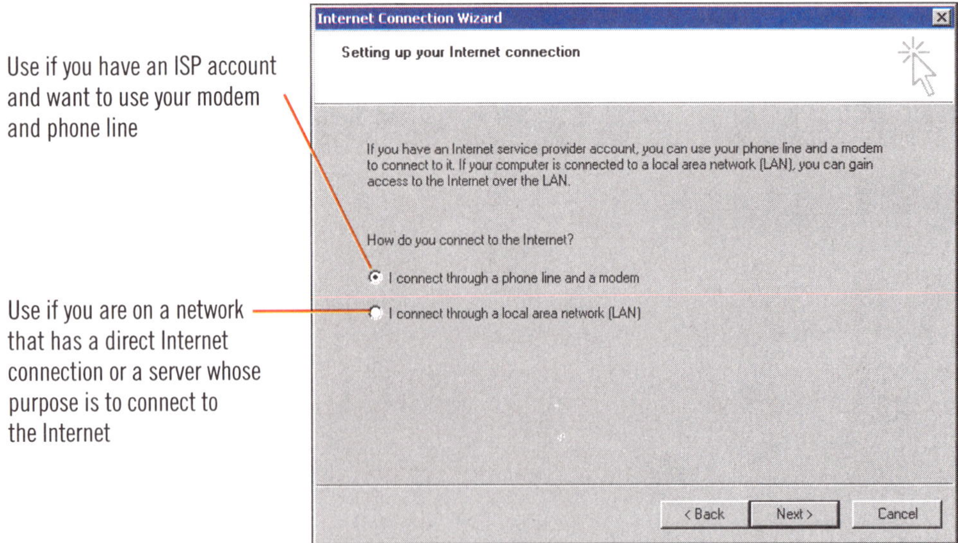

FIGURE I-4: Entering ISP phone information

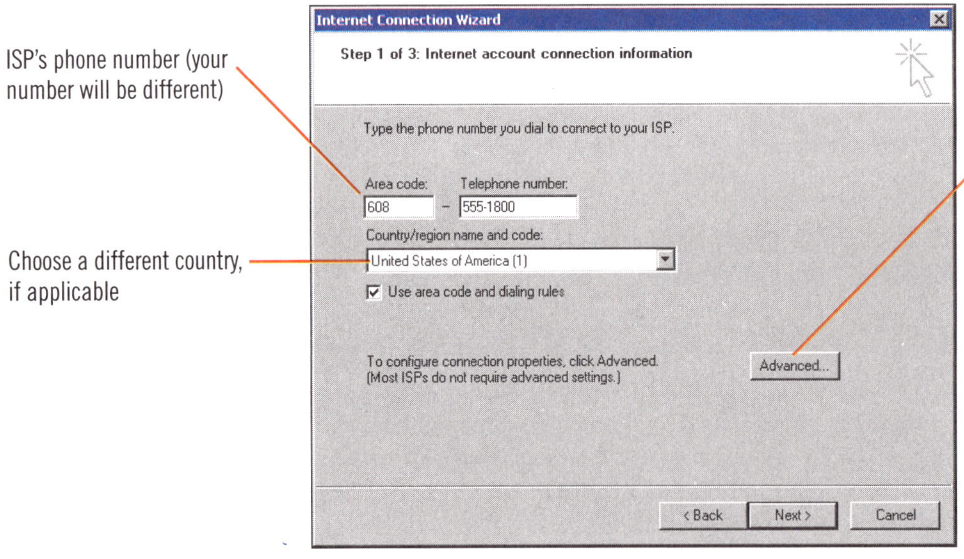

FIGURE I-5: Entering a user name and password

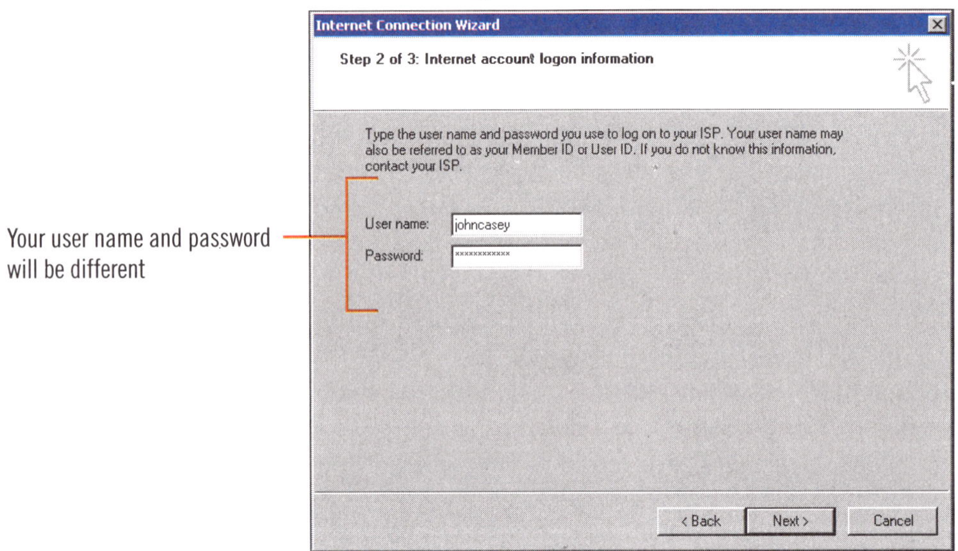

Windows 2000

Using Connection Wizard Advanced Settings

Sometimes your ISP will require specific settings for your Internet connection. This could involve things like specifying the connection type or the ways your computer will be identified on the Internet. The Internet Connection Wizard allows you to configure connection properties manually by clicking the Advanced button when entering your account connection information. If you don't click the Advanced button, you'll complete the Internet Connection Wizard as shown in the previous lesson, "Setting Up a Dial-up Networking Connection." *Complete this lesson only if you stopped at Step 4 in the previous lesson.* John needs to use the Advanced Settings option. The Internet Connection Wizard should be open on your screen.

Trouble?

If you finished creating an Internet connection in the previous lesson, or if you do not need to set up a connection, read through the rest of this lesson without performing the steps.

1. In the Step 1 of 3: Internet account connection information window of the Internet Connection Wizard, click **Advanced**
   The Advanced Connection Properties dialog box opens.
2. Click the **PPP**, **SLIP**, or **C-SLIP option button**
   A **connection type** is the kind of connection between your computer and your ISP's server. Windows 2000 offers two connection types: PPP and SLIP. The preferred and more common connection type today is **Point to Point Protocol**, or **PPP**, which provides error-checking and can cope with noisier phone lines than SLIP. **Serial-Line Internet Protocol**, or **SLIP**, is a basic connection type that runs well on most systems but has no error-checking or security features. **Compressed Serial Line Internet Protocol**, or **C-SLIP**, is similar to SLIP but adds the feature of data compression to speed up data transfer. Most ISPs use a PPP connection, but some require SLIP or C-SLIP; check your ISP documentation to see which one to use.
3. Click the appropriate **Logon Procedure option button**
   Some ISPs require you to log on before you can use the service. In some cases, you must log on manually, providing the information required by your ISP when you attempt to connect. In other cases, you can use a **logon script**, a program that runs on your computer and logs you on to the service automatically.

Trouble?

If you don't need to use a logon script, skip Step 4.

4. If you need to use a logon script, click **Browse**, locate and select the logon script specified by your documentation, then click **Open**
   By default, Windows 2000 stores logon scripts in the C:\Program Files\Accessories folder. Your ISP's documentation will tell you which logon script file to use or will provide you with a different one. John's is shown in Figure I-6.
5. In the Advanced Connection Properties dialog box, click the **Addresses tab**, click the appropriate IP address option; then if you selected the second option, enter the IP address
   An **Internet Protocol**, or **IP**, is a unique address that identifies a server on the Internet. Usually your ISP automatically assigns you one when you log on, because you are only a temporary user of the address (only over the period of time that you are logged on).
6. Click the appropriate **DNS server address option button**; then if you selected the second option, enter the DNS numbers
   The **Domain Name System**, or **DNS**, is a database service that helps computers look up the names of other computers and locate their corresponding IP addresses. If your ISP documentation provides you with a primary and secondary DNS server address, enter them here, as John does in Figure I-7.
7. Click **OK**, then return to the previous lesson and resume with Step 5

FIGURE I-6: Choosing a connection type and logon procedure

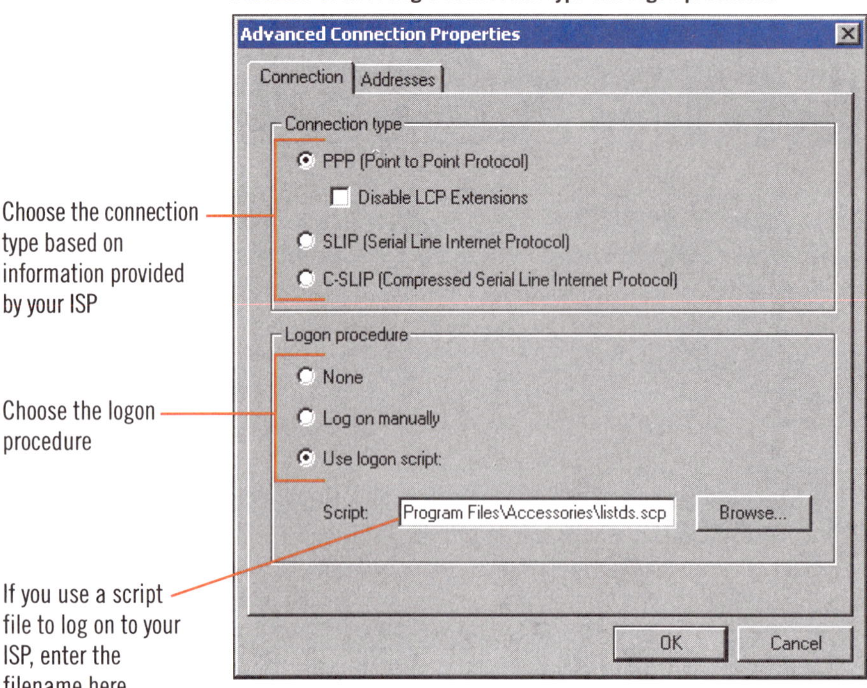

FIGURE I-7: Entering IP and DNS information

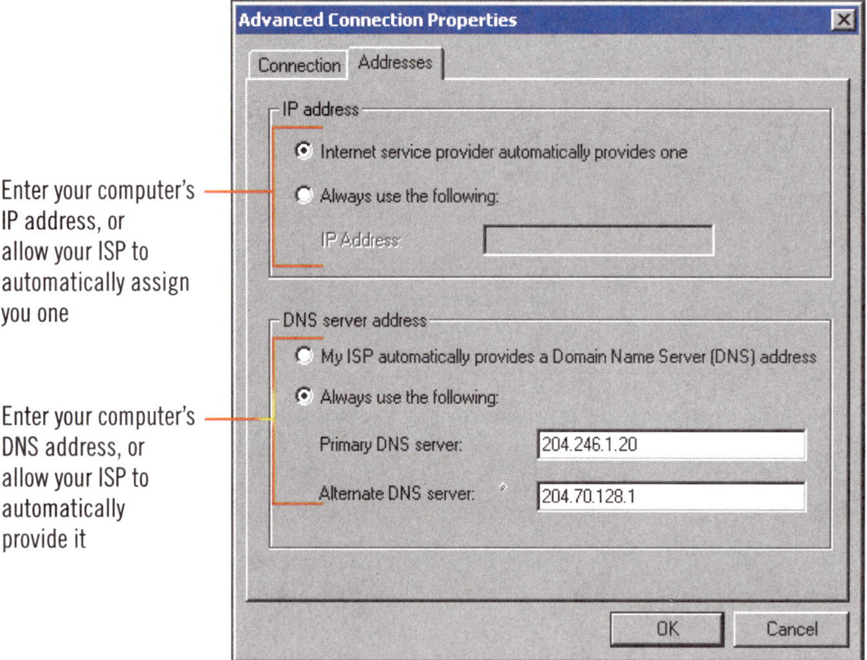

Connecting to a Dial-Up Service

Once you have established a Dial-up Networking connection, you are ready to use it to connect to the Internet or another network or computer. You can have more than one dial-up networking service, in which case multiple icons appear in the Dial-up Networking window. One connection might provide your business Internet service, another might be for home or family use, and another might access a university or institutional account. John decides to test the connection he just set up.

Steps

QuickTip

You can also open the Dial-Up Networking window by opening the Control Panel and then double-clicking the Network and Dial-up Connections icon.

Trouble?

Remember that the Password box displays asterisks to hide your password from unauthorized passers-by.

Trouble?

If a Pre-Dial Terminal Screen dialog box opens after you click Connect, click Continue.

Trouble?

If you don't see a pop-up menu with the items Disconnect and Status, you right-clicked the clock, the taskbar, or some other icon instead of the Connection icon. Click outside the pop-up menu to close it, then repeat Step 7.

1. Click the **Start button**, point to **Settings**, then click **Network and Dial-Up Connections**
   The Network and Dial-up Connections window, shown in Figure I-8, displays icons for each Dial-Up Networking connection you have. If a connection is not currently enabled, the icon will be grayed out.
2. Double-click the **connection you just created** (it will have the same name you entered in the Internet Connection Wizard)
3. Make sure your user name and password are correct in the Connect To dialog box; if they are not correct, type them in the appropriate boxes before you proceed
   John's Connect dialog box is shown in Figure I-9; yours will reflect the information you entered in the wizard, and the name in the title bar will reflect the name of your connection.
4. Click **Dial**
5. Wait as your modem connects
   The Connecting dialog box appears and identifies the steps of establishing a connection. First it uses your modem to dial the number, then it verifies your user name and password, and finally it establishes a connection. A Connection Established dialog box (or something similar) may open indicating that you are connected to your ISP.
6. Click the **Close button** on the Network and Dial-up Connections window
   A connection icon appears on your taskbar to indicate you are connected. You can now start your Internet browser to view Web pages, check your e-mail, or use any of the other Windows 2000 communications features.
7. Right-click the **connection icon** on the taskbar
8. Click **Status**
   The Status dialog box opens, giving you current information on your connection and details about your Internet settings, as shown in Figure I-10.
9. Click the **Disconnect button** to disconnect your computer from the Internet

FIGURE I-8: Network and Dial-up Connections window

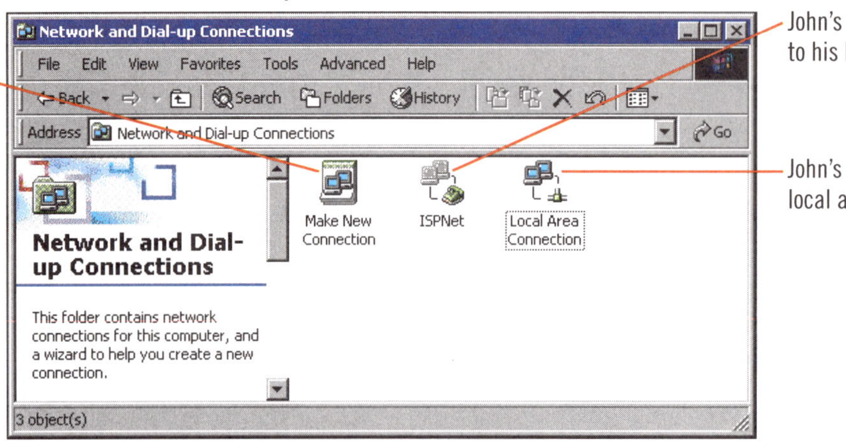

FIGURE I-9: Connecting to a dial-up server

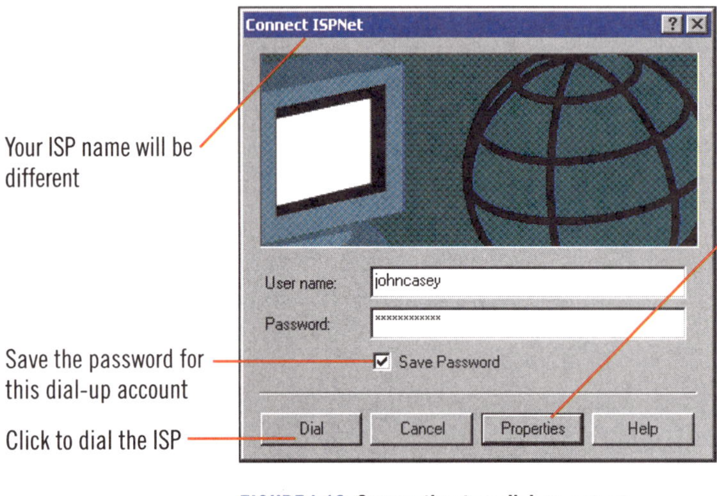

FIGURE I-10: Connecting to a dial-up server

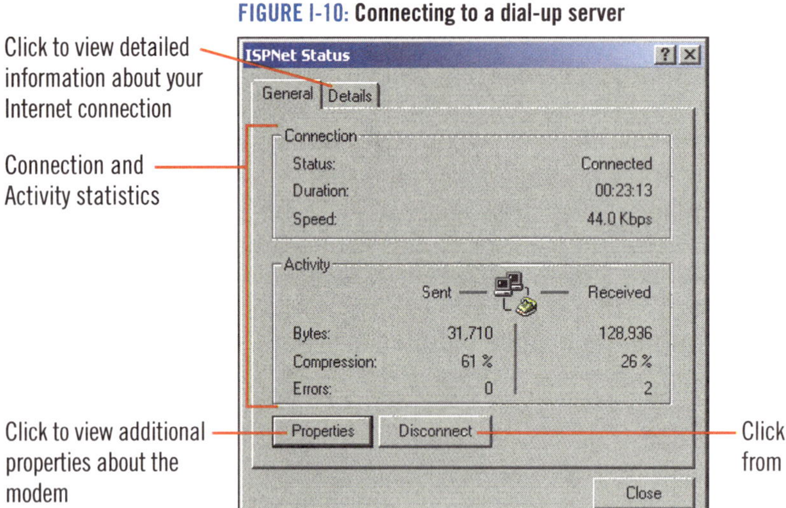

Changing Dial-up Networking settings

You might encounter problems connecting to your dial-up service if the Windows 2000 default settings don't match those of your ISP. You can change the way your dial-up networking connection is configured, or set up, from the Network and Dial-up Connections window. Open the window, right-click the connection you want to modify, and then click Properties. Click the tabs to locate the settings you want to change.

Making an Internet Phone Call with Phone Dialer

Phone Dialer allows you to make calls over a regular phone line or over the Internet. If you're using your modem simply to dial your phone, once the modem connects with the person you're dialing, called the **remote party**, you can pick up your phone and talk. To use the phone dialer in this way, you should have the speaker on your modem turned up, so that you can hear the remote party pick up the phone. Once the remote party picks up the phone, you can pick up the receiver on your end and proceed with the call. You can also make a phone call over the Internet. Using phone dialer in this way, you can make the equivalent of a long-distance call for the cost of a local connection to your ISP. To make an Internet call, you need to have a microphone, sound card, and speakers attached to your computer, and you also need to know the IP address of the computer you're connecting. The remote party must also be using Phone Dialer at the same time you make the call. Once you make a connection, you talk over the computer's microphone and listen to the response from the computer's speakers. John decides to use Phone Dialer to place a long-distance call over the Internet. Your connection to the Internet should still be open.

1. Connect to the Internet, if necessary

Trouble?

If your network administrator has not set up an Internet Directory server on your network, you may see an error message stating that the selected server is not responding. You can ignore this error message and continue with the lesson.

2. Click the **Start button**, point to **Programs**, point to **Accessories**, point to **Communications**, then click **Phone Dialer**

   The Phone Dialer window opens. The left pane lists various folders that contain information on conferences that you can join or users that you can quickly access. The right pane displays details about these selected items. If this is the first time you've used Phone Dialer, these panes are likely to be empty.

3. Have a friend with an Internet connection also start Phone Dialer and then have your friend give you his or her IP address

4. Click **Phone** on the menu bar, then click **Dial**

   The Dial dialog box opens. If you are trying to connect to a user on local area network, you can enter the user's name or the name of the computer on the network. For an Internet call, you need to enter the IP address of the computer.

5. Click the **Internet Call option button** and enter the IP address of the remote party

   See Figure I-11.

Trouble?

If you don't get an answer, check that you have typed the correct IP address and that the remote party is running the Phone Dialer program on his or her end.

6. Click **Place Call**

   Once the remote party accepts the call, you can talk via the Internet Call and Preview box, as shown in Figure I-12.
   You are now connected to the remote party and you can communicate over the phone as you normally would.

7. When you are finished with the phone call, hang up your phone, then click **Disconnect**

FIGURE I-11: Dialing to an IP address on the Internet

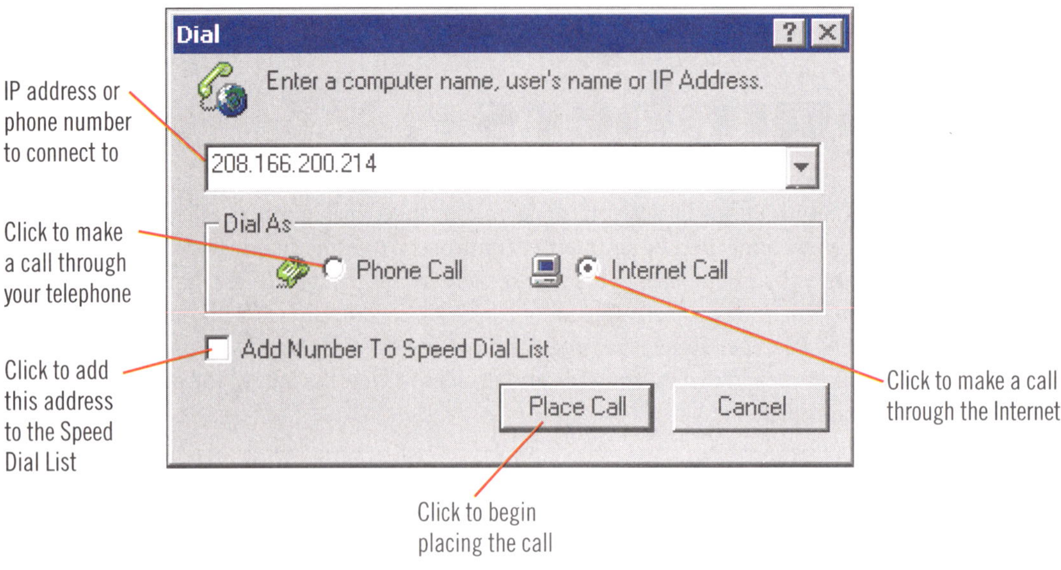

FIGURE I-12: Making a phone call through the Internet

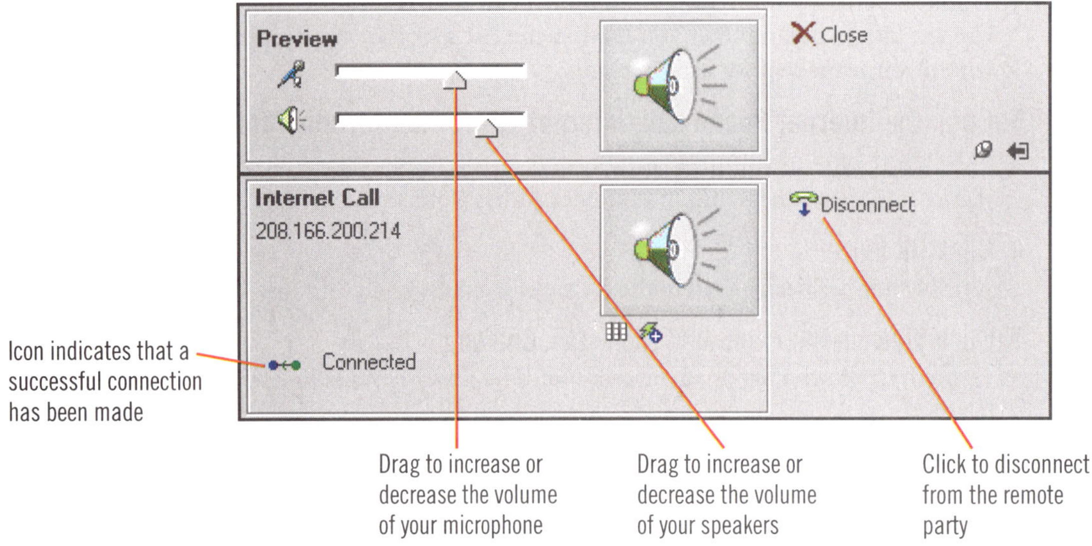

CLUES TO USE

Using video in an Internet call

If you want to use video in your call to share visual information, or just to see the person you're talking with, you can do so with the Phone Dialer. To use this feature, you and the remote party must both have a digital video capture device attached to the computer. If you do, the Phone Dialer program will detect this and give you the option of including video in the connection. Otherwise, you can use the sound recorder to communicate via audio only.

Windows 2000

Managing Phone Numbers

Most phones have speed dial buttons that you can press to dial numbers that you've previously stored. With Phone Dialer, you can store your speed dial numbers, whether they're for a conventional telephone connection or an Internet connection. Another handy feature of Phone Dialer is that you can log your phone calls. This is especially useful for businesses that need to track long-distance calls by client or project. John Casey communicates with one of the Wired Coffee stockholders, Clarence Jones, on a regular basis. He decides to add Clarence's name and IP address on one of the speed dial buttons. He also decides to view the logs of the calls he has already made with Phone Dialer.

1. Click **Phone** on the menu bar, point to **Speed Dial**, then click **Speed Dial List**
   The Edit Speed Dial List dialog box opens, in which you enter a name and phone number for the remote party whose number you want to save.
2. Click **Add**
3. Type a name for the person
   John types the name "Clarence Jones."
4. Type the corresponding **phone number** or **IP address** in the Number or Address box
   Use the automated number you used in the last lesson or the number of a someone with whom you've made prior arrangements.
5. Click the **Internet Phone call**, **Internet call**, or **conference option button** to indicate what type of number this is
   Figure I-13 shows the name and Internet address John entered.
6. Click **OK** twice
   A new entry has been added to the list. See Figure I-14.
7. Click **View** on the menu bar, then click **Call Log**
   Figure I-15 shows a log of all the calls that John Casey has made so far.
8. Close the Call Log window, click **File** on the menu bar, then click **Exit Phone Dialer**
   Phone Dialer closes

QuickTip

You can also add entries to the Speed Dial list by clicking the check box in the Dial dialog box when you first place the call.

FIGURE I-13: Adding a new entry to the Speed Dial List

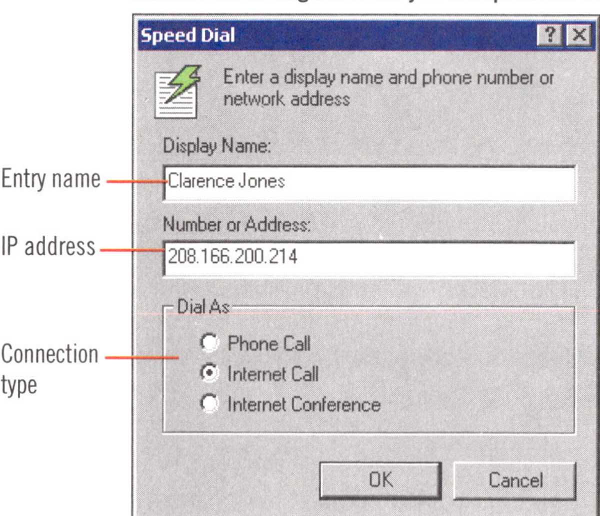

FIGURE I-14: Entries in the Speed Dial list

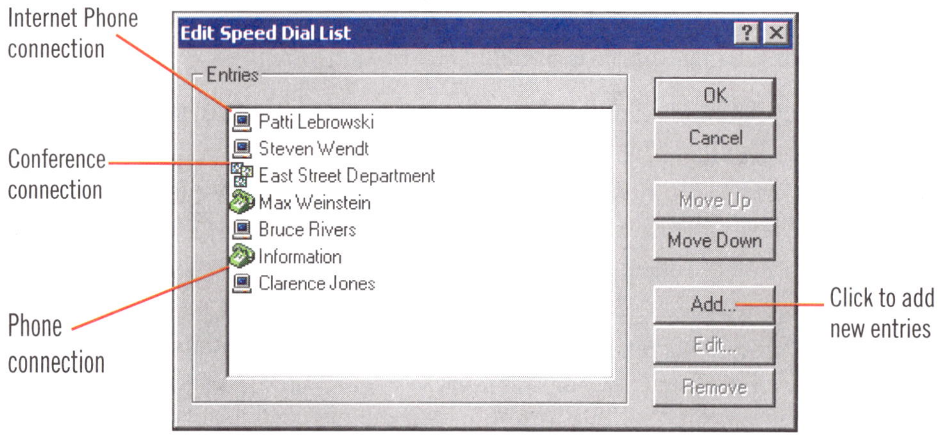

FIGURE I-15: Entries in the phone log

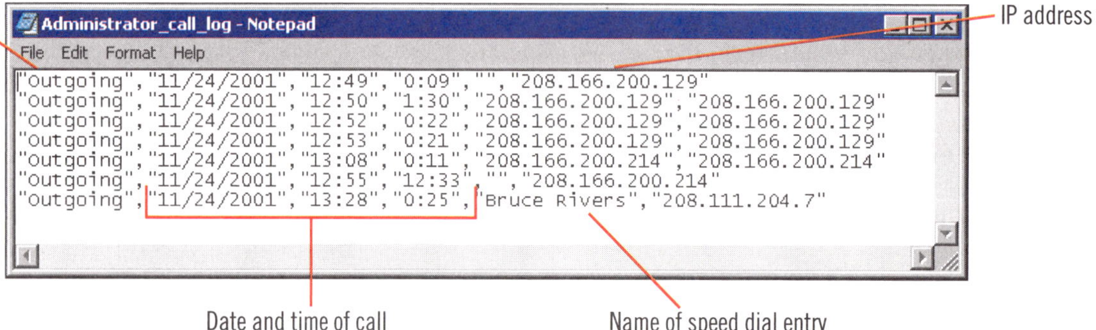

Joining a phone conference with Phone Dialer

If your system or network administrator has set up an Internet Directory server on your network, you can access conference calls involving several parties. To create a conference call, click New Conference from the Phone menu, enter the name of the conference, specify the time that conference will take place, then choose the users who are invited. Note that the network administrator must give your account the permission necessary to create a conference call. To join a conference call, click Join Conference from the Phone menu and then select a conference from a list in the Join Conference dialog box.

Setting Up NetMeeting

Microsoft NetMeeting provides state-of-the-art computer communications features. With NetMeeting, you can talk to others over the Internet as you do on a regular phone; you can use video to see others and let others see you as you converse; you can share programs and files with others; you can collaborate on documents and even share a whiteboard (a drawing canvas); and you can send messages using Chat. The first time you use NetMeeting, you need to set up the NetMeeting service. John Casey would like to be able to use NetMeeting to communicate with his business contacts.

1. Click **Start**, point to **Programs**, point to **Accessories**, point to **Communications**, then click **NetMeeting**
   NetMeeting starts, displaying the setup wizard.
2. Read the opening screen, then click **Next**
3. Enter the requested information, using your real name, e-mail address, and city and state location, then click **Next**
   John enters the information shown in Figure I-16. You don't have to enter anything in the Comments text box if you don't want to.
4. Click the **Server name list arrow**, as shown in Figure I-17, click **Microsoft Internet Directory** or whatever directory server you want to use, then click **Next**
   A **directory server** lists the people you can call using NetMeeting. When you log on to a directory server, your name appears in the list, and others who are also logged on to that server can communicate with you. John chooses the directory server shown in Figure I-17.
5. Click an **option button** to specify the speed of your Internet connection, then click **Next**
   If you want to create a shortcut to NetMeeting on your desktop or Quick Launch bar, leave the corresponding check boxes selected, then click **Next**
6. Click **Next** to tune your audio settings, click **Test** to hear a test sound over your speakers or headphones, click **Stop** after you've chosen the desired sound volume, then click **Next**
7. Adjust the volume of your microphone, click **Next**
8. Click **Finish**
   Continue to the next lesson as NetMeeting starts.

Trouble?

If NetMeeting starts without opening the setup wizard, this is not the first time NetMeeting has been used on your machine. Read through this lesson without performing the steps.

Trouble?

Depending on your computer's hardware, you may see a different set of dialog boxes.

QuickTip

If you need to tune your audio settings again later, click Tools on the NetMeeting menu bar, then click Audio Tuning Wizard and follow the steps.

FIGURE I-16: Entering contact information

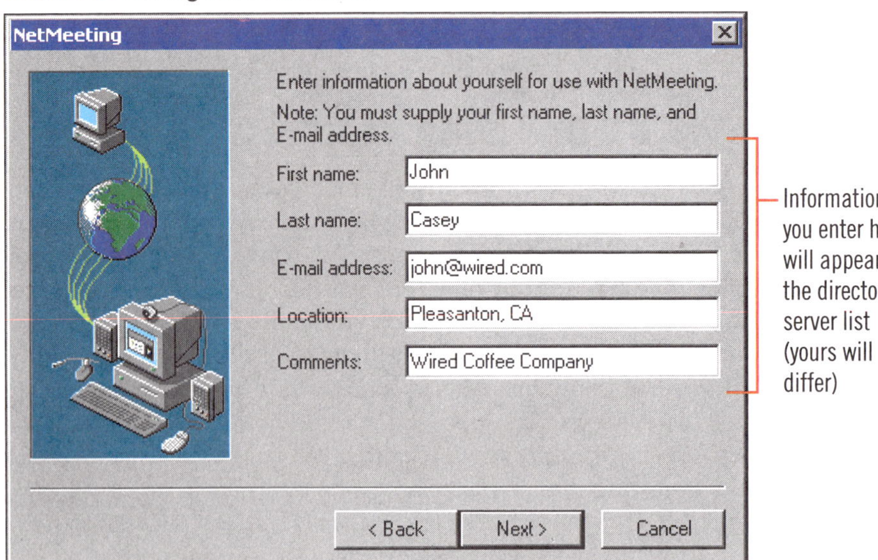

FIGURE I-17: Choosing a directory server

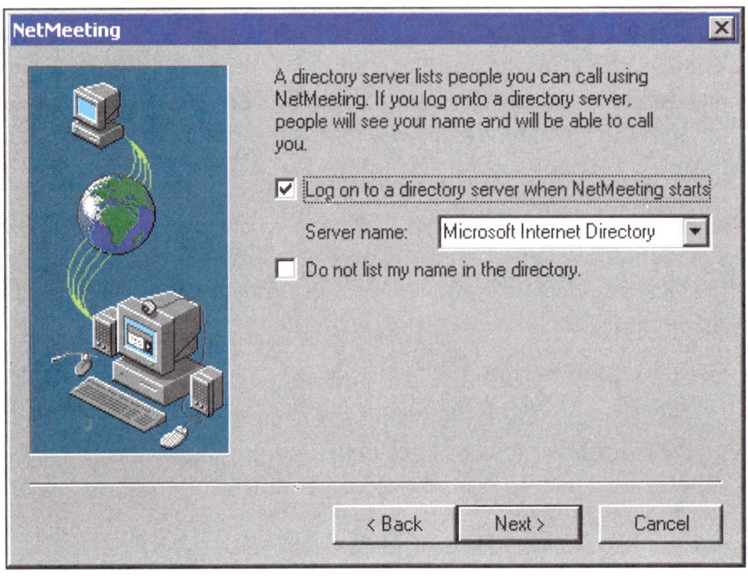

Windows 2000

Contacting Others with NetMeeting

Once NetMeeting is set up on your computer, you can use it to talk over the Internet, using a microphone attached to your computer. You have two communication choices: Chat or Audio and Visual. In Chat, you type messages back and forth. In Audio and Visual, you speak into a microphone and hear the other person's response over your computer's speakers. If you have a video capture device, you can send video to others so they can receive images as well as sound. You can still use Audio and Visual without a video capture device; the remote party will then only hear you. John wants to confer with Bruce Clemons, a Wired Coffee Company stockholder who lives in California, about a stockholders' meeting. *Before attempting this lesson, you should make arrangements with someone else who has a Windows 2000 computer with an Internet connection, a sound card, speakers, and a microphone. That person should start NetMeeting and be logged on to the same directory you chose in the last lesson when you start this lesson.*

Steps

QuickTip

If you don't have access to an Internet directory server, you can click Directory from the Call menu to connect to a Web page that will allow you to sign up for the Microsoft Messenger Service. This is a free service that provides access to an Internet directory among other features.

1. Click **Call** on the NetMeeting menu bar, then click **New Call**
2. Type either the name, e-mail address, computer name, telephone number or IP address of the person you want to contact
   If you connected to this person before, you can also select him or her from the To drop-down list.
3. Click the **Using drop-down list arrow**, then click the type of connection you plan to make
   The Directory option specifies a directory server, the Network option specifies a computer on your network, and the Automatic option allows NetMeeting to determine the type of call for you. As shown in Figure I-18, John has completed the Place a Call dialog box to connect to Bruce Clemons.
4. Click **Call**
   The remote party will see a dialog box telling him or her that you want to connect. If the response is affirmative, you will see the remote party listed in the NetMeeting dialog box, as shown in Figure I-19.
5. Click the **Chat button**, type a message, press **[Enter]**, wait for a response (this may take a few moments), then continue to converse in this manner
   Figure I-20 shows an exchange between John Casey and Bruce Clemons; John started the conversation by asking about the stockholders' meeting, and Bruce responded with a note about the trade show.
6. Click the **Close button** on the Chat window (entitled "Untitled – Chat"), then click **No** when asked whether you want to save the conversation

FIGURE I-18: Placing a NetMeeting Call

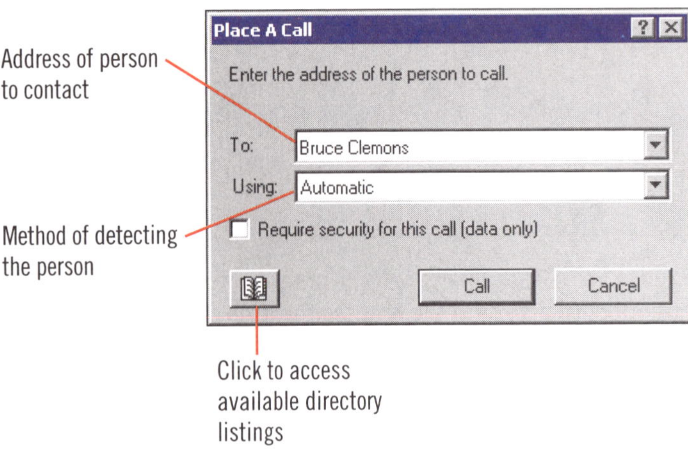

FIGURE I-19: Viewing a connection in NetMeeting

FIGURE I-20: Conducting a chat session in NetMeeting

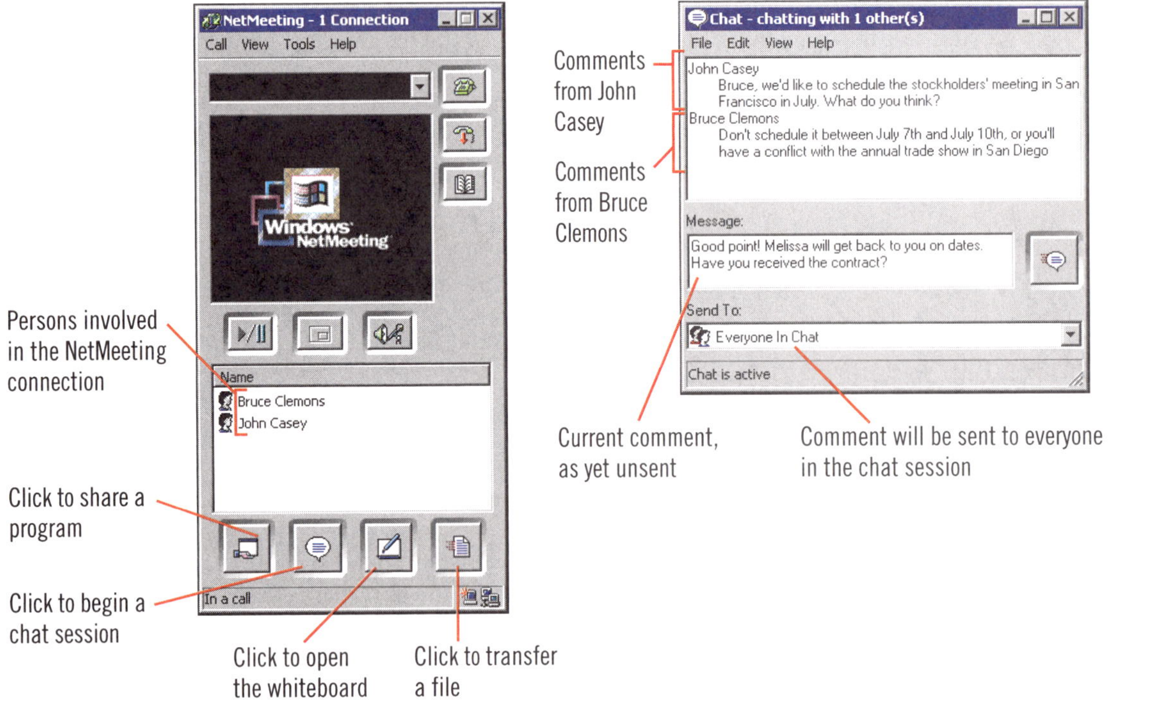

CLUES TO USE

Sharing documents and programs in NetMeeting

You can share your programs and documents with others in the conference by opening the document you want to share in its program window, clicking the Share button in the Chat window, clicking the name of the program in the list of open programs that appears, then clicking the Share button. Others will be able to see your document and the program on their computer screens. They can't work with the document until you give them access to it, which you do by clicking Allow Control button. The user who clicks the program window "takes control" of the program, with the ability to run any of the menu commands or make changes to the document. To discontinue sharing, click the application you want to stop sharing and then click the Unshare button again. Click the Close button to close the window.

Windows 2000

Sharing Graphical Content Using NetMeeting

NetMeeting includes **Whiteboard**, a graphical program that you can use to display and share graphical content. All participants in the NetMeeting can access a shared whiteboard and interactively make changes to the graphics it displays. A whiteboard can have multiple pages, which the users can easily add and delete. You can copy and paste items between the whiteboard and other programs. You can emphasize key points using a highlighter tool or a pointer. Changes to one whiteboard are automatically synchronized with all other whiteboards, unless the user chooses to remove synchronization. John wants to show Bruce a graphic he has found that he thinks will work well with the company logo. He uses NetMeeting to share it with him and get his ideas.

1. Click the **Whiteboard button** in the Chat window
   John pastes the logo image shown in Figure I-21. Because the whiteboards are synchronized, Bruce sees the same thing that John sees.
2. Click the **Remote Pointer On button**
   A pointer appears in the whiteboard. This pointer will also appear on Bruce's whiteboard. As John moves the pointer around the whiteboard, the pointer moves in the same way on Bruce's whiteboard.
3. Click the **Remote Pointer On button** again
   The pointer no longer appears on the whiteboard.
4. Click the **Text button**, then type some sample text on the whiteboard
5. Click the **Pen button**, then drag some sample lines and curves on the whiteboard
   As shown in Figure I-22, John writes the text, "This color needs to be changed" and draws a line pointing to the coffee cup. The same changes and comments appear on Bruce's whiteboard. Any edits that Bruce makes on his whiteboard will be shown to John.
6. Click **File** on the Whiteboard menu bar, then click **Exit** to close the whiteboard, but do not save any changes
7. Click **Call** on the NetMeeting menu bar, click **Exit**, then click **Yes** to end the meeting
   NetMeeting closes.

QuickTip

You can save the contents of the whiteboard by clicking File and Save As from the menu. You would then have a permanent record of the changes you made during the NetMeeting.

FIGURE I-21: Opening a NetMeeting whiteboard

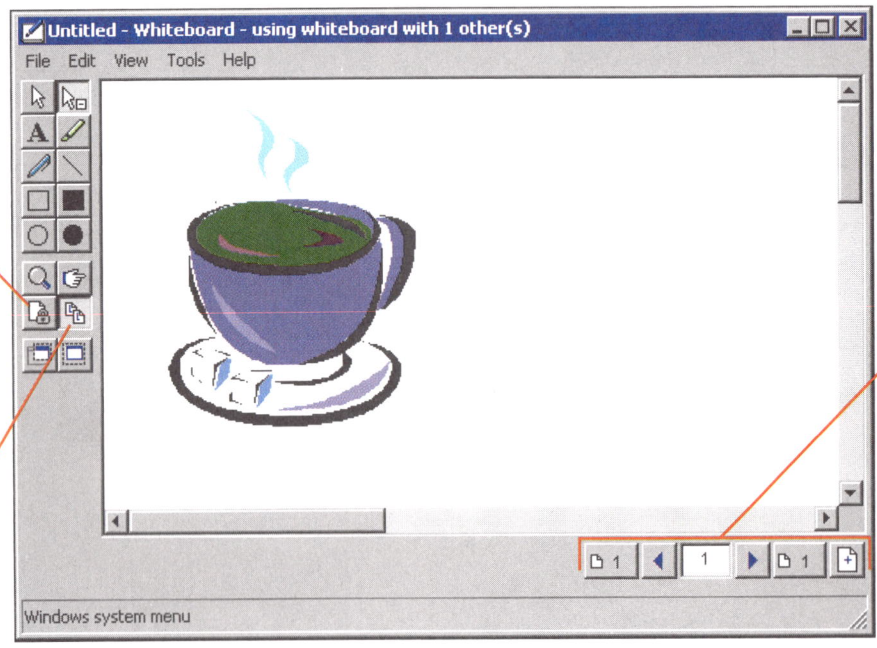

FIGURE I-22: Editing a whiteboard

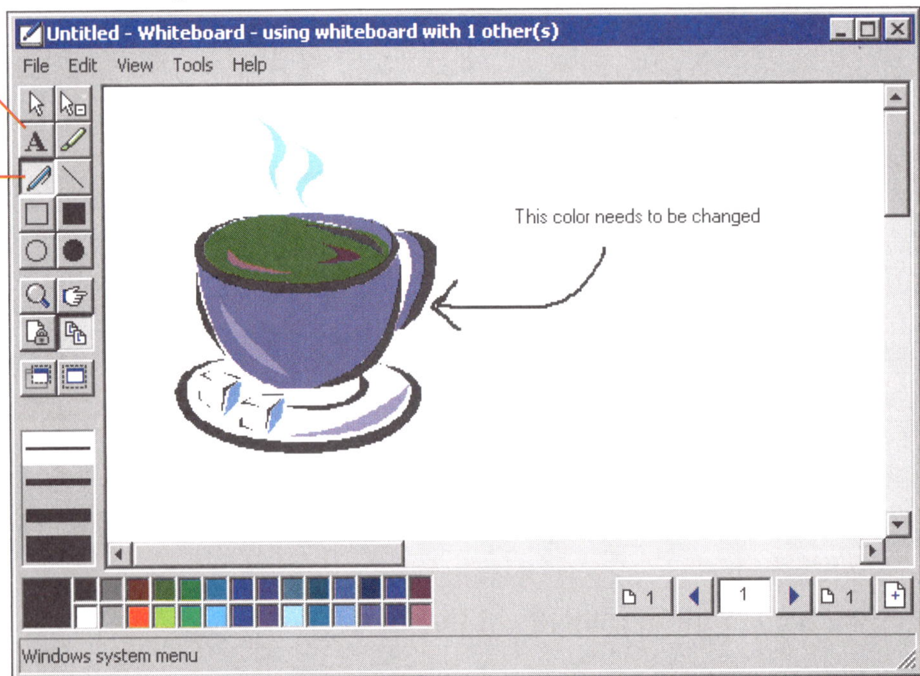

Working with Whiteboard

Whiteboard bears some resemblance to the Windows 2000 Paint program and provides some additional features. One of these is the capability to create and save multiple pages. To add a new page to the whiteboard, click the Insert New Page button . To move between the pages, click the Previous Page and Next Page buttons. By default, the whiteboard is synchronized among all members of the NetMeeting. If you want to break the synchronization (to work on your own for a while), click the Synchronize and Unsynchronize button . Finally, if you want to prevent other users from altering the contents of your whiteboard, click the Lock and Unlock button .

Practice

Concepts Review

Label each of the elements of the screen shown in Figure I-23.

FIGURE I-23

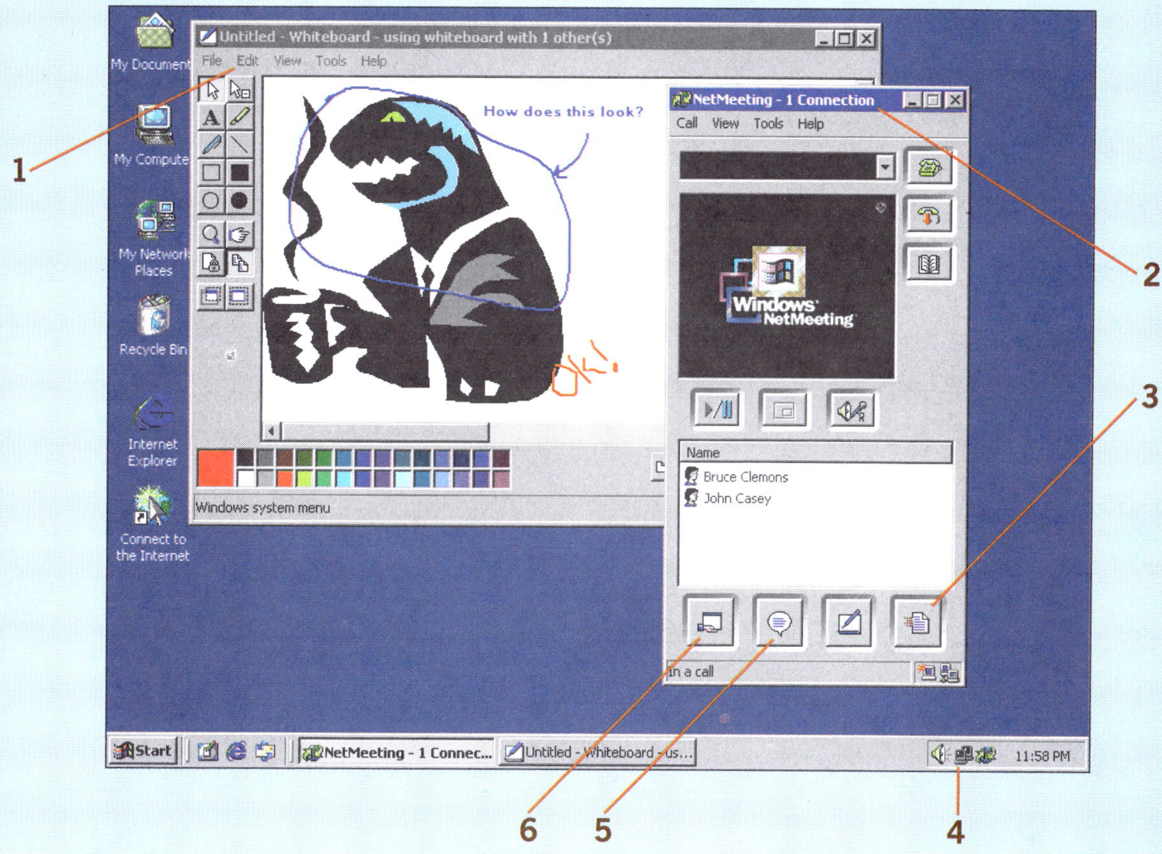

Match each of the terms with the statement that describes its function.

7. Provides a completely digital path from one computer to another
8. Accessory that allows you to dial phone numbers from your computer
9. Service that allows users who share common interests to come together electronically and exchange messages on a specific topic
10. Common server connection type that you use to connect to an Internet server
11. A window in NetMeeting that you can use to share graphic content
12. Allows you to talk to others over the Internet
13. Program that runs on your computer that automatically logs you on to an Internet service

a. Microsoft NetMeeting
b. ISDN
c. forum
d. PPP
e. logon script
f. Whiteboard
g. Phone Dialer

Select the best answer from the list of choices.

14. Under what circumstances are you most likely to need to establish a dial-up networking connection?
- **a.** On a university computer
- **b.** On a home computer
- **c.** On a computer at IBM headquarters
- **d.** On a computer at the Library of Congress

15. What connection possibilities are likely to exist for a home computer?
- **a.** ISDN or DSL line
- **b.** High-speed satellite connection
- **c.** Phone line
- **d.** Both a and c

16. With NetMeeting you can
- **a.** talk with others over the Internet.
- **b.** share a document.
- **c.** save a text file of a conversation.
- **d.** All of the above.

17. If you need to keep track of calls you make to clients, which accessory should you use?
- **a.** NetMeeting
- **b.** Chat
- **c.** Connection Wizard
- **d.** Phone Dialer

Skills Review

1. Set up a Dial-up Networking connection.
- **a.** Start the Internet Connection Wizard.
- **b.** Assume you have an existing Internet service over the phone line and that you have to set up the connection manually.
- **c.** Enter your ISP's phone number, and then your user name and password.

2. Use Connection Wizard advanced settings.
- **a.** In the first step of the Internet Connection Wizard, click the Advanced button.
- **b.** Select the connection type that your ISP requires.
- **c.** Choose the appropriate logon procedure.
- **d.** Enter the required IP and DNS address information.
- **e.** Finish the Connection Wizard by following the prompts.

3. **Connect to a dial-up service.**
   a. Open the Network and Dial-up Connections window, then double-click the connection you want to use.
   b. Verify your user name and password, and then click Dial.
   c. Print an image of your screen with the Status dialog box open and showing the General dialog sheet. (To print a copy of the screen, press [Print Screen] to make a copy of the screen, start Paint, click Edit on the menu bar, click Paste to paste the screen into Paint, then click Yes to paste the large image, if necessary. Click File on the menu bar, click Print, then click Print in the Print dialog box.)
   d. Disconnect from your service and close any open windows.

4. **Make an Internet phone call with Phone Dialer.**
   a. Click the Start button, point to Programs, point to Accessories, point to Communications, then click Phone Dialer.
   b. Dial the IP address of a colleague.
   c. Print an image of your screen showing the active phone connection.
   d. Disconnect from the remote party.

5. **Manage phone numbers.**
   a. From Phone Dialer, open the Edit Speed Dial List dialog box and enter the name and phone number, or IP address for the remote party.
   b. Repeat Step a for a phone number (not an IP address) that you call frequently.
   c. Print an image of your screen showing the Speed Dial list with your new entries (refer to Step 3c for screen printing instructions).
   d. Click View on the menu bar, then click Call Log to open the log of the calls you've made. Print out the contents of the window.

6. **Set up NetMeeting.**
   a. Click the Start button, point to Programs, point to Accessories, point to Communications, then click NetMeeting.
   b. If prompted, proceed through the setup procedure.

7. **Contact others with NetMeeting.**
   a. Click Call on the NetMeeting menu, then click New Call.
   b. In the Place a call dialog box, enter the name of a remote party you want to contact and the type of call you want to make.
   c. Click the Chat button. Type a message and press [Enter], and then wait for a response.
   d. Close the Chat window, then click Yes to save the contents as a text file.
   e. Print the contents of your Chat window (refer to Step 3c for screen printing instructions).

8. **Share graphical content using NetMeeting.**
   a. Click the Whiteboard button to open a whiteboard with the remote party in your NetMeeting.
   b. Use the whiteboard tools to draw an image, include text on the image.
   c. Save the contents of your whiteboard to a file.
   d. Print the contents of the whiteboard and then close the whiteboard.
   e. Close your NetMeeting connection.

Independent Challenges

1. You run a small office machines repair business, Tech-One. You would like to establish a connection to the Internet from your office, but you aren't sure what service you should use. You want e-mail and Internet service, and later on you might need the capability to publish your own Web page. You decide to research some of the local ISPs for the best service.

To complete this independent challenge:

a. Using the local Yellow Pages, look up the term "Internet Service Provider," "Internet On-Line Service Provider," or something similar. Select three ISPs that might meet your needs.
b. Call each ISP and ask about the services they provide, their rates, and their technical support availability.
c. Write a one-page report that compares the three ISPs you chose, and in the final paragraph, indicate which ISP you would choose and why.

2. You work at a small pet shop supply company, PetWorld, and because you have some experience with computers and the Internet, your manager has asked that you establish an Internet connection for the company.

To complete this independent challenge:

a. Use the Internet Connection Wizard to establish a new Internet connection with an ISP. Name this connection *PetWorld*.
b. Open the Dial-up Networking window and use the connection you just created to dial in to your service.
c. Print an image of your screen (refer to Step 3c in the Skills Review for screen printing instructions) with the Dial-up Networking window open. Draw a circle around the connection icon in the taskbar to show you are connected.

3. You are a financial service advisor for Point Financial Services, but you work in a regional office. You place frequent long-distance calls to your company's headquarters, and you would like to be able to use your computer to make those calls via the Internet.

To complete this independent challenge:

a. Start Phone Dialer and enter the IP address of a colleague you want to call.
b. Make sure that your colleague is running Phone Dialer at the time you want to make the call.
c. Call this number and then print an image of your screen (refer to Step 3c in the Skills Review for screen printing instructions), showing the call in action.
d. Print the log file showing the call you made.

4. You are a student at Midwest University, and you will be collaborating with another student on a project this semester. Because you commute to the university from a distance, you want to be able to work on the project at your home computer while communicating efficiently with your partner.

To complete this independent challenge:

a. Select a student in your class who has access to a Windows 2000 computer with an Internet connection.
b. Choose a time for conferencing.
c. At the appointed time, start NetMeeting and call your partner over the Internet.
d. Use Chat to communicate about your project.
e. Open one of your software programs (such as Microsoft Word), create a document for your project (such as a short project proposal), and share the document with your partner.
f. Print an image of the screen (refer to Step 3c in the Skills Review for screen printing instructions) showing the shared document in the NetMeeting window.
g. Save and print your Chat conversation.

▶ Visual Workshop

Re-create the screen shown in Figure I-24, which displays a NetMeeting conference. You will not be able to duplicate the exact window because you have a different user name than that shown in the figure. Observe these guidelines in creating this window:

- You will need to arrange a time to call a recipient who has NetMeeting.
- Your name and the name of the recipient will be different.
- Your directory server might be different.
- Duplicate the messages.

When you have duplicated this window, create a hard copy of your screen (refer to Step 3c in the Skills Review for screen printing instructions).

FIGURE I-24

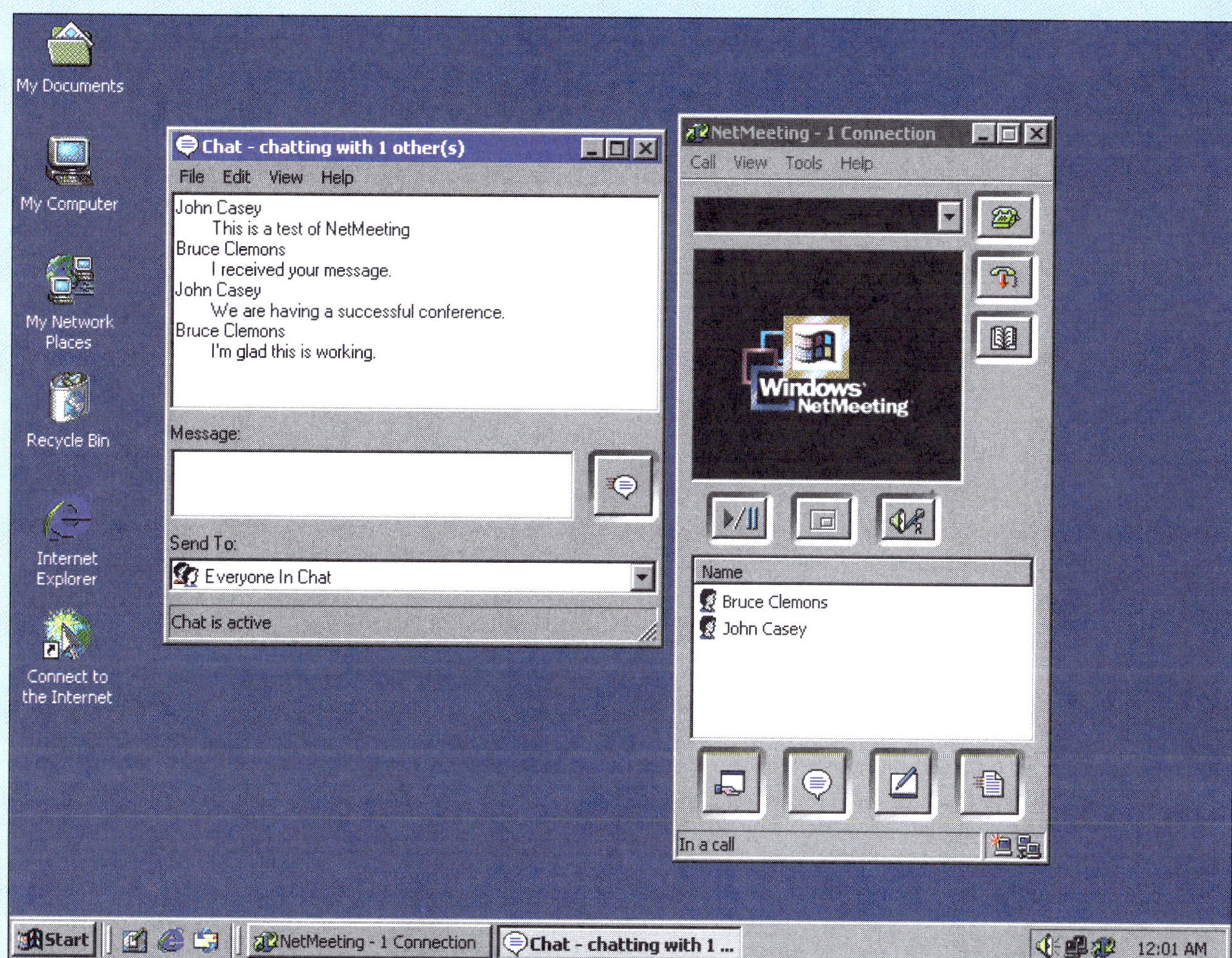

Creating a Docucentric Desktop

Objectives

- Create a document object
- Create a Start menu group
- Work with the Desktop folder
- Send a document to a different location
- Open a document with a different program
- Create and use a scrap
- Create a printer shortcut
- Remove desktop objects

Document is another word for **file**, the electronic data (such as a resume or spreadsheet) that you create with a program. The Windows 2000 interface is **docucentric** because the emphasis is on documents rather than on programs. This is an important distinction. With older operating systems, if you wanted to edit a resume, you would first locate and start your word processor, and then you would locate and open your resume file. In a docucentric environment, you can open your resume without worrying about its exact location on your hard disk or even the program that created it. The operating system locates the file and starts the program you need. John Casey wants to modify his desktop to get better access to the documents he uses most often. If you are in a restricted network environment, you might not be able to complete this unit.

Windows 2000

Creating a Document Object

In a docucentric environment such as Windows 2000, creating a document is easy. Not only can you create a document right from your desktop, but you can also place an icon on the desktop to quickly access that document in the future. This can save time with documents you access often. Instead of having to start a program, search through your computer's folders to find the document, and then open it each time, you can simply double-click an icon on the desktop. One of the documents that John uses on a regular basis is a memo in which he jots down notes as the work day progresses (things to do, calls to make, meetings to attend, errands to run, and so on). He decides to create a document to record his daily notes. Because he wants the memo to be easy to access, John decides to place the document on his desktop. If your network is restricted so you can't place objects on the desktop, you won't be able to do the steps in this unit, but you can read it to familiarize yourself with the concepts. If you are in a lab that does allow you to place icons on the desktop, be sure to restore your desktop to its original appearance when you finish your work. Your first step in this lesson is to check two settings on your computer that will make completing this unit easier.

1. Click the **Show Desktop button**.
2. Double-click the **My Computer icon**, click **Tools** on the menu bar, click **Folder Options**, then click the **View tab**
3. Be sure the **Hide file extensions for known file types check box** is selected (click it if it is not), click **OK**, then close My Computer
   By hiding the file extensions, you don't have to worry about including them when you type the names of your files.
4. Right-click the **desktop**, point to **New**, then click **Text Document**, as shown in Figure J-1
   An icon for a new text document is placed on your desktop, ready for you to name.
5. Type **Daily Memo** to name the text document you just created, then press **[Enter]**
   The icon on the desktop is a **document icon**. You can distinguish an icon that represents a shortcut from an icon that represents the actual document by the small arrow in the lower-left corner of a shortcut icon. It is important that you understand this difference, because you can delete a shortcut icon without removing the object it represents, but if you delete a document icon from the desktop, the document itself is deleted (or moved to the Recycle Bin).
6. Double-click the **Daily Memo icon**
   Windows 2000 knows that this is a text document, so it automatically starts Notepad, a program that comes with Windows 2000, and opens the Daily Memo document. Notepad is useful when you want to enter text without graphics or much formatting.
7. Type the text shown in Figure J-2, click the **Close button** on the Notepad program window, then click **Yes** when prompted to save changes
   Notepad closes. The Daily Memo icon remains on John's desktop, so to open the memo, he can simply double-click the icon. He does not have to start Notepad first, nor does he have to search for the document on the hard drive.

Trouble?

If your Notepad window scrolls to the right as you type, click Format on the menu bar, then click Word Wrap.

FIGURE J-1: Creating a new text document on the desktop

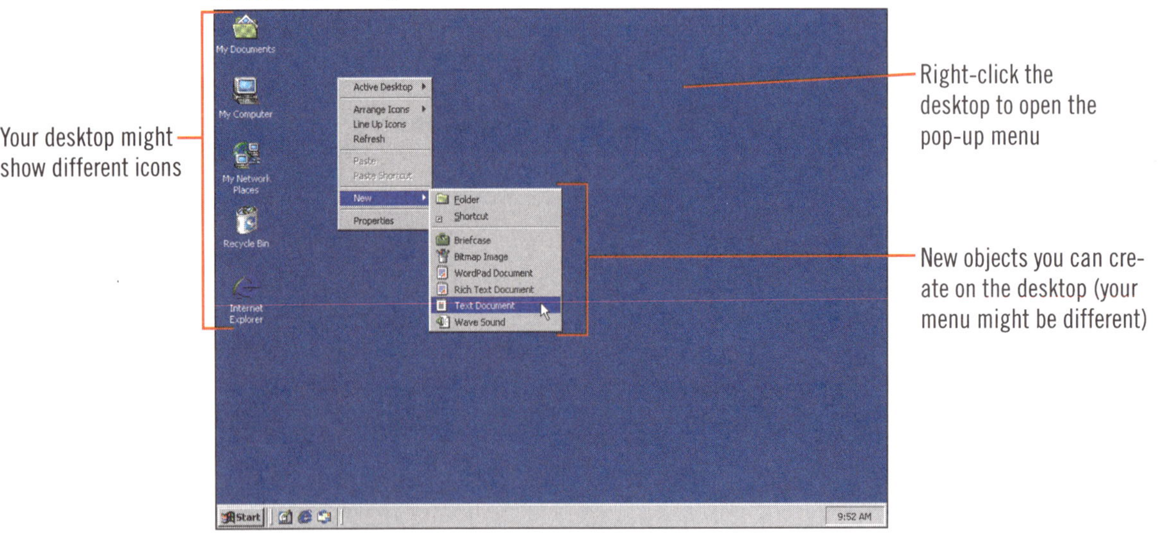

FIGURE J-2: Daily memo document on the desktop

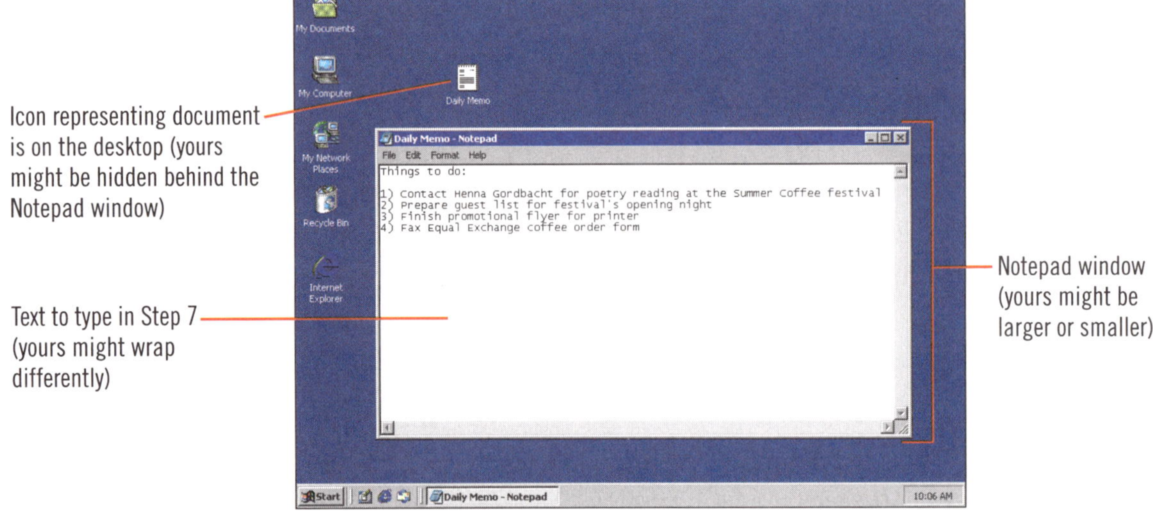

Creating shortcut icons on the desktop

You can place a shortcut to any document on your desktop by right-clicking the desktop, pointing to New, then clicking Shortcut on the pop-up menu. Enter the folder and drive location of the document using the Browse button, click Next, use the name provided or type a name for the shortcut in the dialog box, and then click Finish.

Creating a Start Menu Group

A docucentric environment offers many ways for you to access your documents. You can, for example, modify your Start menu so that it lists your documents in addition to the programs you have installed on your computer. The Start menu is organized into different groups, such as the Programs group and the Settings group. You can create your own groups to better organize the tasks you perform and the documents you work with. John would like to be able to access his Daily Memo document and other documents like it directly from the Start menu. He decides to add a new group to his Start menu called "Memos." Then he'll create a shortcut to the daily memo on the desktop, and finally he'll add that shortcut to the new Memos group on his Start menu.

Steps

1. Right-click the **Start button** on the taskbar, then click **Explore**
   Windows Explorer opens with the Start Menu folder in the left pane.
2. If necessary, resize the Windows Explorer window or drag the Daily Memo icon so you can see both, as shown in Figure J-3
3. Click **File** on the Windows Explorer menu bar, point to **New**, then click **Folder**
   A new folder is placed in the right pane, ready for you to name.
4. Type **Memos**, then press **[Enter]**
   This folder represents a new Memos group on the Start Menu.
5. On the desktop, right-click the **Daily Memo icon**, then click **Create Shortcut**
   An icon for the shortcut appears on the desktop.
6. Drag the **Shortcut to Daily Memo icon** (you might have to move the Windows Explorer window to see it) to the Memos folder, as shown in Figure J-4
7. Click the **Close button** on the Windows Explorer program window
   Windows Explorer closes.
8. Click the **Start button** on the taskbar, then point to **Memos**
   The new Memos group with the Daily Memo shortcut appears on the Start menu, as shown in Figure J-5.
9. Click away from the Start menu to close it without choosing a command

Trouble?

If your right pane displays the icons differently than in Figure J-3, click View on the menu bar, then click Large Icons. Your window will look slightly different if you have Web view enabled.

FIGURE J-3: Preparing to add a group to the Start menu

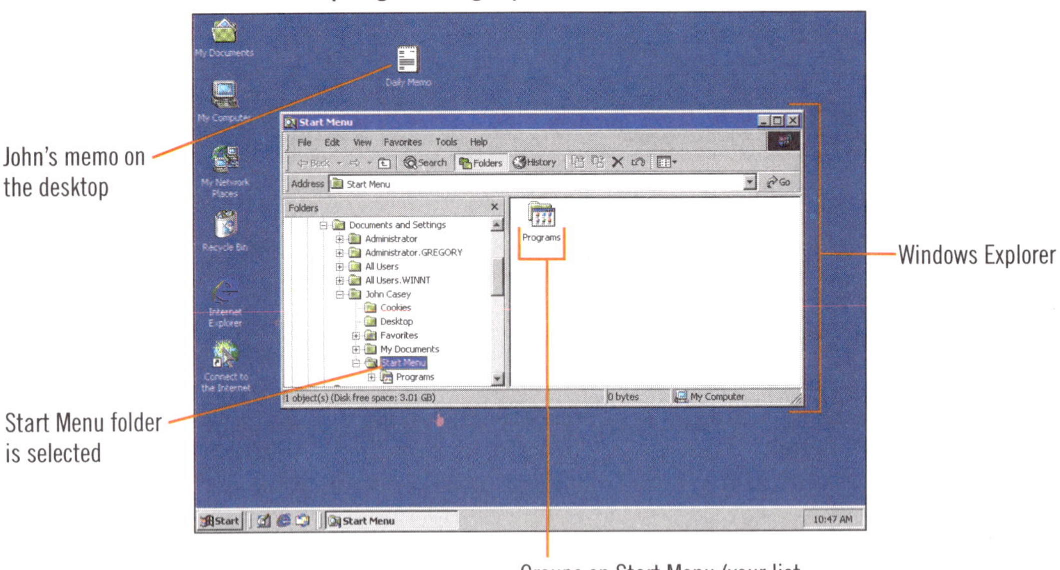

FIGURE J-4: Adding a shortcut to the Memos folder

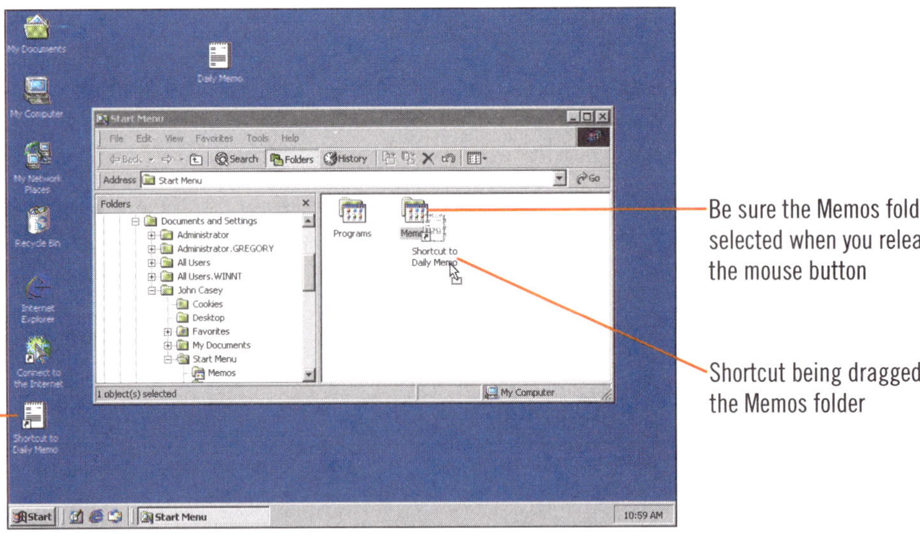

FIGURE J-5: Accessing the Memos folder shortcut

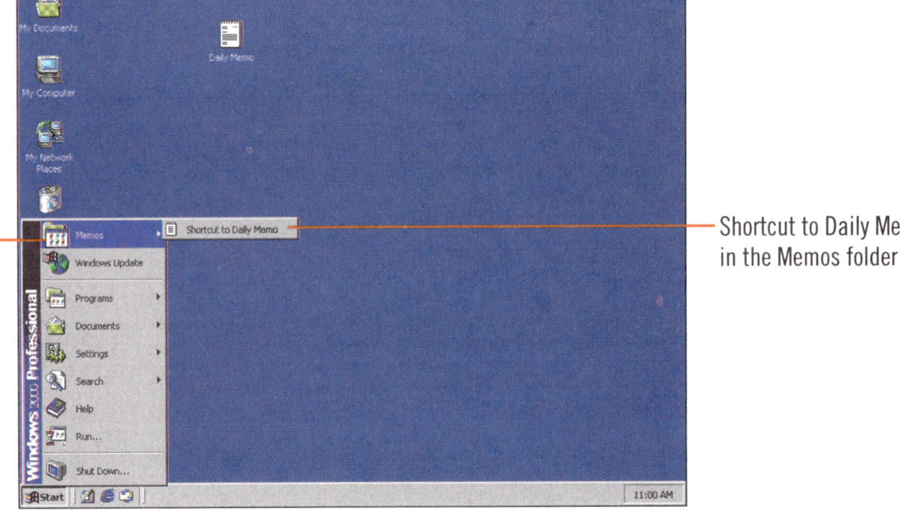

Working with the Desktop Folder

The contents of the Start menu are determined by contents of the Start Menu folder on your computer. Likewise, the contents of the desktop are determined by contents of the Desktop folder on your computer. When you add an object to the desktop, the object is added to the desktop folder, and vice versa; when you add an object to the Desktop folder, the object appears on the desktop. To customize your desktop, you can work directly on the desktop or you can start Windows Explorer, locate and open the Desktop folder, and then add or change objects in the Desktop folder. Any changes you make in the Desktop folder are reflected on the desktop itself. Table J-1 shows a list of other common Windows 2000 objects and their corresponding folders. John wants to add a new document to his desktop. This document will be the start of a letter he is writing to The Beanery regarding an overdue shipment.

1. Right-click the **Start button** on the taskbar, then click **Explore**
   Windows Explorer opens showing the contents of the Start Menu folder.

2. Click the **Desktop folder icon** in the left pane of Windows Explorer (you may have to scroll to see it)
   The Desktop folder on the computer shown in Figure J-6 is located in the Documents and Settings\John Casey folder on the C: drive. The Desktop folder shows the contents of the desktop (with the exception of objects that are part of the desktop, such as My Computer and the Recycle Bin). Notice that it contains the Daily Memo file you created earlier.

Trouble?

If you can't find the Desktop folder, ask your instructor or technical support person for assistance. On some systems, this folder is hidden, so to view it, you must click Tools on the menu bar, click Folder Options, click the View tab, click the Show hidden files and folders option button, and then click OK.

3. Click **File** on the menu bar, point to **New**, then click **Text Document**
   An icon for a new document is placed in the Desktop folder, ready to be named.

4. Type **Beanery Memo**, then press **[Enter]**

5. Double-click the **Beanery Memo icon**, then enter the text shown in Figure J-7

6. Click the **Close button** on the Notepad window, then click **Yes** when prompted to save changes
   The Beanery Memo file is saved and Notepad closes.

7. Click the **Close button** on the Windows Explorer window
   Figure J-8 shows the icon for the new Beanery Memo file that you placed on your desktop using Windows Explorer.

Trouble?

Don't worry if your Beanery Memo file appears in a different location on the desktop.

TABLE J-1: Desktop objects and their folders

desktop object	folder
Windows 2000 desktop	C:\Documents and Settings*Username*\Desktop
My Documents	C:\Documents and Settings*Username*\My Documents
Entries in the Start menu	C:\Documents and Settings*Username*\Start Menu

FIGURE J-6: **Viewing the Desktop folder in Windows Explorer**

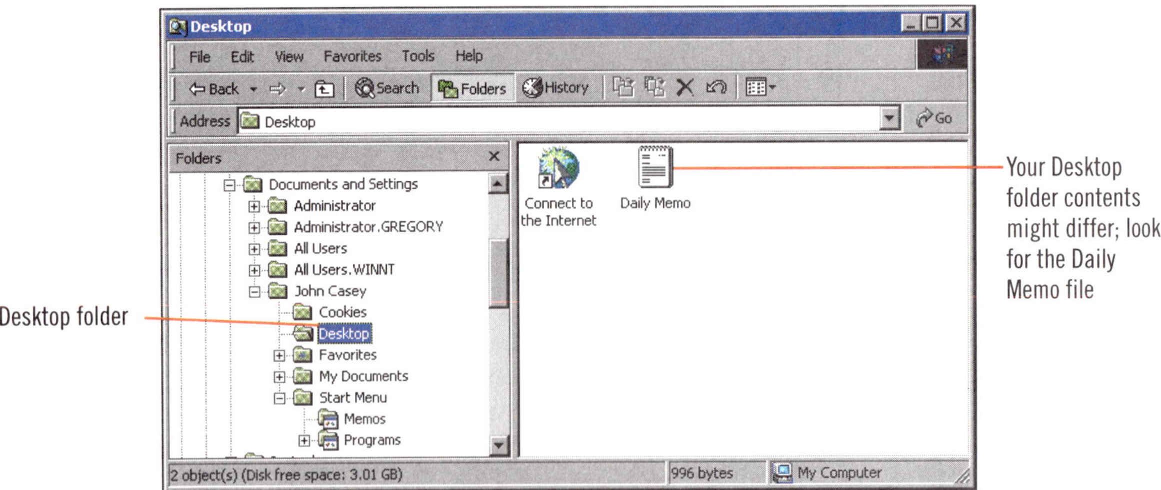

FIGURE J-7: **Notepad window with John's new memo**

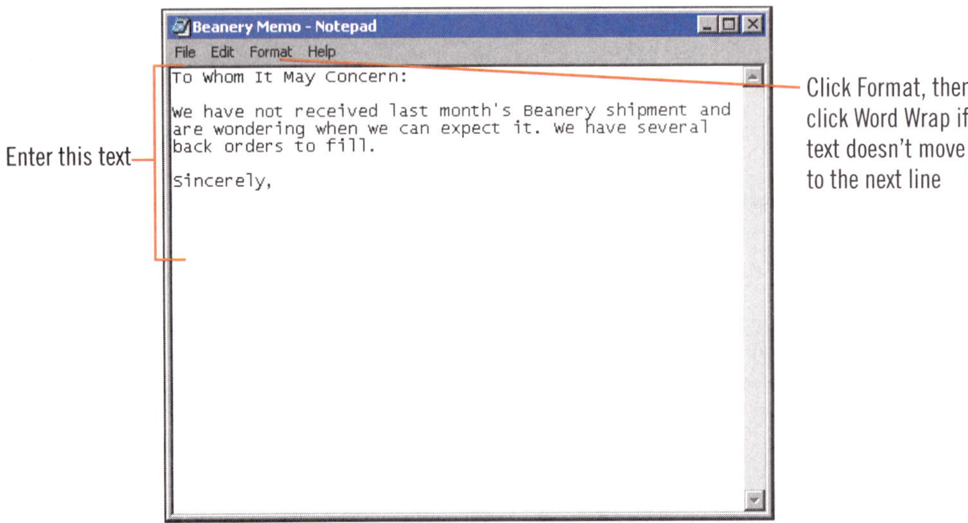

FIGURE J-8: **Icon representing the document you created using Windows Explorer**

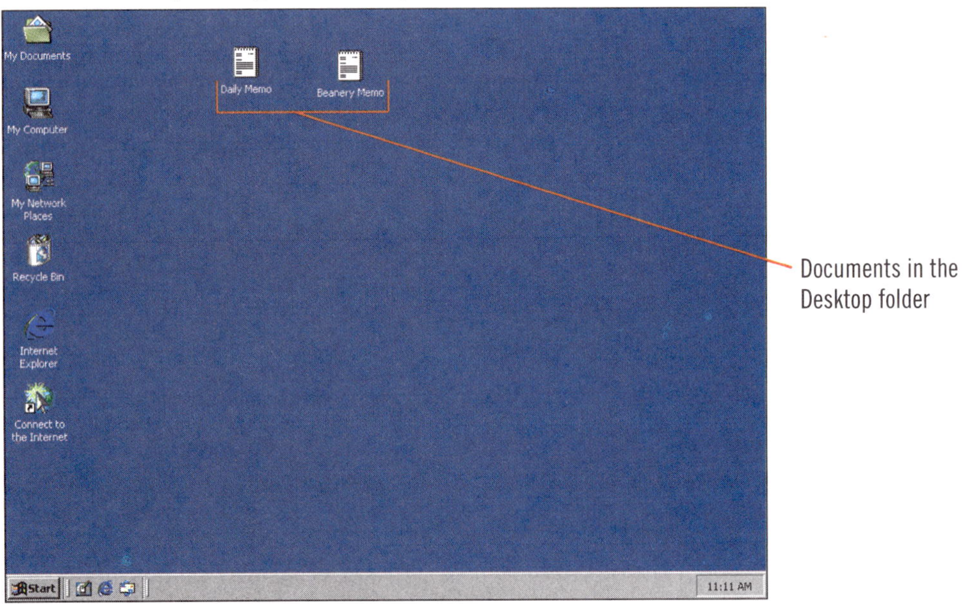

Sending a Document to a Different Location

The Windows 2000 **Send To command** provides another way to manage your documents efficiently. Located on the pop-up menu of any desktop object, the Send To command lets you send a document to a new destination. You simply right-click the document, click Send To, then click the destination you want, like a floppy drive, a printer, folder or a program. If the location you want isn't available in the Send To list, you can add it to the SendTo folder. The SendTo folder is a hidden folder located by the Desktop and Start Menu folders. When you add shortcuts that point to folders and drives on your computer, those shortcuts appear as items on the Send To menu. John would like to be able to send a desktop memo to the Memos group on the Start menu, so he adds this option to the SendTo folder.

1. Right-click the **Start button** on the taskbar, then click **Explore**
   Windows Explorer opens showing the contents of the Start Menu folder.

2. Click **Tools** on the menu bar, click **Folder Options**, click the **View** tab, click the **Show hidden files and folders option button**, then click **OK**

3. Click the **Memos folder** in the left pane, click **Edit** on the menu bar, then click **Copy**
   The Memos group is copied to the Clipboard so that you can paste it into the SendTo folder.

4. Click the **SendTo folder** in the left pane, click **Edit** on the menu bar, then click **Paste Shortcut**
   A shortcut for the Memos group appears in the SendTo folder, as shown in Figure J-9.

5. Right-click the new shortcut, click **Rename**, type **Memos**, then press **[Enter]**
   Renaming the shortcut allows you to see "Memos" when you click the Send To command, rather than "Shortcut to Memos Group."

6. Click the **Close button** on the Windows Explorer program window
   Windows Explorer closes. Now, any time John creates a new memo on his desktop, he can easily send it to the Memos group, which will allow him to open it from the Start menu in the future.

7. Right-click the **Beanery Memo** on the desktop, point to **Send To**, then click **Memos**, as shown in Figure J-10

8. Click the **Start button**, then point to **Memos**
   John's Beanery memo has been placed in the Memos group of the Start menu. See Figure J-11.

9. Click a **blank area of the desktop** to close the Start menu

QuickTip

Send To moves files if destination drive is the same, or copies them if it's different.

Trouble?

You might have to scroll to see the SendTo folder. If you can't locate it, see your instructor or technical support person for assistance.

FIGURE J-9: Adding an option to the SendTo folder

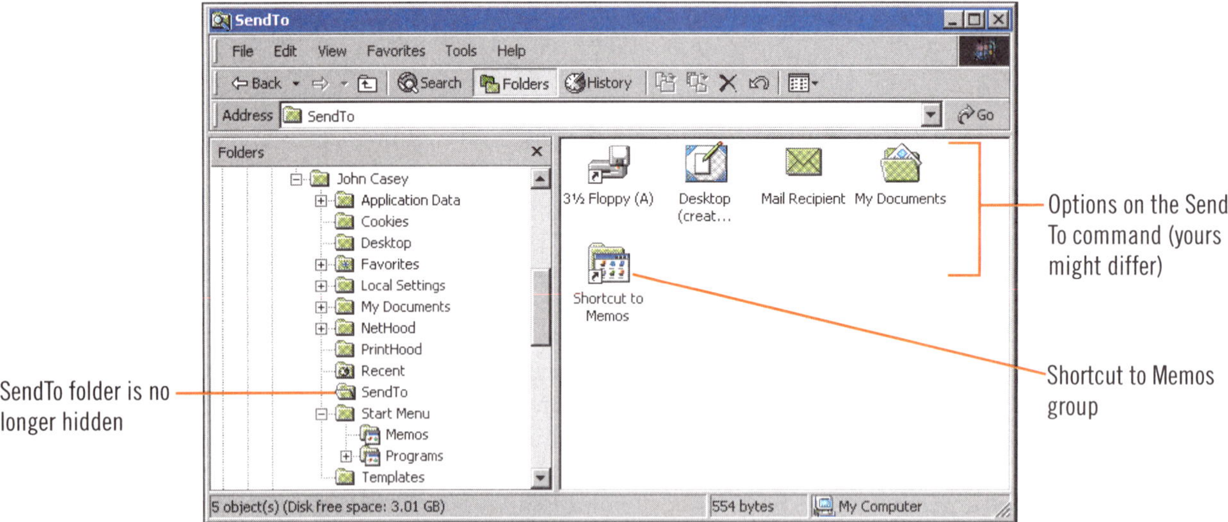

FIGURE J-10: Memos group appears on the Send To menu

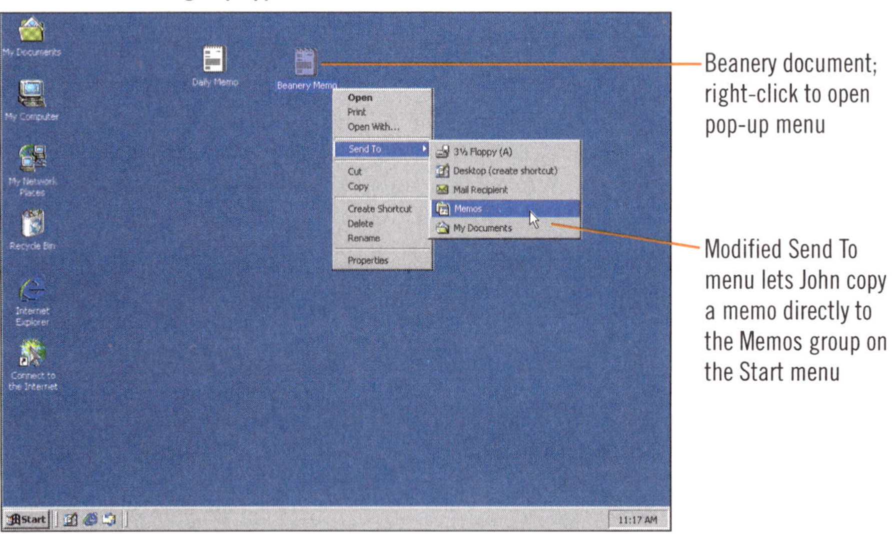

FIGURE J-11: Document in Memos group

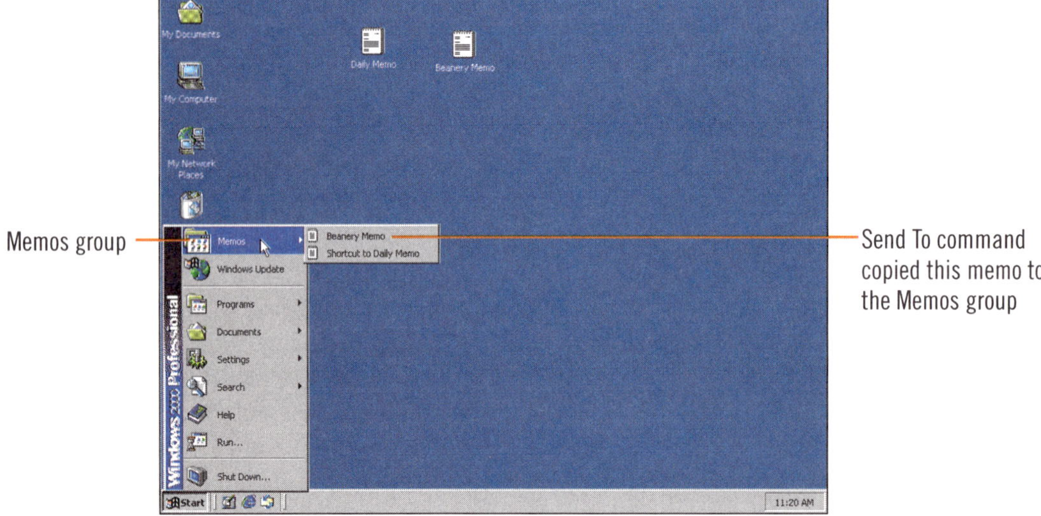

Windows 2000

Opening a Document with a Different Program

Most documents on your desktop are associated with a specific program. For example, if you double-click a document whose filename ends with the three-letter extension "txt," Windows 2000 automatically opens the document with Notepad, a text editor. There are situations, though, when you need to open a document with a program other than the one Windows 2000 chooses, or when you want to choose a different default program. For example, you might want to open a text document in WordPad rather than Notepad so you can add special fonts and graphics. To do this, you can use the Open With command to choose a different application. John would like to have the option of opening his text memos with WordPad when he needs to format them more professionally. To allow for this option, he uses the Open With command to open the file with WordPad.

Steps

Trouble?

Depending on how Windows 2000 has been set up on your system, you may see the submenu shown in Figure J-13. Once you open a file with an alternate application, Windows 2000 automatically adds that application to the Open With list. If this is the case, simply click WordPad from the list of applications.

1. Right-click the **Beanery Memo icon** on the desktop, then click **Open With**
   The Open With dialog box opens, as shown in Figure J-12. Windows displays a list of registered programs installed on your computer. You can click one of the programs in this list, or you can click the Other button to search for a program not in the list. If you click the Always use this program to open these files check box, the selected program will become the default program for this type of file.
2. Click **WordPad** from the list of programs, then click **OK**
   The Beanery Memo document opens in WordPad.
3. Click **View** on the menu bar, then click **Options**
4. Click the **Wrap to window option button**, then click **OK**
   The text of the Beanery Memo wraps to the window, as shown in Figure J-14.

File extensions

The program Windows 2000 uses to open a document depends on a three-letter extension to the document's filename, called a **file extension**. You might have never seen a document's file extension because your system might be set up to hide it. The file extension for many text files is ".txt" (pronounced "dot t-x-t"), and many graphics files have the extension ".bmp" (pronounced "dot b-m-p"). This means that the full name for your Daily Memo file is Daily Memo.txt. If you want to change the program Windows 2000 automatically starts with a given file extension, open My Computer, click Tools, then click Folder Options. Click the File Types tab to see the list of the file extensions Windows 2000 recognizes and the programs associated with each of them, and make changes as appropriate.

FIGURE J-12: Choosing a different program to open a text file

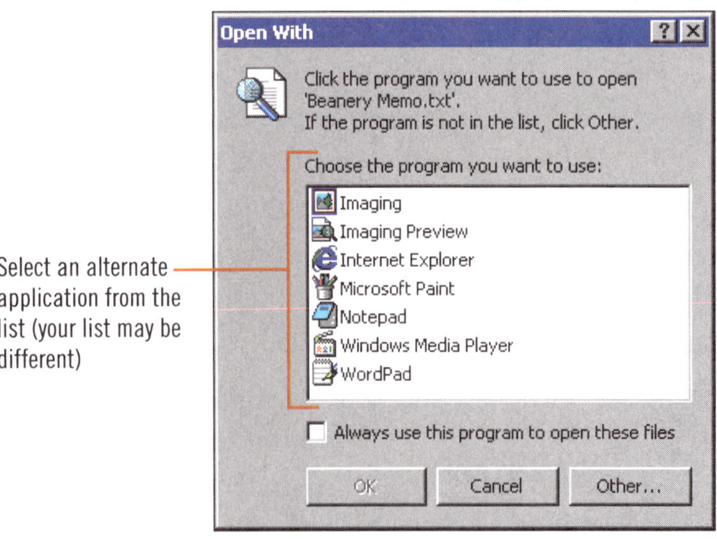

Select an alternate application from the list (your list may be different)

FIGURE J-13: Windows 2000 automatically adds WordPad to the Open With menu

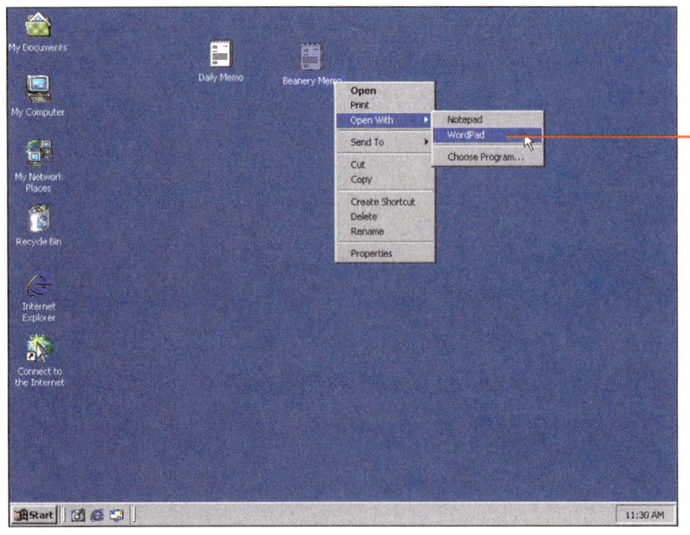

Once you open a text file using WordPad, this option is automatically added to the Open With menu

FIGURE J-14: Beanery Memo in WordPad

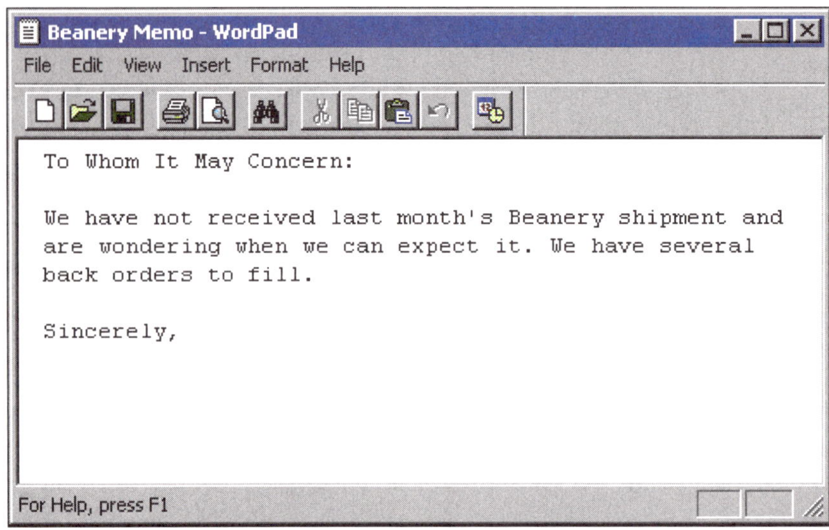

Creating and Using a Scrap

There are certain text or graphic items that you include in almost every document you create, such as your return mailing address, signature, or company logo. Windows 2000 allows you to save such items in special documents called **scraps** that you can quickly and easily insert into your documents. John includes his mailing address in many of the notes he writes. He decides to create a scrap containing his address and place it on his desktop so he can easily drag it into a document whenever he needs it. Then he'll use the scrap in another document, to test it.

Steps

1. With the WordPad document you created in the previous lesson still open, click at the end of the document, if necessary, then type the new text shown in Figure J-15

Trouble?

If you don't see the desktop, resize the WordPad window.

2. Select the lines you just typed (include the blank line)
   You should be able to see the WordPad window and a blank area of the desktop.

QuickTip

If you want to create a document scrap without leaving the selected text or graphic in the original document, hold down the Shift key when you drag your selection to the desktop.

3. Drag the selected text to the desktop
   The selected text is placed as a document scrap on the desktop, as shown in Figure J-16.
4. Click the **Close button** [X] to close the WordPad window, then click **Yes** twice when prompted to save changes
5. Click the **Start button** on the taskbar, point to **Programs**, point to **Accessories**, click **WordPad**, then resize the WordPad window as necessary so that you can see the document scrap on the desktop
   A new document opens in WordPad.
6. Drag the **document scrap** into the WordPad window, as shown in Figure J-17
   The contents of the document scrap are placed at the beginning of the new WordPad document. In dropping the scrap into your document, you did not remove it from the desktop, so you can use it again.

QuickTip

You can create document scraps for many Windows 2000 programs besides WordPad. For example, you can create a Paint scrap containing a company logo.

7. Click the **Close button** [X] to exit WordPad, then click **No** when prompted to save your changes
   John doesn't need to save this document because he was only using it to test his scrap. WordPad closes.

FIGURE J-15: John's revised memo in WordPad

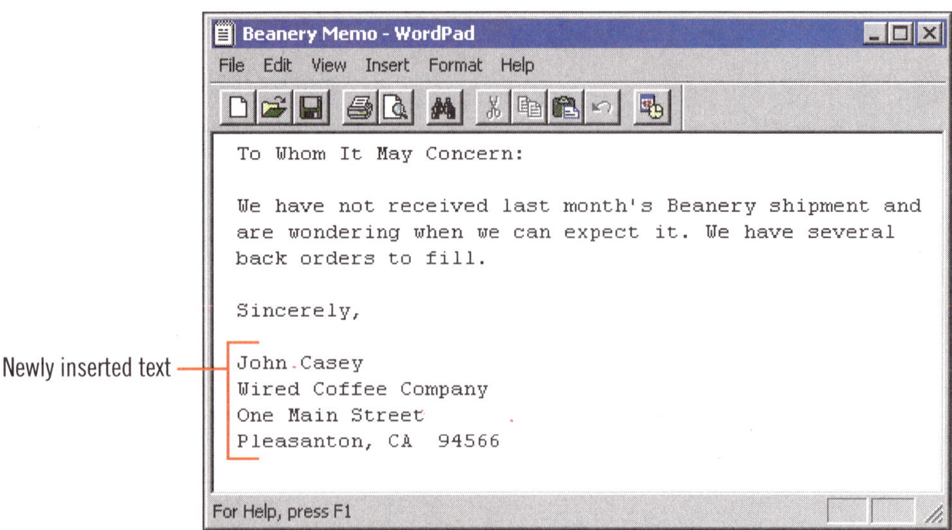

FIGURE J-16: John's memo and the document scrap

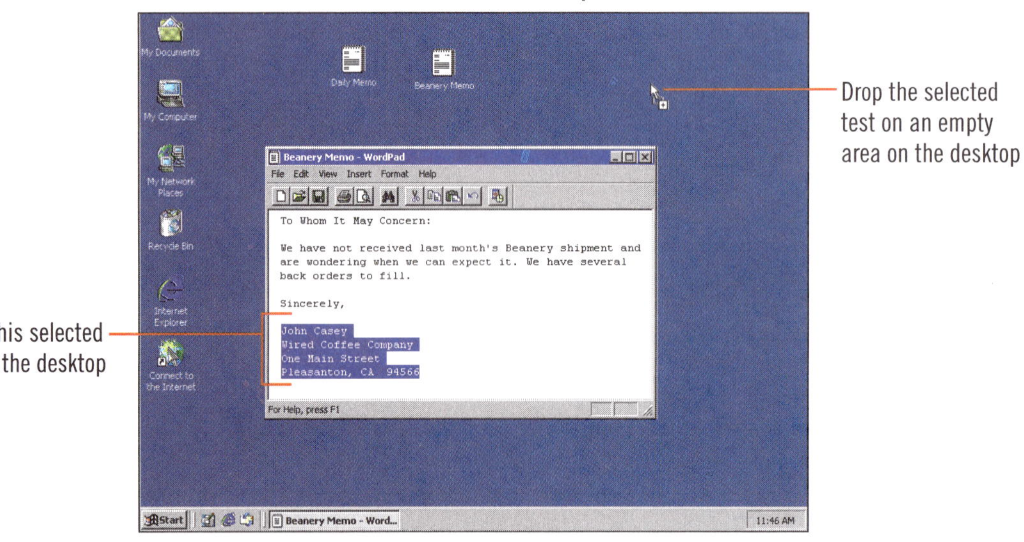

FIGURE J-17: Inserting a document scrap into a document

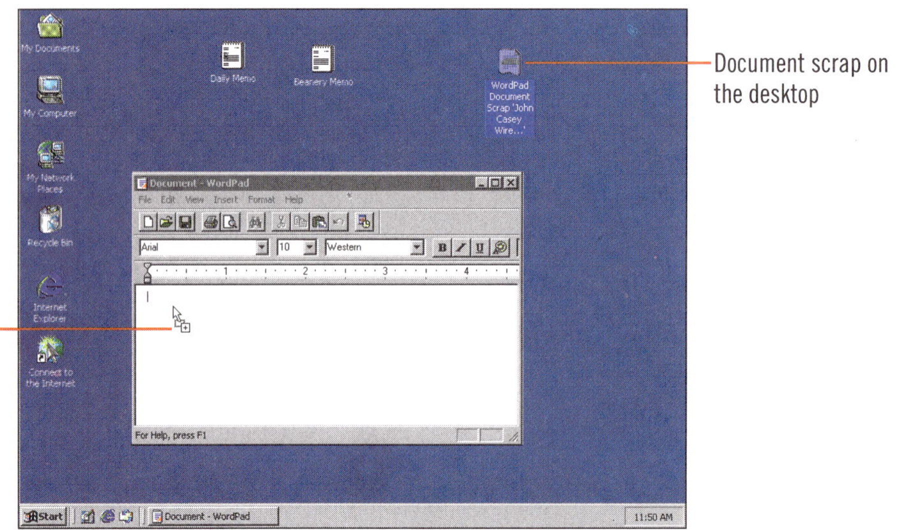

Windows 2000

Creating a Printer Shortcut

In addition to placing documents and shortcuts to documents on the desktop, you can also place shortcuts to resources on your computer, such as drives or printers. Once such a shortcut is on your desktop, you can access that resource almost instantaneously. For example, if you regularly use your floppy drive, you might want to create a shortcut to it on the desktop. Then you don't have to go through My Computer to view its contents; you can simply double-click the shortcut. John decides to place a shortcut to his printer on his desktop. He can then print any document by dragging its icon to the printer shortcut icon. He'll experiment with this by printing his Daily Memo document.

Steps

1. Click the **Start button** on the taskbar, point to **Settings**, then click **Printers**
   The Printers window opens.
2. Point to your default printer, then press and hold down the right mouse button
   This type of printing works only with the default printer.
3. Drag the printer icon to the desktop as shown in Figure J-18, then release the right mouse button
4. Click **Create Shortcut(s) Here**
   A shortcut to your printer appears on the desktop, as shown in Figure J-19. Your shortcut might look different, depending on the printer you are using.
5. Click the **Close button** in the Printers window
6. Drag the **Daily Memo icon** to the printer shortcut icon, as shown in Figure J-20
   Windows opens the Daily Memo document briefly in Notepad, prints it, and then closes it again so quickly that you might not notice it unless you are watching carefully. John is pleased that he can print his documents without even opening them.

Trouble?

If you receive an error message, you might have created a shortcut to a non-default printer. See your instructor or technical support person for assistance.

FIGURE J-18: Creating a printer shortcut on the desktop

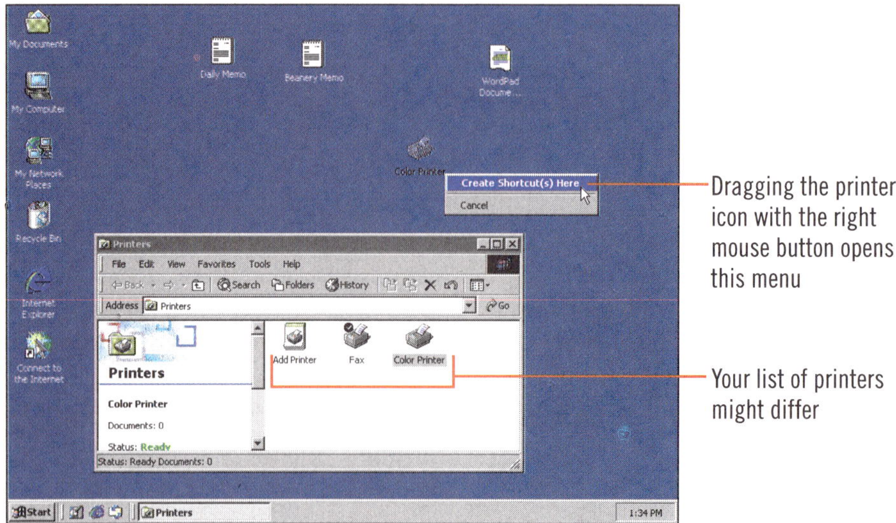

Dragging the printer icon with the right mouse button opens this menu

Your list of printers might differ

FIGURE J-19: Printer shortcut

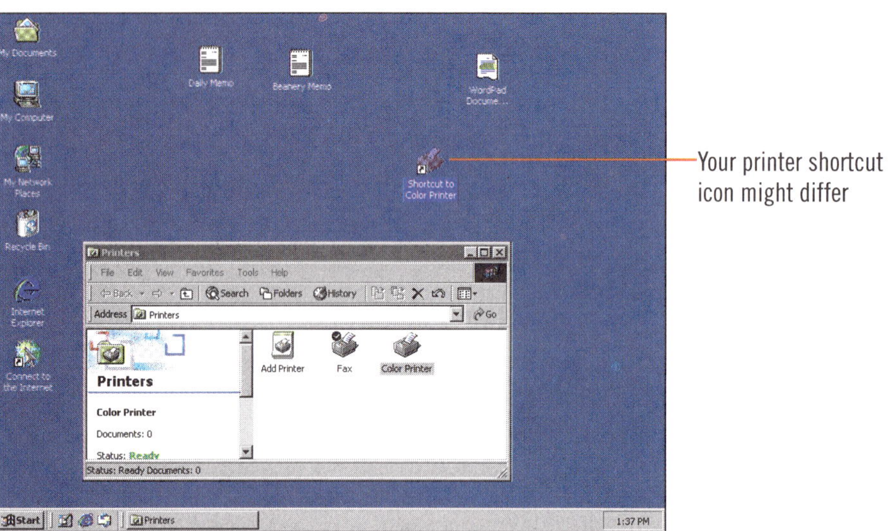

Your printer shortcut icon might differ

FIGURE J-20: Printing a document using the printer shortcut icon

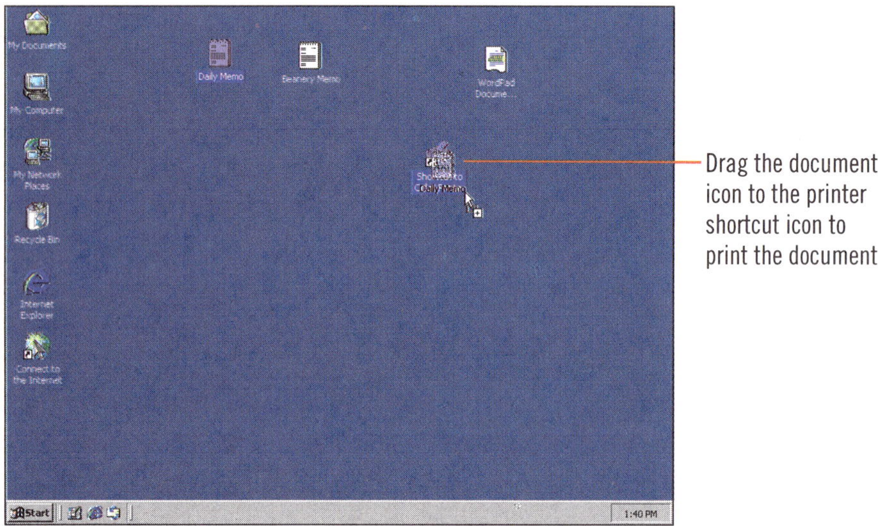

Drag the document icon to the printer shortcut icon to print the document

Removing Desktop Objects

Windows Explorer can be an excellent tool for the creation and also the removal of parts of your desktop and menus. Rather than using different tools to delete the items you created in this unit, you can use one tool, Windows Explorer, to remove all of the items and return your desktop to its original state. Remove all the modifications you made to the desktop so the next user has a clean desktop.

Steps

1. Right-click the **Start button** on the taskbar, then click **Explore**
   Windows Explorer opens showing the contents of the Start Menu folder.
2. Right-click the **Memos folder** in the left pane, click **Delete** from the pop-up menu, as shown in Figure J-21, then click **Yes** when prompted
   The selected item is moved to the Recycle Bin.
3. Click the **SendTo folder** in the left pane
   The right pane now shows the contents of the SendTo folder. The shortcut you created, Memos, should be visible.
4. Click the **Memos shortcut**, click the **Delete button** on the toolbar, then click **Yes** to confirm the deletion
   The shortcut you created is removed from the SendTo folder.
5. Click the **Desktop folder** in the left pane, click the **Daily Memo document** in the right, press and hold down **[Ctrl]**, click the **document scrap**, click the **shortcut to the printer**, click the **Beanery Memo document**, then release **[Ctrl]**
   All four items are selected, as shown in Figure J-22.
6. Click the **Delete button** on the toolbar, then click the **Yes button** to confirm the deletion
   The four desktop items you created are removed from the Desktop folder and the desktop.
7. Close Windows Explorer
   The desktop should now look as it did before you started this unit.

Trouble?

If your Start Menu, Desktop, and SendTo folders are in different locations, see your instructor or technical support person for assistance.

QuickTip

To select a contiguous group of files, you can press and hold down [Shift], click the first file, then click the last file in the list; the two files you clicked and all files in between should be selected.

FIGURE J-21: Deleting the Memos folder from the Start Menu folder

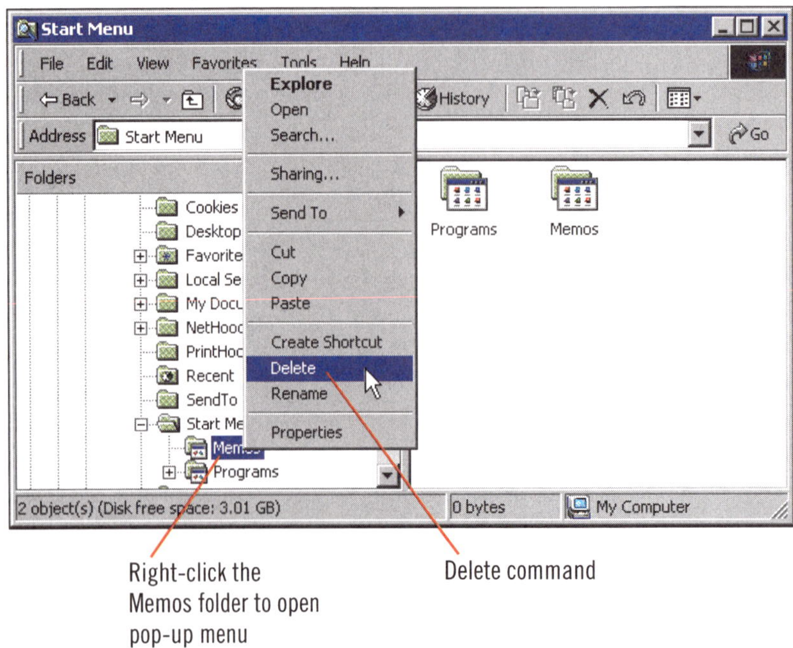

FIGURE J-22: Selected desktop items to delete

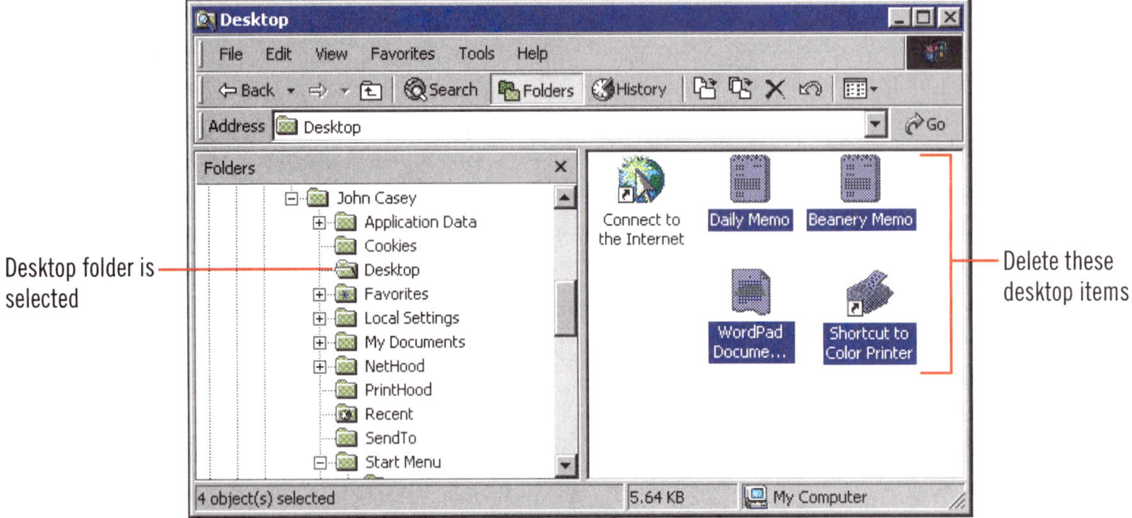

CLUES TO USE

Using Undo in Windows Explorer

Windows 2000 keeps track of all the changes you've made to your folders and documents from the start of your computer session. You can use Windows Explorer to undo all of your work quickly and restore the folders to their original state. Windows 2000 keeps track of the actions you did even when Windows Explorer was not running. To take advantage of this feature, click Edit on the Windows Explorer menu bar, then click Undo. By repeating this command, you will eventually undo every document and folder action that you took in a computer session.

Practice

▶ Concepts Review

Label each of the elements of the screen shown in Figure J-23.

FIGURE J-23

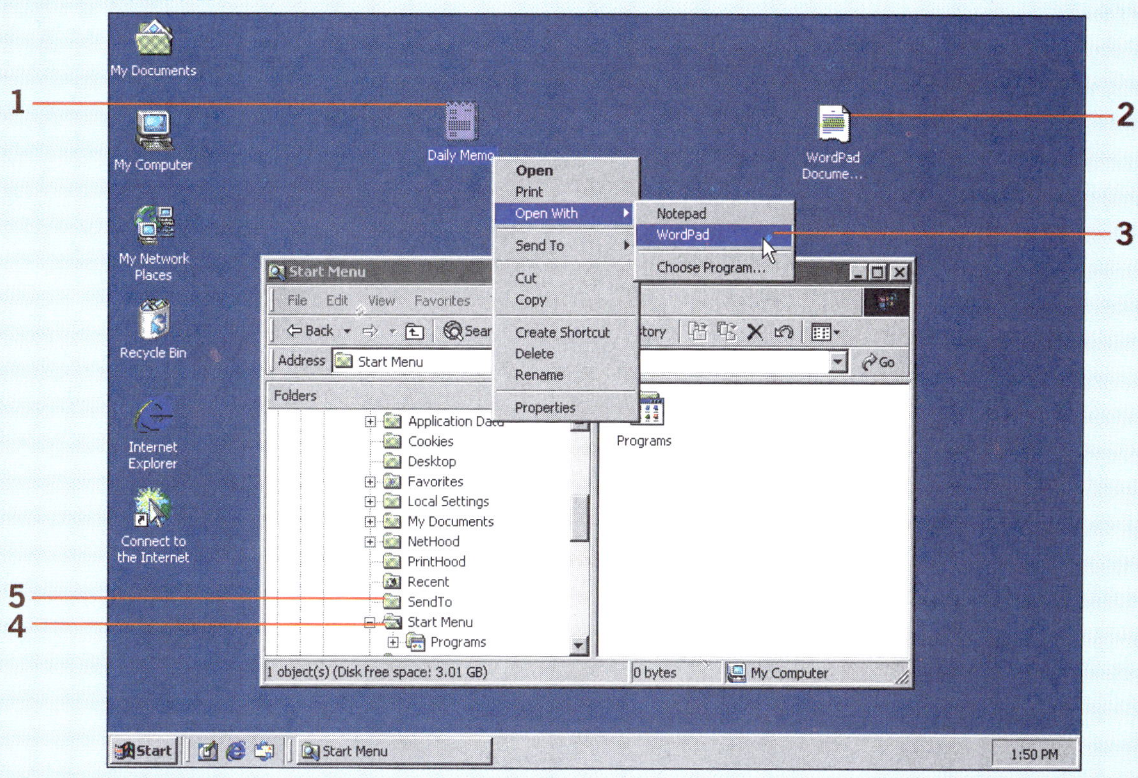

Match each of the terms with the statement that best describes its function.

6. **Scrap**
7. **Docucentric**
8. **Notepad**
9. **File extension**
10. **Windows Explorer**
11. **Send To**
12. **Icon with a small arrow**
13. **Icon without a small arrow**

a. Emphasis on documents rather than software
b. A command that redirects a document to a drive, printer, folder, or program
c. A program that you can use to modify both the desktop and the Start menu
d. A piece of a document
e. Program that Windows 2000 uses to open text documents
f. Icons on the desktop that target objects stored in different locations on your computer
g. Icons on the desktop that represent actual documents or objects located on the desktop
h. Part of a filename that indicates the program associated with the file

Select the best answer from the list of choices.

14. Which of the following is NOT an aspect of a docucentric interface?
- **a.** The ability to create documents without starting programs
- **b.** The ability to access documents from several locations
- **c.** The ability to create documents from the desktop
- **d.** The ability to create documents only from within programs

15. To create a text document on your desktop, you should
- **a.** right-click the desktop, then click Insert Text.
- **b.** right-click the desktop, point to New, then click Text Document.
- **c.** click the Start button, then click Text document.
- **d.** Open Windows Explorer, click File, click New, then click Text Document.

16. If you set it up properly, you can use the Send To command to send documents to
- **a.** a floppy drive.
- **b.** a program.
- **c.** a printer.
- **d.** All of the above.

17. To quickly open a text document with WordPad, you can use
- **a.** a document scrap.
- **b.** the Open With command.
- **c.** the Start menu.
- **d.** the Desktop folder.

18. To create a document scrap on the desktop for selected text in a WordPad document,
- **a.** right-click the selection, click New, then click Scrap.
- **b.** right-click the selection, click Send To, then click Scrap.
- **c.** drag the selection to the desktop.
- **d.** drag the selection to the scraps folder in Windows Explorer.

19. The part of the filename that indicates the default program for the document is called
- **a.** the title bar.
- **b.** the file extension.
- **c.** the document attribute.
- **d.** All of the above.

Skills Review

1. Create a document object.
- **a.** Right-click an open area on the desktop.
- **b.** Point to New.
- **c.** Click Text Document from the pop-up menu.
- **d.** Type **My Address** for the document name.

e. Press [Enter].
f. Double-click the document icon to open it in Notepad.
g. Type your name, address, and phone number in the document.
h. Resize the Notepad window so you can see the text you typed and the icon for the document on the desktop, then print a copy of your text document on the desktop (Press the Print Screen key to make a copy of the screen, start Paint, click Edit on the menu bar, click Paste to paste the screen into Paint, click Yes to paste the large image, if necessary, click File on the menu bar, click Print, then click Print in the Print dialog box.)
i. Click the Close button to exit Notepad.
j. Click Yes when prompted to save the document.

2. Create a Start menu group.

a. Right-click the Start button on the taskbar.
b. Click Explore.
c. Click File, point to New, then click Folder from the Windows Explorer menu bar.
d. Type **Work Documents** then press [Enter].
e. Create a hard copy of your Windows Explorer window (refer to Step 1h for screen printing instructions).
f. Click the Close button.
g. Click the Start button on the taskbar and verify that the Work Documents group has been added to the Start menu.

3. Work with the Desktop folder.

a. Right-click the Start button on the taskbar.
b. Click Explore from the pop-up menu.
c. In the right pane, click the Desktop folder.
d. Click File, point to New, then click Folder.
e. Type **Important Memos** as the folder name.
f. Press [Enter].
g. Resize the Windows Explorer window so you can see the new folder on the desktop and in Windows Explorer, then print a copy of your screen (refer to Step 1h for screen printing instructions).
h. Close Windows Explorer.

4. Send a document to a different location.

a. Right-click the Start button on your taskbar, then click Explore from the pop-up menu.
b. Click the Work Documents folder in the right pane, click Edit on the menu bar, then click Copy.
c. Click the SendTo folder in the left pane (you may have to change your folder options to view it, if it's hidden).
d. Click Edit on the menu bar, then click Paste Shortcut.
e. Click the Shortcut to Work Documents icon, click File, then click Rename.
f. Type **Work Documents**, then press [Enter].
g. Create a hard copy of your screen (refer to Step 1h for screen printing instructions).
h. Click the Close button on the Windows Explorer window.
i. On the desktop, right-click the Important Memos folder, click Send To from the pop-up menu, then click Work Documents.
j. Click the Start button on the taskbar, then click the Work Documents folder to verify that the Important Memos folder has been placed on the Start menu. Print your screen (refer to Step 1h for screen printing instructions).

5. Open a document with a different program.

a. Right-click an empty spot on the desktop, click New, then click Bitmap Image.
b. Open the bitmap image document and draw a simple figure. Save, then close the image.
c. Right-click the image file, then click Open With. If Imaging appears as an option in the submenu, click Choose Program.

d. Print a screen shot of the Open With dialog box (refer to Step 1h for screen printing instructions).
e. Select Imaging from the list of programs, then click OK.
f. Print your screen, showing your drawing in the Imaging window.
g. Close the window and delete the image file from your desktop.

6. **Create and use a scrap.**
   a. Type your school's address into a WordPad document. Select the text you just typed, then drag the text to the desktop.
   b. Create a hard copy of your screen showing both the WordPad window and the scrap icon on the desktop using the steps listed at the beginning of the Skills Review.
   c. Click the Close button to exit WordPad. Do not save the document.
   d. Create a new WordPad document, then drag the scrap into the document.
   e. Print the document from WordPad.
   f. Close WordPad without saving the document.
   g. Click the scrap icon on the desktop, then press [Delete] to remove it from the desktop.
7. **Create a printer shortcut.**
   a. Click the Start button, point to Settings, then click Printers.
   b. Using the right mouse button, drag the printer icon to the desktop, then release the right mouse button.
   c. Close the Printers window.
   d. Drag the My Address document, which should still be on the desktop, over the printer icon you created.
   e. Create a hard copy of your window showing both the My Address document icon and the printer icon on the desktop (refer to Step 1h for screen printing instructions).
   f. Right-click the printer icon, click Delete on the pop-up menu, then click Yes to confirm the deletion.
8. **Remove desktop objects.**
   a. Right-click the Start button.
   b. Click Explore from the pop-up menu.
   c. Click the Work Documents folder in the right pane.
   d. Click File on the menu bar, click Delete, then click Yes to confirm the deletion.
   e. Click the SendTo folder in the left pane.
   f. Select the Work Documents icon in the right pane.
   g. Click File, click Delete, then click Yes to confirm the deletion.
   h. Click the Desktop folder in the left pane.
   i. Click the My Address text document, click File, click Delete, then click Yes to confirm the deletion.
   j. Click the Important Memos folder, click File, click Delete, then click Yes to confirm the deletion.
   k. Close Windows Explorer.

Independent Challenges

1. You are a graphic artist at MJ & G Associates. You would like to be able to create quick and easy Paint documents to record the ideas that occur to you throughout the day. You decide to take advantage of the ability of Windows 2000 to create such objects directly on the desktop.

To complete this independent challenge:

a. Right-click the desktop, point to New, then click Bitmap Image.
b. Name the new Paint file *Idea Sketches*.
c. Double-click the Paint file to open it. If Paint does not open, you might need to configure Windows 2000 so that it associates a bitmap image with Paint. See your instructor or technical support person for assistance.

d. Draw a simple sketch and save it.
e. Print the sketch.
f. Close Paint.
g. Create a hard copy of your desktop (refer to Step 1h in the Skills Review for screen printing instructions).
h. Remove any changes you made to the desktop using the techniques in this unit.

2. You work as a receptionist in a church office. You want to make it easier to print the documents you've placed on your desktop. You decide to use drag-and-drop techniques to create a shortcut to your printer on your desktop.

To complete this independent challenge:

a. Double-click the My Computer icon on your desktop.
b. Double-click the Control Panel icon and then double-click the Printers folder in the My Computer window.
c. Right-click your default printer from the list of printers and, while holding down the right mouse button, drag it to an empty space on your desktop.
d. When Windows 2000 asks whether you want to create a shortcut, click Yes. An icon representing the shortcut to your printer appears on the desktop.
e. Create a hard copy of your desktop (refer to Step 1h in the Skills Review for screen printing instructions).
f. Test the shortcut to your printer by creating a text document on your desktop and dragging the text document icon to the printer icon.
g. Remove any changes you made to the desktop using the techniques in this unit.

3. You have been diagnosed with carpal tunnel syndrome and are trying to find ways to minimize your wrist actions. You like the idea of placing objects on your computer's Start Menu but need to avoid too much dragging action with the mouse. You decide to add the Start Menu folder to the Send To command so you can easily move documents to the Start Menu.

To complete this independent challenge:

a. Right-click the Start button and click Explore from the pop-up menu.
b. Copy the Start Menu folder to the Clipboard.
c. Paste a shortcut to the Desktop folder in the SendTo folder (you may have to change your folder options to view this hidden folder).
d. Create a hard copy of Windows Explorer (refer to Step 1h in the Skills Review for screen printing instructions).
e. Close Windows Explorer.
f. Right-click an object on the desktop to verify that the Send To command has been changed. Print the screen (refer to Step 1h in the Skills Review for screen printing instructions).
g. Remove any changes you made to the desktop using the techniques in this unit.

4. You're the owner of a small bookstore that is being expanded to make room for a coffee bar for your customers. You love the Wired Coffee Company and decide to feature only their blends. Because you will be visiting their Web site frequently to place orders and get updates, you decide to add a shortcut icon to your desktop for the Wired Coffee Company Web site.

To complete this independent challenge:

a. First create a new shortcut on the desktop: right-click the desktop, point to New, then click Shortcut.
b. In the Command line box, type the Wired Coffee Company URL, which is **http:/www.course.com/illustrated/wired/**, then press [Enter].
c. Name your shortcut *Wired.*
d. Create a hard copy of your desktop with the new Wired shortcut (refer to Step 1h in Skills Review for screen printing instructions).
e. Connect to the Wired Coffee Company Web site using the shortcut icon.
f. Print the first page of the Web site.
g. Remove the Wired shortcut from your desktop.

Visual Workshop

Re-create the screen shown in Figure J-24, which displays three desktop objects: one to a text document named Phone Numbers, one to a bitmap image object named Company Logo, and finally, a shortcut to a printer. When you have created the necessary objects and duplicated this desktop, create a hard copy of your screen (refer to Step 1h in the Skills Review for screen printing instructions), then delete the icons from the desktop. (*Hint*: To delete icons from the desktop, you can select them and press [Delete]. You can select multiple desktop objects that are grouped together by dragging a selection box around them. Try this technique to delete the three icons you created for this visual workshop.)

FIGURE J-24

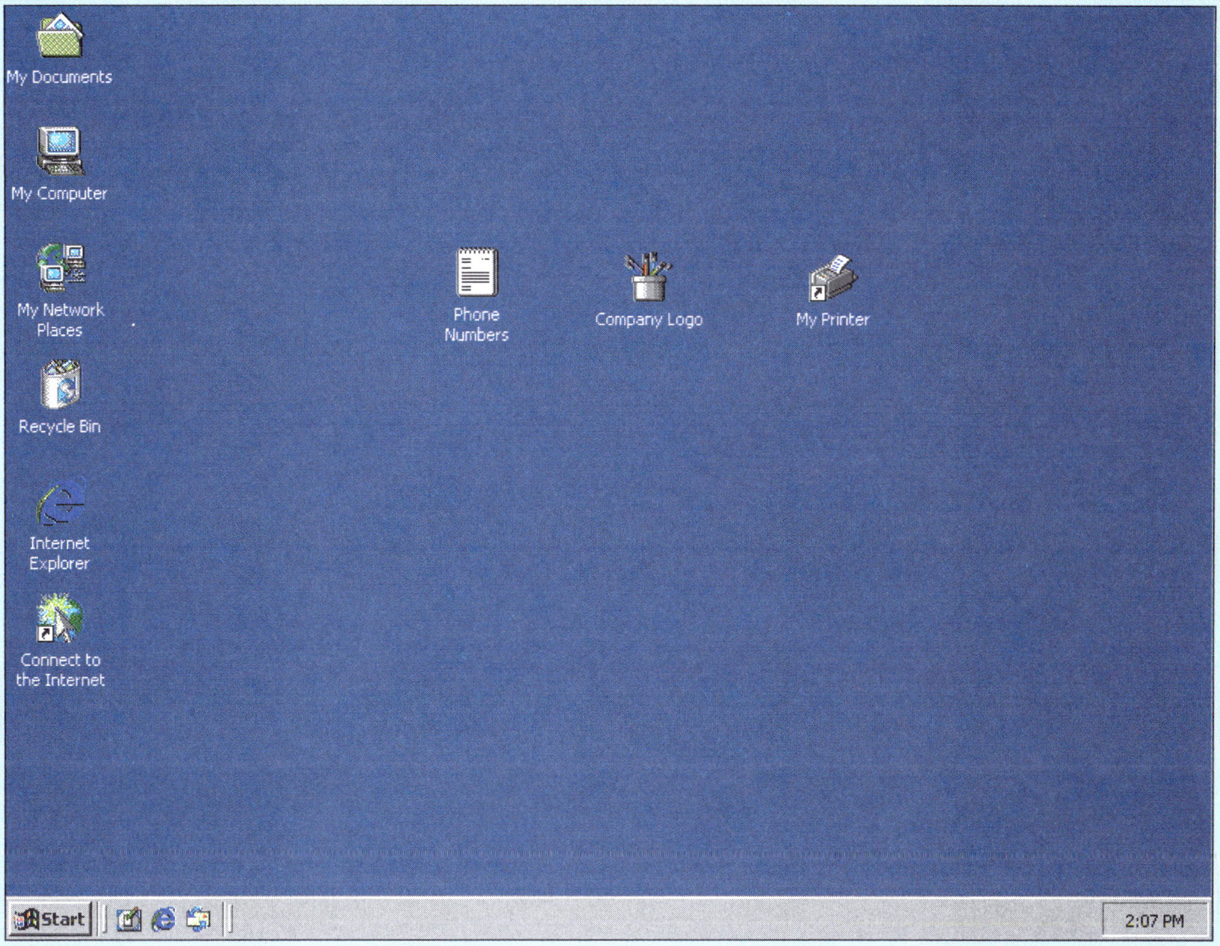

Sharing
Information Among Programs

Objectives

- Understand object linking and embedding
- Embed a new object
- Embed an existing file
- Edit an embedded object
- Embed a video clip
- Modify a video clip
- Link an object
- Update a link

When you are preparing a document, you can supplement text with pictures and other visuals to make your document more interesting. Charts, tables, and pictures, when combined with text, can convey your message much more effectively than text alone. Windows 2000 makes it easy to insert a file (or part of a file) that was created in one program into a file that was created in a different program. The ability to share files and information among different programs is called **object linking and embedding** (**OLE**, pronounced "oh-lay"). With OLE, you can work with a document in WordPad and at the same time, take advantage of the specialized tools in a program such as Paint or Microsoft Excel. In this unit, John Casey will use OLE to place a picture of his signature and a picture of his company logo in a sales promotion document. He will also use OLE to insert a video clip in a promotional document and to link a picture to a flier.

Understanding Object Linking and Embedding

Object linking and embedding involves sharing information between two programs. The information, often referred to as an **object**, can be a picture from a graphics program, a chart from a spreadsheet program, a video clip, text, or almost anything else you can create on a computer. The program that creates the object is called the **source program**; the program that creates the file where you want to insert the object is called the **destination program**. Likewise, the file that originally contains the object is called the **source file**, and the file where you want to insert the object is called the **destination file**. Both embedding and linking involve inserting an object into a destination file; they differ in where their respective objects are stored. With **embedding**, a copy of the object becomes part of the destination file. If you want to edit the object, you make changes in that destination file. With **linking**, the object appears in the destination file, but it is stored in the source file. There are not two copies of the same object; rather, the object exists in the source file and a representation of the object exists in the destination file. If you want to edit the object, you make changes in the source file or its representation in the destination file, and the changes will be reflected in the other file the next time you open it. Figure K-1 illustrates the process of embedding an object into a document, and Figure K-2 illustrates the process of linking an object to a document. Table K-1 can help you decide whether to embed or link an object. John wants to explore the benefits of sharing information between programs.

By using OLE, John will be able to do the following:

Access features from other programs

With OLE, John can put information from one program into another. For example, he can insert a picture into WordPad (a word-processing program) by using Paint (a drawing program).

Edit data easily

When you embed or link an object, you can edit the object directly in the embedded program. For example, if John embeds or links a Paint drawing into a WordPad document, he can edit the drawing from WordPad while using Paint tools.

Update to the latest information

Some of your document may contain objects from source files that other users access, such as financial information or artwork. If you insert the object with a link, Windows 2000 will update the object automatically if a user changes the source file. For example, John can link a Paint drawing to his WordPad document. If someone changes the Paint drawing, John's WordPad document is updated with the changes the next time he opens the document in WordPad.

Save space

When you link an object to a document, a representation of the object, which takes up less disk space than the object itself, appears in the document. The actual object is stored in the source file; and the destination file stays small. Embedding, on the other hand, can require more disk space because the object is actually copied to the destination file. John can use linking to keep the file size of his documents small, thereby saving disk space on his computer.

FIGURE K-1: Embedding an object

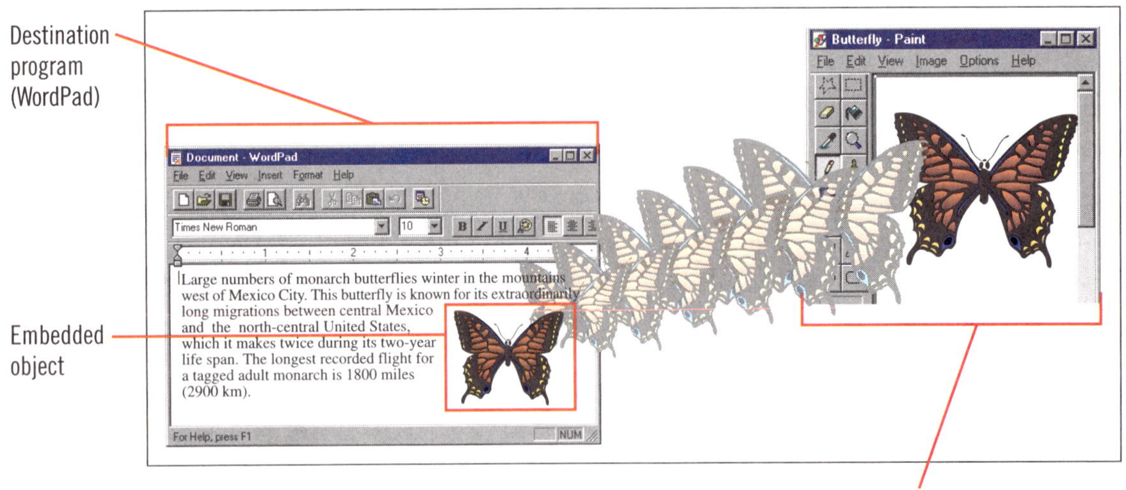

FIGURE K-2: Linking an object

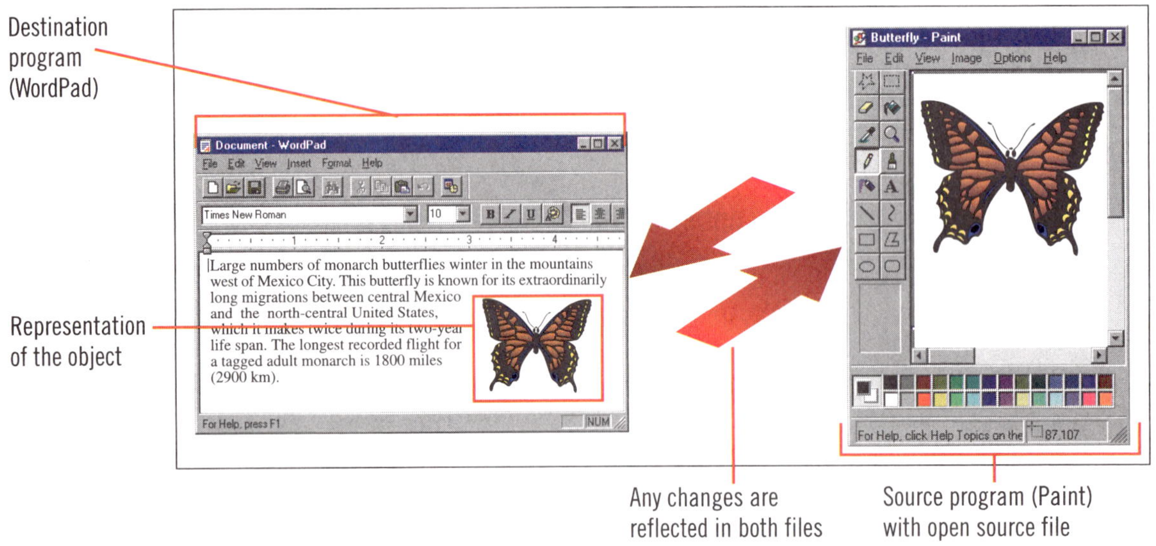

TABLE K-1: Embedding vs. linking

situation	action
You are the only user of an object and you want it to be part of your document	Embed
You want to access the object in its source program, even if the original file is not available	Embed
You want to update the object manually while working in the destination program	Embed
You always want an updated object	Link
The object's source file is on a network where others can change or access it	Link
You want to keep your document file size small	Link

Windows 2000

Embedding a New Object

Sometimes an application isn't designed to handle the data you need to display. For example, if you wanted to include a picture in a WordPad document, which is not designed for drawing, you could start Paint, create a picture in Paint, copy it, switch to WordPad, and paste the picture into your document. With Windows 2000, however, you don't have to start Paint. When you embed a Paint object into your WordPad document, Paint automatically starts in the WordPad program window, so you can create and edit the drawing without leaving WordPad. Embedding can be done with the Insert Object command and, in some situations, the Copy and Paste commands. John wants to create a picture of his signature and place the picture at the bottom of a sales document.

Steps

1. Click the **Start button** on the taskbar, point to **Programs**, point to **Accessories**, then click **WordPad**
2. Open the file **WIN K-1** from the drive and folder that contains your Project Disk, then save it as **Sales Promotion** to your Project Disk
3. Click the **Maximize button** in the WordPad window if necessary, then click **one line below the phrase "Sincerely yours,"**
4. Click **Insert** on the menu bar, then click **Object**
   The Insert Object dialog box, shown in Figure K-3, lets you select an object type and specify whether to create a new object or insert an object from a file that already exists.
5. Click the **Create New option button** to select it if necessary
6. In the Object Type list box, scroll to and click **Paintbrush Picture**, then click **OK**
   An empty Paint canvas appears inside a selection box (gray slanted lines) in the WordPad document, and Paint's menus and tools are available. Though it appears that you have switched to Paint (the source program), the title bar confirms that you are still in WordPad. As long as the Paint object is selected, however, you can use the Paint tools as if you were in the stand-alone Paint program.
7. Click the **Pencil tool** on the Tool Box, then drag in the Paint object to draw the name **John**, as shown in Figure K-4
   If you don't like how a line appears, use the Undo command on the Edit menu.
8. Click outside of the drawing area to exit Paint
   The source program closes and the embedded Paint object becomes part of your document; it is a graphic object that can be moved or resized just like any other object. Sizing handles appear around the embedded object, indicating that it is currently selected.
9. Click away from the object to deselect it, then click the **Save button** on the toolbar
   Compare your screen to Figure K-5.

Trouble?

If the file WIN K-1 doesn't appear in the list of files, click the File of Type list arrow, then click Word for Windows.

QuickTip

To delete an object in the destination program, click the object, then press [Delete].

FIGURE K-3: Insert Object dialog box

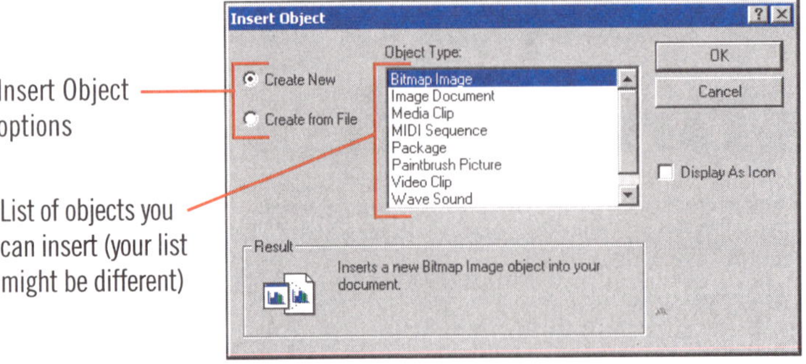

FIGURE K-4: Embedded Paint Object

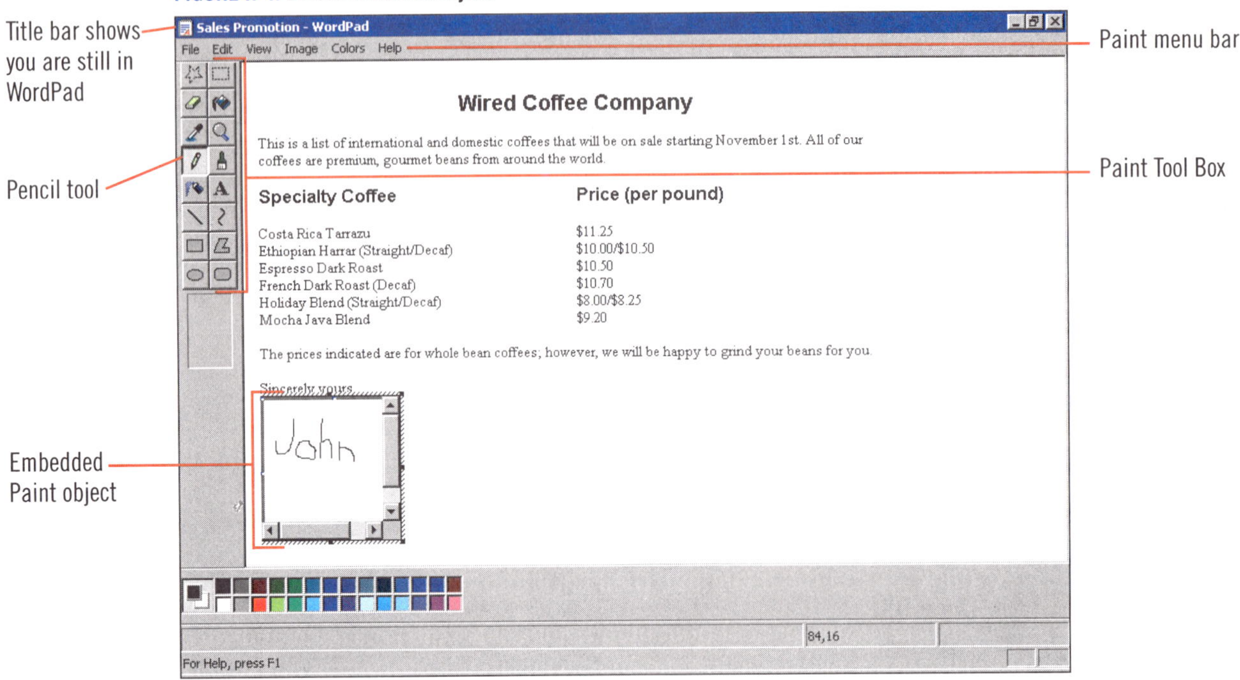

FIGURE K-5: WordPad document with Paint object

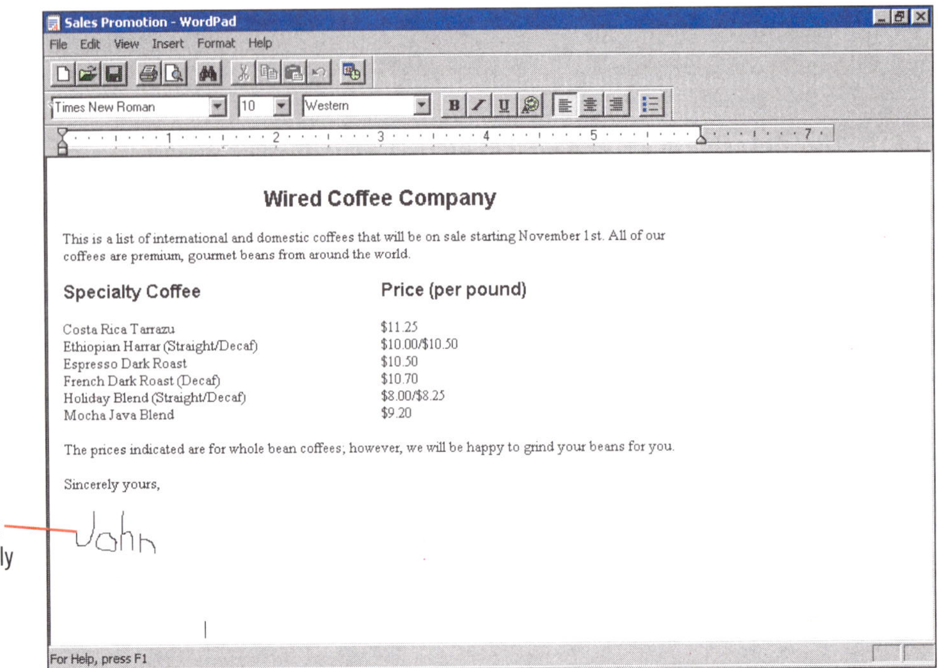

Windows 2000

Embedding an Existing File

In addition to creating and embedding an object from scratch, you can also embed an existing file. When you embed an existing file into a document, a copy of the file is stored in the destination document as an object. The original file remains unchanged, and the object becomes part of the document. John wants to embed the company logo into his sales document.

Steps 1 2 3 4

1. In the WordPad document, click in the **blank line above the title "Wired Coffee Company"** (scroll if necessary)
   This places the insertion point where John wants the company logo to appear.
2. Click **Insert** on the menu bar, then click **Object**
   The Insert Object dialog box opens.
3. Click the **Create from File option button**
   The Object Type list box changes to the File text box.
4. Click **Browse**, click the **Look in list arrow**, locate the drive and folder that contains your Project Disk, open the Unit K folder, click **Wired Coffee Logo**, then click **Open**
   As shown in Figure K-6, the full path name appears in the File text box. The object type for Wired Coffee Logo is a bitmap image. A **bitmap image (BMP)** is a common file format for pictures that are used by drawing programs.
5. Click **OK**
   The embedded object is inserted into the WordPad document. Compare your screen to Figure K-7. Sizing handles appear around the embedded object, indicating it is selected. **Sizing handles** are the small black boxes around the edge of a selected object. In WordPad, as in other Windows programs, sizing handles are used to change the shape and size of an object.
6. Click the **Save button** on the toolbar

QuickTip

To insert an icon in place of an object, click the Display As Icon check box to select it in the Insert Object dialog box. To view the object, double-click the icon.

QuickTip

When you insert an existing file into a document, the source program for the embedded object does not start. You can start the source program by double-clicking the object.

FIGURE K-6: Insert Object dialog box

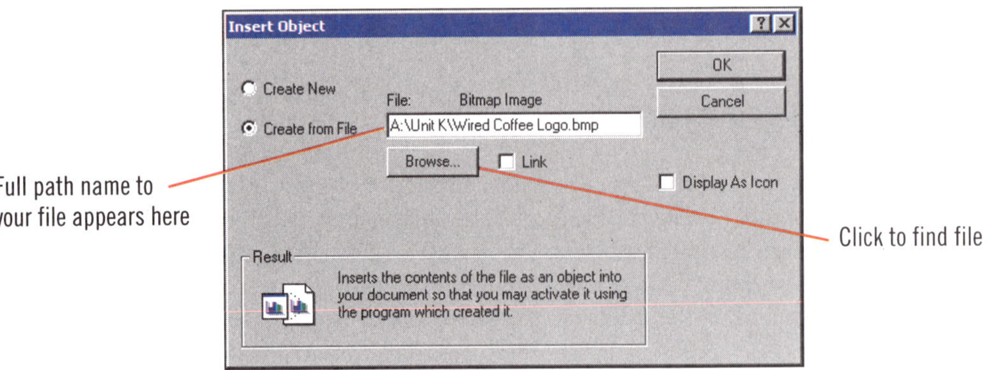

FIGURE K-7: WordPad document with embedded object

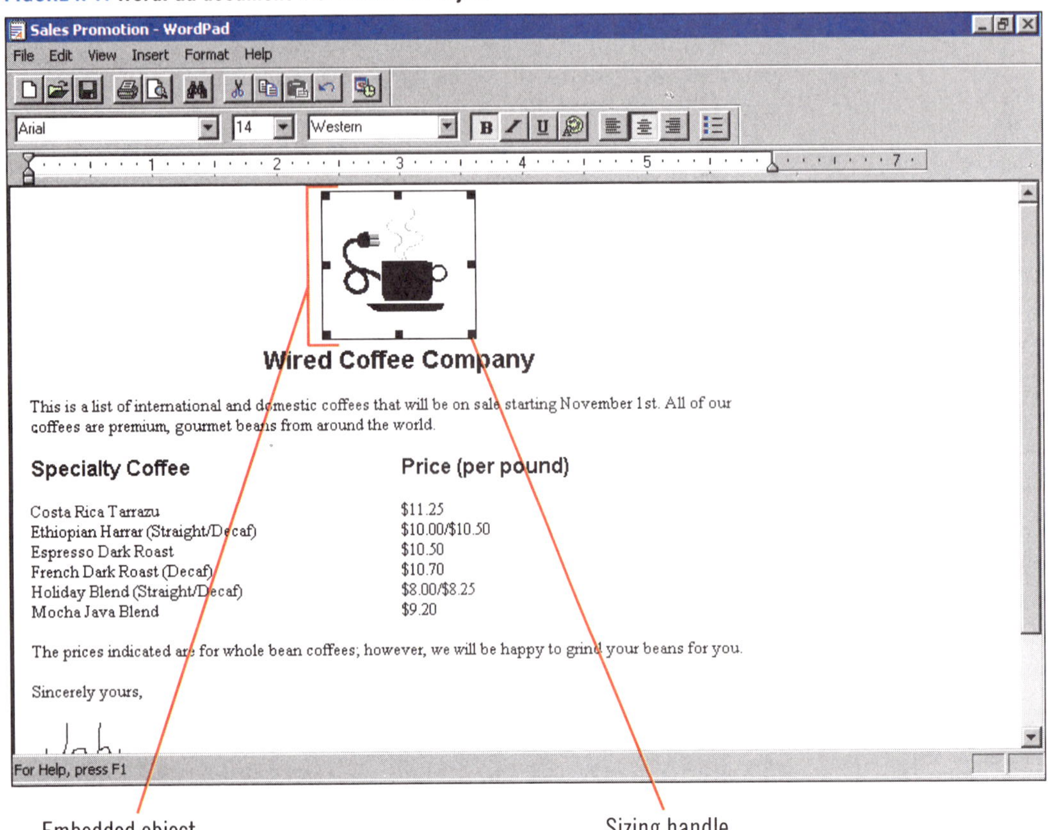

Viewing object properties

You can click Object Properties on the Edit menu to examine an object's properties, such as type, size, and location. The General tab appears with the object information, including the object's type and original location. You can also change the appearance of an object with the View tab in the Object Properties dialog box. An embedded object can appear as editable information, such as a picture or chart, or as an icon. By default, an object appears as editable information, but you can change an object to appear as an icon in order to save disk space.

Editing an Embedded Object

To edit or change the information in an embedded object, you can double-click the object in the destination file. Windows 2000 locates the object's source program and starts it within the destination program. You can then use tools and features of the source program to edit the object. When you're done, you click outside the object and the source program closes. John wants to enlarge and add color to the Wired Coffee Logo in the sales document.

1. Double-click the **Wired Coffee logo**
   The source program (Paint) opens within the WordPad document. If you can't see the entire object in WordPad, scroll bars will appear around it, so you might need to resize the viewing area of the object in WordPad.
2. If necessary, position the sizing pointer over the lower-right sizing handle of the embedded object, then drag the **sizing handle** to match Figure K-8
   As you drag the sizing handles of an embedded object, the border size of the object changes.
3. Click the **Fill With Color button** on the Paint Tool Box
4. Click the **third color cell (from the left) in the second row** of the Paint Color Box
   The Foreground color in the Paint Color Box changes to red, as shown in Figure K-9.
5. Position the mouse pointer over the Paint object
   Notice that the pointer changes to when you move it in the Paint object.
6. Click the tip of inside the coffee cup
   The Fill With Color tool fills only the area inside the lines. If you fill the wrong area, use the Undo command to reverse the action and try again.
7. Click the **seventh color cell in the second row** of the Paint Color Box, then click the tip of inside the saucer below the cup
   The saucer is filled with blue.
8. Click outside the object to exit Paint, then click to the **right of the embedded object**
   Paint closes and the object is deselected. Compare your screen to Figure K-10. The changes you made to the embedded object appear only in this document. If you opened the Wired Coffee Logo in Paint, you would see that it is still black and white.
9. Click the **Save button** on the toolbar

FIGURE K-8: Editing an embedded object in Paint

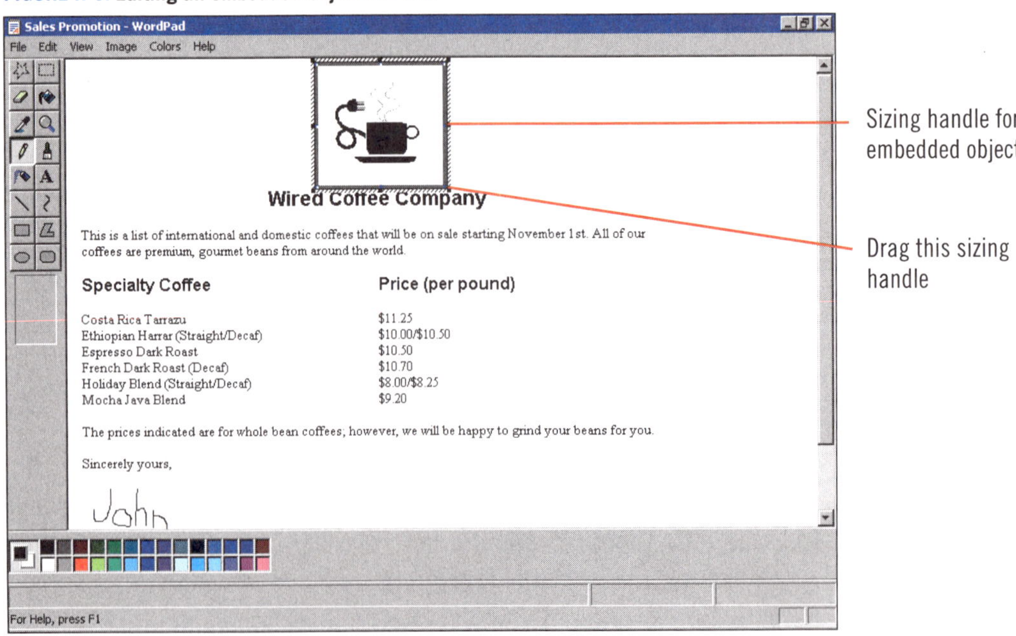

FIGURE K-9: Paint Color box

Foreground color preview box

Click this color for the saucer

Click this color for the cup

FIGURE K-10: WordPad document with edited object

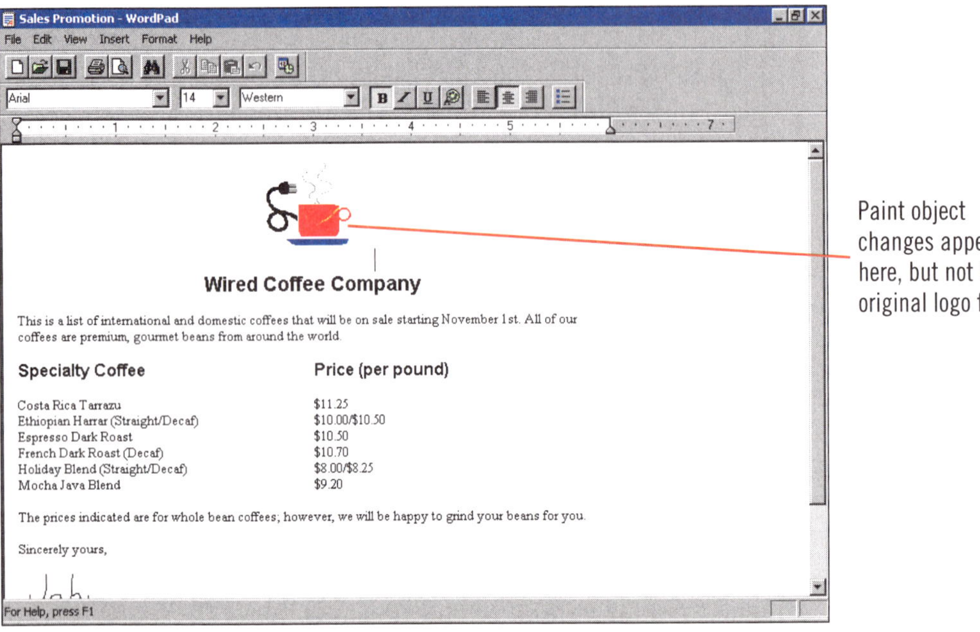

Saving an embedded object

If you have changed an embedded object and you decide to save the object not only in the destination program but also in a separate file, you can save a copy of the embedded object. For example, to save a copy of the color Wired Coffee logo in a separate file, you would select the image, click Edit on the WordPad menu bar, point to Bitmap Image Object, then click Open. The Paint program opens with the company logo in a separate Paint window that is in front of the WordPad window. Click File on the menu bar, click Save Copy As, then save the file. To exit Paint and return to WordPad, click File on the menu bar, then click Exit & Return to Sales Promotion.

Windows 2000

Embedding a Video Clip

With Windows 2000, you can transform a simple document into a multimedia document by adding a video or sound clip. You can play back the clip with Media Player, an accessory that comes with Windows 2000 that plays audio, video, or animation files, and controls the settings for multimedia hardware devices. See Table K-2 for a description of the Media Player media types. To hear the sound on a video clip that has audio, you need to have a sound card and speakers. You can still play a video without a sound card or speakers, but you won't get any sound. John wants to insert a video clip into a WordPad document in order to promote international coffee.

QuickTip

To open a file with a specific program, right-click the file in Windows Explorer, click Open With, then double-click the program you want to use.

1. In WordPad, open the file **WIN K-2** from the Unit K folder on your Project Disk, then save it as **Global Coffee** to your Project Disk
   WordPad closes the Sales Promotion document and opens the new document.
2. In the Global Coffee document, click in the **second blank line below the title "Wired Coffee Company"**
   This places the insertion point where John wants the video to appear.
3. Click **Insert** on the menu bar, then click **Object**
   The Insert Object dialog box opens.
4. Click the **Create from File option button**
   The Object Type list box changes to the File text box.
5. Click **Browse**, click the **Look in list arrow**, locate the drive and folder that contains your Project Disk, click **Globe**, then click **Open**
   The full path name of the video clip object appears in the File text box. The file's object type, Video Clip, appears above the File text box.
6. Click **OK**
   The video clip is embedded in the WordPad document. Sizing handles appear around the embedded object, as shown in Figure K-11.

Trouble?

If the video clip ends before you click the Pause button, you will see that the Pause button changes back to the Play button. Double-click the globe or click the Play button to start the video clip again, then click the Pause button.

7. Double-click the **video clip object** to play it, then quickly click the **Pause button** on the Control Bar
   The video clip plays until you pause it, as shown in Figure K-12, or until it reaches the end of the video clip. When you play a video clip, a Control Bar appears with playback buttons, such as Play, Stop, and Pause, that are similar to those on a VCR.
8. Drag the **slider** all the way to the left to rewind the video
9. Click the **Play button** on the Control Bar
   The video plays from the beginning until the end, then stops. The Control bar then closes.

FIGURE K-11: WordPad document with video clip

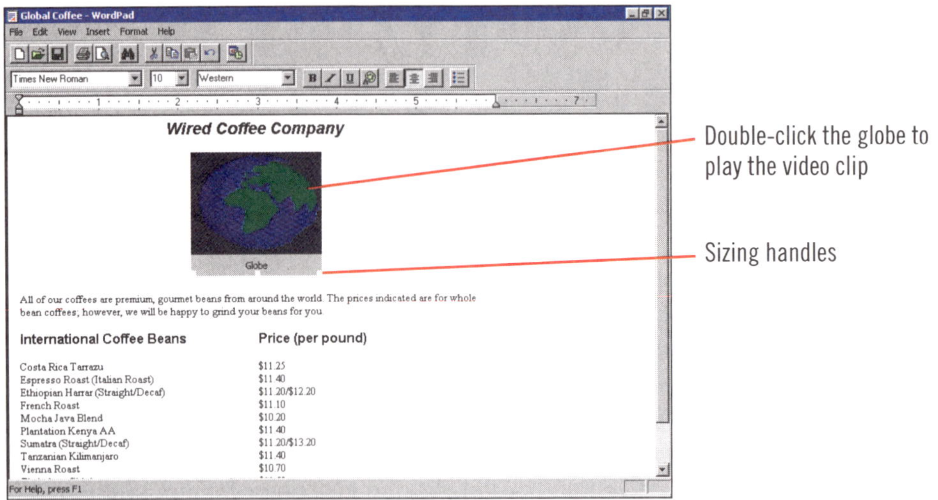

FIGURE K-12: Embedded video clip with Control Bar

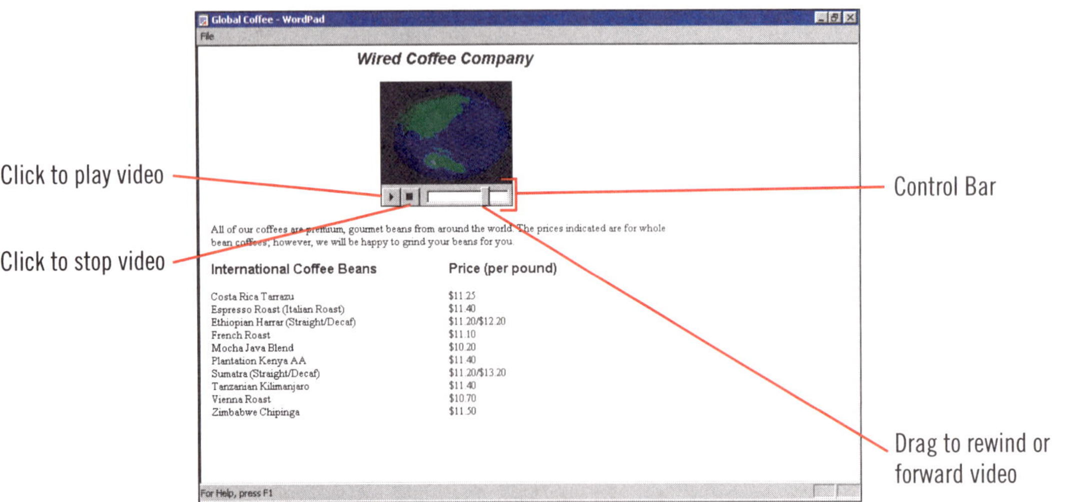

TABLE K-2: Media Player media types

media type	media format	hardware	description
Video	Video for Windows or ActiveMovie	None	Continuous digital video
Animation	Video for Windows	None	A series of graphic images
Audio	CD Audio	Sound card and speakers	A series of sound waves
Musical Instrument Device Interface (MIDI)	MIDI Sequencer	Sound card and speakers	Electronic instructions to play sheet music

Inserting a sound

You can insert a new or existing sound into a document in the same way that you insert a video clip. To insert a sound, click Insert on the menu bar, click Object, then click the Wave Sound object type or browse to select a sound in the Object dialog box. The Sound Recorder embedded program opens. Sound Recorder allows you to adjust volume and speed, add echo, play in reverse, and mix sound elements to create the effect you want. When you exit Sound Recorder, a small speaker icon appears in your document. Before you can play a sound, you need to install a sound card and speakers.

Windows 2000

Modifying a Video Clip

After you insert a video clip, you can edit it or modify its playback options. Media Player offers basic editing capabilities to select, cut, copy, and paste segments of a video clip. Media Player also allows you to set the video clip to automatically repeat or rewind, to display the Control Bar, and to set display and playback options. You can buy specialized software for advanced editing, recording, or compressing of video clips. John wants to modify the playback options of the Globe video clip so that it repeats and so that the Control Bar does not appear.

Steps 1 2 3 4

1. Right-click the **Globe video clip object**, point to **Video Clip Object**, then click **Edit**
   The Media Player menus and toolbar open in WordPad, as shown in Figure K-13. John changes the playback options of the Globe video clip for a better look in the document.
2. Click **Edit** on the menu bar, then click **Options**
   The Options dialog box opens, as shown in Figure K-14.
3. Click the **Control Bar On Playback check box** to deselect it, if necessary
   The Control Bar On Playback option appears deselected, and the Control Bar will not appear when you play the video clip.
4. Click the **Auto Repeat check box** to select it, if necessary
   The Auto Repeat option appears checked, and the video will repeat when it is done playing.
5. Click **OK**
   The video clip appears without the Control Bar.
6. Click the **Play button** on the Media Player toolbar
   The video clip plays without the Control Bar and automatically repeats until you click the Stop button.
7. Click the **Stop button** on the Media Player toolbar
   Because the settings you specified will apply to all files played using the Media Player, you should restore the original settings.
8. Click **Edit** on the menu bar, click **Options**, click the **Auto Repeat check box** to deselect it, click the **Control Bar On Playback check box** to select it, type **Globe** in the Caption text box, then click **OK**
9. Click a **blank area of the WordPad window** to exit Media Player, click the **Save button** on the WordPad toolbar, then click the **Close button** in the WordPad window

QuickTip

To start Media Player separately, click the Start button on the taskbar, point to Programs, point to Accessories, point to Entertainment, then click Windows Media Player.

FIGURE K-13: Embedded Media Player program in WordPad

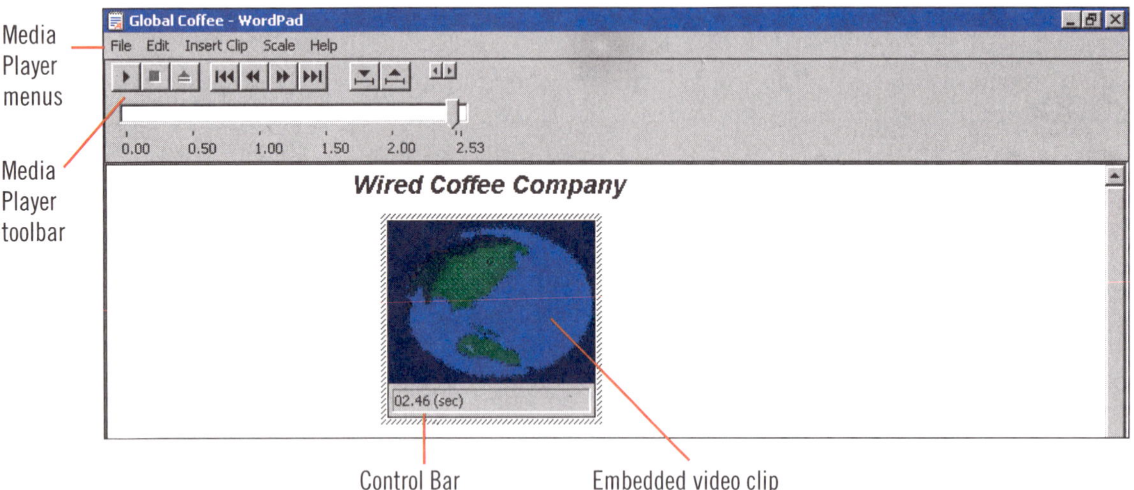

FIGURE K-14: Options dialog box

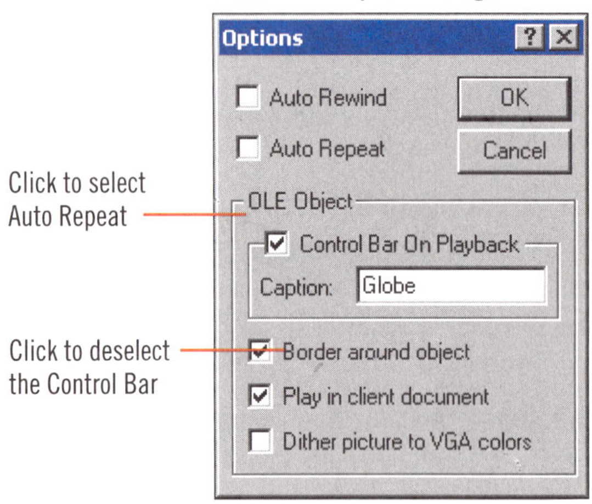

CLUES TO USE

Playing a video or sound in Windows Explorer

You can play a video or sound directly from Windows Explorer without opening the Windows Media Player program. To play a video or sound in Windows Explorer, start Windows Explorer, display the folder with the video or sound you want to play, then click the video or sound file. The Windows Media Player program appears on the left side of the right pane with the video or sound ready to play, as shown in Figure K-15. Click the Play button on the Control Bar to play the video or sound.

FIGURE K-15: Playing a video clip in Windows Explorer

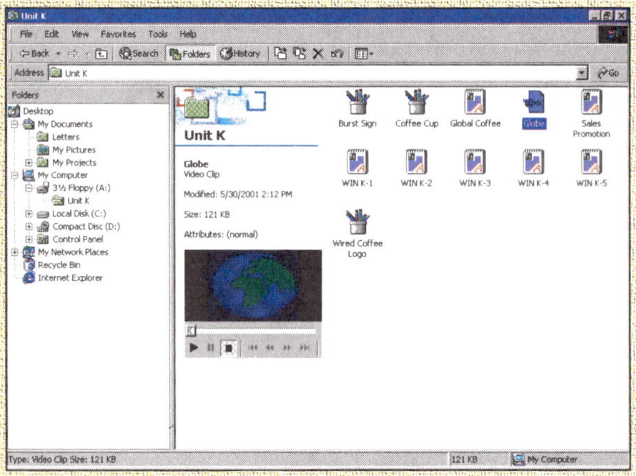

Windows 2000

Linking an Object

When you want to keep source and destination files in synch with each other, you can link the source file that created the object with the destination file that displays the object. Unlike an embedded object, which is stored directly in the destination file, a linked object remains stored in its source file. Only a representation of the object appears in the destination file. You can edit the object itself in the source file, or you can edit its representation in the destination file—either way, changes you make will be updated in the other file the next time you open the other file. John wants to link a picture of a coffee cup to an informational flier he is creating, so that if he decides to change the picture, it will be changed in the flier as well.

Trouble?

If the file WIN K-3 doesn't appear in the list of files, click the File of Type list arrow, then click Word for Windows.

1. Click the **Start button**, point to **Programs**, point to **Accessories**, click **Paint**, open the file **Coffee Cup** from the Unit K folder on your Project Disk, save it as **Coffee Cup Image** to your Project Disk, then exit Paint
   Saving the file with a new name will keep the original file intact.
2. Click the **Start button**, point to **Programs**, point to **Accessories**, click **WordPad**, open the document **WIN K-3** from the drive and folder that contains your Project Disk, then save it as **Roasting Flier** to your Project Disk
3. In the WordPad document, click **two lines below the title "Wired Coffee Company"**
4. Click **Insert** on the menu bar, click **Object**, then click the **Create from File option button**
   The Insert Object dialog box opens.
5. Click **Browse**, click the **Look in list arrow**, locate the drive and folder that contains your Project Disk, click **Coffee Cup Image**, then click **Open**
   So far you have done the same steps that you would do for embedding; however, John wants to link the two files so when he changes the coffee cup image in Paint or in the destination file, the revisions are seen in all of the documents linked to the source file.
6. Click the **Link check box**, as shown in Figure K-16, then click **OK**
   The linked object appears on the WordPad page, as shown in Figure K-17. The linked object looks just like an embedded object; the difference is that any changes you make will affect both files.
7. Click **Edit** on the menu bar, then click **Links**
   The Links dialog box opens, as shown in Figure K-18. In this dialog box, you can open the source file, change the source file, or break the link. You can also check or change the way linked objects are updated; the default setting is automatic.
8. In the Update section, click the **Manual option button**
   This changes the update status of the object so that it will be updated with changes made to the source object only when you choose. For supported programs, you can set a linked object to be updated automatically when the source file is revised and saved, or manually when you click Update Now in the Links dialog box. If a source object is located on a removable disk, it's a good idea to change the update status to manual.
9. Click **Close**, then click the **Save button** on the WordPad toolbar
   The Links dialog box closes, and your changes are saved to disk.

FIGURE K-16: Insert Object dialog box

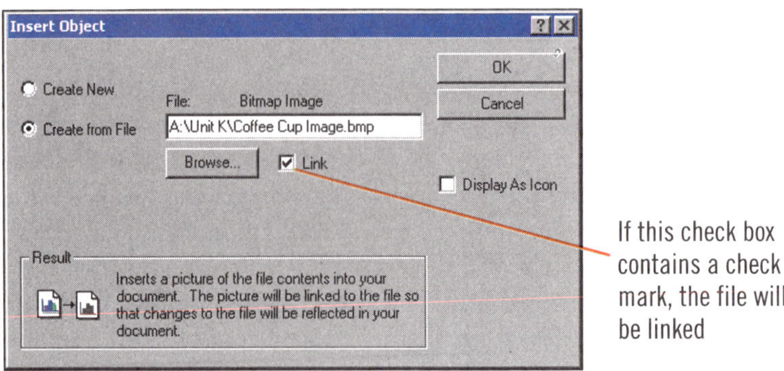

FIGURE K-17: WordPad document with linked object

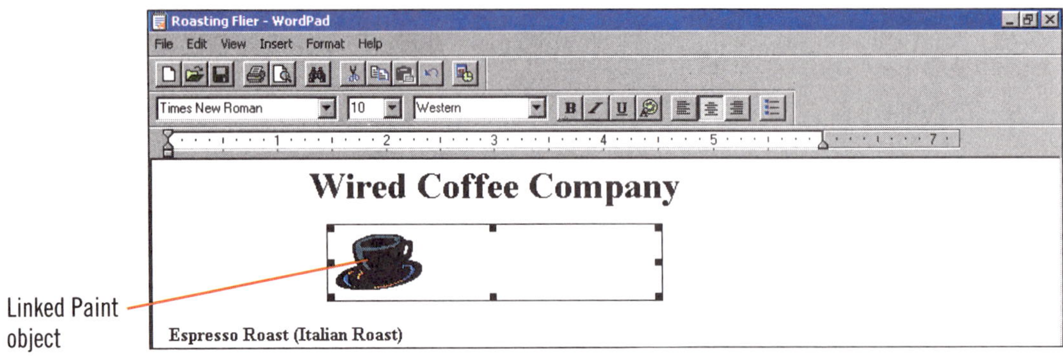

FIGURE K-18: Links dialog box

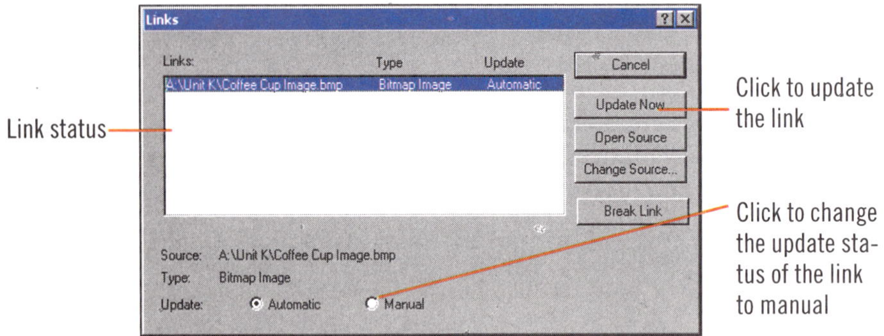

Linking objects by copying and pasting

You can link files by copying and pasting. For example, if you want to link a chart from a Microsoft Excel file to a Word document, you can open the Excel file, select the chart, click Copy, open the Word document, click Edit on the menu bar, click Paste Special, click the Paste Link option button, then click OK.

Updating a Link

When you want to edit a linked object, you can double-click it in the destination file, just as you do with embedded objects, or you can start the source program, open the source file, and make and save your changes. When you double-click a linked object in the destination file, the source program and source file open in a separate window from the destination file. Remember that the object is only represented in the destination file, so any changes you want to make to the object are done in the source file, whether you access it by double-clicking the object in the destination file or by opening it in the source program. John wants to add some text to the coffee cup image. He'll open the linked Paint object, add some information, then update the linked object in WordPad.

Steps

QuickTip

To open a linked object, the object's source program and source file must be available on your computer or network.

Trouble?

If you can't see the Fonts toolbar, click View on the menu bar, then click Text Toolbar.

1. Click the **Start button**, point to **Programs**, point to **Accessories**, click **Paint**, then open the file **Coffee Cup Image** from the Unit K folder on your Project Disk
   Paint starts, displaying the linked file.
2. Click the **Maximize button** in the Paint program window if necessary, click the **Text button** on the Paint Tool Box, then drag to create a text box, as shown in Figure K-19
   The text box appears with an insertion point and the Fonts toolbar.
3. Click the **Font list arrow** on the Fonts toolbar, click **Arial Black** or a similar font, click the **Font Size list arrow**, then click **12**
4. Click the **text box**, then type **A great cup of coffee is all in the roasting!**
   The text automatically wraps inside the text box. When the text box appears, you can edit the text. Press [Backspace] to correct any mistakes.
5. Click **away from the text box** within the object
   When you deselect the text box, the text becomes part of the image. Compare your screen to Figure K-20.
6. Click the **Close button** in the Paint window, then click **Yes** to save the changes
   Paint closes and the WordPad window appears.
7. Click the **linked object** to select it if necessary, click **Edit** on the menu bar, then click **Links**
   The Links dialog box opens.
8. Click **Update Now**, then click **Close**
   The linked object in the Roasting Flier is updated with the changes you made to the source file in Paint, as shown in Figure K-21.
9. Click the **Close button** in the WordPad window, then click **Yes** to save the changes

FIGURE K-19: Paint object with text box

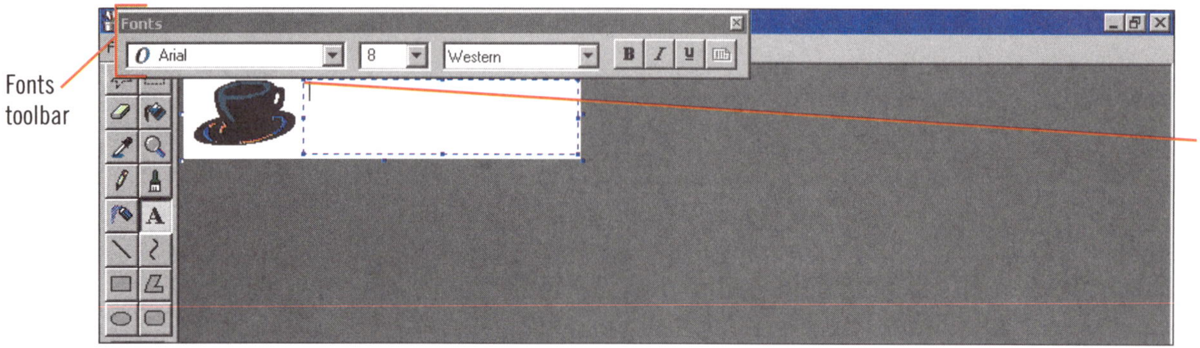

FIGURE K-20: Paint object with new text

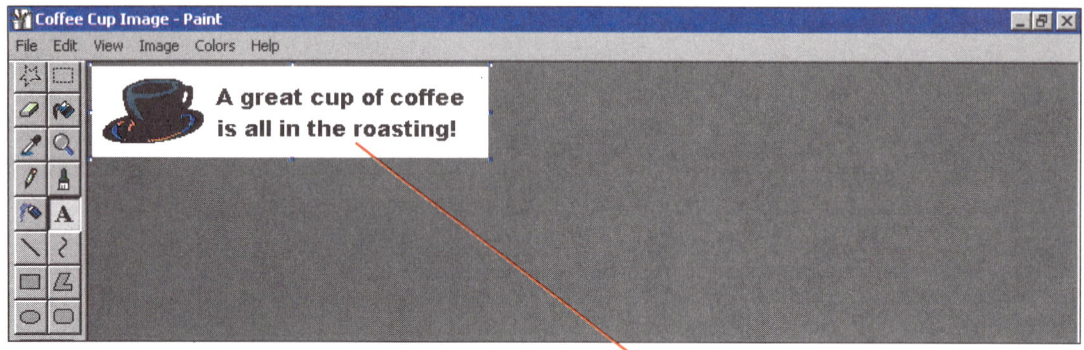

FIGURE K-21: WordPad document with updated object

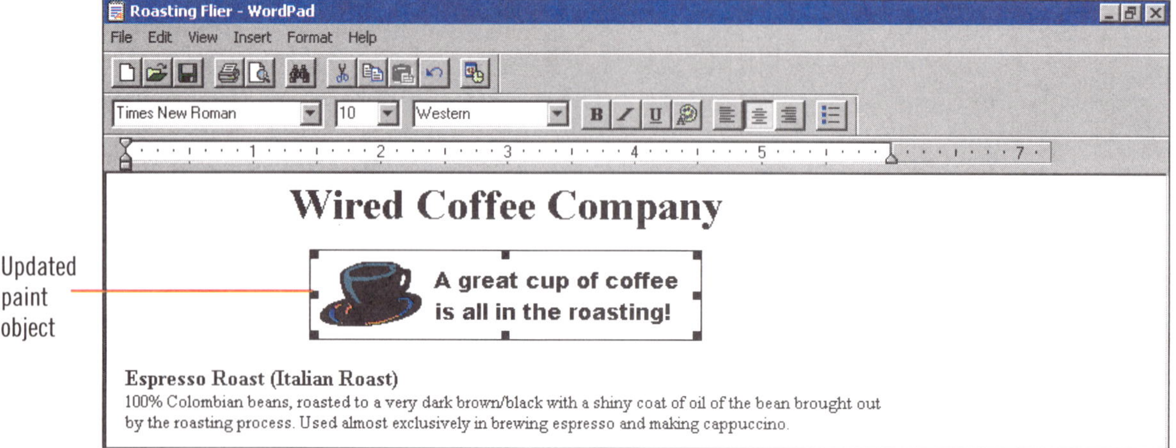

Finding, changing, and breaking a linked object

Instead of opening a linked object from the source file to make changes, you can open a linked object from the destination file using the Open Source button in the Links dialog box. The Open Source button finds the source file containing the linked object and opens that file. After making changes, you exit and return to the destination file. The Links dialog box keeps track of the source file location. You can change the linked source to a different file by using the Change Source command, or you can disregard a link by using the Break Link command.

Practice

▶ Concepts Review

Label each of the elements of the screen shown in Figure K-22.

FIGURE K-22

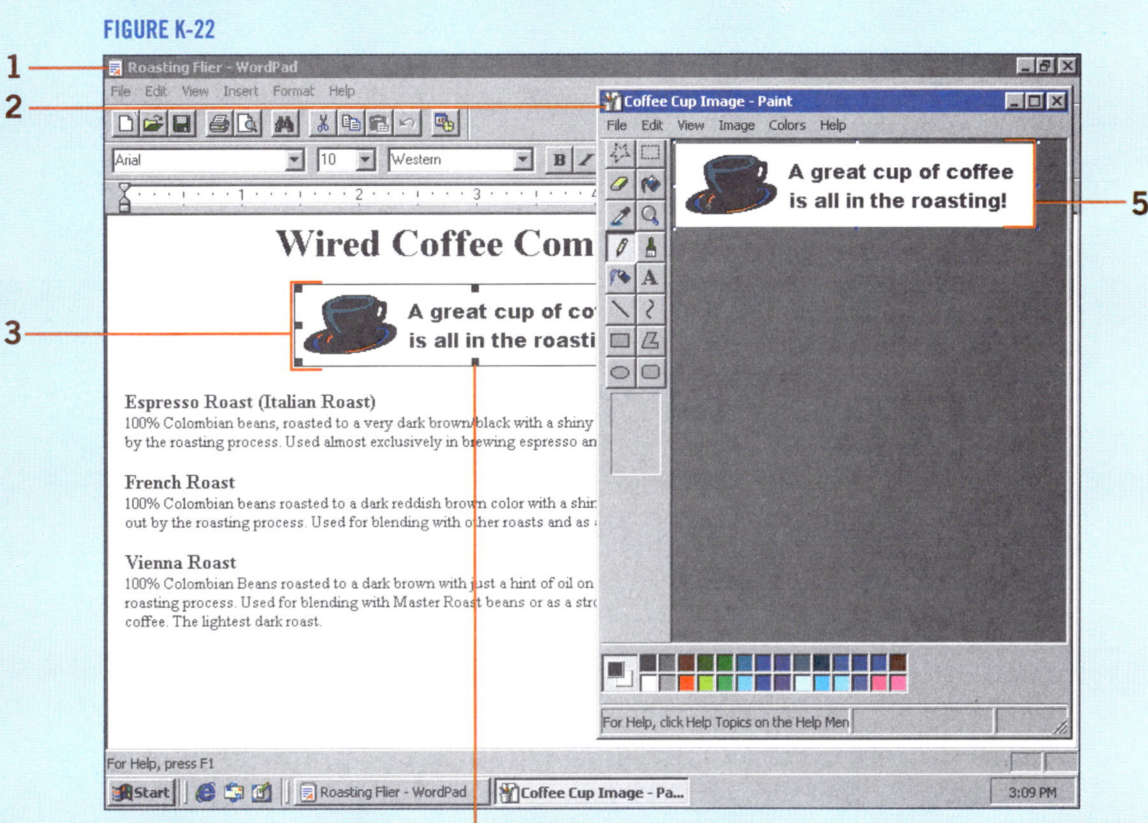

Match each of the terms with the statement that describes its function.

6. An object created in one program and stored in another
7. The place where an embedded object is stored
8. The WordPad menu command you use to embed a file
9. WordPad menu command you use to check the status of a document's links
10. The place where a linked object is stored
11. The connection between an object from a source file and the respective destination file

a. Object
b. Embedded object
c. Links
d. Link
e. Destination file
f. Source file

Select the best answer from the list of choices.

12. Which of the following objects can be embedded into WordPad?
- **a.** Video clip
- **b.** Picture
- **c.** Microsoft Excel chart
- **d.** All of the above

13. Which type of object is stored only in its source file?
- **a.** A linked object
- **b.** An embedded object
- **c.** A text placeholder
- **d.** None of the above

14. Which program would you most likely use to create an embedded object that resembles a drawing?
- **a.** Media Player
- **b.** Microsoft Word
- **c.** Microsoft Paint
- **d.** Microsoft Excel

15. Each of the following is true about embedded objects, EXCEPT:
- **a.** Embedded objects can be edited from the destination file.
- **b.** Embedded objects are stored in the destination file.
- **c.** Embedded objects are displayed in the destination file.
- **d.** Embedded objects are stored in the source file.

16. Each of the following is false about linked objects, EXCEPT:
- **a.** To edit a linked object, you must open its source file.
- **b.** A linked object is an independent object embedded directly into a document.
- **c.** You can access a linked object even when the source file is not available.
- **d.** A linked object substantially increases your destination file size.

17. Which of the following is NOT true about updating a link?
- **a.** You can manually update a link.
- **b.** You can update a linked object even when the link is broken.
- **c.** When you link an object, the default setting for updating is "automatic."
- **d.** An automatic link updates when the source file is saved.

18. Which command on the Edit menu can you use to update a link?
- **a.** Links
- **b.** Paste Special
- **c.** Object
- **d.** Object Properties

► Skills Review

1. **Embed a new object.**
   a. Start WordPad.
   b. Open the file WIN K-4 from the Unit K folder on your Project Disk.
   c. Save the document as *Company Memo* to your Project Disk.
   d. Click the first blank line below the phrase "Sincerely yours".
   e. Click Insert on the menu bar, then click Object.
   f. Click the Paintbrush Picture object type, then click OK.
   g. Use the Pencil tool to draw the signature **John** in the embedded object.
   h. Click outside the existing to exit Paint.
   i. Save the WordPad document.

2. **Embed an existing file.**
   a. Click the blank line above the title at the top of the WordPad document.
   b. Click Insert on the menu bar, then click Object.
   c. Click the Create from File option button, click Browse, then locate the drive and folder that contains your Project files.
   d. Click the file Wired Coffee Logo.
   e. Click Open, then click OK.
   f. Click away from the object to deselect it.
   g. Save the WordPad document.

3. **Edit an embedded object.**
   a. Double-click the Wired Coffee Company Logo at the top of the WordPad document.
   b. Use the Rounded Rectangle tool to draw a rectangle around the Wired Coffee Company Logo in the embedded object.
   c. Click the Fill With Color tool, choose a color, then click a blank area inside the rectangle to change the background to a different color.
   d. Click outside the object to exit Paint.
   e. Save the WordPad document.

4. **Embed a video clip.**
   a. Click the second blank line below the title in the WordPad document.
   b. Click Insert on the menu bar, click Object, click the Create from File option button, then click Browse.
   c. Locate the drive and folder that contains your Project Disk, then click the Globe video clip file.
   d. Click Open, then click OK.
   e. Play the video clip.
   f. Save the WordPad document.

5. **Modify a video clip.**
   a. Right-click the video clip, point to Video Clip Object, then click Edit.
   b. Click Edit on the menu bar, then click Options.
   c. Click the Control Bar On Playback check box to deselect it.
   d. Click the Auto Repeat check box to select it, then click OK.
   e. Play the video clip, then stop it.

- **f.** Click Edit on the menu bar, then click Options.
- **g.** Click the Control Bar On Playback check box to select it.
- **h.** Type **Globe** in the Caption text box.
- **i.** Click the Auto Repeat check box to deselect it.
- **j.** Click OK.
- **k.** Click outside the object to exit Media Player.
- **l.** Save the WordPad document.
- **m.** Exit WordPad.

6. Link an object.

- **a.** Start Paint.
- **b.** Open the file Burst Sign from the drive and folder that contains your Project files.
- **c.** Save the file as *Burst Sign Image* to your Project Disk.
- **d.** Exit Paint.
- **e.** Start WordPad.
- **f.** Open the file WIN K-5 from the drive and folder that contains your Project files.
- **g.** Save the document as *Holiday Sale* to your Project Disk.
- **h.** Click the second blank line below the title of the WordPad document.
- **i.** Click Insert on the menu bar, Click Object, click the Create from File option button, then click Browse.
- **j.** Locate the drive and folder that contains your Project Disk, click the file Burst Sign Image, then click Open.
- **k.** Click the Link check box to select it, then click OK.
- **l.** Click Edit on the menu bar, click Links, click the Manual option button, then click Close.
- **m.** Save the document.

7. Update a link.

- **a.** Start Paint.
- **b.** Open the file Burst Sign Image from the drive and folder that contains your Project files.
- **c.** Click the Text tool, then drag to create a text box inside the burst sign.
- **d.** Type **Sale** (do not click outside the text box yet).
- **e.** Click the Font Size list arrow on the Fonts toolbar, then click 18, or a similar font size that matches the text in the burst.
- **f.** Click outside the text box.
- **g.** Save your changes to the file, then exit Paint.
- **h.** Make sure the Burst image is selected in the WordPad document, click Edit on the menu bar, then click Links.
- **i.** Click Update Now, then click Close.
- **j.** Save and print the document.
- **k.** Close WordPad.

Independent Challenges

1. You opened a small arts and craft store called Stamp By Me. You want to create a flier that contains sales and promotional information for the next three months.
To complete this independent challenge:

a. Start Paint, open the WIN K-6 file from the drive and folder that contain your Project files, then create a sales logo for the store. You can create your own or use the Text tool and the Rectangle tool to place the name of the store inside a rectangle.
b. Save the image as *Sales Logo* to your Project Disk, then close Paint.
c. Start WordPad.
d. Enter store information, including the name, address, city, state, zip, phone number, and store hours of the arts and craft store.
e. Enter store specials. They can include *Buy one, get one of equal or lesser value at 50% discount*, *25% off*, or anything else.
f. Create a list of important dates such as the following: *January 5, Introduction to Stamping, March 2, Introduction to Stamping*, and *March 19, Masking, Reverse Images, and Other Tricks.*
g. Format the information in the document.
h. Above the name of the arts and craft store, embed the Sales Logo image from your Project Disk.
i. Embed a new bitmap image of your signature at the bottom of the document.
j. Close Paint and return to WordPad.
k. Proofread your flier and correct any errors.
l. Print the flier.
m. Save the flier as *Stamp By Me* to your Project Disk.
n. Close WordPad.

2. You are the owner of Hiezer Bakery. In an attempt to increase sales to businesses, you want to create a new catering menu with pastries and desserts. Using WordPad, enter and format text, then embed and edit a drawing to make the menu appealing.
To complete this independent challenge:

a. Start Paint, open the WIN K-7 file from the drive and folder that contain your Project Files then create a menu sign for the bakery. Add appropriate text using the Text tool.
b. Save the image as *Menu Sign* to your Project Disk, then close Paint.
c. Start WordPad.
d. Create a menu with descriptions of at least five items.
e. Format the menu information to make it readable and attractive.
f. Embed the Menu Sign file from your Project Disk at the top of your menu.
g. Edit the embedded object from WordPad so that it contains the text *Now offering catering!* inside a circle.
h. Proofread your document and correct any errors.
i. Save the document as *Hiezer Menu* to your Project Disk.
j. Print the document.
k. Close WordPad.
l. Open Paint, then open and print the Menu Sign file.
m. Close Paint.

3. You are the director of sales at Classified Collectibles, a large distributor of stamps, pins, coins, and other rare items. You are seeking rights to distribute Olympic memorabilia to retail stores across the country. Write a letter to persuade the United States Olympic Committee to grant you the exclusive rights. Assume the following facts:

- The company currently distributes United States collectible stamps and coins.
- The company currently distributes 15,000 items through 25 distribution centers in the United States.
- There are four direct-sales centers with toll-free numbers.

To complete this independent challenge:

a. Start Paint, then open the WIN K-8 file from the drive and folder that contain your Project Files.
b. Create a logo for Classified Collectibles using the Ellipse tool. (To make perfect circles, press [Shift] while you drag the Ellipse tool.) The logo can be similar to the Olympic rings logo, or you can use other tools to make it quite different.
c. Save the image as *Classified Collectibles Logo* to your Project Disk, then close Paint.
d. Start WordPad.
e. Write a letter to convince the Olympic Committee to award you the contract, and format the letter as needed.
f. Save the WordPad file as *Olympic Letter* to your Project Disk.
g. Link the Classified Collectibles Logo file on your Project Disk to your document.
h. Start Paint and open the Classified Collectibles Logo file.
i. Add the text *Classified Collectibles* to the logo, then exit Paint.
j. Update the linked file in your WordPad document.
k. Print the document.
l. Save the file, then close WordPad.

4. You are the president of Garfield Graffiti Removal, Inc., a company that specializes in the removal of graffiti. The company's patented RemoveX system removes paint from all types of surfaces. After removing the paint, GGRI restores surfaces with PreventX, a special clear coating that makes graffiti easier to clean up in the future. Write a letter to persuade the Los Angeles City Council to award GGRI the contract to remove graffiti from city property.

To complete this independent challenge:

a. Start Paint, then open the WIN K-9 file from the drive and folder that contain your Project Files.
b. Create a logo for GGRI.
c. Save the logo as *GGRI Logo* to your Project Disk, then close Paint.
d. Start WordPad.
e. Write a letter to convince the city council to award GGRI the contract, and format the letter as needed.
f. Save the document as *LA Graffiti* to your Project Disk.
g. Link the file GGRI Logo on your Project Disk to your letter.
h. Start Paint and open the GGRI Logo.
i. Add graffiti to the GGRI Logo using the Airbrush tool (the fifth tool in the left column), then close Paint.
j. Update the linked file in your document.
k. Print the document.
l. Save the file, then close WordPad.

▶ Visual Workshop

Create a document that looks like the example in Figure K-23. Use WordPad as the destination program and Paint as the source program; use linking to save disk space. Save the document as *Accident Report* to your Project Disk. Print the document.

FIGURE K-23

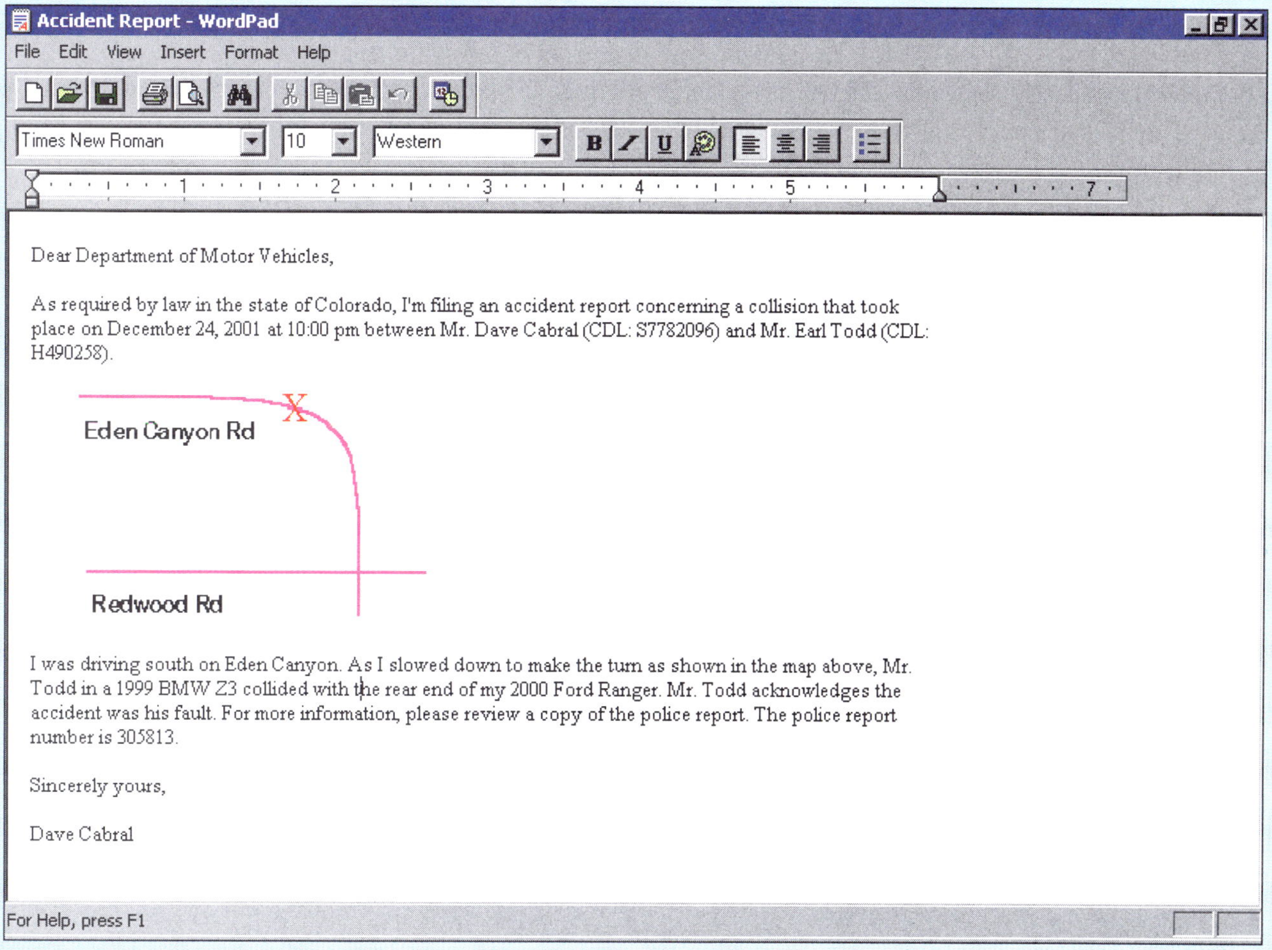

Unit L

Managing Hardware

Objectives

- Understand Plug and Play hardware
- Install a printer
- View printer properties
- Manage printers and print jobs
- Install hardware devices
- View system hardware
- View hardware settings
- Remove hardware devices

A **hardware device** is any physical object that you plug into your computer. This device can be, for example, a network card or a sound card that you install inside your computer, or it can be a printer or a scanner that you plug into the outside of the computer. Windows 2000 makes it easy to manage your hardware. In this unit, you will learn how to install hardware automatically with Windows 2000, install a printer using the Add Printer Wizard, manage multiple printers and print jobs, view hardware properties with the Device Manager, and uninstall hardware quickly and easily. John Casey uses Windows 2000 to install, manage, and remove different computer hardware devices and to learn about plug and play hardware in the process.

Understanding Plug and Play Hardware

Windows 2000 includes Plug and Play support for hardware, making it easy to install and uninstall devices quickly. With **Plug and Play** support, you simply plug the device in, and Windows 2000 handles the task of setting the device to work with your existing hardware and resolving any system conflicts. With Plug and Play, you can be confident that any new devices will work together properly and that your computer will restart correctly after you install or uninstall hardware. Plug and Play works with Power Options in the Control Panel to be sure that your system runs efficiently while you are installing or removing hardware devices. The **Power Options** control the power supply to the devices attached to your computer, supplying power to those that you are using and conserving power for those that you are not. Windows 2000 will automatically manage the power for devices. John wants to install a new printer, so he decides to learn about Plug and Play devices. Plug and Play supports only those devices that indicate that they are Plug and Play compatible, as shown in Figure L-1.

To install a Plug and Play device, John learns that it's necessary to complete the following steps:

Gather your original Windows 2000 CD-ROMs, the hardware device that you want to install, and the disks that come with the device.

If you want to install a hardware device, such as a network card or a sound card that you install inside your computer, you need to turn off your computer before you can physically install the device. If you want to install a hardware device, such as a printer, that plugs into the outside of your computer, you can use the Add/Remove Hardware utility program in the Control Panel without having to turn off your computer.

Follow the manufacturer's instructions to plug the new device into your computer.

Turn on your computer or start the Add/Remove Hardware utility program in the Control Panel.

Windows 2000 detects the new device and might ask you to insert a Windows 2000 disk or the disk that comes with the device into the appropriate drive. If Windows 2000 doesn't recognize a hardware change as your computer turns on, the hardware might not be Plug and Play compatible.

Follow the instructions on the screen until a message indicates that you are finished. Windows 2000 automatically notifies all other devices of the new device so there are no conflicts and manages the power requirements of your hardware and peripherals, shutting them down or conserving power when you are not using them. And, if you are working in another program when you install or uninstall a device, Plug and Play lets you know that it is about to change your computer configuration and warns you to save your work.

Windows 2000

Editing Text in a WordPad Document

One of the major advantages of using a word processor is that you can **edit**, or change the contents of a document, without having to retype it. You can also move whole sections of a document from one place to another using the Cut and Paste commands. John wants to add a greeting and change the price for a pound of coffee in the Coffee Menu document. He also wants to change the order of the menu items, so that the coffees are listed in alphabetical order.

Steps

1. Press ↓ three times or click in the **line just above "Specialty Coffees"**
   Figure B-5 shows the insertion point where you want to insert new text. Repositioning the insertion point in a document (called **navigating**) is an important skill to learn. In addition to the arrow keys, WordPad offers another set of keys and key combinations, as shown in Table B-1, that enable you to navigate a document quickly.

Trouble?

If you make a mistake while typing, press [Backspace] (which deletes the character to the left of the insertion point) until you have deleted your mistake, then retype the text.

2. Type **Welcome to the taste tantalizing coffee selections offered to you by Wired Coffee Company. You will find a variety of specialty coffees, including Single-Origin, Blends, Dark Roasts, and Decaffeinated.**, then press **[Enter]**
   WordPad automatically puts the text that won't fit on the current line onto the next line, using a feature called **wordwrap**.
3. In the price of the Breakfast Blend coffee, click to the right of the last digit, **0**
   This number needs to be changed from "11.90" to "11.00".
4. Press **[Backspace]** twice, then type **00**
   Now John wants to rearrange the list so that the coffees are listed in alphabetical order. The fourth coffee in the list (Espresso Dark Roast) needs to be moved so it comes before the third (Ethiopian Harrar). To do this, John first has to select the entire line so that he can move the text up the list. You can select text three different ways. You can drag the mouse to highlight the text you want to select. If you need to select just a word, you can double-click it. If you need to select a line or paragraph, you can position the pointer to the left of the first character in the line or paragraph, then click once to select a line or twice to select an entire paragraph.
5. Position the pointer to the left of the first character in the line "Espresso Dark Roast"
   The pointer changes from I to ↖.

QuickTip

To select the entire paragraph, you can triple-click anywhere in the paragraph.

6. Click once
   The entire line is selected. Now, John can move the line.
7. Click the **Cut button** on the toolbar
   When selected text is **cut** from a document, Windows removes it from the document and places it on the **Clipboard**, a temporary storage place where it remains available to be pasted somewhere else. When text is **copied**, a copy of it is placed on the Clipboard to be pasted in another location, but the text also remains in its original place in the document.
8. Press ↑ once to move up one line in the list
   This is where John wants to paste the line he cut. Selections you paste are inserted at the location of the insertion point.
9. Click the **Paste button** on the toolbar, then click the **Save button** on the toolbar
   Figure B-6 shows the line pasted into the list. The coffees are now in alphabetical order and the changes you made to the file are saved.

FIGURE B-3: Open dialog box

Click an icon in the Places bar to open a common location on your computer or network

Type filename here; AutoComplete suggests possible matches with previous filenames

Click to specify the location of file to open

List of files and folders stored in the selected location (such as the My Documents folder); your list may be different

Click to open selected file

Select type of file here

FIGURE B-4: Save As dialog box

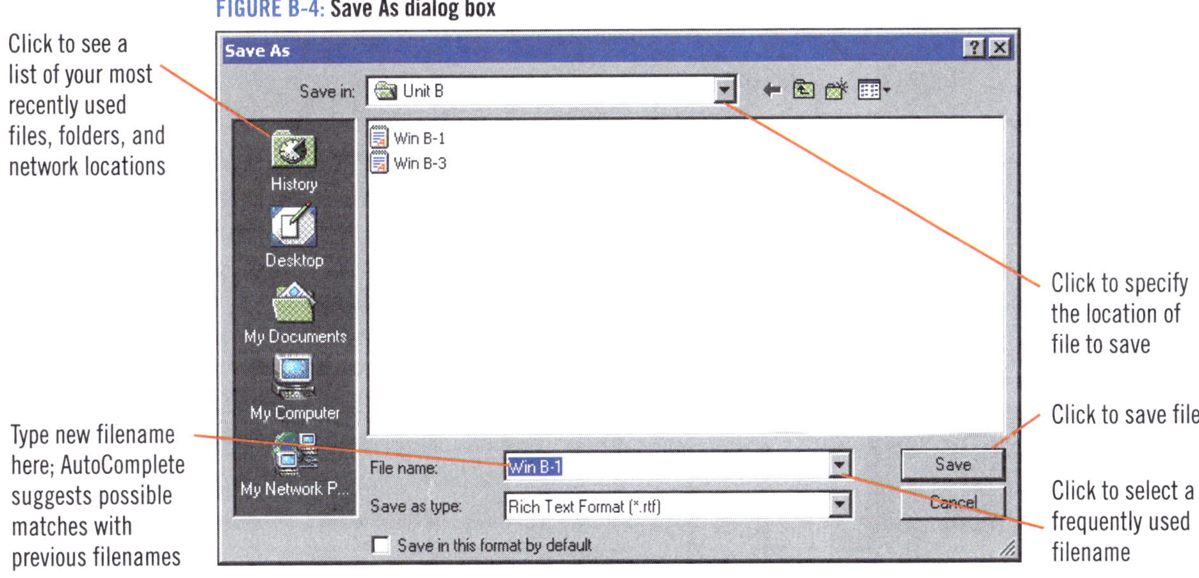

Click to see a list of your most recently used files, folders, and network locations

Type new filename here; AutoComplete suggests possible matches with previous filenames

Click to specify the location of file to save

Click to save file

Click to select a frequently used filename

About saving files

Until you save them, the documents you create are stored in the computer's **Random Access Memory (RAM)**. RAM is a temporary storage space that is erased when the computer is turned off. To store a document permanently, you must save it as a file to a disk. A **file** is a collection of information that has a unique name, distinguishing it from other files. You can save files to a **floppy disk** that you insert into the disk drive of your computer (usually the A: or B: drive) or a **hard disk**, which is built into the computer (usually the C: drive). This book assumes that you will save all of your files to your Project Disk, which your instructor or technical support person has provided to you. Windows 2000 lets you save files using names that have up to 255 characters, including spaces.

Opening and Saving a WordPad Document

A **document** is the piece of work you create using a word-processing program. You can use WordPad to create documents such as letters, memos, and resumes. When you start WordPad, a blank document appears in the work area of the WordPad window, known as the **document window**. You can enter new information to create a new document and save the result as a file, or you can open an existing file and save the document with any changes you made. To prevent any accidental changes to the original document, you can save the document with a new name. This makes a copy of the document, so you can make changes to the new document and leave the original file unaltered. John wants to open an existing WordPad document that contains the text of the coffee menu rather than typing the menu from scratch. He needs to open the document and save it with a new name before making any changes to it, so that the original file remains intact.

QuickTip

Make sure you have made a copy of your Project Disk, to protect the original. If you need assistance, contact your instructor or technical support person.

Trouble?

If a list of files doesn't appear in the file list, click the Files of Type list arrow, then click Text Document or Word for Windows 6.0.

QuickTip

To provide a consistent place to store all your files, Windows 2000 saves and opens all your documents to and from the My Documents folder on your desktop unless you choose a different location.

QuickTip

When an existing document is open, you can click the New button on the toolbar to create a blank new document.

1. **Insert a copy of your Project Disk into the appropriate floppy drive, click the Open button on the WordPad toolbar**

   The Open dialog box opens, as shown in Figure B-3. In this dialog box, you locate and choose the file you wish to open. You can click icons in the **Places bar** on the left side of the dialog box to navigate to common locations or recently used files and folders on your computer or network. The file John created is stored on your Project Disk.

2. **Click the Look in list arrow, click the drive that contains your Project Disk, then click the Unit B Folder**

   A list of the files in this folder on the Project Disk appears in the file list. You can select a file in the file list or type the name of the file you want in the File name text box. When you type a name, **AutoComplete** suggests possible matches with previous filename entries. You can continue to type or click the File name list arrow, then click a matching filename from the list. The list is constrained by the Files of Type list, which means you will see different lists depending on the file type you select.

3. **In the file list click Win B-1, then click Open**

   The file named Win B-1 opens. This is a menu for the coffee company.

4. **Click File on the menu bar, then click Save As**

   The Save As dialog box opens, as shown in Figure B-4. The Save As command allows you to save an existing document under a new name and also in a different folder or drive location.

5. **If Win B-1 is not already selected, click in the File name text box, then select the entire filename by dragging the mouse pointer over it**

   In WordPad, as in most other Windows programs, you must select text in order to modify it. When you select text, the selection appears **highlighted** (white text on a black background) to indicate that it has been selected. Any action you now take will be performed on the selected text.

6. **Type Coffee Menu to replace the selected text**

   As soon as you start typing, the selected text is replaced by the text you are typing. It's a good idea to use descriptive names for your files so you can identify their contents more easily.

7. **Click Save**

   The file is saved under the new name, Coffee Menu, in the same folder and drive location as the Win B-1 file. The original file, called Win B-1, is automatically closed, and the new filename appears in the title bar of the WordPad window.

FIGURE B-1: Starting WordPad using the Start menu

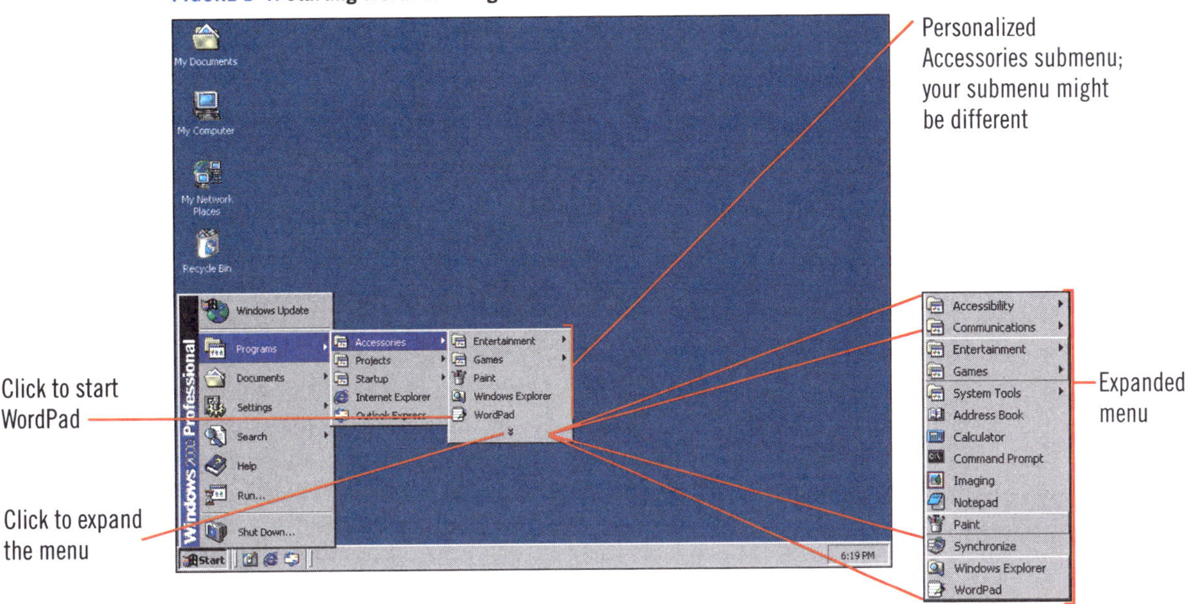

FIGURE B-2: Windows desktop with the WordPad window open

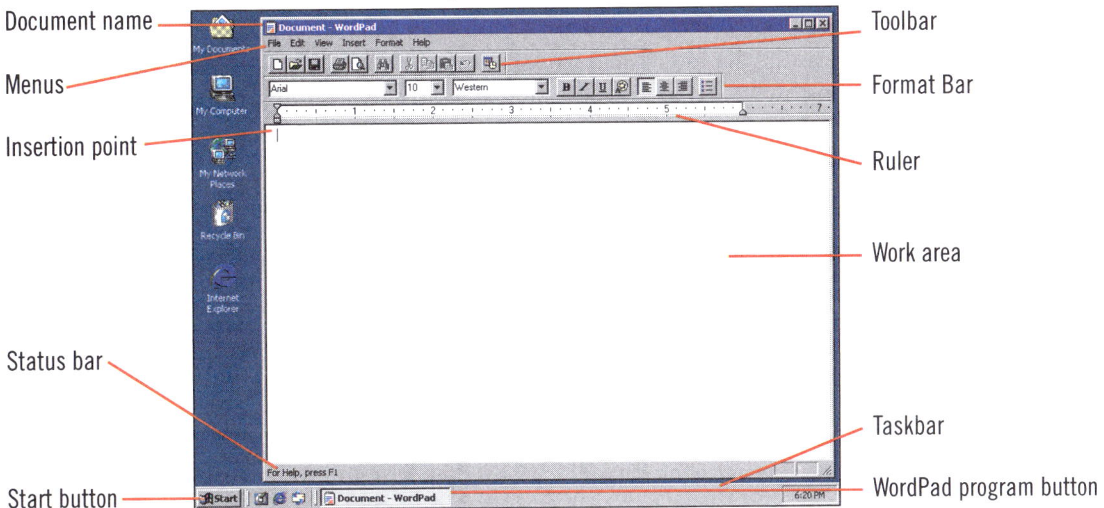

Creating documents in other languages

You can install multiple languages on your computer, such as Hebrew, Arabic, Japanese, Korean, French, Spanish, German, and many others. You can choose which language you want to use when you create a document. Then Windows 2000 makes the characters for that language available, so you can start writing. You can create documents in other languages using WordPad and NotePad, word-processing accessories that come with Windows 2000. To install additional languages, click the Start button, point to Settings, click Control Panel, double-click Regional Options, click the General tab, and then click the check box next to the language group you want to install. To complete the installation, you must insert the Windows 2000 CD-ROM. To add an input locale and keyboard layout, click the Input Locales tab in the Regional Options dialog box, click Add, and then click the locale and layout you want. Once you have added one or more input locale(s), an input locale indicator appears in the status area of the taskbar. The indicator displays the first two letters of the current input language (such as EN for English). You can compose documents that contain more than one language. Any recipients of multilanguage documents must also have the same languages installed on their computer to read and edit the documents. To compose a document using multiple languages, click the input locale indicator on the taskbar, click the language you want to use in the list that opens, and then type your message.

Starting a Program

A **Windows program** (also called an application), is software designed to run on the Windows operating system. All Windows accessories are located on the Accessories submenu of the Programs submenu. John wants to use **WordPad**, a word-processing accessory that comes with Windows, to prepare the text of his new coffee menu, so he needs to start this program.

Steps

QuickTip

If a single arrow appears at the top or bottom of the Programs submenu, point to the arrow to scroll up or down the menu to view more elements.

Trouble?

If the Toolbar, Format Bar, ruler, or status bar does not appear, click View on the menu bar, then click the element (without a check mark) you want to view.

1. Click the **Start button** on the taskbar
   The Start menu opens.
2. Point to **Programs** on the Start menu
   The Programs submenu opens, listing the programs and categories for programs installed on your computer. WordPad is on the Accessories submenu.
3. Point to **Accessories** on the Programs submenu
   The Accessories submenu opens, as shown in Figure B-1. The Accessories submenu lists a personalized menu of the programs you have used most recently. To reduce the number of elements on the Programs submenus and customize your Windows environment, Windows keeps track of which programs you use and hides the programs you have not used recently.
4. Click the **More menu items indicator** at the bottom of the Accessories submenu, if necessary
   The full Accessories submenu appears. Locate the WordPad item on this submenu.
5. Click **WordPad** on the Accessories submenu
   The mouse pointer briefly changes to an hourglass, indicating that you are to wait while Windows starts the WordPad program. The WordPad window then appears on your desktop, as shown in Figure B-2. The WordPad window includes two toolbars, the **Toolbar** and the **Format Bar**, as well as a ruler, a work area, and a status bar. A blinking cursor, known as the **insertion point**, appears in the work area of the WordPad window, indicating where new text will be inserted. The WordPad program button appears in the taskbar, indicating that the WordPad program is now running.
6. Click the **Maximize button** in the WordPad window
   WordPad expands to fill the screen.

Working with Windows Programs

Objectives

- Start a program
- Open and save a WordPad document
- Edit text in a WordPad document
- Format text in a WordPad document
- Use Paint
- Copy data between programs
- Print a document
- Play a video clip
- Play a sound

Now that you know how to work with common Windows graphical elements, you're ready to work with programs. Windows comes with several **accessories,** built-in programs that, while not as feature-rich as many programs sold separately, are extremely useful for completing basic tasks. In this unit, you will work with some of these accessories. John Casey is the owner of Wired Coffee Company, a growing company that uses Windows 2000. John needs to prepare a new coffee menu, so he will use two Windows accessories, WordPad and Paint, to create it. He will use another accessory, Windows Media Player, to play video and sound clips on his computer.

▶ Visual Workshop

Re-create the screen shown in Figure A-16, which shows the Windows desktop with My Documents and My Computer open. Print the screen. (See Independent Challenge 2, Step d for screen printing instructions.)

FIGURE A-16

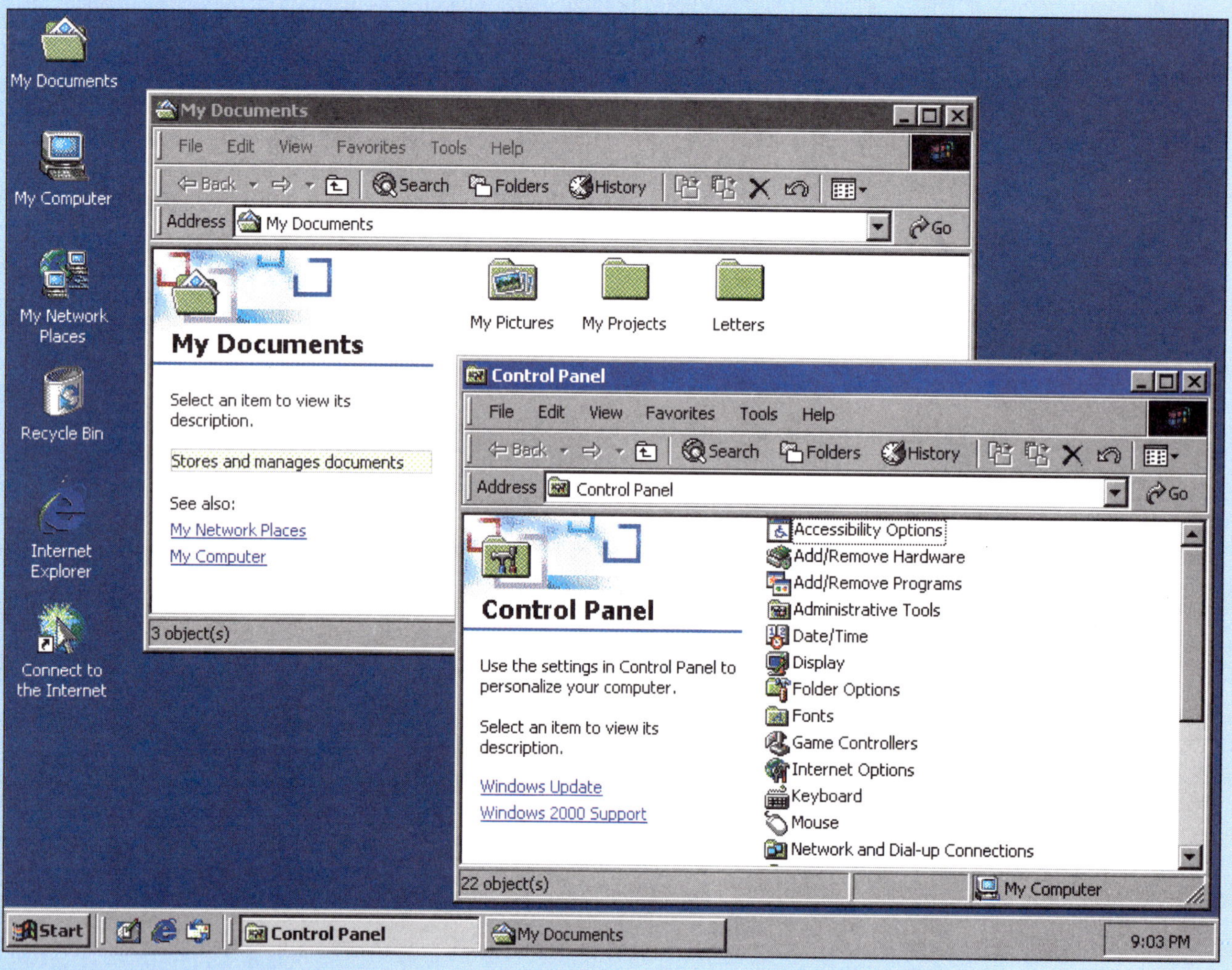

FIGURE L-1: Computer with attached printer

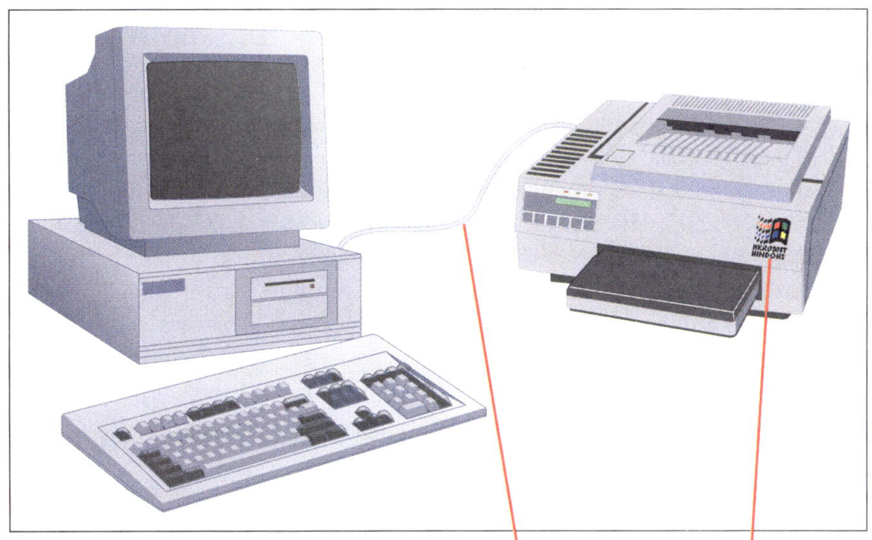

Printer is plugged into the computer via a cable

Logo indicates device is plug-and-play compatible

Getting system information

In Windows 2000, you can use the System Information tool to collect and display your system configuration data, as shown in Figure L-2. Support technicians require specific information about your computer so that they can resolve your system problem. You can use System Information to quickly find the data they need. To open the System Information window, click the Start button on the taskbar, point to Programs, point to Accessories, point to System Tools, then click System Information. For information about working in the System Information window, click Action on the menu bar, and then click Help.

FIGURE L-2: System Information window

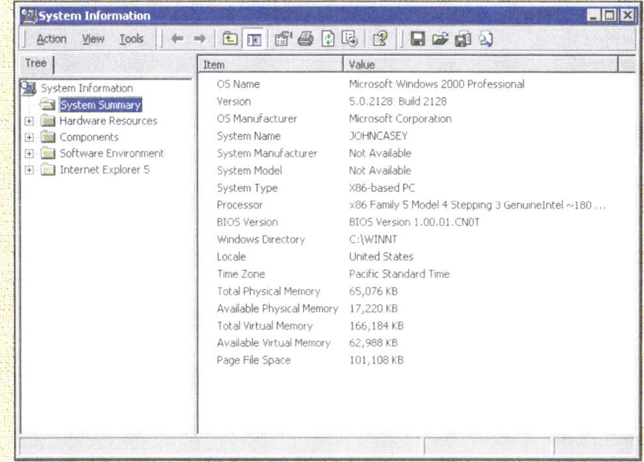

Windows 2000

Installing a Printer

The Add Printer Wizard makes installing a printer quick and easy. This wizard asks a series of questions to help you install either a network or local printer, establish a connection, and print a test page to make sure that the printer works properly. If the printer does not work properly, Windows 2000 starts an automated troubleshooter to help you fix the problem. John purchased a new HP OfficeJet printer and wants to install it. In this lesson, you won't physically install a new printer, but you'll go through the wizard to install the appropriate software for a printer. Normally you would turn off your computer, physically connect your printer to your computer, and then turn your computer back on. Windows 2000 would then automatically detect your printer using Plug and Play support and start the wizard.

Steps 1 2 3 4

QuickTip

To start the Add Printer Wizard, you can also double-click the Printers icon in the Control Panel, then double-click the Add Printer icon, or double-click the Add/Remove Hardware icon in the Control Panel.

1. Click the **Start button** on the taskbar, point to **Settings**, then click **Printers**
   The Printers window opens, as shown in Figure L-3.
2. Double-click the **Add Printer icon**, then click **Next**
   The wizard asks you to specify whether you are installing a local or a network printer. A **local printer** is a printer that is directly connected to your computer, and a **network printer** is one that is connected to a network to which you have access. The local printer option is already selected.
3. Click the **Automatically detect and install my Plug and Play printer check box** to deselect it, if necessary, then click **Next**
   Because an actual printer is not connected to your computer, you do not want this feature to be active; if you were actually installing a printer, you would turn on the feature so that Windows could automatically complete the installation for you. The wizard asks which port you want to use with this printer. A **port** is the location on the back of your computer where you connect the printer cable. You can connect the cable to either a printer port, which is labeled LPT1 or LPT2, or to a communications port, which is labeled COM1 or COM2. For this lesson, it does not matter whether the port is actually in use; if you were actually installing a printer, you would choose an unused port.
4. Click **LPT1** or **LPT2**, then click **Next**
   The wizard asks you to select a printer.

Trouble?

If an HP OfficeJet printer is already installed on your computer, select another printer.

5. Press **[H]**, click **HP** in the Manufacturers list if necessary, click **HP OfficeJet** in the Printers list, as shown in Figure L-4, click **Next**, then click the **No option button** if necessary
   The wizard asks you to type a name for the printer and whether you want the printer to be the default printer. HP OfficeJet appears as the printer name, and the No option button is selected. If you have access to several printers, the **default printer** is the printer that you use most often. When you start a print job without specifying a particular printer, the job is sent to the default printer. A black dot with a checkmark appears, as shown in Figure L-3.
6. Click **Next**, click the **Do not share this printer option button**, then click **Next**
   The wizard asks if you want to print a test page.

Trouble?

If the Windows 2000 installation CD-ROM is not available, click Cancel, then click OK in Step 7 to cancel the operation. For the remaining lessons, you will need to use a printer that is currently installed on your computer.

7. Click the **No option button**, click **Next**, then click **Finish**
   Because you are just practicing and are not actually installing a printer, you do not need a test page. Normally, printing a test page is important to make sure the printer is working properly.
8. If necessary, insert the Windows 2000 installation CD-ROM into the appropriate drive, then click **OK**
   Windows 2000 needs to install the appropriate printer driver from the CD-ROM to complete the printer installation and to test the printer.
9. If necessary, click the **Close button** in the Windows 2000 CD-ROM window
   Upon completion, the HP OfficeJet printer icon appears in the Printers window, as shown in Figure L-5.

FIGURE L-3: Printers window

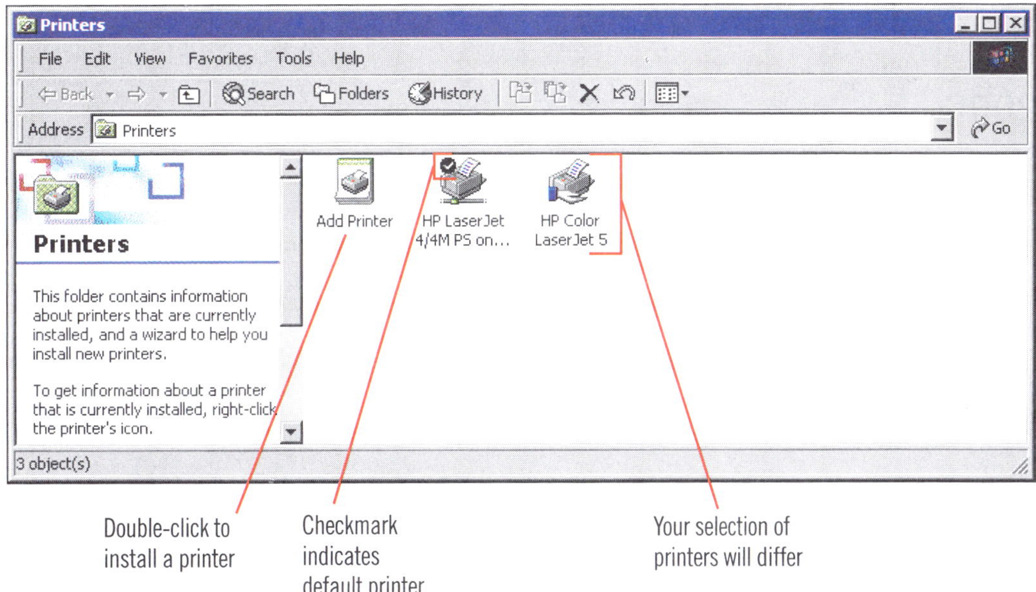

FIGURE L-4: Add Printer Wizard dialog box

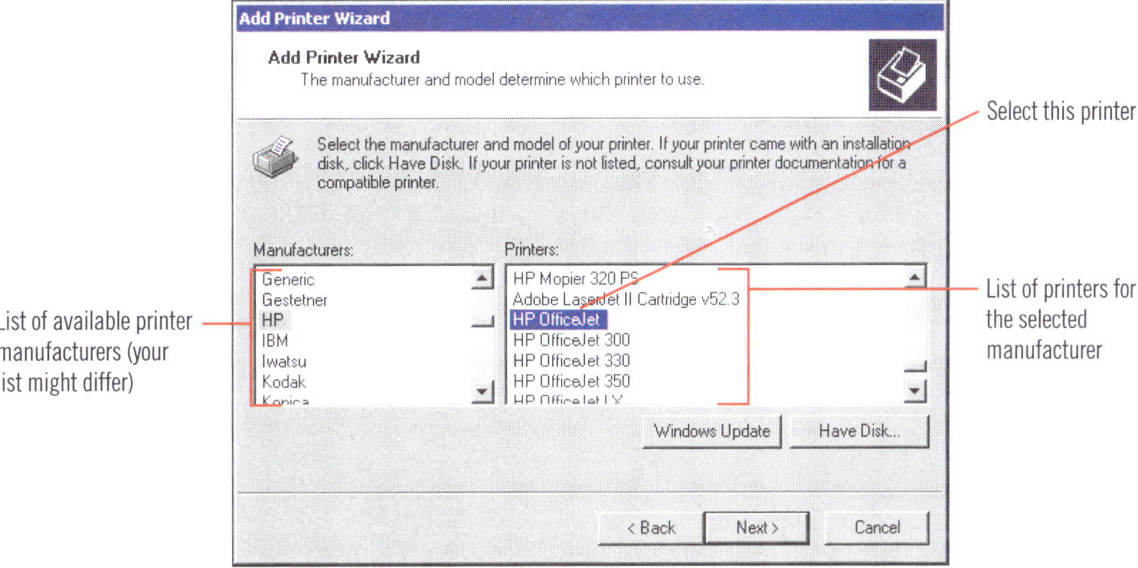

FIGURE L-5: Printers window with new printer

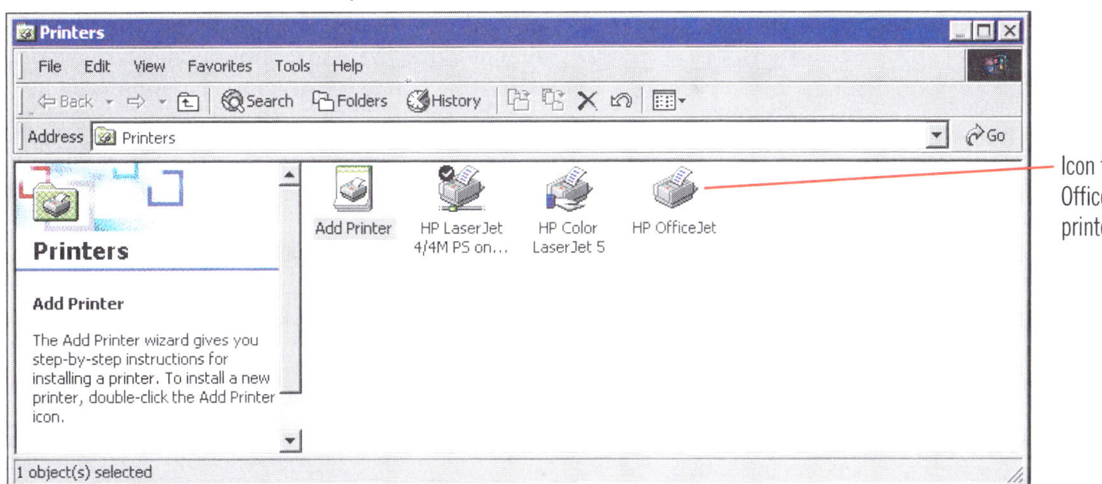

Viewing Printer Properties

A printer is one of the most common hardware devices that computer users install. Viewing printer properties gives you information about a printer's computer connection or network location, related software, paper options, graphics settings, and installed fonts. John wants to view the printer properties of the printer he just installed to make sure that the settings are correct.

1. In the Printers window, click the **HP OfficeJet icon**
   Information about the selected printer appears in the left side of the Printers window, as shown in Figure L-6. Every installed printer on your computer is represented by an icon in the Printers window. When you select a printer icon, status information for that printer, such as number of documents to be printed, whether the printer is ready to print, and the waiting time to print a document, appears in the Printers window. When a printer icon in the window appears with a cable, it indicates a network printer. When a printer icon appears without a cable, it indicates a local printer. When a printer icon appears with a hand, it indicates a **shared printer**, a printer that is directly connected to your computer and is shared with other network users.
2. In the Printers window, right-click the **HP OfficeJet printer icon** or a different printer icon if you did not install the HP OfficeJet printer in the previous lesson, then click **Properties** in the shortcut menu
   The Printer Properties dialog box opens with the General tab in front, as shown in Figure L-7. Table L-1 describes the Printer Properties tabs in the dialog box; your tabs might differ.
3. Click **Print Test Page**
   A dialog box opens, asking if the test page printed correctly.
4. Click **Yes**
5. Click the **Ports tab**
   The Ports tab shows a printer's local connection.
6. Click the **Advanced tab**
   The Advanced tab shows a printer's current driver and gives you specific printing options from which you can choose. When you install a hardware device, Windows 2000 installs related software, known as a **driver**, that allows the hardware to communicate with Windows 2000 and other software programs. To maximize hardware performance, it is important to use the driver that matches the printer.
7. Click **OK**
   The Printers window appears.

QuickTip

To install an updated driver for the selected printer, click New Driver on the Advanced tab, click Next, click Have Disk, insert the disk containing the driver, click Browse, double-click the icon for the drive and folder containing the driver, then click OK.

FIGURE L-6: Printers window

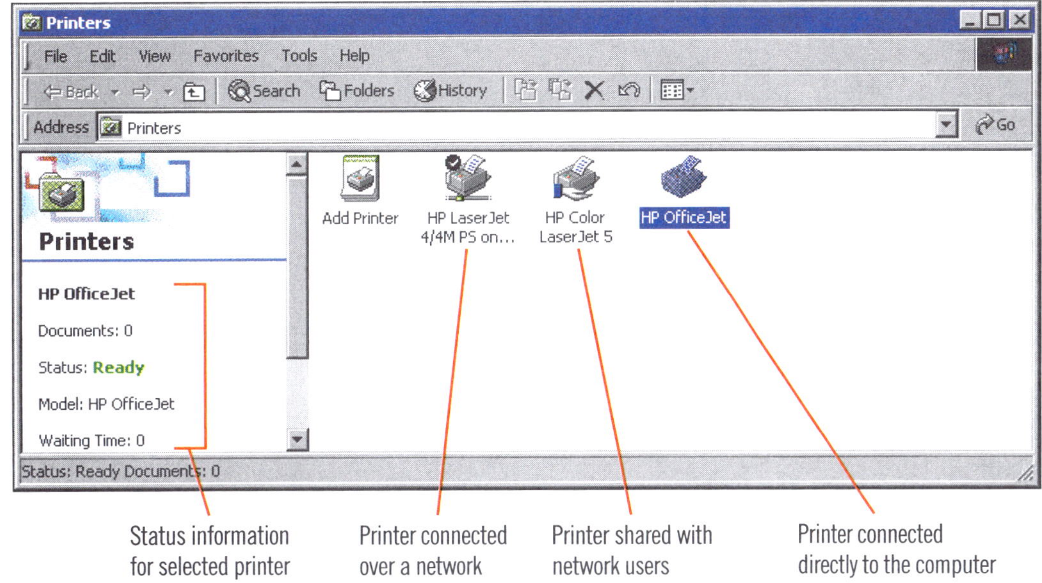

FIGURE L-7: General tab of Printer Properties dialog box

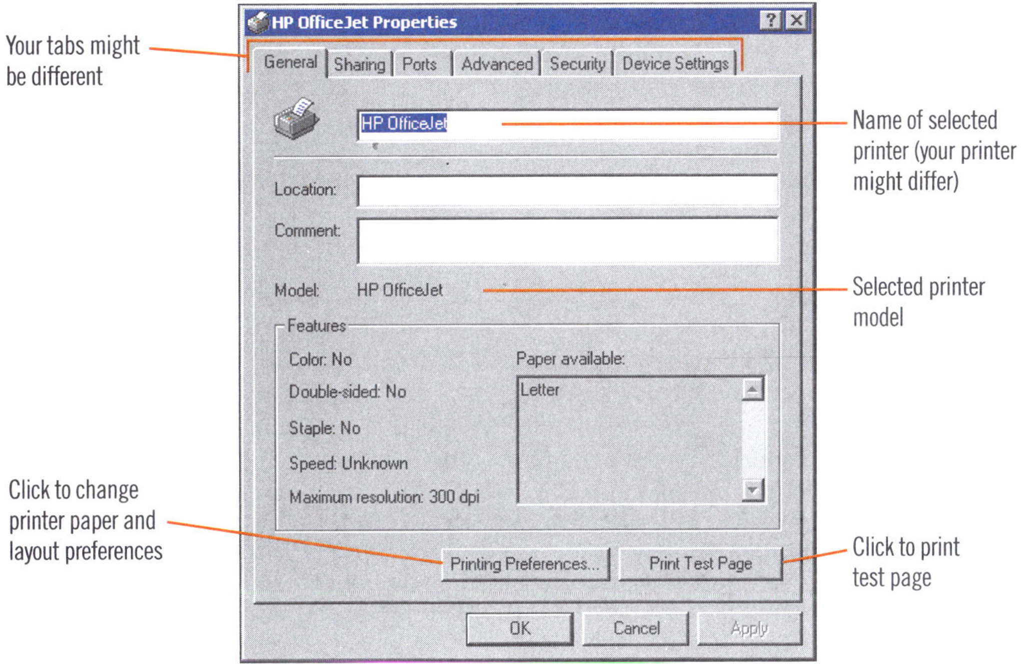

TABLE L-1: Tabs in the Printer Properties dialog box

tab	description
General	Lists general information about the printer and allows you to print a test page
Sharing	Allows you to share the printer over a network
Ports	Lists the printer's connection port and software drivers
Advanced	Lists software drivers and allows you to change printer options
Security	Allows you to manage permission settings to access a printer
Device Settings	Allows you to change printer memory and related settings

Windows 2000

Managing Printers and Print Jobs

When you want to check the status of a printer or manage multiple print jobs, you can double-click the appropriate printer icon in the Printers window. A window opens showing the **print queue**, which is the list of documents to be printed. You can use this window to cancel print jobs, temporarily pause print jobs, view printer properties, and so on. With **deferred printing**, you can send a job to be printed even if your computer is not connected to a printer. To do this, you pause printing, and the document waits in the print queue until you connect a printer to the computer and turn off pause printing. John wants to learn how to manage the printer and print jobs. Because you are not actually printing to a real printer, you will use deferred printing in this lesson.

Steps

1. Insert your Project Disk into the appropriate disk drive
2. In the Printers window, right-click the **HP OfficeJet icon**, then click **Pause Printing**
   This prevents the computer from attempting to send a print job to the printer. Not all printers have an offline mode. When a printer is offline, the printer's icon dims.
3. Double-click the **My Computer icon** on the desktop, double-click the **icon for the drive containing your Project Disk**, double-click the Unit L folder, then drag and resize the open windows so you can see both the window for the Project Disk and the HP OfficeJet icon in the Printers window
   Compare your screen to Figure L-8.
4. Click **Edit** on the menu bar of the window displaying Unit L files, click **Select All**, drag the **files** to the HP OfficeJet icon in the Printers window, then click **Yes** to confirm multiple print jobs
   When you drag the documents over the printer icon, a plus sign appears indicating that it is safe to release the mouse button. When a printer is not paused, a printer icon appears on the taskbar next to the clock, indicating that a job has been sent to be printed. Because you do not actually have this printer attached to your computer (and the printer has been paused anyway), nothing will print; the job simply waits in the print queue until you either delete the job or connect a printer to your computer.
5. Double-click the **HP OfficeJet icon** in the Printers window
   The HP OfficeJet window opens, as shown in Figure L-9. The HP OfficeJet window displays the printer status in the title bar and the print jobs currently in the queue. The documents are listed in the order in which they will be printed.
6. In the HP OfficeJet window, click **Burst Sign**, click **Document** on the menu bar, then click **Pause**
   The printing status of the selected document is changed to paused. If your printer were not paused, you would use this command to pause printing of individual documents in the print queue. Then, when you wanted to print this document, you would click Document on the menu bar and click Resume.
7. Click **Printer** on the menu bar, click **Cancel All Documents**, then click **Yes**
   This deletes all of the print jobs from the queue.
8. Click the **Close button** for all the open windows

QuickTip

To view jobs that have been sent to a network printer, you need to double-click the printer's icon in the Printers window of a computer that is physically connected to the network printer.

QuickTip

You can delete a single document from the print queue by selecting the document, clicking Document on the menu bar, then clicking Cancel Printing.

FIGURE L-8: Preparing to drag files to print

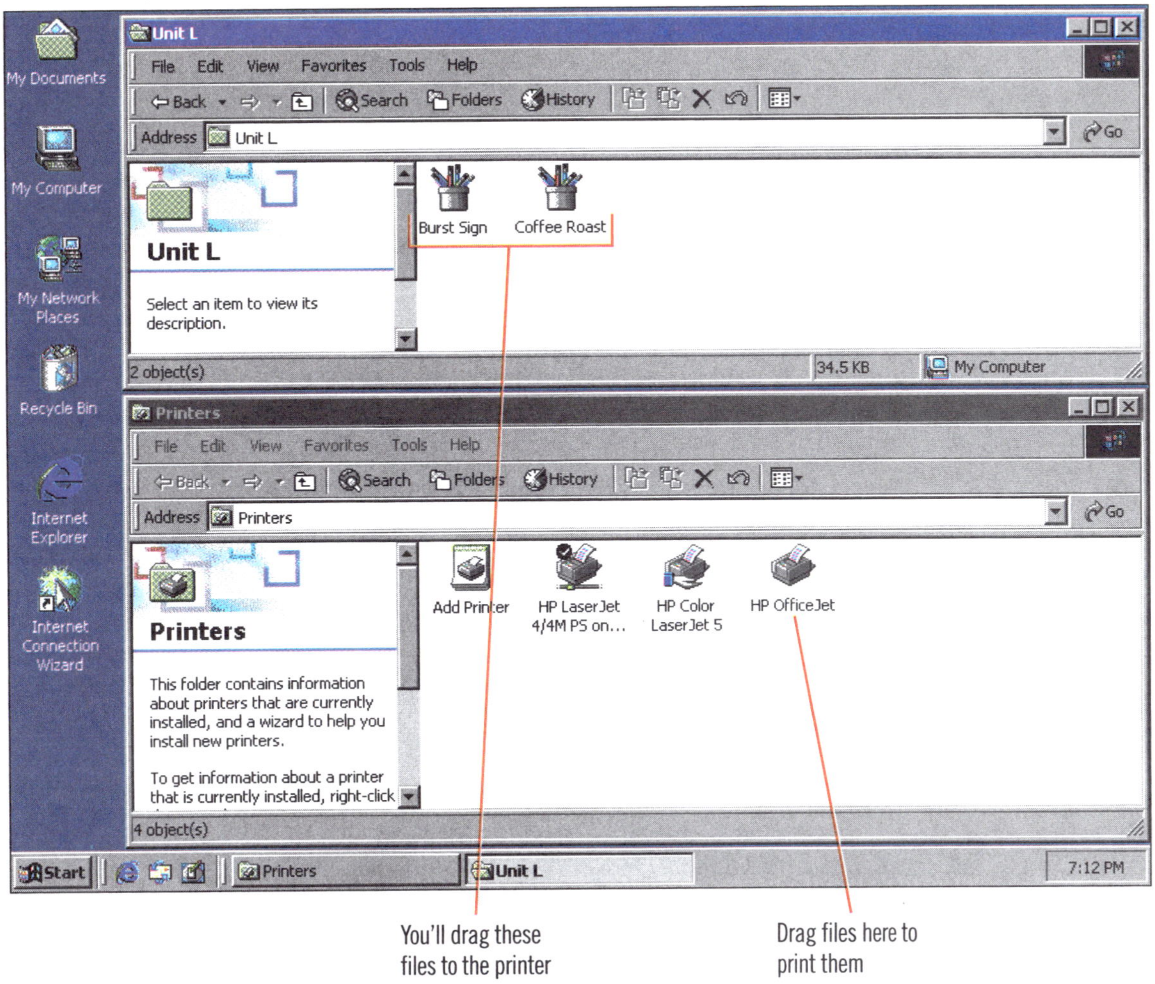

You'll drag these files to the printer

Drag files here to print them

FIGURE L-9: HP OfficeJet window

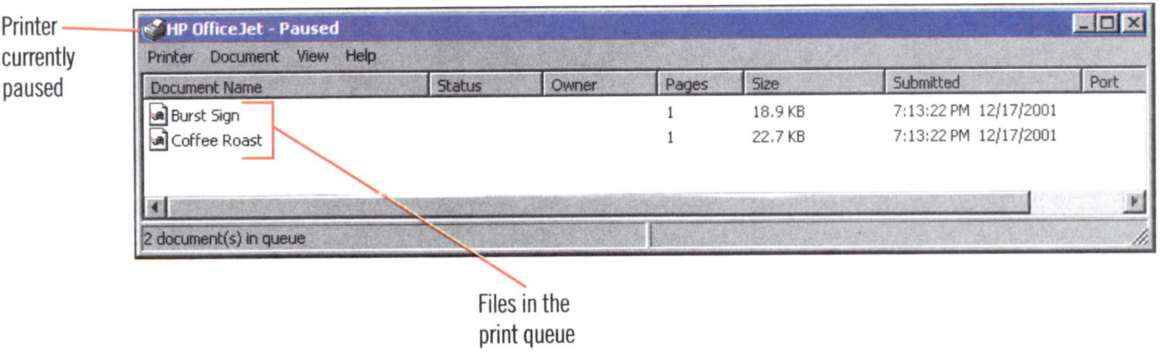

Adding a separator page to print jobs

When you work in a network environment in which many different users are printing to the same printer, adding a separator page to your documents can be helpful. A **separator** (or **banner**) **page** lists the name, author, date, and time of the print job. You can set up separator pages only to a printer attached directly to your computer; in a network, the network administrator would make the change. To add a separator page to print jobs, right-click the printer icon, click Properties, click the Advanced tab, click Separator Page, click Browse, then select the file that you want to use as a custom separator page.

Windows 2000

Installing Hardware Devices

The Add/Remove Hardware Wizard makes installing hardware devices easy by asking a series of questions to help you set up the software that is necessary for the new hardware device to work properly on your computer. John uses the Add/Remove Hardware Wizard to install support software for a hardware device (an imaging device) he just connected to his computer. In this lesson, you won't physically install a new hardware device, but you'll go through the wizard to install the appropriate software for the hardware device. Normally, you would turn off your computer, physically connect the new hardware to your computer, then turn your computer back on. Windows 2000 would then automatically detect your new hardware device using Plug and Play support and start the wizard.

Steps 1 2 3 4

1. Close any open programs, click the **Start button** on the taskbar, point to **Settings**, then click **Control Panel**
   The Control Panel window opens.
2. Double-click the **Add/Remove Hardware icon**, then click **Next**
   The wizard asks if you want to add or troubleshoot a device, or uninstall or unplug a device. The Add/Troubleshoot a device option is already selected.
3. Click **Next**
   Wait while Windows 2000 searches your computer for new Plug and Play devices. Next, the wizard asks you to add a new device or to select the installed device that you want to troubleshoot.
4. Click **Add a new device**, as shown in Figure L-10, then click **Next**
5. Click the **No, I want to select the hardware from a list option button**, then click **Next**
   Because an actual hardware device is not connected to your computer, you want this feature to be active; if you were actually installing a hardware device, you would let Windows search for the new hardware device. The wizard asks you to select the type of hardware for which you want to install the support software, as shown in Figure L-11.
6. Click **Imaging devices**, then click **Next**
   The wizard asks you to select a make and model for the new hardware. Devices are listed alphabetically. The default manufacturer is Agfa, and the default model is Agfa ePhoto 1280 Digital Camera.
7. Click **Next** to accept the default, click **Automatic Port Select**, then click **Next**
   The wizard asks you to enter a name for the device.
8. Click **Next** to accept the default device name, then click **Finish** to install the software
9. If necessary, insert the required Windows 2000 installation CD-ROM into the appropriate drive, click **OK**, then click the **Close button** in the Windows 2000 CD-ROM window
   Windows 2000 needs to install the appropriate driver to complete the installation. You then return to the Control Panel.

Trouble?

To start the Add/Remove Hardware Wizard, you can also click Hardware Wizard on the Hardware tab in the System Properties dialog box.

Trouble?

If the Windows 2000 installation CD-ROM is not available, click OK, then click Cancel.

FIGURE L-10: Add/Remove Hardware Wizard dialog box

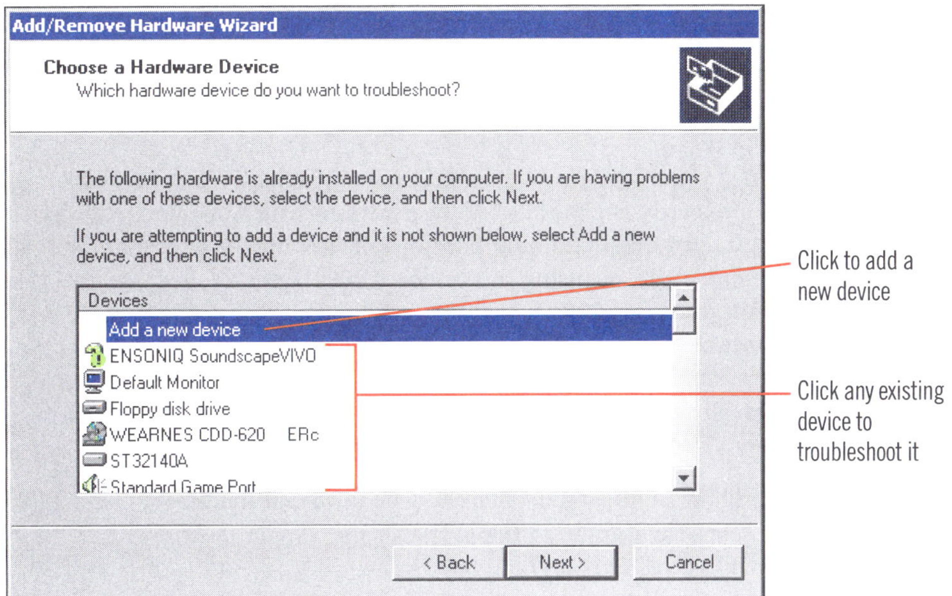

FIGURE L-11: Choosing a hardware device to install

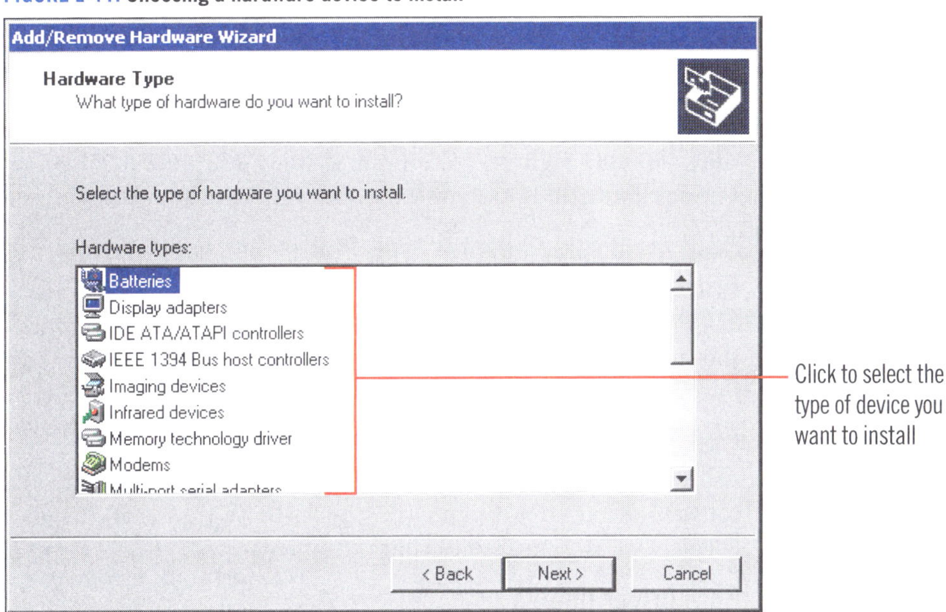

CLUES TO USE

Creating a hardware profile

You can customize your computer by creating a **hardware profile,** a list of settings that specify which devices to start when you start your computer. Hardware profiles are especially useful if you have a laptop or portable computer. When you first install Windows 2000, a hardware profile called Profile 1 (for laptops, the profiles would be Docked Profile or Undocked Profile) is created. By default, every device that is installed on your computer at the time you install Windows 2000 is enabled in the Profile 1 hardware profile. To create a hardware profile, double-click the System icon in the Control Panel, click the Hardware tab, click Hardware Profiles, click Profile 1 in the Available hardware profiles section, click Copy, type a name for the new profile, then click OK. Once you create a hardware profile, you can use Device Manager to disable and enable devices that are in the profile. When you disable a device in a hardware profile, the device drivers for the device are not loaded when you start your computer. If there is more than one hardware profile, you can designate a default profile that will be used every time you start your computer. You can also have Windows 2000 ask you which profile to use every time you start your computer.

Windows 2000

Viewing System Hardware

When you install a new operating system, such as Windows 2000, it is important to make sure that you are using the latest software drivers with your system hardware. If you are not using the latest software drivers, your hardware devices might not work to full capacity. You can view your system hardware using a Windows 2000 utility called Device Manager. With the Device Manager, you can determine the software driver versions that are being used with your system hardware. After viewing your software driver version numbers, you can call the manufacturer to determine the latest versions. John wants to make sure that he is using the latest software driver version of the display adapter for his monitor.

Trouble?

If a specific device is conflicting with some other device, its icon is marked by an exclamation point within a yellow circle, as shown in Figure L-12.

1. In the Control Panel, double-click the **System icon** (you might have to scroll to see it), click the **Hardware tab** in the System Properties dialog box, then click **Device Manager**

   The Device Manager window opens, as shown in Figure L-12. Device Manager provides you with a list of the hardware types, also known as **hardware classes**, that are attached to your computer. To see the specific devices within a hardware type, you click the plus sign next to the hardware device type. Once you select a specific device within a hardware device type, you can investigate the properties of the hardware device. On his computer, John uses an older **display adapter**, a hardware device that allows a computer to communicate with its monitor, so he decides to learn its properties.

2. Click the **plus sign** next to the Display adapters icon

   The display expands to show the name of the display adapter attached to your computer.

QuickTip

To disable a hardware device, you can click the hardware device in the Device Manager, click the Disable button on the toolbar, then click Yes. To enable the device, you can click the Enable button on the toolbar.

3. Click the **display adapter type** that is connected to your computer, then click the **Properties button** on the toolbar

   The Properties dialog box for your display adaptor type opens with the General tab in front, showing identification and status information about the display adapter. Table L-2 describes the options available in each of the tabs.

4. Click the **Driver tab**

   As shown in Figure L-13, you can click Driver Details to learn the current version of the software driver, or you can click Update Driver to install the latest driver for the display adapter that is connected to your computer.

5. Click **Driver Details**

   Details for the current driver are shown in the Driver Details dialog box, including the driver file version number.

QuickTip

To view hardware devices by what they are connected to, click View on the menu bar, then click Devices by connection.

6. Click **OK**, then click **OK**

7. Click the **minus sign** next to the Display adapters icon

   The list of display adapters collapses. Leave the Device Manager open as you continue to the next lesson.

FIGURE L-12: Device Manager window

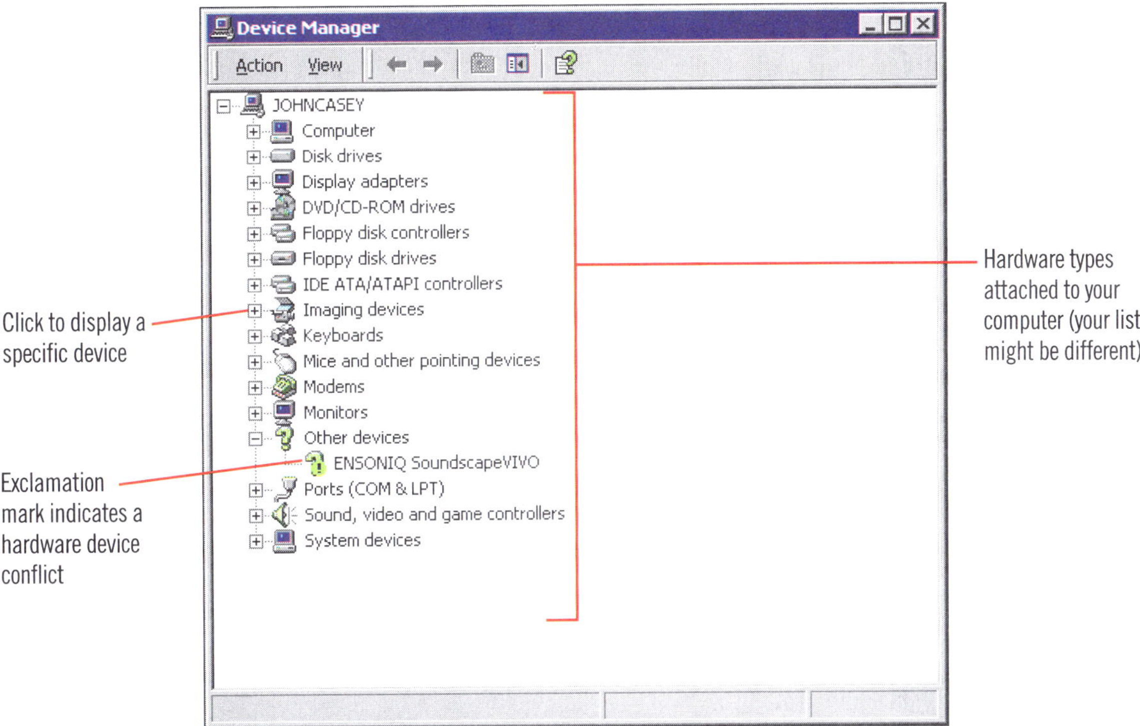

FIGURE L-13: Display Adapter Properties dialog box

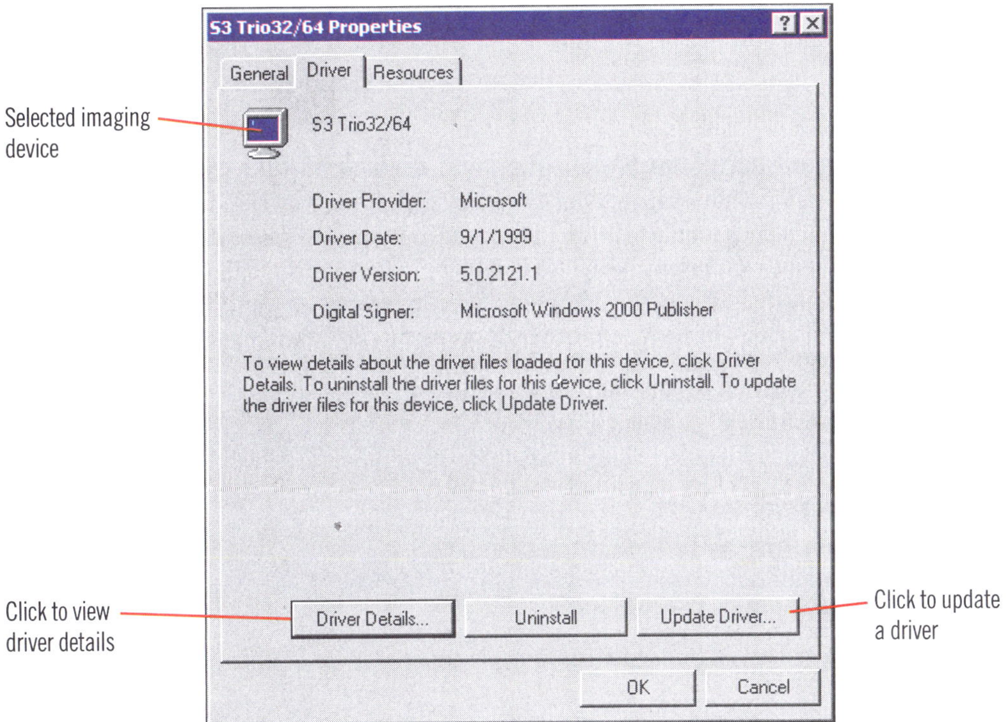

TABLE L-2: Tabs in the Display Adapter Properties dialog box

tab	description
General	Lists general status and usage information about the hardware device
Driver	Lists the software drivers related to the hardware device
Resources	Lists the memory settings related to the hardware device

Viewing Hardware Settings

One reason you might want to view hardware settings is if you plan to install any legacy hardware. **Legacy hardware** is any device that is not designed for Windows 98 or 2000 plug-and-play support. If you have a hardware device that is not designed for Plug and Play, then it is important to find out current hardware resource settings to avoid **conflicts**, two devices with the same resource settings, during installation. Before you actually place a legacy hardware device into your computer, you should browse through the devices currently attached to your computer system and ensure that your computer has the available resources to install the hardware device. With the Device Manager, you can view the device resources that are being used with your system hardware and determine whether your computer has the available resources to install a legacy or Plug and Play hardware device. Generally, you cannot install non-Plug and Play hardware without performing some manual setup with the Device Manager. John has an old scanner and wants to examine current hardware resource settings to determine whether he can install the legacy hardware.

QuickTip

To scan for any hardware changes in the Device Manager, click the Scan for hardware changes button on the toolbar.

QuickTip

To get additional information about Device Manager, click the Help button on the toolbar.

1. **In the Device Manager window, click View on the menu bar, then click Resources by connection**

2. **Click the plus sign ⊞ next to the Interrupt request (IRQ) icon**

   The Device Manager displays the resource settings currently in use and the hardware that is using each resource, as shown in Figure L-14. Each installed device requires a communication line called an **interrupt request line (IRQ)**, which allows the hardware device to communicate with your computer's software. Each device must have its own IRQ. If two devices attempt to share an IRQ, you will have an IRQ conflict, and neither device will work properly.

3. **Drag the scroll bar to the bottom of the window, if necessary**

   Take note of the available IRQs on your computer. Any IRQ number between 0 and 15 that is not listed is available. When you install a legacy hardware device, the device's instructions might ask you to provide an IRQ setting. When prompted by the device instructions, provide an IRQ that is not already in use. Instead of writing down your computer resource information on paper, you can print a system summary report.

4. **Click View on the menu bar, then click Print**

   The Print dialog box opens, as shown in Figure L-15. Table L-3 describes the report options available in the Print dialog box. Before you print, make sure that an available printer is selected.

5. **Click Print**

   Figure L-16 shows the first part of the summary report. If you are having trouble installing a hardware device, a technical support person might ask you questions that this summary report will help you answer.

6. **Click the Close button ☒ in the Device Manager window, then click OK to close the System Properties dialog box**

CLUES TO USE

Using the hardware troubleshooter

Hardware conflict can occur when two or more devices try to use the same IRQ. In many cases, one of the devices will not work. If you have a conflict, you can use the hardware troubleshooter. To use the troubleshooter, click Help on the Start menu, click the Contents tab, click the Troubleshooting and Maintenance book, click the Windows 2000 Troubleshooters book, click the Hardware link in the right pane of the Help window, click Next at the bottom of the right pane, then follow the instructions and suggestions listed.

FIGURE L-14: Device Manager window in Resources by connection view

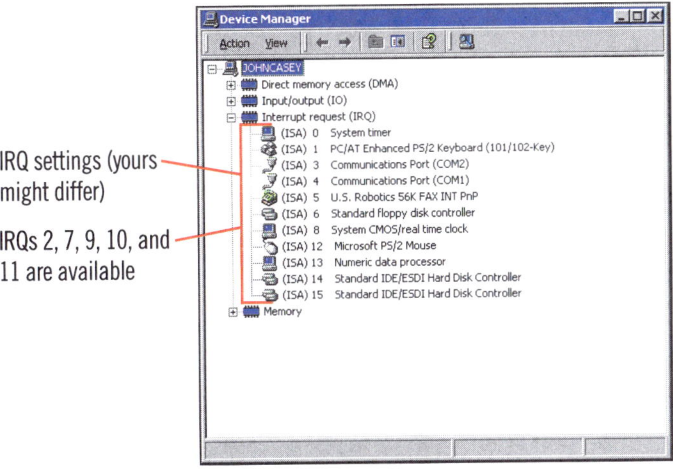

FIGURE L-15: Print dialog box

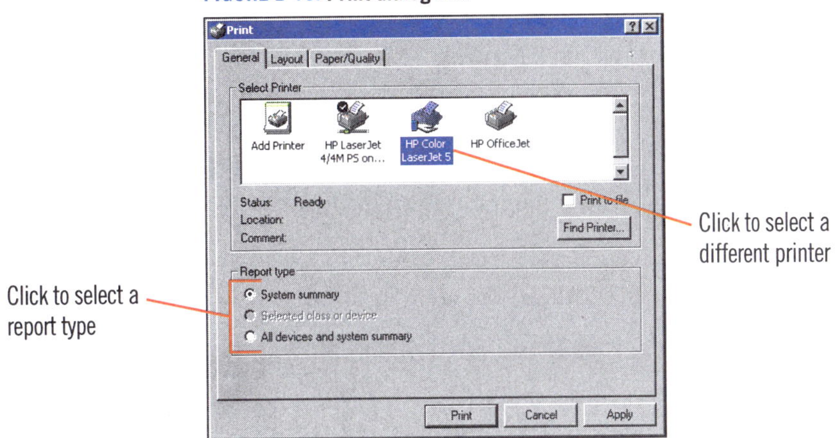

FIGURE L-16: Summary report

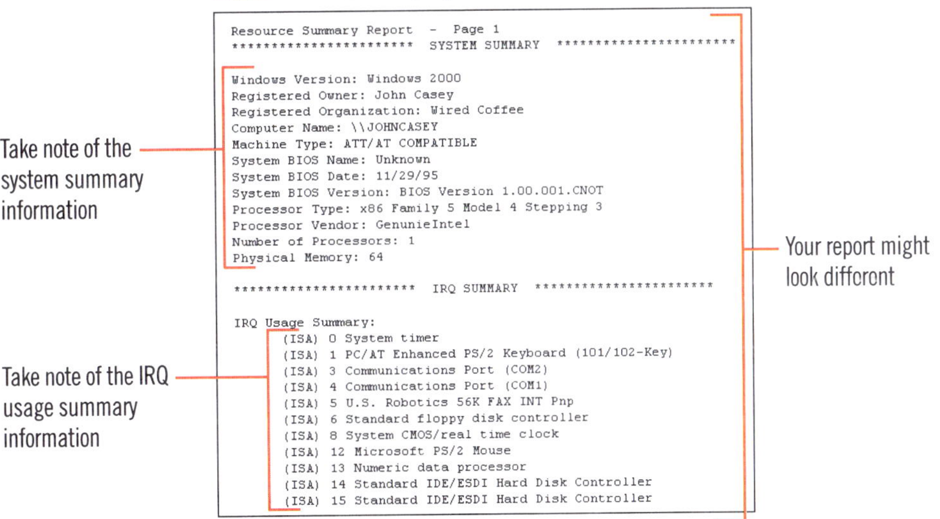

```
Resource Summary Report  -  Page 1
*********************** SYSTEM SUMMARY ***********************

Windows Version: Windows 2000
Registered Owner: John Casey
Registered Organization: Wired Coffee
Computer Name: \\JOHNCASEY
Machine Type: ATT/AT COMPATIBLE
System BIOS Name: Unknown
System BIOS Date: 11/29/95
System BIOS Version: BIOS Version 1.00.001.CNOT
Processor Type: x86 Family 5 Model 4 Stepping 3
Processor Vendor: GenuineIntel
Number of Processors: 1
Physical Memory: 64

*********************** IRQ SUMMARY ***********************

IRQ Usage Summary:
      (ISA) 0 System timer
      (ISA) 1 PC/AT Enhanced PS/2 Keyboard (101/102-Key)
      (ISA) 3 Communications Port (COM2)
      (ISA) 4 Communications Port (COM1)
      (ISA) 5 U.S. Robotics 56K FAX INT Pnp
      (ISA) 6 Standard floppy disk controller
      (ISA) 8 System CMOS/real time clock
      (ISA) 12 Microsoft PS/2 Mouse
      (ISA) 13 Numeric data processor
      (ISA) 14 Standard IDE/ESDI Hard Disk Controller
      (ISA) 15 Standard IDE/ESDI Hard Disk Controller
```


TABLE L-3: Print dialog box report types

report types	description
System summary	Prints general system, IRQ, port, memory, and DMA channel usage information about your computer
Selected class or device	Prints device type, resource, and driver information
All devices and system summary	Prints general system, IRQ, port, memory, DMA channel usage, and driver information for all devices on your computer

Windows 2000

Removing Hardware Devices

If you no longer use a hardware device or you have an older hardware device that you want to upgrade, you need to remove the hardware device drivers and related software before you remove the physical hardware device from your computer. Windows 2000 makes it easy to remove device drivers. In the same way you can use the Add/Remove Hardware Wizard to install a hardware device, you can also use the wizard to remove a hardware device. The Add/Remove Hardware Wizard walks you through the process and removes the device drivers and related software. Just as you can use the Printers window to install a printer, you can remove a printer in the Printers window as well. John decides not to connect the digital camera and printer he installed to his computer after all, so he needs to delete both drivers.

Steps

QuickTip

To delete a hardware device in the Device Manager, click the plus sign next to the hardware type that contains the device you want to remove, select the device, then click the Uninstall button on the toolbar.

1. In the Control Panel, double-click the **Add/Remove Hardware icon**, as shown in Figure L-17, then click **Next**
2. Click the **Uninstall/Unplug a device option button**, then click **Next**
   The wizard asks you to select a removal task, as shown in Figure L-18.
3. Click the **Uninstall a device option button**, then click **Next**
   The wizard asks you to select the device you want to remove.
4. Click the **scroll down arrow**, click **Agfa ePhoto 1280 Digital Camera**, then click **Next**
5. Click the **Yes, I want to uninstall this device option button**, click **Next**, then click **Finish**
   The Agfa digital camera hardware device is removed.
6. Double-click the **Printers icon** in the Control Panel
   The Printers window opens.
7. Click the **HP OfficeJet icon**
   The HP OfficeJet icon appears highlighted in the Printers window, as shown in Figure L-19.
8. Click the **Delete button** on the toolbar, then click **Yes** to confirm the delete
9. Click the **Close button** in the Printers window

Trouble?

If a printer contains a print job, Windows 2000 ignores the Delete command. You need to purge all print jobs before you can delete a printer.

FIGURE L-17: Control Panel window

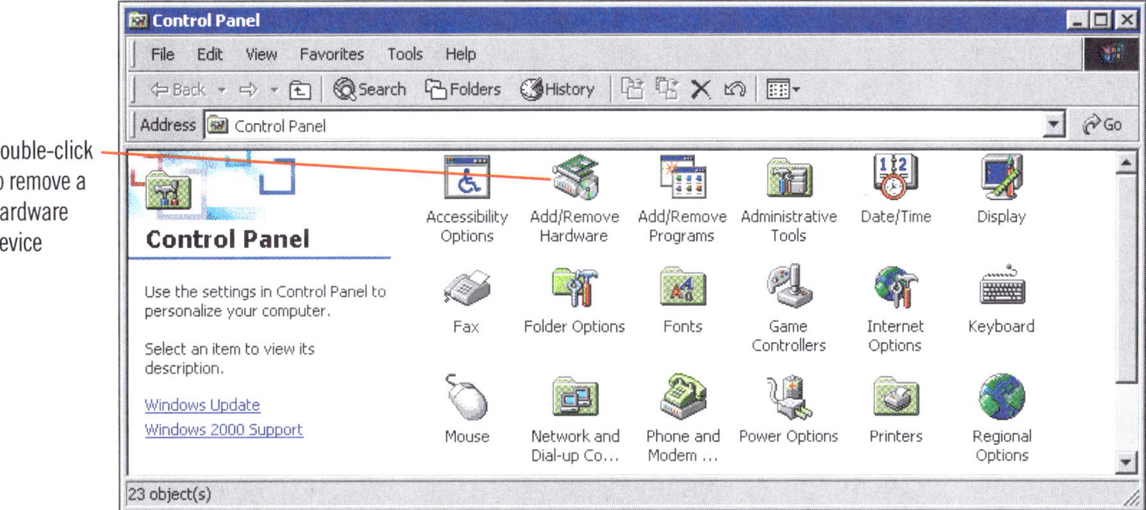

FIGURE L-18: Add/Remove Hardware Wizard dialog box

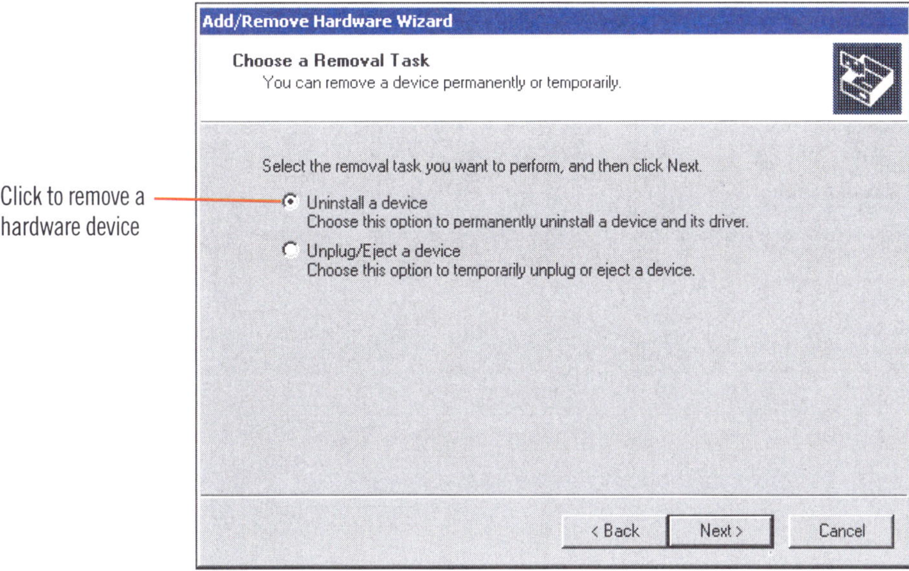

FIGURE L-19: Printers window

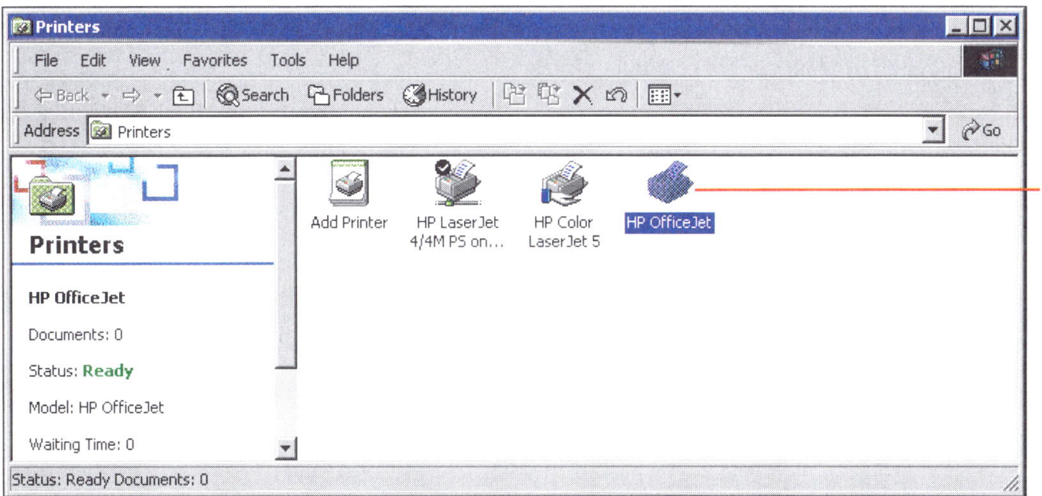

Practice

▶ Concepts Review

Label each of the elements of the screen shown in Figure L-20.

FIGURE L-20

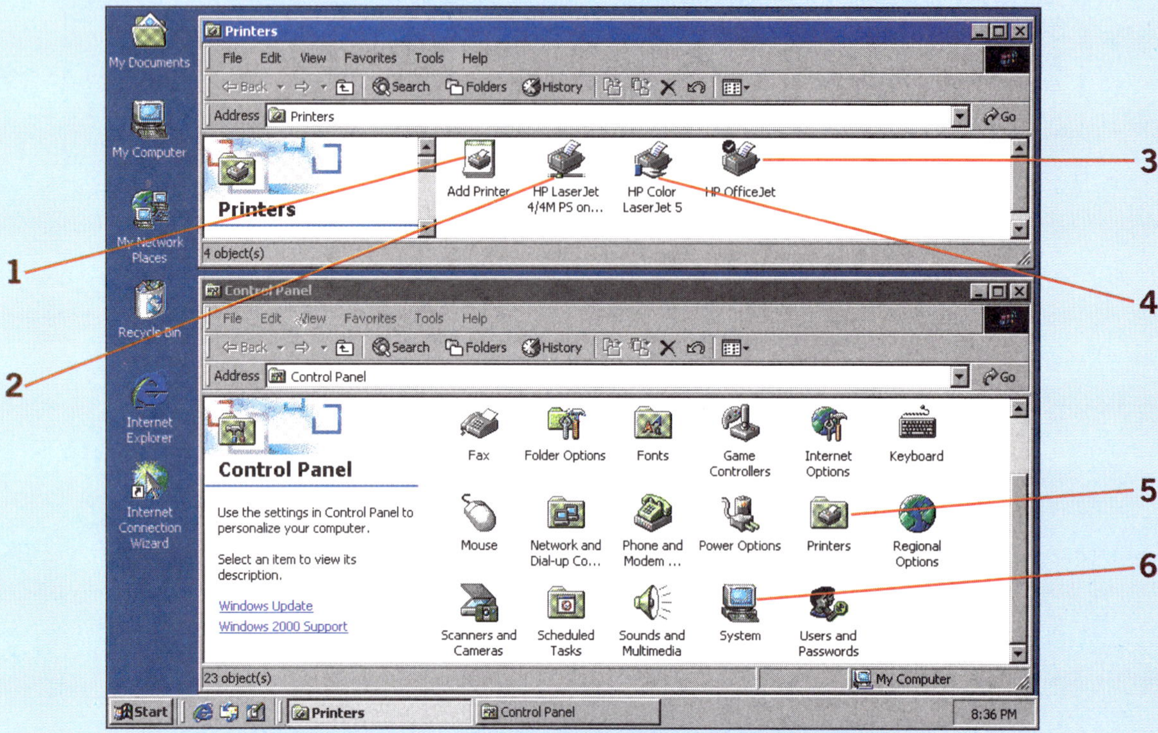

Match each of the terms with the statement that describes its function.

7. Location on a computer where you connect a cable
8. Location where you find device drivers
9. Hardware designed for Windows 98 or 2000
10. Location where you find printer drivers
11. How a device communicates
12. Hardware designed for pre-Windows 98 or 2000

a. Advanced tab of Printer Properties dialog box
b. Plug and Play device
c. Port
d. Drivers tab of Properties dialog box
e. Legacy device
f. IRQ

Select the best answer from the list of choices.

13. Which of the following is a way to print a document?
- **a.** Select the Print command from a program
- **b.** Right-click a document, then click Print
- **c.** Drag a document to the printer icon
- **d.** All of the above

14. When right-clicking a printer icon, which of the following can you NOT do?
- **a.** Open the printer's window
- **b.** Set the printer as the default printer
- **c.** Delete the printer
- **d.** Close the printer's window

15. Which tab in the Printer Properties dialog box do you click to check printing preferences?
- **a.** The General tab
- **b.** The Ports tab
- **c.** The Advanced tab
- **d.** The Device tab

16. Which of the following commands is NOT a way to stop a print job that is currently in progress?
- **a.** Cancel All Documents
- **b.** Pause Printing
- **c.** Cancel Printing
- **d.** Stop Printing

17. Which tab in the System Properties dialog box do you click to open the Device Manager?
- **a.** The General tab.
- **b.** The Hardware tab.
- **c.** The User Profiles tab.
- **d.** The Advanced tab.

18. Which of the following is NOT a system report?
- **a.** System summary
- **b.** All device and system summary
- **c.** Class or device summary
- **d.** Selected class or device

19. What does IRQ stand for?
- **a.** Interrupt result queue
- **b.** Interrupt request queue
- **c.** Interrupt response queue
- **d.** Interpreted request queue

Skills Review

1. Install a printer.

a. Click the Start button, point to Settings, then click Printers.
b. Double-click the Add Printer icon.
c. Click Next.
d. Click the Automatically detect and install my Plug and Play printer check box to deselect it, then click Next.
e. Click an open port (COM or LPT), then click Next.
f. Click Xerox as the manufacturer, click Xerox Document Centre 220 as the model, then click Next.
g. Click the No option button, click Next, click the Do not share this printer option button, then click Next.
h. Click the No option button, click Next, then click Finish.
i. If necessary, insert a Windows 2000 CD-ROM into the appropriate drive, then click OK.
j. If necessary, close the Windows 2000 CD-ROM window.

2. View printer properties.

a. Right-click a printer icon, then click Properties.
b. Click Print Test Page, then click OK.
c. Click the available tabs to view the various printer properties.
d. Click OK.

3. Manage printers and print jobs.

a. Right-click the Xerox Document Centre 220 icon, then click Pause Printing.
b. Double-click the My Computer icon on the desktop.
c. Insert your Project Disk in the appropriate floppy drive, then double-click the Unit L folder.
d. Right-click an empty area of the taskbar, then click Tile Windows Horizontally.
e. Locate and click the Burst Sign document.
f. Hold down [Shift], then click the Coffee Roast document.
g. Drag the files to the Xerox Document Centre 220 icon in the Printers window, then click Yes.
h. Double-click the Xerox Document Centre 220 icon.
i. Click Printer on the menu bar, then click Cancel All Documents, then click Yes.
j. Click the Close button in all of the open windows.

4. Install hardware devices.

a. Click the Start button, point to Settings, then click Control Panel.
b. Double-click the Add/Remove Hardware icon, then click Next.
c. Click Next, click Add a new device, then click Next.
d. Click the No, I want to select the hardware from a list option button, then click Next.
e. Click System Device, then click Next.
f. Make sure Microsoft Corporation and Full screen video driver for console are selected, then click Next.
g. Click Next, then click Finish.
h. If necessary, insert a Windows 2000 CD-ROM, then click OK.
i. If necessary, close the Windows 2000 CD-ROM window.
j. Click No if prompted to restart your computer.

5. View system hardware.

a. Double-click the System icon in the Control Panel (you might have to scroll to see it).
b. Click the Hardware tab, then click Device Manager.
c. Click + next to the DVD/CD-ROMS icon.
d. Click a DVD or CD-ROM device.
e. Click the Properties button on the toolbar.
f. Click the Properties tab.
g. Click the Driver tab.
h. Click OK.
i. Click – next to the system devices icon.

6. View hardware settings.

a. Click View on the menu bar, then click Resources by connection.
b. Click the plus sign next to the Interrupt request (IRQ) icon.
c. Click View on the menu bar, the click Print.
d. Click Print.
e. Click the Close button in the Device Manager.
f. Click OK.

7. Remove hardware devices.

a. Double-click the Add/Remove Hardware icon in the Control Panel, then click Next.
b. Click the Uninstall/Unplug a device option button, then click Next.
c. Click the Uninstall a device option button, then click Next.
d. Click Full screen video driver for console device, then click Next.
e. Click the Yes, I want to uninstall this device option button, click Next, then click Finish.
f. Double-click the Printers icon in the Control Panel.
g. Click the Xerox Document Centre 220 icon.
h. Click the Delete button on the toolbar, then click Yes.
i. Click the Close button in the Printers window.

Independent Challenges

1. You are an administrator at the U.S. Geological Survey and are in charge of creating earthquake reports on seismic activity in California. Your boss recently approved the purchase of a new color printer to help you create better reports. You want to install the color printer on your computer.

To complete this independent challenge:

a. Start the Add Printer Wizard.
b. Install a new printer, assuming the following about the installation: it's a local printer, the manufacturer is Tektronix, and the printer model is Tektronix Phaser IIPX.
c. Choose an open port (LPT or COM).
d. Do not set the printer as default.
e. Do not print a test page.
f. Open the Printer Properties dialog box, verify that the port and printer assignments are correct, then click OK.
g. Print the screen. (Press the Print Screen key to make a copy of the screen, open Paint, click Edit on the menu bar, click Paste to paste the screen into Paint, then click Yes to paste the large image if necessary. Click File on the menu bar, click Print, then click Print in the Print dialog box.)
h. Delete the printer you just added.
i. Close all open windows.

2. You are the director of a youth center called Hosanna Homes for troubled teens. Half of your funding comes from the state and the other half comes from donations. At the end of the month, you need to send a report to the state indicating the status of each teen at the home. You also send a report to donors to let them know what happened during the month. For this challenge, create several reports, print the documents, and manage the print jobs.

To complete this independent challenge:

a. Use a real, working printer that is attached to your computer.
b. Pause printing. Get permission from your instructor or technical support person to do this.
c. Assume the following information about the youth center:
Hosanna Homes ID: 251523
35 Live Oak Ranch Road
Livermore, TX 82510
d. Using WordPad, create a file named *June 2001 State* on your Project Disk, then enter the following information:
State of Texas Protective Services

Name	**Age**	**Level**	**Number of Days**
Maura Colligan	**16**	**4**	**30**
Brian Hubbard	**17**	**5**	**30**
Jill Meyer	**16**	**3**	**30**
David Smith	**17**	**4**	**30**
Earl Todd	**15**	**1**	**16**

e. Print the document on the chosen printer.

f. Open a new WordPad window and create a file named *June 2001 Donor* on your Project Disk, then enter the following information:
Dear Donor,
During the month, Hosanna Homes received a new teenager at the ranch. His name is Earl Todd. He is 15 years old. His hobbies are playing football and basketball, and drawing sports pictures.
Hosanna Homes is in need of sports and recreational equipment. If you or anyone you know has any equipment to donate, please contact me at the main office.
Thank you for all your support.
[Your name], Director

g. Send the document to the chosen printer.
h. Cancel the print job June 2001 State.
i. Choose the Pause Printing command to turn off Pause Printing and print the job June 2001 Donor.
j. Open the printer window, then check the status of the printer.
k. Open the file June 2001 State in the WordPad window, change the number of days for Earl Todd from 16 to 18, then save the file.
l. Print the file, then close all open windows.

3. You are the owner of Lasting Impressions, a photography studio that specializes in wedding and location photography. To increase revenues and streamline production, you want to add the ability to take digital wedding photos for your photography clients. Before you invest in the hardware and software needed to take digital wedding photos, you decide to install a digital camera device and check your computer's hardware properties.

To complete this independent challenge:

a. Open the Control Panel.
b. Open the Scanners and Cameras Properties dialog box.
c. Click Add.
d. Install a Kodak digital camera.
e. Display the properties for this device.
f. Print the screen. (See Independent Challenge 1, Step g for screen printing instructions.)
g. Remove the Kodak digital camera.
h. Close open windows.

4. You are an engineer at Denson Engineering, a company that specializes in technical drawings. You want to install a special hardware device to create 35mm slides for a technical presentation that you have developed with some of your drawings. During the installation of the legacy hardware, you encountered some problems. When you called technical support, the representative asked you to print a resource summary report to help diagnose the problem.

To complete this independent challenge:

a. Open the Control Panel.
b. Open the System Properties dialog box.
c. Open the Device Manager window.
d. View the IRQ resources.
e. Print a resource summary report.
f. Close the Device Manager window, then cancel the System properties.
g. Close open windows.

Visual Workshop

Create the screen shown in Figure L-21, which displays information about a keyboard. Your keyboard results will differ from the ones shown here. Print the screen (see Independent Challenge 1, Step g for screen printing instructions).

FIGURE L-21

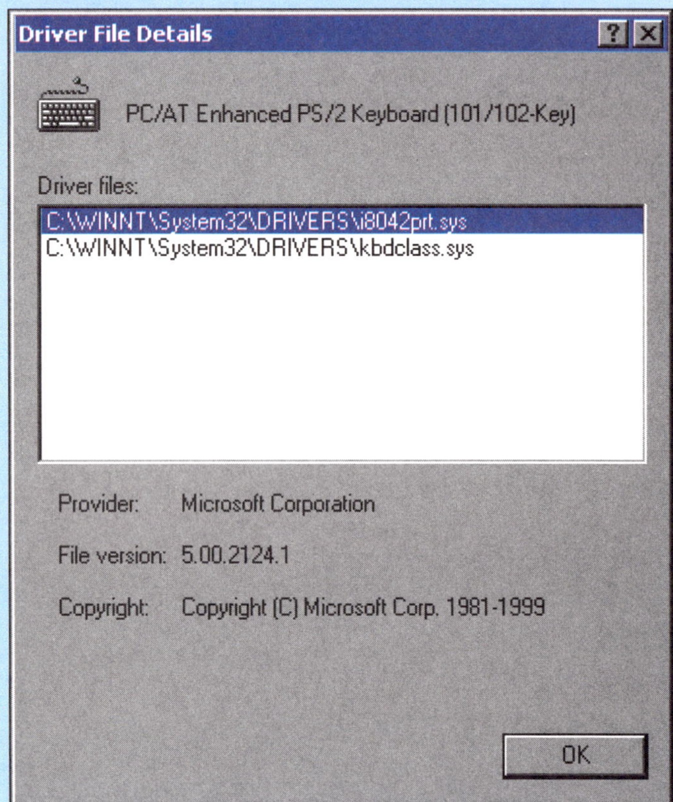

Unit M

Maintaining

Your Computer

Objectives

- Make an emergency repair disk
- Format a disk
- Copy a disk
- Find and repair disk errors
- Defragment a disk
- Clean up a disk
- Add and remove a program
- Enter DOS commands

Windows 2000 offers a number of useful tools for managing routine tasks such as installing and removing programs, formatting, copying, and repairing disks. Windows 2000 also provides tools to find and fix disk problems, speed up disk access, and clean up disk space. By periodically finding and repairing disk errors, you can keep your files in good working condition and prevent disk problems that might cause you to lose your work. In addition, you can also work with the DOS operating system alongside your Windows 2000 operating system. In this unit, John Casey creates an emergency repair disk, performs several routine disk management tasks, and uses DOS commands to view his hard disk drive directory.

Windows 2000

Making an Emergency Repair Disk

An **emergency repair disk** contains a set of utilities and tools that help you troubleshoot your computer in an emergency, such as a power outage. Having an emergency repair disk is a good idea in the event a problem with your hard disk prevents you from starting your computer. You can create an emergency repair disk using a Windows 2000 program called Backup. To use emergency repair on a system that may be preventing you from starting your computer, you start your computer from the Windows 2000 Setup disks or the CD, choose the repair option during setup, choose the type of repair, and start the repair process. During the repair process, you use the emergency repair disk to help reconstruct your system, run diagnostic programs, and fix any problems. John did not create an emergency repair disk when he installed Windows 2000. Now he wants to create one. To complete this lesson, you'll need a blank disk or one that does not contain files you want to keep, because creating an emergency disk removes all existing files on that disk.

1. Click the **Start button** on the taskbar, point to **Programs**, point to **Accessories**, point to **System Tools**, then click **Backup**
   The Backup window opens, as shown in Figure M-1. The emergency repair disk is one of the recovery tools that comes with the Backup program.

QuickTip

You can also reinstall Windows 2000 over a damaged Windows 2000 system. If you reinstall your system, you might lose changes that have been made to your system.

2. Click the **Emergency Repair Disk button**
   The Emergency Repair Diskette dialog box opens, as shown in Figure M-2.
3. Click the **Also backup the registry to the repair directory check box** to select it
   The **registry** is a Windows 2000 database file with information about your computer's configuration. The registry contains information that Windows 2000 continually references during operation, such as the programs and hardware devices installed, the types of documents each program can create, and property settings for folders and program icons.
4. Remove your Project Disk from the appropriate drive on your computer
   This process will remove any files on your disk, so do not use your Project Disk or any disk that has files that you want to keep.
5. Insert a formatted floppy disk into the appropriate drive on your computer
   Make sure the disk is blank or does not contain files you want to keep because creating an emergency disk removes all existing files on that disk.
6. Click **OK**
   A progress meter appears, showing the status of the repair disk utility saving the updated repair information. When the progress meter reaches 100%, the emergency repair disk is complete.

QuickTip

Because the emergency repair disk contains information about a specific computer, it should be used only with the system on which it was created.

7. Remove the emergency repair disk from the appropriate drive on your computer, then label the floppy disk **Windows 2000 Emergency Repair Disk** and note the current date
   You should store your repair disk in a safe place. Then, if your computer is having trouble starting, you can restart your computer from the Windows 2000 Setup disks or the CD, choose the repair option during setup, choose the type of repair, start the repair process, insert the emergency repair disk into the floppy drive as requested, and then restart your computer to complete the repair process.
8. Click **OK**
9. Click the **Close button** in the Backup window

FIGURE M-1: Backup window with the Welcome tab in front

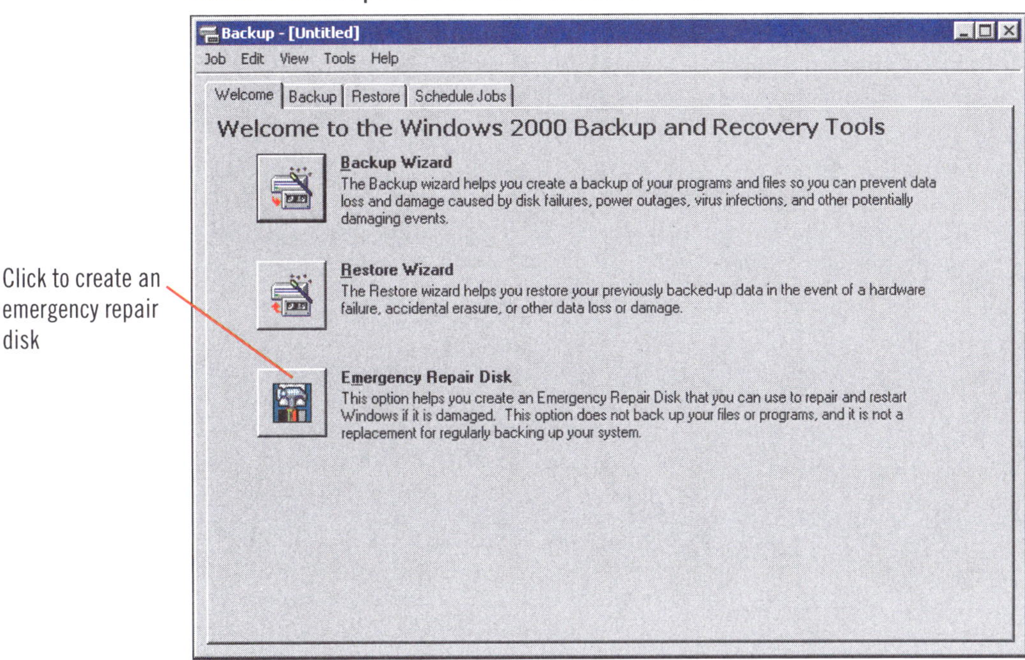

FIGURE M-2: Emergency Repair Diskette dialog box

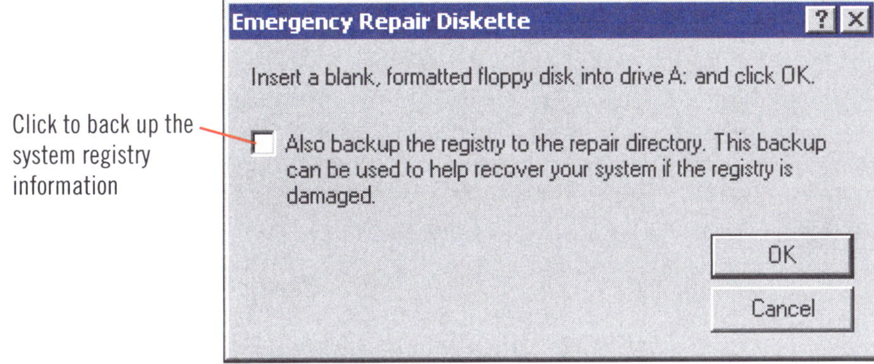

Specifying a default operating system

If you have more than one operating system on your computer, you can set which one you want to use as the default when you start your computer. To specify the default operating system for startup, double-click the System icon in the Control Panel, click the Advanced tab, then click Startup and Recovery. In the Default operating system list, click the operating system you want to start if you do not select one from the list displayed during startup. In the Display list of operating systems for box, type the number of seconds the list should be displayed before the default operating system starts automatically. During a system failure, you can indicate how you want the system to respond. You can select options to write an event to the system log, send an administrative alert, or automatically reboot. If you are an advanced user, you can specify the type of debugging information you want the system to collect.

Windows 2000

Formatting a Disk

Formatting a disk prepares it so that you can store information on it. Formatting removes all information from the disk, so you should never format a disk that has files you want to keep. Disks are usually formatted before you buy them, so you don't need to format a new disk before you can use it; however, formatting is still a quick way to erase old files from a floppy disk and to scan a disk for errors. When you format a disk, all files on the disk must be closed for the process to run. John wants to make a copy of the Project Disk for safe keeping, but first he needs to format the disk to which he will copy. To complete this lesson, use a blank disk or a disk that does not contain files you want to keep.

Steps

1. Click the **Start button** on the taskbar, point to **Programs**, point to **Accessories**, then click **Windows Explorer**

Trouble?

Formatting removes all the files on your disk, so do not use your Project Disk or any disk that has files you want to keep.

2. Insert a floppy disk into the appropriate drive on your computer
   Make sure the disk you are using does not contain any files you want to keep.
3. Locate and then click the **drive icon containing your floppy disk** in the left pane of Windows Explorer
   Disks and drives appear under the My Computer icon in the left pane of Windows Explorer. The icon representing the 3½" disk drive is highlighted and the files on the disk drive appear in the right pane of Windows Explorer. Review the files on your floppy disk to make sure they are ones you don't want to keep.
4. Right-click the **drive icon containing your floppy disk** in the left pane of Windows Explorer, then click **Format** on the pop-up menu
   The Format dialog box opens, as shown in Figure M-3. See Table M-1 for information about format types and file systems. If the disk has any files on it, formatting will remove the files. The fastest way to format a floppy disk is with the **Quick Format** option. This option simply formats a previously formatted disk, removing all files from it. The **Full Format** option (which you choose by deselecting the Quick Format check box) removes all files from any floppy disk (previously formatted or not), and also scans the disk for bad sectors. You should choose Quick Format only if you are sure that your disk is not damaged.
5. In the Format Options area, click the **Quick Format check box** to select it

QuickTip

If your computer uses the FAT file system, the label can contain up to 11 characters. If your computer uses NTFS, the limit is 32 characters.

6. Click in the **Volume label text box**, then type **Backup**
7. Click **Start**, then click **OK** to close the Warning dialog box
   A progress meter appears at the bottom of the dialog box. After a few moments, the Format Complete dialog box opens.
8. Click **OK** to close the Format Complete dialog box, click **Close** to close the Format dialog box, then remove the formatted disk from the appropriate drive on your computer
   You will use this formatted disk in the next lesson to make a copy of your Project Disk.

FIGURE M-3: Format dialog box

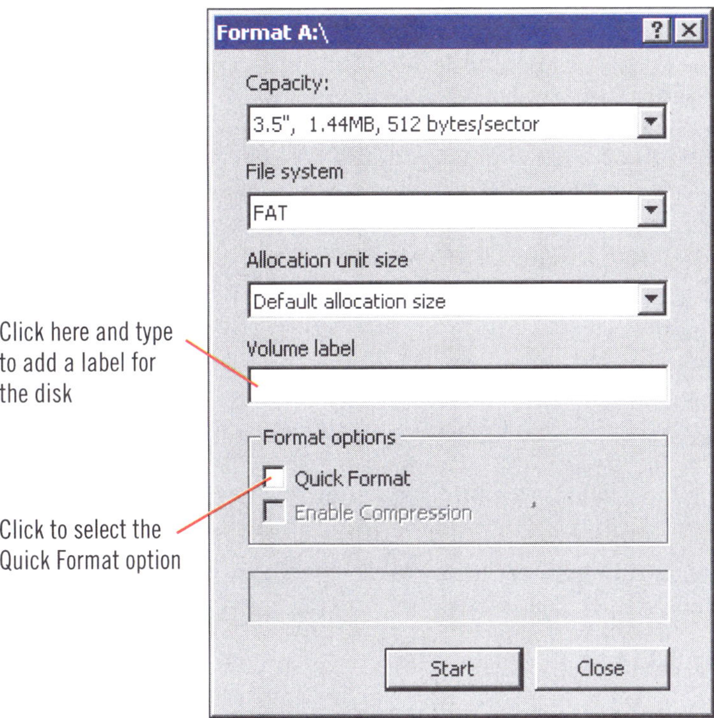

TABLE M-1: Format types

format settings	description
Capacity	Specifies how much data the disk or partition can hold. The physical size, storage size, and sector size.
File System	Displays the file system for the disk. A file system is the overall structure in which files are named, stored, and organized. NTFS and FAT are types of file systems.
Allocation Unit Size	Specifies the disk allocation unit size. The Default Allocation Size is typically selected. This option is meaningful for hard drives.

Using file compression to maximize disk space

If your hard disk drive is formatted as an NTFS volume (NTFS is a Windows 2000 file system), you can compress individual files, entire folders, or a hard disk drive and all it contains. Compression increases the effective capacity of the file, folder, or volume. Compressed files look and act like ordinary files, making them easy to work with. Once you compress a folder, Windows 2000 compresses files that you add to the folder, without requiring any special action by you. When you read a file from a compressed disk, the file automatically expands. You can identify a compressed file by viewing its property dialog box; or to more easily distinguish between compressed and uncompressed files, you can display them with different colors (use the Windows Explorer Options command). To compress files or folders, start Windows Explorer, select the files or folder that you want to compress, click File on the menu bar, click Properties, click Advanced, click the Compress contents to save disk space check box to select it, and then click OK. Because NTFS is not available for floppy disks, you can't use Windows 2000 file compression to increase the capacity of floppy disks.

Windows 2000

Copying a Disk

One way to protect the information on a disk from possible problems is to copy the disk, placing copies of all the files on it to another disk. Then, if information goes bad on a disk, you still have the copied information. You can use one disk drive to copy information from one disk to another. Windows 2000 manages the process for you. John wants to make a copy of a floppy disk. He'll copy it to the disk he formatted in the previous lesson.

Trouble?

If your project files are stored on a network or hard disk drive, substitute any disk that has files on it for the Project Disk.

1. Right-click the **drive icon containing your Project Disk** in the left pane of Windows Explorer
   The icon representing the 3½" disk drive is highlighted, and the pop-up menu for the left pane opens, as shown in Figure M-4.
2. Click **Copy Disk** on the pop-up menu
   The Copy Disk dialog box opens, as shown in Figure M-5. On the left side of the dialog box, you select the **source drive** from which you want to copy. On the right side, you select the **destination drive** to which you want to copy. Both the disk you are copying from (the Project Disk) and the disk you are copying to (the disk you formatted in the previous lesson) are 3½" floppy disks, so the drive shown is the same. When you copy disks, the disks must be the same type (3½" or 5¼"), size (1.44 MB or 1.2 MB), and not write protected. The 3½" Floppy (A:) or (B:) icons on both sides of the dialog box are selected by default; no additional drives appear because this computer does not contain additional floppy disk drives.
3. Click **Start**
4. Insert your Project Disk into the appropriate drive on your computer, then click **OK** in the Copy Disk message dialog box
   A progress meter appears with the status message "Reading source disk." After reading the source disk, a Copy Disk message dialog box opens, asking you to insert a destination disk.
5. Remove your Project Disk, label the blank formatted disk labeled "Copy of Project Disk" from the previous lesson and insert it into the same drive, then click **OK**
   The progress meter continues with the status message "Writing to destination disk." Upon completion, the status message "Copy completed successfully." appears.
6. Click **Close**
   Now that he has a copy of his disk, John can perform maintenance operations on his disk without worrying about losing any information. Leave the "Copy of Project Disk" disk in the floppy drive for the next lesson.

FIGURE M-4: Windows Explorer with pop-up menu

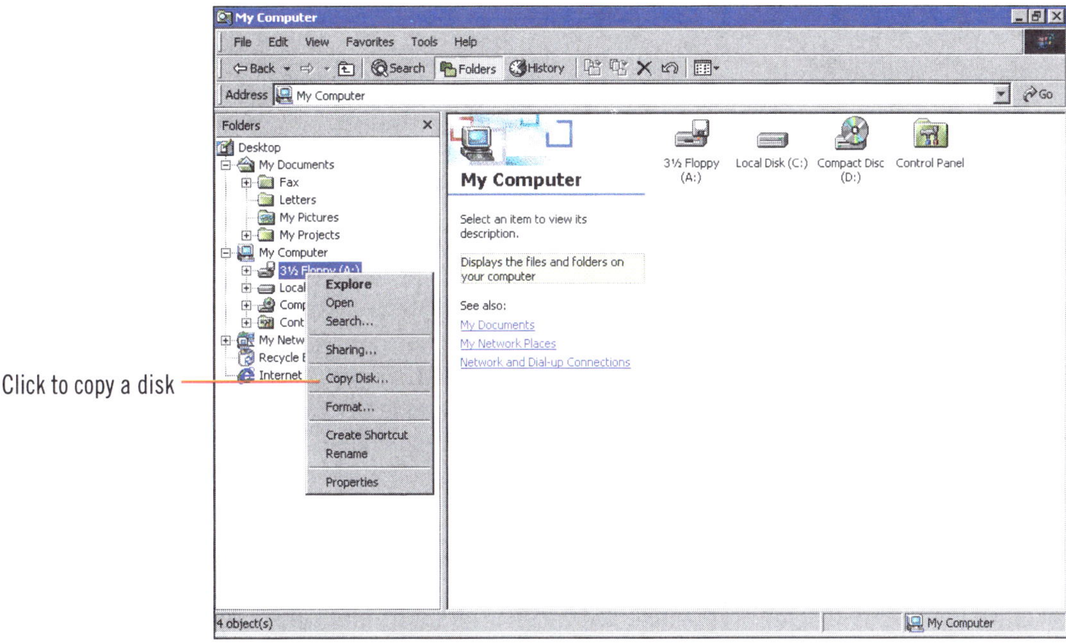

FIGURE M-5: Copy Disk dialog box

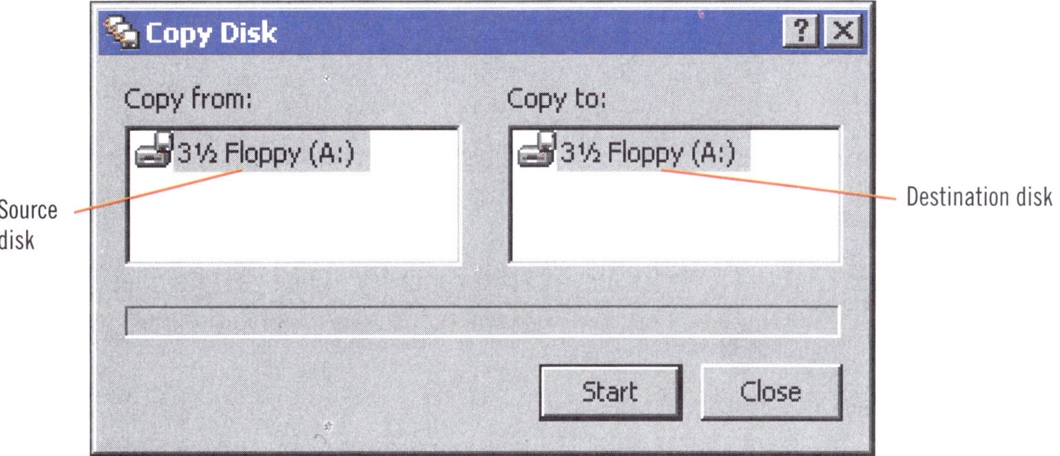

Synchronizing files between computers

If you want to work on files that are copied onto two different computers (such as your work computer and your home computer), you can **synchronize** the files, to keep the various copies updated between computers, using a Windows 2000 feature called **My Briefcase**. To use My Briefcase, drag the files you want to copy to your other computer from Windows Explorer to the My Briefcase icon. The My Briefcase icon appears on the desktop if you chose the Portable option during Windows 2000 Setup. Then drag the My Briefcase icon to the icon for the floppy drive, and remove the floppy disk. You can now insert the floppy disk into a different computer. If you edit the files, you will need to synchronize them when you return to your main computer by reinserting the floppy disk, double-clicking the My Briefcase icon, then clicking Update All on the Briefcase menu. This copies the new versions of your files from the floppy disk to the hard disk.

Windows 2000

Finding and Repairing Disk Errors

Sometimes an unexpected power loss or program error can create inaccessible file segments that take up space on a hard disk or a floppy disk. The **Check Disk** program that comes with Windows 2000 helps you find and repair damaged sections of a disk. Check Disk can also be used to find physical disk errors (**bad sectors**). The program doesn't physically repair your media, but it moves data away from any bad sectors it finds. To keep your floppy or hard disk drive working properly, you should run Check Disk from time to time. When you run Check Disk, all files must be closed for the process to run. John wants to make sure his disk has no problems, so he runs Check Disk. For this lesson, use the copy of your Project Disk that you made in the previous lesson.

1. In Windows Explorer, right-click the **drive icon containing the copy of your Project Disk** in the left pane, then click **Properties** on the pop-up menu
   The Properties dialog box opens.
2. Click the **Tools tab**
   The Properties dialog box appears with the Tools tab in front, as shown in Figure M-6.
3. In the Error-checking area, click **Check Now**
   The Check Disk dialog box opens, as shown in Figure M-7.
4. Click the **Automatically fix file system errors check box** to select it
   With this option checked, Check Disk repairs most errors automatically using predetermined settings.
5. Click the **Scan for and attempt recovery of bad sectors check box** to select it
   With this option checked, Check Disk makes corrections for any unreadable or bad sectors on the disk.
6. Click **Start**
   A progress meter appears, displaying scanning status. After a few moments, the Check Disk Results dialog box opens.
7. Click **OK** to close the Disk Check Complete dialog box, then click **OK** to close the Properties dialog box
8. Click the **Close button** in Windows Explorer
9. Remove the copy of your Project Disk from the appropriate drive on your computer, then insert your original Project Disk

QuickTip

For Help, click the Help button ? in the title bar, and then click any item to display a Help screen.

Trouble?

If a hard disk drive is currently in use, a message asks if you want to reschedule the disk cleaning for the next time you restart your computer.

FIGURE M-6: Properties dialog box with Tools tab in front

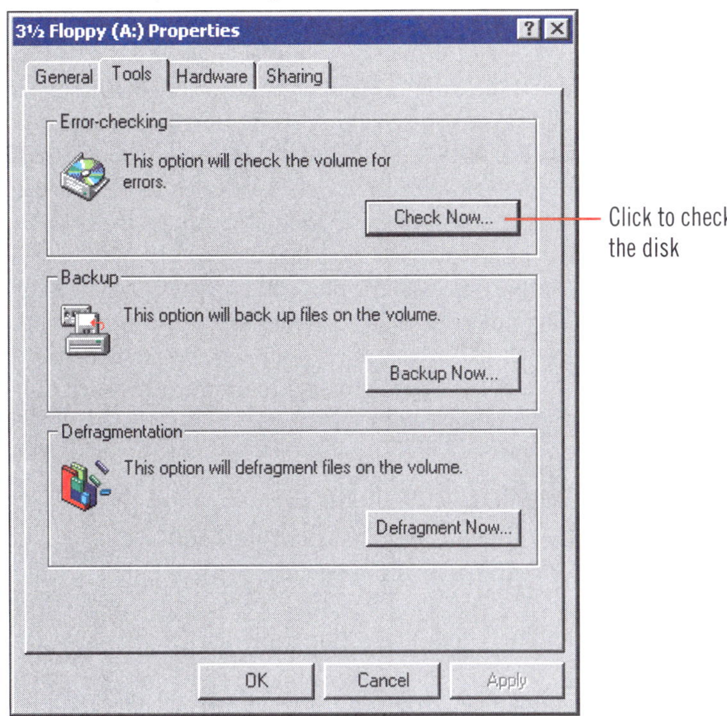

FIGURE M-7: Check Disk dialog box

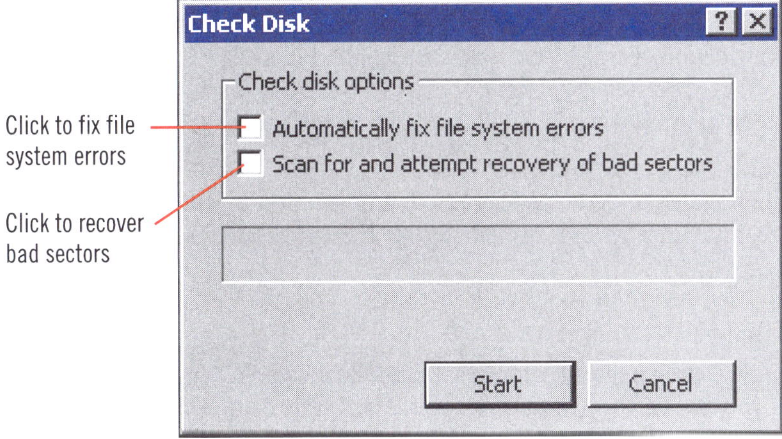

Using Windows Report Tool

Windows Report Tool collects information about your computer that can be used by technical support staff to diagnose and troubleshoot problems on your computer. To start Windows Report Tool, click the Start button on the taskbar, click Run, type "winrep", then click OK. In the Windows Report Tool window, type the problem description, expected result, and steps to reproduce the problem. You can click the Change System File Selections link to specify the file information you want to collect. You can also click Options on the menu bar, then click User Information to include user information as needed. When you are done entering information, click Next, select a folder in which to store the file, type a name for the file, then click Save. Upon completion, click Cancel to close the program. If your technical support provider offers e-mail support, you can save the report as a text file on your computer and send it as an attachment in an e-mail with your support request.

Defragmenting a Disk

When you delete files from a disk, the empty space that results might be fragmented over different areas of the disk. When you create a new file on a fragmented disk, parts of the file are stored in these empty spaces; thus, a single file might be broken into many parts. A file that is broken up in this way is called a **fragmented file**. To retrieve a fragmented file, the computer must search many areas on the disk, which lengthens retrieval time. You can use the Disk Defragmenter, a Windows 2000 program, to place all of the parts of a file in one **contiguous**, or adjacent, location. This procedure, which efficiently arranges all the files and unused space, is called **optimization**. Optimization helps your programs run faster and your files to open more quickly. For best results, you should run Check Disk to check for errors on your disk before you start the disk defragmentation process. John uses Disk Defragmenter to optimize his hard disk; the program doesn't allow you to defragment a floppy disk.

1. Click the **Start button** on the taskbar, point to **Programs**, point to **Accessories**, point to **System Tools**, then click **Disk Defragmenter**
   The Disk Defragmenter dialog box opens.

QuickTip
To start Disk Defragmenter from the Properties dialog box, double-click the System icon in the Control Panel, click the Tools tab, then click Defragment Now.

2. Click the **hard disk drive** (typically the C: drive)

3. Click **Analyze**
   The analyzing process can take a few minutes, depending on the extent of the fragmentation on your disk. You can monitor the process with the progress meter. Upon completion, the Analysis Complete dialog box opens.

QuickTip
To temporarily stop Disk Defragmenter, click Pause, then click Resume when you are ready.

4. Click **View Report**
   The View Report dialog box opens, as shown in Figure M-8.

5. In the File information box, click the **down scroll arrow** to display the file fragmentation statistics
   The file fragmentation statistics provide information on the total number of files, average file size, total number of fragmented files and excess file fragments, and average fragments per file.

QuickTip
To print the analysis report, click Print in the Analysis Report dialog box, then click Print again.

6. Click **Close**
   The Disk Defragmenter window appears, as shown in Figure M-9. The Analysis display shows you the defragmentation process. Different colored lines, each representing a disk section known as a **cluster**, appear in the Analysis display. The colored lines tell you the defragmentation status of your hard disk drive, and the legend at the bottom of the window explains how to interpret the colors.

7. Click **Defragment**
   The defragmentation process can take several minutes or more, depending on the extent of the fragmentation on your disk. You can monitor the process with the progress meter. The Disk Defragmenter window opens, as shown in Figure M-10. The Defragmentation display shows you the result of the defragmentation process.

Trouble?
If you are working in a lab, see your instructor or technical support person for authorization to defragment your hard disk drive.

8. When the defragmentation is complete, click **Close**, then click the **Close button** [X] in the Defragmentation window
   Your disk is now optimized.

QuickTip
To customize the Defragmentation window, click View on the menu bar, then click Customize.

FIGURE M-8: Analysis Report dialog box

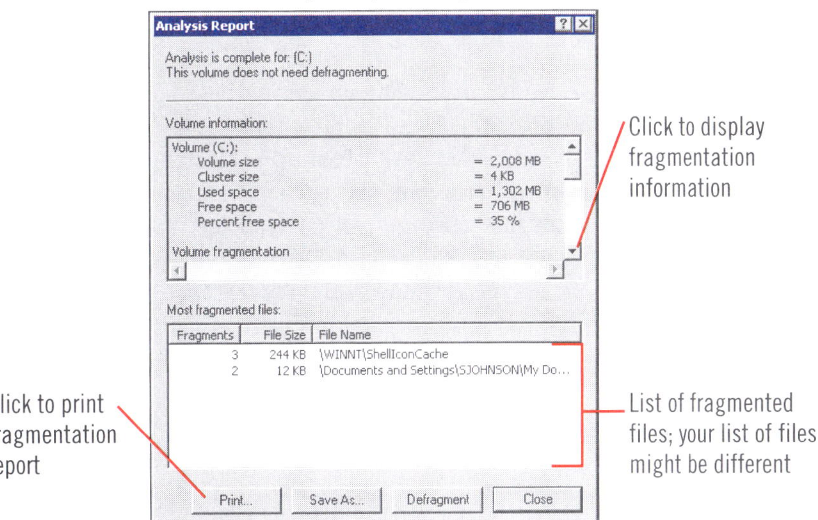

FIGURE M-9: Disk Defragmenter window

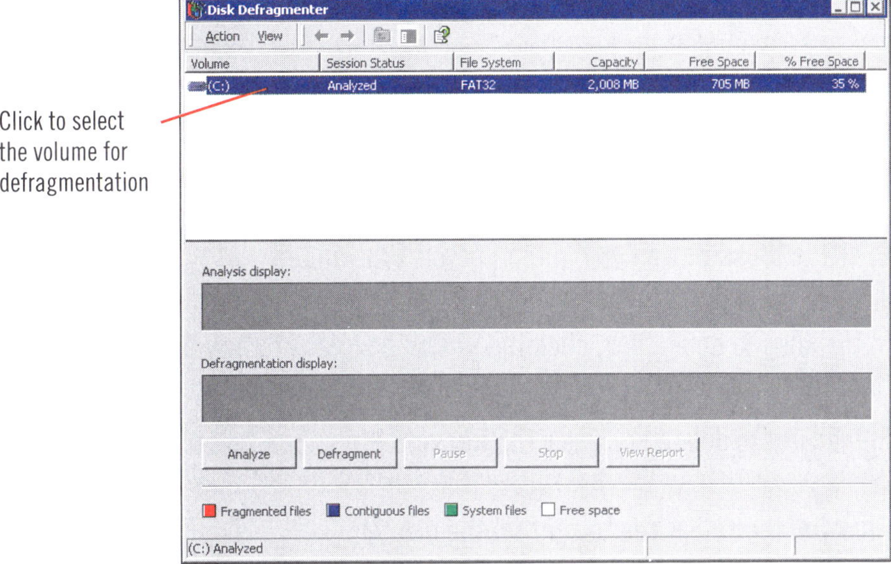

FIGURE M-10: Defragmentation process

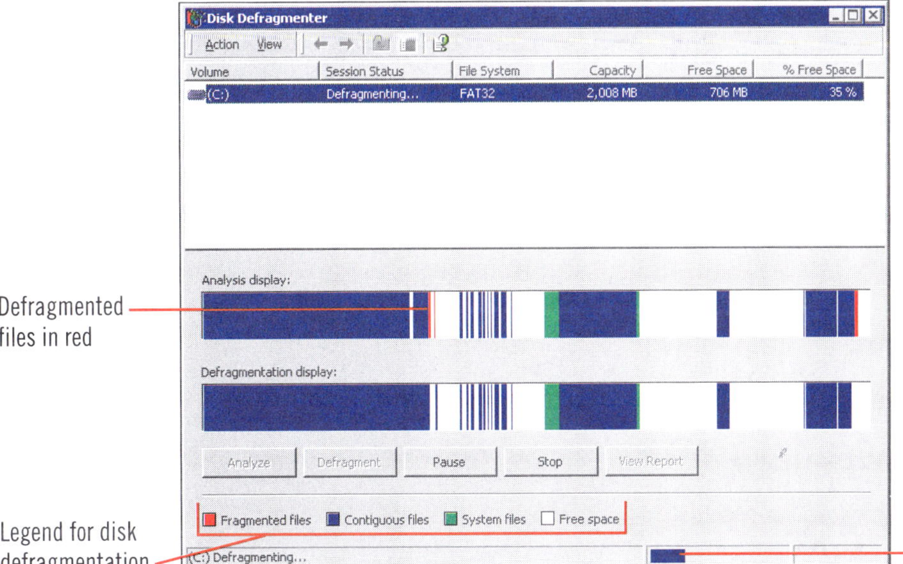

Windows 2000

Cleaning Up a Disk

Cleaning up a disk involves removing unneeded files to make room for other files on your computer; this can be difficult if you don't know the significance of each file. You can use a Windows 2000 program called **Disk Cleanup** to clean up your hard disk drive safely and effectively. Disk Cleanup searches your drive, then lists temporary files, Internet cache files, and unnecessary program files that you can safely delete. You can also empty the Recycle Bin. You can select the types of files you want Disk Cleanup to delete. Before you select and delete files, make sure you will not need them in the future. Disk Cleanup also gives you the option to remove Windows 2000 components and installed programs that you no longer use. John decides to clean up a disk.

Steps 1 2 3 4

QuickTip

You can also start Disk Cleanup using the Run command. To start Disk Cleanup, click the Start button, click Run, type "cleanmgr", then click OK.

1. Click the **Start button** on the taskbar, point to **Programs**, point to **Accessories**, point to **System Tools**, then click **Disk Cleanup**
   The Select Drive dialog box opens, as shown in Figure M-11.
2. Click the **drive list arrow**, click the **hard disk drive** for the computer, then click **OK**
   The Disk Cleanup dialog box opens and calculates how much disk space you will be able to free on (C:), then the Disk Cleanup for (C:) dialog box opens, as shown in Figure M-12. Your list of files to delete might be different.
3. In the Files to delete list, click **Recycle Bin** (not the check box), then click **View Files**
   The Recycle Bin window opens, listing the files currently stored in the Recycle Bin.
4. Click the **Close button** [X] in the Recycle Bin window
   The Disk Cleanup for (C:) dialog box opens.
5. In the Files to delete box, click the **check box next to any item with a check mark** (be sure to scroll through the entire list) to deselect them
6. In the Files to delete box, click the **Recycle Bin check box** to select it
   The check mark indicates that you want to delete all the files.

Trouble?

If you are working in a lab, check with your instructor or technical support person to authorize deletion of Recycle Bin files; if you do not receive authorization, click Cancel to close the dialog box.

7. Click **OK**, then click **Yes** to confirm the deletion
   The Disk Cleanup for (C:) dialog box opens and a progress meter appears, displaying deletion status. After a few moments, the progress meter closes.

FIGURE M-11: Select Drive dialog box

FIGURE M-12: Disk Cleanup for (C:) dialog box

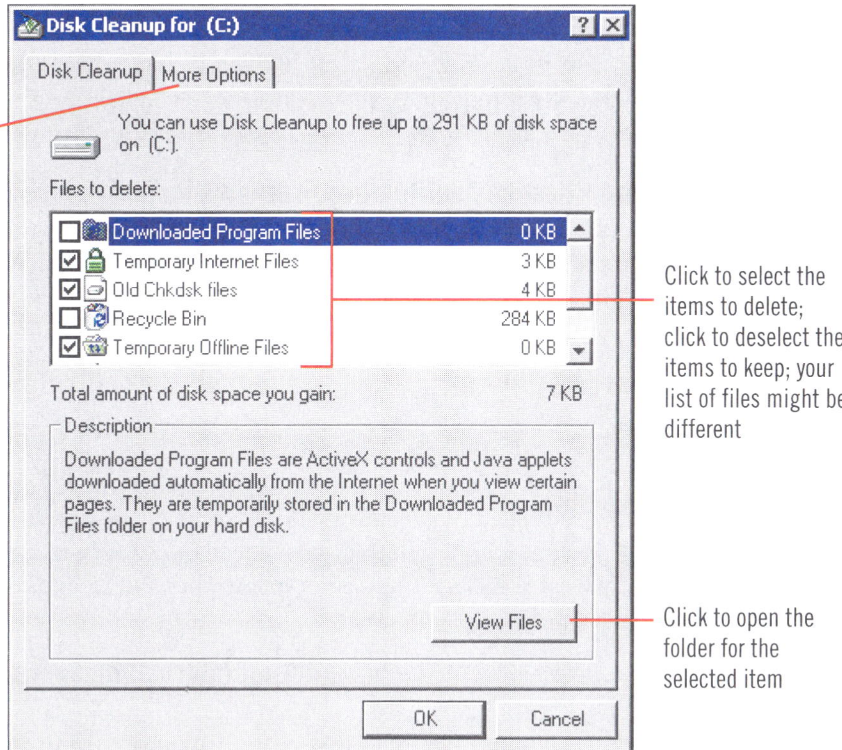

Managing your computer's performance

You can adjust Windows 2000 to improve its performance by changing the way Windows 2000 manages system processing and memory. You can set Windows 2000 to give a greater proportion of processor time to the program in which you are currently working, known as a **foreground process**. The greater the processor time, the faster response time you receive from the program in which you are currently working. If you have **background processes**, such as printing or disk backup that you want to run while you work, you might want to have Windows 2000 share processor time equally between background and foreground programs. To optimize performance for foreground and background processes, double-click the System icon in the Control Panel, click the Advanced tab, click Performance Options, then click the Applications option button to optimize for foreground processes or click the Background services option button to optimize for background processes. When your computer is running low on RAM and more is needed immediately to complete your current task, Windows 2000 uses hard disk drive space to simulate system RAM. This is known as **virtual memory**. For processes that require a lot of RAM, you can optimize virtual memory use by allocating more available space on your hard disk drive. In the Performance Options dialog box, click Change, then enter the initial size and maximum size you want to allocate for virtual memory use.

Adding and Removing a Program

The ability to add and remove programs gives you the flexibility to use the programs you need, when you need them, and maximize the free space on your hard drive. If you do not use a program very often and want to free up some space on your hard drive, you can remove the program. You can always reinstall it if you need it again. Windows 2000 comes with many programs; a typical installation installs only the most common programs, leaving it to you to install or remove others as needed. You can use Add/Remove Programs to add Windows 2000 components you chose not to include in the original installation, programs, or Windows updates and new features from the Internet. John needs more space on his hard drive, so he decides to remove a Windows component and then reinstall it later when he needs the component again.

1. Click the **Start button** on the taskbar, point to **Settings**, then click **Control Panel**
   The Control Panel opens.

QuickTip

For a currently installed program, you can click Change/Remove to modify or delete a program installation.

2. Double-click the **Add/Remove Programs icon**
   The Add/Remove Programs window opens, as shown in Figure M-13. At the same time, the Setup program searches for currently installed programs on your computer (this may take a few moments).
3. Click **Add/Remove Windows Components**
   The Windows Components Wizard dialog box opens, and the wizard searches for components installed on your computer. The Components list shows all the components of Windows 2000, as shown in Figure M-14. Each component contains one or more parts that you can install or remove. A blank box means that none of the parts of that component are installed, a shaded box means that only some of the parts of the component are installed, and a white box with a check means that all of the parts of that component are installed. To display what is included in a component, click the component name (not the check box), then click Details.
4. In the Components list, click **Internet Information Services (IIS)** (not the check box), then click **Details**
   The Internet Information Services (IIS) dialog box opens, listing the parts of this component. The check boxes indicate which parts are currently installed on your computer.
5. Click **Cancel**
   The Windows Components Wizard dialog box opens.

Trouble?

See your instructor or technical support person for authorization to remove this component.

6. Click **Add/Remove Windows Components**, the **Indexing Service check box** (or another component indicated by your instructor or technical support person) to deselect it, click **Next**, then click **Finish**
   A status bar appears, indicating progress. The component is removed from the computer.

Trouble?

See your instructor or technical support person if you do not have the Windows 2000 installation CD-ROM.

7. Click the **Indexing Service check box** (or another component indicated by your instructor or technical support person) to select it, click **Next**, then click **Finish**
8. If necessary, insert the Windows 2000 installation disk or CD-ROM into the appropriate drive, click OK then remove the installation CD-ROM when the installation is complete
9. Click **Close** in the Add/Remove Programs window, then click the **Close button** in the Control Panel

FIGURE M-13: Add/Remove Programs window

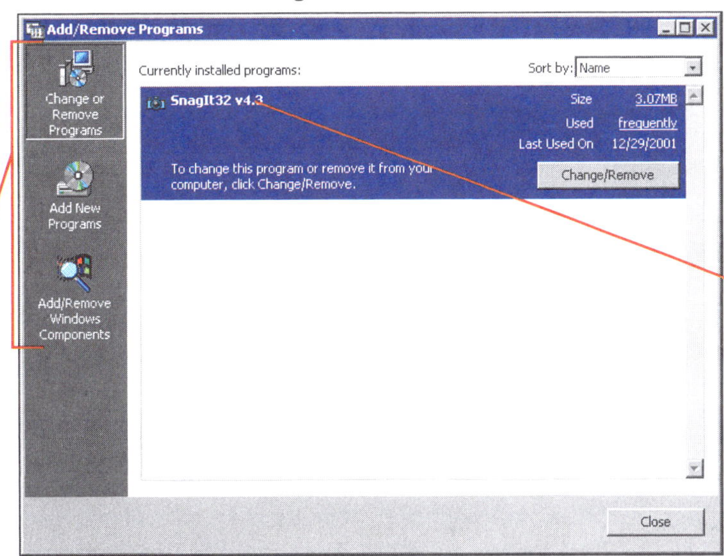

Click to choose the type of program to add, remove, or change

Currently installed program; your list might be different

FIGURE M-14: Windows Components Wizard dialog box

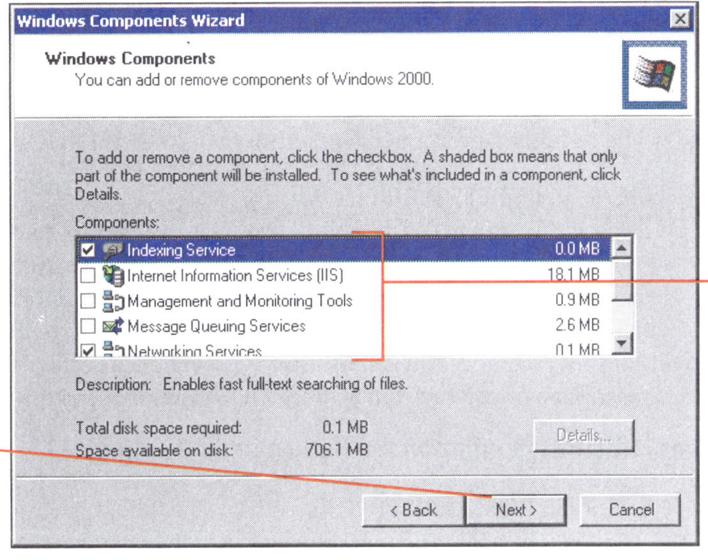

Click to select the components to add; click to deselect the components to remove; your list of files might be different

Click to add or remove a component

More on adding and removing programs

You can use Windows 2000 to install or uninstall programs that are not included on the Windows 2000 installation disks. In the Control Panel, double-click the Add/Remove Programs icon. To install a program, click Add New Programs, click CD or Floppy, and then follow the dialog box instructions. To add features from Microsoft Windows Update, click Add New Programs, click Windows Update, and then follow the instructions on the Web site to locate and add new Windows features, system updates, and device drivers. You should avoid using Windows Explorer to remove a program because program files and other information could be located in unexpected places and you might not find everything. Instead, use the Change or Remove Programs feature to make sure all of the program files are removed. To remove or change an installed program, click Change or Remove Programs, click the program in the list box and then click the Change/Remove button. In some cases, you will need the program installation disk or disks.

Windows 2000

Entering DOS Commands

Besides running Windows 2000 programs, you can also enter commands and run programs written in Windows 3.1 and MS-DOS. **DOS** stands for disk operating system. DOS employs a **command-line interface** through which you must type commands at a **command prompt** to run different tasks. A character such as a > or $ appears at the beginning of a command prompt. Each DOS command has a strict set of rules called a **command syntax** that you must follow when expressing a command. Table M-2 shows a list of common DOS commands and their syntax. You can also start Windows 2000 programs from within DOS; for example, you can type "explorer" at the command prompt to start Windows Explorer. For some tasks, John prefers to enter commands at the DOS prompt. He decides to start DOS on his computer and run a few simple commands.

QuickTip

To display a list of MS-DOS commands, click the Start button, click Help, click the Reference book on the Contents tab, then click MS-DOS Commands.

1. Click the **Start button** on the taskbar, point to **Programs**, point to **Accessories**, then click **Command Prompt**

   The Command Prompt window opens, displaying the DOS command prompt, as shown in Figure M-15. The command prompt indicates the current directory, in this case the hard drive directory. You can view the contents of the current directory using the dir command.

2. Type **cd windows**, then press **[Enter]**

   DOS changes from accessing the hard drive (C:) directory to accessing the Windows directory. The command prompt changes from C:\> to C:\WINDOWS>.

3. Type **dir /p**, then press **[Enter]**

   DOS displays the contents of the Windows directory. The "/p" part of what you typed is called an **argument**, part of the syntax that gives DOS more information about what you want it to do. By adding the optional /p argument to the dir command, DOS displays the contents of the directory one screen at a time. Figure M-16 shows the first screenful, also called the **output**, or results of the command. You can continue viewing the directory listing one page at a time by pressing any key, or you can return to the DOS prompt at any time by pressing [Ctrl][C].

QuickTip

To view information about a particular DOS command, type the command name followed by /?, then press [Enter] at the DOS command prompt.

4. Press **[Ctrl][C]** to return to the DOS command prompt

5. Type **exit**, then press **[Enter]**

   The DOS window closes and you return to Windows 2000.

FIGURE M-15: Command Prompt window

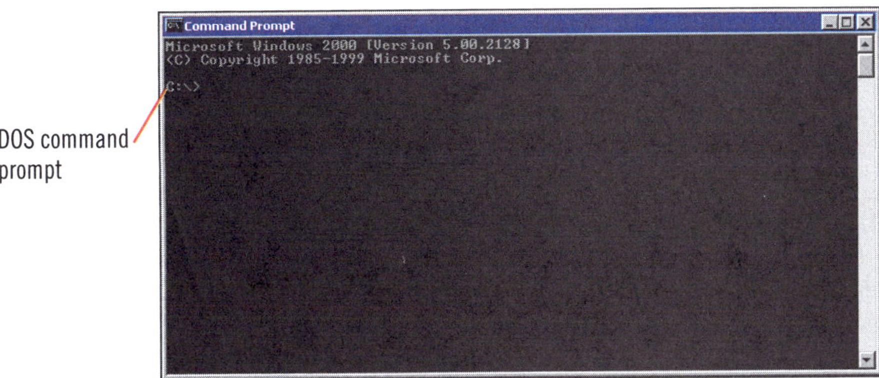

FIGURE M-16: Results of the dir/p command

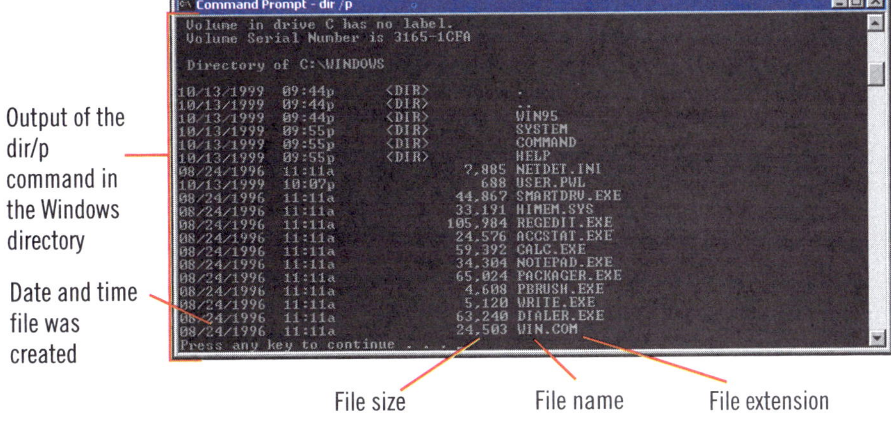

TABLE M-2: Common DOS commands (arguments are in italics)

command	purpose
cd *foldername*	Opens the folder named foldername
dir /p	Lists the contents of the current folder, one screen at a time if you use the /p argument
dir at*.doc	The asterisk is a wildcard and represents any number of characters in a filename. The command matches atback.doc, ati.doc, and atlm.doc
exit	Closes the DOS window
more *filename*	Displays the contents of a file one screen of output at a time
type *filename*	Displays the contents of the text file named filename

Controlling the appearance of the Command Prompt window

Windows 2000 gives you several options for controlling the appearance of the Command Prompt window. Windows 2000 includes a Control Panel program called Console that enables you to change the appearance of the Command Prompt window. To open the Console, right-click the Command Prompt window title bar, then click Properties. In the Console Windows Properties dialog box, you can click the Options tab to change the cursor size and display options, click the Font tab to change font sizes and styles, click the Layout tab to change the window size and position and screen buffer size, and click the Colors tab to change screen text, screen background, popup text, and popup background colors.

Practice

Concepts Review

Label each of the elements of the screen shown in Figure M-17.

FIGURE M-17

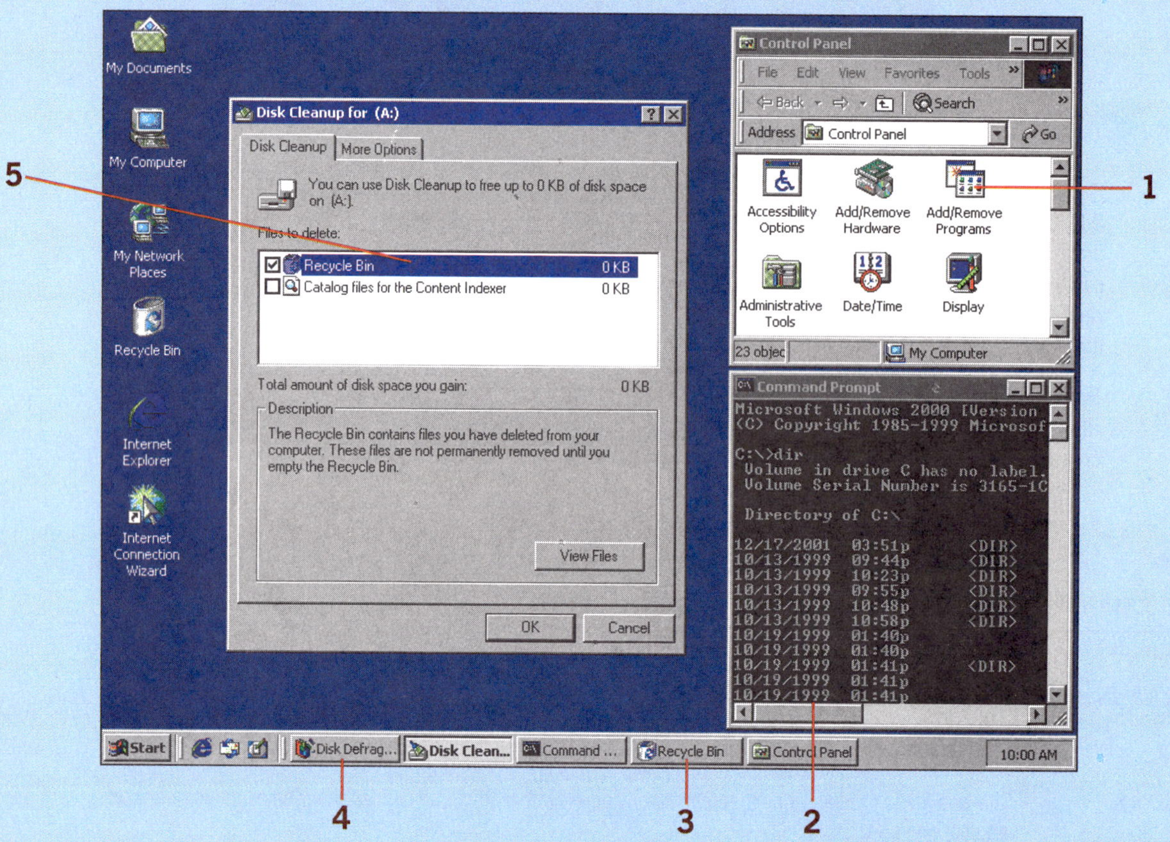

Match each of the terms with the statement that describes its function.

6. Starts your computer if you are having computer problems
7. Optimizes disk access
8. Deletes files
9. Stores files
10. Finds and repairs disk errors

a. Disk Cleanup
b. Check Disk
c. Disk Defragmenter
d. Emergency repair disk
e. Formatted disk

Select the best answer from the list of choices.

11. Which option performs a disk format that removes all files from a disk and scans the disk for bad sectors?
    a. Check Quick Format
    b. Uncheck Quick Format
    c. Check Full Format
    d. Uncheck Full Format

12. Which Windows 2000 file system allows you to compress files and folders?
    a. FAT
    b. FAT32
    c. NTFS
    d. NTFS32

13. When copying a floppy disk, the disks that you use do NOT need to be
    a. formatted.
    b. the same size.
    c. the same type.
    d. non-write protected.

14. Which of the following is NOT a Check Disk function?
    a. Finds damaged sections of a disk
    b. Moves data away from damaged sections of a disk
    c. Repairs damaged sections of a disk
    d. Physically repairs damaged media

15. Disk defragmentation arranges
    a. data files.
    b. unused disk space.
    c. system files.
    d. All of the above.

16. Which of the following is NOT a Disk Cleanup file type?
    a. Old system files
    b. Old Checkdsk files
    c. Offline files
    d. Temporary Internet files

17. When installing a Windows 2000 component, which icon do you double-click in the Control Panel?
    a. System icon
    b. Multimedia icon
    c. Add/Remove Programs icon
    d. Add/Remove Hardware icon

18. **When you type the DOS command *more text.txt,* DOS**
    - **a.** displays the contents of the file text.txt.
    - **b.** finds the file text.txt.
    - **c.** displays the contents of the file text.txt one screen at a time.
    - **d.** displays more information about the file text.txt.

Skills Review

1. **Make an emergency repair disk.**
    - **a.** Click the Start button, point to Programs, point to Accessories, point to System Tools, then click Backup.
    - **b.** Click the Emergency Repair Disk button.
    - **c.** Click the Also backup the registry to the repair directory check box to select it.
    - **d.** Remove your Project Disk from the appropriate drive.
    - **e.** Insert a blank disk into the same drive (you can reuse the startup disk from the unit, but not your Project Disk).
    - **f.** Click OK.
    - **g.** Remove the emergency repair disk from the appropriate drive, then label the floppy disk "Windows 2000 Emergency Repair Disk" and note the current date.
    - **h.** Click OK, then click the Close button.

2. **Format a disk.**
    - **a.** Click the Start button, point to Programs, point to Accessories, then click Windows Explorer.
    - **b.** Insert a blank disk in the floppy drive (you can reuse "Copy of Project Disk" that you created in this unit).
    - **c.** Right-click the drive icon containing your floppy disk, then click Format.
    - **d.** Click the Quick Format check box to deselect it, click Start, then click OK.
    - **e.** Click OK, then click Close.
    - **f.** Remove the formatted disk from the floppy drive.

3. **Copy a disk.**
    - **a.** Insert your Project Disk into the floppy drive.
    - **b.** In Windows Explorer, right-click the drive icon containing your Project Disk, then click Copy Disk.
    - **c.** Click the drive icon containing your Project Disk, click Start, then click OK.
    - **d.** Remove the floppy disk, then insert the blank disk you just formatted (not your Project Disk) into the floppy drive.
    - **e.** Click OK, then click Close.

4. **Find and repair disk errors.**
    - **a.** In Windows Explorer, right-click the drive containing the copy of your Project Disk, then click Properties.
    - **b.** Click the Tools tab, then click Check Now.
    - **c.** Click the Automatically fix file system errors check box to select it.
    - **d.** Click the Scan for and attempt recovery of bad sectors check box to select it.
    - **e.** Click Start.
    - **f.** Click OK twice, then click the Close button.
    - **g.** Remove the copy of your Project Disk from the appropriate drive on your computer, then insert your original Project Disk.

5. Defragment a disk.

a. Click the Start button on the taskbar, point to Programs, point to Accessories, point to System Tools, then click Disk Defragmenter.
b. Click the hard disk drive (typically the C: drive).
c. Click Defragment.
d. Click View Report, click Print, then click Print again.
e. Click Close, then click the Close button.

6. Clean up a disk.

a. Click the Start button, point to Programs, point to Accessories, point to System Tools, then click Disk Cleanup.
b. Click the drive list arrow, click the hard disk drive for the computer, then click OK.
c. Click Temporary Internet Files, then click View Files.
d. Click the Close button in the Content window.
e. Click the check box next to any item with a check mark (be sure to scroll through the entire list) to deselect them.
f. Click the Temporary Internet Files check box to select it.
g. Click OK, then click Yes.

7. Add and remove a program.

a. Click the Start button, point to Programs, point to Settings, then click Control Panel.
b. Double-click the Add/Remove Programs icon.
c. Click Add/Remove Windows Components.
d. Click Network Services (not the check box), then click Details.
e. Click the RIP Listener check box (or another component indicated by your instructor or technical support person) to deselect it click OK, click Next, then click Finish (if necessary, use the Windows installation CD).
f. Click Add/Remove Windows Components, click Network Services, then click Details.
g. Click the RIP Listener check box (or another component indicated by your instructor or technical support person) to select it, click Next, then click Finish.
h. Click Close, then click the Close button.

8. Enter DOS commands.

a. Click the Start button, point to Programs, point to Accessories, then click Command Prompt.
b. Type **cd program files**, then press [Enter].
c. Type **dir /w**, then press [Enter].
d. Type **exlt**, then press [ENTER].

► Independent Challenges

1. You are the network administrator at Franklin International Group, a family of insurance companies and services. Recently, the head office has been beset by a series of power outages. To ensure that they will be able to start Windows 2000 in the event of a problem, you want to create emergency repair disks for them to use. You decide to create one emergency startup disk and then make copies.

To complete this independent challenge:

a. Format a blank floppy disk (or one that does not have any files that you want to keep) using the Full Format and the label *Startup*. You can use the startup disk you created in this unit. Do not use your Project Disk.

b. Create an emergency repair disk.
c. Make a disk copy of the emergency repair disk. You can use the disk from this unit if you want, but not your Project Disk.
d. Label both disks for easy identification.

2. You are the network administrator at Robotz, Inc., a toy company that specializes in the production and distribution of robots. You want employees to update their computer systems with the latest Windows 2000 programs and components. You decide to check out the Windows Update Web site and determine which programs and components you want the employees to install. To do this, you'll need to establish a connection to the Internet.

To do this:

a. Start the Add/Remove Programs utility in the Control Panel.
b. Click Add New Programs, then click Windows Update to start your Web browser and access the Windows Update Web site. Connect to the Internet as necessary.
c. Click the Support Information link.
d. Click the Frequently Asked Questions link, then read the Web page.
e. Click the Known Issues link, then read the Web page.
f. Click the Product Update link.
g. Print the Web page with the software updates for your Windows system.
h. Close your Web browser and disconnect from the Internet.

3. You are a course developer at EZSoft Inc., a computer training company that specializes in training beginner-to expert-level software users. You are developing a new course on maintaining a computer. You are currently working on a lesson to teach students how to check and speed up disks by using the Windows 2000 system tools Check Disk and Disk Defragmenter. To complete the lesson, write down the steps to use Check Disk and Disk Defragmenter and take screen shots for the production staff. Create a WordPad document on a floppy disk with steps that explain how to check and defragment a disk.

To complete this independent challenge:

a. Insert a blank floppy disk into the appropriate drive. You can use one of the disks from the unit, but not your Project Disk.
b. Open WordPad, then create a document called *Win Tools Training* on the floppy disk that instructs students on how to use the Check Disk and Disk Defragmenter system tool. Print the document, then close WordPad.
c. Follow the steps in the WordPad document to check and defragment the hard disk drive (see your instructor or technical support person for authorization to defragment your hard disk drive), and take screen shots of the Check Disk and Disk Defragmenter window as you go through the material. Print the Screen. (Press the Print Screen key to make a copy of the screen, open Paint, click Edit on the menu bar, click Paste to paste the screen into Paint, then click Yes to paste the large image if necessary. Click File on the menu bar, click Print, then click Print again.)

4. You are an employee at an insurance firm. You've used several DOS programs for many years. Since installing Windows 2000, one of your DOS programs has been behaving erratically. To get help, you call your vendor's technical support help desk. To help figure out the problem, the technical support operator asks you to display the autoexec.bat file through a DOS window one screen at a time.

To complete this independent challenge:

a. Click the Start button on the taskbar, point to Programs, point to Accessories, then click Command Prompt.
b. Type **cd c:** at the DOS prompt, then press [Enter].
c. Type **more autoexec.bat** at the DOS prompt, then press [Enter].
d. Press [Spacebar] to advance to the next screen.
e. Print the screen (see Independent Challenge 3, Step c for screen printing instructions).
f. Type **exit** to return to Windows 2000.

► Visual Workshop

Re-create the screen shown in Figure M-18, which displays the results from a defragmentation of the C: drive (see your instructor or technical support person for authorization to defragment your hard disk drive). If the C: drive is not available or you don't have authorization, re-create the customization of the Disk Defragmenter window. Your results will differ from the ones shown here. The defragmentation can take a few minutes. Print the screen (see Independent Challenge 3, Step c for screen printing instructions).

FIGURE M-18

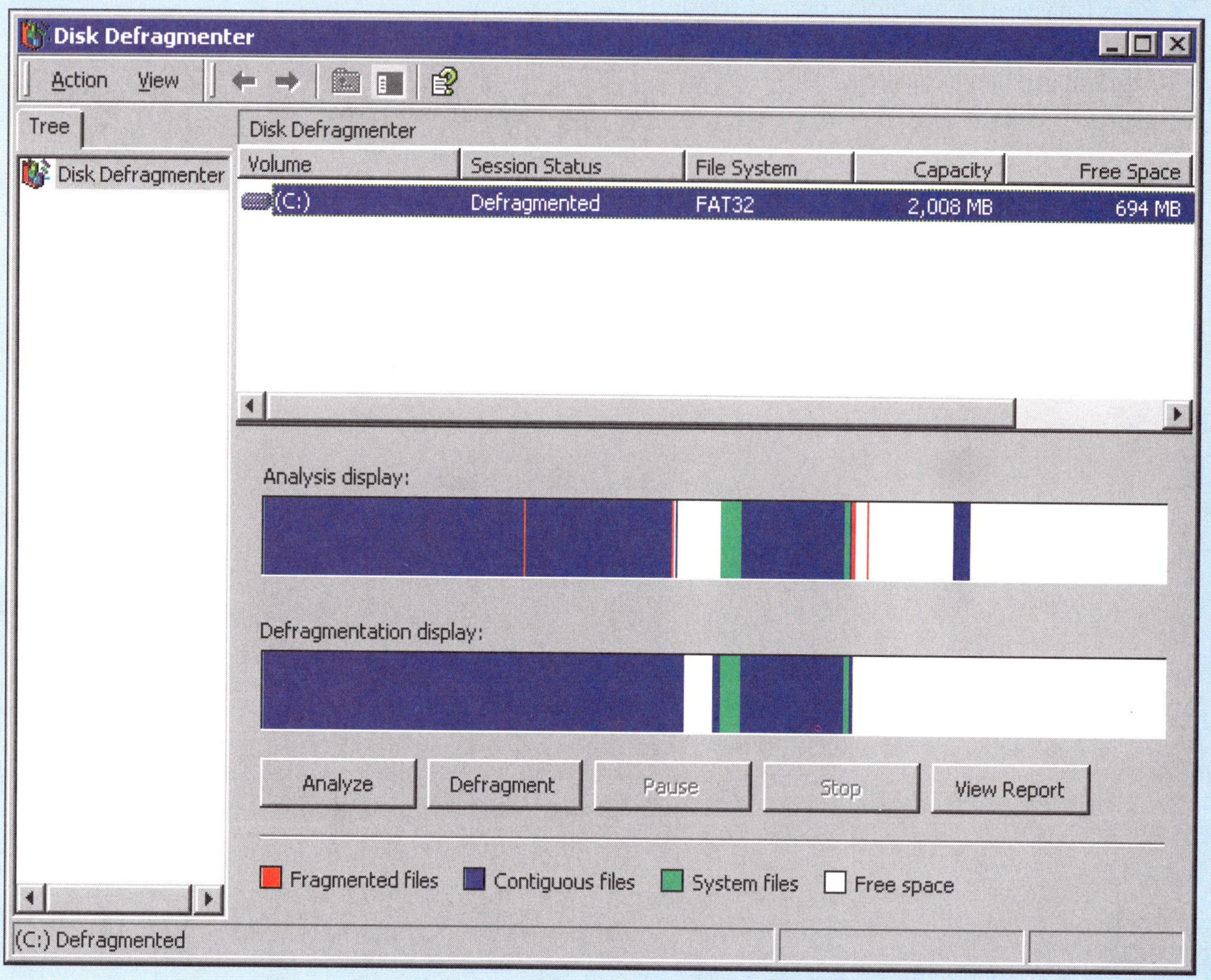

Disk Defragmenter
Action View
Tree
Disk Defragmenter

Volume	Session Status	File System	Capacity	Free Space
(C:)	Defragmented	FAT32	2,008 MB	694 MB

Analysis display:
Defragmentation display:
Analyze | Defragment | Pause | Stop | View Report
Fragmented files | Contiguous files | System files | Free space
(C:) Defragmented

Backing Up Your Files

Objectives

- Develop a backup strategy
- Copy files to a hard drive
- Start Backup
- Select files for a backup
- Perform a normal backup
- View and print a backup report
- Perform an incremental backup
- Restore a backed up file
- Delete a backup job

You should make backup copies of your files. The term **back up** (or **backup**, when referring to the noun or adjective) usually refers to the process of using a special software program designed to read your data quickly, compress it into a small, efficient space, then store it on a medium, such as a set of disks or a tape cartridge. Windows 2000 includes a program called Backup. Using Backup has several advantages over simply copying files to a floppy disk; these include compressing files as it copies them so you can fit more onto a floppy disk and splitting a large file across two or more floppies, something you cannot do with the Copy command. Also, in an emergency, Backup offers several data-recovery aids to help you locate and restore important files quickly. John uses Backup to back up important files on a floppy disk.

Windows 2000

Developing a Backup Strategy

The **backup medium** that you use to store backed up files from a hard drive is usually a set of floppy or zip disks, or a tape cartridge designed to store computer data. Zip disks and tape cartridges are large capacity backup media that require special hardware, a zip or tape drive, on your computer, but this extra expense may be worthwhile if you depend on your computer for business. With Backup, you can back up files from a local or network hard drive to a floppy disk, a zip disk, a network drive, or a tape drive that is attached to your computer, as shown in Figure N-1. This unit assumes you are using a floppy disk as your backup medium and focuses primarily on backup strategies using floppies. Before you back up files, it is a good idea to develop a backup strategy. A **backup strategy** is a method for regularly backing up your work that balances trade-offs between safety, time, and media space. For example, if safety were your only concern, you could back up your entire hard drive every hour. But you would not have any time to work, and you would spend a fortune on backup tapes. If spending minimal time and money on backups were your only concern, you might back up only a few crucial files once a month. The best choice is a balance between the two extremes. John wants to explore the different methods of backing up files in order to develop a backup strategy. See Table N-1 for a description of a weekly backup strategy.

These are some of the different methods for backing up files with Backup:

A **normal backup** copies all selected files to the backup medium, regardless of when the files were last changed, and clears the archive attribute for each file in order to mark the file as backed up. An **archive attribute** is a Windows marker indicating whether a file needs to be backed up.

An **incremental backup** copies only the files that have changed since your most recent normal or incremental backup. It also clears the archive attribute for each file that is backed up. Therefore, the first incremental backup after a normal backup copies all files that have changed since the normal backup, and the second incremental backup copies only those files that have changed since the first incremental backup, and so on.

A **differential backup** copies only the selected files that have changed since your most recent normal or incremental backup. Unlike incremental backups, however, the archive attribute is not cleared during a differential backup. Therefore, successive differential backups copy all the files that have changed since the last normal or incremental backup, not just the ones that have changed since the last differential backup. Differential backups take longer than incremental backups and require more disk or tape space.

A **copy backup** copies all selected files, like a normal backup, but it does not clear the archive attribute. Therefore, you can use it to perform a special backup without affecting your normal backup routine.

A **daily backup** copies all selected files that were changed on the day the backup is done. It does not clear the archive attribute. You can use daily backups to save your day's work without affecting your normal backup routine.

FIGURE N-1 : Computer with floppy, zip, and tape drives

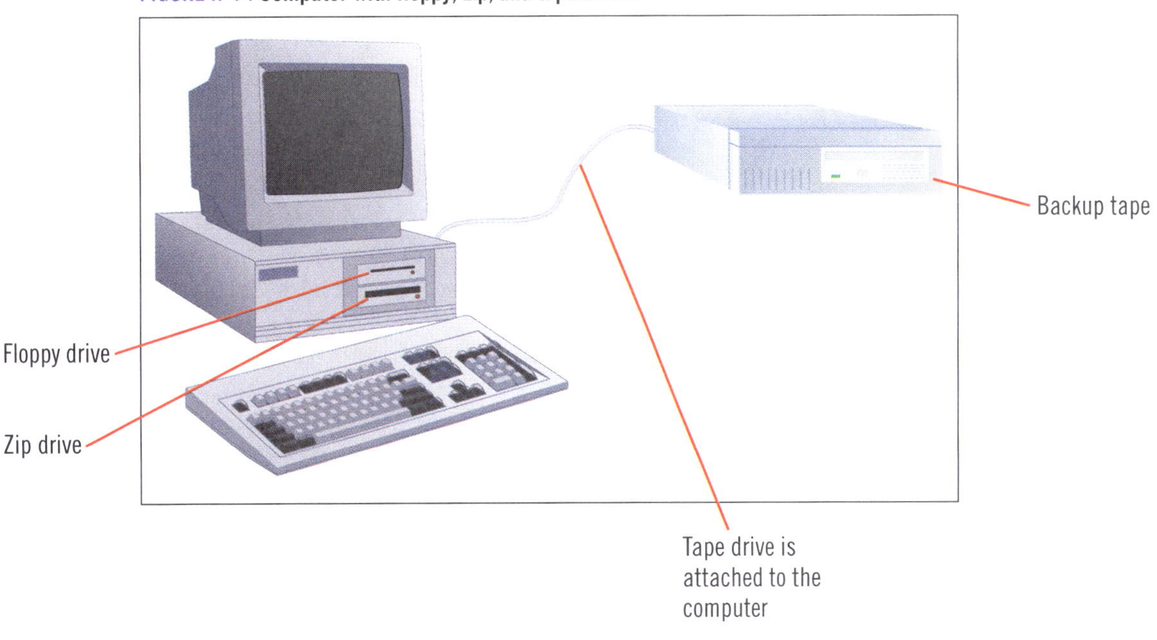

TABLE N-1: Example of a weekly backup strategy

day	tasks to do
Monday, Week 1	Label your medium (floppy disk or tape); if your backup requires more than one medium, label and number all the media in advance so you can recognize them easily; insert your first medium into the backup device and perform a normal backup with the Backup everything on my computer option
Tuesday, Week 1	Reinsert the medium you used for the normal backup and perform an incremental backup; the incremental backup is automatically appended to the normal backup
Wednesday through Friday, Week 1	Perform incremental backups; each subsequent incremental backup is appended to the previous backup; if you need more than one medium, you will be prompted to insert another one; after your Thursday backup, you will have a complete rotation set
Monday through Friday, Week 2	Repeat the cycle with a second set of media
Monday through Friday, Week 3	Repeat the cycle with the first set of media; continue rotating in this fashion

Rotating your backups

For extra security, it is a good idea to rotate backup tapes or disks. For example, if you do a complete normal backup once a week and incremental backups on the intervening days, you might want to keep one week's worth of backup on one tape or set of disks and then use a different tape or set of disks the following week. If your original storage medium and your backup tape or set of disks are both damaged, you will still be able to restore files from the previous time period's backup. The file you restore probably will not be the most current versions, but you will be better off than if you had to re-create everything from scratch. If possible, store your backup tape or disks away from your computers. That way, if you experience a fire or theft, you will not necessarily lose both your originals and your backups.

Windows 2000

Copying Files to a Hard Drive

Backup is designed to back up the contents of a hard drive (or several hard drives) onto a backup medium. It is unable to back up files from one floppy disk to another. So that you have some files to back up, this unit begins by having you copy the files from your Project Disk to a hard disk. As you proceed through the lessons, you will back up the files you copied onto the hard disk to a different blank floppy disk. If you do not have access to a hard drive, you might not be able to complete this unit; if this is the case, check with your instructor or technical support person about backing up different files that are already on a network drive. John prepares to back up his files. In this lesson, you will copy the files on your Project Disk to the C: drive so you can begin to back them up in the next lesson. First you'll create a new folder for the files in the My Documents folder.

1. Insert your Project Disk into the appropriate floppy drive, click the **Start button** on the taskbar, point to **Programs**, point to **Accessories**, then click **Windows Explorer**
2. In the left pane of Windows Explorer, locate the My Documents folder icon, then, if a ⊞ appears next to the icon, click the ⊞ to expand the folder; if a ⊟ is next to the icon, the folder is already expanded
3. In the left pane of Windows Explorer, click the **My Documents folder icon**, click **File** on the menu bar, point to **New**, click **Folder**, type **John's Backup**, then press **[Enter]**
   The new John's Backup folder appears in the list of folders and files in the My Documents folder. You will use this folder to store your Project Disk files temporarily.
4. In the left pane of Windows Explorer, click the ⊞ **next to the My Computer icon**, click the ⊞ **next to the floppy drive icon containing your Project Disk**, then click the **Unit N folder**
   Windows Explorer displays the contents of the floppy disk in the right pane, as shown in Figure N-2.
5. Click **Edit** on the menu bar, click **Select All**, then click the **Copy To button** on the Windows Explorer toolbar
   The Browse For Folder dialog box opens.
6. Scroll the list if necessary, click the ⊞ **next to the My Documents icon** (do not click if a ⊟ appears next to the icon), then click the **John's Backup folder icon**
   The Browse For Folder dialog box opens, as shown in Figure N-3.
7. Click **OK**
   The Project Disk files are copied from the floppy disk to John's Backup folder.
8. In the left pane of Windows Explorer, click the **John's Backup folder icon**
   Windows Explorer displays the files in John's Backup folder in the right pane, as shown in Figure N-4. You are now ready to use Backup.
9. Click the **Close button** in the Windows Explorer window

Trouble?

If you make a mistake typing the folder name, select the folder name and then retype your text.

QuickTip

To copy files quickly from one disk to another, such as from a floppy disk to a hard disk, you can drag the selected files from the right pane of Windows Explorer to a folder or disk in the left pane.

FIGURE N-2: Windows Explorer

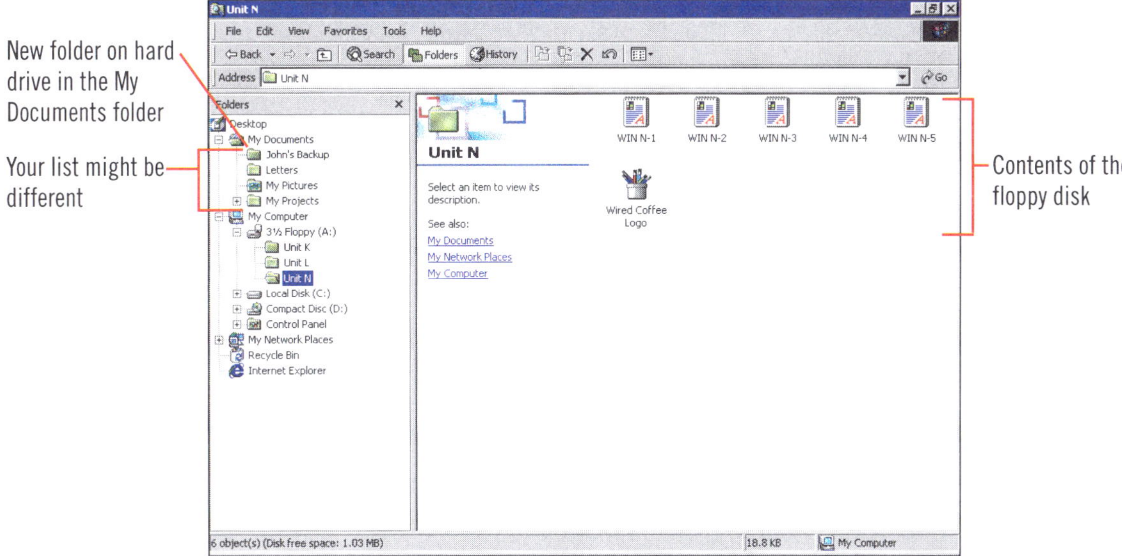

FIGURE N-3: Browse for Folder dialog box

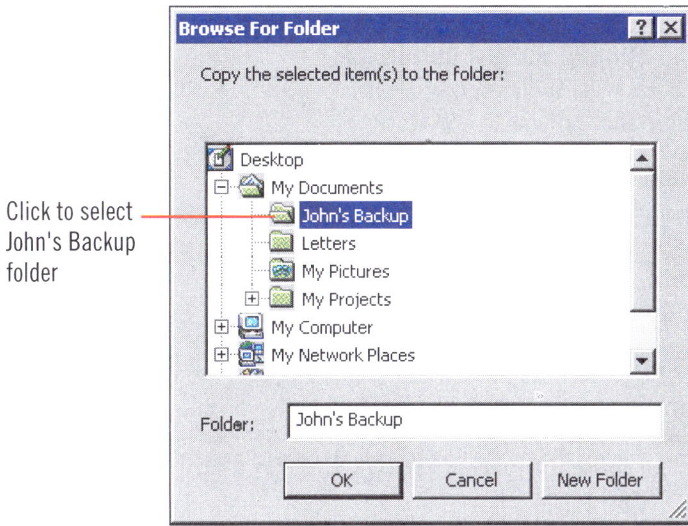

FIGURE N-4: Windows Explorer with John's Backup folder

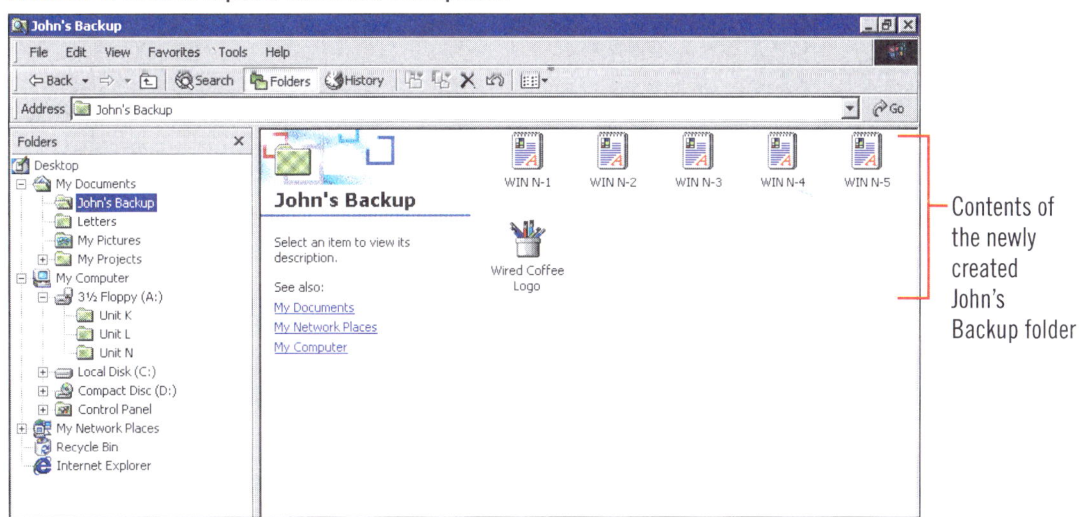

Windows 2000

Starting Backup

Now that you have files on the hard drive to back up, you can use Backup. Because backups take time, you should not back up all of the files on your computer every time you perform a backup. For example, because you can easily reinstall your program files from their original program disks, you do not need to back them up as often as your document files. An effective backup strategy begins with a complete normal backup, which backs up all files on your system, and continues with incremental backups, which back up only the files that have changed since your last backup. Ask yourself how much work can you afford to lose. If you can afford to lose the work accomplished in one day, back up once a day. If your work does not change much during the week, back up once a week. John starts Backup to do a normal backup of his important files on the hard drive.

Steps

1. Click the **Start button** on the taskbar, point to **Programs**, point to **Accessories**, point to **System Tools**, then click **Backup**
   The Backup window opens with the Welcome tab in front, as shown in Figure N-5. The Welcome tab contains options to create a new backup, restore backed up files, or create an emergency repair disk.
2. Click the **Backup Wizard button**
   The Backup Wizard dialog box opens. The Backup Wizard walks you through the process of backing up files on your computer.
3. Click **Next**
   The next step in the Backup Wizard, as shown in Figure N-6, is specifying the items you want to back up. You can back up every file on your computer, selected files, drives, or network data, or only the System State data. The **System State data** is a collection of system-specific data, such as the registry and boot files, that can be backed up and restored.
4. Click the **Back up selected files, drives, or network data option button**
5. Click **Next**
   Leave the Backup Wizard dialog box open and continue to the next lesson, where you will select the files to back up.

QuickTip

You can only back up the System State data on a local computer. You cannot back up the System State data on a remote computer using a communication line.

FIGURE N-5: Backup window with Welcome tab in front

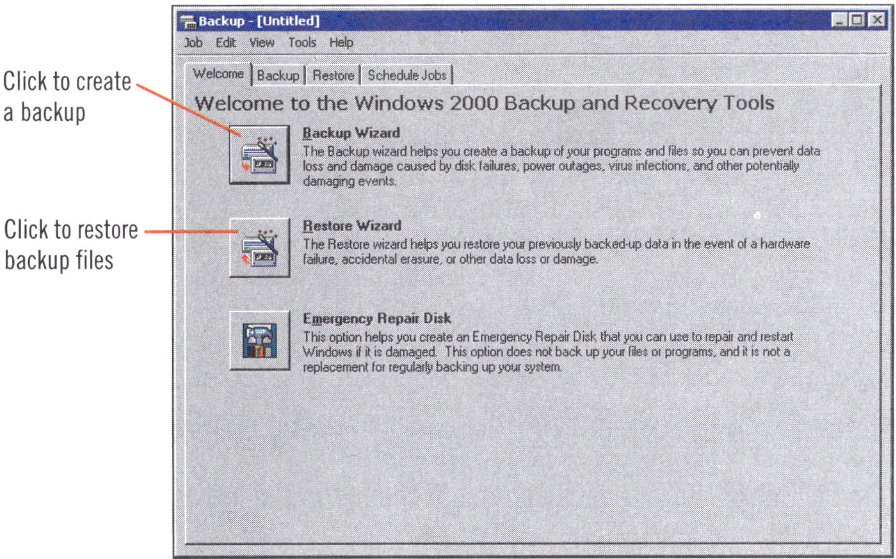

FIGURE N-6: Choosing what to back up

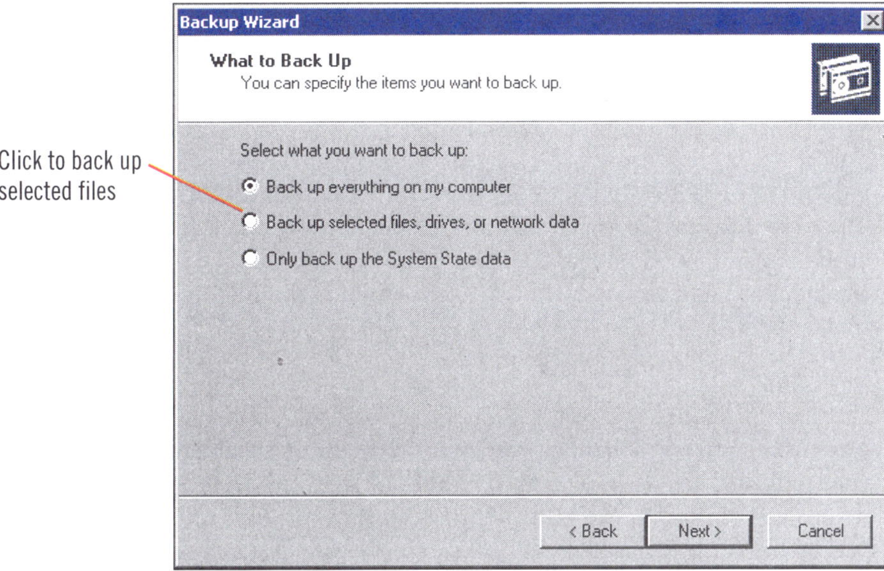

Understanding permissions to back up files and folders

You must have certain permissions to back up files and folders. If you are an administrator or a backup operator in a local group, you can back up any file and folder on the computer to which the local group applies. However, if you are not an administrator or a backup operator, and you want to back up files, then you must be the owner of the files and folders you want to back up, or you must have one or more of the following permissions for the files and folders you want to back up: Read, Read and Execute, Modify, or Full Control. You can also restrict access to a backup file by selecting Allow only the owner and the Administrator access to the backup data in the Backup Job Information dialog box. If you select this option, only an administrator or the person who created the backup file will be able to restore the files and folders. You can use Backup to back up and restore data on either FAT or NTFS volumes. However, if you have backed up data from an NTFS volume used in Windows 2000, it is recommended that you restore the data to an NTFS volume used in Windows 2000 instead of Windows NT 4.0, or you could lose data as well as some file and folder features.

Windows 2000

Selecting Files for a Backup

When backing up only some of the files on your disk, you need to display and then select the folders and files that you want to back up in the Backup window. Working in this window is similar to working in Windows Explorer. To display or hide the folders located on your hard drive, click the [+] (plus sign) or [−] (minus sign) to the left of the drive or folder icon. In addition, there is a check box to the left of each storage device, folder, or file on your computer. After using [+] and [−] to display and hide the appropriate files, you click this check box to select the folders and files you want to back up. John needs to select the files he wants to back up.

Steps

1. In the Backup Wizard dialog box, click the [+] **to the left of the My Documents icon** in the What to back up list
   The My Documents icon expands to display all the folders and files it contains. See Table N-2 for information concerning the display of drives and folders.
2. In the What to back up list, click the **John's Backup folder icon** (do not click the check box)
   The folders and files stored in the John's Backup folder appear in the right pane. To back up all the files in a folder, click the check box next to the folder in the left pane. To back up a specific file, click the check box next to the file in the right pane.
3. In the What to back up list, click the **John's Backup folder check box** to select it
   The folders and files in the John's Backup folder appear checked, as shown in Figure N-7; all of the files in the John's Backup folder will be backed up. The shaded check box beside the My Documents icon indicates that only some of the folders and files in that drive are selected.
4. Click **Next**
   The Backup Wizard asks you to select a backup destination, as shown in Figure N-8 (the place where you will store your backed up files). If you don't have a tape device installed on your computer, the backup media type File is selected by default and grayed out. The default destination for the backup is the floppy A: drive; your drive might be different. The default backup file name is "Backup.bfk" (bfk is the extension for all backup files).
5. If necessary, insert your Project Disk into the appropriate drive on your computer, then edit the backup location and filename to A:\Backup.bkf (where A is your floppy drive)
6. Click **Next**
   The Backup Wizard dialog box displays the current back up settings. In the next lesson, you will actually perform the backup.

Trouble?

If the drive shown is not the same as your Project Disk, click Browse, click the Look in list arrow, click the floppy drive containing your Project Disk, then click Open to select the appropriate drive on your computer.

FIGURE N-7: Choosing items to back up

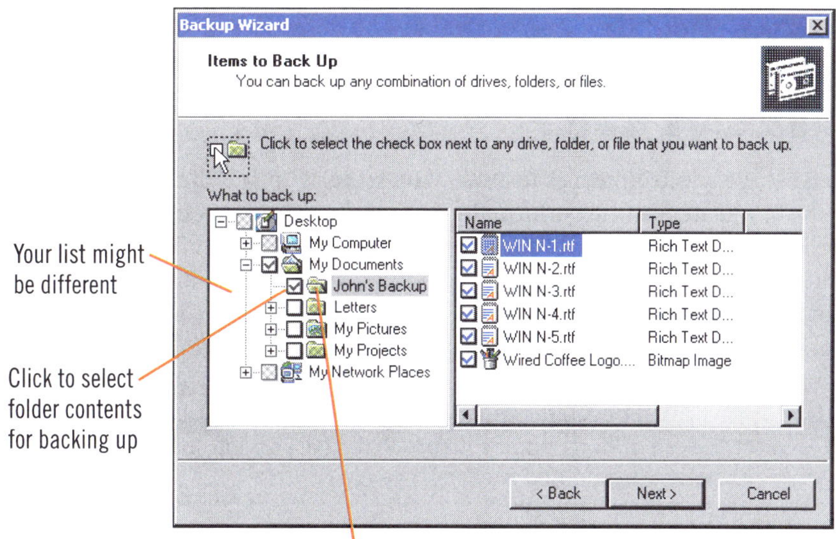

FIGURE N-8: Choosing where to store the backup

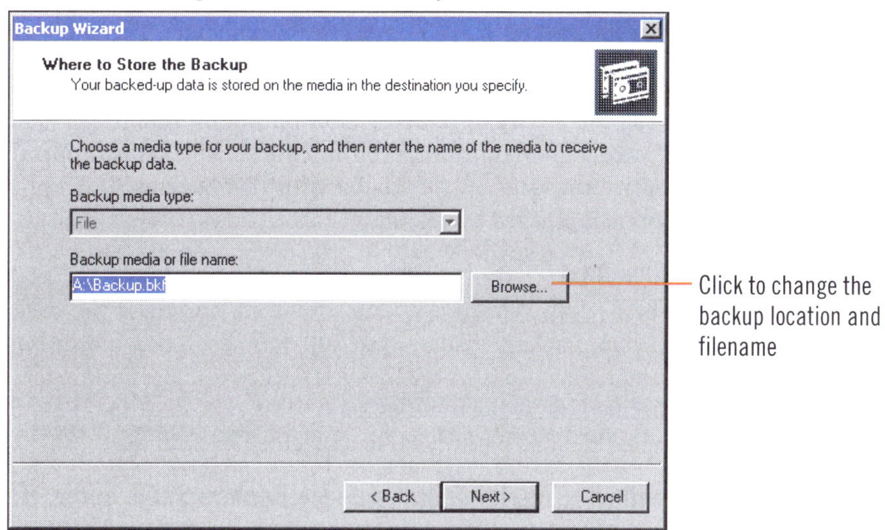

TABLE N-2: Displaying drive and folder contents

folder selection	item	function
[+]	**A plus sign to the left of a drive or folder**	All the folders it contains are hidden
[−]	**A minus sign to the left of a drive or folder**	All the folders it contains are displayed
	No sign to the left of a drive or folder	The folder does not contain any folders, although it may contain files
[blue checked box]	**A blue checked box to the left of a drive or folder**	All the folders and files it contains are selected for backup
[gray checked box]	**A gray checked box to the left of a drive or folder**	Only some of the folders and files it contains are selected for backup
[unchecked box]	**An unchecked box to the left of a drive or folder**	None of the folders and files it contains are selected for backup

Windows 2000

Performing a Normal Backup

Once you have selected the files that you want to back up and the destination where you want to store them, you are ready to perform the backup. During the backup, Backup compresses the files you selected and copies them to the floppy. When a file does not fit on a floppy, Backup splits the file, fitting what it can on the current floppy and then prompting you to insert the next floppy. Depending on the number and size of your files and the backup device you are using, the backup can take a few minutes to a few hours to complete. If you are planning to back up large amounts of information, such as your entire hard drive, it is best to start the backup at the end of the day and use a tape or zip drive if possible so you do not have to swap multiple floppy disks. John is ready to select backup options, enter a name for the backup job, and start the backup.

Steps 1 2 3 4

1. In the Backup Wizard dialog box, click **Advanced**
   The Backup Wizard asks you to select the type of backup operation to perform, as shown in Figure N-9. The Normal backup option is selected by default.
2. Click **Next**
   The Backup Wizard asks you to select options that will compare original and backup files after the backup, and compress the backup data. This is done to verify that the data was successfully backed up and to compress the backed up data to save space.
3. Click the **Verify data after backup check box** to select it, then click **Next**
   The Backup Wizard asks you to choose whether to append this backup to the media or replace the data on the media with this backup. The Append this backup to the media option is selected by default.
4. Click **Next**
   The Backup Wizard asks you to enter a name for the backup job. When you perform a backup, Backup creates a **backup job**, also known as a **backup set**, which contains the compressed copies of the files you backed up. The backup job is stored in the backup file you specified in the previous lesson (in this case, Backup.bfk on the floppy drive). You can store more than one backup job in a specified backup file.
5. In the Backup label box, type **My Backup Set 1**, press **[Tab]**, type **My Backup Disk 1**, then click **Next**
   The Backup Wizard asks you to select the option to run the backup now or schedule it for later. The Now option is selected by default.
6. Click **Next**
   The Backup Wizard displays a summary of the current backup settings, as shown in Figure N-10.
7. Click **Finish**
   The Backup Progress dialog box opens with a progress meter that indicates the current backup status. If the backup requires more than one floppy disk, a dialog box appears asking you to insert another disk. Upon completion, the Backup Progress dialog box opens, indicating that the operation is complete, as shown in Figure N-11.
8. Click **Close**
   The Backup window appears.

Trouble?

If the Use hardware compression option is grayed out, the option is not available.

QuickTip

To schedule a backup using a calendar, click the Schedule Jobs tab, select the day, click Add Job, then follow the Backup Wizard instructions.

FIGURE N-9: Choosing the type of backup

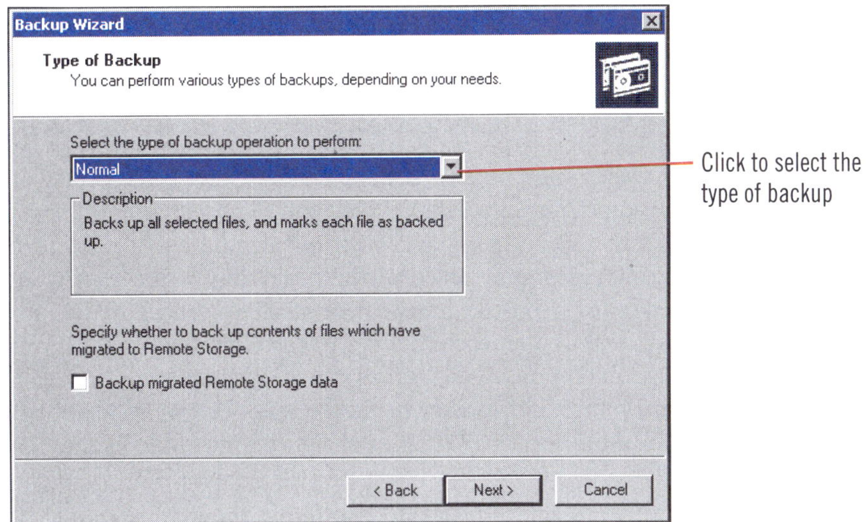

FIGURE N-10: Completing the Backup Wizard

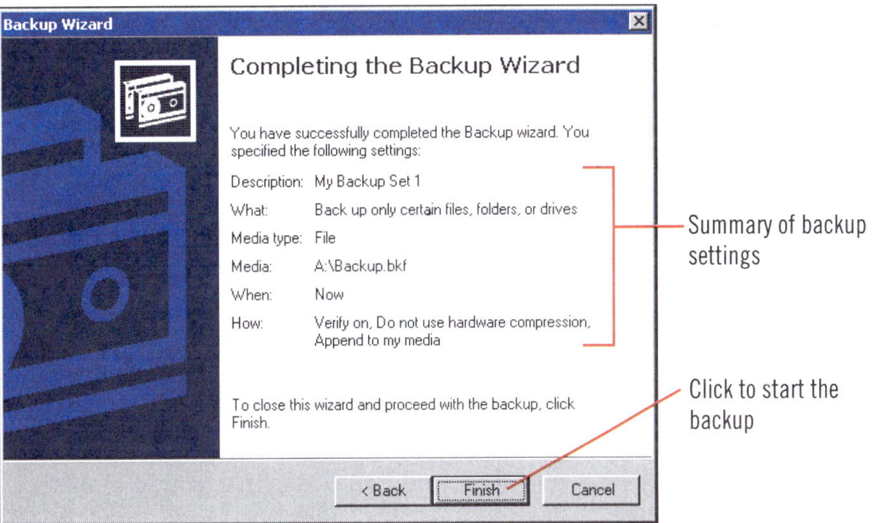

FIGURE N-11: Backup Progress dialog box

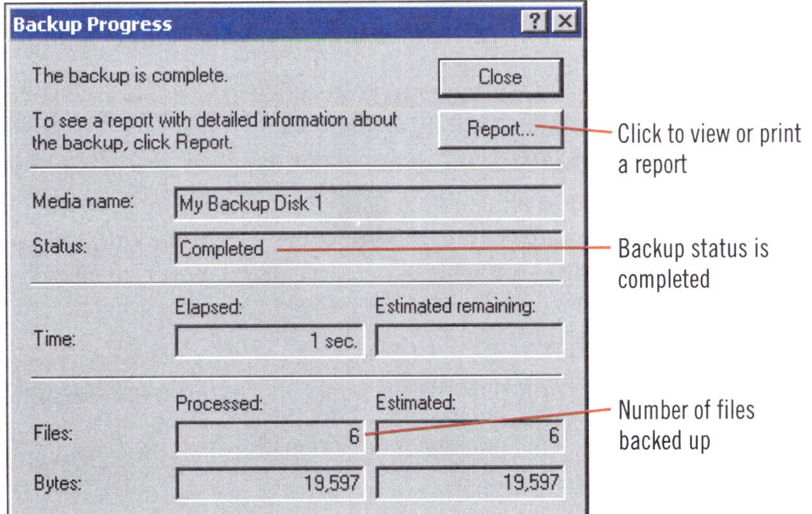

Viewing and Printing a Backup Report

After performing a backup, Backup creates a report with status information about the backup. The backup report is created in Notepad (a text program that comes with Windows 2000) and saved in the Backup program folder on your hard drive. Each time you perform a backup, the report information is added to the beginning of the backup report file in order to create a backup history. To make it easier to manage your backup jobs, it is important to view and print a backup report after each backup. To customize your report, you can use the Report tab in the Backup Job Options dialog box to specify the items you want to include in your backup report. John wants to view the backup report, change a report option, and then print a copy. Then he finds he needs to make a change to one of the files he has backed up.

1. Click **Tools** on the Backup menu bar, then click **Report**
   The Backup Reports dialog box opens with a list of backup reports performed on this computer, identified by report date, time, and backup job name. When you perform a backup immediately, instead of scheduling it for later, Backup uses Interactive for the backup job name instead of the backup job name you assigned.

QuickTip

Each Backup session (starting and exiting Backup) creates a new backup report file in Notepad.

2. Click the backup report with the current time and date you just created (the top entry), then click **View**
   Notepad opens, as shown in Figure N-12. The report lists the type of operation and the media name; the backup set number, description, and type; the backup job start time, end time, date, number of processed files, size (in bytes) of the processed files, and backup time. Notice that the report does not include names of the files that were backed up.
3. Click **File** on the menu bar, click **Print**, then click **Print** in the Print dialog box
4. Click the **Close button** in the Notepad window, then click **Cancel** to close the Backup Reports dialog box
   The Backup window remains open.
5. Click **Tools** on the Backup menu bar, click **Options**, then click the **Backup Log tab**
   The Backup Job Options dialog box opens with the Backup Log tab in front, as shown in Figure N-13. See Table N-3 for a description of the Options dialog box tabs.
6. Click the **Detailed option button**, then click **OK**
   Now when you perform the incremental backup in the next lesson, the report will list the files that were backed up.
7. Leave the Backup window open, click the **Start button** on the taskbar, point to **Programs**, point to **Accessories**, click **WordPad**, then open the document **WIN N-1** from the John's Backup folder in the My Documents folder on your hard drive
   Make sure you open the document from the correct location (the John's Backup folder in the My Documents on the hard drive), not from your Project Disk. The WordPad window appears with the WIN N-1 document. This is the file you will change for the backup in the next lesson.
8. In the first paragraph, select the word **November**, then type **October**
9. Click the **Save button** on the toolbar, then click the **Close button** in the WordPad window
   Leave Backup open, then continue to the next lesson.

FIGURE N-12: Backup report in Notepad

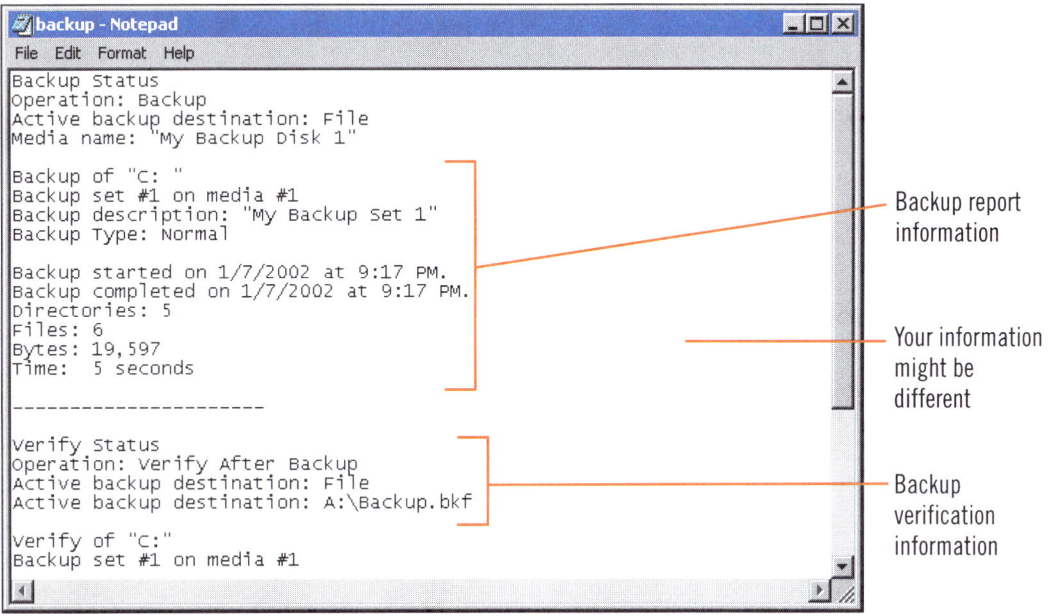

FIGURE N-13: Options dialog box

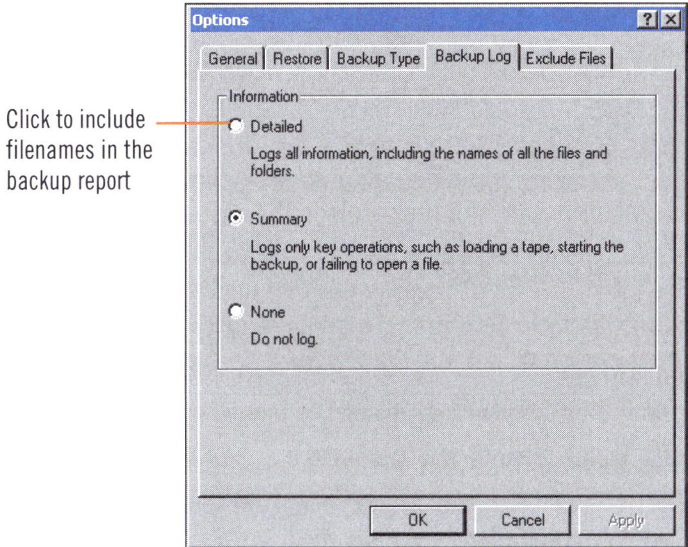

TABLE N-3: Options dialog box tabs

tab	description
General	Allows you to verify that data is successfully backed up, specify how to handle media that already contain backups, and select different types of alert messages
Restore	Allows you to specify how to restore files
Backup Type	Allows you to specify the default backup type when you start a backup
Backup Log	Allows you to specify the items you want to include in your backup report
Exclude Files	Allows you to add or remove files of a specified type to or from a backup

Windows 2000

Performing an Incremental Backup

When you perform an incremental backup, Backup backs up only the files that have changed since the last backup. This saves you having to re-do the entire backup every time. Files created after the date of the initial incremental backup set and files that have been renamed are not included in the incremental backup unless you select them before you start the backup operation. John completed a complete backup of all his files, but it does not include the current version of the file he just changed. John performs an incremental backup to include the change he just made to the WIN N-1 file.

Steps 1 2 3 4

1. In the Backup window, click the **Backup tab**
   The Backup window opens. If you have already performed a backup and want to use similar settings, you can use the Backup tab to perform a quick backup. The Backup tab allows you to select the files you want to back up, change backup options, and then start the backup process.
2. Click the ⊞ **(plus sign) to the left of the My Documents icon**, then click the **John's Backup folder check box** to select it
   The Backup window appears with John's Backup folder selected, as shown in Figure N-14. When a folder is selected with a blue check mark, all the files in the folder are selected.
3. Click **Start Backup**
   The Backup Progress dialog box opens.
4. In the Backup description box, select the text, type **My Backup Set 2**, press **[Tab]** twice, then type **My Backup Disk 1**
   This new job name will distinguish this backup from the complete backup you performed earlier.
5. Click **Advanced**
   The Advanced Backup Options dialog box opens.
6. Click the **Backup Type list arrow**, click **Incremental**, click **OK**, then click **Start Backup**
   The Backup Progress dialog box opens with a progress meter indicating current backup status. The file that changed since the last backup is backed up. Upon completion, a message dialog box opens indicating that the operation is finished.
7. In the Backup Progress dialog box, click **Report**, then drag the **scroll box** to the bottom of the NotePad window
   Notepad opens with the backup report, as shown in Figure N-15. The name of the changed file appears in the backup report.
8. Click the **Close button** ☒ in the NotePad window, then click **Close** to close the Backup Progress dialog box
9. Click **Tools** on the menu bar, click **Options**, click the **Backup Log tab**, click the **Summary option button**, then click **OK**
   This restores the report options to the original settings.

QuickTip

To compress backup data to a tape, click the If possible, compress the backup data to save space check box to select it in the Advanced Backup Options dialog box.

FIGURE N-14: Backup window with the Backup tab in front

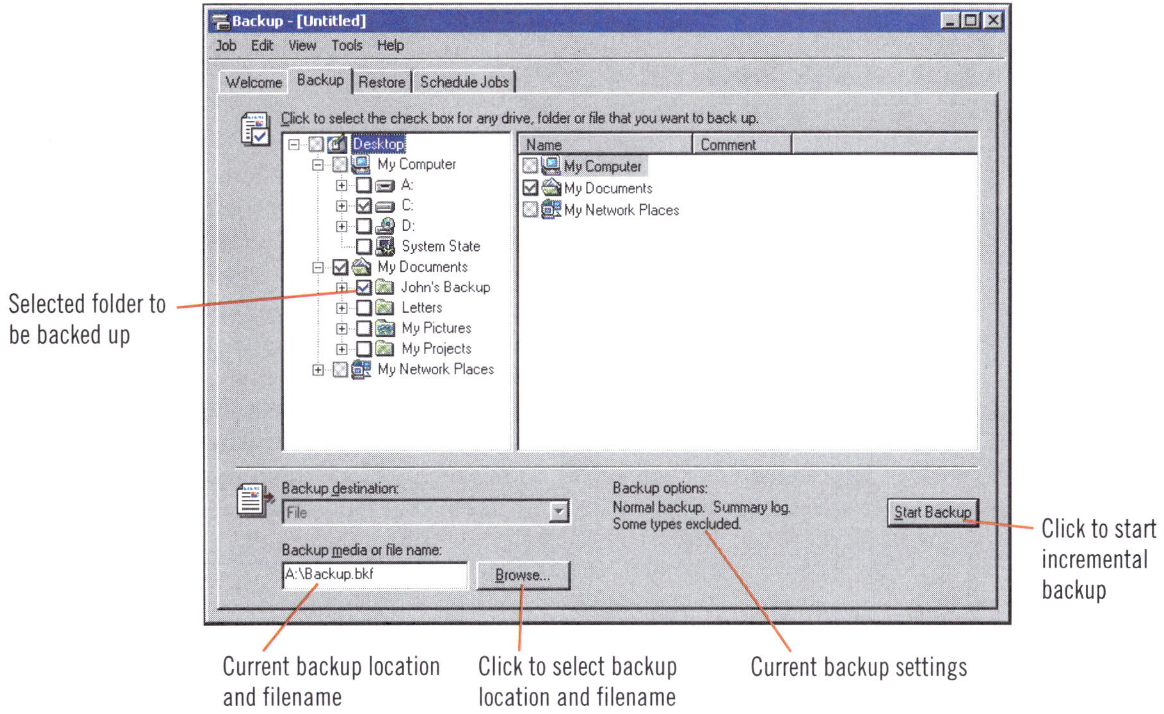

FIGURE N-15: Backup report in Notepad

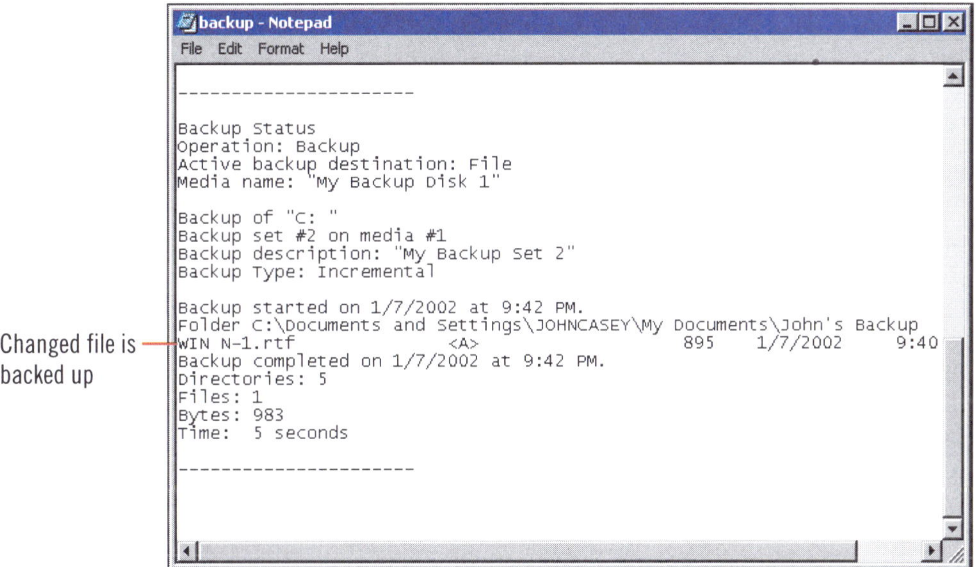

Using a tape drive to back up files

Using a tape drive can make backing up large amounts of information, such as an entire hard drive, fast and easy. Before you use a tape drive with Backup, make sure the tape drive is compatible with Backup. For a complete list of compatible tape drives, click Help Topics on the Help menu in the Backup window. After connecting the tape drive to your computer and loading a tape cartridge into the tape drive, you can click the Restore tab, then right-click the tape media to retension, format or erase a tape cartridge to back up your files. To format a tape cartridge, you need to have a DC-2000-type tape drive, which requires that you format a tape before you use it.

Restoring a Backed Up File

The real value in backing up your files becomes apparent if you lose or damage some files or need information from a document that has changed a great deal over time. You can restore a single file, several files, or an entire hard drive. Using the Restore Wizard, you can specify which files you want to restore and where you want them to be placed. When you create a backup set with the Use the catalogs on the media option selected in the General tab of the Options dialog box (it is selected by default), a **catalog**, or index of the backed up files, is built and stored on the backup medium. When you store the catalog on the backup medium, it speeds up the process when you want to restore files. Instead of re-creating the catalog, the Restore function opens the catalog on the backup medium. However, if you want to restore data from several tapes, and the tape with the catalog is missing, or you want to restore data from media that is damaged, you should not select the Use the catalogs on the media option. A co-worker at Wired Coffee needs the original WIN N-1 file, so he asks John to restore that file onto the hard drive.

Trouble?

If you are restoring the System State data, and you do not designate an alternate location for the restored data, Backup will erase the System State data that is currently on your computer and replace it with the System State data you are restoring.

Trouble?

If you see a folder icon with a question mark in the Restore tab window, you need to right-click the backup set icon, then click Catalog to update the catalog on the backup medium.

1. In the Backup window, click the **Welcome tab**, click the **Restore Wizard button**, then click **Next**
   The Restore Wizard opens, and then asks you to specify the files you want to restore.
2. In the What to restore list, click the **+ (plus sign) to the left of the File icon**, click the **+ to the left of the My Backup Disk 1 icon**, then click the **My Backup Disk icon**
   The Restore Wizard appears with a list of backup sets in the Backup.bkp file, as shown in Figure N-16.
3. In the What to restore list, click the hard drive (C:) icon for Set 1, click the **+ to the left of the hard drive (C:) icon for Set 1**, then click the **+ to the left of each folder icon** until John's Backup folder appears
4. In the What to restore list, click the **John's Backup folder** (scroll to see it if necessary), then click the **WIN N-1 file check box** in the Contents list to select it
   The selected file appears checked, as shown in Figure N-17.
5. Click **Next**, then click **Advanced**
   The Restore Wizard asks you to select a destination for the restored files and folders.
6. Click **Next** to restore the file in its original location
   The Restore Wizard asks you to choose how you want to restore files that are already on disk.
7. Click the **Always replace the file on disk option button**, then click **Next**
   The Restore Wizard asks you to select the special restore option you want to use.
8. Click **Next**, click **Finish**, then click **OK** to confirm the location and name of the backup file you want to restore (in this case, A:\Backup.bkf)
   The Restore Progress dialog box opens with a progress meter indicating current status. Upon completion, the Restore Progress dialog box opens, indicating that the operation is complete. Notice the number of files processed, or restored, is one.
9. Click **Close** to return to the Backup window
   The previous version of the WIN N-1 file is restored. John could check this by opening the restored file in WordPad.

FIGURE N-16: Restore Wizard dialog box

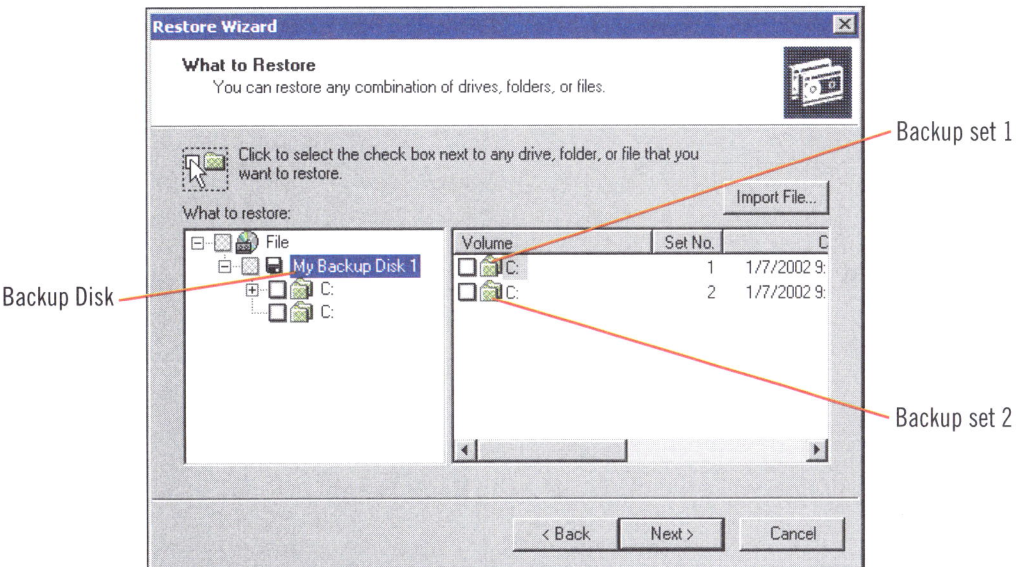

FIGURE N-17: Restore Wizard dialog box

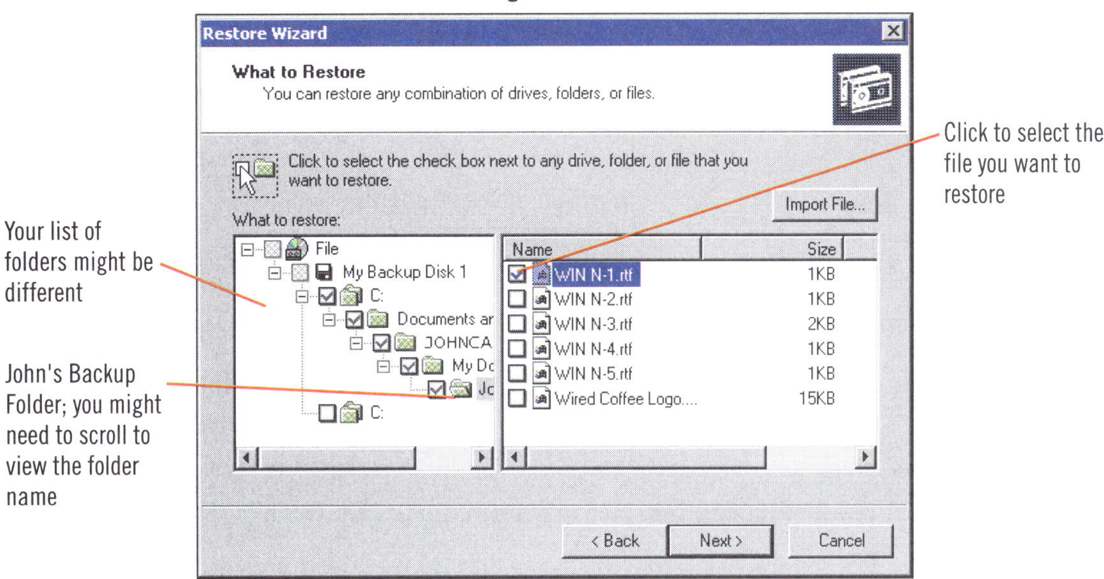

CLUES TO USE

Excluding file types from a backup

When you want to backup all but a few files of a specific type on your computer, its more efficient to backup all the files on your computer and then exclude the ones you don't want to backup instead of selecting the individual files you want. To exclude file types from a backup, click Tools on the menu bar, click Options, click the Exclude Files tab, then click Add new under the Files excluded for all users list if you want to exclude files that are owned by all users, or click Add new under the Files excluded for user list if you want to exclude only files that you own. In the Add Excluded Files dialog box, click the file type in Registered file type to exclude a registered file type or enter a period and then the one, two, or three letter file extension in Custom file mask to exclude a custom file type. Type a path in the Applies to path text box if you want to restrict the excluded file type to a specific folder or hard disk drive, then click OK. If you restrict excluded files to a specific path (folder), the files will be restricted from all subfolders of that path unless you click the Applies to all subfolders check box to deselect it.

Deleting a Backup Job

After backing up files for a while, you might find a number of unneeded backup jobs accumulating in Backup. You can delete these jobs quickly and easily from within Backup. When you delete a backup job, such as My Backup Set 1, only the backup job is deleted, but the backup file, such as Backup.bfk, remains in the backup location. If you want to delete the backup file, drag the file icon into the Recycle Bin as you would any other Windows file. John deletes old backup jobs from Backup.

Steps

1. In the Backup window, click the **Restore tab**
2. Right-click the **My Backup Disk 1 icon**, as shown in Figure N-18
3. Click **Delete catalog** on the pop-up menu
   Both backup sets in this catalog are deleted.
4. Click the **Close button** [X] in the Backup window
5. Click the **Start button** on the taskbar, point to **Programs**, point to **Accessories**, then click **Windows Explorer**
   You can use Windows Explorer to delete the John's Backup folder and backup files in order to restore your drives to their original state.
6. Click the [+] **next to the My Documents folder**, if necessary, click the **John's Backup folder**, press **[Delete]**, then click **Yes** in the Confirm Folder Delete dialog box
7. Click the [+] **next to the My Computer icon**, locate the **floppy drive** containing your Project Disk with the backup file, then click the **floppy drive icon**
   Windows Explorer displays the contents of the floppy disk in the right pane.
8. Click the **Backup file**, press **[Delete]**, then click **Yes** to confirm the deletion
9. Click the **Close button** [X] in the Windows Explorer window
   Now the backup jobs and John's Backup folder are deleted.

FIGURE N-18: Backup window with the Restore tab in front

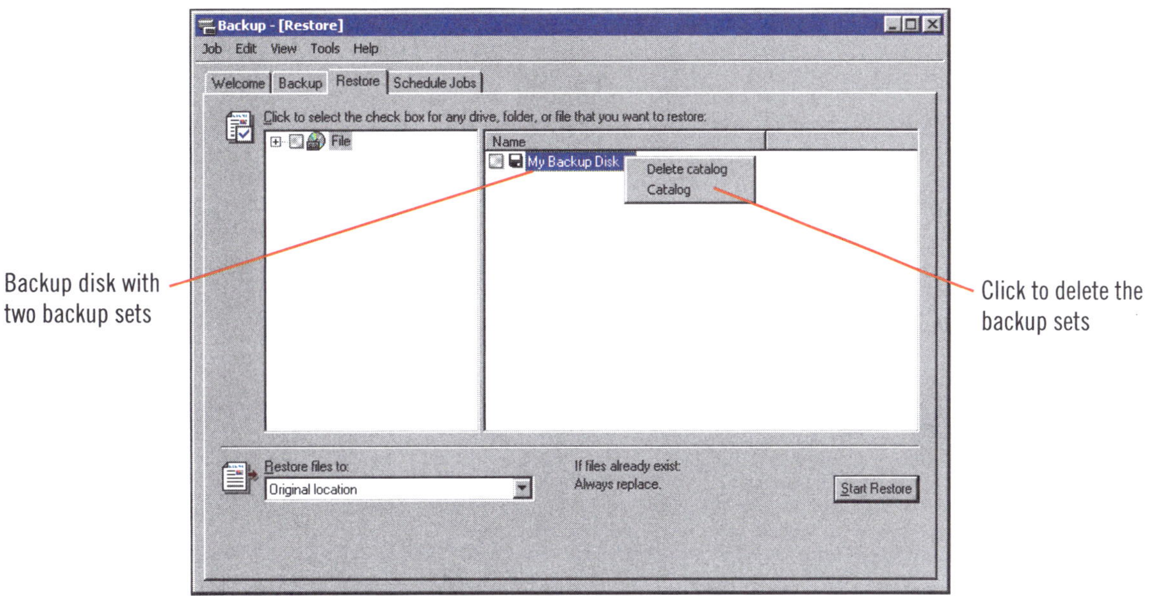

Using batch files to back up data

You can perform backup operations from batch files using the ntbackup command followed by various command line parameters. Using the ntbackup command, you can back up entire folders only. You cannot designate individual files for backup. However, you can designate a backup selection file (.bks file) from the command line, which contains a list of files you want to back up. You must use the GUI version of the Backup utility to create backup selection files. The ntbackup command does not support the use of wildcard characters. For example, typing *.txt will not back up files with a .txt. To create a batch file, open Wordpad, type the DOS commands you want to execute, then save the file with a .bat extension. An example of a DOS command to perform a backup is `ntbackup backup "@C:\ntbackup\batch.bks "/j "My Backup 1" /t "Batch Backup 1" / n "Batch Backup 2"` This example will perform a backup using the backup type that is specified in the Backup program. It will use the backup selection file named batch.bks, located in the C:\NTBackup\ directory to choose which files to backup. The backup job will be named "My Backup 1" and it will overwrite the tape named *Batch Backup 1* with the new name "Batch Backup 2."

Practice

▶ Concepts Review

Label each of the elements of the screen shown in Figure N-19.

FIGURE N-19

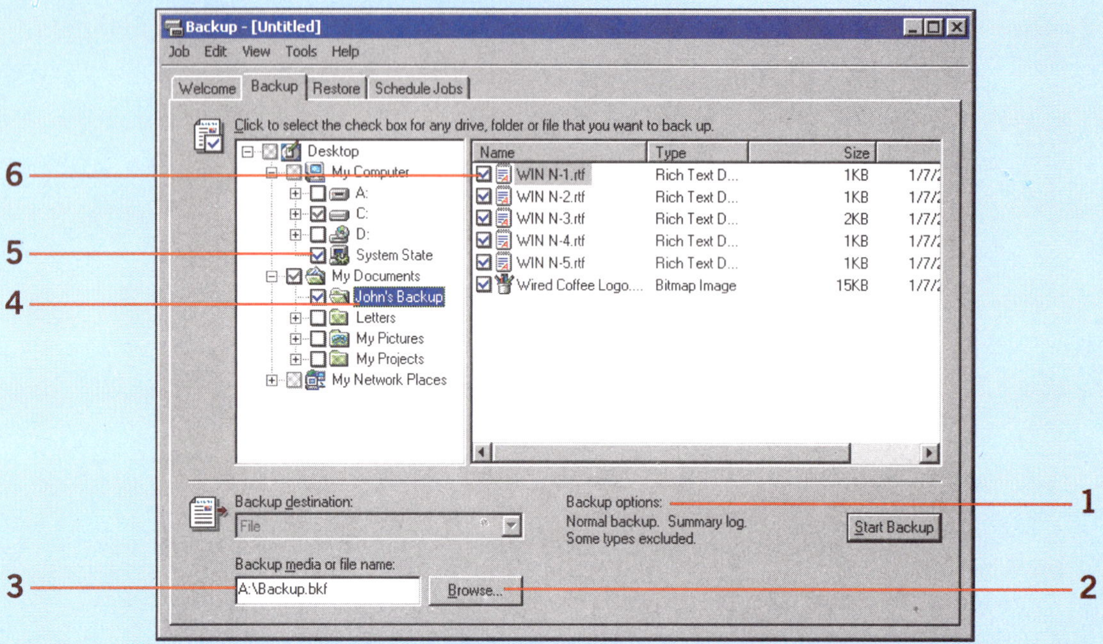

Match each of the terms with the statement that describes its function.

7. **Backs up files**
8. **Retrieves files**
9. **Clears archive attributes**
10. **Saves backup jobs**
11. **Verifies a backup**
12. **Does not clear archived attributes**

a. A backup option
b. Backup Wizard
c. Normal backup
d. Restore Wizard
e. A backup job
f. Differential backup

Select the best answer from the list of choices.

13. Which of the following is NOT an advantage of Backup?
- a. Compresses files as it copies them
- b. Backs up floppy to floppy
- c. Splits large files across two or more floppies
- d. Automatically detects tape drives

14. Which of the following is something you CANNOT do with Backup?
- a. Back up files
- b. Modify files
- c. Verify files
- d. Restore files

15. A gray checkmark indicates that
- a. all of the folders and files are selected.
- b. some of the files are selected.
- c. some of the folders and files are selected.
- d. all of the files are selected.

16. Which backup type copies only files that have changed since the last backup?
- a. Daily
- b. Normal
- c. Incremental
- d. System State data

Skills Review

1. **Copy files to a hard drive.**
   a. Insert your Project Disk into the appropriate floppy drive.
   b. Click the Start button on the taskbar, point to Programs, point to Accessories, then click Windows Explorer.
   c. Click the My Documents icon, click File on the menu bar, point to New, then click Folder.
   d. Type **Backup Files**, then press [Enter].
   e. Click the + next to the My Computer icon, click the + next to the floppy drive icon containing your Project Disk, then click the Unit N folder.
   f. Click Edit on the menu bar, click Select All, then drag the files from your Project Disk to the Backup Files folder.
   g. Close Windows Explorer.
2. **Start Backup.**
   a. Click the Start button, point to Programs, point to Accessories, point to System Tools, then click Backup.
   b. Click the Backup Wizard button, then click Next.
   c. Click the Back up selected files, drives, or network data option button, then click Next.
3. **Select files for a backup.**
   a. In the What to back up list, click the + to the left of the My Documents icon.
   b. Click the Backup Files folder icon, click the Backup Files folder check box to select it, then click Next.
   c. If necessary, insert your Project Disk into the appropriate drive on your computer.
   d. Click Browse, select the floppy drive containing your Project Disk, type **Wiredbkup** in the File name text box, then click Open.
   e. Click Next.
4. **Perform a normal backup.**
   a. In the Backup Wizard dialog box, click Advanced, then click Next.
   b. Click the Verify data after backup check box to select it, click Next, then click Next again.
   c. Type **Wired Backup Set 1**, press [Tab], type **Wired Backup Disk 1**, then click Next.
   d. Click Next, Click Finish, then click Close.
5. **View and print a backup report.**
   a. Click Tools on the menu bar, then click Report.
   b. Click the backup report with the current time and date you just created, then click View.
   c. Click File on the menu bar, click Print, then click Print in the Print dialog box.
   d. Click the Close button in the Notepad window, then click Cancel.
   e. Click Tools on the menu bar, click Options, then click the Backup Log tab.
   f. Click the Detailed option button, then click OK.
   g. Click the Start button, point to Programs, point to Accessories, then click Paint.
   h. Open the file Wired Coffee Logo from the Backup Files folder.
   i. Add the text **Great Coffee!** to the image, save the file, then exit Paint.
6. **Perform an incremental backup.**
   a. Click the Backup tab.
   b. Click the + to the left of the My Documents icon, then click the Backup Files folder check box to select it.
   c. Click Start Backup.
   d. In the Backup description text box, type **Wired Backup Set 2**, press [Tab] twice, then type **Wired Backup Disk 1**.
   e. Click Advanced.
   f. Click the Backup Type list arrow, click Differential, click OK, then click Start Backup.
   g. Click Report, then drag the scroll box to the bottom of the NotePad window to read the report status.
   h. Click the Close button in the NotePad window, then click Close.

i. Click Tools on the menu bar, click Options, click the Backup Log tab, click the Summary option button, then click OK.

7. Restore a backed up file.

a. Click the Welcome tab, click the Restore Wizard button, then click Next.

b. Click the + to the left of the File icon, click the + to the left of the Wired Backup Disk 1 icon, then click the Wired Backup Disk 1 icon.

c. Click the hard drive (C:) icon for Set 1, click the + to the left of the hard drive (C:) icon for Set 1, then click the + to the left of each folder icon until Backup Files folder appears.

d. Click the Backup Files folder (scroll to see it, if necessary), then click the Wired Coffee Logo file check box.

e. Click Next, click Advanced, click Next, click the Always replace the file on disk option button, then click Next.

f. Click Next, click Finish, click OK, then click Close.

8. Delete a backup job.

a. Click the Restore tab.

b. Right-click the Wired Backup Disk 1 icon, then click Delete catalog.

c. Click the Close button in the Backup window.

d. Click the Start button, point to Programs, point to Accessories, then click Windows Explorer.

e. Click the + next to the My Documents folder, click Backup Files folder, press [Delete], then click Yes.

f. Click the + next to the My Computer icon, click the floppy drive containing your Project Disk, click the Wiredbkup file, press [Delete], then click Yes.

g. Click the Close button in the Windows Explorer window.

Independent Challenges

1. You are the owner of Buds and Petals, Inc., a company that specializes in freeze-dried flowers. To grow your business, you attend craft fairs to sell arrangements and build a mailing list. After each fair, you send letters to those who purchased arrangements, and information to those who request it. For this independent challenge, create a thank-you letter, a sample customized letter, an arrangement and pricing information document, then back up the files on your Project Disk.

To complete this independent challenge:

a. Using Windows Explorer, create a folder named *Customers* in the My Documents folder.

b. Using WordPad, create the following documents in the Customers folder:
- A thank-you letter you can customize for each customer
- A sample thank-you letter with name and address information
- An arrangement and pricing information sheet

c. Start Backup, then insert your Project Disk into the appropriate drive.

d. Start the backup and create a new backup job.

e. Select the files that you created in WordPad, then back up the files to your Project Disk as *Buds and Petals*.

f. Save the backup job as *Fair BKUP 1*, perform a normal backup, then print a report.

g. Change and save the arrangement and pricing information sheet document, then perform an incremental backup.

h. Delete the backup jobs, then using Windows Explorer, delete the Customers folder and the backup file on your Project Disk.

2. You are an associate at Andersen, Williams & Barnes law firm. You are currently helping two partners create a California corporation. To create a new corporation, you need to fill out corporation forms for the state, create by-laws, and hold board meetings. For this independent challenge, create the documents necessary to create a corporation, and then back up the documents on your Project Disk.

In this challenge, you will create your own information. Assume the following facts about the corporation:
- Corporation name: IntSoft, Inc.
- Business: Develop testing tools for Windows software developers

- Ownership: Dorian Golu, 6,000 shares (60%); and John Yokela, 4,000 shares (40%)
- Address: 722 Main Street, Suite 100, Silicon Valley, CA 90028

To complete this independent challenge:

a. Using Windows Explorer, create a folder named *IntSoft 02* in the My Documents folder.
b. Using WordPad, create the following documents in the IntSoft 02 folder:
- A document stating the above information called *INTAOI*
- Board meeting minutes, called *INT BM 001*, stating all the steps to create the corporation have been taken
- A bill for services called *INT Bill 001*

c. Start Backup, then insert your Project Disk into the appropriate drive.
d. Start the backup, create a new backup job, then back up the selected files that you created in WordPad.
e. Back up the files to your Project Disk as *Important*, then save the backup job as *INT BKUP 1*.
f. Select the files that you created with WordPad, then perform the normal backup and print a report.
g. Add billing information to INT Bill 001, save the document, then perform an incremental backup.
h. Save the backup job as *INT BKUP 2*, then restore the changed file and verify that the incremental backup stored the latest version.
i. Delete the backup jobs, then using Windows Explorer, delete the IntSoft 02 folder and the backup file on your Project Disk.

3. You are a graphic artist for Zero Gravity Designs, Inc., a company that specializes in logos. A real estate developer asks you to create a logo for his company, called Syntec, Inc. For this independent challenge, create several different logos in Paint, then back up the logo files on your Project Disk. After getting comments on the designs, make changes, then back up the documents. After making so many changes, compare your backups with your current files.

To complete this independent challenge:

a. Using Windows Explorer, create a folder named *Syntec* in the My Documents folder.
b. Using Paint, create several Paint documents with different logo designs, then save them in the Syntec folder.
c. Start Backup, then insert your Project Disk into the appropriate drive.
d. Start the backup, create a new backup job, then back up the selected files that you created in Paint.
e. Back up the files to your Project Disk as *Syntec Files*, then save the backup job as *SYN BKUP 1*.
f. Select the files that you created with Paint, then perform the normal backup.
g. Revise several designs, save the documents, then perform an incremental backup.
h. Save the backup job as *SYN BKUP 2*, print a report, then delete the backup jobs.
i. Using Windows Explorer, delete the Syntec folder and the backup file on your Project Disk.

4. After retiring from the police force, you decide to start a company, called Safety One, Inc., that specializes in gun safety training programs for police academies and the general public. To get the company started, you need to create an introductory gun safety class. You decide to create a class outline and a letter, then back up the documents on your Project Disk. After getting comments on the outline, you'll make changes, then back up the documents. After saving your changes, you'll restore the original document.

To complete this independent challenge:

a. Using Windows Explorer, create a folder named *Safety 1* in the My Documents folder.
b. Using WordPad, create the following documents in the Safety 1 folder.
- An outline called *GS 101 Outline* for the Gun Safety 101 class
- A letter called *GS Comments* to friends at the police department asking for comments on the outline

c. Start Backup, then insert your Project Disk into the appropriate drive.
d. Start the backup, create a new backup job, then back up the selected files that you created in WordPad.
e. Back up the files to your Project Disk as *Safety One*, then save the backup job as *SO BKUP 1*.
f. Select the files that you created with WordPad, then perform the normal backup and print a report.
g. Revise the *GS 101 Outline* document, then save the document.
h. Perform a differential backup, then save the backup job as *SO BKUP 2*.
i. Restore the GS 101 Outline document from the *SO BKUP 1* backup job, print a report, then delete the backup jobs.
j. Using Windows Explorer, delete the Safety 1 folder and the backup file on your Project Disk.

► Visual Workshop

Re-create the screen shown in Figure N-20, which displays the Notepad window with a backup report. Your hard drive folders might be different. Print the report in Notepad or Print the Screen. (Press the Print Screen key to make a copy of the screen, open Paint, click Edit on the menu bar, click Paste to paste the screen into Paint, then click Yes to paste the large image if necessary. Click File on the menu bar, click Print, then click Print in the Print dialog box.)

FIGURE N-20

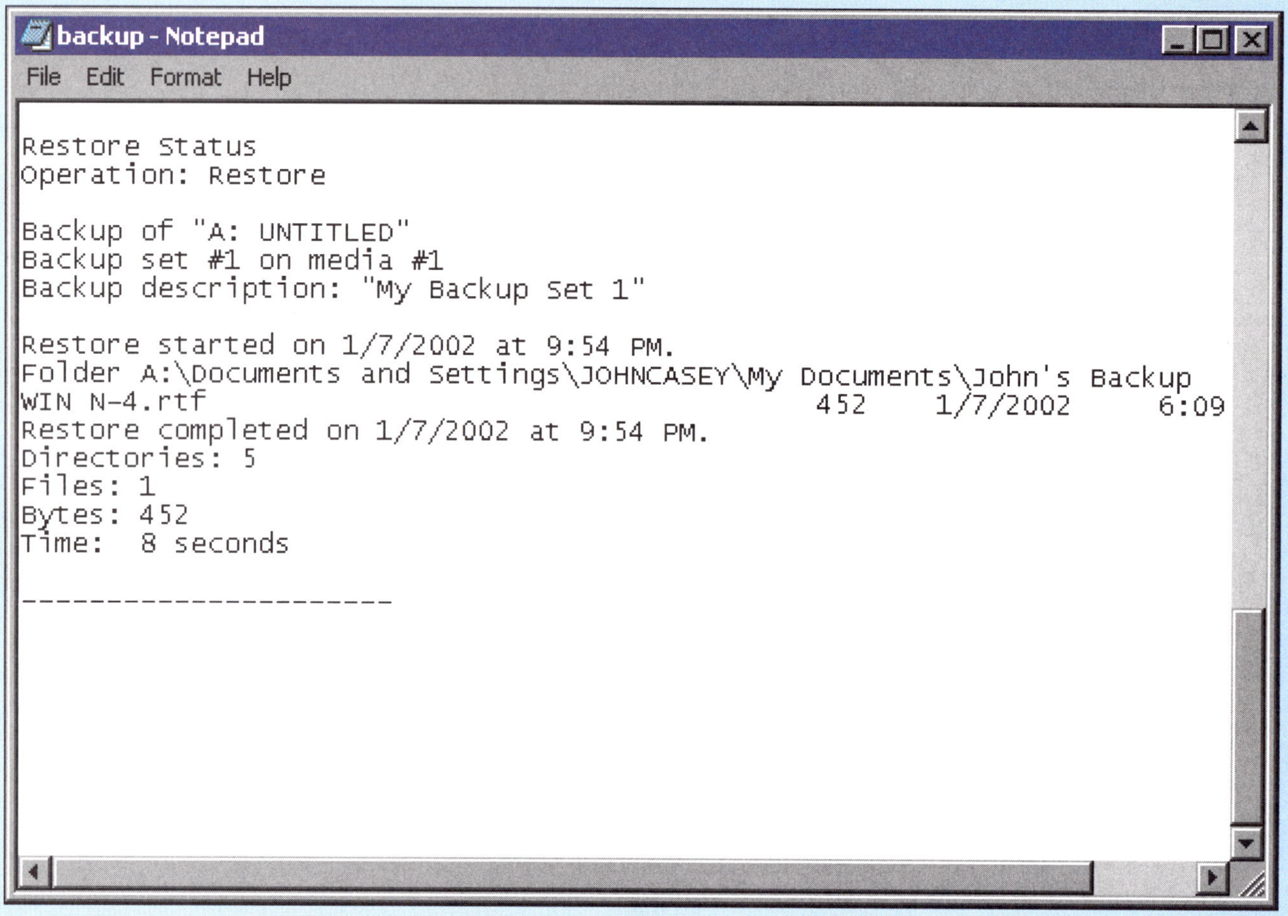

backup - Notepad

File Edit Format Help

```
Restore Status
Operation: Restore

Backup of "A: UNTITLED"
Backup set #1 on media #1
Backup description: "My Backup Set 1"

Restore started on 1/7/2002 at 9:54 PM.
Folder A:\Documents and Settings\JOHNCASEY\My Documents\John's Backup
WIN N-4.rtf                                            452    1/7/2002     6:09
Restore completed on 1/7/2002 at 9:54 PM.
Directories: 5
Files: 1
Bytes: 452
Time:  8 seconds

----------------------
```

Windows 2000

Administering Your Computer

Objectives

- Explore Windows 2000 administrative tools
- Monitor activity with Event Viewer
- Manage an event log
- Create a performance chart
- Set up an alert
- View Computer Manager tools
- Understand disk file systems
- Manage disks
- View and save system information

If you have purchased a computer and set it up in your home, you are that computer's administrator. Computers on a network in an institution such as a university are managed by one or more system or network administrators, who have the task of ensuring that the network and its services are reliable, fast, and secure. Although most network administration takes place on the server end, clients must also be administered. Windows 2000 includes administrative tools that make it easy to ensure that client computers are operating as they should. John Casey is considering setting up a few computers for patrons to use while relaxing at Wired Coffee. He wants to understand more about how those computers would need to be administered and secured. He asks his system administrator, Margaret Kolbe, to assist him in understanding Windows 2000 administrative tools.

Windows 2000

Exploring Windows 2000 Administrative Tools

Windows 2000 offers a set of administrative tools that help you administer your computer and ensure its smooth operation. The Administrative Tools window, opened from the Control Panel, provides tools that allow you to configure administrative settings for local and remote computers. Margaret explains that many Windows 2000 users won't ever have to open the Administrative Tools window, but that computers open to the public will probably require more maintenance. She suggests, therefore, that John open this window to see the tools available to him.

1. Click the **Start button** on the taskbar
2. Point to **Settings**
3. Click **Control Panel**
4. Double-click the **Administrative Tools icon**
   Figure O-1 shows the tools available on John's computer. See Table O-1 for a description of each tool. You will work with some of these tools in the lessons that follow.

Trouble?

Your Administrative Tools window might show other tools or fewer tools if your network administrator has installed additional administrative tools on or removed tools from your computer.

TABLE O-1: Administrative tools

icon	tool	description
	Computer Management	Manages disks and provides access to other tools to manage local and remote computers
	Event Viewer	Displays monitoring and troubleshooting messages from Windows and other programs
	Local Security Policy	Modifies local security policy, such as user rights and audit policies
	Performance	Displays graphs of system performance and configures data logs and alerts
	Services	Displays, starts, and stops services provided to users by your computer

FIGURE O-1: Viewing the Administrative Tools window

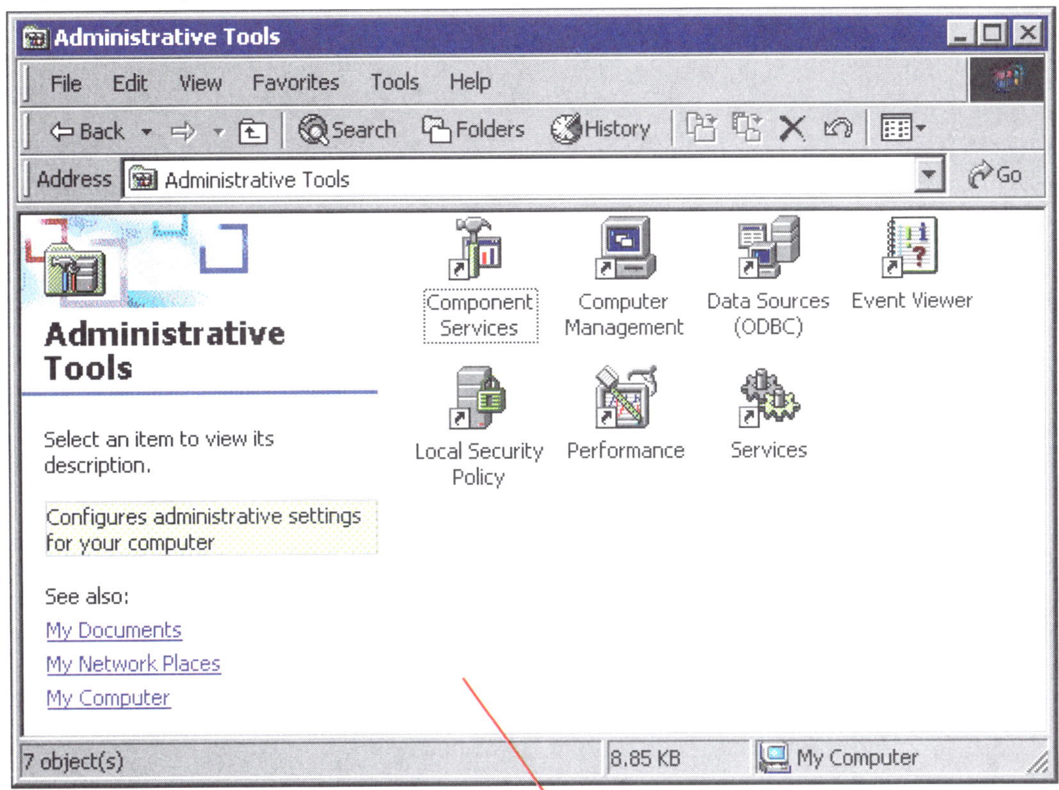

Network security

Security on a network is the degree to which data and resources on the computer are protected from system failure or unauthorized intrusion. One way a network administrator ensures security is by assigning rights to individual users or groups of users. Thus, a user on a client computer running Windows 2000 that has physical access to a network cannot access network files or resources until the administrator has granted rights to that computer and user. For example, the ability to access administrative tools is assigned only to certain groups. If you are a user in a group that does not have the right to use administrative tools, you might not be able to perform all the steps in this unit or even see some of the tools in Figure O-1.

Monitoring Activity with Event Viewer

Every time you start Windows 2000, an event-logging service starts that notes any unusual event that occurs, such as a failed logon, the installation of a new driver for a hardware device, the failure of a device or service to start, or a network interruption. For some critical events, such as when your disk is full, a warning message appears on your screen. Most events, however, don't require immediate attention, so Windows 2000 logs them in an event log file that you can view using the Event Viewer tool. Event Viewer maintains three logs: System, for events logged by Windows 2000 operating system components, Security, for security and audit events (such as who logged on), and Application, for program events. When you are troubleshooting problems on your computer, you can use the Event Viewer logs to monitor what activity took place. Margaret suggests John open Event Viewer to see what sorts of activities have been logged on the computer.

QuickTip

Once you have selected a log from the left pane, you can click View on the toolbar to open a menu of viewing options, including the option of choosing which columns to display or the order in which they appear.

Trouble?

If your Security log is blank, you are not on a network, you don't have the rights to view this log, or there have been no security breaches.

1. **From the Administrative Tools window, double-click the Event Viewer icon**
   The Event Viewer window opens. The left pane of the window displays the three types of logs maintained by your computer. From the Action menu, you can run commands to save these logs to files or open additional log files (perhaps from other computers on the network).

2. **In the left pane, click System Log if necessary**
   The log for System events appears in the right pane of the Event Viewer window. Figure O-2 shows the System Log window for John's computer. Your log will show different events. You can click any column header to resort the list; by default, items are sorted by date, with the most recent even listed first. The first column, Type, identifies the nature or severity of the event: for example, indicates a normal event, warns that the event might indicate a problem, and indicates a more serious error that resulted in the loss of a function or data. See Table O-2 for a description of each column.

3. **Double-click one of the events in the right pane**
   The Event Properties window for the event you double-clicked opens, showing details of the event. Figure O-3 shows the Event Properties window for a network connection error. Additionally, a description appears, and in some cases a data section at the bottom of the window. Some events generate **binary data** that experienced computer technicians can evaluate to better interpret the event.

4. **Click either the up arrow or down arrow button**
   Another event description appears in the window.

5. **Click the Close button to close the Event Properties window**

6. **Click Security Log in the left pane**
   If your computer has experienced any security events (such as a user trying to log on using an incorrect password), those events will be listed in the right pane.

7. **Click Application Log in the left pane**
   The right pane lists all of the events associated with the operation of the various applications on your system. This could include the installation of new programs or errors that have caused your programs to fail.

8. **Click System Log to return to the System Log**

FIGURE O-2: System Event log

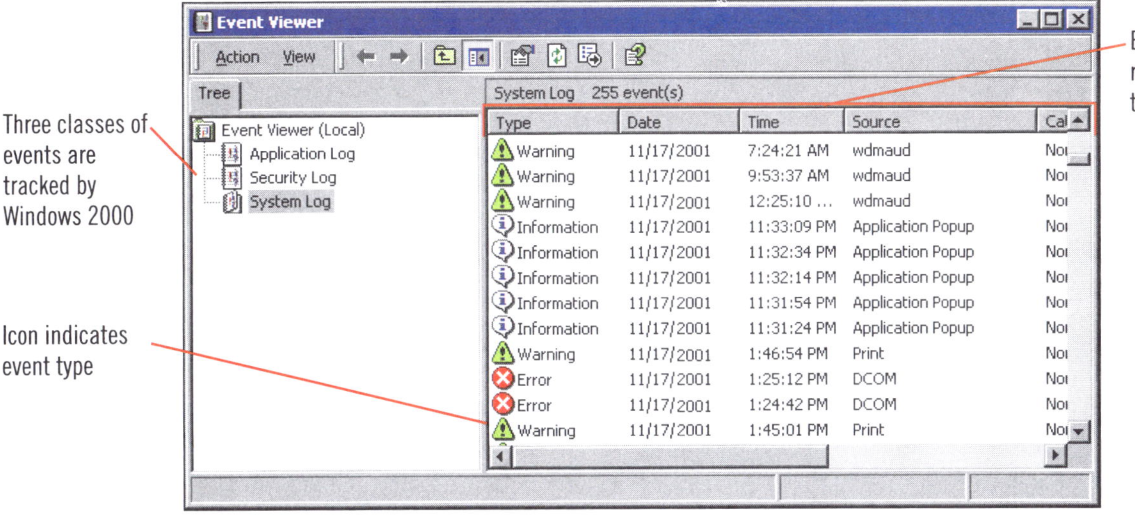

FIGURE O-3: Viewing event details

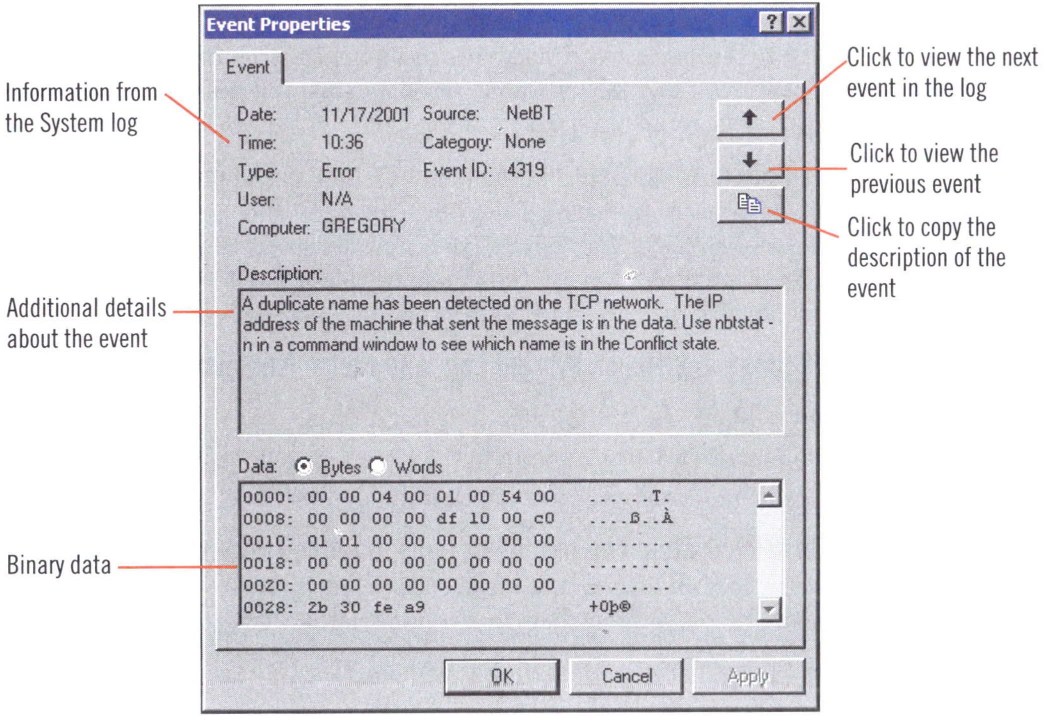

TABLE O-2: Event Viewer columns

column	description
Type	Identifies the nature of the event, such as informational, a warning, or an error
Date and Time	Point when an event occurred, based on the computer's clock
Source	The object, such as the program, computer, or user, that logged the event
Category	Event classification, if applicable, such as Logon/Logoff
Event	Number that identifies the specific event type; this number helps technical support personnel track events in the system
User	User associated with the event, if applicable; the user is not responsible for most events, so the User entry is often N/A
Computer	Name of the computer where the event occurred

Managing an Event Log

Event logs grow in size as you work on your computer, but Event Viewer provides tools that help you view just the information you need and store the information you want to save for later. For example, you can apply a **filter** that allows you to view only events matching specified criteria, such as all events associated with a certain user. You can also search for a specific event using similar criteria. You probably don't want your active log to include events that happened long ago. With Event Viewer, you can **archive**, or save, your log periodically and then clear the events you've archived. Most administrators archive event logs on a regular schedule. Margaret wants John to see how he might filter and locate events. John also wants to archive his System Log and then clear the events to prevent the list from becoming too long. In this lesson, you will practice the first few steps of clearing a log, but you will not actually complete the procedure because your system administrator might want the logs to remain intact. The System Log should still be open in the Event Viewer window.

Steps

1. Click **View** on the menu bar, then click **Filter**
   The System Log Properties dialog box opens, as shown in Figure O-4, with the Filter tab in front. You can deselect the Event types check boxes to view only events of a certain type; you can view events in a specified time period, or you can view events from a specified source, category, user, computer, or ID number.

2. Click **Cancel**, click **View** on the menu bar, then click **Find**
   The Find in Local System Log dialog box, shown in Figure O-5, allows you to search through all types of events or only certain types. You can specify a source, category, ID, computer, user, or description when searching for a particular event. Once you've specified what you are looking for, you click the Find Next button.

3. Click **Close**, right-click **System Log**, and then click **Save Log File As**

4. Insert a blank, formatted disk into the A: drive, click the **Save in list arrow**, click **3-1/2 Floppy (A:)**, type **System** in the File name box, then click the **Save button**
   Once you have saved a log, you can clear it.

5. Right-click **System Log** in the left pane, and then click **Clear All Events**
   A message asks if you want to archive the events before clearing the log. Because you just archived the log, you don't have to save events again.

6. Click Cancel to close Event Viewer without affecting the System log
   Because this is simply a practice, you will not actually clear the log. If you had clicked Yes, Event Viewer would have emptied the log, giving you the opportunity to save the log to a file. If you had clicked No, Event Viewer would have emptied the log without saving the log contents to a file.

7. Click the **Close button** in the Event Viewer window title bar
   The Event Viewer window closes, and you return to the Administrative Tools window.

Trouble?

If your System Log is larger than the capacity of your disk, a message appears telling you there isn't enough space on the disk. Click the OK button and skip Steps 6–8.

Trouble?

If you don't have the necessary rights, you won't be able to clear event logs. Skip to Step 8.

QuickTip

You can open the log you archived by using the Open Log File command on the Action menu in the Event Viewer window.

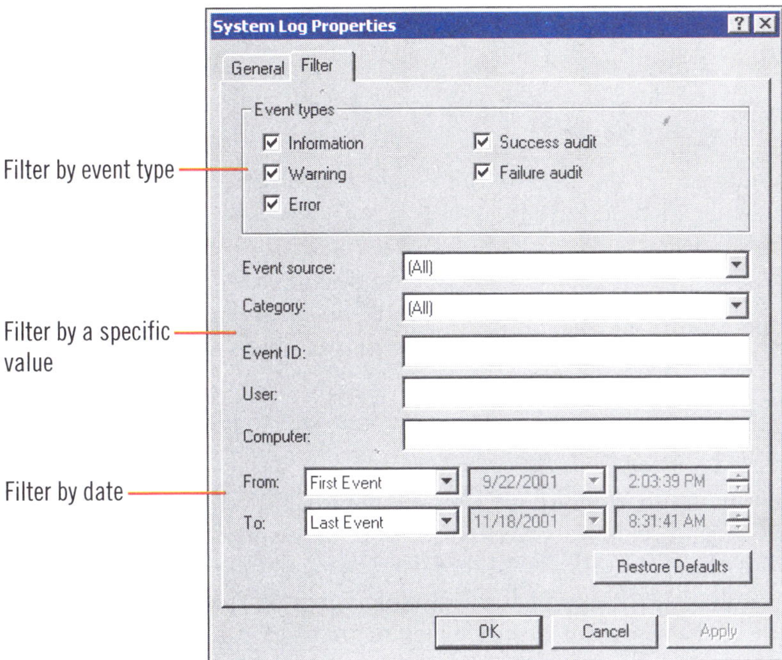

FIGURE O-4: Filtering an event log

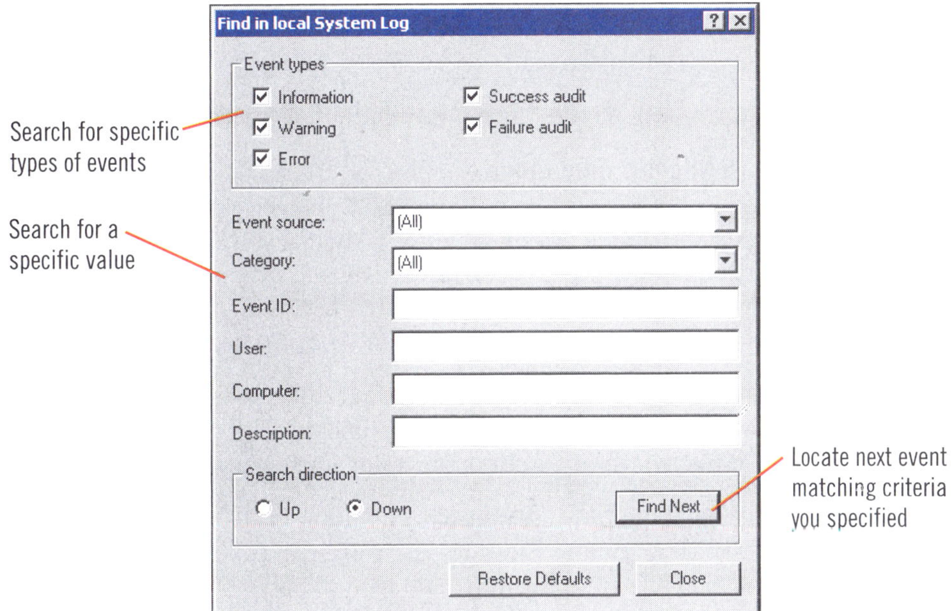

FIGURE O-5: Find in local System Log dialog box

Changing log settings

You can control how any log in the Event Viewer collects data by defining a maximum log size (the default is 512K) and instructing Event Viewer how to handle an event log that has reached its maximum size. Only users with administrative rights can change log settings. When the log is selected in the Event Viewer window, you can click the Properties button on the toolbar to open the Log Properties dialog box, which allows you to change log settings. In addition to specifying a maximum log size, you can also choose from three log options when the log is full: new events can automatically overwrite the oldest events, new events can overwrite only events older than a specified number of days, or you can set Event Viewer not to overwrite events, in which case you must manually clear a full log before it can resume logging events.

Windows 2000

Creating a Performance Chart

Systems administrators use **performance charts** to observe how a computer's processes are behaving over time. The Performance Monitor tool allows you to create performance charts that enable you to view items such as your browser's activity, your computer's memory use, or the amount of congestion on a device. Each item you examine has a set of **counters** associated with it that provide specific numeric information. Margaret suggests that John create a performance chart documenting the activities of the computer's processor.

Steps

1. In the Administrative Tools window, double-click the **Performance icon**
   The Performance window opens. In this window, you can record and chart the performance of various objects in your computer, such as your computer's processor or hard disk. The right pane displays the chart that will give you a graphical picture of the object's performance. From the left pane you can create log files that record the performance values in text format.
2. If necessary, click the **View Chart button** located in the right pane above the empty chart, then click the **Add button**
   The Add Counters dialog box opens, displaying a list of performance objects and their counters that you can select to chart. See Figure O-6. You'll want to chart one of the counters associated with the computer's processor.
3. If necessary, click the **Performance Object list arrow**, then click **Processor**
4. Click **%Privileged Time** in the Counter list, then click **Add**
   The %Privileged Time counter monitors the percentage of the time the processor spends working with hardware, system memory, and other privileged system components. A value of 100% indicates that the processor is completely occupied with running these types of tasks. The Performance Monitor immediately begins charting this counter, though you may not be able to see the chart if the Add Counters dialog box obscures it on your screen.
5. Click **%Processor Time** in the Counter list, then click **Add**
   This counter measures the percentage of time that the processor is executing a "non-idle thread;" it is a primary indicator of processor activity for any type of process.
6. Click **%User Time**, then click **Add**
   The %User Time counter measures the percentage of time the processor works in user mode, responding to requests from user applications.
7. Click **Close** in the Add Counters dialog box
   A red bar moves across the screen and the counters you specified appear as colored lines on the chart.
8. Double-click on any blank area of the desktop
   Watch how the measure of processor time jumps up when activity occurs. Figure O-7 shows how a performance chart of these three counters might appear on a typical computer.
9. Click the **Stop button** on the System Monitor toolbar
   The performance counters stop tracking events.

QuickTip

If you aren't sure what a counter measures, click Explain to open a pane that displays explanatory information.

QuickTip

To show processor use in a performance chart, disable screen savers, as they take up processor resources and give your chart a distorted view of processor performance.

QuickTip

Limit the number of counters on a given chart to just a few, or your chart will have too many lines to be readable.

FIGURE 0-6: Selecting performance counters to chart

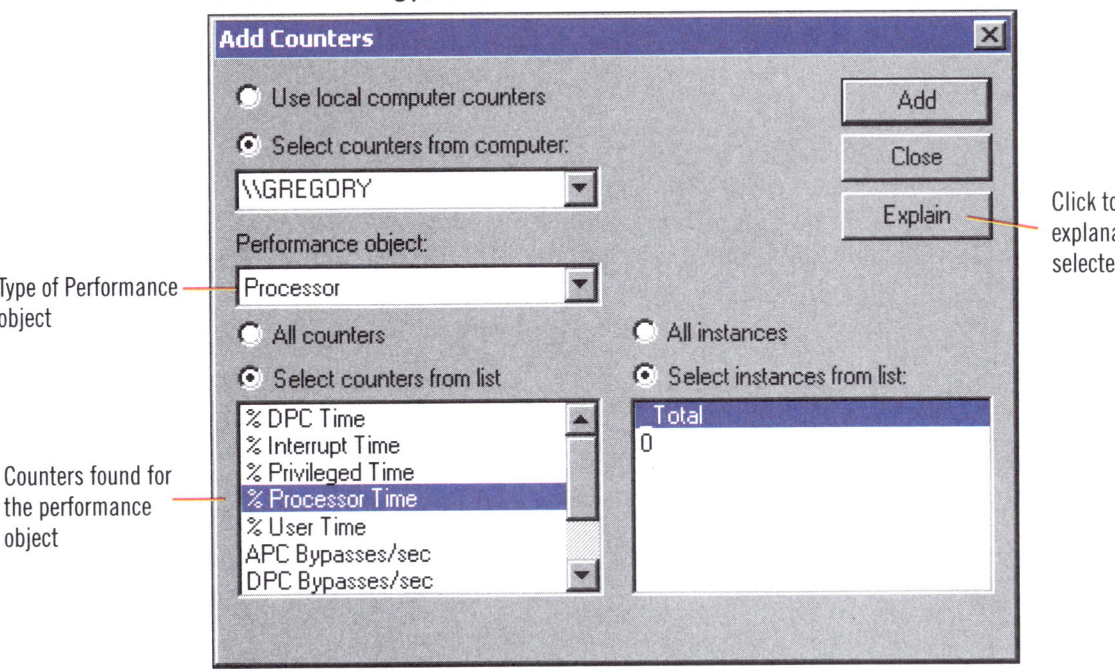

FIGURE 0-7: Charting processor performance

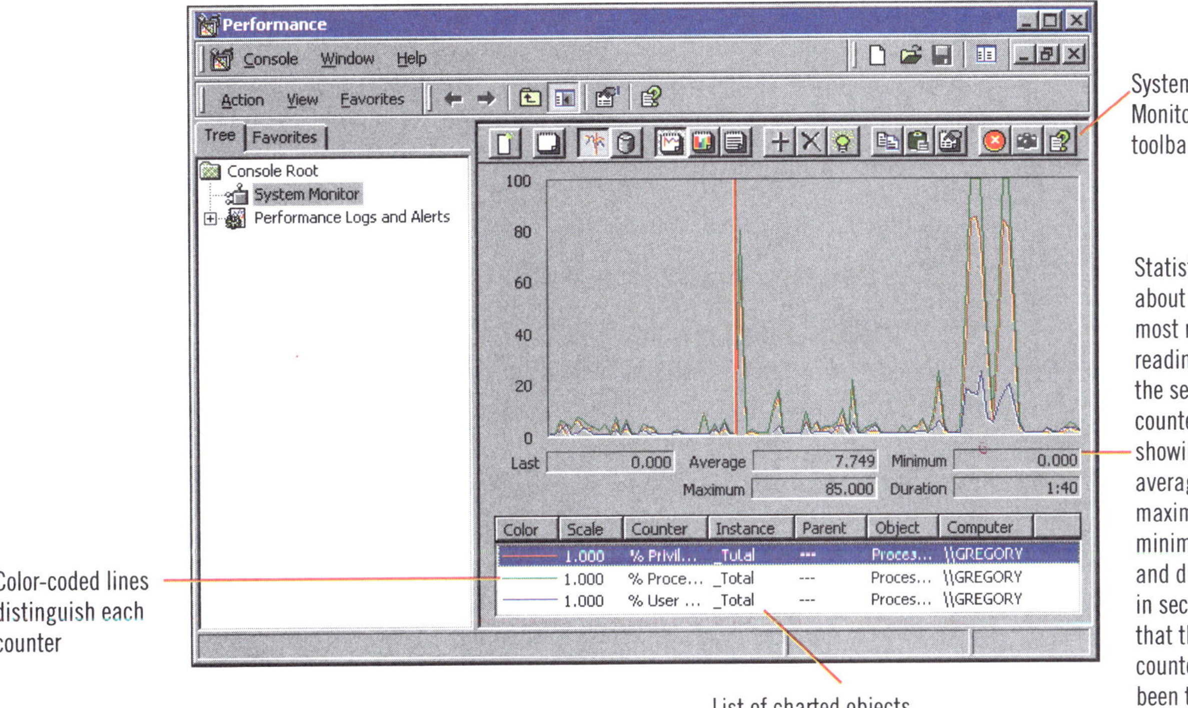

Baseline charts

Performance charts include statistics about each counter you select, but unless you know how your system should perform, these statistics might not be very meaningful. For this reason, administrators create **baseline charts**, charts made when the computer or network is running at a normal level. When there are problems, the administrator can create another performance chart that can be compared to the baseline chart. By regularly creating and comparing performance charts, administrators can anticipate and then prevent problems.

Windows 2000

Setting Up an Alert

In addition to creating performance charts, you can also use the Performance window to create user alerts. An **alert** is a warning that is automatically generated when a counter value exceeds or falls short of a threshold value you have specified. Margaret suggests John set up an alert to monitor the use of the computer's processor. The alert could be tripped whenever the percentage of the time the processor is in use exceeds a certain threshold. Margaret suggests a threshold value of 75%.

Steps

1. In the Performance window, click the **Performance Logs and Alerts icon** in the left pane, then click **Alerts** in the Performance Logs and Alerts list that opens in the right pane
2. Click **Action** on the toolbar, then click **New Alert Settings**
   The New Alert Settings dialog box opens. Each alert requires a specific name, so you'll first have to give it a name to identify it to the performance monitor.
3. Type **Alert Test** in the Name box, then click **OK**
   The Alert Test dialog box opens. From this dialog box, you specify which counters you want to track, and under what conditions the alert will be triggered.
4. Click **Add** in the Alert Test dialog box
   The Select Counters dialog box opens.
5. If necessary, click the **Performance Object list arrow**, then click **Processor**
6. Click **% Processor Time**, click **Add**, then click **Close**
7. Click the **Alert when the value is list arrow**, click **Over**, then type **75** in the Limit box
   Figure O-8 shows the Alert Test dialog box so that an alert will be added to the alert log when processor time exceeds 75%. If you wanted to monitor other counters, you would repeat Steps 4–7 for each counter.
8. Click **OK**
   Figure O-9 shows the Alert Test you just created. It appears green when it is running and red when it is not. If a counter matches the alert condition, the date and time of the event are recorded in the Application Log, which you can view from Event Viewer.
9. Right-click the **Alert Test icon**, click **Delete**, click **OK** if you are asked if you are sure, then close the Performance window
   You return to the Administrative Tools window.

QuickTip

Your system can record up to 1,000 alert events, after which the oldest events are discarded as new events occur.

FIGURE 0-8: Creating an alert

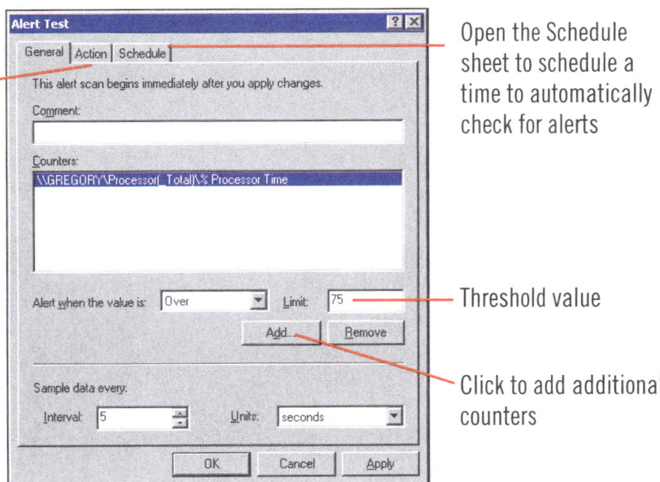

FIGURE 0-9: Running the alert

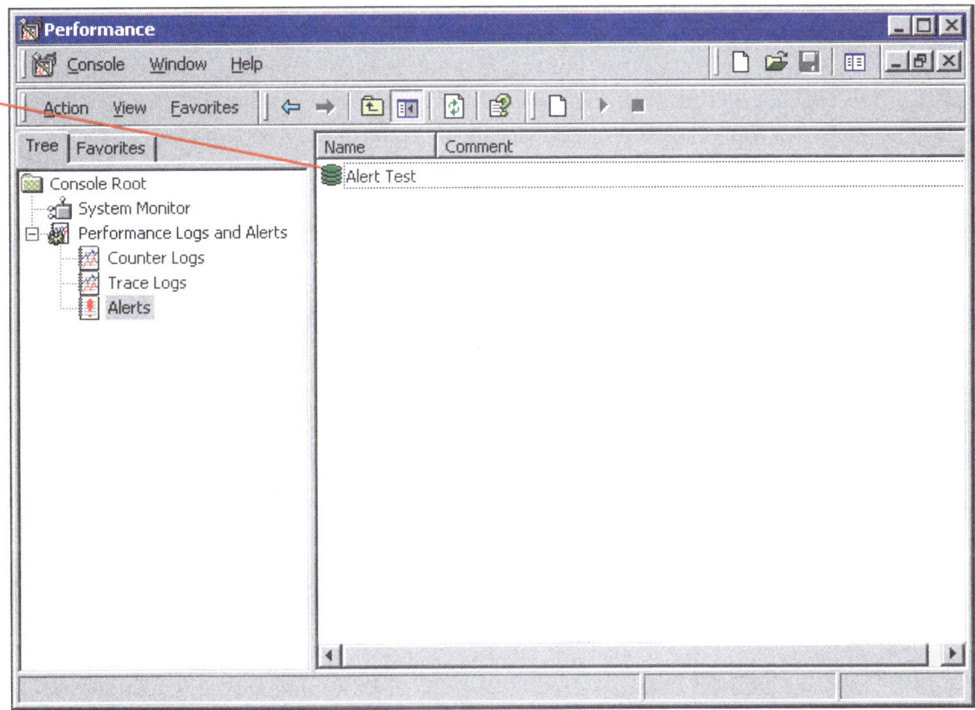

Alert actions and schedules

The Action tab in the selected alert's dialog box allows you to specify what action you want to take when your system triggers an alert. By default, the system logs an entry in the application event log when it triggers an alert. You can also specify that the system send a message to the network administrator, that performance data be collected, or that a specific program be run. To run a program, you click the Browse button and specify the program path. You can also schedule alerts using the Schedule tab in the selected alert's dialog box. Your system will scan for an alert at the times or intervals you specify.

Viewing Computer Manager Tools

Windows 2000 consolidates computer management utilities, including those you've already used, into a single window, called the **Computer Management** window, that provides easy access to a specific computer's administrative tools. Margaret suggests you practice using Computer Manager by viewing the Application Log to see how your alert was monitored.

Steps

1. From the Administrative Tools window, double-click the **Computer Management** icon

   The Computer Management window opens, as shown in Figure O-10. The Computer Management window uses a two-pane view that is similar to Windows Explorer. The left pane lists the hierarchy of tools; you navigate the tools using the familiar ⊞ and ⊟ icons that expand and contract the tool display. The hierarchy of tools in the left pane of the Computer Management window is called a **console tree** and appears on the Tree tab; each main category of tools is called a **node**. The three nodes in the Computer Management window are System Tools, Storage, and Services and Applications. You perform an administrative task by first selecting a tool in the console tree (you might need to navigate the hierarchy first). The selected tool appears in the right pane, and you can use the toolbars and menus that appear to take appropriate action with the tool. Both the Event Viewer and Performance tools are available from this window.

2. If System Tools is preceded by a plus box ⊞ in the console tree, click ⊞ next to **System Tools** to view the tools in the System Tools node

3. If Event Viewer is preceded by plus box ⊞ in the console tree, click ⊞ next to **Event Viewer** to view the event logs

4. Click **Application**

   Application events appear in the right pane. Margaret asks you to note that the Computer Management window gives you quick access to most system tools from one consolidated location.

5. Double-click the second **Information event** in the Application Log list.

   If you have been working through the lessons without pausing, the Application Log should show two Information events. Figure O-11 shows the second event; it notes that the conditions of the Alert Test have been met.

6. Click **Cancel** to close the Event Properties dialog box

   You return to the Computer Management window. Notice that the System Tools node lists the Performance Logs and Alerts tools a little further down.

FIGURE O-10: Computer Management window

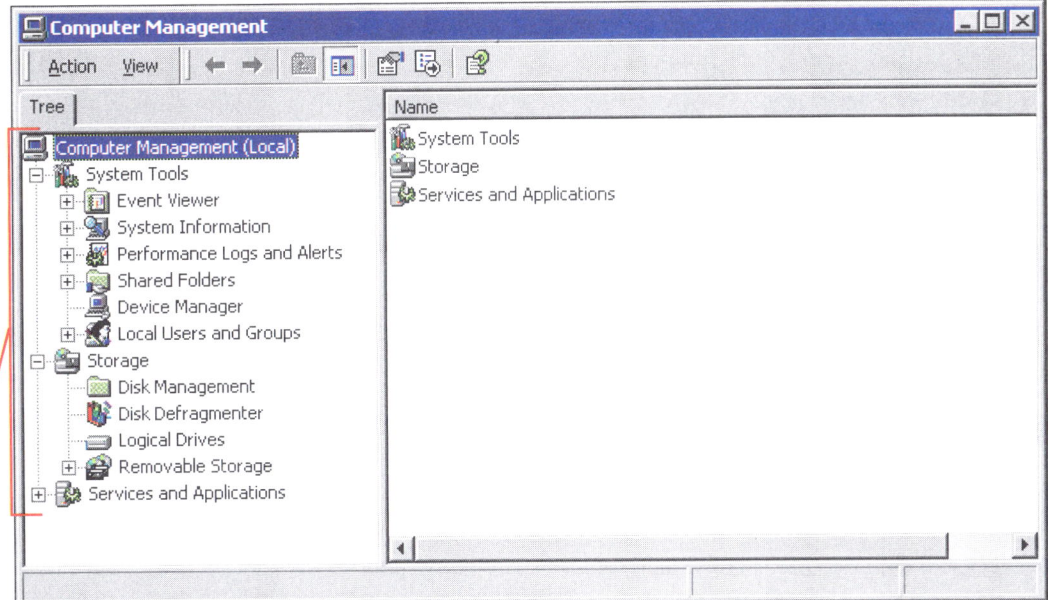

The Computer Management window organizes many of the Window 2000 administrative tools into one list

FIGURE O-11: Viewing an alert event

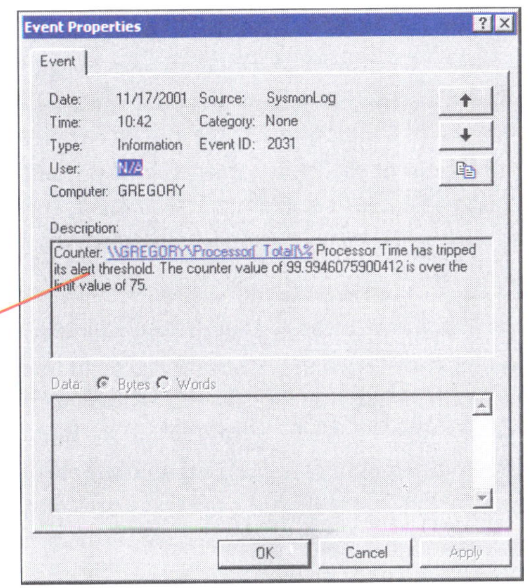

Description of the event that the alert conditions have been met

Customizing the Computer Management window

You can modify the Computer Management window by adding your own console. You create a "container" and then add tools to that container, called **snap-ins**. A **container** is any item on the console tree to which you add objects. The container appears with the familiar [+] and [−] icons that you click to view or hide items within that container. The most basic container is the folder, though you can add other types of containers. Before you create a console, you should identify the tasks the console will perform, the components to be administered, and the snap-ins and controls that are needed to perform the task. You can add snap-ins using the Add/Remove Snap-In command, which offers a set of snap-ins. The Microsoft Web site created by Microsoft employees and outside developers offers still more.

Understanding Disk File Systems

A disk must be formatted with a **file system** that allows it to work with the operating system to store, manage, and access data. Two of the most common file systems are FAT (or FAT32, an improvement on FAT technology) and NTFS. Disks on DOS, Windows 3.1, or Windows 98 computers use the FAT file system. NTFS improves on some of the shortcomings of FAT disks that make them less desirable on a network. Table O-3 describes the major differences between these two file systems. Which file system are your disks most likely to use and why? That depends on the type of disk, whether your computer is on a network, and your computer's role as a resource on the network. Margaret explains the features of file systems to John.

There are important differences between FAT and NTFS file systems:

FAT

When you format a disk with the FAT file system, a formatting program divides the disk into storage compartments. First it creates a series of rings, called **tracks**, around the circumference of the disk. Then it divides the tracks into equal parts, like pieces of pie, to form **sectors**, as shown in Figure O-12. The number of sectors and tracks depends on the size of the disk.

Although the physical surface of a disk is made of tracks and sectors, a file is stored in clusters. A **cluster**, also called an **allocation unit**, is one or more sectors of storage space—it represents the minimum amount of space that an operating system reserves when saving the contents of a file to a disk. Thus, a file might be stored in more than one cluster. Each cluster is identified by a unique number; the first two clusters, shown in yellow, are reserved by the operating system. The operating system maintains a **file allocation table** (or **FAT**) on each disk that lists the clusters on the disk and records the status of each cluster: whether it is occupied (and by which file), available, or defective. Each cluster in a file "remembers" its order in the chain of clusters—and each cluster points to the next one until the last cluster, which marks the end of the file.

NTFS

NTFS features a built-in security system that does not allow users to access the disk unless they have a user account and password with the necessary rights and permissions. NTFS protects disks from damage by automatically redirecting data from a bad sector to a good sector without requiring you to run a disk-checking utility. Given the reliability and the built-in repair mechanisms of NTFS disks, only rarely do they require maintenance. This is an example of **fault tolerance**, the ability of a disk to resist damage—a critical issue with disks on a network computer.

TABLE O-3: NTFS improvements on the FAT file system

feature	FAT	NTFS
Security	Vulnerable to "hackers"—unauthorized users who break into other people's files	Includes built-in security measures that only allow people who have permission to access files
Recoverability	Likely to fail if a sector containing system data is lost, because they store critical system files in single sectors	Highly reliable because it uses **redundant storage**—it stores everything in vital sectors twice, so if a disk error in a vital sector occurs, NTFS can access file system data from the redundant sector
File size	Designed for small disks (originally less than 1 MB in size); can handle a maximum file size of 4 GB	Handles files up to 64 GB in size

FIGURE 0-12: Files stored in clusters

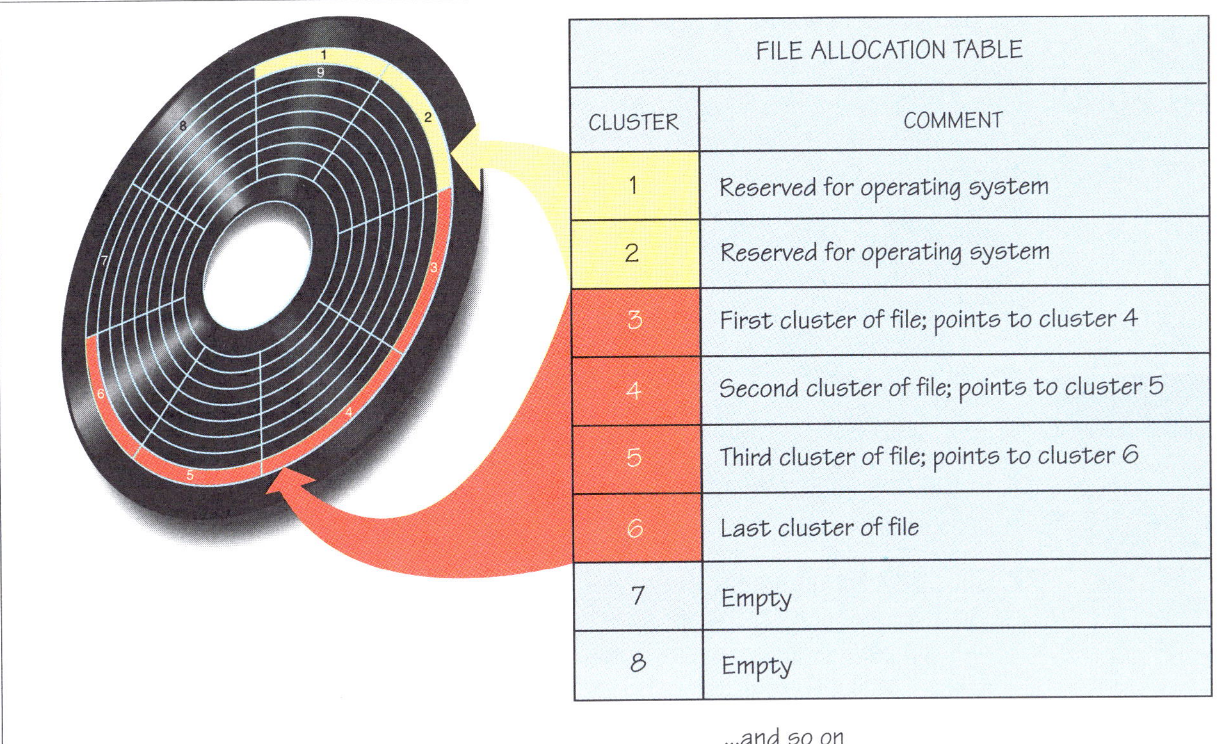

Selecting a file system

Floppy disks must be formatted with the FAT file system because NTFS does not support floppy disks. If you are running Windows 2000 on a stand-alone computer, you can choose either FAT or NTFS, but in most cases, the file system has already been chosen for you, either by the person who originally set up the computer or the manufacturer from whom you purchased the computer. If your computer is a client on a Windows 2000 network, it is more likely that your hard disk uses NTFS. Because NTFS is more suited to network demands, such as a high level of security and resistance to system failure, network administrators format network disks with NTFS whenever possible. Sometimes, however, users on a network want or need to use a non-Windows 2000 operating system. Also, a user might need a computer that is capable of running either Windows 2000 or Windows 98. The disks on that computer would then be formatted with FAT.

Managing Disks

The Storage node in the Computer Management window helps you manage your disks. The Disk Management tool is a graphical tool for managing disks. It allows you to partition unallocated portions of your disks into **volumes**, or designated storage areas that can span part of one or more disks. A volume on a disk is assigned its own drive letter. Thus, the same physical disk might contain two drives. Each drive can use a different file system—so you might have a single disk partitioned into two volumes, each with its own file system. Figure O-13 shows how you might partition a single hard disk in two different ways: first with a single NTFS volume, and second with one NTFS volume and one FAT volume. The Disk Defragmenter utility is also available in the Storage node, as well as a list of logical drives. Margaret suggests that John view the storage tools.

Steps

1. In the Computer Management window, click the **plus sign** ⊞ next to the Storage node, if necessary
2. Click **Disk Management**

   The disks on your computer appear in the right pane. The top right pane of the window displays your computer's volumes and the bottom right pane offers a graphic display of the breakdown of space on each disk, allowing you to see how your disks are partitioned. Figure O-14 displays a computer with a hard disk and a CD-ROM disk. The hard disk, labeled Disk 0, has only one FAT drive, named C:, and no unallocated space. The CD-ROM drive is labeled drive D:.
3. Click the **Settings button**

   The View Setting dialog box opens, as shown in Figure 0-15, allowing you to change the color or pattern of any disk region displayed in the Disk Management window. Refer to the Item list in Figure O-15 to identify the disk regions that you might see on your drives. System administrators use many of the items in this list to create drives that are extremely reliable for data storage.
4. Click **Cancel** to close the View Settings dialog box

Partitioning a disk

If you have a computer at home, its disks are most likely already partitioned, and partitioning those disks further can be laborious if there is no available free space (space that is not yet part of a partition). If, however, you have the necessary rights on a computer whose disk or disks have available unallocated space, you can partition your disk. You right-click an unallocated region of a disk in the Disk Management pane, then click Create Partition. You then follow the Create Partition Wizard directions that appear on your screen. This wizard helps you format your new drive so you can store data on it.

FIGURE O-13: A hard disk, partitioned two different ways

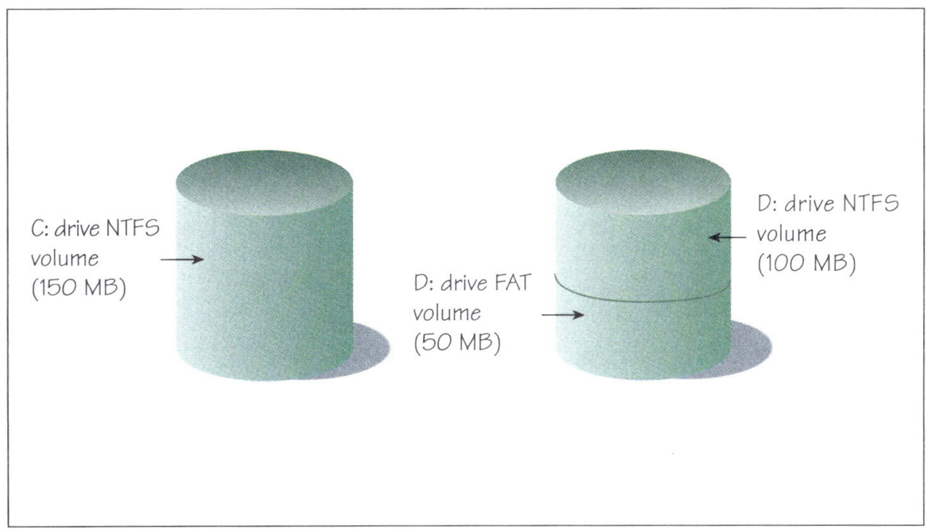

FIGURE O-14: Computer Management window

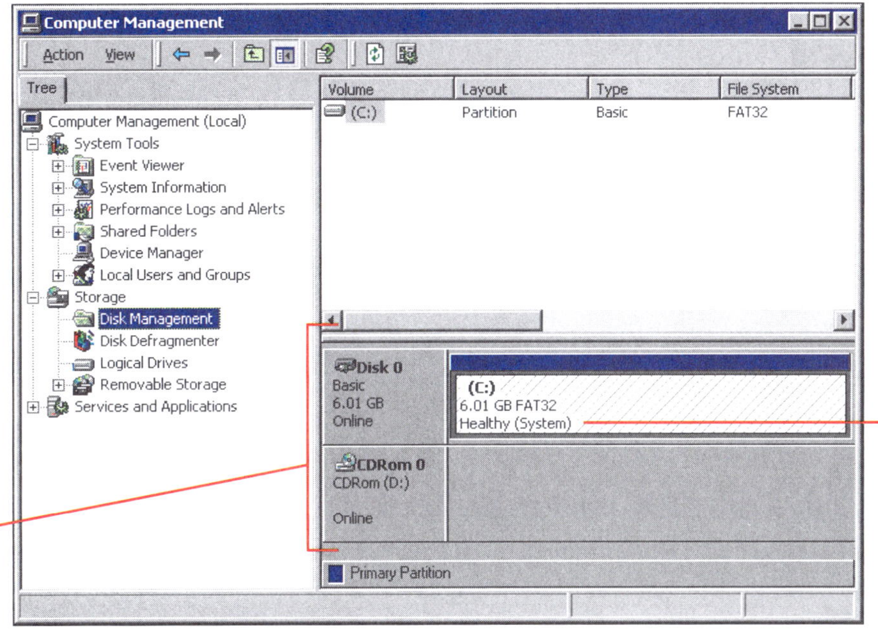

There are two drives on the system

Drive is formatted using the FAT32 file system

FIGURE O-15: View Settings dialog box

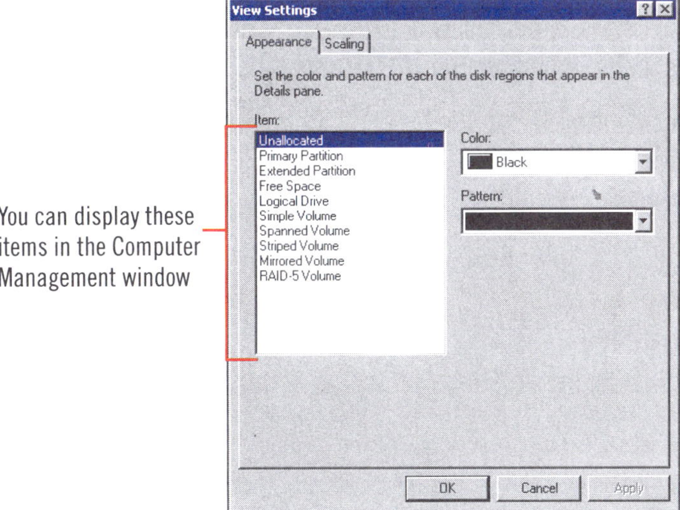

You can display these items in the Computer Management window

Viewing and Saving System Information

At times you need basic information about your computer. Perhaps you are on the phone with a technical support service and you need to be able to identify system settings. Windows 2000 pulls all the information about your system together in the System Information node, which features five folders that include a system summary, and information on hardware resources, components, software environment, and Internet Explorer settings. System administrators often keep a printed diagnostic report next to each computer on a network so they have access to diagnostic information when they most need it—that is, when the computer isn't working. You can create a printed report that you file near the computer or you can save a text report on a floppy disk stored next to the computer. You can report on only a single folder or on all the information in the System Information node. Margaret suggests that John learn how to find and view basic information about Windows 2000 computers and then save some of that information in a text file. She suggests he save a record of his hardware resources on a floppy disk so that if his computer does fail, he has access to information about the system.

1. If System Tools is preceded by a plus sign ⊞ in the console tree of the Computer Management window, click ⊞ next to System Information to view the folders in the System Information node
2. Click **System Summary**
   The System Summary displays basic information about your computer in the right pane, as shown in Figure O-16.
3. If Hardware Resources is preceded by ⊞ in the console tree, click ⊞ next to Hardware Resources
4. Right-click **Hardware Resources**, then click **Save as Text File**
   The Save As dialog box opens.
5. Click the **Save in list arrow**, then select the drive containing your Project Disk
6. Type **Test Report** in the File name box
7. Click **Save**
   The system gathers hardware resources information and saves it as a text file. This might take a few moments; creating a file of system information can be time-consuming.
8. Click the **Start** button, then point to **Programs**, **Accessories**, click **Notepad**, click **Open** from the File menu, then open the **Test Report** file to note its contents
9. Click the **Close** button ☒ in the Notepad, Computer Management, and Administrative Tools windows
   All three windows close.

QuickTip

To save a report on all your system information, you right-click System Information in the console tree and click Save as Text File. You can right-click many folders in the Computer Management window to access a similar save command that allows you to generate reports.

FIGURE O-16: Viewing the System Summary

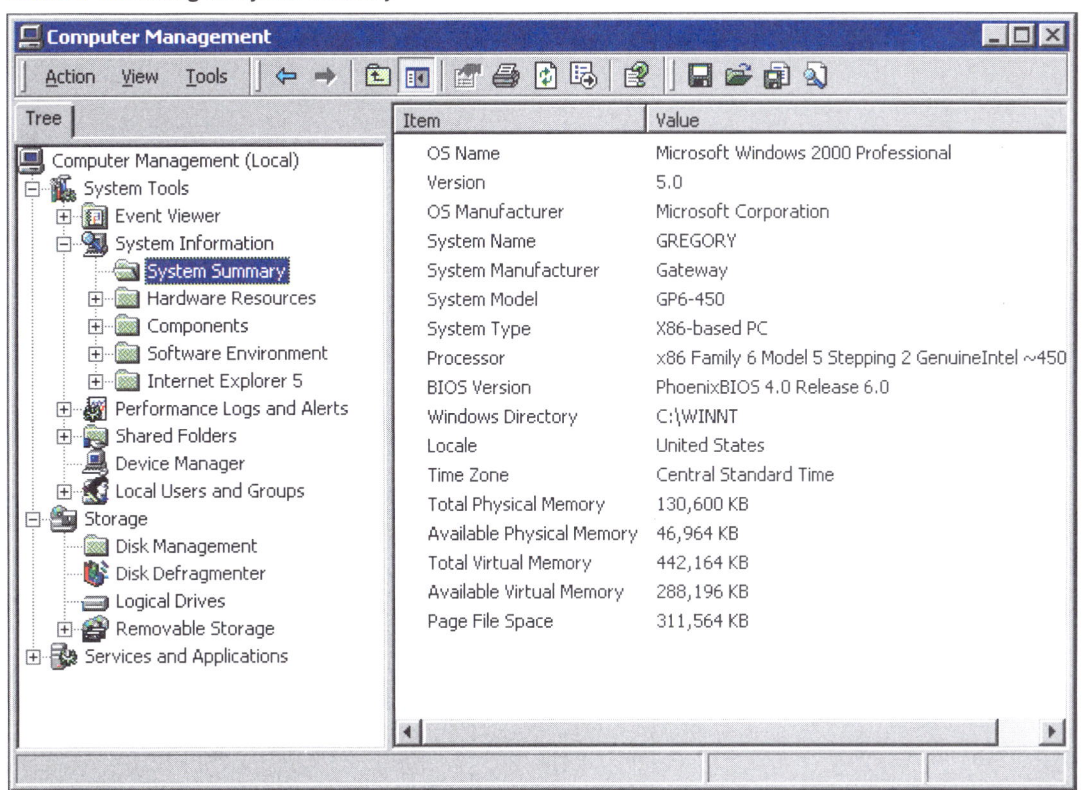

Practice

▶ Concepts Review

Label each of the elements of the screen shown in Figure O-17.

FIGURE O-17

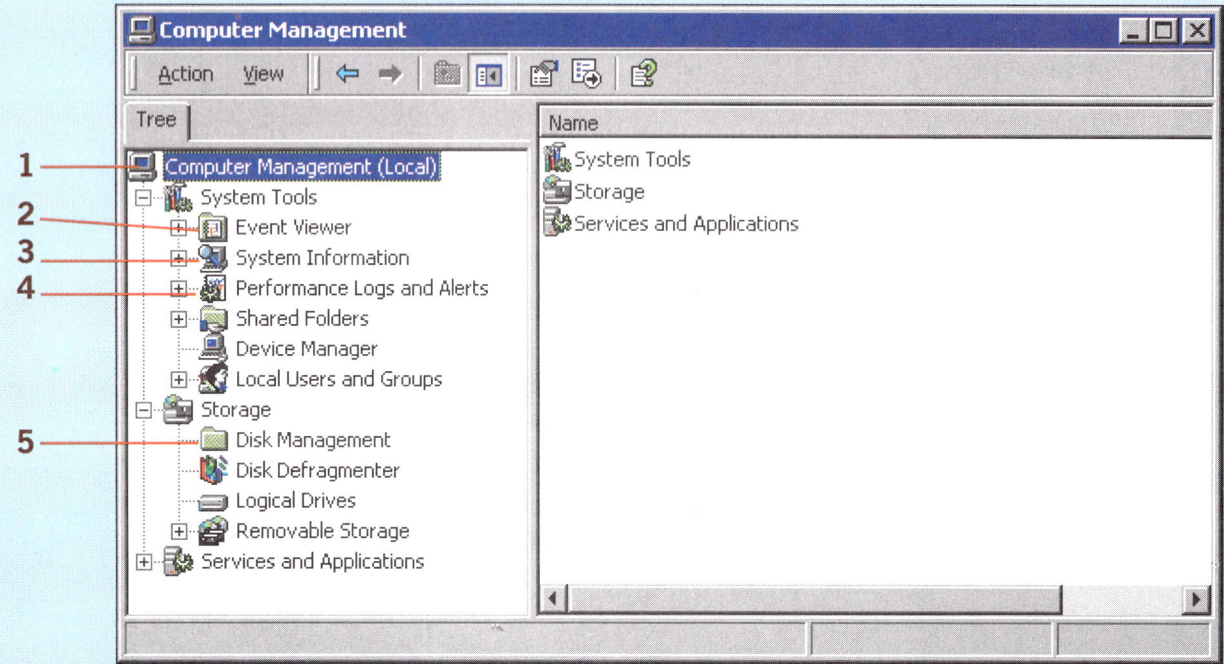

Match each of the following terms with the statement that best describes its function.

6. Performance Monitor	**a.** Allows you to examine System, Security, and Application Logs
7. NTFS	**b.** Allows you to log an alert
8. Disk Administrator	**c.** Uses redundant storage
9. Volume	**d.** Allows you to create a partition
10. Counter	**e.** When a computer or network is running at a normal level
11. FAT	**f.** Storage space that can span one or more disks
12. Baseline	**g.** Designed for small disks
13. Event Viewer	**h.** Numerical information about the performance of an item on your computer

Select the best answer from the list of choices.

14. The Windows 2000 Computer Management window contains tools that allow you to

- **a.** install new programs.
- **b.** change your display settings.
- **c.** view but not change system information.
- **d.** track performance data.

15. If you want your computer to create an alert when your processor is running at 85%, which tool should you use?

- **a.** Disk Administrator
- **b.** Event Viewer
- **c.** Performance Monitor
- **d.** User Manager

16. If an alert threshold value is reached, Windows 2000 will
- **a.** add an alert event to the Event Log.
- **b.** send e-mail to the network administrator.
- **c.** shut down the computer.
- **d.** print a diagnostic report.

17. To interpret a performance chart, an administrator should compare it to
- **a.** a Windows 2000 diagnostic report.
- **b.** the Event Viewer System Log.
- **c.** list of volumes in Disk Administrator.
- **d.** a baseline chart.

18. What is a counter?
- **a.** An object such as a processor or physical disk
- **b.** A program you can run when an alert reaches a threshold value
- **c.** A numeric value that measures the performance of an object
- **d.** A red bar on the Performance Monitor chart that indicates an object's status

Skills Review

1. Explore Windows 2000 administrative tools.
- **a.** Click the Start button, point to Settings, then click Control Panel.
- **b.** Double-click the Administrative Tools icon.
- **c.** Print an image of the screen. (To print a copy of the screen, press [Print Screen] to make a copy of the screen, start Paint, click Edit on the menu bar, click Paste, click Yes to paste the large image if necessary, click File on the menu bar, click Print, then click Print again.)
- **d.** On the printout, write a sentence that tells whether you have all the administrative tools that come with Windows 2000. If you are missing any, write which ones. If you have additional tools, circle them on your printout. (You could use the text tool from within Paint to type your comments on the figure.)

2. Monitor activity with Event Viewer.
- **a.** Start Event Viewer, then click the Application Log icon to open the Application Log. If this log is empty, use another log, such as the System Log.
- **b.** Maximize the Event Viewer window.
- **c.** Print the visible entries in the Application Log (refer to Step 1e for screen printing instructions).
- **d.** Double-click one of the entries to view a description of that event in the Event Properties window.
- **e.** On your printout, draw an arrow to the event whose details you are examining.
- **f.** Write in the margin a note describing that event, based on what you learned in the Event Detail window.

3. Manage an event log.
- **a.** Click View on the menu bar, then click Filter.
- **b.** Deselect all the Event types check boxes, except for Error, and then click the OK button. The log should now show only events that resulted in errors. Print the contents of the log (refer to Step 1e for screen printing instructions).
- **c.** View details on two of the error events and describe them on the back of your printout.
- **d.** Click View, click Filter, click the Restore Defaults button, then click the OK button. All events are now visible.
- **e.** Click View and then click Find.
- **f.** Click the Event source list arrow, then click one of the programs in the list.
- **g.** Click the Find Next button. (The first event matching your criteria is selected in the event log.)
- **h.** Double-click the event you just found and then write on the back of your printout a description of the event.
- **i.** Archive the Application Log to your floppy disk.
- **j.** Close Event Viewer.

4. Create a performance chart.
- **a.** Start Performance Monitor, then click the View Chart button.
- **b.** Click the Add counter button, click the Object list arrow, then click Memory.
- **c.** Click Available Bytes and then click the Add button.

d. Click Committed Bytes and then click the Add button.
e. Click the Close button.
f. Allow the chart to generate for a few minutes, and then print your chart (refer to Step 1e for screen printing instructions).
g. On your printout, label the two lines in your chart. Then write a sentence stating whether you have more available bytes than committed bytes or less.

5. Set up an alert.

a. Click the Alerts icon in the Performance window, then click Action and New Alert Settings from the menu.
b. Type Alert Test 2 in the New Alert Settings text box, then click OK.
c. Click the Add button, then click Processor in the Object list.
d. Click %Processor Time in the Counter list.
e. Click the Add button, then Click the Close button.
f. Click the Over option button, type 85 in the Limit text box, then click the OK button.
g. In the Event Log, open the item from the log of application events indicating that the alert conditions have been met.
h. Print the contents of your screen (refer to Step 1e for screen printing instructions).
i. Return to the Performance window and delete the alert you just created.
j. Close Performance Monitor.

6. View Computer Manager tools.

a. Open the Computer Manager window in the Administrative Tools window.
b. Open the Event Viewer folder.
c. Create a printout of your application event log as it appears in the Computer Management window.

7. Manage disks.

a. Start Disk Management from the Computer Management window.
b. Print the contents of the screen (refer to Step 1e for screen printing instructions).
c. On the back of your printout, write the number of FAT volumes you have and the number of NTFS volumes.
d. Write several sentences describing how physical disk space is used on your computer Disk Configuration view.
e. Explain why your computer's disks might be configured the way they are (consider the advantages of NTFS over FAT in a network environment).

8. View and save system information.

a. Open the Computer Management window and using the System Information tool, answer the following questions
- What version of Windows 2000 are you using? To whom is it registered? (*Hint*: Use the System Summary folder.)
- What is your BIOS version?
- What processor is your computer using?
- What is the available physical memory on your computer?
- What device is using IRQ 3? (*Hint*: Use the IRQs subfolder within the Hardware Resources folder.)
- What are your startup programs? (*Hint*: Use the Startup Programs subfolder of the Software Environment folder.)

Independent Challenges

1. You own a small bakery and you just purchased a Windows 2000 computer to help manage inventory, payroll, and other accounting procedures. The vendor from whom you purchased the machine advised you to create some printed documentation about your new system to refer to in case of computer trouble. You decide to use Windows 2000 Administrative Tools to create a complete report on your system. Rather than print it, however, you will save it on a floppy disk. You also decide to create a baseline chart using Performance Monitor that indicates how the computer performs in normal circumstances.

To complete this independent challenge:

a. Start the Windows 2000 Computer Management window, then open the System Summary folder.

b. Click Action, then click Save As Text File.
c. Save the report on a blank floppy disk with the name *Complete Report*.
d. Open Performance Monitor and create a chart with two Memory counters: %Committed Bytes in Use and Cache Bytes. Print the chart (refer to Step 1e in the Skills Review for screen printing instructions).
e. Use the Explain button to learn more about the two counters you charted. On the back of your printout, write a short description of both counters.

2. You own a small resumé preparation business. You are considering buying a new hard disk for your Windows 2000 computer, which you use to produce and store clients' resumes. Before you shop, you want to produce documentation on your current disk setup. You can then take your findings to different computer vendors so that the sales representatives have the information they need to advise you. You'll use both Disk Administrator and Windows 2000 Diagnostics to find the information you need.

To complete this independent challenge:

a. Open the Computer Management window, then open the Disk Management folder.
b. Create a printout of your disk configuration (refer to Step 1e in the Skills Review for screen printing instructions).
c. Open the System Summary folder, then create a report of information on the Drives folder (located in the Storage subfolder of the Components folder).
d. Close the Computer Manager.

3. You are the systems administrator for the Research and Development Department at Herrera Pharmaceuticals. One of the R&D specialists has been having problems with her computer. You decide to start by examining the event logs, particularly the System Log. You also want to check the log settings to make sure the log is collecting data properly.

To complete this independent challenge:

a. Start Event Viewer, open the System Log, then use the Filter feature to view only Error and Warning events. Print the list (refer to Step 1e in the Skills Review for screen printing instructions).
b. Check Event Viewer settings using the Properties command on the Auction menu. On the printout, write a summary of the current settings.
c. Archive the System Log to your floppy disk, naming it System 2.
d. Turn off the Filter feature, then close Event Viewer.

4. In college, you and some friends have joined forces with a supplier of sweaters, blankets, and other hand-made wares from Peru. You and your friends have arranged with your university's union to sell the wares on your university's pedestrian mall. You've been handling your company's computing needs on a stand-alone Windows 2000, and you are concerned because your computer runs rather slowly. You decide to run some tests on the processor and memory and gather some information about how you might improve your computer's performance before you start shopping.

To complete the independent challenge:

a. Go to the library and learn about what controls the speed of a computer. Study the functions of memory and processors and how they relate. Use the Internet, trade magazines about computers, or computer text books as your sources.
b. Use Performance Monitor to create two performance charts, one on memory and one on your computer's processor. Use three counters for each chart. Use the Explain button to learn more about the counters you chose.
c. Print the performance charts you created (refer to Step 1e in the Skills Review for screen printing instructions). On the back of each printout, describe the counters you chose.
d. Use the Computer Management window to learn more about your current processor and memory. The System Summary and Hardware Resources folders should be useful.
e. Write a one-page report summarizing what you have learned about computer speed and how it relates to your system.

► Visual Workshop

Re-create and print the screen shown in Figure O-18, which displays a Performance Monitor report (refer to Step 1e in the Skills Review for screen printing instructions). Don't worry if your numbers don't match the numbers shown.

FIGURE O-18

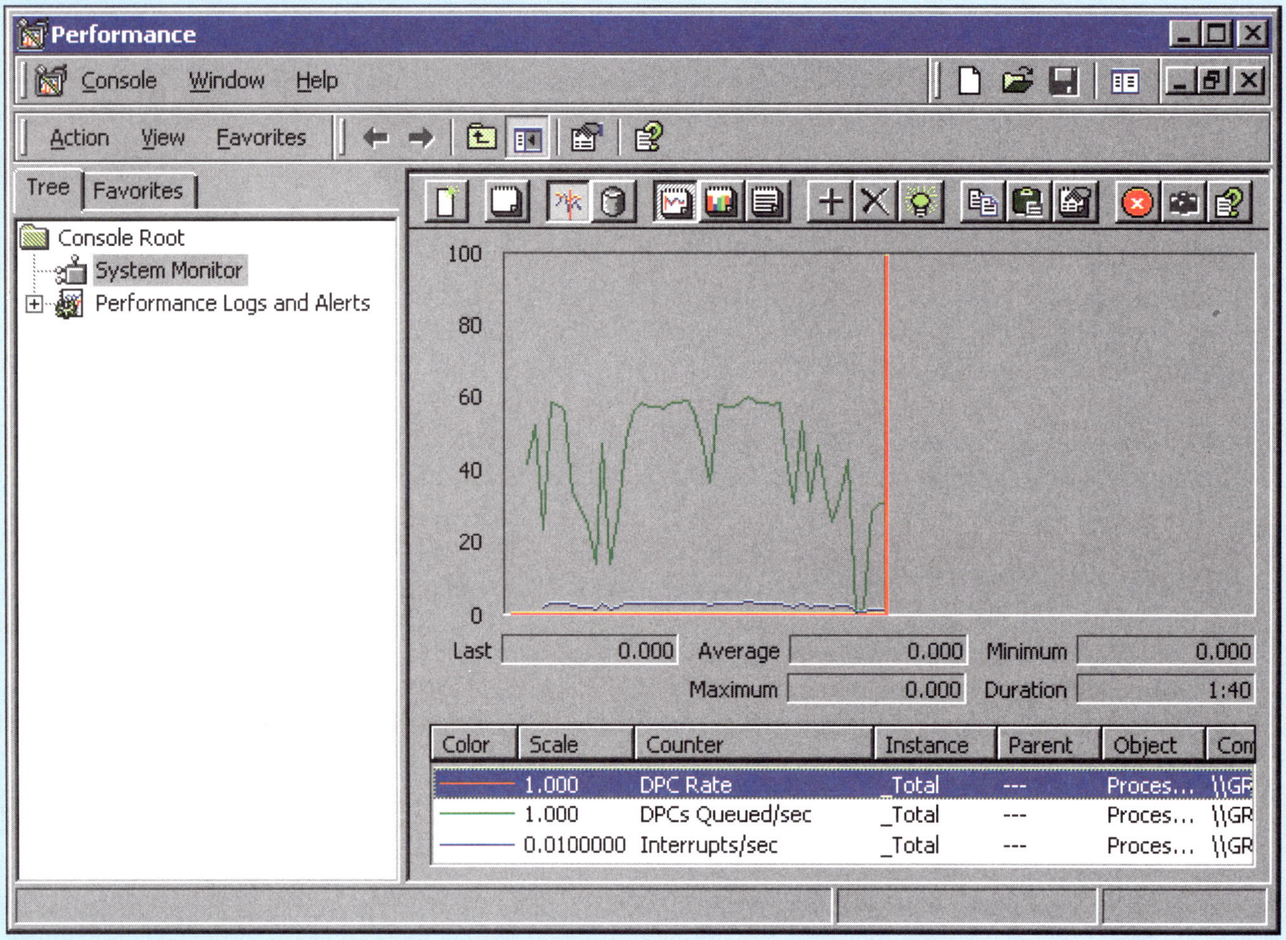

Glossary

Accessibility Wizard A series of dialog boxes that guides you through steps to configure Windows 2000 for vision, hearing, and mobility needs.

Accessories Built-in programs that come with Windows 2000 that you can use for day-to-day tasks.

Active Desktop The desktop that allows you to access the Internet and view Active Desktop items directly from it. *See also* Active Desktop item, Desktop.

Active Desktop item An element you can place on the desktop to access or display content from the Internet.

Active Directory A catalog of information, including people, computers, shared folders, and printers on a network.

Active program The program that is currently running.

Active window A window that you are currently using; if a window is active, its title bar changes color to differentiate it from other windows, and its program button on the taskbar appears indented.

Adapter A device that connects a computer to a network.

Address bar A bar that displays the address of the current Web page or the contents of a local or network computer drive.

Address Book An electronic database where you can store detailed information about a person or company.

Alert A warning that is automatically generated when a counter value exceeds or falls short of a threshold value you have specified. *See also* Counter.

Allocation unit *See* Cluster.

Application log A list of program events maintained by the Event Viewer.

Archive The process to save a copy of the logs produced by the Event Viewer.

Archive attribute A Windows marker indicating whether a file needs to be backed up.

Argument The part of the syntax of a DOS command that gives DOS specific information about what you want it to do.

Article A newsgroup message.

Auto hide A feature that automatically hides the taskbar when you are not using it.

AutoComplete A File name feature in the Open and Save dialog boxes that suggests possible matches with previous filename entries in the File name text box.

Automatic caching An offline file option that makes every file someone opens from a shared folder available for offline access.

Back up The process you perform to save your data quickly and compress it into a small space on a set of disks or a tape cartridge. *See also* Backup.

Background The surface of your desktop on which icons and windows appear; you can customize its appearance using the Display Properties dialog box.

Background process The processing time that programs, such as printing or disk backup, require while you run a foreground process. *See also* Foreground process.

Backup A Windows 2000 accessory for backing up files; also, the results of backing up your data.

Backup medium A set of floppy or zip disks, or a tape cartridge designed to store computer data.

Backup set A file that Backup creates when you perform a back up.

Backup strategy The process in which you select a backup method by evaluating tradeoffs among safety, time, and media space.

Bad sector A physical disk error.

Baseline chart A chart that system administrators create when the computer or network is running at a normal level, in order to compare with other charts.

Binary data Internal computer software programming code that experienced computer technicians can evaluate to better interpret the event.

Binding A connection that enables communications among the adapters, protocols, and services installed in Windows 2000.

Bitmap Image A common file format for graphic images.

Bitmapped character A character that consists of small dots organized to form it.

Bookmark A reference point in a document to which you want to create a link.

Briefcase A Windows 2000 accessory that synchronizes or updates files between two different computers.

Browser A program, such as Microsoft Internet Explorer, designed to access the Internet. *See also* Web browser.

Bullet mark An indicator that shows an option is enabled.

Cache A reserved portion of disk space on a computer.

Cascading menu An additional list of commands available from a menu item with an arrow next to it. Pointing to the arrow displays the list of commands, also known as a submenu.

Catalog An index of the backed up files that is built and stored on the backup medium.

Center A Display Properties option that positions the wallpaper picture or pattern in the center of the desktop screen.

Channel A specialized Web page that delivers content from the Internet.

Chat rooms Services that allow users who share common interests to come together electronically and exchange messages on a specific topic.

Check Disk A Windows 2000 accessory that checks for and then marks or repairs damaged sections of a disk.

Check mark An indicator that shows a feature is enabled.

Click To press and release the left mouse button once.

Client A computer that accesses shared resources on a server.

Client/server network A network setup that provides all users on a network a central location for accessing shared files.

Clipboard A temporary storage space in RAM that contains information that has been cut or copied.

Close To exit a program or remove a window from the desktop. The Close button usually appears in the upper-right corner of a window.

Cluster A section of a disk.

Command A directive that provides access to a program's features.

Command-line interface An interface in which you perform operations by typing commands at a command prompt.

Command prompt A character such as > or $ that appears at the beginning of a line and that signals the user to enter commands.

Command syntax A set of rules that you follow to write a command.

Compressed Serial Line Internet Protocol (C-SLIP) A dial-up connection type that is similar to SLIP, but adds the feature of data compression to speed up data transfer. *See also* Serial-Line Internet Protocol.

Computer management A Windows 2000 utility that provides easy access to a specific computer's administrative tools.

Configured The way a program or device on a computer is set up.

Conflict Two devices with the same resource settings.

Connection type The type of connection between a computer and an ISP's server. Windows 2000 offers two connection types: PPP and SLIP.

Console tree The hierarchy of tools in the left pane of the Computer Management window.

Contact Information about a person or company with whom you communicate; in Outlook Express, contacts are stored in the Address Book.

Contact group A group of contacts that you can organize together; in Outlook Express, contact groups are stored in the Address Book.

Contacts list A list in Outlook Express that displays the contacts and contact groups in the Address Book.

Container An item on the console tree to which you add objects. *See also* Console tree.

Context-sensitive help Help that relates to the task on which you are currently working.

Contiguous The process to place all of the parts of a file in one adjacent location.

Control bar A bar in Windows Media Player that contains buttons to play all or part of a video or sound clip.

Control Panel A Windows utility for changing computer settings.

Conversation thread A collection of newsgroup messages that consists of the original message on a particular topic along with any responses.

Copy To copy data to another location while leaving it in the original location.

Copy backup A Backup type that copies all selected files, like a normal backup, but does not clear the archive attribute.

Counter A performance chart item that provides specific numeric information. *See also* Performance chart.

Criteria A set of information on which to make a decision.

Cut To remove data and place it on the Clipboard to be pasted in another location.

Cut and paste To move information from one place to another using the Clipboard as the temporary storage area.

Daily backup A Backup type that copies all selected files that changed on the day the backup was done.

Default printer The printer that you use most often.

Deferred printing A print job that waits in the print queue with the printer paused.

Defragment A feature that allows you to rewrite the files on your disk to contiguous blocks rather than in random blocks.

Delete To remove a file or folder that is placed in the Recycle Bin, then removed from the disk.

Desktop An on-screen version of a desk that provides a workspace for different computing tasks. *See also* Active Desktop.

Destination program The program where you store an embedded object.

Destination drive When copying files, the drive to which you want to copy.

Destination file When linking, the file where you store a representation of a linked object.

Device Manager A Windows 2000 utility that allows you to view system hardware.

Dialog box A window that requests information. Many dialog boxes have options you must choose before Windows or a program can carry out a command.

Differential backup A type of backup that copies only selected files that have changed since the most recent normal or incremental backup.

Directory server A computer that maintains a list of people logged on to the NetMeeting service.

Disk Cleanup A Windows 2000 accessory that deletes temporary, Internet cache, and unnecessary program files.

Disk Defragmenter A Windows 2000 accessory that restores fragmented files in one location.

Disk label A name that you assign to a disk by using the Properties dialog box.

Display adapter A hardware device that allows a computer to communicate with its monitor.

Display pane The bottom pane of Outlook Express that displays the e-mail message selected in the preview pane. *See also* Preview pane.

Docucentric An interface in which the emphasis is on the documents rather than on the software applications.

Document A file that you create in a program such as WordPad.

Document icon An icon on the desktop that represents a document.

Document window The part of a program window that displays the current document.

Domain A collection of computers that the person managing the network creates to group computers that are used for the same tasks together and to simplify the set up and maintenance of the network.

Domain Name System (DNS) A database service that helps computers look up the names of other computers and locate their corresponding IP addresses.

DOS Short for Disk Operating System, the standard operating system for PCs prior to Microsoft Windows.

Double-click To press and release the left mouse button twice quickly.

Download The process by which you access and display a Web page from the Internet.

Drag To press and hold the left mouse button while moving the mouse in order to move an item or text to a new location.

Driver Software that allows a hardware device (e.g., a printer) to communicate with Windows and other software applications.

Edit To change the contents of a file without having to re-create it.

Electronic mail (e-mail) A system used to send and receive messages electronically.

Embedding Inserting an object created in one program into a document created in another program.

Emergency repair disk A disk that contains a set of utilities and tools that help repair a computer in an emergency.

Explorer Bar The pane on the left side of the screen in Windows Explorer that displays all objects available to the computer.

Favorite A shortcut to a Web address.

Fault tolerance The ability of a disk to resist damage—a critical issue with disks on a network computer.

File An electronic collection of information that has a unique name, distinguishing it from other files.

File allocation table A list of information about the status of the various sections of a disk that is maintained by the operating system.

File extension In a filename, three-letter extension, such as doc or bmp, that an operating system uses to determine the file type.

File hierarchy A logical structure for folders and files that mimics how you would organize files and folders in a filing cabinet.

File management The process of organizing and keeping track of files and folders.

File sharing A networking option that allows many people to work on the same file without the need for creating or storing multiple copies.

File system A format applied to a disk to make it compatible with the operating system in storing, managing, and accessing data.

Filter The process of retrieving newsgroup messages from a particular person, about a specific subject, of a certain length, or older than a number of days.

Floppy disk A disk that you insert into the disk drive of your computer and on which you can save files.

Folder A storage location for files and/or other folders that helps you organize your disks.

Folders list A list that displays folders where Outlook Express stores e-mail messages.

Foreground process The processing time that the program in which you are currently working requires.

Forums Services that allow users who share common interests to come together electronically and exchange messages on a specific topic.

Fragmented file A file that is broken up and stored on different parts of a disk.

Frame A separate window within a Web page.

Full Format A Disk Copy option that removes all files from any floppy disk (previously formatted or not) and scans the disk for bad sectors.

Full permission A file setting that allows the user to edit and save changes to the file.

Graphical user interface (GUI) An environment made up of meaningful symbols, words, and windows that controls the basic operation of a computer and the programs that run on it.

Hard copy Paper output resulting from a print job. *See also* Printout.

Hard disk A disk (usually drive C) that is built into the computer and on which you store programs and files.

Hardware class A list of hardware types.

Hardware device A physical object that you plug into a computer.

Hardware profile A list of settings that specify which hardware devices to start when you start a computer.

Hibernation A state in which a computer saves everything in memory on disk and shuts down.

Highlight To shade text or graphics with a different color by dragging the mouse or pressing a keyboard combination, in order to select the text or graphic. *See also* Select.

Hits A list of matched sites produced by search engine request. *See also* Search engine.

Home page The first Web page that appears when you open a Web browser.

Horizontal scroll bar A bar that moves your view from right to left through a window.

Hyperlink Highlighted words, phrases, and graphics that you click to open other Web pages. *See also* Link.

Icon A graphical representation of a file or another screen element.

Incremental backup A backup option that backs up only the files that have changed since your last backup. *See also* Backup.

Ingoing connection A network connection that enables a computer to be contacted by other computers.

Insertion point The blinking vertical line in a document window that indicates where text will appear when you type.

Internet A collection of networks that connects computers all over the world using phone lines, coaxial cables, fiber-optic cables, satellites, and other telecommunications media. *See also* Network.

Internet account A service account that allows you to access the features of the Internet.

Internet Protocol (IP) A unique address that identifies a server on the Internet.

Internet service provider (ISP) A company that provides access to the Internet.

Interrupt Request Line (IRQ) A software setting that allows a hardware device to communicate with your computer's software.

ISDN lines Wires that provide a completely digital path from one computer to another.

Keyword A word you submit to a search engine that is compared with words found on various Web sites on the Internet. *See also* Search engine.

Keyboard shortcut A keyboard alternative for executing a menu command; for example, [Ctrl][X] for Cut.

Legacy hardware Any hardware device, such as a mouse or printer, that is not designed for Windows 95 Plug and Play.

Link An element in a hypertext document that moves you to another place in the document. *See also* Hyperlink.

Linking The process of connecting an object in one program to a document in a second program without actually removing the object from its original location.

Links bar A bar that displays link buttons to Web pages on the Internet or documents on a local or network drive.

Local area network (LAN) A group of computers and other devices in a limited area connected by a communications link that allows one device to interact with another device on the network.

Local printer A printer connected directly to a computer.

Logon script A program that runs on your computer automatically to log you on to a dial-up networking service.

Manual caching An offline file option that enables offline access for selected documents in a shared folder.

Mapping The process by which you assign drive letters to network folders, making them appear as extra drives.

Margin The extra space around the edges of a document.

Maximize To enlarge a window so it fills the entire screen. Usually, the Maximize button is located in the upper-right corner of a window.

Media Player A Windows accessory that plays video, sound, or animation files.

Menu A list of available commands in a program.

Menu bar A bar at the top of the program window that organizes commands into groups of related operations.

Message flag An icon associated with an e-mail message that helps you determine the status or priority of the message.

Minimize To reduce the size of a window. The Minimize button is usually located in the upper-right corner of a window. Clicking the Minimize button shrinks the window to a button on the taskbar.

Most Frequently Used List A list of the most frequently used files organized by type.

Mouse A hand-held input device that you roll on your desk to position the mouse pointer on the Windows desktop. *See also* Mouse pointer.

Mouse buttons The buttons (right and left) on the mouse that you use to make selections and issue commands.

Mouse pointer The arrow-shaped cursor on the screen that follows the movement of the mouse as you roll the mouse on your desk and which you can use to select items, choose commands, and start programs. The shape of the mouse pointer changes depending on the program and the task being executed.

Multitasking The ability to run several programs at once and easily switch among them.

My Computer A window that displays the devices and folders available on your computer.

My Network Places An icon on the Windows 2000 desktop that lists the computers on the network.

Navigate To reposition the insertion point in a document.

Navigation bar A bar in Windows Media Player that contains buttons to move backward and forward between open video or sound clip files and start your Web browser and open media Web sites on the Internet.

Network Two or more computers connected together in order to exchange and share data, programs, and hardware.

Network and Dial-up Connection A network connection using a direct cable or modem.

Network folder A folder on a network that is made available to other computers on the network.

Network interface card (NIC) An adapter card inserted into a slot in the back of a computer that connects to the network.

Network operating system The software that creates, maintains, and controls the operations of a network.

Network printer A printer made available to other computers on a network.

News server A computer located on the Internet where articles on different topics are stored.

Newsgroup Online discussion groups about a particular topic, usually in an e-mail format.

Node A category of tools in the left pane of the Computer Management window. *See also* Console tree.

Normal backup A Backup type that backs up all selected files, regardless of when the files were last changed.

Object A picture, chat, video clip, text, or almost anything you can create on a computer.

Object Linking and Embedding (OLE) The process of placing and working with common objects in different programs.

Offline When the connection to the Internet is disconnected.

Offline file A version of a shared file from a network stored on a local drive.

Offline viewing When a Web page is copied to a local drive for viewing later, when the Internet connection is disconnected.

Online services Companies that sell communications services such as e-mail, Internet access, Web page storage space, and newsgroup access. *See also* Internet service provider.

OpenType character A character that is based on a mathematical equation so the curves are smooth and the corners are sharp.

Operating system A program that controls the basic operation of your computer and the programs you run on it.

Optimization The procedure to rearrange fragmented files into one location on a disk.

Outgoing connection A network connection that contacts a remote access server by using a cable or modem to establish a connection with a computer.

Outlook Express Start Page A page that displays tools you can use to read e-mail, compose e-mail messages, download the latest newsgroup messages, read newsgroup messages, enter and edit Address Book information, and find people on the Internet.

Output The results of a DOS command.

Pane A part of a window that divides the window into two or more sections.

Pattern A design that appears as your desktop background.

Peer-to-peer network A network setup that enables two or more computers to link together without designating a central server.

Performance chart A chart that system administrators use to observe how a computer's processes are behaving over time.

Permission A user setting, such as Read or Full, that designates what a user can and cannot do to a file.

Personalized menu A customized menu that keeps track of which programs you use and hides the programs you have not used recently.

Places bar A bar on the left side of the Open and Save dialog box that organizes navigation buttons to common locations or recently used files and folders on your computer or network.

Plug and Play Hardware device designed for quick and easy installation with Windows 2000.

Point To move the mouse pointer to position it over an item on the desktop.

Point to Point Protocol (PPP) Common dial-up networking connection type that provides error-checking and the ability to cope with noisy phone lines.

Pop-up menu The menu that appears when you right-click an item.

Port The location on the back of a computer where you connect the printer cable.

Power options A feature that controls the power supply to the devices attached to your computer.

Preview pane The top pane of Outlook Express that displays a list of all of the messages in your Inbox. *See also* Display pane.

Print Preview A feature that shows the layout and formatting of a document before you print it.

Print queue The order in which a printer prints documents.

Printout A document printed on paper.

Program Task-oriented software, such as Microsoft Access, Corel WordPerfect, and Microsoft Word, that you use for a particular kind of work, such as word processing or database management.

Program button The button that appears on the taskbar that represents a program that is minimized but still running.

Properties The characteristics of a specific element (such as the mouse, keyboard, or desktop display) that you can customize.

Protocol A language that the computer uses to communicate with other computers on the network.

Proxy server An Internet connection option that provides a secure barrier between your network and the Internet.

Quick Format A Disk Copy option that formats a previously formatted disk and removes all files from it.

Quick Launch toolbar A toolbar located next to the Start button on the taskbar that contains buttons to quickly start Internet-related programs and show the desktop.

Random access memory (RAM) The memory that programs use to perform necessary tasks while the computer is on, and when you turn the computer off, all information in RAM is lost.

Read permission A file setting that allows the user to view the file but not to make changes.

Recycle Bin An icon that appears on the desktop and which represents a temporary storage area on your hard drive for deleted files. Files remain in the Recycle Bin until you empty it or you restore the file(s).

Redundant storage A process where NTFS, a Windows 2000 file system, stores data in vital sectors twice, so if a disk error in a vital sector occurs, NTFS can access file system data from the redundant sector.

Registry A Windows 2000 database file, which contains information about your computer's configuration.

Remote party The recipient of a call you place with Phone Dialer or NetMeeting.

Restore To reduce the window to its previous size before it was maximized. The Restore button usually is located in the upper-right corner of a maximized window.

Right-click To press and release the right mouse button once quickly.

Scheme A combination of color, fonts, or character designs for window elements.

Scraps Sections of documents you can save, place on your desktop, and paste into other documents.

Screen font A font that consists of bitmapped characters. *See also* Bitmapped characters.

Screen saver A moving pattern that fills your screen after your computer has not been used for a specified amount of time.

ScreenTip A description of a toolbar button that appears on your screen when you position the mouse pointer over the button.

Scroll bar A bar that appears at the bottom and/or right edge of a window whose contents are not entirely visible and which contains a scroll box and two scroll arrows.

Scroll box A box located in the vertical and horizontal scroll bars that indicates your relative position in a window. *See also* Horizontal scroll bar *and* Vertical scroll bar.

Search engine A program on the Web that allows you to search through a collection of information found on the Internet. *See also* Keyword.

Sector A track divided into equal parts, like pieces of pie. *See also* Track.

Security The network feature that protects a computer from system failure or unauthorized intrusion.

Security log A list of security and audit events, such as who logged on, maintained by the Event Viewer.

Seek bar A bar in Windows Media Player that you drag backward or forward to play different parts of a video or sound clip.

Select To click and highlight an item in order to perform some action on it. *See also* Highlight.

Send To command A command that lets you send a document to a new location.

Separator page A printed page that reports the name, owner, date, and time of a print job.

Serial-Line Internet Protocol (SLIP) A basic dial-up connection type that runs well on most systems but has no error checking or security features.

Server A computer that stores and shares resources, such as programs, files, and folders, with other users on a network.

Service The network component that allows you to share resources on your computer, such as files and printers, with other networked computers.

Shared printer A printer made available to computers on a network.

Shortcut A link that you can place in any location that gives you instant access to a particular file, folder, or program on your hard disk or on a network.

Shut down The action you perform when you are finished working with Windows and after which it is safe to turn off your computer.

Sizing handles The small black boxes that appear around the edge of an object when it is selected, that allow you to resize the object.

Snap-in A tool that you add to a container in the Computer Management window. *See also* Container.

Source drive The drive from which you want to copy.

Source file The file where you store a linked object.

Source program The program where you create or insert an object.

Standby A state in which a monitor and hard disks turn off after standing idle for a set time.

Start button A button on the taskbar that you use to start programs, find and open files, access Windows Help, and more.

Start menu A list of commands that allows you to start a program, open a document, change a Windows setting, find a file, or display help information.

Status bar The area along the bottom of the window that displays information about the open document or Web page.

Status indicator A graphic (the Internet Explorer logo) that spins to indicate a new Web page is loading in Internet Explorer.

Streaming media A high-quality continuous video and sound playback.

Stretch A Display properties option that displays the wallpaper picture or pattern enlarged across the desktop screen.

Submenu *See* Cascading menu.

Synchronize To save the latest version of an offline Web page to a local drive.

System log A list of events logged by Windows 2000 operating system components.

System state data A collection of system-specific data, such as the registry and boot files, that can be backed up and restored.

Tab A section at the top of the dialog box that separates options into related categories.

Task Scheduler A Windows accessory that enables you to schedule tasks to run at specific times.

Taskbar A bar at the bottom of the screen that contains the Start button and the Quick Launch toolbar, and shows which programs are running.

Tile A Display Properties option that displays the wallpaper picture or pattern consecutively across the desktop screen.

Title bar The area along the top of the window that contains the filename and the program used to create it.

Tip of the day An area on the Outlook Express Start Page that displays a different Outlook Express tip each time you start the program.

Toggle A button that acts as an on/off switch.

Toolbar A bar that contains buttons that allow you to activate a command quickly.

Track A ring around the circumference of a hard or floppy disk.

Uniform Resource Locator (URL) Another name for a Web address. *See also* Web address.

Vertical scroll bar A bar that moves your view up and down through a window.

Virtual memory A process by which Windows 2000 uses hard disk drive space to simulate system RAM.

Virtual Private Network A secure network connection over the Internet.

Volume A designated storage area that can span part of one or more disks.

Wallpaper An image that you display as your desktop background.

Web address A unique address on the Internet where you can locate a Web page. *See also* Uniform Resource Locator.

Web browser A program that retrieves and displays Web pages. *See also* Browser.

Web page A document that contains highlighted words, phrases, and graphics that link the document to other documents on the Internet.

Web server A computer on the Internet that hosts Web sites, making them available to the World Wide Web.

Web site A computer on the Internet that contains Web pages.

Whiteboard A graphical program in NetMeeting that you can use to display and share graphical content.

Wide area network (WAN) A group of computers and other devices spread out over a large area connected by a communications link that allows one device to interact with another device on the network.

Window A rectangular frame on a screen that might contain icons, the contents of a file, or other usable data.

Windows Explorer A Windows 2000 program that lets you manage files, folders, and shortcuts; more powerful than My Computer and allows you to work with more than one computer, folder, or file at a time.

Windows Help An online book stored on your computer, complete with an index and a table of contents, that provides information on the features and tasks associated with a Windows program.

Windows Media Player A Windows accessory that plays video, sound, and mixed-media files.

Wizard A series of dialog boxes that guides you through steps to complete a task and prompts you for information.

WordPad A word-processing accessory that comes with Windows 2000.

Wordwrap A feature that automatically places text that will not fit on one line onto the next line.

Workgroup A group of computers within a network that shares resources, such as files and printers.

Workstation *See* Clients.

World Wide Web (Web, or WWW) The part of the Internet that consists of Web sites located on different computers around the world.

Index

Index

C

▶ D

Index

▶G

Index

Index

►O

►P

Q

R

Index

▶T

▶U

Index

► Z